Programming Microsoft® ADO.NET 2.0 Applications: Advanced Topics

Glenn Johnson

PUBLISHED BY
Microsoft Press
A Division of Microsoft Corporation
One Microsoft Way
Redmond, Washington 98052-6399

Library of Congress Control Number 2005934090

Printed and bound in the United States of America.

1 2 3 4 5 6 7 8 9 QWT 8 7 6 5

Distributed in Canada by H.B. Fenn and Company Ltd.

A CIP catalogue record for this book is available from the British Library.

Microsoft Press books are available through booksellers and distributors worldwide. For further information about international editions, contact your local Microsoft Corporation office or contact Microsoft Press International directly at fax (425) 936-7329. Visit our Web site at www.microsoft.com/mspress. Send comments to *mspinput@microsoft.com*.

Acquisitions Editor: Ben Ryan
Project Editor: Kathleen Atkins
Technical Editor: Kurt Meyer
Copy Editor: Ina Chang
Indexer: William S. Meyers

Body Part No. X11-50066

I dedicate this book to my lovely wife, Susan Johnson, a source of love, happiness, and stability even in the most trying times. Sue, your love, wit, and perspective have provided me with the guidance that I have needed in life. I am looking forward to our rapidly approaching 25th wedding anniversary and the many more wonderful years that follow. I love you, Sue.

Contents at a Glance

Table of Contents

Foreword

Pretty much every enterprise application uses databases. A large part of the code base of these applications is devoted to accessing and manipulating data stored in those databases. Accordingly, a large portion of the time and effort put into creating a new application is spent in the data-access space. That makes the data-access space a critical area that can be targeted by development tools to streamline the development process.

It's interesting to see how development tools change focus over time from one tier to another. Sometimes it's all about the presentation layer and how to make it really easy to build great-looking desktop applications and Web browser–based applications for use over the Web or the company intranet. Other times it's all about communications. Emphasis at still other times has been on data access and the data-access tier in general. The fact that the Internet has connected the whole world has changed the way we think about applications. Most recently a whole lot of new tools and technologies have been created to support our new environments.

When development tools and environments concentrated on data access in the past, they did it in different ways. For example, the folks who created languages and environments such as COBOL and xBase-like tools (among which are DBase and FoxPro) included data access as an intrinsic part of the infrastructure. These tools were created at different times and with different goals in mind but arose from many of the same ideas. You could declare the shapes of the records for the different entities in the system right in the language and use language primitives to scan, manipulate, and store those records.

Other tools used a different approach to the problem. Many data-access technologies were created around a programming interface instead of a language, making them usable from different languages at the cost of language integration. These APIs came in backend-specific flavors, such as Oracle's OCI or Sybase's CTLIB, or they came in backend-agnostic versions, such as the well-known ODBC.

We have our own cut of data-access history here at Microsoft. We've gone multiple ways: from DBLIB, a Microsoft SQL Server–specific API, to ODBC, an API designed to isolate developers from the backend specifics, to OLEDB, which aimed to enable "universal data access" over any data source out there, to ADO, a high-level API that simplifies the use of the powerful-but-complex OLEDB.

The evolution continues, and the expectation now is that you don't get separate support for any given task in isolation, be it data access, presentation, communications, or anything else that applications need to do. The software development community expects integrated application frameworks that address entire problem spaces.

In the Microsoft .NET Framework, data access happens through an API-based technology named ADO.NET. The entire .NET Framework is designed as a highly integrated and consistent set of classes. ADO.NET follows that design by providing classes for dealing with database connections, commands, and results in a way that fits nicely within the rest of the framework and within the Integrated Development Environment (the Visual Studio IDE).

ADO.NET is designed around a primary principle: *simplicity*. We wanted to make sure that every behavior exposed by the ADO.NET data-access framework is obvious and consistent. We made sure that you won't find surprises down the path because of some obscure limitation of the database or the data-access driver. In retrospect, I think that this concern for simplicity has helped make ADO.NET such a successful technology.

That very same clarity, however, brings some challenges to the table. By making everything explicit throughout the API, we ask our users to manually create and compose different elements of the API in a way that's appropriate for a given task. That requirement provides a lot of flexibility and avoids surprises for developers (because we don't do anything we weren't asked for), but also makes it harder to learn how to use ADO.NET.

To master ADO.NET, you need to learn the basics first. Many books and white papers describe ADO.NET, and MSDN publishes a lot of material that can help you get started with the technology. However, once you go through the initial steps, the real-world issues and requirements start to show up. What are the characteristics of the "connected" and "disconnected" patterns? How do you make sure your application is secure? What's the best way of leveraging the internal workings of connection management to maximize application performance?

I love the book you're holding in your hands because it tackles those issues, the hard ones that come up when you're solving real problems. When you're writing an application, you'll run into most if not all of these issues, and I find this book to be the right reference to review to make sure you leave no loose ends in the work you do.

Pablo Castro
ADO.NET Technical Lead
Microsoft Corporation

Acknowledgments

To Kathleen Atkins, whose professionalism shone even as deadlines neared, thank you for your wonderful feedback and overwhelming interest in making this book successful.

Thanks to Kurt Meyer, whose technical perspective and guidance ensured consistency and conciseness in this book's text and sample code.

Pablo Castro, you are an amazing person. I always find your seminars provide an insightful perspective on real-world problems, with astounding solutions. Thank you very much for providing the foreword for this book.

Thanks to Ina Chang for her careful copy editing.

I would like to thank Lynn Finnel for her help and truly interesting advice and comments.

Thanks to Robert Lyon for his time and effort in helping to ensure the technical accuracy of this book.

I'd like to thank Ben Ryan for convincing me to write another book.

I would like to thank the Microsoft DataWorks, Visual Studio .NET, and SQL Server teams for providing the most flexible and powerful data access technologies in the world.

To everyone at Microsoft Press who has played a role in getting my book to the public, thank you for your hard work, and thanks for making this book venture a positive experience for me.

Introduction

Microsoft ADO.NET 2.0 represents a major improvement in data access capabilities. You'll see little resemblance between the object model in the original release of ADO included in Microsoft Visual Studio 6 and the improved object model in the new release included in Visual Studio 2005. ADO.NET 2.0 contains many changes that simplify development by requiring less code, and it has new capabilities that enable you to write more database-agnostic code, which means you will have a much easier time writing code without knowledge of the database server that will be used.

This book dives deep into advanced implementations of the new and old ADO.NET features that make up the current release. Complex problems rarely have a single solution, so I offer a comparative analysis whenever possible to highlight the benefits and drawbacks of several possible solutions.

Who This Book Is For

Although this book does cover advanced topics, readers are not expected to be advanced programmers, but it is important that you have solid programming skills and experience using Visual Studio. Every chapter starts by laying the foundation for the topic covered in the chapter. To help you understand the topics covered later in the book, the first two chapters even give you an overview of the ADO.NET classes. If you understand the need to store data in a database and have had some experience using any version of ADO, this book is for you.

If you are already familiar with the material covered in a given chapter, then by all means, skip ahead as needed, and don't forget that in many cases the index can direct you straight to the solution for a problem that you are trying to solve.

How This Book Is Organized

This book is probably best used as a reference that provides ideas for and solutions to the problems that you encounter when working with data, but I have connected topics in each chapter so you can also get a more comprehensive view by reading the book sequentially. You can follow cross-references to other chapters as needed to strengthen your understanding of the given topic.

Conventions

Throughout this book, names of classes, properties, variables, and other program elements are in italics. Structured Query Language (SQL) statements such as the WHERE clause are in uppercase.

Microsoft Visual Basic and C# code samples are shown together in the following format.

Visual Basic

```
Visual Basic version of cool code here
```

C#

```
C# version of cool code here
```

Output, or code that is shown for reading purposes only (that is, anything you are not expected to type), is presented in a screened format, as follows.

Sample Output

```
Item      Cost
 1      123.45
 2        2.99
 3       83.21
 4      543.56
```

System Requirements

You'll need the following hardware and software to build and run the code samples for this book:

- Microsoft Windows XP Professional with Service Pack 2 (SP2), Windows Server 2003 with Service Pack 1 (SP1), or Windows 2000 with Service Pack 4 (SP4).
- Visual Studio 2005 Standard Edition or Professional Edition. (The latter is required for Chapter 9 sample code.)
- Microsoft SQL Server 2005 Express (included with Visual Studio 2005) and/or Microsoft SQL Server 2005. (See the next section.)
- 600 MHz Pentium or compatible processor (1 GHz Pentium recommended).
- 192 MB RAM (256 MB or more recommended).
- 800 x 600 or higher resolution video monitor with at least 256 colors (1024 x 768 High Color 16-bit recommended).
- DVD-ROM drive.
- Microsoft Mouse or compatible pointing device.

SQL Server 2005 vs. SQL Server 2005 Express Edition

I have tried to use SQL Server 2005 Express Edition (SQL Server Express) where possible because it's easy to use. Further, SQL Server Express makes it easy to set up standalone samples because the database files can simply be included in the project. Some chapters use SQL

Server 2005 because the features being covered are not available in SQL Server Express or because they are easier to use in SQL Server 2005.

The following table shows which release of SQL Server 2005 is used in the sample code, using these entries:

- *N/A* Not applicable; database access not required
- *Yes* Used in the code sample
- *No* Not usable for the code sample
- *Possible* Can optionally be used in place of the other version but requires connection string change

SQL Server Edition Used for Sample Code

Chapter and Topics	SQL Server 2005	SQL Server 2005 Express Edition
1: Overview of ADO.NET Disconnected Classes	N/A	N/A
2: Overview of ADO.NET Connected Classes	Yes, Possible	Yes, Possible
3: ADO.NET Trace Logging	Yes	No
4: Advanced Connectivity to the Data Store a. *ConnectionStringBuilder* b. Asynchronous access c. Connection pooling/failover d. *StatisticsTest*	 a. Possible b. Yes c. Yes d. Possible	 a. Yes b. Possible c. No d. Yes
5: Working with Disconnected Data	Possible	Yes
6: Working with Relational Disconnected Data	Possible	Yes
7: Working with the Windows Data Grid Control	Possible	Yes
8: Working with the Web Data Grid Control	Possible	Yes
9: Working with the SQLCLR	Yes	No
10: Understanding Transactions	Possible	Yes
11: Retrieving Metadata	Possible	Yes
12: Data Caching for Performance a. *SqlDependency* b. *SqlCacheDependency* c. *CommandNotification*	 a. Yes b. Yes c. Yes	 a. No b. Possible c. No
13: Implementing Security a. Security b. *PartialTrust* c. *EncryptedWebSite* d. *SqlInjection*	 a. N/A b. Possible c. Possible d. Possible	 a. N/A b. Yes c. Yes d. Yes

SQL Server Edition Used for Sample Code

Chapter and Topics	SQL Server 2005	SQL Server 2005 Express Edition
14: Working with Large Objects (LOBs, BLOBs, and CLOBs)	Possible	Yes
15: Working with XML Data	Possible	Yes

Configuring SQL Server 2005 Express Edition

This book requires that you have access to SQL Server 2005 Express Edition (and/or SQL Server 2005) to create and use the Northwind Traders and the Pubs sample databases. If you are using SQL Server 2005 Express, log in as Administrator on your computer, and follow these steps to grant access to the user account that you will use for performing the exercises.

1. On the Windows Start menu, click All Programs, Accessories, Command Prompt to open a command prompt window.
2. In the command prompt window, type the following command:

   ```
   sqlcmd -S YourServer\SQLExpress -E
   ```

   Replace *YourServer* with the name of your computer. You can find the name of your computer by running the *hostname* command in the command prompt window before running the *sqlcmd* command.
3. At the 1> prompt, type the following command, including the square brackets, and then press Enter:

   ```
   SP_GRANTLOGIN [YourServer\UserName]
   ```

   Replace *YourServer* with the name of your computer, and replace *UserName* with the name of the user account that you will be using.
4. At the 2> prompt, type the following command, and then press Enter:

   ```
   GO
   ```

   If you see an error message, make sure that you typed the SP_GRANTLOGIN command correctly, including the square brackets.
5. At the 1> prompt, type the following command, including the square brackets, and then press Enter:

   ```
   SP_ADDSRVROLEMEMBER [YourServer\UserName], dbcreator
   ```

6. At the 2> prompt, type the following command, and then press Enter:

   ```
   GO
   ```

   If you see an error message, make sure that you typed the SP_ADDSRVROLEMEMBER command correctly, including the square brackets.

7. At the 1> prompt, type the following command, and then press Enter:

   ```
   EXIT
   ```

8. Close the command prompt window.

Prerelease Software

This book was reviewed and tested against the September 2005 release of Visual Studio 2005 and SQL Server 2005. The September release was the last preview before the final release of Visual Studio 2005 and SQL Server 2005. This book is expected to be fully compatible with the final release of Visual Studio 2005. If there are any changes or corrections for this book, they will be collected and added to a Microsoft Knowledge Base article. See the "Support for This Book" section in this Introduction for more information.

Technology Updates

As technologies related to this book are updated, links to additional information will be added to the Microsoft Press Technology Updates Web page. Visit this page periodically for updates on Visual Studio 2005 and other technologies.

http://www.microsoft.com/mspress/updates/

Code Samples

All of the code samples discussed in this book can be downloaded from the book's companion content page at the following address:

http://www.microsoft.com/mspress/companion/0-7356-2141-1/

Also, be sure to visit my Web site for additional materials and information:

http://GJTT.com

Support for This Book

Every effort has been made to ensure the accuracy of this book and of the companion content. As corrections or changes are collected, they will be added to a Microsoft Knowledge Base article. To view the list of known corrections for this book, visit the following article:

http://support.microsoft.com/kb/905043

Microsoft Press provides support for books and companion content at the following Web site:

http://www.microsoft.com/learning/support/books/

Questions and Comments

If you have comments, questions, or ideas regarding the book or the companion content, or questions that are not answered by visiting the sites above, please send Microsoft Press e-mail at *mspinput@microsoft.com*, or send postal mail to:

Microsoft Press

Attn: *Programming Microsoft ADO.NET 2.0 Applications: Advanced Topics* Editor

One Microsoft Way

Redmond, WA 98052-6399

Please note that Microsoft software product support is not offered through the preceding addresses.

Chapter 1

Overview of ADO.NET Disconnected Classes

The ADO.NET class hierarchy can be split into two categories: connected and disconnected objects. Figure 1-1 shows the principal connected and disconnected classes. This chapter describes the disconnected classes that are shown in the diagram and many other classes of this category as well. I cover the disconnected classes in detail because these classes can be used without your ever creating a connection to a data store. In Chapter 2, I'll discuss the connected classes in detail.

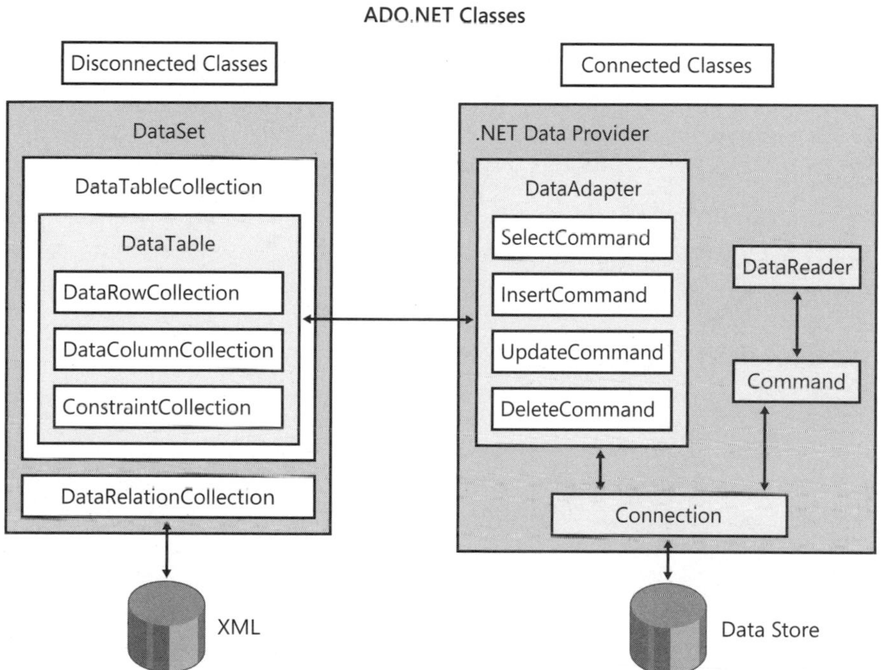

Figure 1-1 The more familiar disconnected and connected classes

The classes shown in Figure 1-1 existed in previous versions of ADO.NET, but these are the primary ADO.NET classes, so knowing them well is important if you want to successfully implement an ADO.NET solution. In ADO.NET 2.0, the primary classes have additional methods and properties to improve functionality and performance of your code.

The disconnected data access classes are instantiated within the client application and (as I said earlier) can be used without ever connecting to a data store. Because you must use the

DataTable object when you're using disconnected classes, this chapter begins by covering it and the objects that the *DataTable* object works with closely. Next I'll discuss the *DataSet* object in detail. Finally I'll describe the *DataTableReader* object, an ADO.NET object that is new in version 2.0.

Getting Started with the *DataTable* Object

The *DataTable* object represents tabular data as an in-memory table of rows, columns, and constraints. You must use the *DataTable* object to perform any disconnected data access. You can create a *DataTable* object explicitly by creating an instance of the *DataTable* class, adding *DataColumn* objects that define the data to be held, and adding *DataRow* objects containing the data. The following code, which creates a table for storing car information, demonstrates the creation of a *DataTable*:

Visual Basic

```
'Create the DataTable named "Auto"
Dim auto As New DataTable("Auto")
```

C#

```
//Create the DataTable named "Auto"
DataTable auto = new DataTable ("Auto");
```

This code creates an empty *DataTable* for which the *TableName* property is *Auto*. You can use the *TableName* property to access this *DataTable* when this *DataTable* is in a *DataTableCollection* (as detailed later in this chapter).

Adding *DataColumn* Objects to Create a Schema

The *DataTable* object is of little use until it has a schema. You create the schema by adding *DataColumn* objects and setting the constraints of each column. Constraints help maintain data integrity by limiting the data that can be placed in the column. The following code adds *DataColumn* objects to the auto *DataTable* object:

Visual Basic

```
'Add the DataColumn object using all properties
Dim vin As New DataColumn("Vin")
vin.DataType = GetType(String)
vin.MaxLength = 23
vin.Unique = True
vin.AllowDBNull = False
vin.Caption = "VIN"
auto.Columns.Add(vin)
'Add the DataColumn using defaults
Dim make As New DataColumn("Make") 'default is String
make.MaxLength = 35 'default is -1
make.AllowDBNull = False 'default is True
auto.Columns.Add(make)
Dim year As New DataColumn("Year",GetType(Integer))
```

```
year.AllowDBNull = False
auto.Columns.Add(year)
'Derived column using expression
Dim yearMake As New DataColumn("Year and Make")
yearMake.MaxLength = 70
yearMake.Expression = "Year + ' ' + Make"
auto.Columns.Add(yearMake)
```

C#

```
//Add the DataColumn using all properties
DataColumn vin = new DataColumn("Vin");
vin.DataType = typeof(string);
vin.MaxLength = 23;
vin.Unique = true;
vin.AllowDBNull = false;
vin.Caption = "VIN";
auto.Columns.Add(vin);
//Add the DataColumn using defaults
DataColumn make = new DataColumn("Make");
make.MaxLength = 35;
make.AllowDBNull = false;
auto.Columns.Add(make);
DataColumn year = new DataColumn("Year", typeof(int));
year.AllowDBNull = false;
auto.Columns.Add(year);
//Derived column using expression
DataColumn yearMake = new DataColumn("Year and Make");
yearMake.DataType = typeof(string);
yearMake.MaxLength = 70;
yearMake.Expression = "Year + ' ' + Make";
auto.Columns.Add(yearMake);
```

With the addition of each *DataColumn* object, the column's name is specified in the constructor. The *DataType* property is set to *string* for all of the *DataColumn* objects except the *year*, which is set to an integer (int) to limit this column to numeric data. The *MaxLength* property limits the length of the string data. Setting the *Unique* property to *true* creates an index to prevent duplication of entries. The *AllowDBNull* property is set to false to ensure that the column is populated with data. The *Caption* property isn't really a constraint; it's a string that holds the column heading when this *DataTable* object is used with graphic data grid controls. The *yearMake DataColumn* object demonstrates the creation of a calculated column, in this case by assigning an expression. Adding a calculated column is especially beneficial when data is available but not in the correct format.

Notice that some of the *DataColumn* objects were created without specifying values for all of the properties. The default values for the common properties are as follows:

- *DataType* Default is the string type.
- *MaxLength* Default is −1, which means that no check for maximum length is performed.
- *Unique* Default is *false*, which allows the existence of duplicate values.

- *AllowDBNull* Default is *true*, which means the *DataColumn* does not need to have a value.
- *Caption* Default is the *DataColumn* object's *Name* property value.

Creating Primary Key Columns

The primary key of a *DataTable* object consists of a column or columns that make up a unique identity for each data row. In the previous example, the vehicle identification might be considered to be a unique key from which data for a given auto can be retrieved. In other situations, getting a unique key might require combining two or more fields. For example, a sales order might contain sales order details. The primary key for each of the sales order detail rows might be the combination of the order number and the line number. The *PrimaryKey* property must be set to an array of *DataColumn* objects to accommodate composite (multiple) keys. The following code shows how to set the *PrimaryKey* property for the *auto DataTable* object:

Visual Basic

```
'Set the Primary Key
auto.PrimaryKey = new DataColumn (){vin}
```

C#

```
//Set the Primary Key
auto.PrimaryKey = new DataColumn [] {vin};
```

Creating *DataRow* Objects to Hold Data

After the *DataTable* object is created and contains *DataColumn* objects, you can populate the *DataTable* object by adding *DataRow* objects. A *DataRow* object can be created only in the context of a *DataTable* because the *DataRow* must conform to constraints of the *DataTable* object's columns.

Adding Data to the *DataTable*

The *DataTable* object contains a *Rows* collection, which contains a collection of *DataRow* objects. There are several ways to insert data into the *Rows* collection.

The *Rows* collection has an *Add* method that accepts a *DataRow*. The *Add* method is overloaded to accept an array of objects instead of a *DataRow* object. If an array of objects is passed to the *Add* method, the array object count must match the quantity of *DataColumn* objects that the *DataTable* has.

The *DataTable* object also contains a *Load* method, which can be used to update existing *DataRow* objects or load new *DataRow* objects. The *DataTable* requires the *PrimaryKey* property to be set so that the *DataTable* object can locate the *DataRow* that is to be updated. The

Load method accepts an array of objects and a *LoadOption* enumeration value. The possible values for the *LoadOption* enumeration are shown in Table 1-1.

Table 1-1 *LoadOption* Enumeration Members

LoadOption Member	Description
OverwriteChanges	Overwrites the original *DataRowVersion* and the current *DataRowVersion* and changes the *RowState* to *Unchanged*. New rows have a *RowState* of *Unchanged* as well.
PreserveChanges (default)	Overwrites the original *DataRowVersion* but does not modify the current *DataRowVersion*. New rows have a *RowState* of *Unchanged* as well.
Upsert	Overwrites the current *DataRowVersion* but does not modify the original *DataRowVersion*. New rows have a *RowState* of *Added*. Rows that had a *RowState* of *Unchanged* have a *RowState* of *Unchanged* if the current *DataRowVersion* is the same as the original *DataRowVersion*, but if they are different, the *RowState* is *Modified*.

The following code snippet demonstrates the methods of creating and adding data into the auto *DataTable*:

Visual Basic

```
'Add new DataRow by creating the DataRow first
Dim newAuto As DataRow = auto.NewRow()
newAuto ("Vin") = "123456789ABCD "
newAuto ("Make") = "Ford"
newAuto ("Year") = 2002
auto.Rows.Add(newAuto)
'Add new DataRow by simply passing the values
auto.Rows.Add("987654321XYZ", "Buick", 2001)
'Load DataRow, replacing existing contents, if existing
auto.LoadDataRow(new object() _
   { "987654321XYZ", "Jeep", 2002 },LoadOption.OverwriteChanges)
```

C#

```
//Add New DataRow by creating the DataRow first
DataRow newAuto = auto.NewRow();
newAuto ["Vin"] = "123456789ABCD";
newAuto ["Make"] = "Ford";
newAuto ["Year"] = 2002;
auto.Rows.Add(newAuto);
//Add New DataRow by simply adding the values
auto.Rows.Add("987654321XYZ", "Buick", 2001);
//Load DataRow, replacing existing contents, if existing
auto.LoadDataRow(new object[]
   { "987654321XYZ", "Jeep", 2002 },LoadOption.OverwriteChanges);
```

This code adds new *DataRow* objects to the *auto DataTable*. The first example explicitly creates a new *DataRow* using the *NewRow* method on the *auto DataTable*. The next example adds a new *DataRow* by simply passing the values into the *auto.Rows.Add* method. Remember that nothing has been permanently stored to a database. We'll cover sending updates in Chapter 2.

Viewing the State of the *DataRow* Object Using *DataRowState*

The *DataRow* goes through a series of states that can be viewed and filtered at any time. You can retrieve the current state of the *DataRow* from the *RowState* property, which contains a *DataRowState* enumeration. The *DataRowState* values are described in Table 1-2.

Table 1-2 *RowState* Enumeration Members

RowState Value	Description
Detached	The *DataRow* has been created but not added to a *DataTable*.
Added	The *DataRow* has been created and added to the *DataTable*.
Unchanged	The *DataRow* has not changed since the last call to the *AcceptChanges* method. When the *AcceptChanges* method is called, the *DataRow* changes to this state.
Modified	The *DataRow* has been modified since the last time the *AcceptChanges* method was called.
Deleted	The *DataRow* has been deleted using the *Delete* method of the *DataRow*.

You can view the *RowState* property of the *DataRow* at any time to determine the current state of the *DataRow*. Figure 1-2 shows the *RowState* transitions at different times in the *DataRow* object's life.

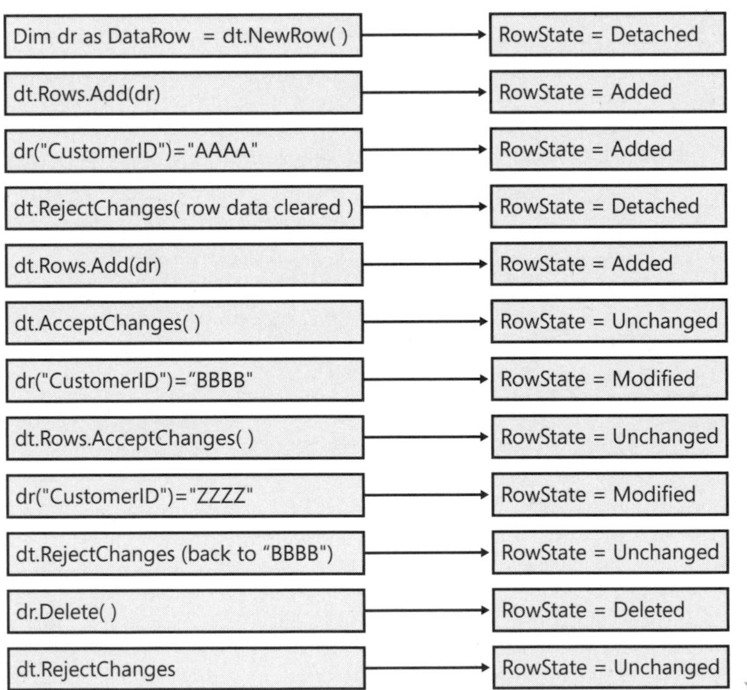

Figure 1-2 The *RowState* as it changes during the lifetime of a *DataRow* object

Notice that after the CustomerID is assigned a value of "AAAA", the *RowState* does not change to *Modified*. The *RowState* is still *Added* because *RowState* is an indicator of an action required to send an update of this data to the database. The fact that "AAAA" was placed into the CustomerID is not as important as the fact that the *DataRow* needs to be added to the database.

Managing Multiple Copies of Data Using the *DataRowVersion*

The *DataRow* can hold up to three versions of data: Original, Current, and Proposed. When the *DataRow* is loaded, it contains a single copy of the data. At that time, only the Current version exists. When the *DataRow* is placed into edit mode by the *BeginEdit* method, changes to the data are placed in a second instance of the data, called the Proposed version. When the *EndEdit* method is executed, the Current version becomes the Original version, the Proposed version becomes the Current version, and the Proposed version no longer exists. After *EndEdit* is called, there are two instances of the *DataRow* data, the Original and the Current versions. If the *BeginEdit* method is called again, the Current version of the data is copied to a third instance of the data, which is the Proposed version. Once again, calling the *EndEdit* method causes the Proposed version to become the Current version and the Proposed version to no longer exist.

When you retrieve data from the *DataRow*, the *DataRowVersion* can be specified as well. Table 1-3 describes the *DataRowVersion* enumeration members that you can specify.

Table 1-3 *DataRowVersion* Enumeration Members

DataRowVersion Value	Description
Current	The current value of the *DataRow*, even after changes have been made. This version exists in all situations, except when the *DataRowState* is *Deleted*. If the *DataRowState* is *Deleted*, an exception is thrown.
Default	If the *DataRowState* is *Added* or *Modified*, the default version is Current. If the *DataRowState* is *Deleted*, an exception is thrown. If the *BeginEdit* method has been executed, the version is Proposed.
Original	The value that was originally loaded into the *DataRow*, or the value at the time the last *AcceptChanges* method was executed. Note that this version is not populated until the *DataRowState* becomes *Modified*, *Unchanged*, or *Deleted*. If the *DataRowState* is *Deleted*, this information is retrievable. If the *DataRowState* is *Added*, a *VersionNotFoundException* is thrown.
Proposed	The value at the time of editing the *DataRow*. If the *DataRowState* is *Deleted*, an exception is thrown. If the *BeginEdit* method has not been explicitly executed or if *BeginEdit* was implicitly executed via editing a detached *DataRow* (an orphaned *DataRow* object that has not been added to a *DataTable* object), a *VersionNotFoundException* is thrown.

The *DataRow* contains the *HasVersion* method that can be used to query for the existence of a particular *DataRowVersion*. Using the *HasVersion* method means that you can check for the existence of a *DataRowVersion* before attempting to retrieve a version that does not exist. The following code snippet demonstrates how to retrieve a string using the *RowState* and the *DataRowVersion*. This sample uses the *HasVersion* method to retrieve the *DataRow* version information without throwing an exception.

Visual Basic

```
Private Function GetDataRowInfo( _
ByVal row As DataRow, ByVal columnName As String) _
   As String

   Dim retVal As String = String.Format( _
      "RowState: {0} " + VbCrLf, row.RowState)

   Dim versionString As String
   For Each versionString In [Enum].GetNames(GetType(DataRowVersion))
      Dim version As DataRowVersion = _
         CType([Enum].Parse(GetType(DataRowVersion), versionString), _
         DataRowVersion)

      If (row.HasVersion(version)) Then
         retVal += String.Format( _
            "Version: {0} Value: {1}" + vbCrLf, _
            version, row(columnName, version))
      Else
         retVal += String.Format( _
            "Version: {0} does not exist." + VbCrLf, _
            version)
      End If
   Next
   Return retVal
End Function
```

C#

```
private string GetDataRowInfo(DataRow row, string columnName)
{
   string retVal=string.Format(
      "RowState: {0} \r\n",
      row.RowState);

   foreach (string versionString in Enum.GetNames(typeof (DataRowVersion)))
   {
      DataRowVersion version = (
         DataRowVersion)Enum.Parse(
            typeof(DataRowVersion),versionString);

      if (row.HasVersion(version))
      {
         retVal += string.Format(
            "Version: {0} Value: {1} \r\n",
            version, row[columnName, version]);
      }
      else
      {
         retVal += string.Format(
```

```
            "Version: {0} does not exist.\r\n",
            version);
        }
    }
    return retVal;
}
```

Resetting the Slate Using the *AcceptChanges* and *RejectChanges* Methods

You can use the *AcceptChanges* method to reset the *DataRow* state to *Unchanged*. This method exists on the *DataRow*, *DataTable*, and *DataSet* objects. (I'll cover the *DataSet* object later in this chapter.) In a typical data environment (after data has been loaded), the *DataRow* state of the loaded rows is set to *Added*. Calling *AcceptChanges* on the *DataTable* resets the *RowState* of all of the *DataRow* objects to *Unchanged*. Next, if you modify the *DataRow* objects, their *RowState* changes to *Modified*. When it is time to save the data, you can easily query the *DataTable* object for its changes by using the *DataTable* object's *GetChanges* method. This method returns a *DataTable* that is populated only with the *DataRow* objects that have changed since the last time that *AcceptChanges* was executed. Only these changes need to be sent to the data store. After the changes have been successfully sent to the data store, you must change the state of the *DataRow* objects to *Unchanged*, which essentially indicates that the *DataRow* objects are in sync with the data store. You use the *AcceptChanges* method for this purpose. Note that executing the *AcceptChanges* method also causes the *DataRow* object's *Current DataRowVersion* to be copied to the *DataRow* object's *Original* version.

You use the *RejectChanges* method to roll back the *DataRow* to the point in time when you last called the *AcceptChanges* method. You cannot roll back to a point in time that is earlier than the last time *AcceptChanges* was called because the *AcceptChanges* method overwrites the Original *DataRowVersion*. In other words, you can call the *RejectChanges* method to roll back any changes you didn't accept. Note that both *AcceptChanges* and *RejectChanges* typically reset the *RowState* to *Unchanged*, but *RejectChanges* also copies the *DataRow* object's *Original DataRowVersion* to the *DataRow* object's *Current DataRowVersion*. Also, if the *RowState* was set to *Added* before you called *RejectChanges*, the *RowState* becomes *Detached* because the *AcceptChanges* method has never been executed on a *DataRow* that has a *RowState* of *Added*, so an Original *DataRowVersion* does not exist.

Using *SetAdded* and *SetModified* to Change the *RowState*

The *DataRow* contains the *SetAdded* and *SetModified* methods, which allow the *DataRow* object to be forcibly set to *Added* or *Modified*, respectively. These operations are useful when you want to force a *DataRow* to be stored in a data store that is different from the data store from which the *DataRow* was originally loaded. These methods can be executed only on *DataRow* objects whose *RowState* is *Unchanged*. An attempt to execute these methods on a *DataRow* object with a different *RowState* throws the exception called *InvalidOperationException*.

If the *SetAdded* method is executed, the *DataRow* object discards its *Original DataRowVersion* because *DataRow* objects that have a *RowState* of *Added* never contain an *Original DataRowVersion*.

If the *SetModified* method is executed, the *DataRow* object's *RowState* is simply changed to *Modified* without modifying the *Original* or *Current DataRowVersion*.

Deleting the *DataRow*, and What About Undeleting?

The *DataRow* contains a *Delete* method, which you can use to set the *RowState* of the *DataRow* to *Deleted*. *DataRow* objects that have a *RowState* of *Deleted* indicate rows that need to be deleted from the data store. When the *DataRow* object is deleted, the *Current* and *Proposed DataRowVersion* are discarded, but the *Original DataRowVersion* remains. The *DataRow* is not formally removed from the *DataTable* until the *AcceptChanges* method has been executed.

Sometimes you need to undelete a *DataRow*. The *DataRow* object doesn't have an *UnDelete* method, but you can use the *RejectChanges* method to perform an effective undelete in some situations. Be aware that executing the *RejectChanges* method copies the *Original DataRowVersion* to the *Current DataRowVersion*. This effectively restores the *DataRow* object to its state at the time the last *AcceptChanges* method was executed, but any subsequent changes that were made to the data prior to deleting are also discarded.

Enumerating the *DataTable*

It is possible to loop through the rows and columns of the *DataTable* by using a *foreach* statement. The following code shows how the rows and columns of a *DataTable* can be enumerated.

Visual Basic

```
Dim buffer As System.Text.StringBuilder
buffer = New System.Text.StringBuilder()
For Each dc As DataColumn In auto.Columns
    buffer.Append( _
        String.Format("{0,15} ", dc.ColumnName))
Next
buffer.Append(vbCrLf)
For Each dr As DataRow In auto.Rows
    For Each dc As DataColumn In auto.Columns
        buffer.Append( _
            String.Format("{0,15} ", dr(dc)))
    Next
    buffer.Append(vbCrLf)
Next
TextBox1.Text = buffer.ToString()
```

C#

```
System.Text.StringBuilder buffer;
buffer = new System.Text.StringBuilder();
foreach (DataColumn dc in auto.Columns)
{
```

```
    buffer.Append(
        string.Format("{0,15} ",dc.ColumnName));
}
buffer.Append("\r\n");
foreach (DataRow dr in auto.Rows)
{
    foreach( DataColumn dc in auto.Columns)
    {
        buffer.Append(
            string.Format("{0,15} ", dr[dc]));
    }
    buffer.Append("\r\n");
}
textBox1.Text = buffer.ToString();
```

The code begins by simply collecting the column names to use as a header and places this information into the *StringBuilder* called *buffer*. After the header is rendered into the buffer, the table rows and columns are enumerated, and all values are placed into the buffer. Code such as this can be used to generically walk a *DataTable* and perform an action on all of the data. Figure 1-3 shows the output of this code. (The TextBox font is set to Courier New to get the columns to line up.)

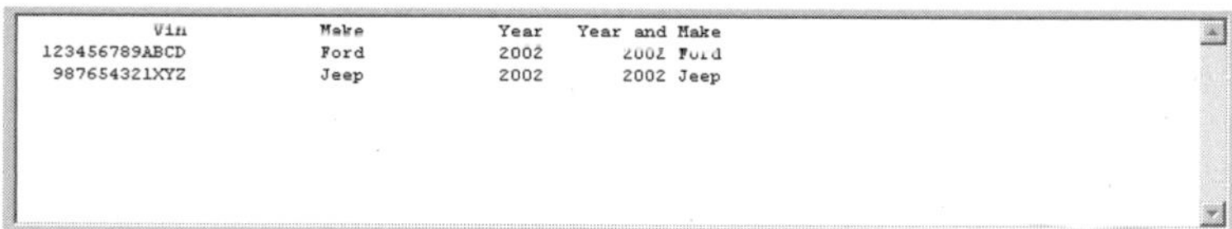

Figure 1-3 The output when enumerating the *DataTable* object's rows and columns

Copying and Cloning the *DataTable*

Sometimes you want to create a full copy of a *DataTable*. You can do this by using the *DataTable* object's *Copy* method, which copies the *DataTable* object's schema and data. The following code snippet shows how to invoke the *Copy* method.

Visual Basic

```
Dim copy as DataTable = auto.Copy( )
```

C#

```
DataTable copy = auto.Copy( );
```

On some occasions you might need a copy of the *DataTable* schema without data. To copy just the schema without data, you can invoke the *DataTable* object's *Clone* method. This method is commonly used when an empty copy of the *DataTable* is required; at a later time, *DataRow* objects can be added. The following code shows the *Clone* method.

Visual Basic

```
Dim clone as DataTable = auto.Clone( )
```

C#

```
DataTable clone = auto.Clone( );
```

Importing *DataRow* Objects into a *DataTable*

After cloning a *DataTable*, you might need to copy certain *DataRow* objects from one *DataTable* to another. The *DataTable* contains an *ImportRow* method, which you can use to copy a *DataRow* from a *DataTable* that has the same schema. The *ImportRow* method is useful in situations where the *Current* and *Original DataRowVersion* must be maintained. For example, after editing a *DataTable*, you might want to copy the changed *DataRow* objects to a different *DataTable* but maintain the *Original* and *Current DataRowVersion*. The *ImportRow* method on the *DataTable* object imports the *DataRow* objects as long as a *DataRow* with the same *PrimaryKey* does not exist. (If a duplicate *DataRow* exists, a *ConstraintException* is thrown.) The following code snippet shows the process for cloning the *DataTable* and then copying a single *DataRow* to the cloned copy.

Visual Basic

```
Dim clone as DataTable = auto.Clone( )
clone.ImportRow(auto.Rows(0))
```

C#

```
DataTable clone = auto.Clone();
clone.ImportRow(auto.Rows[0]);
```

Using the *DataTable* with XML Data

The contents of a *DataTable* can be written to an XML file or stream using the *DataTable* object's *WriteXml* method. If this method is executed with a simple filename, the auto.xml file looks like the following:

XML File

```
<?xml version="1.0" standalone="yes"?>
<DocumentElement>
  <Auto>
    <Vin>123456789ABC</Vin>
    <Make>BMW</Make>
    <Year>2005</Year>
    <Year_x0020_and_x0020_Make>2005 BMW</Year_x0020_and_x0020_Make>
  </Auto>
  <Auto>
    <Vin>123456789DEF</Vin>
    <Make>BMW</Make>
    <Year>2004</Year>
    <Year_x0020_and_x0020_Make>2004 BMW</Year_x0020_and_x0020_Make>
  </Auto>
  <Auto>
    <Vin>999888777ABC</Vin>
    <Make>Ford</Make>
    <Year>2003</Year>
```

```
    <Year_x0020_and_x0020_Make>2003 Ford</Year_x0020_and_x0020_Make>
  </Auto>
  <Auto>
    <Vin>987654321XYZ</Vin>
    <Make>Jeep</Make>
    <Year>2002</Year>
    <Year_x0020_and_x0020_Make>2002 Jeep</Year_x0020_and_x0020_Make>
  </Auto>
</DocumentElement>
```

This example uses a *DocumentElement* as the root element and uses repeating *Auto* elements for each *DataRow*. The data for each *DataRow* is nested as elements within each *Auto* element. Also notice that an XML element name cannot have spaces, so *Year and Make* were automatically converted to *Year_x0020_and_x0020_Make*.

You can tune the XML output by providing an XML schema or by setting properties on the *DataTable* and its objects. To change the name of the repeating element for the *DataRow* objects from *Auto* to *Car*, you can change the *DataTable* object's *TableName*. To change the *Vin*, *Make*, and *Year* to XML attributes, you can set each *DataColumn* object's *ColumnMapping* property to *MappingType.Attribute*. The "Year and Make" column is a calculated column, so its data does not need to be stored. To prevent the "Year and Make" column from storing its data, set its *ColumnMapping* property to *MappingType.Hidden*. Table 1-6 describes the *MappingType* enumeration members and the following snippets show the necessary code and the resulting XML file contents.

Visual Basic

```
auto.TableName = "Car"
auto.Columns("Vin").ColumnMapping = MappingType.Attribute
auto.Columns("Make").ColumnMapping = MappingType.Attribute
auto.Columns("Year").ColumnMapping = MappingType.Attribute
auto.Columns("Year and Make").ColumnMapping = MappingType.Hidden
```

C#

```
auto.TableName = "Car";
auto.Columns["Vin"].ColumnMapping = MappingType.Attribute;
auto.Columns["Make"].ColumnMapping = MappingType.Attribute;
auto.Columns["Year"].ColumnMapping = MappingType.Attribute;
auto.Columns["Year and Make"].ColumnMapping = MappingType.Hidden;
```

XML

```
<?xml version="1.0" standalone="yes"?>
<DocumentElement>
  <Car Vin="123456789ABC" Make="BMW" Year="2005" />
  <Car Vin="123456789DEF" Make="BMW" Year="2004" />
  <Car Vin="999888777ABC" Make="Ford" Year="2003" />
  <Car Vin="987654321XYZ" Make="Jeep" Year="2002" />
</DocumentElement>
```

The resulting XML file is quite compact, but one problem is that the data types aren't saved, so all data is considered to be string data. The solution is to store the XML schema with the data, which you can do by including the *XmlWriteMode.WriteSchema* enumeration when you are saving, as shown here:

Visual Basic

```
auto.WriteXml("C:\auto.xml", XmlWriteMode.WriteSchema)
```

C#

```
auto.WriteXml(@"C:\auto.xml", XmlWriteMode.WriteSchema);
```

XML File

```
<?xml version="1.0" standalone="yes"?>
<DocumentElement>
  <xs:schema id="NewDataSet" xmlns=""
   xmlns:xs="http://www.w3.org/2001/XMLSchema"
   xmlns:msdata="urn:schemas-microsoft-com:xml-msdata">
    <xs:element name="NewDataSet" msdata:IsDataSet="true"
   msdata:MainDataTable="Car" msdata:Locale="en-US">
      <xs:complexType>
        <xs:choice minOccurs="0" maxOccurs="unbounded">
          <xs:element name="Car">
            <xs:complexType>
              <xs:attribute name="Vin" msdata:Caption="VIN" use="required">
                <xs:simpleType>
                  <xs:restriction base="xs:string">
                    <xs:maxLength value="23" />
                  </xs:restriction>
                </xs:simpleType>
              </xs:attribute>
              <xs:attribute name="Make" use="required">
                <xs:simpleType>
                  <xs:restriction base="xs:string">
                    <xs:maxLength value="35" />
                  </xs:restriction>
                </xs:simpleType>
              </xs:attribute>
              <xs:attribute name="Year" type="xs:int" use="required" />
              <xs:attribute name="Year_x0020_and_x0020_Make"
                 msdata:ReadOnly="true"
                 msdata:Expression="Year + ' ' + Make" use="prohibited">
                <xs:simpleType>
                  <xs:restriction base="xs:string">
                    <xs:maxLength value="70" />
                  </xs:restriction>
                </xs:simpleType>
              </xs:attribute>
            </xs:complexType>
          </xs:element>
        </xs:choice>
      </xs:complexType>
      <xs:unique msdata:TableNamespace="" name="Constraint1"
         msdata:PrimaryKey="true">
```

```
        <xs:selector xpath=".//Car" />
        <xs:field xpath="@Vin" />
      </xs:unique>
    </xs:element>
  </xs:schema>
  <Car Vin="123456789ABC" Make="BMW" Year="2005" />
  <Car Vin="123456789DEF" Make="BMW" Year="2004" />
  <Car Vin="999888777ABC" Make="Ford" Year="2003" />
  <Car Vin="987654321XYZ" Make="Jeep" Year="2002" />
</DocumentElement>
```

With the XML schema included in the file, the data types are defined. Notice that the XML schema also includes the maximum length settings for *Vin* and *Make*. A *DataTable* can be loaded with this XML file, and the resulting *DataTable* will be the same as the *DataTable* that was saved to the file. The following code snippet reads the XML file into a new *DataTable* object.

Visual Basic

```
Dim xmlTable as new DataTable()
xmlTable.ReadXml("C:\auto.xml")
```

C#

```
DataTable xmlTable = new DataTable();
xmlTable.ReadXml(@"C:\auto.xml");
```

Although the data for the "Year and Make" column was not saved, the column data is populated because this column is calculated and the schema contains the expression to re-create this column data.

Using the *DataView* as a Window into a *DataTable*

The *DataView* object provides a window into a *DataTable*. The *DataView* object can be sorted and filtered. A *DataTable* can have many *DataView* objects assigned to it, allowing the data to be viewed in many different ways without requiring it to be re-read from the database. The *Sort*, *RowFilter*, and *RowStateFilter* properties on the *DataView* object can be combined as needed. You can use the *DataView* object's *AllowDelete*, *AllowEdit*, and *AllowNew* properties to constrain user input.

Internally, the *DataView* object is essentially an index. You can provide a sort definition to sort the index in a certain order, and you can provide a filter to simply filter the index entries.

Ordering Data Using the *Sort* Property

The *Sort* property requires a sort expression. The default order for the sort is ascending, but you can specify *ASC* or *DESC* with a comma-separated list of columns to be sorted. The following code snippet shows how a *DataView* is created on the *auto DataTable* with a compound sort on the *Make* column in ascending order and on the *Year* column in descending order.

Visual Basic

```
Dim view as new DataView(auto)
view.Sort = "Make ASC, Year DESC"
```

C#

```
DataView view = new DataView(auto);
view.Sort = "Make ASC, Year DESC";
```

Narrowing the Search Using the *RowFilter* and *RowStateFilter* Properties

The filters comprise a *RowFilter* and a *RowStateFilter*. The *RowFilter* is set to a SQL WHERE clause without the word *"WHERE"*. The following code shows a filter on the *Make* column for cars beginning with the letter B and on the *Year* column for cars newer than 2003.

Visual Basic

```
Dim view as new DataView(auto)
view.RowFilter = "Make like 'B%' and Year > 2003"
```

C#

```
DataView view = new DataView(auto);
view.RowFilter = "Make like 'B%' and Year > 2003";
```

The *RowStateFilter* provides a filter base on the *DataRow* object's *RowState* property. This filter provides an extremely easy method of retrieving specific version information within the *DataTable*. The *RowStateFilter* requires the use of *DataViewRowState* enumeration values, which are shown in Table 1-4. The *DataViewRowState* enumeration is a bit-flag enumeration, which means you can use the OR operator on the enumeration members. For example, the default *RowState* filter value is set to display multiple states by using the OR operator to combine the *Unchanged*, *Added*, and *ModifiedCurrent* enumeration values.

Table 1-4 *DataViewRowState* Enumeration Members

DataViewRowState Value	Description
Added	Retrieves the *Current DataRowVersion* of *DataRow* objects that have a *RowState* of *Added.*
CurrentRows	Retrieves all *DataRow* objects that have a *Current DataRowVersion.*
Deleted	Retrieves the *Original DataRowVersion* of *DataRow* objects that have a *RowState* of *Deleted.*
ModifiedCurrent	Retrieves the *Current DataRowVersion* of *DataRow* objects that have a *RowState* of *Modified.*
ModifiedOriginal	Retrieves the *Original DataRowVersion* of *DataRow* objects that have a *RowState* of *Modified.*
None	Clears the *RowStateFilter* property.
OriginalRows	Retrieves the *DataRow* objects that have an *Original DataRowVersion.*
Unchanged	Retrieves *DataRow* objects that have a *RowState* of *Unchanged.*

The following code sample shows the use of the *RowStateFilter* to retrieve the *DataRow* objects that have a *RowState* of *Deleted*.

Visual Basic

```
Dim view as new DataView(auto)
view.RowFilter = "Make like 'B%' and Year > 2003"
view.RowStateFilter = DataViewRowState.Deleted
```

C#

```
DataView view = new DataView(auto);
view.RowFilter = "Make like 'B%' and Year > 2003";
view.RowStateFilter = DataViewRowState.Deleted;
```

Enumerating the *DataView*

The procedure for walking the *DataView* is similar to that for enumerating the *DataTable*, except the objects are different. The following code can be used to enumerate the rows and columns of a *DataView*.

Visual Basic

```
Dim view as new DataView(auto)
view.RowFilter = "Make like 'B%' and Year > 2003"
view.RowStateFilter = DataViewRowState.Deleted
Dim buffer As New System.Text.StringBuilder()
For Each dc As DataColumn In auto.Columns
    buffer.Append( _
        String.Format("{0,15} ", dc.ColumnName))
Next
buffer.Append(vbCrLf)
For Each dr As DataRowView In view
    For Each dc As DataColumn In auto.Columns
        buffer.Append( _
            String.Format("{0,15} ", dr.Row(dc)))
    Next
    buffer.Append(vbCrLf)
Next
TextBox1.Text = buffer.ToString()
```

C#

```
DataView view = new DataView(auto);
view.Sort = "Make ASC, Year DESC";
view.RowFilter = "Make like 'B%' and Year > 2003";

System.Text.StringBuilder buffer;
buffer = new System.Text.StringBuilder();
foreach (DataColumn dc in auto.Columns)
{
   buffer.Append(
      string.Format("{0,15} ", dc.ColumnName));
}
buffer.Append("\r\n");
foreach (DataRowView dr in view)
{
```

```
   foreach (DataColumn dc in auto.Columns)
   {
      buffer.Append(
         string.Format("{0,15} ", dr.Row[dc]));
   }
   buffer.Append("\r\n");
}
textBox1.Text = buffer.ToString();
```

This code creates a *DataView* based on the *Make*, beginning with the letter "B" and the *Year* being greater than 2003, sorted by *Make* ascending and *Year* descending, and formats the enumeration in a text box.

Exporting a *DataView* to a New *DataTable*

A *DataView* object can be used to export data from one *DataTable* object to another. This can be especially useful when a user-defined set of filters is applied and the user wants to convert the view that is seen into a new *DataTable*. Exporting to a new *DataTable* is done with the *DataView* object's *ToTable* method, as shown here.

Visual Basic

```
'here is the method signature
'Public Function ToTable(tableName as String, distinct as Boolean, _
'        ParamArray columnNames() as String) as System.Data.DataTable
Dim export as DataTable = view.ToTable( _
"MyAutoTable", true, "Vin", "Make", "Year")
```

C#

```
//here is the method signature
//DataTable DataView.ToTable(string tableName,
//         bool distinct, params string[] columns)
DataTable export = view.ToTable(
"MyAutoTable", true, "Vin", "Make", "Year");
```

This code snippet exports the data that is seen in the *DataView* called *"view"* to a new *DataTable* object named *"MyAutoTable"*. The boolean *true* is used to indicate whether the distinct values (which filter out duplicate values) or all values should be shown. The last parameters are an array of strings that represent the columns to include in the output.

Using a *DataSet* Object to Work with Lots of Data

The *DataSet* is a memory-based relational representation of data and is the primary disconnected data object. Conceptually, you can think of the *DataSet* as an in-memory relational database, but it is simply cached data and doesn't provide any of the transactional properties (atomicity, consistency, isolation, durability) that are essential to today's relational databases. The *DataSet* contains a collection of *DataTable* and *DataRelation* objects, as shown in Figure 1-4. The *DataTable* objects can contain unique and foreign key constraints to enforce data integrity. The *DataSet* also provides methods for cloning the *DataSet* schema, copying the *DataSet*, merging with other *DataSet* objects, and retrieving changes from the *DataSet*.

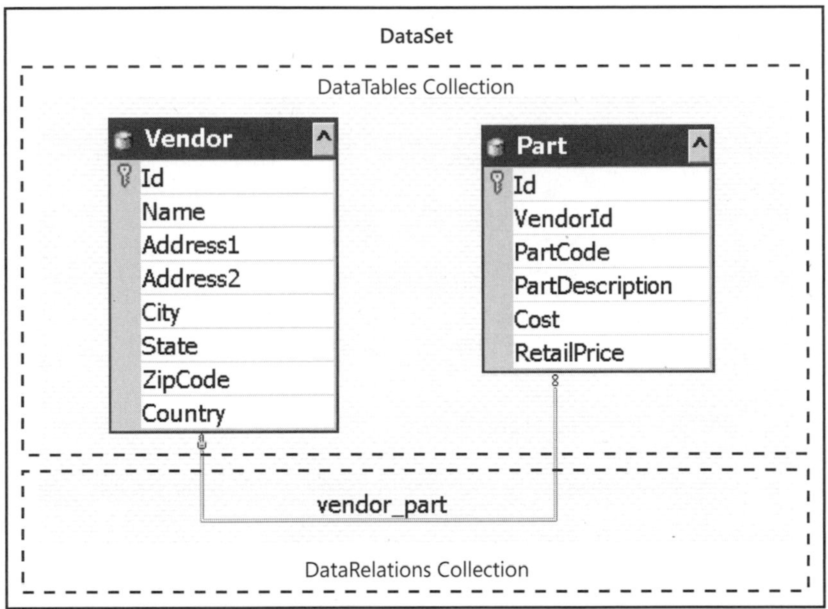

Figure 1-4 The *DataSet* object contains a collection of *DataTable* and *DataRelation* objects.

You can create the *DataSet* schema programmatically or by providing an XML schema definition. The following code demonstrates the creation of a simple *DataSet* containing a *DataTable* for vendors and a *DataTable* for parts. The two *DataTable* objects are joined using a *DataRelation* named *vendor_part*. (The *DataRelation* is discussed in more detail in the next section.)

Visual Basic

```
Dim vendorData as new DataSet("VendorData")

Dim vendor as DataTable = vendorData.Tables.Add("Vendor")
vendor.Columns.Add("Id", GetType(Guid))
vendor.Columns.Add("Name", GetType(string))
vendor.Columns.Add("Address1", GetType(string))
vendor.Columns.Add("Address2", GetType(string))
vendor.Columns.Add("City", GetType(string))
vendor.Columns.Add("State", GetType(string))
vendor.Columns.Add("ZipCode", GetType(string))
vendor.Columns.Add("Country", GetType(string))
vendor.PrimaryKey = new DataColumn() { vendor.Columns("Id") }

Dim part as DataTable = vendorData.Tables.Add("Part")
part.Columns.Add("Id", GetType(Guid))
part.Columns.Add("VendorId", GetType(Guid))
part.Columns.Add("PartCode", GetType(string))
part.Columns.Add("PartDescription", GetType(string))
part.Columns.Add("Cost", GetType(decimal))
```

```
part.Columns.Add("RetailPrice", GetType(decimal))
part.PrimaryKey = new DataColumn() { part.Columns("Id") }

vendorData.Relations.Add( _
   "vendor_part", _
   vendor.Columns("Id"), _
   part.Columns("VendorId"))
```

C#

```
DataSet vendorData = new DataSet("VendorData");

DataTable vendor = vendorData.Tables.Add("Vendor");
vendor.Columns.Add("Id", typeof(Guid));
vendor.Columns.Add("Name", typeof(string));
vendor.Columns.Add("Address1", typeof(string));
vendor.Columns.Add("Address2", typeof(string));
vendor.Columns.Add("City", typeof(string));
vendor.Columns.Add("State", typeof(string));
vendor.Columns.Add("ZipCode", typeof(string));
vendor.Columns.Add("Country", typeof(string));
vendor.PrimaryKey = new DataColumn[] { vendor.Columns["Id"] };

DataTable part = vendorData.Tables.Add("Part");
part.Columns.Add("Id", typeof(Guid));
part.Columns.Add("VendorId", typeof(Guid));
part.Columns.Add("PartCode", typeof(string));
part.Columns.Add("PartDescription", typeof(string));
part.Columns.Add("Cost", typeof(decimal));
part.Columns.Add("RetailPrice", typeof(decimal));
part.PrimaryKey = new DataColumn[] { part.Columns["Id"] };

vendorData.Relations.Add(
   "vendor_part",
   vendor.Columns["Id"],
   part.Columns["VendorId"]);
```

Being More Specific with Typed *DataSet* Objects

The previous code created a schema for a *DataSet*. Accessing the *DataTable* named *vendor* would require code like this:

Visual Basic

```
Dim vendorTable as DataTable = vendorData.Tables("Vendor")
```

C#

```
DataTable vendorTable = vendorData.Tables["Vendor"];
```

What happens if the table name is spelled incorrectly? An exception is thrown, but not until runtime. A better approach is to create a new, specialized *DataSet* class that inherits from *DataSet*, adding a property for each of the tables. For example, a specialized *DataSet* class might contain a property called *Vendor* that can be accessed as follows:

Visual Basic

```
Dim vendorTable as DataTable = vendorData.Vendor
```

C#

```
DataTable vendorTable = vendorData.Vendor;
```

Using the preceding syntax, a compile error is generated if *Vendor* is not spelled correctly. Also, the chances of incorrect spelling are significantly reduced because Visual Studio's IntelliSense displays the *Vendor* property for quick selection when the line of code is being typed. The standard *DataSet* class is an untyped *DataSet*, whereas the specialized *DataSet* is a typed *DataSet*.

You can create a typed *DataSet* class manually, but it's usually better to provide an XML schema definition (XSD) file that can be used to generate the typed *DataSet* class. Visual Studio contains a tool called the DataSet Editor that you can use to graphically create and modify an XSD file which in turn can be used to generate the typed *DataSet* class. You can invoke the DataSet Editor by adding a *DataSet* file to a Visual Studio project: right-click the project, choose Add, choose New Item, and select the DataSet template. After you add the DataSet template to the project, the template will be open for you to edit using the DataSet Editor. Figure 1-5 shows the files that are created when the DataSet template is added to a project. Notice that you must select the Show All Files button to see these files. One of the files has a .cs extension, which is the extension for a C# source code file. A Visual Basic application would have a file with a .vb extension. The source code file contains the specialized typed *DataSet* code, which is generated automatically by the DataSet Editor.

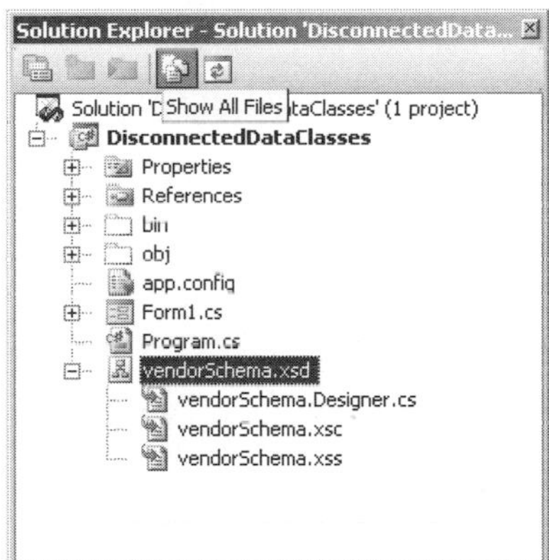

Figure 1-5 The DataSet template contains an XML schema definition and generates source code to create a typed *DataSet*.

Navigating the Family Tree with *DataRelation* Objects

The *DataRelation* objects are used to join *DataTable* objects that are in the same *DataSet*. Joining *DataTable* objects creates a path from one *DataTable* object to another. This *DataRelation* can be traversed programmatically from parent *DataTable* to child *DataTable* or from child

DataTable to parent *DataTable*, which enables navigation between the *DataTable* objects. The following code example populates the *vendor* and *part DataTable* objects and then demonstrates *DataRelation* object navigation, first from parent to child and then from child to parent, using the previously declared *vendor_part* DataRelation.

Visual Basic

```
Dim vendorRow as DataRow = nothing
vendorRow = vendor.NewRow()
Dim vendorId as Guid = Guid.NewGuid()
vendorRow("Id") = vendorId
vendorRow("Name") = "Tailspin Toys"
vendor.Rows.Add(vendorRow)

Dim partRow as DataRow = nothing
partRow = part.NewRow()
partRow("Id") = Guid.NewGuid()
partRow("VendorId") = vendorId
partRow("PartCode") = "WGT1"
partRow("PartDescription") = "Widget 1 Description"
partRow("Cost") = 10.00
partRow("RetailPrice") = 12.32
part.Rows.Add(partRow)

partRow = part.NewRow()
partRow("Id") = Guid.NewGuid()
partRow("VendorId") = vendorId
partRow("PartCode") = "WGT2"
partRow("PartDescription") = "Widget 2 Description"
partRow("Cost") = 9.00
partRow("RetailPrice") = 11.32
part.Rows.Add(partRow)

'Navigate parent to children
Dim parts as DataRow() = vendorRow.GetChildRows("vendor_part")
for each dr as DataRow in parts
   textBox1.AppendText("Part: " + dr("PartCode") +vbcrlf)
Next

'Navigate child to parent
Dim parentRow as DataRow  = part.Rows(1).GetParentRow("vendor_part")
textBox1.AppendText("Vendor: " + parentRow("Name") + vbcrlf)
```

C#

```
DataRow vendorRow = null;
vendorRow = vendor.NewRow();
Guid vendorId = Guid.NewGuid();
vendorRow["Id"] = vendorId;
vendorRow["Name"] = "Tailspin Toys";
vendor.Rows.Add(vendorRow);

DataRow partRow = null;
partRow = part.NewRow();
partRow["Id"] = Guid.NewGuid();
partRow["VendorId"] = vendorId;
```

```
partRow["PartCode"] = "WGT1";
partRow["PartDescription"] = "Widget 1 Description";
partRow["Cost"] = 10.00;
partRow["RetailPrice"] = 12.32;
part.Rows.Add(partRow);

partRow = part.NewRow();
partRow["Id"] = Guid.NewGuid();
partRow["VendorId"] = vendorId;
partRow["PartCode"] = "WGT2";
partRow["PartDescription"] = "Widget 2 Description";
partRow["Cost"] = 9.00;
partRow["RetailPrice"] = 11.32;
part.Rows.Add(partRow);

//Navigate parent to children
DataRow[] parts = vendorRow.GetChildRows("vendor_part");
foreach (DataRow dr in parts)
{
   textBox1.AppendText("Part: " + dr["PartCode"] +"\r\n");
}

//Navigate child to parent
DataRow parentRow = part.Rows[1].GetParentRow("vendor_part");
textBox1.AppendText("Vendor: " + parentRow["Name"] + "\r\n");
```

Creating Primary and Foreign Key Constraints

You can create a *DataRelation* object with or without unique and foreign key constraints for the sole purpose of navigating between parent and child *DataTable* objects. The *DataRelation* object also contains a constructor that allows for the creation of a unique constraint on the parent *DataTable* object and a foreign key constraint on the child *DataTable* object. These constraints are used to enforce data integrity by ensuring that a parent *DataRow* object exists for any child *DataRow* object that is to be created, and that a parent *DataRow* object can't be deleted if it has child *DataRow* objects. The following code demonstrates the creation of the *DataRelation* named *vendor_part*, passing *true* to create constraints if they don't already exist.

> **Note** If a foreign key constraint is set to a *DataColumn* object that allows nulls, this child *DataRow* can exist without having a parent *DataRow* object. In some situations, this might be desired or required, but in other situations it might not. Be sure to verify the *AllowDbNull* property of the *DataColumn* objects that are being used as foreign keys.

Visual Basic

```
vendorData.Relations.Add( _
   "vendor_part", _
   vendor.Columns("Id"), _
   part.Columns("VendorId"), True)
```

C#

```
vendorData.Relations.Add(
   "vendor_part",
   vendor.Columns["Id"],
   part.Columns["VendorId"], true);
```

Cascading Deletes and Cascading Updates

A foreign key constraint ensures that a child *DataRow* object cannot be added unless a valid parent *DataRow* object exists and that a parent *DataRow* object cannot be deleted if the parent still has child *DataRow* objects. In some situations, it is desirable to force the deletion of the child *DataRow* objects when the parent *DataRow* object is deleted. You can do this by setting the *DeleteRule* on the *ForeignKeyConstraint* to *Cascade*. As it turns out, *Cascade* is the default setting. Table 1-5 describes the other members of the *Rule* enumeration.

As with deleting, on some occasions you'll want to cascade changes to a unique key in the parent *DataRow* object to the child *DataRow* object's foreign key. You can set the *ChangeRule* to a member of the *Rule* enumeration to get the appropriate behavior.

Table 1-5 *Rule* Enumeration Members

Rule Value	Description
Cascade	Default. Deletes or updates the child *DataRow* objects when the *DataRow* object is deleted or its unique key is changed.
None	Throws an *InvalidConstraintException* if the parent *DataRow* object is deleted or its unique key is changed.
SetDefault	Sets the foreign key column(s) value to the default value of the *DataColumn* object(s) if the parent *DataRow* object is deleted or its unique key is changed.
SetNull	Sets the foreign key column(s) value to *DbNull* if the parent *DataRow* object is deleted or its unique key is changed.

The default setting for the *ForeignKeyConstraint* object's *DeleteRule* is *Rule.Cascade*. The following code snippet shows how to force an *InvalidConstraintException* exception to be thrown when a parent that has children is deleted or when a child is being added that has no parent.

Visual Basic

```
Dim fk as ForeignKeyConstraint = part.Constraints("vendor_part")
fk.DeleteRule = Rule.None
```

C#

```
ForeignKeyConstraint fk =
   (ForeignKeyConstraint)part.Constraints("vendor_part");
fk.DeleteRule = Rule.None;
```

Serializing and Deserializing *DataSet* Objects

A populated *DataSet* can be saved, or serialized, as XML or as binary data to a stream or file. The *DataSet* can also be loaded, or deserialized, with XML or binary data from a stream or file. The data stream can be transferred across a network over many protocols, including HTTP. This section looks at the various methods of transferring data.

Serializing the *DataSet* Object as XML

You can easily serialize a populated *DataSet* to an XML file by executing the *DataSet* object's *WriteXml* method. The following code snippet uses the populated *vendorData DataSet* that was created earlier in this chapter and writes the contents to an XML file. The resulting XML file contents are also shown.

Visual Basic

```
vendorData.WriteXml("c:\vendors.xml", XmlWriteMode.IgnoreSchema)
```

C#

```
vendorData.WriteXml(@"c:\vendors.xml", XmlWriteMode.IgnoreSchema);
```

XML

```
<?xml version="1.0" standalone="yes"?>
<VendorData>
  <Vendor>
    <Id>d9625cfa-f176-4521-98f5-f577a8bc2c00</Id>
    <Name>Tailspin Toys</Name>
  </Vendor>
  <Part>
    <Id>df84fa52-5aa3-4c08-b5ba-54163eb1ea3a</Id>
    <VendorId>d9625cfa-f176-4521-98f5-f577a8bc2c00</VendorId>
    <PartCode>WGT1</PartCode>
    <PartDescription>Widget 1 Description</PartDescription>
    <Cost>10</Cost>
    <RetailPrice>12.32</RetailPrice>
  </Part>
  <Part>
    <Id>c411676a-ec53-496c-bdbd-04b4d58124d0</Id>
    <VendorId>d9625cfa-f176-4521-98f5-f577a8bc2c00</VendorId>
    <PartCode>WGT2</PartCode>
    <PartDescription>Widget 2 Description</PartDescription>
    <Cost>9</Cost>
    <RetailPrice>11.32</RetailPrice>
  </Part>
</VendorData>
```

Notice that the XML document is well formed and that its root node is called *VendorData*. You can set the name of the root node by changing the *DataSet* object's *DataSetName* property. This property can be changed at any time, but notice that the code on page 19 that created the *DataSet* passed a *DataSetName* to the constructor of the *DataSet* object.

The *DataRow* objects have been represented as repeating elements in the XML. For example, the single *vendor DataRow* object is represented in the XML file by the single *Vendor* element, while the two *part DataRow* objects are represented in the XML file by the two *Part* elements. Also notice that the column data is represented as elements within the element for the *DataRow*. You can change the format of the column data by assigning a new value to the *ColumnMapping* property of the *DataColumn* objects. Table 1-6 shows the available settings.

Table 1-6 *MappingType* Enumeration Members

MappingType Value	Description
Attribute	The column data is placed into an XML attribute.
Element	The default. The column data is placed into an XML element.
Hidden	The column data is not sent to the XML file.
SimpleContent	The column data is stored as text within the row element tags. In other words, the data is stored as text like the *Element* setting, but without the *Element* tags.

Another formatting option is to nest the *Part* elements inside the *Vendor* that owns the parts. You can do this by setting the *Nested* property of the *DataRelation* object to *true*. The following code snippet shows how the XML format can be changed substantially–first by nesting the data and then setting all of the *DataColumn* objects except those with a data type of *Guid* (globally unique identifier) to *Attribute*. The resulting XML file is also shown.

Visual Basic

```
vendorData.Relations("vendor_part").Nested = True
For Each dt As DataTable In vendorData.Tables
    For Each dc As DataColumn In dt.Columns
        If Not (dc.DataType.Equals(GetType(Guid))) Then
            dc.ColumnMapping = MappingType.Attribute
        End If
    Next
Next
```

C#

```
vendorData.Relations["vendor_part"].Nested = true;
foreach (DataTable dt in vendorData)
{
   foreach (DataColumn dc in dt.Columns)
   {
      if(dc.DataType != typeof(Guid))
      {
         dc.ColumnMapping = MappingType.Attribute;
      }
   }
}
```

XML

```
<?xml version="1.0" standalone="yes"?>
<VendorData>
  <Vendor Name="Tailspin Toys">
    <Id>33323c89-213e-4168-924d-72262a7a3f5a</Id>
    <Part PartCode="WGT1" PartDescription="Widget 1 Description"
      Cost="10" RetailPrice="12.32">
      <Id>e28d9624-9e97-4106-a175-309b95952a8f</Id>
      <VendorId>33323c89-213e-4168-924d-72262a7a3f5a</VendorId>
    </Part>
    <Part PartCode="WGT2" PartDescription="Widget 2 Description"
      Cost="9" RetailPrice="11.32">
      <Id>07be7d2c-acba-40da-a1b7-78db3b774566</Id>
      <VendorId>33323c89-213e-4168-924d-72262a7a3f5a</VendorId>
    </Part>
  </Vendor>
</VendorData>
```

In the example, the XML file is being written, but the XML file contains no information that describes the data types of the data. When not specified, the default data type for all data is string. If the XML file is read into a new *DataSet*, all data, including *DateTime* data and numeric data, is loaded as string data. One fix is to store the data type information with the XML file. You do this by storing the schema definition with the XML file. The following code shows how to specify the *XmlWriteMode* to include the schema definition within the XML file.

Visual Basic

```
vendorData.WriteXml("c:\vendors.xml", XmlWriteMode.WriteSchema)
```

C#

```
vendorData.WriteXml(@"c:\vendors.xml", XmlWriteMode.WriteSchema);
```

XML

```
<?xml version="1.0" standalone="yes"?>
<VendorData>
  <xs:schema id="VendorData" xmlns=""
    xmlns:xs="http://www.w3.org/2001/XMLSchema"
    xmlns:msdata="urn:schemas-microsoft-com:xml-msdata">
    <xs:element name="VendorData" msdata:IsDataSet="true">
      <xs:complexType>
        <xs:choice minOccurs="0" maxOccurs="unbounded">
          <xs:element name="Vendor">
            <xs:complexType>
              <xs:sequence>
                <xs:element name="Id" msdata:DataType="System.Guid,
                  mscorlib, Version=2.0.3600.0, Culture=neutral,
                  PublicKeyToken=b77a5c561934e089" type="xs:anyType"
                  msdata:Ordinal="0" />
              </xs:sequence>
              <xs:attribute name="Name" type="xs:string" />
              <xs:attribute name="Address1" type="xs:string" />
              <xs:attribute name="Address2" type="xs:string" />
              <xs:attribute name="City" type="xs:string" />
```

```
            <xs:attribute name="State" type="xs:string" />
            <xs:attribute name="ZipCode" type="xs:string" />
            <xs:attribute name="Country" type="xs:string" />
          </xs:complexType>
        </xs:element>
        <xs:element name="Part">
          <xs:complexType>
            <xs:sequence>
              <xs:element name="Id" msdata:DataType="System.Guid,
                mscorlib, Version=2.0.3600.0, Culture=neutral,
                PublicKeyToken=b77a5c561934e089" type="xs:anyType"
                msdata:Ordinal="0" />
              <xs:element name="VendorId" msdata:DataType="System.Guid,
                mscorlib, Version=2.0.3600.0, Culture=neutral,
                PublicKeyToken=b77a5c561934e089" type="xs:anyType"
                minOccurs="0" msdata:Ordinal="1" />
            </xs:sequence>
            <xs:attribute name="PartCode" type="xs:string" />
            <xs:attribute name="PartDescription" type="xs:string" />
            <xs:attribute name="Cost" type="xs:decimal" />
            <xs:attribute name="RetailPrice" type="xs:decimal" />
          </xs:complexType>
        </xs:element>
      </xs:choice>
    </xs:complexType>
    <xs:unique name="Constraint1" msdata:PrimaryKey="true">
      <xs:selector xpath=".//Vendor" />
      <xs:field xpath="Id" />
    </xs:unique>
    <xs:unique name="Part_Constraint1"
      msdata:ConstraintName="Constraint1"
      msdata:PrimaryKey="true">
      <xs:selector xpath=".//Part" />
      <xs:field xpath="Id" />
    </xs:unique>
    <xs:keyref name="vendor_part" refer="Constraint1">
      <xs:selector xpath=".//Part" />
      <xs:field xpath="VendorId" />
    </xs:keyref>
  </xs:element>
</xs:schema>
<Vendor Name="Tailspin Toys">
  <Id>f6cb3b63-6d1a-4941-abe8-b81b5b2357c4</Id>
</Vendor>
<Part PartCode="WGT1" PartDescription="Widget 1 Description"
  Cost="10" RetailPrice="12.32">
  <Id>d7263a61-f9de-4d27-9d29-5167e95317d0</Id>
  <VendorId>f6cb3b63-6d1a-4941-abe8-b81b5b2357c4</VendorId>
</Part>
<Part PartCode="WGT2" PartDescription="Widget 2 Description"
  Cost="9" RetailPrice="11.32">
  <Id>310a89d1-60dd-4b06-b368-453ed210f670</Id>
  <VendorId>f6cb3b63-6d1a-4941-abe8-b81b5b2357c4</VendorId>
</Part>
</VendorData>
```

When the *XmlWriteMode* is set to WriteSchema, the resulting XML file is substantially larger. When few files are being generated for this data, this approach is acceptable. But if many files are being created, it might be better to create a separate XSD file that can be loaded before the data. You can use the *DataSet* object's *WriteXmlSchema* method to extract the XML schema definition to a separate file, as shown here.

Visual Basic

```
vendorData.WriteXmlSchema("c:\vendorSchema.xsd")
```

C#

```
vendorData.WriteXmlSchema(@"c:\vendorSchema.xsd");
```

Serializing a Changed DataSet Object as a *DiffGram*

A *DiffGram* is an XML document that contains all of the data from your *DataSet* object, including the original *DataRow* object information. A *DataSet* object can be serialized as a *DiffGram* by simply setting the *XmlWriteMode* to *DiffGram* as shown in the following snippet.

Visual Basic

```
vendorData.WriteXml("c:\vendors.xml", XmlWriteMode.DiffGram)
```

C#

```
vendorData.WriteXml(@"c:\vendors.xml", XmlWriteMode.DiffGram);
```

Where is the *DiffGram* useful? Picture this: you are writing an application that occasionally connects to a database to synchronize your disconnected *DataSet* object with the current information that is contained in the database. When you are not connected to the database, you want your *DataSet* object to be stored locally. All of the previous examples of serializing a *DataSet* object stored the current data, but not the original data. This means that when you deserialize the data, you will have lost the information needed to find the changed *DataRow* objects that should be sent back to the database

The *DiffGram* contains all of the *DataRowVersion* information as shown in the following XML document. Notice that *Part1* has been modified, and its status is indicated as such. Also notice that the bottom of the XML document contains the "before" information for *DataRow* objects that have been modified or deleted. This XML document also shows *Part2* as being deleted because *Part2* has "before" information but not current information. *Part3* is an inserted *DataRow* object as indicated, so this DataRow object has no "before" information.

XML

```
<?xml version="1.0" standalone="yes"?>
<diffgr:diffgram xmlns:msdata="urn:schemas-microsoft-com:xml-msdata"
    xmlns:diffgr="urn:schemas-microsoft-com:xml-diffgram-v1">
  <VendorData>
    <Vendor diffgr:id="Vendor1" msdata:rowOrder="0" Name="Tailspin Toys">
      <Id>0ad3358e-38a6-4648-ba68-209bb212e7a3</Id>
      <Part diffgr:id="Part1" msdata:rowOrder="0" diffgr:hasChanges="modified"
          PartCode="WGT1" PartDescription="Widget 1 Description"
```

```
          Cost="12" RetailPrice="12.32">
        <Id>ec52f9d2-392f-4870-8003-497d658076ec</Id>
        <VendorId>0ad3358e-38a6-4648-ba68-209bb212e7a3</VendorId>
      </Part>
      <Part diffgr:id="Part3" msdata:rowOrder="2" diffgr:hasChanges="inserted"
          PartCode="WGT3" PartDescription="Widget 3 Description"
          Cost="8" RetailPrice="10.02">
        <Id>3c34b25f-336a-4e42-a9c8-bfba177056a3</Id>
        <VendorId>0ad3358e-38a6-4648-ba68-209bb212e7a3</VendorId>
      </Part>
    </Vendor>
  </VendorData>
  <diffgr:before>
    <Part diffgr:id="Part1" msdata:rowOrder="0"
          PartCode="WGT1" PartDescription="Widget 1 Description"
          Cost="10" RetailPrice="12.32">
      <Id>ec52f9d2-392f-4870-8003-497d658076ec</Id>
      <VendorId>0ad3358e-38a6-4648-ba68-209bb212e7a3</VendorId>
    </Part>
    <Part diffgr:id="Part2" diffgr:parentId="Vendor1" msdata:rowOrder="1"
          PartCode="WGT2" PartDescription="Widget 2 Description"
          Cost="9" RetailPrice="11.32">
      <Id>e4bf3db0-7a8a-404e-84a2-4b7e4c588ffa</Id>
      <VendorId>0ad3358e-38a6-4648-ba68-209bb212e7a3</VendorId>
    </Part>
  </diffgr:before>
</diffgr:diffgram>
```

Deserializing a *DataSet* from XML

You can easily deserialize XML into a *DataSet* from a file or stream. Remember that when a schema is not provided, all XML data is treated as string data, so you should first load the schema if it is in a separate file. The following code can be used to read the schema file and load the XML file.

Visual Basic

```
Dim vendorData as new DataSet()
vendorData.ReadXmlSchema("c:\vendorSchema.xsd")
vendorData.ReadXml("c:\vendors.xml", XmlReadMode.IgnoreSchema)
```

C#

```
DataSet vendorData = new DataSet();
vendorData.ReadXmlSchema(@"c:\vendorSchema.xsd");
vendorData.ReadXml(@"c:\vendors.xml", XmlReadMode.IgnoreSchema);
```

In the preceding example, the *XmlReadMode* is set to *IgnoreSchema*. This means that if the XML data file contains an XML schema definition, it is ignored. Table 1-7 lists the other options of the *XmlReadMode* enumeration.

Table 1-7 *XmlReadMode* Enumeration Members

XmlReadMode Value	Description
Auto	The XML source is examined by the *ReadXml* method and the appropriate mode is selected.
DiffGram	If the *XmlFile* contains a *DiffGram*, the changes are applied to the *DataSet* using the same semantics that the *Merge* method uses. *Merge* is covered in more detail in the next section.
Fragment	Reads the XML as a fragment. Fragments can contain multiple root elements. *FOR XML* in SQL Server is an example of something that produces fragments.
IgnoreSchema	Ignores any schema that is defined within the XML data file.
InferSchema	The XML file is read, and the schema (*DataTable* objects and *DataColumn* objects) is created based on the data. If the *DataSet* currently has a schema, the existing schema is used and extended to accommodate tables and columns that existing in XML document but don't exist in the *DataSet* object. All data types of all *DataColumn* objects are a string.
InferTypedSchema	The XML file is read, and the schema is created based on the data. An attempt is made to identify the data type of each column, but if the data type cannot be identified, it will be a string.
ReadSchema	Reads the XML file and looks for an embedded schema. If the *DataSet* already has *DataTable* objects with the same name, an exception is thrown. All other existing tables will remain.

Inferring a schema simply means that the *DataSet* attempts to create a schema for the data by looking for patterns of XML elements and attributes.

Serializing the *DataSet* Object as Binary Data

Although the *DataSet* can be serialized as XML, in many situations the size of the XML file causes problems with resources such as memory and drive space or bandwidth when you move this data across the network. If XML is not required, the *DataSet* can be serialized as a binary file. The code snippet that appears at the top of the next page writes to a binary file the contents of the *vendorData DataSet* that we previously defined and populated.

In this example code, a *BinaryFormatter* object is created and is used to create the binary file. Opening the binary file using the Visual Studio hex editor would reveal that the binary file contains embedded XML, as shown in Figure 1-6. We'll refer to this file as the BinaryXml file. The size of this small sample is 4186 bytes. Adding the line of code that follows Figure 1-6 on the next page to the beginning of the code sample causes the file to be saved with true binary data.

Visual Basic

```
'Added the following Imports statements to the top of the file
Imports System.Runtime.Serialization.Formatters.Binary
Imports System.IO
...
Dim fs as new FileStream( _
    "c:\vendorData.bin",FileMode.Create)
Dim fmt as new BinaryFormatter()
fmt.Serialize(fs, vendorData)
fs.Close( )
```

C#

```
//Added the following using statements to the top of the file
using System.Runtime.Serialization.Formatters.Binary;
using System.IO;
...
FileStream fs = new FileStream(
   @"c:\vendorData.bin",FileMode.Create);
BinaryFormatter fmt = new BinaryFormatter();
fmt.Serialize(fs, vendorData);
fs.Close( );
```


```
00000000  00 01 00 00 00 FF FF FF  FF 01 00 00 00 00 00 00  ................
00000010  00 0C 02 00 00 00 51 53  79 73 74 65 6D 2E 44 61  ......QSystem.Da
00000020  74 61 2C 20 56 65 72 73  69 6F 6E 3D 32 2E 30 2E  ta, Version=2.0.
00000030  33 36 30 30 2E 30 2C 20  43 75 6C 74 75 72 65 3D  3600.0, Culture=
00000040  6E 65 75 74 72 61 6C 2C  20 50 75 62 6C 69 63 4B  neutral, PublicK
00000050  65 79 54 6F 6B 65 6E 3D  62 37 37 61 35 63 35 36  eyToken=b77a5c56
00000060  31 39 33 34 65 30 38 39  05 01 00 00 00 13 53 79  1934e089......Sy
00000070  73 74 65 6D 2E 44 61 74  61 2E 44 61 74 61 53 65  stem.Data.DataSe
00000080  74 03 00 00 00 17 44 61  74 61 53 65 74 2E 52 65  t.....DataSet.Re
00000090  6D 6F 74 69 6E 67 56 65  72 73 69 6F 6E 09 58 6D  motingVersion.Xm
000000a0  6C 53 63 68 65 6D 61 0B  58 6D 6C 44 69 66 66 47  lSchema.XmlDiffG
000000b0  72 61 6D 03 01 01 0E 53  79 73 74 65 6D 2E 56 65  ram....System.Ve
000000c0  72 73 69 6F 6E 02 00 00  00 09 03 00 00 00 06 04  rsion...........
000000d0  00 00 00 FF 16 3C 3F 78  6D 6C 20 76 65 72 73 69  .....<?xml versi
000000e0  6F 6E 3D 22 31 2E 30 22  20 65 6E 63 6F 64 69 6E  on="1.0" encodin
000000f0  67 3D 22 75 74 66 2D 31  36 22 3F 3E 0D 0A 3C 78  g="utf-16"?>..<x
00000100  73 3A 73 63 68 65 6D 61  20 69 64 3D 22 56 65 6E  s:schema id="Ven
00000110  64 6F 72 44 61 74 61 22  20 78 6D 6C 6E 73 3D 22  dorData" xmlns="
00000120  22 20 78 6D 6C 6E 73 3A  78 73 3D 22 68 74 74 70  " xmlns:xs="http
00000130  3A 2F 2F 77 77 77 2E 77  33 2E 6F 72 67 2F 32 30  ://www.w3.org/20
00000140  30 31 2F 58 4D 4C 53 63  68 65 6D 61 22 20 78 6D  01/XMLSchema" xm
00000150  6C 6E 73 3A 6D 73 64 61  74 61 3D 22 75 72 6E 3A  lns:msdata="urn:
00000160  73 63 68 65 6D 61 73 2D  6D 69 63 72 6F 73 6F 66  schemas-microsof
00000170  74 2D 63 6F 6D 3A 78 6D  6C 2D 6D 73 64 61 74 61  t-com:xml-msdata
00000180  22 3E 0D 0A 20 20 3C 78  73 3A 65 6C 65 6D 65 6E  ">..  <xs:elemen
00000190  74 20 6E 61 6D 65 3D 22  56 65 6E 64 6F 72 44 61  t name="VendorDa
000001a0  74 61 22 20 6D 73 64 61  74 61 3A 49 73 44 61 74  ta" msdata:IsDat
000001b0  61 53 65 74 3D 22 74 72  75 65 22 3E 0D 0A 20 20  aSet="true">..
000001c0  20 20 3C 78 73 3A 63 6F  6D 70 6C 65 78 54 79 70    <xs:complexTyp
000001d0  65 3E 0D 0A 20 20 20 20  20 20 3C 78 73 3A 63 68  e>..      <xs:ch
000001e0  6F 69 63 65 20 6D 69 6E  4F 63 63 75 72 73 3D 22  oice minOccurs="
000001f0  30 22 20 6D 61 78 4F 63  63 75 72 73 3D 22 75 6E  0" maxOccurs="un
00000200  62 6F 75 6E 64 65 64 22  3E 0D 0A 20 20 20 20 20  bounded">..
00000210  20 20 20 3C 78 73 3A 65  6C 65 6D 65 6E 74 20 6E     <xs:element n
00000220  61 6D 65 3D 22 56 65 6E  64 6F 72 22 3E 0D 0A 20  ame="Vendor">..
```


Figure 1-6 The *DataSet* is serialized to a binary file, but the binary file contains embedded XML.

Visual Basic

```
vendorData.RemotingFormat = SerializationFormat.Binary
```

C#

```
vendorData.RemotingFormat = SerializationFormat.Binary;
```

We can then run the code, with the results shown in Figure 1-7. We'll refer to this file as the TrueBinary file. The size of this small *DataSet* object is more than 20,000 bytes. This file was supposed to get smaller, but the initial overhead to create the TrueBinary file was more than 20,000 bytes, compared with about 3400 bytes of initial overhead for the BinaryXml file. With 10,000 vendors and 20,000 parts, the BinaryXml file size grows to 7,938,982 bytes and the TrueBinary file grows to only 1,973,401 bytes. This means that small objects might not benefit from changing the *RemotingFormat* property to *Binary*, while large objects will be about one-fourth the size, or four times faster.

> **Note** The *DataTable* also contains the *RemotingFormat* property, which can be used when only a single *DataTable* is to be saved as binary data.


```
00000000  00 01 00 00 00 FF FF FF  FF 01 00 00 00 00 00 00  ................
00000010  00 0C 02 00 00 00 51 53  79 73 74 65 6D 2E 44 61  ......QSystem.Da
00000020  74 61 2C 20 56 65 72 73  69 6F 6E 3D 32 2E 30 2E  ta, Version=2.0.
00000030  33 36 30 30 2E 30 2C 20  43 75 6C 74 75 72 65 3D  3600.0, Culture=
00000040  6E 65 75 74 72 61 6C 2C  20 50 75 62 6C 69 63 4B  neutral, PublicK
00000050  65 79 54 6F 6B 65 6E 3D  62 37 37 61 35 63 35 36  eyToken=b77a5c56
00000060  31 39 33 34 65 30 38 39  05 01 00 00 00 13 53 79  1934e089......Sy
00000070  73 74 65 6D 2E 44 61 74  61 2E 44 61 74 61 53 65  stem.Data.DataSe
00000080  74 2B 00 00 00 17 44 61  74 61 53 65 74 2E 52 65  t+....DataSet.Re
00000090  6D 6F 74 69 6E 67 56 65  72 73 69 6F 6E 16 44 61  motingVersion.Da
000000a0  74 61 53 65 74 2E 52 65  6D 6F 74 69 6E 67 46 6F  taSet.RemotingFo
000000b0  72 6D 61 74 13 44 61 74  61 53 65 74 2E 44 61 74  rmat.DataSet.Dat
000000c0  61 53 65 74 4E 61 6D 65  11 44 61 74 61 53 65 74  aSetName.DataSet
000000d0  2E 4E 61 6D 65 73 70 61  63 65 0E 44 61 74 61 53  .Namespace.DataS
000000e0  65 74 2E 50 72 65 66 69  78 15 44 61 74 61 53 65  et.Prefix.DataSe
000000f0  74 2E 43 61 73 65 53 65  6E 73 69 74 69 76 65 12  t.CaseSensitive.
00000100  44 61 74 61 53 65 74 2E  4C 6F 63 61 6C 65 4C 43  DataSet.LocaleLC
00000110  49 44 1A 44 61 74 61 53  65 74 2E 45 6E 66 6F 72  ID.DataSet.Enfor
00000120  63 65 43 6F 6E 73 74 72  61 69 6E 74 73 1A 44 61  ceConstraints.Da
00000130  74 61 53 65 74 2E 45 78  74 65 6E 64 65 64 50 72  taSet.ExtendedPr
00000140  6F 70 65 72 74 69 65 73  14 44 61 74 61 53 65 74  operties.DataSet
00000150  2E 54 61 62 6C 65 73 2E  43 6F 75 6E 74 10 44 61  .Tables.Count.Da
00000160  74 61 53 65 74 2E 54 61  62 6C 65 73 5F 30 10 44  taSet.Tables_0.D
00000170  61 74 61 53 65 74 2E 54  61 62 6C 65 73 5F 31 17  ataSet.Tables_1.
00000180  44 61 74 61 54 61 62 6C  65 5F 30 2E 43 6F 6E 73  DataTable_0.Cons
00000190  74 72 61 69 6E 74 73 17  44 61 74 61 54 61 62 6C  traints.DataTabl
000001a0  65 5F 31 2E 43 6F 6E 73  74 72 61 69 6E 74 73 11  e_1.Constraints.
000001b0  44 61 74 61 53 65 74 2E  52 65 6C 61 74 69 6F 6E  DataSet.Relation
000001c0  73 23 44 61 74 61 54 61  62 6C 65 5F 30 2E 44 61  s#DataTable_0.Da
000001d0  74 61 43 6F 6C 75 6D 6E  5F 30 2E 45 78 70 72 65  taColumn_0.Expre
000001e0  73 73 69 6F 6E 23 44 61  74 61 54 61 62 6C 65 5F  ssion#DataTable_
000001f0  30 2E 44 61 74 61 43 6F  6C 75 6D 6E 5F 31 2E 45  0.DataColumn_1.E
00000200  78 70 72 65 73 73 69 6F  6E 23 44 61 74 61 54 61  xpression#DataTa
```


Figure 1-7 After we set *RemotingFormat* to binary data, the binary file no longer contains embedded XML.

Deserializing a *DataSet* from Binary Data

The binary data file we saved in the previous example can easily be deserialized into a *DataSet* from a file or stream. The *BinaryFormatter* stores the schema automatically, so there is no need to load a schema first. The *BinaryFormatter* automatically identifies the file as having been saved as *BinaryXml* or *TrueBinary*. The following code can be used to load the binary file.

Visual Basic

```
Dim vendorData as DataSet
Dim fs as new FileStream( _
   "c:\vendorData.bin", FileMode.Open)
Dim fmt as new BinaryFormatter()
vendorData = CType(fmt.Deserialize(fs),DataSet)
fs.Close()
```

C#

```
DataSet vendorData;
FileStream fs = new FileStream(
   @"c:\vendorData.bin", FileMode.Open);
BinaryFormatter fmt = new BinaryFormatter();
vendorData = (DataSet)fmt.Deserialize(fs);
fs.Close();
```

Using *Merge* to Combine *DataSet* Data

On many occasions, data available in one *DataSet* must be combined with another *DataSet*. For example, a sales application might need to combine serialized *DataSet* objects received by e-mail from a number of salespeople. Even internally within an application, you might want to create a copy of *DataTable* objects that the user can edit, and based on the user clicking Update, the modified data can be merged back to the original *DataSet*.

The *DataSet* contains a method called *Merge* that can be used to combine data from multiple *DataSet* objects. The *Merge* method has several overloads to allow data to be merged from *DataSet*, *DataTable*, or *DataRow* objects. The following code example demonstrates using the *Merge* method to combine changes from one *DataSet* into another *DataSet*.

Visual Basic

```
'Create an initial DataSet
Dim masterData As New DataSet("Sales")
Dim person As DataTable = masterData.Tables.Add("Person")
person.Columns.Add("Id", GetType(Guid))
person.Columns.Add("Name", GetType(String))
person.PrimaryKey = New DataColumn() {person.Columns("Id")}
person.Rows.Add(Guid.NewGuid(), "Joe")
'Create a temp DataSet and make changes
Dim tempData As DataSet = masterData.Copy()
'get Joe's info
Dim tempPerson As DataTable = tempData.Tables("Person")
Dim joe As DataRow = tempPerson.Select("Name='Joe'")(0)
Dim joeId As Guid = CType(joe("Id"), Guid)
'Modify joe's name
joe("Name") = "Joe in Sales"
'Create an Order table and add orders for Joe
Dim order As DataTable = tempData.Tables.Add("Order")
order.Columns.Add("Id", GetType(Guid))
order.Columns.Add("PersonId", GetType(Guid))
order.Columns.Add("Amount", GetType(Decimal))
order.PrimaryKey = New DataColumn() {order.Columns("Id")}
order.Rows.Add(Guid.NewGuid(), joeId, 100)
'Now merge back to master
masterData.Merge(tempData, False, MissingSchemaAction.AddWithKey)
```

C#

```
//Create an initial DataSet
DataSet masterData = new DataSet("Sales");
DataTable person = masterData.Tables.Add("Person");
person.Columns.Add("Id", typeof(Guid));
person.Columns.Add("Name", typeof(string));
person.PrimaryKey = new DataColumn[] { person.Columns["Id"] };
person.Rows.Add(Guid.NewGuid(), "Joe");
//Create a temp DataSet and make changes
DataSet tempData = masterData.Copy();
//get Joe's info
DataTable tempPerson = tempData.Tables["Person"];
DataRow joe = tempPerson.Select("Name='Joe'")[0];
```

```
Guid joeId = (Guid)joe["Id"];
//Modify joe's name
joe["Name"] = "Joe in Sales";
//Create an Order table and add orders for Joe
DataTable order = tempData.Tables.Add("Order");
order.Columns.Add("Id", typeof(Guid));
order.Columns.Add("PersonId", typeof(Guid));
order.Columns.Add("Amount", typeof(decimal));
order.PrimaryKey = new DataColumn[] { order.Columns["Id"] };
order.Rows.Add(Guid.NewGuid(), joeId, 100);
//Now merge back to master
masterData.Merge(tempData, false, MissingSchemaAction.AddWithKey);
```

This code creates a *DataSet* that contains a single *DataTable* object, called *Person*. A person named Joe was added to the *Person DataTable* object. The *DataRowState* for Joe's *DataRow* is *Added*. Next, the code copies the *masterData DataSet* object to a *DataSet* object called *tempData*. The code modifies the *tempData DataSet* object by changing Joe's name to *Joe in Sales*, and then it creates a new *DataTable* object called *Order* and adds an order.

The *Merge* method on *masterData*, which takes three parameters, is then called. The first parameter is the *tempData* object. The second parameter is a Boolean called *preserveChanges*, which specifies whether updates from the *tempData DataSet* should overwrite changes made in the *masterData* object. For example, Joe's *DataRowState* in the *masterData DataSet* is not *Unchanged*, so if the *preserveChanges* setting is *true*, Joe's name change (to *Joe in Sales*) will not be merged into *masterData*. The last parameter is a *MissingSchemaAction* enumeration member. The *AddSchemaWithKey* is selected, which means the *Sales DataTable* and its data are added to *masterData*. Table 1-8 describes the enumeration members.

Table 1-8 *MissingSchemaAction* Enumeration Members

MissingSchemaAction Value	Description
Add	Adds the necessary *DataTable* and *DataColumn* objects to complete the schema.
AddWithPrimaryKey	Adds the necessary *DataTable*, *DataColumn*, and *PrimaryKey* objects to complete the schema.
Error	An exception is thrown if a *DataColumn* does not exist in the *DataSet* that is being updated.
Ignore	Ignores data that resides in *DataColumns* that are not in the *DataSet* being updated.

When you use the *Merge* method, make sure the *DataTable* objects have a primary key. Failure to set the *PrimaryKey* property of the *DataTable* object results in *DataRow* objects being appended rather than existing *DataRow* objects being modified.

Looping Through Data with the *DataTableReader*

The *DataTableReader* class lets you iterate through *DataRow* objects in one or more *DataTable* objects. The *DataTableReader* provides a stable, forward-only, read-only means of looping over *DataRow* objects. You can also use a *DataTableReader* to populate many Windows and Web controls without having to write looping code.

If an underlying *DataRow* is deleted or removed from the *DataTable* before the *DataTableReader* gets to the *DataRow* object, no attempt is made to retrieve the *DataRow* object. If a *DataRow* object that has already been read is deleted or removed, the current position is maintained–there is no resulting shift in position.

If *DataRow* objects are added to the underlying *DataTable* object while the *DataTableReader* is looping, these *DataRow* objects are included in the *DataTableReader* iterations only if the *DataRow* is added after the current position of the *DataTableReader* object. *DataRow* objects that are inserted before the current position of the *DataTableReader* are not included in the iterations.

The *DataTableReader* contains a method called *Read* that is executed to load the *DataTableReader* with the *DataRow* at the current position, and then the position is advanced. If the end of file is reached, the *Read* method returns *null*. Any attempt to execute the *Read* method after the *Read* method returns *null* always returns *null*, even if more *DataRow* objects are added.

The *DataSet* contains a method called *CreateDataReader* that returns an instance of the *DataTableReader* class. If the *DataSet* contains more than one table, the *DataTableReader* object reads the first *DataTable* object in the *DataSet*.

The following code example demonstrates the use of the *DataTableReader* to loop over a *DataTable* and display the *Person* object's *Name* property and then move to the *Part DataTable* and display the *PartName* property to a *TextBox*.

Visual Basic

```
'Create an initial DataSet
Dim masterData As New DataSet("Sales")
Dim person As DataTable = masterData.Tables.Add("Person")
person.Columns.Add("Id", GetType(Guid))
person.Columns.Add("Name", GetType(String))
person.PrimaryKey = New DataColumn() {person.Columns("Id")}
Dim part As DataTable = masterData.Tables.Add("Part")
part.Columns.Add("Id", GetType(Guid))
part.Columns.Add("PartName", GetType(String))
part.PrimaryKey = New DataColumn() {part.Columns("Id")}

For i As Integer = 0 To 100
    person.Rows.Add(Guid.NewGuid(), "Joe " + i.ToString())
    part.Rows.Add(Guid.NewGuid(), "Part " + i.ToString())
Next
'read the data in the DataTable
Dim rd As DataTableReader = masterData.CreateDataReader()
```

```
While (rd.Read())
    TextBox1.AppendText(rd("Name").ToString() + vbcrlf)
End While
rd.NextResult()
While (rd.Read())
    TextBox1.AppendText(rd("PartName").ToString() + vbcrlf)
End While
```

C#

```
//Create an initial DataSet
DataSet masterData = new DataSet("Sales");
DataTable person = masterData.Tables.Add("Person");
person.Columns.Add("Id", typeof(Guid));
person.Columns.Add("Name", typeof(string));
person.PrimaryKey = new DataColumn[] { person.Columns["Id"] };
DataTable part = masterData.Tables.Add("Part");
part.Columns.Add("Id", typeof(Guid));
part.Columns.Add("PartName", typeof(string));
part.PrimaryKey = new DataColumn[] { part.Columns["Id"] };

for (int i = 0; i < 100; i++)
{
   person.Rows.Add(Guid.NewGuid(), "Joe " + i);
   part.Rows.Add(Guid.NewGuid(), "Part " + i);
}
//read the data in the DataTable
DataTableReader rd = masterData.CreateDataReader();
while (rd.Read())
{
  textBox1.AppendText( rd["Name"].ToString() + "\r\n");
}
rd.NextResult();
while (rd.Read())
{
   textBox1.AppendText(rd["PartName"].ToString() + "\r\n");
}
```

The *DataTableReader* class inherits from the *DbDataReader* class. You'll find more information on the properties inherited from the *DbDataReader* in the next chapter.

Summary

This chapter provided a detailed overview of ADO.NET's disconnected classes. When you work with disconnected data, a *DataTable* object is almost always a requirement.

The *DataTable* object contains *DataColumn* objects, which define the schema, and *DataRow* objects, which contain the data. *DataRow* objects have *RowState* and *DataRowVersion* properties.

You use the *RowState* property to indicate whether the *DataRow* should be inserted, updated, or deleted from the data store if the data is ever persisted to a database.

The *DataRow* object can contain up to three copies of its data, based on the *DataRowVersion*. This feature allows the data to be rolled back to its original state, and you can use it when you write code to handle conflict resolution.

The *DataSet* object is an in-memory, relational data representation. The *DataSet* object contains a collection of *DataTable* objects and a collection of *DataRelation* objects.

DataSet and *DataTable* objects can be serialized and deserialized to and from a binary or XML file or stream. Data from other *DataSet*, *DataTable*, and *DataRow* objects can be merged into a *DataSet* object.

You can use the *TableDataReader* to provide stable, forward-only, read-only looping over a *DataTable*. You can also use it to populate many Windows and Web controls.

Chapter 2

Overview of ADO.NET Connected Classes

The ADO.NET libraries contain classes that you can use to transfer data between a data store and the client application. There are many different kinds of data stores, which means you need specialized code to provide the necessary bridge between the disconnected data access classes (discussed in Chapter 1) and a particular data store. This chapter focuses on these specialized classes, starting with the most essential classes, such as *DbConnection* and *DbCommand*. The chapter concludes with the more elaborate classes that have been added in ADO.NET 2.0, such as *DbProviderFactory* and *DbProviderFactories*.

Using Providers to Move Data

The classes that are responsible for the movement of data between the disconnected data classes in the client application and the data store are referred to as *connected classes* or *provider classes*. The Microsoft .NET Framework contains the following providers:

- *OLEDB* Contains classes that provide general-purpose data access to many data sources. You can use this provider to access SQL Server 6.5 and earlier, SyBase, DB2/400, and Microsoft Access.
- *ODBC* Contains classes for general-purpose data access to many data sources. This provider is typically used when no newer provider is available.
- *SQL Server* Contains classes that provide functionality similar to the generic OLEDB provider. The difference is that these classes are tuned for SQL Server 7.0 and later data access. SQL Server 6.5 and earlier must use the OLEDB provider.
- *Oracle* Contains classes for accessing Oracle 8i and later servers. This provider is similar to the OLEDB provider but provides better performance.

You can also use third-party providers, such as DB2 and MySql, which can be downloaded from the Web.

Table 2-1 lists the primary provider classes and interfaces. The classes are subclassed by the provider, which replaces the *Db* prefix with a provider prefix, such as *Sql*, *Oracle*, *Odbc*, or

OleDb. You can use the base classes with factory classes to create client code that is not provider specific. The following sections describe these classes in detail.

Table 2-1 Primary Provider Classes and Interfaces in ADO.NET

Base Classes	*SqlClient* Classes	Generic Interface
DbConnection	*SqlConnection*	*IDbConnection*
DbCommand	*SqlCommand*	*IDbCommand*
DbDataReader	*SqlDataReader*	*IDataReader/IDataRecord*
DbTransaction	*SqlTransaction*	*IDbTransaction*
DbParameter	*SqlParameter*	*IDbDataParameter*
DbParameterCollection	*SqlParameterCollection*	*IDataParameterCollection*
DbDataAdapter	*SqlDataAdapter*	*IDbDataAdapter*
DbCommandBuilder	*SqlCommandBuilder*	
DbConnectionStringBuilder	*SqlConnectionStringBuilder*	
DBDataPermission	*SqlPermission*	

Getting Started with the *DbConnection* Object

You need a valid, open connection object to access a data store. The *DbConnection* class is an abstract class from which the provider inherits to create provider-specific classes. The connection class hierarchy is shown in Figure 2-1.

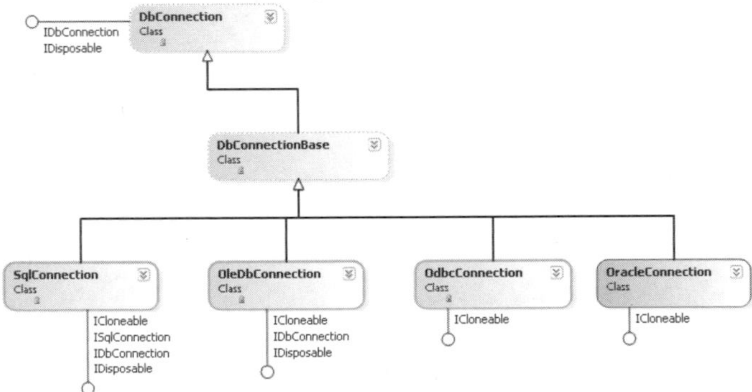

Figure 2-1 The *DbConnection* class hierarchy

You need a valid connection string to create a connection. The following code snippet shows first how to create the connection and then how to assign the connection string. With a valid connection string, you can open the connection and execute commands. When you are finished working with the connection object, you must close the connection to free up the resources being held. Note that you need the pubs sample database to use this connection. The pubs and Northwind sample databases are available from the Microsoft download site and are also included on the sample disc.

Visual Basic

```
Dim connection as DbConnection = new SqlConnection()
connection.ConnectionString = _
   "Server=.;Database=pubs;Trusted_Connection=true"
connection.Open()
'Do lots of cool work here
connection.Close()
```

C#

```
DbConnection connection = new SqlConnection();
connection.ConnectionString =
   "Server=.;Database=pubs;Trusted_Connection=true";
connection.Open();
   //Do lots of cool work here
connection.Close();
```

By creating an instance of the *SqlConnection* class, the *DbConnection* is created using the SQL Server .NET provider. The *ConnectionString* property is initialized to use the local machine (".") and set the startup database to the pubs database. Lastly, the connection uses a trusted connection for authentication when connecting to SQL Server.

Note that the connection string is the same regardless of the programming language used. The following sections explain how to configure a connection string using each of the .NET providers.

Configuring an ODBC Connection String

The connection string can be the most difficult object to set up when you're working with a provider for the first time. Open Database Connectivity (ODBC) is one of the older technologies that the .NET Framework supports, primarily because the .NET Framework is still required to connect to older database products that have ODBC drivers. Table 2-2 describes the most common ODBC connection string settings.

Table 2-2 ODBC Connection String Keywords

Keyword	Description
Driver	The ODBC driver to use for the connection
DSN	A data source name, which can be configured through Control Panel |Administrative Tools| Data Sources (ODBC)
Server	The name of the server to connect to
Trusted_Connection	Specifies that security is based on using the domain account of the currently logged on user
Database	The database to connect to
DBQ	Typically refers to the physical path to a data source

Sample ODBC Connection Strings The following connection string instructs the text driver to treat the files that are located in the C:\Test\MyFolder subdirectory as tables in a database.

```
Driver={Microsoft Text Driver (*.txt; *.csv)};
   DBQ=C:\\Test\\MyFolder;
```

The following connection string instructs the Access driver to open the northwind database file that is located in the C:\Program Files\myApp folder.

```
Driver={Microsoft Access Driver (*.mdb)};
   DBQ=C:\\program files\\myApp\\northwind.mdb
```

The following connection string uses the settings that have been configured as a data source name (DSN) on the current machine.

```
DSN=My Application DataSource
```

The following is a connection to an Oracle database on the ORACLE8i7 servers. The name and password are passed in as well.

```
Driver={Microsoft ODBC for Oracle};
   Server=ORACLE8i7;
   UID=john;
   PWD=s3$W%1Xz
```

The following connection string uses the Excel driver to open the MyBook.xls file.

```
Driver={Microsoft Excel Driver (*.xls)};
   DBQ=C:\\Samples\\MyBook.xls
```

The following connection string uses the SQL Server driver to open the northwind database on MyServer using the passed-in user name and password.

```
DRIVER={SQL Server};
   SERVER=MyServer;
   UID=AppUserAccount;
   PWD=Zx%7$ha;
   DATABASE=northwind;
```

This connection string uses the SQL Server driver to open the northwind database on MyServer using SQL Server's trusted security.

```
DRIVER={SQL Server};
   SERVER=MyServer;
   Trusted_Connection=yes
   DATABASE=northwind;
```

OLEDB Connection String Configuration

Another common but older technology that is used to access databases is Object Linking and Embedding for Databases (OLEDB). Table 2-3 describes the most common OLEDB connection string settings.

Table 2-3 OLEDB Connection String Keywords

Keyword	Description
Data Source	The name of the database or physical location of the database file.
File Name	The physical location of a file that contains the real connection string.
Persist Security Info	If set to *true*, retrieving the connection string returns the complete connection string that was originally provided. If set to *false*, the connection string contains the information that was originally provided, minus the security information.
Provider	The vendor-specific driver to use for connecting to the data store.

Sample OLEDB Connection Strings This connection string uses the settings stored in the MyAppData.udl file. The .udl extension stands for *universal data link*.

```
FILE NAME=C:\Program Files\MyApp\MyAppData.udl
```

This connection string uses the Jet driver, which is the Access driver, and opens the demo database file. Retrieving the connection string from the connection returns the connection that was originally passed in, minus the security information.

```
Provider=Microsoft.Jet.OLEDB.4.0;
   Data Source=C:\Program Files\myApp\demo.mdb;
   Persist Security Info=False
```

SQL Server Connection String Configuration

The SQL Server provider allows you to access SQL Server 7.0 and later. If you need to connect to SQL Server 6.5 and earlier, use the OLEDB provider. Table 2-4 describes the most common SQL Server connection string settings.

Table 2-4 SQL Server Connection String Keywords

Keyword	Description
Data Source, addr, address, network address, server	The name or IP address of the database server.
Failover Partner	Provides support for database mirroring in SQL Server 2005.

Table 2-4 **SQL Server Connection String Keywords**

Keyword	Description
AttachDbFilename, extended properties, initial filename	The full or relative path and name of a file containing the database to be attached to. The path supports the keyword string *|DataDirectory|*, which points to the application's data directory. The database must reside on a local drive. The log filename must be in the format *<database-File-Name>_log.ldf* or it will not be found. If the log file is not found, a new log file is created.
Initial Catalog, database	The name of the database to use.
Integrated Security, trusted_connection	Used to connect to SQL Server using a secure connection, where authentication is through the user's domain account. Can be set to *true*, *false*, or *sspi*. The default is *false*.
Persist Security Info, persistsecurityinfo	If set to *true*, retrieving the connection string returns the complete connection string that was originally provided. If set to *false*, the connection string contains the information that was originally provided, minus the security information. The default is *false*.
User ID, uid, user	The user name to use to connect to the SQL Server when not using a trusted connection.
Password, pwd	The password to use to log in to SQL Server when not using a trusted connection.
Enlist	When set to *true*, the pooler automatically enlists the connection into the caller thread's ongoing transaction context.
Pooling	When set to *true*, causes the request for a new connection to be drawn from the pool. If the pool does not exist, it is created.
Max Pool Size	Specifies the maximum allowed connections in the connection pool. The default is 100.
Min Pool Size	Specifies the minimum number of connections to keep in the pool. The default is 0.
Asynchronous Processing, async	When set to *true*, enables execution of asynchronous commands on the connection. Synchronous commands should use a different connection, to minimize resource usage. The default is *false*.
Connection Reset	Indicates that the database connection will be reset when the connection is removed from the pool. The default is *true*. A setting of *false* results in fewer round-trips to the server when creating a connection, but the connection state is not updated.
MultipleActiveResultSets	When set to *true*, allows for the retrieval of multiple forward-only, read-only result sets on the same connection. The default is false.
Replication	Used by SQL Server for replication.

Table 2-4 **SQL Server Connection String Keywords**

Keyword	Description
Connect Timeout, connection timeout, timeout	The time in seconds to wait while an attempt is made to connect to the data store. The default is 15 seconds.
Encrypt	If *Encrypt* is set to *true* and SQL Server has a certificate installed, all communication between the client and server is SSL encrypted.
Load Balance Timeout, connection lifetime	The maximum time in seconds that a pooled connection should live. The maximum time is checked only when the connection is returned to the pool. This setting is useful in load-balanced cluster configurations to force a balance between a server that is on line and a server that has just started. The default is 0.
Network Library, net, network	The network library DLL to use when connecting to SQL Server. Allowed libraries include dbmssocn (TCP/IP), dbnmpntw (Named Pipes), dbmsrpcn (Multiprotocol), dbmsadsn (AppleTalk), dbmsgnet (VIA), dbmsipcn (Shared Memory), and dbmsspxn (IPX/SPX). The default is dbmssocn (TCP/IP), but if a network is not specified and either "." or "(local)" is specified for the server, shared memory is used as the default.
Packet Size	The size in bytes for each packet that is sent to SQL Server. The default is 8192.
Application Name, app	The name of the application. If not set, this defaults to .NET SQL Client Data Provider.
Current Language, language	The SQL Server language record name.
Workstation ID, wsid	The name of the client computer that is connecting to SQL Server.

Sample SQL Server Connection Strings The following connection string connects to the northwind database on the current computer (localhost) using integrated security. This connection must be made within 30 seconds or an exception is thrown. The security information will not be persisted.

```
Persist Security Info=False;
   Integrated Security=SSPI;
   database=northwind;
   server=localhost;
   Connect Timeout=30
```

This next connection string uses the TCP sockets library (DBMSSOCN) and connects to the MyDbName database on the computer located at IP address 10.1.2.3, using port 1433. Authentication is based on using *MyUsername* as the user name and *x&1W$dF9* as the password.

```
Network Library=DBMSSOCN;
   Data Source=10.1.2.3,1433;
```

```
Initial Catalog=MyDbName;
User ID=myUsername;
Password=x&1W$dF9
```

Attaching to a Local SQL Database File with SQL Express SQL Express is a free database product that is easy to install and use and is based on SQL Server 2005 technology. When you're building small Web sites and single-user applications, SQL Express is a natural choice due to its XCOPY deployment capabilities, reliability, and high-performance engine. In addition, SQL Express databases can easily be attached to SQL Server 2005. SQL Express is installed as part of the default Visual Studio 2005 installation, which makes it an excellent database to use when you're developing applications that are destined to be used on SQL Express or SQL Server 2005. To attach a local database file, you can use the following connection string.

```
Data Source=.\SQLEXPRESS;
   AttachDbFilename=C:\MyApplication\PUBS.MDF;
   Integrated Security=True;
   User Instance=True
```

In this example, the *Data Source* is set to an instance of SQL Express called .\SQLEXPRESS. The database filename is set to the database file located at C:\MyApplication\PUBS.MDF. Note that the log file (PUBS_LOG.LDF) must also exist. Integrated security is used to authenticate with SQL Express; setting *User Instance* to *true* starts an instance of SQL Express using the current user's account.

Although you can use SQL Server to attach to a local file, SQL Server does not work with the *User Instance=True* setting. Also, SQL Server keeps the database attached when your application ends, so the next time you run SQL Server an exception is thrown because the data file is already attached.

AttachDBFile can also understand the keyword |*DataDirectory*| to use the application's data directory. Here is the revised connection string.

```
Data Source=.\SQLEXPRESS;
   AttachDbFilename=|DataDirectory|\PUBS.MDF;
   Integrated Security=True;
   User Instance=True
```

How Is the DataDirectory Resolved? Internally, the System.Data.dll library contains a class called *System.Data.Common.DbConnectionOptions*, which has a method called *ExpandDataDirectory*. This method includes code that resolves the |*DataDirectory*| keyword by executing code that looks something like the following.

Visual Basic

```
Dim path As string = AppDomain.CurrentDomain.GetData("DataDirectory")
If path = string.Empty Then
      path = AppDomain.CurrentDomain.BaseDirectory
End If
Return path
```

C#

```
string path = (string)AppDomain.CurrentDomain.GetData("DataDirectory");
if (path==string.Empty)
{
      path = AppDomain.CurrentDomain.BaseDirectory;
}
return path;
```

What does this mean? Well, first of all, the *ExpandDataDirectory* method tries to get the *DataDirectory* location from the current assembly. The *DataDirectory* is set for every ClickOnce application installed on a local computer. The *DataDirectory* is located in the user's Documents And Settings folder. If a database file (.mdf) and its log file (.ldf) are included in a ClickOnce application and marked as a "data" file, they are copied to this directory on application install. If the ClickOnce application is uninstalled, the application's data directory and the contents of the data directory are destroyed.

Notice that the sample code uses the *BaseDirectory* of *CurrentDomain* if there is no *DataDirectory*. The *BaseDirectory* is the directory that contains the compiled application (bin\Debug). Instead of placing the database file directly in the compiled application folder, it's better to place it in the project folder and set Copy To Output Directory to Copy Always or Copy If Newer.

Storing the Connection String in the Application Configuration File

You can store *connectionStrings* in the machine or application configuration file, which means that the connection strings can be changed without requiring a recompile of the application. You place the *<connectionStrings>* element under the *<configuration>* root element. This section supports the *<add>*, *<remove>*, and *<clear>* tags, as shown here:

XML Application Configuration File

```
<connectionStrings>
   <clear />
   <add name="PubsData"
      providerName="System.Data.SqlClient"
      connectionString=
      "Data Source=.\SQLEXPRESS;
         AttachDbFilename=|DataDirectory|PUBS.MDF;
         Integrated Security=True;
         User Instance=True"/>
</connectionStrings>
```

This example clears the list of *connectionSettings* that may have been defined in the machine configuration file and then adds a new connection string setting called *PubsData*. The *connectionStrings* can be accessed in code by using the static *ConnectionStrings* collection on the *ConfigurationManager* class, as shown in the following code snippet.

Visual Basic

```
'Get the settings from the configuration file
Dim pubs As ConnectionStringSettings
pubs = ConfigurationManager.ConnectionStrings("PubsData")
'name = "PubsData"
```

```
Dim name As String = pubs.Name
'provider = "System.Data.SqlClient"
Dim provider As String = pubs.ProviderName
'cnString = "Data Source=.\SQLEXPRESS;
'   AttachDbFilename=|DataDirectory|PUBS.MDF;
'   Integrated Security=True;
'   User Instance=True"
Dim cnString As String = pubs.ConnectionString
```

C#

```
//Get the settings from the configuration file
ConnectionStringSettings pubs =
   ConfigurationManager.ConnectionStrings["PubsData"];
DbConnection connection = new SqlConnection(pubs.ConnectionString);
//name = "PubsData"
string name = pubs.Name;
//provider = "System.Data.SqlClient"
string provider = pubs.ProviderName;
//cnString = "Data Source=.\SQLEXPRESS;
//   AttachDbFilename=|DataDirectory|\PUBS.MDF;
//   Integrated Security=True;
//   User Instance=True"
string cnString = pubs.ConnectionString;
```

GetSchema Method

The *DbConnection* object contains a method called *GetSchema*, which you can use to query a data store for its schema information. The method can be useful when you need to discover a data store's metadata dynamically. To use the *GetSchema* method, you open a connection, call *GetSchema*, and then close the connection. The following sample code demonstrates the retrieval of the schema information from the pubs database and binding the returned results to a *DataGridView* object. The output of this code is shown in Figure 2-2.

Visual Basic

```
'Get the settings from the configuration file
Dim pubs As ConnectionStringSettings
pubs = ConfigurationManager.ConnectionStrings("PubsData")
Dim connection As DbConnection = New SqlConnection()
connection.ConnectionString = pubs.ConnectionString
connection.Open()
Dim schema As DataTable = connection.GetSchema()
connection.Close()
dataGridView1.DataSource = schema
```

C#

```
//Get the settings from the configuration file
ConnectionStringSettings pubs =
   ConfigurationManager.ConnectionStrings["PubsData"];
DbConnection connection = new SqlConnection(pubs.ConnectionString);
connection.Open();
DataTable schema = connection.GetSchema();
connection.Close();
dataGridView1.DataSource = schema;
```

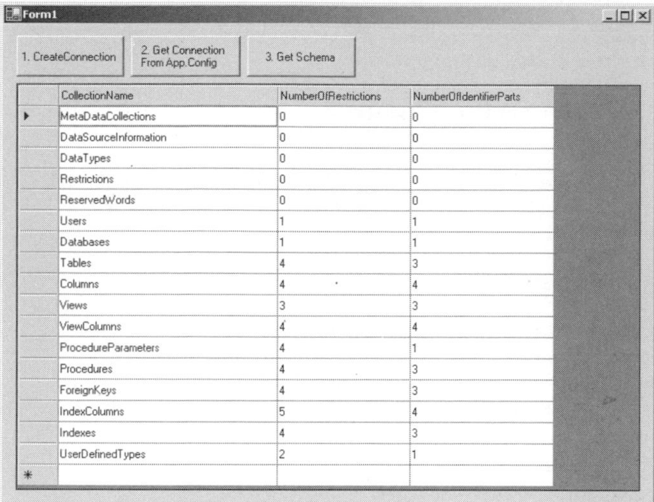

Figure 2-2 The *GetSchema* method provides metadata information.

Notice that the schema is returned as a *DataTable* object that contains three *DataColumn* objects:

- *CollectionName* Identifies the name of a collection that can be queried for more specific information. For example, one of the collection names is *Tables*. If you pass *Tables* to the *GetSchema* method, you receive a list of all of the tables in the database.
- *NumberOfRestrictions* For each collection item, this represents an array of qualifiers that can be used to restrict the scope of the schema information when you request it.
- *NumberOfIdentifierParts* For each collection item, this represents the number of parts that can be joined together to form a fully qualified object name. For example, the *Tables* collection name contains three identifier parts: the database name, the user name, and the name of the *DataTable* itself.

You can use this information to query for more specific information. For the following example, another *DataGridView* object was added to the form and code was added to the *SelectionChanged* event of the first *DataGridView* object, which populates the second *DataGridView* object as you select a different row. The *SelectionChanged* code looks like the following:

Visual Basic

```
Private Sub DataGridView1_SelectionChanged( _
      ByVal sender As System.Object, _
      ByVal e As System.EventArgs) _
      Handles DataGridView1.SelectionChanged
   Dim schema As DataTable = DataGridView1.DataSource
   Dim currentRow As DataRow = _
      schema.Rows(DataGridView1.CurrentCell.RowIndex)
   Dim collectionName As String = currentRow("CollectionName")
   'Get the settings from the configuration file
   Dim pubs As ConnectionStringSettings
```

```
   pubs = ConfigurationManager.ConnectionStrings("PubsData")
   Dim connection As DbConnection = New SqlConnection()
   connection.ConnectionString = pubs.ConnectionString
   connection.Open()
   Dim schema2 As DataTable = connection.GetSchema(collectionName)
   connection.Close()
   DataGridView2.DataSource = schema2
End Sub
```

C#

```
private void dataGridView1_SelectionChanged(object sender, EventArgs e)
{
   DataTable schema = (DataTable)dataGridView1.DataSource;
   DataRow currentRow = schema.Rows[dataGridView1.CurrentCell.RowIndex];
   string collection = (string)currentRow["CollectionName"];
   //Get the settings from the configuration file
   ConnectionStringSettings pubs =
      ConfigurationManager.ConnectionStrings["PubsData"];
   DbConnection connection = new SqlConnection(pubs.ConnectionString);
   connection.Open();
   DataTable schema2 = connection.GetSchema(collection);
   connection.Close();
   dataGridView2.DataSource = schema2;
}
```

The results can be seen in Figure 2-3. Notice that the *Tables CollectionName* is selected, which triggers the *SelectionChanged* event code. The lower *DataGridView* object contains the more specific metadata for the tables in the database. There are four columns, each of which can be used to filter the information when you execute the *GetSchema* method. Also, the fully qualified table name has three parts: the *table_catalog*, the *table_schema*, and the *table_name*. For more information on metadata, refer to Chapter 11, "Retrieving Metadata."

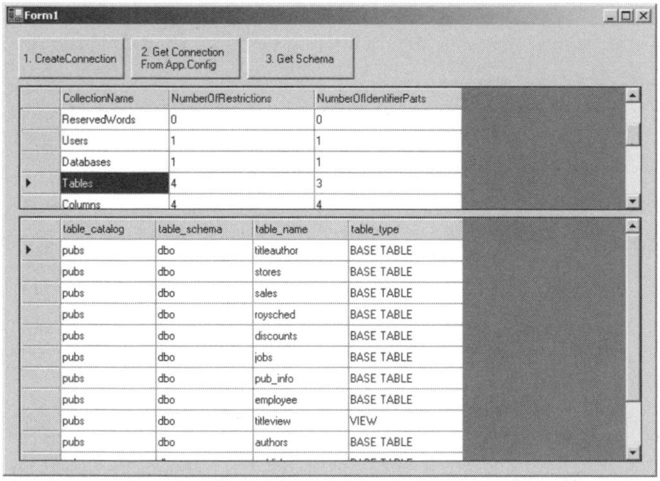

Figure 2-3 The *GetSchema* method is executed again, with *Tables* passed in as a parameter to retrieve more specific metadata for the tables in the database.

DbCommand Object

You use the *DbCommand* object to send a Structured Query Language (SQL) command to the data store. The *DbCommand* can be a Data Manipulation Language (DML) command to retrieve, insert, update, or delete data. The *DbCommand* object can also be a Data Definition Language (DDL) command, which allows you to create tables and modify schema information at the database. The *DbCommand* object requires a valid open connection to issue the command to the data store. A *DbConnection* object can be passed into the *DbCommand* object's constructor or attached to the *DbCommand* object's *Connection* property after the *DbCommand* is created, but the best way to create a *DbCommand* is to use the *CreateCommand* method on the *DbConnection* object. Using the *CreateCommand* method on the *DbConnection* means that provider-specific code is limited to the creation of the *DbConnection*, and the *DbConnection* automatically creates the appropriate provider-specific *DbCommand*.

The *DbCommand* also requires a valid value for its *CommandText* and *CommandType* properties. The following code snippet shows how to create and initialize a *DbCommand*.

Visual Basic

```
Dim pubs As ConnectionStringSettings
pubs = ConfigurationManager.ConnectionStrings("PubsData")
Dim connection As DbConnection = New SqlConnection()
connection.ConnectionString = pubs.ConnectionString
Dim cmd As DbCommand = connection.CreateCommand()
cmd.CommandType = CommandType.StoredProcedure
cmd.CommandText = "uspGetCustomerById"
```

C#

```
ConnectionStringSettings pubs =
   ConfigurationManager.ConnectionStrings["PubsData"];
DbConnection connection =
   new SqlConnection(pubs.ConnectionString);
DbCommand cmd = connection.CreateCommand();
cmd.CommandType = CommandType.StoredProcedure;
cmd.CommandText = "uspGetCustomerById";
```

This code creates a *DbConnection* object that is a *SqlConnection* object. The *DbConnection* object is then used to create a *SqlCommand*, which is assigned to *cmd*. The *DbConnection* must be opened before the command can be executed. This command executes a stored procedure. Notice that the *CommandText* property contains the name of the stored procedure, whereas the *CommandType* property indicates that this is a call to a stored procedure.

DbParameter Objects

Stored procedures typically require parameter values to be passed to them in order to execute. For example, a user-defined stored procedure called *uspGetCustomerById* might require a customer identification to retrieve the appropriate customer. You can create *DbParameter* objects by using the *Parameters.Add* method of the *Command* object, as shown here.

Visual Basic

```
Dim pubs As ConnectionStringSettings
pubs = ConfigurationManager.ConnectionStrings("PubsData")
Dim connection As DbConnection = New SqlConnection()
connection.ConnectionString = pubs.ConnectionString
Dim cmd As DbCommand = connection.CreateCommand()
cmd.CommandType = CommandType.StoredProcedure
cmd.CommandText = "uspGetCustomerById"
Dim parm As DbParameter = cmd.CreateParameter()
parm.ParameterName = "@Id"
parm.Value = "AROUT"
cmd.Parameters.Add(parm)
```

C#

```
ConnectionStringSettings pubs =
   ConfigurationManager.ConnectionStrings["PubsData"];
DbConnection connection = new SqlConnection(pubs.ConnectionString);
DbCommand cmd = connection.CreateCommand();
cmd.CommandType = CommandType.StoredProcedure;
cmd.CommandText = "uspGetCustomerById";
DbParameter parm = cmd.CreateParameter();
parm.ParameterName = "@Id";
parm.Value = "AROUT";
cmd.Parameters.Add(parm);
```

This code creates a *DbConnection* object and a *DbCommand* object. It also configures the *DbCommand* object to execute a stored procedure called *uspGetCustomerById*, which requires a single parameter called *@Id* that is assigned the value "AROUT".

Note The SQL provider requires that the parameter names match the parameter names defined in the stored procedure. The creation of the parameters is therefore not order dependent.

The OLEDB provider on the other hand requires the parameters to be defined in the same order that they are defined in the stored procedure. This means the name assigned to the parameter need not match the name defined in the stored procedure.

You can use the name assigned to the *DbParameter* object to access the parameter through code. For example, to retrieve the value that is currently in the *SqlParameter* called *@Id*, use the following code.

Visual Basic

```
Dim id as String = cmd.Parameters("@Id").Value
```

C#

```
string id = (string)((DbParameter)cmd.Parameters["@Id"]).Value;
```

ExecuteNonQuery Method

You execute a *DbCommand* object differently, depending on the data that is being retrieved or modified. You use the *ExecuteNonQuery* method when you don't expect a command to return any rows–an insert, update, or delete query, for example. This method returns an integer that represents the number of rows affected by the operation. The following example executes a stored procedure to increment the *qty* field in the sales table for sales with *qty* greater that 50, and it returns the number of rows that were updated.

Visual Basic

```
Dim pubs As ConnectionStringSettings
pubs = ConfigurationManager.ConnectionStrings("PubsData")
Dim connection As DbConnection = New SqlConnection()
connection.ConnectionString = pubs.ConnectionString
Dim cmd As DbCommand = connection.CreateCommand()
cmd.CommandType = CommandType.Text
cmd.CommandText = "UPDATE SALES SET qty = qty + 1 WHERE qty > 50"
connection.Open()
Dim count As Integer = cmd.ExecuteNonQuery()
connection.Close()
```

C#

```
ConnectionStringSettings pubs =
   ConfigurationManager.ConnectionStrings["PubsData"];
DbConnection connection = new SqlConnection(pubs.ConnectionString);
DbCommand cmd = connection.CreateCommand();
cmd.CommandType = CommandType.Text;
cmd.CommandText = "UPDATE SALES SET qty = qty + 1 WHERE qty > 50";
connection.Open();
int count = cmd.ExecuteNonQuery();
connection.Close();
```

ExecuteScalar Method

Queries are often expected to return a single row with a single column. In these situations, the results can be treated as a single return value. For example, the following SQL returns a result that consists of a single row with a single column.

```
SELECT COUNT(*) FROM Sales
```

If you use the *ExecuteScalar* method, the .NET runtime will not create an instance of a *DataTable* for the result, which means less resource usage and better performance. The following code shows how to use the *ExecuteScalar* method to easily retrieve the number of rows in the Sales table into a variable called *count*.

Visual Basic

```
Dim pubs As ConnectionStringSettings
pubs = ConfigurationManager.ConnectionStrings("PubsData")
Dim connection As DbConnection = New SqlConnection()
connection.ConnectionString = pubs.ConnectionString
Dim cmd As DbCommand = connection.CreateCommand()
```

```
cmd.CommandType = CommandType.Text
cmd.CommandText = "SELECT COUNT(*) FROM Sales"
connection.Open()
Dim count As Integer = cmd.ExecuteScalar()
connection.Close()
MessageBox.Show(count.ToString())
```

C#

```
ConnectionStringSettings pubs =
   ConfigurationManager.ConnectionStrings["PubsData"];
DbConnection connection = new SqlConnection(pubs.ConnectionString);
DbCommand cmd = connection.CreateCommand();
cmd.CommandType = CommandType.Text;
cmd.CommandText = "SELECT COUNT(*) FROM Sales";
connection.Open();
int count = (int)cmd.ExecuteScalar();
connection.Close();
```

ExecuteReader Method

The *ExecuteReader* method returns a *DbDataReader* instance. The *DbDataReader* object is a forward-only, read-only, server-side cursor. *DbDataReader* objects can be created only by executing one of the *ExecuteReader* methods on the *DbCommand* object. (See the next section for more information on the *DbDataReader*.) The following example uses the *ExecuteReader* method to create a *DbDataReader* object with the selection results and then continuously loops through the results until the end of data has been reached (when the *Read* method returns *false*).

Visual Basic

```
Dim pubs As ConnectionStringSettings
pubs = ConfigurationManager.ConnectionStrings("PubsData")
Dim connection As DbConnection = New SqlConnection()
connection.ConnectionString = pubs.ConnectionString
Dim cmd As DbCommand = connection.CreateCommand()
cmd.CommandType = CommandType.Text
cmd.CommandText = "SELECT stor_id, ord_num FROM Sales"
connection.Open()
Dim rdr As DbDataReader = cmd.ExecuteReader()
While (rdr.Read())
   MessageBox.Show(rdr("stor_id") + ": " + rdr("ord_num"))
End While
connection.Close()
```

C#

```
ConnectionStringSettings pubs =
   ConfigurationManager.ConnectionStrings["PubsData"];
DbConnection connection = new SqlConnection(pubs.ConnectionString);
DbCommand cmd = connection.CreateCommand();
cmd.CommandType = CommandType.Text;
cmd.CommandText = "SELECT stor_id, ord_num FROM Sales";
connection.Open();
DbDataReader rdr = cmd.ExecuteReader();
```

```
while (rdr.Read())
{
   MessageBox.Show((string)rdr["stor_id"] + ": " + (string)rdr["ord_num"]);
}
connection.Close();
```

DbDataReader Object

A *DbDataReader* object provides a high-performance method of retrieving data from the data store. It delivers a forward-only, read-only, server-side cursor. This makes the *DbDataReader* object an ideal choice for populating *ListBox* objects and *DropDownList* objects. When you run reports, you can use the *DbDataReader* object to retrieve the data from the data store. The *DbDataReader* might not be a good choice when you are coding an operation that modifies data and needs to send the changes back to the database. For data modifications, the *DbDataAdapter* object, which is discussed in the next section, might be a better choice.

The *DbDataReader* contains a *Read* method that retrieves data into its buffer. Only one row of data is ever available at a time, which means that the data does not need to be completely read into the application before it is processed. The following code populates a new *DataTable* directly with the list of publishers from the pubs database.

Visual Basic

```
Dim pubs As ConnectionStringSettings
pubs = ConfigurationManager.ConnectionStrings("PubsData")
Dim connection As DbConnection = New SqlConnection()
connection.ConnectionString = pubs.ConnectionString
Dim cmd As DbCommand = connection.CreateCommand()
cmd.CommandType = CommandType.Text
cmd.CommandText = "SELECT pub_id, pub_name FROM publishers"
connection.Open()
Dim rdr As DbDataReader = cmd.ExecuteReader()
Dim publishers As New DataTable()
publishers.Load(rdr, LoadOption.Upsert)
connection.Close()
```

C#

```
ConnectionStringSettings pubs =
   ConfigurationManager.ConnectionStrings["PubsData"];
DbConnection connection = new SqlConnection(pubs.ConnectionString);
DbCommand cmd = connection.CreateCommand();
cmd.CommandType = CommandType.Text;
cmd.CommandText = "SELECT pub_id, pub_name FROM Publishers";
connection.Open();
DbDataReader rdr = cmd.ExecuteReader();
DataTable publishers = new DataTable();
publishers.Load(rdr, LoadOption.Upsert);
connection.Close();
```

Notice that the *DataTable* object's *Load* method contains a *LoadOption* parameter. The *LoadOption* gives you the option of deciding which *DataRowVersion* should get the incoming data. For example, if you load a *DataTable* object, modify the data, and then save the changes back to the database, you might encounter concurrency errors if someone else has modified the data between the time you got the data and the time you attempted to save the data. One option is to load the *DataTable* object again, using the default *PreserveCurrentValues* enumeration value, which loads the original *DataRowVersion* with the data from the database while leaving the current *DataRowVersion* untouched. Next you can simply execute the *Update* method again and the update will succeed.

For this to work properly, the *DataTable* must have a *PrimaryKey* defined. Failure to define a *PrimaryKey* results in duplicate *DataRow* objects being added to the *DataTable* object. The *LoadOption* enumeration members are described in Table 2-5.

Table 2-5 *LoadOption* Enumeration Members

LoadOption Member	Description
OverwriteChanges	Overwrites the original *DataRowVersion* and the current *DataRowVersion* and changes the *RowState* to *Unchanged*. New rows will have a *RowState* of *Unchanged* as well.
PreserveChanges (default)	Overwrites the original *DataRowVersion* but does not modify the current *DataRowVersion*. New rows have a *RowState* of *Unchanged* as well.
Upsert	Overwrites the current *DataRowVersion* but does not modify the original *DataRowVersion*. New rows have a *RowState* of *Added*. Rows that had a *RowState* of *Unchanged* have a *RowState* of *Unchanged* if the current *DataRowVersion* is the same as the original *DataRowVersion*, but if they are different, the *RowState* is *Modified*.

Using Multiple Active Result Sets (MARS) to Execute Multiple Commands on a Connection

Using the *DbDataReader* object is one of the fastest methods to retrieve data from the database, but one of the problems with the *DbDataReader* is that it keeps an open server-side cursor while you are looping through the results of your query. If you try to execute another command while the first command is still executing, you receive an *InvalidOperationException* message stating that "There is already an open DataReader associated with this Connection which must be closed first." You can avoid this exception by setting the *MultipleActiveResultSets* connection string option to *true* when connecting to MARS-enabled hosts, such as SQL Server 2005. For example, the following connection string shows how this setting is added into a new connection string called *PubsDataMars*.

XML Application Configuration File

```
<connectionStrings>
   <clear />
   <add name="PubsData"
      providerName="System.Data.SqlClient"
      connectionString=
      "Data Source=.\SQLEXPRESS;
```

```
         AttachDbFilename=|DataDirectory|PUBS.MDF;
         Integrated Security=True;
         User Instance=True"/>
   <add name="PubsDataMars"
      providerName="System.Data.SqlClient"
      connectionString=
      "Data Source=.\SQLEXPRESS;
         AttachDbFilename=|DataDirectory|PUBS.MDF;
         Integrated Security=True;
         User Instance=True;
         MultipleActiveResultSets=True"/>
</connectionStrings>
```

MARS does not provide any performance gains, but it does simplify your coding efforts. Think of a scenario in which you execute a query to get a list of stores, and while you loop through a list of stores that are returned, you want to execute a second query to get the total quantity of books sold.

MARS is not something that you can't live without. MARS simply makes your programming easier. As a matter of fact, setting *MultipleActiveResultSets = True* in the connection string has a negative performance impact, so you should not turn on MARS arbitrarily.

On a database server without MARS, you could first collect the list of stores into a collection and close the connection. After that, you can loop through the collection to get each store ID and execute a query to get the total quantity of books sold for that store. This means that you loop through the stores twice—once to populate the collection and again to get each store and execute a query to get the store's quantity of book sales. Another solution is simply to create two connections: one for the store list and one for the quantity of books sold query.

Another benefit that MARS provides is that you might have purchased database client licenses that are based on the quantity of connections to the database. Without MARS, you would have to open a separate connection to the database for each command that needs to run at the same time, which means that you might need to purchase more client licenses.

The following code snippet shows how MARS can be used to perform the nested queries for the store list and the quantity of books sold.

Visual Basic

```
Dim pubs As ConnectionStringSettings
pubs = ConfigurationManager.ConnectionStrings("PubsDataMars")
Dim connection As DbConnection = New SqlConnection()
connection.ConnectionString = pubs.ConnectionString
Dim cmd As DbCommand = connection.CreateCommand()
cmd.CommandType = CommandType.Text
cmd.CommandText = "SELECT stor_id, stor_name FROM Stores"
connection.Open()
Dim rdr As DbDataReader = cmd.ExecuteReader()
While rdr.Read()
   Dim salesCmd as DbCommand = connection.CreateCommand()
   salesCmd.CommandType = CommandType.Text
```

```
    salesCmd.CommandText = _
       "SELECT SUM(qty) FROM sales WHERE (stor_id = @storeId)"
    Dim parm as DbParameter  = salesCmd.CreateParameter()
    parm.ParameterName = "@storeId"
    parm.Value = rdr("stor_id")
    salesCmd.Parameters.Add(parm)
    Dim qtySales as object= salesCmd.ExecuteScalar()
    MessageBox.Show(rdr("stor_name").ToString() + ": " + qtySales.ToString())
End while
connection.Close()
```

C#

```
ConnectionStringSettings pubs =
   ConfigurationManager.ConnectionStrings["PubsDataMars"];
DbConnection connection = new SqlConnection(pubs.ConnectionString);
DbCommand cmd = connection.CreateCommand();
cmd.CommandType = CommandType.Text;
cmd.CommandText = "SELECT stor_id, stor_name FROM Stores";
connection.Open();
DbDataReader rdr = cmd.ExecuteReader();
while (rdr.Read())
{
   DbCommand salesCmd = connection.CreateCommand();
   salesCmd.CommandType = CommandType.Text;
   salesCmd.CommandText =
      "SELECT SUM(qty) FROM sales WHERE (stor_id = @storeId)";
   DbParameter parm = salesCmd.CreateParameter();
   parm.ParameterName = "@storeId";
   parm.Value = (string)rdr["stor_id"];
   salesCmd.Parameters.Add(parm);
   object qtySales = salesCmd.ExecuteScalar();
   MessageBox.Show((string)rdr["stor_name"] + ": "
      + qtySales.ToString());
}
connection.Close();
```

Performing Bulk Copy Operations with the *SqlBulkCopy* Object

There are many occasions for which you need to copy large amounts of data from one location to another. Most of the database servers provide a means to copy from one database to another, either by a Windows GUI interface, such as SQL Server's Enterprise Manager, or through a command-line tool, such as SQL Server's Bulk Copy Program (BCP.exe). In addition to using the tools that are provided by the database vendor, you also can write your own bulk copy program using the *SqlBulkCopy* class.

The *SqlBulkCopy* class provides a high performance method for copying data to a table in a SQL Server database. The source of the copy is constrained overloads of the *WriteToServer* method, which can accept an array of *DataRow* objects, an object that implements the *IDbDataReader* interface, a *DataTable* object, or a *DataTable* object and *DataRowState* enumeration value, as shown in Figure 2-4. This variety of parameters means that you can retrieve data from most locations.

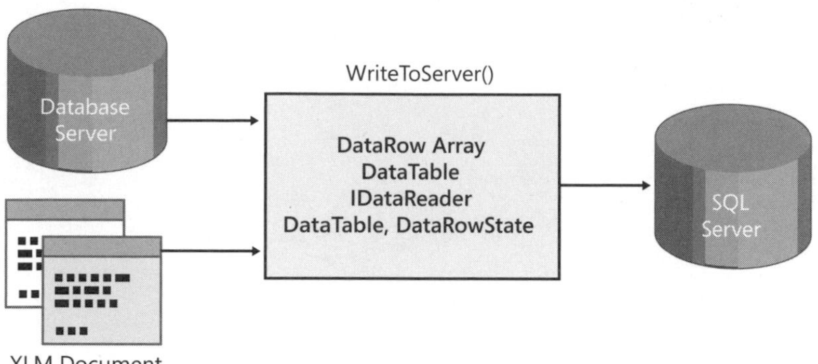

Figure 2-4 The *SqlBulkCopy* object can copy from a variety of sources to a SQL Server table.

The following code shows how you can use a *SqlBulkCopy* object to copy data from the *Store* table in the *pubs* database to the *StoreList* table in a SQL Server database called *BulkCopy*.

Visual Basic

```
Private Sub BtnBulkCopy_Click( _
      ByVal sender As System.Object, _
      ByVal e As System.EventArgs) Handles BtnBulkCopy.Click
   Dim pubs As ConnectionStringSettings
   pubs = ConfigurationManager.ConnectionStrings("PubsData")
   Dim connection As DbConnection = New SqlConnection()
   connection.ConnectionString = pubs.ConnectionString
   Dim bulkCopy As ConnectionStringSettings
   bulkCopy = ConfigurationManager.ConnectionStrings("BulkCopy")
   Dim bulkCopyConnection As DbConnection = New SqlConnection()
   bulkCopyConnection.ConnectionString = bulkCopy.ConnectionString
   Dim cmd As DbCommand = connection.CreateCommand()
   cmd.CommandType = CommandType.Text
   cmd.CommandText = "SELECT stor_name FROM Stores"
   connection.Open()
   bulkCopyConnection.Open()
   Dim rdr As DbDataReader = cmd.ExecuteReader()
   Dim bc As New SqlBulkCopy(bulkCopyConnection)
   bc.DestinationTableName = "StoreList"
   bc.WriteToServer(rdr)
   connection.Close()
   bulkCopyConnection.Close()
   MessageBox.Show("Done with bulk copy")
End Sub
```

C#

```
private void btnBulkCopy_Click(object sender, EventArgs e)
{
   ConnectionStringSettings pubs =
      ConfigurationManager.ConnectionStrings["PubsData"];
   DbConnection connection =
```

```
        new SqlConnection(pubs.ConnectionString);
    ConnectionStringSettings bulkCopy =
        ConfigurationManager.ConnectionStrings["BulkCopy"];
    SqlConnection bulkCopyConnection =
        new SqlConnection(bulkCopy.ConnectionString);
    DbCommand cmd = connection.CreateCommand();
    cmd.CommandType = CommandType.Text;
    cmd.CommandText = "SELECT stor_name FROM Stores";
    connection.Open();
    bulkCopyConnection.Open();
    DbDataReader rdr = cmd.ExecuteReader();
    SqlBulkCopy bc = new SqlBulkCopy(bulkCopyConnection);
    bc.DestinationTableName = "StoreList";
    bc.WriteToServer(rdr);
    connection.Close();
    bulkCopyConnection.Close();
    MessageBox.Show("Done with bulk copy");
}
```

You should consider using the *IDbDataReader* parameter whenever possible to get the best performance with the least resources used. You can decide how much data should be copied based on the query that you use. For example, the preceding code sample retrieved only the store names and could have had a *WHERE* clause to further limit the data.

DbDataAdapter Object

You use the *DbDataAdapter* object to retrieve and update data between a *DataTable* and a data store. The *DbDataAdapter* is derived from the *DataAdapter* class and is the base class of the provider-specific *DbDataAdapter* classes, as shown in Figure 2-5.

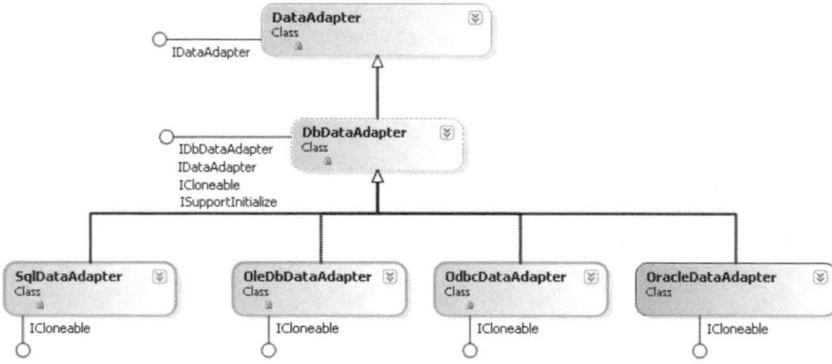

Figure 2-5 The *DbDataAdapter* hierarchy, showing the *DataAdapter* base class and the provider-specific derived classes

The *DbDataAdapter* has a *SelectCommand* property that you use when retrieving the data. The *SelectCommand* must contain a valid *DbCommand* object, which must have a valid connection. Internally, the *SelectCommand* property's *ExecuteReader* method is executed to get a *DbDataReader* object, which is used to populate a *DataTable* object.

The *DbDataAdapter* also has *InsertCommand*, *UpdateCommand*, and *DeleteCommand* properties, which might contain *DbCommand* objects. You use these commands if you want to save *DataTable* changes back to the data store. You need not create these command objects if you only need to read data from the data store, but if you create one of these latter three commands, you must create all four of them.

Using the *Fill* Method

The *Fill* method moves data from the data store to the *DataTable* object that you pass into this method. The *Fill* method has several overloads, some of which accept only a *DataSet* as a parameter. When a *DataSet* is passed to the *Fill* method, a new *DataTable* object is created in the *DataSet* if a source *DataTable* object is not specified.

The following code snippet shows how a *DataTable* can be loaded using the *Fill* method.

Visual Basic

```
Dim pubs As ConnectionStringSettings
pubs = ConfigurationManager.ConnectionStrings("PubsData")
Dim connection As DbConnection = New SqlConnection()
connection.ConnectionString = pubs.ConnectionString
Dim cmd As SqlCommand = Ctype(connection.CreateCommand(),SqlCommand)
cmd.CommandType = CommandType.Text
cmd.CommandText = "SELECT pub_id, pub_name FROM publishers"
Dim pubsDataSet as New DataSet("Pubs")
Dim da as New SqlDataAdapter(cmd)
da.Fill(pubsDataSet, "publishers")
```

C#

```
ConnectionStringSettings pubs =
   ConfigurationManager.ConnectionStrings["PubsData"];
DbConnection connection = new SqlConnection(pubs.ConnectionString);
SqlCommand cmd = (SqlCommand)connection.CreateCommand();
cmd.CommandType = CommandType.Text;
cmd.CommandText = "SELECT pub_id, pub_name FROM Publishers";
DataAdapter da = new SqlDataAdapter(cmd);
DataSet pubsDataSet = new DataSet("Pubs");
da.Fill(pubsDataSet, "publishers");
```

Many developers attempt to use a single *DbDataAdapter* for all of their queries or try to use a single *DbDataAdapter* to execute a SQL statement that returns a result set from multiple tables joined in the SQL query. If you need to store the data changes, you should consider using a separate *DbDataAdapter* for each *DataTable* that is being loaded, as shown in Figure 2-6. If all you need is a read-only *DataTable*, you can simply use a *DbCommand* object and *DbDataReader* object to load the *DataTable*.

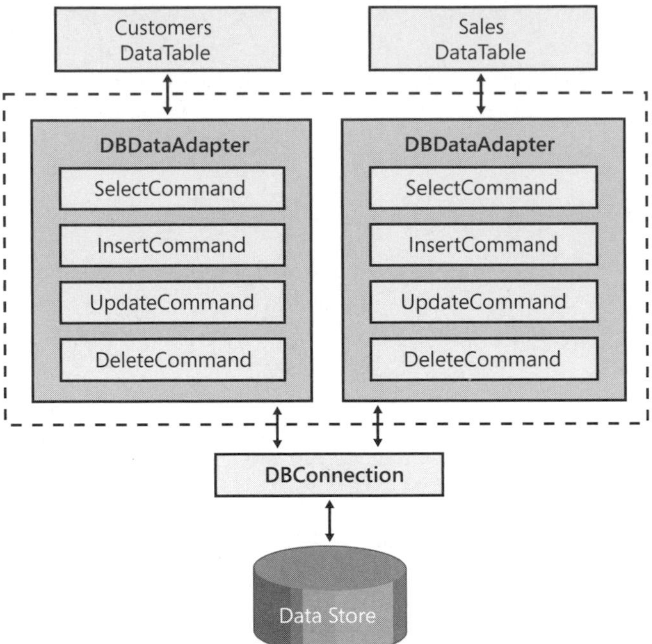

Figure 2-6 The *DbDataAdapter,* which has four *DbCommand* objects, should be used to populate each *DataTable* if the *DataTable* will contain read-write data.

Saving Changes to the Database Using the *Update* Method

The *Update* method saves the *DataTable* modifications to the database by retrieving the changes from the *DataTable* and then using the respective *InsertCommand*, *UpdateCommand*, or *DeleteCommand* to send the appropriate change to the database on a row-by-row basis. The *Update* method retrieves the *DataRow* objects that have changed by looking at the *RowState* property of each row. If the *RowState* is anything but *Unchanged*, the *Update* method sends the change to the database.

For the *Update* method to work, all four commands must be assigned to the *DbDataAdapter*. Normally, this means creating individual *DbCommand* objects for each command. You can easily create the commands by using the *DbDataAdapter* configuration wizard, which starts when a *DbDataAdapter* is dropped onto the form. The wizard can generate stored procedures for all four commands.

Another way to populate the *DbDataAdapter* object's commands is to use the *DbCommand-Builder* object. This object creates the *InsertCommand*, *UpdateCommand*, and *DeleteCommand* as long as a valid *SelectCommand* exists. The *DbDataAdapter* is great for ad hoc changes and demos, but it's generally better to use stored procedures for all database access to eliminate security risk from SQL injection attacks. The following code demonstrates a simple update to the database using the *SqlDataAdapter*, which is the SQL Server–specific version of the *DbDataAdapter*.

Visual Basic

```
Dim pubs As ConnectionStringSettings
pubs = ConfigurationManager.ConnectionStrings("PubsData")
Dim connection As DbConnection = New SqlConnection()
connection.ConnectionString = pubs.ConnectionString
Dim cmd As SqlCommand = CType(connection.CreateCommand(), SqlCommand)
cmd.CommandType = CommandType.Text
cmd.CommandText = "SELECT * FROM publishers"
Dim pubsDataSet As New DataSet("Pubs")
Dim da As New SqlDataAdapter(cmd)
Dim bldr as New SqlCommandBuilder(da)
da.Fill(pubsDataSet, "publishers")
'Modify data here
pubsDataSet.Tables("publishers").Rows(0)("pub_name")="Hello"
pubsDataSet.Tables("publishers").Rows.Add( _
   "9911", "Tailspin Toys","Paris", Nothing, "France")
da.Update(pubsDataSet, "publishers")
MessageBox.Show("Update Complete")
```

C#

```
ConnectionStringSettings pubs =
   ConfigurationManager.ConnectionStrings["PubsData"];
DbConnection connection = new SqlConnection(pubs.ConnectionString);
SqlCommand cmd = (SqlCommand)connection.CreateCommand();
cmd.CommandType = CommandType.Text;
cmd.CommandText = "SELECT * FROM Publishers";
SqlDataAdapter da = new SqlDataAdapter(cmd);
DataSet pubsDataSet = new DataSet("Pubs");
SqlCommandBuilder bldr = new SqlCommandBuilder(da);
da.Fill(pubsDataSet,"publishers");
//Modify data here
pubsDataSet.Tables[0].Rows[0]["pub_name"] = "Hello";
pubsDataSet.Tables["publishers"].Rows.Add(
   "9911", "Tailspin Toys", "Paris", null, "France");
da.Update(pubsDataSet,"publishers");
MessageBox.Show("Update Complete");
```

Note that if you click the button two times, an exception is thrown that indicates that you are trying to insert duplicate rows.

Saving Changes to the Database in Batches

If you use the SQL Profiler tool to view the update commands sent to SQL Server, you will notice that individual insert, update, and delete commands are sent to SQL Server on a row-by-row basis. One way to increase update performance is to send the changes to the database server in batches. You can do this by assigning a value to the *DbDataAdapter* object's *UpdateBatchSize* property. This property defaults to 1, which causes each change to be sent to the server on a row-by-row basis. Setting the value to 0 instructs the *DbDataAdapter* object to create the largest possible batch size for changes, or you can set the value to the number of changes you want to send to the server in each batch. Setting the *UpdateBatchSize* to a number greater than the number of changes that need to be sent is equivalent to setting it to 0.

One way to confirm that the changes are being sent to the database server in batches is to add a *RowUpdated* event to the *DbDataAdapter* object. The event handler method exposes the number of rows affected in the last batch. When the *UpdateBatchSize* is set to 1, the *RecordsAffected* property will always be 1. In the following code snippet, the publishers table contains eight rows. The *pubsDataSet* is filled, and then the *pub_name* field is modified on all eight rows. Before the *Update* method is executed, the *UpdateBatchSize* is changed to 3. When the *Update* method is executed, the changes are sent to the database as a batch of three changes, another batch of three changes, and finally a batch of two changes. This code contains a *RowUpdated* event handler to collect batch information, which is displayed after the *Update* method is executed.

Visual Basic

```
Public WithEvents da As New SqlDataAdapter()
public sb as New System.Text.StringBuilder()

private sub rowUpdated(byval sender as Object, _
      byval e as SqlRowUpdatedEventArgs) handles da.RowUpdated
   sb.Append("Rows: " & e.RecordsAffected.ToString() & vbCrLf)
End Sub

Private Sub btnUpdateBatch_Click(ByVal sender As System.Object, _
      ByVal e As System.EventArgs) Handles btnUpdateBatch.Click
   Dim pubs As ConnectionStringSettings
   pubs = ConfigurationManager.ConnectionStrings("PubsData")
   Dim connection As DbConnection = New SqlConnection()
   connection.ConnectionString = pubs.ConnectionString
   Dim cmd As SqlCommand = CType(connection.CreateCommand(), SqlCommand)
   cmd.CommandType = CommandType.Text
   cmd.CommandText = "SELECT * FROM publishers"
   Dim pubsDataSet As New DataSet("Pubs")
   da.SelectCommand = cmd
   Dim bldr As New SqlCommandBuilder(da)
   da.Fill(pubsDataSet, "publishers")
   'Modify data here
   For Each dr As DataRow In pubsDataSet.Tables("publishers").Rows
      dr("pub_name") = "Updated Toys"
   Next
   da.UpdateBatchSize = 3
   da.Update(pubsDataSet, "publishers")
   MessageBox.Show(sb.ToString())
End Sub
```

C#

```
public SqlDataAdapter da = new SqlDataAdapter();
public System.Text.StringBuilder sb = new System.Text.StringBuilder();

private void rowUpdated(object sender, SqlRowUpdatedEventArgs e )
{
   sb.Append("Rows: " + e.RecordsAffected.ToString() + "\r\n");
}

private void btnUpdateBatch_Click(object sender, EventArgs e)
```

```
{
   //event subscription is normally placed in constructor but is here
   //to encapsulate the sample
   da.RowUpdated+=new SqlRowUpdatedEventHandler(rowUpdated);
   ConnectionStringSettings pubs =
      ConfigurationManager.ConnectionStrings["PubsData"];
   DbConnection connection = new SqlConnection(pubs.ConnectionString);
   SqlCommand cmd = (SqlCommand)connection.CreateCommand();
   cmd.CommandType = CommandType.Text;
   cmd.CommandText = "SELECT * FROM Publishers";
   da.SelectCommand = cmd;
   DataSet pubsDataSet = new DataSet("Pubs");
   SqlCommandBuilder bldr = new SqlCommandBuilder(da);
   da.Fill(pubsDataSet, "publishers");
   //Modify data here
   foreach (DataRow dr in pubsDataSet.Tables["publishers"].Rows)
   {
      dr["pub_name"] = "Updated Toys";
   }
   da.UpdateBatchSize = 3;
   da.Update(pubsDataSet, "publishers");
   //if event subscription is in the constructor, no need to
   //remove it here....
   da.RowUpdated -= new SqlRowUpdatedEventHandler(rowUpdated);
   MessageBox.Show(sb.ToString());
}
```

DbProviderFactory Classes

There are many reasons for writing an application that does not require database provider-specific code. A company might want the flexibility to upgrade from one database product to another, such as moving from Microsoft Access to SQL Server. Or a company might have a retail application that must allow connectivity to any data source. With earlier versions of ADO.NET, you can write a provider-independent application by using generic interfaces. The typical coding might look something like the following:

Visual Basic

```
Public Enum DbProvider
   SqlClient
   OleDb
   Odbc
   Oracle
End Enum

Public Function GetConnection() As IDbConnection
   'Get the provider from the config file
   Dim provider As DbProvider = [Enum].Parse( _
   GetType(DbProvider), _
      ConfigurationSettings.AppSettings("provider").ToString())

   Dim connection As IDbConnection = Nothing
   Select Case (provider)
      Case DbProvider.SqlClient
```

```
            connection = New System.Data.SqlClient.SqlConnection()
        Case DbProvider.OleDb
        connection = New System.Data.OleDb.OleDbConnection()
        Case DbProvider.Odbc
        connection = New System.Data.Odbc.OdbcConnection()
        Case DbProvider.Oracle
        connection = New System.Data.OracleClient.OracleConnection()
    End Select
    Return connection
End Function
```

C#

```
public IDbConnection GetConnection()
{
   // Get the provider from the config file
   DbProvider provider = (DbProvider)Enum.Parse(
      typeof(DbProvider),
      (string)ConfigurationManager.AppSettings["provider"]);

   IDbConnection connection = null;
   switch (provider)
   {
      case DbProvider.SqlClient:
         connection = new System.Data.SqlClient.SqlConnection();
         break;
      case DbProvider.OleDb:
         connection = new System.Data.OleDb.OleDbConnection();
         break;
      case DbProvider.Odbc:
         connection = new System.Data.Odbc.OdbcConnection();
         break;
      case DbProvider.Oracle:
         connection = new System.Data.OracleClient.OracleConnection();
         break;
   }
   return connection;
}
public enum DbProvider
   { SqlClient, OleDb, Odbc, Oracle };
```

XML App.config File

```
<configuration>
    <appSettings>
        <add key="provider" value="SqlClient" />
    </appSettings>
</configuration>
```

One problem with this approach is that you can't create interface instances directly, so provider-specific code exists to determine the type of connection to create. Another problem is that interfaces are immutable by definition, so new features can't be easily added without adding a new interface.

ADO.NET provides base classes from which the provider-specific classes inherit, as shown earlier in Table 2-1. The .NET Framework supports only single inheritance, so this approach has limitations if you want to create your own base class, but for classes that will expand, providing base class inheritance is better than providing interface implementation. Note that interfaces are still provided for backward compatibility.

The preceding code listing addresses only the creation of the connection object. You would duplicate the code if you wanted to create many of the other provider objects, such as the data adapter and command objects. To keep from duplicating this conditional code for each of the provider objects, you can create a factory object that is responsible for creating the appropriate provider objects. This is where the *DbProviderFactory* is used. Each provider must supply a subclass of *DbProviderFactory* that can be used to create instances of its provider classes. For example, you can use the *SqlClientFactory* to create instances of any of the SQL Server classes. Figure 2-7 shows the *DbProviderFactory* and the *SqlClientFactory* classes, along with their properties and methods.

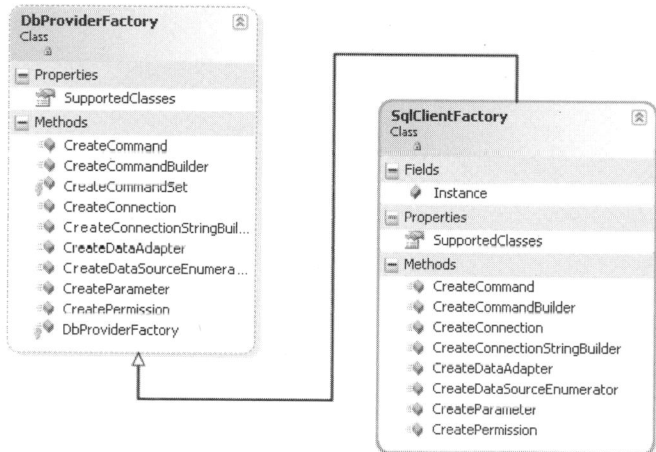

Figure 2-7 The *DbProviderFactory* and the *SqlClientFactory* classes

The provider factory classes are implemented as singletons, where each class provides an "*Instance*" property that is used to access the methods and properties shown in Figure 2-7. For example, you can use the following code to create a new connection using the *SqlClientFactory*.

Visual Basic

```
'Get the singleton instance
Dim factory As DbProviderFactory = SqlClientFactory.Instance

Public Function GetProviderConnection() As DbConnection
   Dim connection As DbConnection = factory.CreateConnection()
   connection.ConnectionString = "Data Source=.\SQLEXPRESS;" _
      & "AttachDbFilename=|DataDirectory|PUBS.MDF;" _
      & "Integrated Security=True;User Instance=True"
   Return connection
End Function
```

C#

```
//Get the singleton instance
DbProviderFactory factory = SqlClientFactory.Instance;

public DbConnection GetProviderConnection()
{
   DbConnection connection = factory.CreateConnection();
   connection.ConnectionString = "Data Source=.\SQLEXPRESS;"
      + "AttachDbFilename=|DataDirectory|PUBS.MDF;"
      + "Integrated Security=True;User Instance=True";
   return connection;
}
```

You can use the factory variable to create any of the other SQL Server–specific objects. Note that the *SqlDataReader* is created indirectly, by creating a *SqlCommand* and then using the *ExecuteReader* method, as shown in the following code snippet.

Visual Basic

```
Private Function GetData(ByVal commandText As String, _
      ByVal commandType As CommandType) As DataTable
   'get SqlDbCommand
   Dim command As DbCommand = factory.CreateCommand()
   command.Connection = GetProviderConnection()
   If (command.Connection Is Nothing) Then
      Return Nothing
   End If
   command.CommandText = commandText
   command.CommandType = commandType
   command.Connection.Open()
   Dim dataTable As DataTable = New DataTable()
   'Get SqlDataReader and populate data table
   dataTable.Load(command.ExecuteReader())
   command.Connection.Close()
   Return dataTable
End Function
```

C#

```
private DataTable GetData(string commandText, CommandType commandType)
{
   //get SqlDbCommand
   DbCommand command = factory.CreateCommand();
   command.Connection = GetProviderConnection();
   if (command.Connection == null) return null;
   command.CommandText = commandText;
   command.CommandType = commandType;
   command.Connection.Open();
   DataTable dataTable = new DataTable();
   //Get SqlDataReader and populate data table
   dataTable.Load(command.ExecuteReader());
   command.Connection.Close();
   return dataTable;
}
```

This code snippet uses the factory variable to create a *DbCommand*, which is then used to create the *DbDataReader*.

DbProviderFactories Class

You can use the *DbProviderFactory* object's subclasses to obtain a provider factory that can create any of the provider-specific objects, but it sure would be nice to retrieve a list of the provider factories that are available on a machine, or within an application. To query for the list of available factories, you can use the *DbProviderFactories* class. This class is a factory for obtaining factories. It contains a method called *GetFactoryClasses* that returns a *DataTable* that is populated with information describing all available providers. Retrieving the list of providers can be easily demonstrated by creating a Windows form and adding a *Button* and a *DataGridView* control. Add the following code to the *click* event of the button.

Visual Basic

```
Dim  providersList as DataTable = nothing

Private Sub Button1_Click(ByVal sender As System.Object, _
      ByVal e As System.EventArgs) Handles Button1.Click
   providersList = DbProviderFactories.GetFactoryClasses()
   DataGridView1.DataSource = providersList
End Sub
```

C#

```
DataTable providersList = null;
private void button1_Click(object sender, EventArgs e)
{
   providersList = DbProviderFactories.GetFactoryClasses();
   dataGridView1.DataSource = providersList;
}
```

When this simple application is run and the button is clicked, the screen shown in Figure 2-8 is displayed.

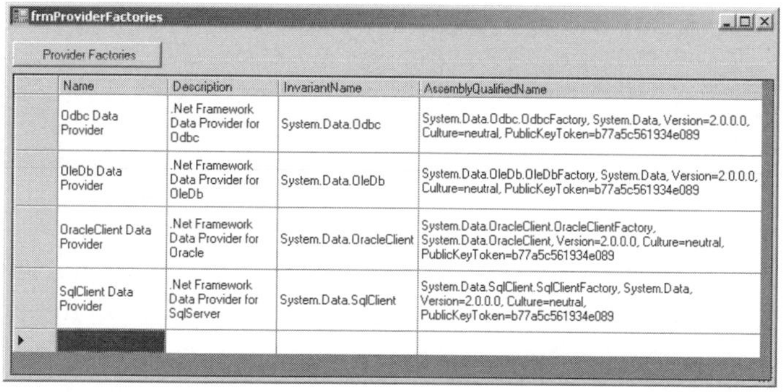

frmProviderFactories

Provider Factories

Name	Description	InvariantName	AssemblyQualifiedName
Odbc Data Provider	.Net Framework Data Provider for Odbc	System.Data.Odbc	System.Data.Odbc.OdbcFactory, System.Data, Version=2.0.0.0, Culture=neutral, PublicKeyToken=b77a5c561934e089
OleDb Data Provider	.Net Framework Data Provider for OleDb	System.Data.OleDb	System.Data.OleDb.OleDbFactory, System.Data, Version=2.0.0.0, Culture=neutral, PublicKeyToken=b77a5c561934e089
OracleClient Data Provider	.Net Framework Data Provider for Oracle	System.Data.OracleClient	System.Data.OracleClient.OracleClientFactory, System.Data.OracleClient, Version=2.0.0.0, Culture=neutral, PublicKeyToken=b77a5c561934e089
SqlClient Data Provider	.Net Framework Data Provider for SqlServer	System.Data.SqlClient	System.Data.SqlClient.SqlClientFactory, System.Data, Version=2.0.0.0, Culture=neutral, PublicKeyToken=b77a5c561934e089

Figure 2-8 The provider factory classes that are available on this computer

The invariant column contains a string that you can use to retrieve a specific provider. The name and description provide information that you can use to display a friendly provider list to an application user. The assembly names listed are fully qualified. Any provider on the list must be located within the application's probing path. This means that the .NET runtime must be able to locate the provider. In most situations, the provider library is installed in the Global Assembly Cache (GAC) or the application folder.

The provider list shown in Figure 2-8 is from the Machine.config file, which by default contains the following provider information within the *<configuration>* root element:

Machine.config File

```
<system.data>
  <DbProviderFactories>
    <add name="Odbc Data Provider"
      invariant="System.Data.Odbc"
      description=".Net Framework Data Provider for Odbc"
      type="System.Data.Odbc.OdbcFactory, System.Data, Version=2.0.0.0,
      Culture=neutral, PublicKeyToken=b77a5c561934e089" />
    <add name="OleDb Data Provider"
      invariant="System.Data.OleDb"
      description=".Net Framework Data Provider for OleDb"
      type="System.Data.OleDb.OleDbFactory, System.Data, Version=2.0.0.0,
      Culture=neutral, PublicKeyToken=b77a5c561934e089" />
    <add name="OracleClient Data Provider"
      invariant="System.Data.OracleClient"
      description=".Net Framework Data Provider for Oracle"
      type="System.Data.OracleClient.OracleClientFactory,
      System.Data.OracleClient, Version=2.0.0.0, Culture=neutral,
      PublicKeyToken=b77a5c561934e089" />
    <add name="SqlClient Data Provider"
      invariant="System.Data.SqlClient"
      description=".Net Framework Data Provider for SqlServer"
      type="System.Data.SqlClient.SqlClientFactory, System.Data,
      Version=2.0.0.0, Culture=neutral, PublicKeyToken=b77a5c561934e089" />
    <add name="SQL Server CE Data Provider"
      invariant="Microsoft.SqlServerCe.Client"
      description=".NET Framework Data Provider for Microsoft SQL Server 2005
      Mobile Edition"
      type="Microsoft.SqlServerCe.Client.SqlCeClientFactory,
      Microsoft.SqlServerCe.Client, Version=2.0.0.0, Culture=neutral,
      PublicKeyToken=b77a5c561934e089" />
  </DbProviderFactories>
</system.data>
```

Notice that *DbDatabaseProviderFactories* uses the *<add>* element. Using the *<add>* element, you can add more providers to the Machine.config file or the application's configuration file. You can also use the *<remove>* tag to remove providers from the default Machine.config list. For example, the following is a sample App.config file that removes the *Odbc* provider from the defaults defined in Machine.config.

App.config File

```
<configuration>
  <system.data>
    <DbProviderFactories>
        <remove invariant="System.Data.Odbc" />
    </DbProviderFactories>
  </system.data>
</configuration>
```

If very few specific providers (such as SQL Server and Oracle) are required, you can use the *<clear>* element to remove all of the providers in the Machine.config file and then use the *<add>* element to add the desired providers back into the list. The following example clears the provider list and adds the SQL Server provider back into the list.

App.config File

```
<configuration>
  <system.data>
    <DbProviderFactories>
        <clear/>
        <add name="SqlClient Data Provider"
          invariant="System.Data.SqlClient"
          description=".Net Framework Data Provider for SqlServer"
          type="System.Data.SqlClient.SqlClientFactory, System.Data,
          Version=2.0.0.0, Culture=neutral,
          PublicKeyToken=b77a5c561934e089" />
    </DbProviderFactories>
  </system.data>
</configuration>
```

Enumerating Data Sources

Sometimes you want to display a list of the available data sources for a given provider. For example, if an application allows data to be read from one SQL Server and written to a different SQL Server, it might require a dialog box for selecting from a list of available SQL Servers for the source and destination servers. We can add an event to the previous sample Windows application that will fire when the user double-clicks a row. We can add code to the *event* method that uses the selected provider to obtain a list of data sources for that provider. With the list of data sources, we can display a dialog box to prompt the user to select a data source. Here is the required code.

Visual Basic

```
'code in frmProviderFactories.vb
Private Sub DataGridView1_RowHeaderMouseDoubleClick( _
      ByVal sender As System.Object, _
      ByVal e As System.Windows.Forms.DataGridViewCellMouseEventArgs) _
      Handles DataGridView1.RowHeaderMouseDoubleClick
   Dim providerRow As DataRow = providersList.DefaultView(e.RowIndex).Row
   Dim factory As DbProviderFactory = _
      DbProviderFactories.GetFactory(providerRow)
   'get SQL Server instances
   Dim sources As DataTable = _
```

```
      factory.CreateDataSourceEnumerator().GetDataSources()
   Dim f As frmSources = New frmSources()
   f.DataSources = sources
   If f.ShowDialog() <> DialogResult.OK Then
      Return
   End If
   'get selected dataRow
   Dim selectedSource As DataRow = f.SelectedSource
End Sub

'code in frmProviderFactories.vb
Public Class frmSources
   Public Property DataSources() As DataTable
      Get
         Return DataGridView1.DataSource
      End Get
      Set(ByVal Value As DataTable)
         DataGridView1.DataSource = Value
      End Set
   End Property

   Public Property SelectedSource() As DataRow
      Get
         Return _SelectedSource
      End Get
      Set(ByVal value As DataRow)
         _SelectedSource = value
      End Set
   End Property
   Private _SelectedSource As DataRow = nothing

   Private Sub DataGridView1_MouseDoubleClick(ByVal sender As System.Object, _
         ByVal e As System.Windows.Forms.MouseEventArgs) _
         Handles DataGridView1.MouseDoubleClick
      SelectedSource = _
         DataGridView1.DataSource.DefaultView( _
         DataGridView1.CurrentCell.RowIndex).Row
      DialogResult = DialogResult.OK
   End Sub
End Class
```

C#

```
//code in frmProviderFactories.cs
private void dataGridView1_RowHeaderMouseDoubleClick(
   object sender, DataGridViewCellMouseEventArgs e)
{
   DataRow providerRow = providersList.DefaultView[e.RowIndex].Row;
   DbProviderFactory factory = DbProviderFactories.GetFactory(providerRow);
   //get SQL Server instances
   DataTable sources =
      factory.CreateDataSourceEnumerator().GetDataSources();
   frmSources f = new frmSources();
   f.DataSources = sources;
   if (f.ShowDialog() != DialogResult.OK)
   {
```

```
        return;
    }
    //get selected dataRow
    DataRow selectedSource = f.SelectedSource;
}

//code in frmSources.cs
namespace Chapter2
{
    public partial class frmSources : Form
    {
        public frmSources()
        {
            InitializeComponent();
        }

        public DataTable DataSources
        {
            get { return dataGridView1.DataSource as DataTable; }
            set { dataGridView1.DataSource = value; }
        }

        public DataRow SelectedSource
        {
            get { return selectedSource; }
            set { selectedSource = value; }
        }
        DataRow selectedSource;

        private void dataGridView1_MouseDoubleClick(
            object sender, MouseEventArgs e)
        {
            SelectedSource = ((DataTable)dataGridView1.DataSource)
                .DefaultView[dataGridView1.CurrentCell.RowIndex].Row;
            DialogResult = DialogResult.OK;
        }
    }
}
```

Using *DbException* to Catch Provider Exceptions

All provider-specific exceptions inherit from a common base class called *DbException*. When you are working with a provider-neutral coding model, your try catch block can simply catch *DbException* generically instead of trying to catch each provider-specific exception.

Summary

Connected classes, also known as provider classes, are responsible for movement of data between the data store and the disconnected classes. A valid *DbConnection* object is required to use most of the primary provider classes.

SQL Express is an excellent database server for development because the .mdf database file can be placed into the project and the file can be configured to be copied to the output folder every time the application is built and run.

You use the *DbCommand* object to send an SQL command to a data store. You can also create parameters and pass them to the *DbCommand* object.

The *DbDataReader* object provides a high-performance method of retrieving data from a data store by delivering a forward-only, read-only, server-side cursor.

The *SqlBulkCopy* object can be used to copy data from a number of sources to a SQL Server table.

You can use the *DbDataAdapter* object to retrieve and update data between a *DataTable* and a data store. The *DbDataAdapter* can contain a single *SelectCommand* for read-only data, or it can contain a *SelectCommand*, *InsertCommand*, *UpdateCommand*, and *DeleteCommand* for fully updatable data.

The *DbProviderFactory* object helps you create provider-independent code, which might be necessary when the data store needs to be quickly changeable.

You can use the *DbProviderFactories* object to obtain a list of the provider factories that are available on a computer.

Chapter 3

ADO.NET Trace Logging

Trace logging provides a detailed record of system and application events when activities such as a disk I/O operation or a committed transaction occur. Tracing of data access activities is vastly improved in ADO.NET 2.0 with the ADO.NET Event Tracing for Windows (ETW) provider. ETW is a tracing mechanism that you can use in drivers as well as applications. ETW can log about 20,000 entries per second with only 5 percent CPU load, even while logging from multiple processes concurrently. ETW can easily be turned on and off at runtime. The ETW output can be consumed by third-party tools, including the logparser.exe utility that is included in the Microsoft Internet Information Service (IIS) 6.0 Resource Kit.

This chapter starts by explaining the procedure to set up tracing; it then covers the LogMan.exe command-line utility, which comes with the operating system and is part of the Performance Logs And Alerts services. We also explore the Performance Logs And Alerts snap-in, which provides a graphical means for creating and controlling traces. Finally, we look at how to use tracing to diagnose problems.

Setting Up Tracing

The first step in setting up tracing within ADO.NET is to register the AdoNetDiag.dll component. You do this by adding a single registry value. Open the registry editor using regedit.exe and locate the following key:

```
HKLM\Software\Microsoft\BidInterface\Loader
```

If this key does not exist, add it. Next add the following string value in the *Loader* key (where *xxxxx* is the current build number), if it doesn't already exist.

```
Name=":Path"
Value="C:\WINDOWS\Microsoft.NET\Framework\v2.0.xxxxx\AdoNetDiag.dll"
```

If the key and string value did not already exist, you must restart your machine to get this setting to work properly. This component makes any class library that is instrumented for data tracing look like an ETW provider.

Next you must configure AdoNetDiag.dll so that it shows up on both the public provider list and the Windows Management Instrumentation (WMI) provider list. You do this by compiling a Managed Object Format (MOF) file using the mofcomp.exe utility. The MOF file contains statements that add objects into the WMI repository. These objects describe the events being exposed by the AdoNetDiag.dll component. The MOF file is located in the same folder as the AdoNetDiag.dll component and can be configured using the following command:

```
mofcomp adonetdiag.mof
```

One way to verify that the MOF file has properly added the object to the WMI repository is to use the WMI CIM Studio (available as a download from Microsoft). You can view the event trace classes in the WMI tree, as shown in Figure 3-1. (Notice that the providers have a *Bid2Etw_* prefix.)

> **Note** Prior to the Visual Studio 2005 release, there were versions of the adonetdiag.mof file that did not include the SQL Native Client (Bid2Etw_SQLNCLI_1) information. If the SQL Native Client does not show in your list, you can use the AdoNetDiag.mof file that is included in the Chapter 3 sample files.

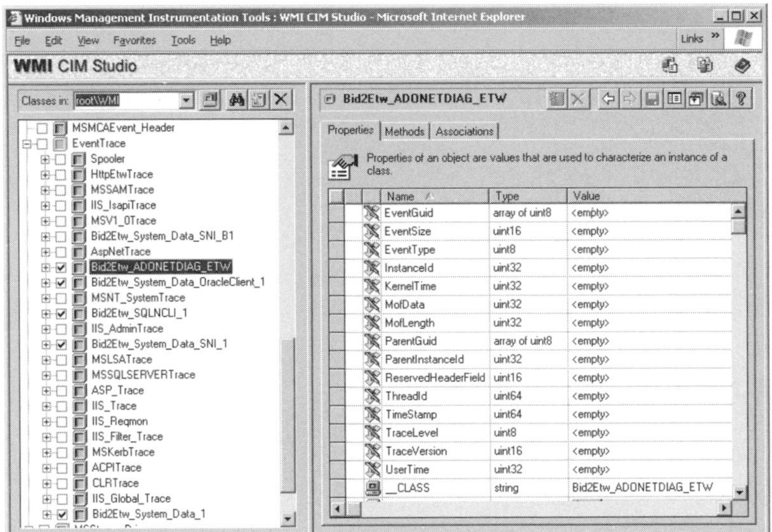

Figure 3-1 I checked the items that were added by running the mofcomp.exe utility.

Another way to verify that the mofcomp command worked properly is to run the following Log Manager command:

```
Logman query providers
```

This command lists all of the providers that are registered. Table 3-1 lists the providers that should have been registered as a result.

Table 3-1 ADO.NET Registered WMI Providers

Provider	GUID	Description
System.Data.1	*{914ABDE2-171E-C600-3348-C514171DE148}*	Provider for events in the System.Data.dll component
System.Data.SNI.1	*{C9996FA5-C06F-F20C-8A20-69B3BA392315}*	Provider for SQL Server Network Interface (SNI) events in the System.Data.dll component
SQLNCLI.1	*{BA798F36-2325-EC5B-ECF8-76958A2AF9B5}*	Provider for the SQL Native Client and its SNI events
System.Data.OracleClient.1	*{DCD90923-4953-20C2-8708-01976FB15287}*	Provider for events in System.OracleClient.dll
ADONETDIAG.ETW	*{7ACDCAC8-8947-F88A-E51A-24018F5129EF}*	Provider for events in the ETW Adapter

Using the logman.exe Utility

You can use the Log Manager (logman.exe) tool to perform all logging activities. This tool is a command-line utility that has a -? switch for viewing the command syntax and listing the switches. To turn on tracing, use the following command:

```
logman start MyTrace -pf ProviderList.txt -ct perf -o C:\Perflogs\Out.etl -ets
```

This command begins with *start MyTrace*, which starts a trace that is arbitrarily called *MyTrace*. The command specifies *-pf ProviderList.txt*, which dictates the use of a list of providers included in the file ProviderList.txt. The next part of the command is *-ct perf*, which means use the high-performance clock type, as opposed to using the low-resolution *-ct system* setting. The next part of the command is *-o C:\Perflogs\Out.etl*, which identifies the output location as Out.etl (the .etl extension stands for Event Trace Log). Note that C:\Perflogs is specified as the path because the file needs to be placed in a folder that the providers have access to, and this is the default location for output files when running Performance Monitor. The last part of the command is *-ets*, which means that this is an ad hoc trace collection and the trace collection's definition will not be persisted.

The contents of the ProviderList.txt file are as follows. Notice that the Oracle provider is not included because none of the examples uses Oracle.

ProviderList.txt File

```
"ADONETDIAG.ETW"                          0x2  0x0   ADONETDIAG.ETW
{914ABDE2-171E-C600-3348-C514171DE148} 0x2  0x0   System.Data.1
"System.Data.SNI.1"                       0x2  0x0   System.Data.SNI.1
"SQLNCLI.1"                               0x2  0x0   SQLNCLI.1
```

Table 3-2 describes the elements of the ProviderList.txt file. Notice that the file contains an example using a GUID and an example using a name as the provider identification. Also notice that having a control bit value of *0x2* means that a regular trace is done, without enter/exit or other advanced information.

Table 3-2 ProviderList.txt Contents

Item	Description
Provider	Can be a GUID that identifies the ETW provider, delimited by curly braces { }. Can also be the provider name delimited by double quotation marks " ". The ProviderList.txt file listing shows examples of both.
Control Bits	Flag mask that can be used to filter the trace. Bits can be set as follows and can be ORed together. The default value is 0x0006 if 0x0000 is specified. ■ **0x0002** Regular trace ■ **0x0004** Show execution flow with enter/leave. For System.Data.1: ■ **0x0080** Advanced output; adds TDS Packet Data Read/Written ■ **0x1000** Add connection pooling information to the trace log.
Logging Level	Typically used to control the verboseness of the output. With data providers, the following values can be supplied. ■ **0x0000** Normal ■ **0x0040** Disables tracing on this component. ■ **0x0080** Convert Unicode output to ASCII to reduce the output size.
Provider Name	The name of the provider, which is required by ETW but ignored by the logman utility.

When the trace is running, the Out.etl file is populated with data from the providers. Running a simple application that populates a *DataSet* object can produce lots of data. Here is a simple program that generates some output data. If you haven't already done so, turn on tracing using the logman command shown on page 77, and then simply create a console application and insert the code that follows.

Visual Basic

```
Imports System
Imports System.Data
Imports System.Data.SqlClient

Public Class MyApp
   Public Shared Sub Main()
      Dim cnSettings As SqlConnectionStringBuilder
      Dim cn As SqlConnection
      Dim da As SqlDataAdapter
      Dim cmdBld As SqlCommandBuilder
      Dim ds As DataSet

      cnSettings = New SqlConnectionStringBuilder( _
        "Data Source=.\SQLEXPRESS;" _
        + "AttachDbFilename=|DataDirectory|NORTHWND.MDF;" _
        + "Integrated Security=True;User Instance=True")
      cn = New SqlConnection(cnSettings.ConnectionString)
      da = New SqlDataAdapter("Select * from Products", cn)
      cmdBld = New SqlCommandBuilder(da)
      ds = New DataSet()
      da.Fill(ds, "Products")
      For Each dr As DataRow In ds.Tables("Products").Rows
         dr("UnitPrice") = dr("UnitPrice") * 1.1
      Next
      da.Update(ds, "Products")
   End Sub
End Class
```

C#

```
using System;
using System.Data;
using System.Data.SqlClient;

namespace Tracing
{
   static class Program
   {
      static void Main()
      {
         SqlConnectionStringBuilder cnSettings;
         SqlConnection cn;
         SqlDataAdapter da;
         SqlCommandBuilder cmdBld;
         DataSet ds;
         cnSettings = new SqlConnectionStringBuilder(
           @"Data Source=.\SQLEXPRESS;"
           + "AttachDbFilename=|DataDirectory|NORTHWND.MDF;"
           + "Integrated Security=True;User Instance=True");
         cn = new SqlConnection(cnSettings.ConnectionString);
         da = new SqlDataAdapter("Select * from Products", cn);
         cmdBld = new SqlCommandBuilder(da);
```

```
            ds = new DataSet();
            da.Fill(ds, "Products");
            foreach (DataRow dr in ds.Tables["Products"].Rows)
            {
               dr["UnitPrice"] = (decimal)dr["UnitPrice"] * (decimal)1.1;
            }
            da.Update(ds, "Products");
         }
      }
   }
```

After you compile this program, run it from the command prompt to keep Microsoft Visual Studio's Server Explorer from adding data into the trace output. You can then run the following command to turn off the trace.

```
Logman stop MyTrace -ets
```

This command simply stops the trace called *MyTrace* that was started earlier. The output file will contain binary trace information that must be converted to a readable format.

Performance Logs And Alerts Snap-in

The previous example used the *start* command to create an ad hoc trace, but you can use the *create* command to create a trace that is controllable from the Performance Logs And Alerts snap-in, which is also known as Performance Monitor. To get access to the high-performance WMI events from within Performance Monitor, start Performance Monitor by executing the following command from the Run menu.

```
perfmon.exe  /wmi
```

Open the Performance Logs And Alerts tree to see the Trace Logs node. Right-click the Trace Logs node and click New Log Settings. After specifying a name, on the General tab select the four providers from the non-system providers list. On the Log Files tab, uncheck the End File Names With option and select the Overwrite Existing Log File option. Also click the Configure button to change the filename to *Out.etl* and the location to *C:\PerfLogs*. On the Schedule tab, select Manually for both the Start Log and Stop Log options. Figure 3-2 shows the screen layout for setting up this trace collection.

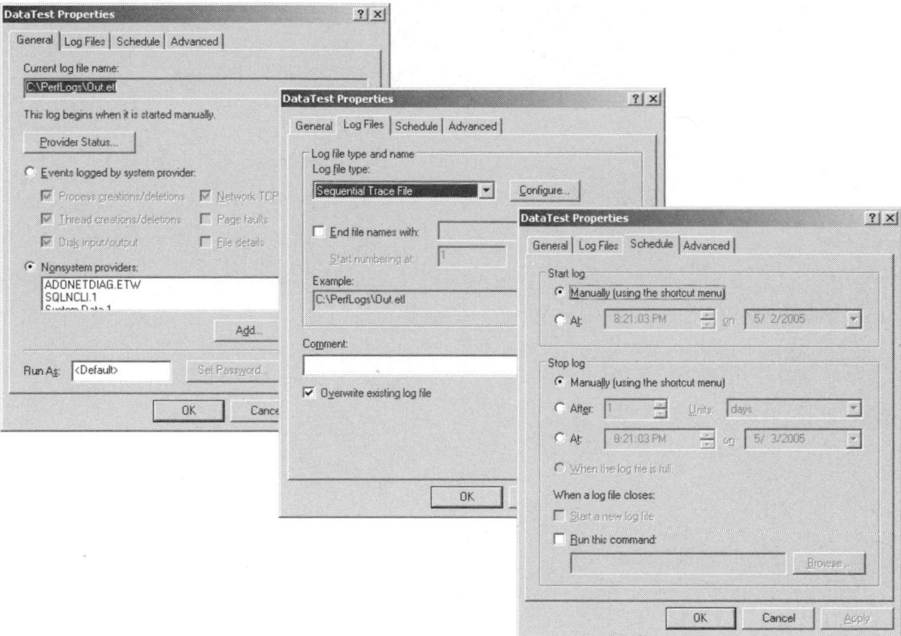

Figure 3-2 Creating a new trace collection using Performance Monitor

After you create the trace collection, it is available within Performance Monitor, as shown in Figure 3-3. You can also move the trace settings from one computer to another by saving the settings as an HTML object file on one machine and using the Load Settings From menu option on the target machine to load the HTML settings file from the first machine.

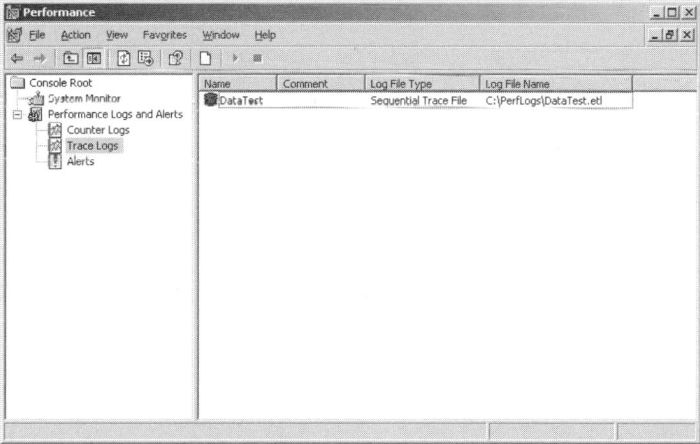

Figure 3-3 Using the Performance Logs And Alerts snap-in to control the trace collections

The summary file provides an at-a-glance display of the numbers of events captured by each provider. This file is useful when you want to quickly check to see if a change to your application has caused additional events to be logged. The summary file should look like the example in the following section.

Working with Event Trace Log Files

The trace output is an Event Trace Log (.etl) file, but this is a binary file that can be difficult to work with, so let's use the following command to convert this file into something that's easier to work with–a comma-separated value (.csv) file.

```
TraceRpt /y C:\Perflogs\Out.etl
```

This command produces a summary file called summary.txt and a detailed log file called dumpfile.csv. We use the */y* switch to silently answer yes to any prompts that might be displayed.

Summary.txt File

```
Files Processed:
   Out.etl
Total Buffers Processed 7
Total Events  Processed 2624
Total Events  Lost      0
Start Time              Saturday, April 30, 2005
End Time                Saturday, April 30, 2005
Elapsed Time            10 sec
+----------------------------------------------------------------------------+
|Event Count   Event Name     Event Type        Guid                         |
+----------------------------------------------------------------------------+
|        1   EventTrace        Header  {68fdd900-4a3e-11d1-84f4-0000f80464e3}|
|        6   AdoNetDiag        TextW   {7acdcac9-8947-f88a-e51a-24018f5129ef}|
|      685   System.Data       TextW   {914abde3-171e-c600-3348-c514171de148}|
|     1807   System.Data.SNI   TextA   {c9996fa6-c06f-f20c-8a20-69b3ba392315}|
|       85   SQLNCLI           TextA   {ba798f37-2325-ec5b-ecf8-76958a2af9b5}|
|       40   SQLNCLI           TextW   {ba798f37-2325-ec5b-ecf8-76958a2af9b5}|
+----------------------------------------------------------------------------+
```

Note that the results can vary, depending on the control settings you use and whether other applications (such as Reporting Services) are running.

The detailed log file contains granular log information. This information is in column format, as described in Table 3-3.

Table 3-3 DumpFile.csv File Format

Column	Description
Event Name	Name of the event provider.
Event Type	Either TextW (Unicode) or TextA (ASCII) for data providers.

Table 3-3 DumpFile.csv File Format

Column	Description
TID	Thread identifier.
Clock Time	Event timestamp that specifies the time the event occurred. The time is in Integer8 format, which is a 64-bit value that holds the number of 100-nanosecond intervals that have occurred since 12:00 a.m., January 1, 1601.
Kernel (ms)	Processor time in milliseconds that the event was in kernel mode. The value is in clock ticks, which are 10-millisecond intervals. The time is from when the current thread started to when the event tracer fires the event.
User (ms)	Processor time in milliseconds that the event was in user mode. The value is in clock ticks, which are 10-millisecond intervals. The time is from when the current thread started to when the event tracer fires the event.
User Data	Data that the provider added about the trace point.

Our example used *0x2* in the control bits to provide basic output information. The intent was to start with a small amount of data. The following excerpt is a small part of the user data where the connection string and command text are being set.

Dumpfile.csv User Data Excerpt

```
"<prov.DbConnectionHelper.ConnectionString_Set|API> 1#  'Data
 Source=.\SQLEXPRESS;AttachDbFilename=|DataDirectory|NORTHWND.MDF;Integrated
 Security=True;User Instance=True'"
"<sc.SqlCommand.set_CommandText|API> 1#  '"
"Select * from Products"
"'"
"<sc.SqlCommand.set_Connection|API> 1#  1#"
"<ds.DataSet.DataSet|API> 1#"
```

If the control bits were set to *0x6* (or *0x0*, which uses *0x6* as a default setting), the summary.txt file would show that many more events were logged and the dumpfile.csv would contain enter events and leave events. The enter and leave events also contain a nest level number that is used to match the enter and the leave event. The following is a small part of the dumpfile.csv that shows enter and leave events.

Dumpfile.csv User Data Export with Enter/Leave Events

```
"<prov.DbConnectionHelper.ConnectionString_Set|API> 1#
 'Data Source=.\SQLEXPRESS;AttachDbFilename=|DataDirectory|NORTHWND.MDF;
 Integrated Security=True;User Instance=True'"
"<sc.SqlCommand.set_CommandText|API> 1#  '"
"Select * from Products"
"'"
"<sc.SqlCommand.set_Connection|API> 1#  1#"
"<ds.DataSet.DataSet|API> 1#"
"<ds.DataTableCollection.DataTableCollection|INFO> 1#  dataSet=1"
"enter_01 <comm.DbDataAdapter.Fill|API> 1#  dataSet  srcTable='Products'"
"enter_02 <comm.DbDataAdapter.Fill|API> 1#  dataSet  startRecord  maxRecords
 srcTable  command  behavior=16{ds.CommandBehavior}"
```

```
"enter_03 <sc.SqlConnection.Open|API> 1#"
"enter_04 <SNIInitialize|API|SNI> pmo: 00000000{void}"
"enter_05 <SNIInitializeEx|API|SNI> pmo: 00000000{void}"
"enter_06 <SNIxInitialize|API|SNI>"
. . . other events . . .
"leave_06"
. . . other events . . .
"leave_05"
. . . other events . . .
"leave_04"
. . . other events . . .
"leave_03"
. . . other events . . .
"leave_02"
. . . other events . . .
"leave_01"
```

Notice that the user data contains bracketed information that helps you understand the program flow. The bracketed information is in the following format:

<*abbreviated namespace.classname.methodname|keyword*> parameters

The abbreviated namespace saves space in the output. The abbreviations are defined in Table 3-4.

Table 3-4 Namespace Abbreviations

Namespace	Abbreviation
System.Data	*ds*
System.Data.Common	*comm*
System.Data.Odbc	*odbc*
System.Data.OleDb	*oledb*
System.Data.OracleClient	*ora*
System.Data.ProviderBase	*prov*
System.Data.SqlCient	*sc*

The keyword is used to define the category of the event that is being logged. Table 3-5 describes the keywords that are generated by the data providers.

Table 3-5 Keywords

Keyword	Description
ADV	Advanced trace point events.
API	Public member that is called.
CATCH	Code is in a caught exception.
CPOOL	Connection pool events.
ERR	Error event.
INFO	Information event.

Table 3-5 Keywords

Keyword	Description
ODBC	Code is in the ODBC API.
OLEDB	Code is in the OLEDB API.
RET	A return value.
SNI	Code is in SQL Server Networking Interface (SNI).
THROW	A new exception is being thrown. This does not include an exception being rethrown.
WARN	Warning.

The parameter contains the syntax *1#* (number and pound symbol) to identify the instance of the class; this information makes it easier to work with traces that involve multiple instances.

Using the LogParser Utility

The LogParser utility is a command-line tool that can convert several different input file types into several output file types. LogParser is part of the IIS 6.0 Resource Kit, which is a free download from Microsoft's Web site. LogParser comes as two files; LogParser.exe is the command-line utility, and LogParser.dll is a set of COM objects that support scripting. These files are independent of each other, so you don't need to register the LogParser.dll file in order to run the LogParser.exe utility.

One use for the LogParser is to browse the dumpfile.csv in a *DataGrid*. Figure 3-4 shows the output when the following command is executed:

```
logparser.exe "SELECT * from c:\perflogs\dumpfile.csv" -o:DATAGRID
```

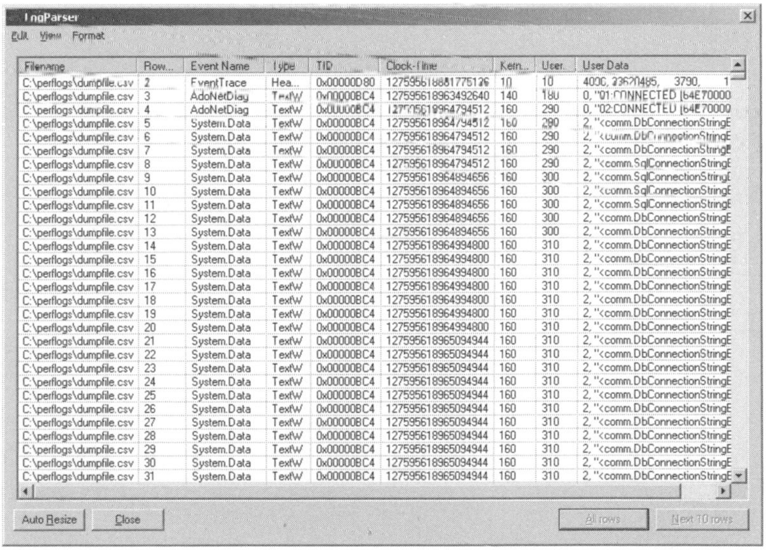

Figure 3-4 Using the LogParser.exe command-line utility to display a .csv file in a *DataGrid*

Notice that this tool lets you supply SQL queries to the source, and the output will contain the result. For example, you can supply a *WHERE* clause that looks for events that took place on a specific thread by using the following SQL command:

```
"SELECT * from c:\perflogs\dumpfile.csv WHERE TID='0x00000BC4'"
```

This is especially useful when you are trying to troubleshoot a problem in a production environment and you only want to see the events that took place on your thread.

Using Tracing as a Diagnostic Tool

Tracing is especially useful as a diagnostic tool when you are trying to troubleshoot a problem and you don't have the source code. For example, let's say you installed your application on a machine that will be used for final testing before the application goes to production. You need to make sure that the code being tested is the same code that will be pushed to production, but when you compile the application for release, there is no source code on the machine.

The problem is that the database was not copied to the testing machine, but this might not be readily apparent based on the user-friendly (developer-unfriendly) error message that was displayed. You can use the console application that we used to create trace output earlier in this chapter and simulate the problem by renaming or deleting the database before running the application.

To troubleshoot this problem, you simply start the trace before running the application and stop the trace after the problem occurs. We can start the Performance Monitor trace that we defined earlier in this chapter and then start the problem application. After the exception is thrown, stop the trace and convert the Out.etl file to dumpfile.csv by using the TraceRpt.exe utility. Finally, run the LogParser.exe command-line utility with a filter on events that are exceptions. The LogParser command looks like the following:

```
LogParser.exe
   "SELECT * from c:\perflogs\dumpfile.csv WHERE [User Data] like '%|ERR|%'"
       -o:DATAGRID
```

In the LogParser *DataGrid*, only two events are listed as exceptions. The user data in the following event clearly explains that there is a problem locating the database.

```
"<comm.ADP.TraceException|ERR|CATCH> 'System.Data.SqlClient.SqlException: An attempt to
attach an auto-
named database for file C:\Projects\Chapter3\CS\Tracing\bin\Debug\NORTHWND.MDF failed. A
 database with the same name exists or specified file cannot be opened  or it is located
 on UNC share. ,    at System.Data.SqlClient.SqlInternalConnection.OnError(SqlException e
xception  Boolean breakConnection) ,    at System.Data.SqlClient.TdsParser.ThrowException
AndWarning(TdsParserStateObject stateObj) ,    at System.Data.SqlClient.TdsParser.Run(Run
Behavior runBehavior  SqlCommand cmdHandler  SqlDataReader dataStream  BulkCopySimpleRes
ultSet bulkCopyHandler  TdsParserStateObject stateObj) ,    at System.Data.SqlClient.SqlI
nternalConnectionTds.CompleteLogin(Boolean enlistOK) ,    at System.Data.SqlClient.SqlInt
ernalConnectionTds.OpenLoginEnlist(SqlConnection owningObject  SqlConnectionString conne
ctionOptions  String newPassword  Boolean redirectedUserInstance) ,    at System.Data.Sql
Client.SqlInternalConnectionTds..ctor(SqlConnectionString connectionOptions  Object prov
iderInfo  String newPassword  SqlConnection owningObject  Boolean redirectedUserInstance
) ,    at System.Data.SqlClient.SqlConnectionFactory.CreateConnection(DbConnectionOptions
 options  Object poolGroupProviderInfo  DbConnectionPool pool  DbConnection owningConnec
tion) ,    at System.Data.ProviderBase.DbConnectionFactory.CreatePooledConnection(DbConne
ction owningConnection  DbConnectionPool pool  DbConnectionOptions options) ,    at Syste
m.Data.ProviderBase.DbConnectionPool.CreateObject(DbConnection owningObject)'"
```

Summary

Tracing can provide detailed information about application flow as well as performance.

You can set up tracing by registering the AdoNetDiag.dll component. You can use the Log-Man.exe command-line utility to create, control, and modify trace collections. The Performance Logs And Alerts snap-in provides a graphical means for creating and controlling traces.

The output of a trace is an .etl file, which is a binary file that can be converted to a .csv file by running the TraceRpt.exe command-line utility. The output of the TraceRpt.exe utility is a file called summary.txt and a file called dumptrace.csv. The summary.txt file contains event counts, and the dumptrace.csv file contains detailed information that can be consumed by third-party applications, such as the LogParser.exe utility that is included with the IIS 6.0 Resource Kit.

You can use tracing to diagnose problems by starting the trace, running the application until it breaks, stopping the trace, and running reports or tools to filter the data.

Chapter 4

Advanced Connectivity to the Data Store

Chapter 2 explained how to create a *DbConnection* object and communicate to the data store as quickly and easily as possible. This chapter explores some of the more advanced connectivity options and best practices by looking at connection pooling, clustered connections, and asynchronous access. But first we examine the *ConnectionStringBuilder* object, which we use throughout this chapter when implementing these advanced options.

Building Accurate Connection Strings

You'll often want to prompt the user for information that will be used to build a connection string. For example, when the user starts your application for the first time or before you grant the user the ability to export data from one database server to another, you might want to prompt the user for a SQL Server computer name, the database name, a user name, and password. How can you possibly ensure that the user has typed everything correctly? Also, how can you prevent a user from breaching security by injecting other settings into that information?

After a user enters information into your application, you normally build a connection string using code that looks something like the following snippet (which builds a connection string based on the data source name that is typed into the txtDataSource text box).

Visual Basic

```
Public Function GetConnectionString() As String
   Return String.Format( _
      "AttachDbFilename=|DataDirectory|PUBS.MDF;" _
      & "integrated security=true;User Instance=true;" _
      & "Data Source={0};", _
      txtDataSource.Text)
End Function
```

C#

```
public string GetConnectionString()
{
   return string.Format(
      "AttachDbFilename=|DataDirectory|PUBS.MDF;"
      + "integrated security=true;User Instance=true;"
      + "Data Source={0};",
      txtDataSource.Text);
}
```

One of the biggest problems with this code is that the user can insert a keyword separator (the semicolon) into the password field and then type additional keywords and values. For example, if the user types ".\SQLEXPRESS;Database=Joe", the database file that is being attached is mounted as Joe on the server while the application is running; if the user types "*.\SQLEXPRESS;Database=Joe;User Instance=false;*", the database file is permanently mounted on the database server as Joe. We can easily create an example of this by placing a button and a text box on a Windows form and adding the following code to the button click event handler.

Visual Basic

```
Private Sub btnConnectionStringTest_Click( _
      ByVal sender As System.Object, _
      ByVal e As System.EventArgs) Handles btnConnectionStringTest.Click
   MessageBox.Show(GetConnectionString())
   Dim cn As SqlConnection = New SqlConnection(GetConnectionString())
   Try
      cn.Open()
      Dim cmd As SqlCommand = New SqlCommand("Select DB_NAME()", cn)
      MessageBox.Show(cmd.ExecuteScalar().ToString())
   Catch xcp As Exception
      MessageBox.Show(xcp.Message)
   Finally
      cn.Close()
   End Try
End Sub
```

C#

```
private void btnConnectionStringTest_Click(object sender, EventArgs e)
{
   MessageBox.Show(GetConnectionString());
   SqlConnection cn = new SqlConnection(GetConnectionString());
   try
   {
      cn.Open();
      SqlCommand cmd = new SqlCommand("Select DB_NAME()",cn);
      MessageBox.Show(cmd.ExecuteScalar().ToString());
   }
   catch (Exception xcp)
   {
      MessageBox.Show(xcp.Message);
   }
   finally
   {
      cn.Close();
   }
}
```

In this example, if the user types "*.\SQLEXPRESS*" in the text box and clicks the button, a message box showing the resulting connection string is displayed. The button can be clicked several times without any problem. If the user types "*.\SQLEXPRESS;Database=Joe;User Instance=false;*" in the text box and clicks the button, the pubs database file is mounted as a permanent database called Joe. If the user types "*.\SQLEXPRESS*" in the text box and clicks the button again, an exception is thrown that indicates that the pubs database is already in use.

I always try to set up Microsoft SQL Server to use integrated Windows authentication. If you set up SQL Server to use SQL Server authentication, a user can potentially bypass a user name and password in the connection string by adding *";Integrated Security=true"*. If this succeeds, the user will have the permissions that the process login has.

Another problem with this approach to building the connection string is that there is no checking of this string. For example, if a user incorrectly types one of the keywords, he won't realize it until it's time to open the connection. For example, if he types *"Integrated_Security=true"* in the connection string, he won't find out that the underscore should be a space until the code attempts to open the connection.

The solution to these problems is to use a *ConnectionStringBuilder* object. The *ConnectionStringBuilder* properly adds quotation marks around each value to keep someone from typing the semicolon command separator and adding new keywords and values. The *ConnectionStringBuilder* has a constructor that accepts a connection string through which you can initialize the *ConnectionStringBuilder* object. After the object has been initialized, the properties are available for reading and writing. The following code shows the use of the *SqlConnectionStringBuilder* object.

Visual Basic

```
Private Sub button1__Click( _
      ByVal sender As System.Object,  _
      ByVal e As System.EventArgs) _
      Handles btnConnectionStringBuilderTest.Click
   Dim bld as SqlConnectionStringBuilder = new SqlConnectionStringBuilder( _
      "AttachDbFilename=|DataDirectory|PUBS.MDF;" _
      + "integrated security=true;User Instance=true;")
   bld.DataSource = txtDataSource.Text
   MessageBox.Show(bld.ConnectionString)
   Dim cn as SqlConnection = new SqlConnection(bld.ConnectionString)
   try
      cn.Open()
      Dim cmd as SqlCommand = new SqlCommand("Select DB_NAME()", cn)
      MessageBox.Show(cmd.ExecuteScalar().ToString())
   catch xcp as Exception
      MessageBox.Show(xcp.Message)
   finally
      cn.Close()
   end try
End Sub
```

C#

```
private void button1_Click(object sender, EventArgs e)
{
   SqlConnectionStringBuilder bld = new SqlConnectionStringBuilder(
      "AttachDbFilename=|DataDirectory|PUBS.MDF;"
      + "integrated security=true;User Instance=true;");
```

```
   bld.DataSource = txtDataSource.Text;
   MessageBox.Show(bld.ConnectionString);
   SqlConnection cn = new SqlConnection(bld.ConnectionString);
   try
   {
      cn.Open();
      SqlCommand cmd = new SqlCommand("Select DB_NAME()", cn);
      MessageBox.Show(cmd.ExecuteScalar().ToString());
   }
   catch (Exception xcp)
   {
      MessageBox.Show(xcp.Message);
   }
   finally
   {
      cn.Close();
   }
}
```

In our example, if the user types "*.\SQLEXPRESS;Database=Joe;User Instance=false;*" in the text box, here is the resulting connection string:

```
Data Source=".\SQLEXPRESS;Database=Joe;User Instance=false;"
;AttachDbFilename=|DataDirectory|PUBS.MDF;Integrated Security=True;
User Instance=True
```

Notice the quotation marks around "*.\SQLEXPRESS;Database=Joe;User Instance=false;*". They indicate that the process uses this string as the *DataSource* when locating the server. The end result is that this code generates a timeout exception because the process cannot find a server named "*.\SQLEXPRESS;Database=Joe;User Instance=false;*".

The *ConnectionStringBuilder* also validates connection string information for proper key names. If the connection string contains an invalid key, such as *abc=def*, an *ArgumentException* is thrown. The *ConnectionStringBuilder* also contains an *Add* method, which you can use to pass key and value pairs as needed. The *Add* method also validates the keys that are added.

Provider-Independent Data Access

The *ConnectionStringBuilder* also plays an important role in the creation of database platform-independent code. For example, if you save a proper connection string in the application's configuration file, you can create and validate a provider-specific *ConnectionStringBuilder* object at run time. Notice that even though the following code example does not use any provider-specific classes, the provider-specific connection string is validated by the *DbConnectionStringBuilder* when *pubs.ConnectionString* is assigned to *bld.ConnectionString*.

App.Config File

```
<?xml version="1.0" encoding="utf-8" ?>
<configuration>
   <connectionStrings>
      <clear />
```

```
    <add name="PubsData"
      connectionString="Data Source=.\SQLEXPRESS;
      AttachDbFilename=|DataDirectory|PUBS.MDF;
      Integrated Security=True;
      User Instance=True"
      providerName="System.Data.SqlClient" />
  </connectionStrings>
</configuration>
```

Visual Basic

```
Private Sub btnGenericDatabaseAccess_Click( _
    ByVal sender As System.Object,  _
    ByVal e As System.EventArgs) _
    Handles btnGenericDatabaseAccess.Click
  Dim pubs as ConnectionStringSettings = _
    ConfigurationManager.ConnectionStrings("PubsData")
  Dim factory as DbProviderFactory = _
    DbProviderFactories.GetFactory(pubs.ProviderName)
  Dim bld as DbConnectionStringBuilder = _
    factory.CreateConnectionStringBuilder()
  bld.ConnectionString=pubs.ConnectionString
  Dim cn as DbConnection = factory.CreateConnection()
  cn.ConnectionString = bld.ConnectionString
  Dim da as DbDataAdapter = factory.CreateDataAdapter()
  Dim cmd as DbCommand =  factory.CreateCommand()
  cmd.CommandText= "Select * from authors"
  cmd.CommandType = CommandType.Text
  cmd.Connection = cn
  da.SelectCommand = cmd
  Dim cmdBld as DbCommandBuilder = factory.CreateCommandBuilder()
  cmdBld.DataAdapter = da
  Dim ds as DataSet = new DataSet()
  da.Fill(ds, "authors")
  dataGridView1.DataSource = ds
  dataGridView1.DataMember = "authors"
End Sub
```

C#

```
private void btnGenericDatabaseAccess_Click(object sender, EventArgs e)
{
  ConnectionStringSettings pubs =
    ConfigurationManager.ConnectionStrings["PubsData"];
  DbProviderFactory factory =
    DbProviderFactories.GetFactory(pubs.ProviderName);
  DbConnectionStringBuilder bld =
    factory.CreateConnectionStringBuilder();
  bld.ConnectionString=pubs.ConnectionString;
  DbConnection cn = factory.CreateConnection();
  cn.ConnectionString = bld.ConnectionString;
  DbDataAdapter da = factory.CreateDataAdapter();
  DbCommand cmd =  factory.CreateCommand();
  cmd.CommandText= "Select * from authors";
  cmd.CommandType = CommandType.Text;
  cmd.Connection = cn;
  da.SelectCommand = cmd;
```

```
    DbCommandBuilder cmdBld = factory.CreateCommandBuilder();
    cmdBld.DataAdapter = da;
    DataSet ds = new DataSet();
    da.Fill(ds, "authors");
    dataGridView1.DataSource = ds;
    dataGridView1.DataMember = "authors";
}
```

Connection Pooling

Picture this: Your application is running great—executing code quickly on your local machine, displaying its opening screen—when the user clicks on an icon that requires database access to retrieve some relatively trivial information. The application pauses for 2 to 3 seconds before the information is displayed. Why the relatively long delay? The delay occurs while your application is opening a connection to the database.

Creating and Opening Connections

Creating and opening a connection to a data store can be a time-consuming and resource-intensive proposition. One of the most common solutions to this problem has been to immediately open a connection to the data store when the application is starting and hold the connection open until the application is closed. Unfortunately, this approach means that the data store maintains connections for long periods of time, even if the user is in a part of the application that doesn't need data store connectivity. The problem grows significantly on multi-user systems, such as multi-tier and Web-based systems, because a separate connection might be required on a user-by-user basis from a single machine to the data store. We can easily get into a situation where every user has one or more open connections to the database and the database is consuming too many resources just managing connections. Ideally, we want the data store to spend most of its time delivering data and as little time as possible maintaining connections. This is where connection pooling can help.

Connection pooling is the reuse of existing active connections instead of creating new connections when a request is made to the database. It involves the use of a connection manager that is responsible for maintaining a list, or pool, of available connections. When the connection manager receives a request for a new connection, it checks its pool for available connections. If a connection is available, it is returned. If no connections are available and the maximum pool size has not been reached, a new connection is created and returned. If the maximum pool size has been reached, the connection request is added to the queue and the next available connection is returned, as long as the connection timeout has not been reached.

Connection pooling is controlled by parameters placed into the connection string. Table 4-1 lists the parameters that affect pooling.

Table 4-1 Parameters That Affect Pooling

Parameter	Description
Connection Timeout	The time in seconds to wait while a connection to the data store is attempted. The default is 15 seconds.
Min Pool Size	The minimum amount of pooled connections to keep in the pool. The default is 0. It's usually good to set this to a low number, such as 5, when your application requires consistent, fast response—even if the application is inactive for long periods.
Max Pool Size	The maximum allowed connections in the connection pool. The default is 100, which is usually more than enough for most Web site applications.
Pooling	A value of *true* causes the request for a new connection to be drawn from the pool. If the pool does not exist, it is created. The default is *true*.
Connection Reset	Indicates that the database connection will be reset when the connection is removed from the pool. The default is *true*. A value of *false* results in fewer roundtrips to the server when creating a connection, but the connection state is not updated.
Load Balancing Timeout, Connection Lifetime	The maximum time in seconds that a pooled connection should live. The maximum time is checked only when the connection is returned to the pool. This setting is useful in load-balanced cluster configurations to force a balance between a server that is online and a server that has just started. The default is 0.
Enlist	When this value is *true*, the connection is automatically enlisted into the creation thread's current transaction context. The default is *true*.

To implement connection pooling, you must follow a few rules:

- The connection string must be the same for every user or service that will participate in the pool. Remember that each character must match in terms of lowercase and uppercase as well.
- The user ID must be the same for every user or service that will participate in the pool. Even if you specify *integrated security=true*, the Windows user account of the process will be used to determine pool membership.
- The process ID must be the same. It has never been possible to share connections across processes, and this limitation extends to pooling.

Where's the Pool?

Connection pooling is a client-side technology. The database has no idea that there might be one or more connection pools involved in your application. Client-side means that the connection pooling takes place on the machine that is initiating the *DbConnection* object's *Open* statement.

When Is the Pool Created?

The connection pool group is an object that manages the connection pools for a specific ADO.NET provider. When the first connection is instantiated, a connection pool group is created. However, the first connection pool is not created until the first connection is opened.

How Long Will the Connection Stay in the Pool?

A connection is removed from the pool of available connections for use and then returned to the pool of available connections. By default, when a connection is returned to the connection pool, it has an idle lifetime of 4 to 8 minutes (a time that is set somewhat randomly). This means the connection pool does not continue to hold on to idle connections indefinitely. If you want to make sure that at least one connection is available when your application is idle for long periods, you can set the connection string's *Min Pool Size* to one or more.

Load-Balancing Timeout (AKA Connection Lifetime)

The connection string has a setting called the *Load Balancing Timeout*, formerly known as the *Connection Lifetime*. *Connection Lifetime* still exists for backward compatibility, but the new name better describes this setting's intended use. You should use this setting only in an environment with clustered servers because it is meant to aid in load balancing database connections. This setting is examined only when the connection is closed. If the connection stays open longer than its *Load Balancing Timeout* setting, the connection is destroyed. Otherwise, it is added back into the pool.

Look at this scenario where we can use the *Load Balancing Timeout* setting to solve a problem. Let's say two database servers are clustered together and they appear heavily loaded, so a third database server is added. The original databases still seem overloaded and the new server has few or no connections.

What happened? Connection pooling was doing its job by maintaining connections to the existing database servers. To solve the problem, we can specify a *Load Balancing Timeout* setting that essentially throws out some of the perfectly good connections so the new connection can go to a newly added database server. The tradeoff is some loss of performance because connections occasionally have to be re-created, but the connections will potentially go to a new server.

Exceeding the Pool Size

The default maximum connection pool size is 100. You can modify this by changing the *Max Pool Size* connection string setting, although the default setting is fine for most scenarios. How do you know if you need to change this value? You can use Performance Monitor to watch the *NumberOfPooledConnections*. If the maximum pool size is reached, any new requests for a connection are blocked until a connection frees up or the *Connection Timeout* connection string setting expires. The *Connection Timeout* setting has a default value of 15 seconds. If you exceed the Connection Timeout value, an *InvalidOperationException* is thrown:

```
Timeout expired.  The timeout period elapsed prior to obtaining a connection from the
pool.  This may have occurred because all pooled connections were in use and max pool
size was reached.
```

This same exception is thrown if you try to connect to a database server and the server cannot be reached or if the server is found but the database service is down.

Are You Exceeding the Pool Size Due to Connection Leaks?

Your application might need a larger *Max Pool Size* if you have a large Web application with hundreds of users hitting the site at the same time. If that's the case, by all means increase the *Max Pool Size* connection string setting.

If you are watching your application in Performance Monitor and notice that the *NumberOfPooledConnections* continues to rise uncontrollably, you might be suffering from connection leaks. A connection leak occurs when you open a connection but never close it. In some cases where you have code that closes the connection, if an exception occurs before you reach that line of code, you might never close the connection. The following code shows an example of this.

Visual Basic

```
Imports System.Data
Imports System.Data.SqlClient
Imports System.Configuration

Public Class Form1
   Private Sub Button1_Click( _
         ByVal sender As System.Object, _
         ByVal e As System.EventArgs) Handles Button1.Click
      Try
         ConnectionLeak()
      Catch ex As Exception
         'do something cool to recover
      End Try
      MessageBox.Show("Done")
   End Sub
```

```
   Public Sub ConnectionLeak()
      Dim cnSettings As SqlConnectionStringBuilder
      cnSettings = New SqlConnectionStringBuilder( _
      "Data Source=.;" _
         + "Database=PUBS;" _
         + "Integrated Security=True;" _
         + "Min Pool Size=3;Max Pool Size=5")

      Dim cn As SqlConnection = New SqlConnection(cnSettings.ConnectionString)
      cn.Open()
      Dim cmd As SqlCommand = cn.CreateCommand()
      cmd.CommandText = "raiserror ('Simulate an error in sql', 17,1)"
      cmd.ExecuteNonQuery()  'throws the SqlException
      cn.Close() 'Calls connection close, but this code is not reached
   End Sub
End Class
```

C#

```
using System;
using System.Windows.Forms;
using System.Configuration;
using System.Data.SqlClient;

namespace ConnectionPooling
{
   public partial class Form1 : Form
   {
      public Form1() { InitializeComponent(); }
      private void button1_Click(object sender, EventArgs e)
      {
         try { ConnectionLeak(); }
         catch (SqlException)
         {
            //do something cool to recover
         }
         MessageBox.Show("Done");
      }
      public void ConnectionLeak()
      {
         SqlConnectionStringBuilder cnSettings;
         cnSettings = new SqlConnectionStringBuilder(
            @"Data Source=.;"
               + "Database=PUBS;"
               + "Integrated Security=True;"
               + "Min Pool Size=3;Max Pool Size=5");
         SqlConnection cn = new SqlConnection(cnSettings.ConnectionString);
         cn.Open();
         SqlCommand cmd = cn.CreateCommand();
         cmd.CommandText = "raiserror ('Simulate an error in sql', 17,1)";
         cmd.ExecuteNonQuery();  //throws the SqlException
         cn.Close(); //Calls connection close, but this code is not reached
      }
   }
}
```

As you can see, every time the button is clicked a *SqlException* is thrown and immediately bubbles up to the calling method. This means the *Close* method is not executed in the *ConnectionLeak* method. Depending on when garbage collection takes place, you might be able to continue clicking the button and not exceed the maximum pool size, but if this code is hit frequently, it won't take long to get an *InvalidOperationException* (timeout expired) because you exceeded the maximum pool size.

You can use Performance Monitor to identify orphaned connections by watching the *NumberOfReclaimedConnections* while the application is running. Figure 4-1 shows the *NumberOfReclaimedConnections* rising each time the button is clicked.

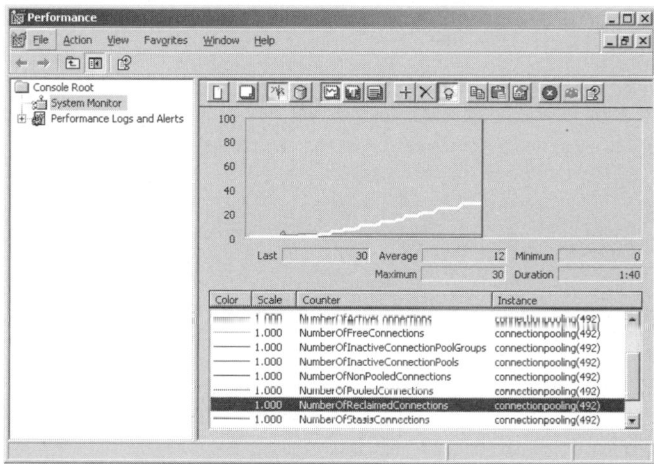

Figure 4-1 *NumberOfReclaimedConnections* rises due to connection not being closed.

Goodbye, *Close* Method; Hello, *Using* Block

To solve the problem in the previous code sample, you must rewrite your code to ensure that the *Close* or *Dispose* method is always called. You can do this by implementing a *try/catch/finally* block or a *using* block. The following code shows the *ConnectionLeak* method rewritten, implementing *using* blocks to solve the problem.

Visual Basic

```
Public Sub NoConnectionLeak()
   Dim cnSettings As SqlConnectionStringBuilder
   cnSettings = New SqlConnectionStringBuilder( _
   "Data Source=.;" _
      + "Database=PUBS;" _
      + "Integrated Security=True;" _
      + "Min Pool Size=3;Max Pool Size=5")
   Using cn As SqlConnection = New SqlConnection(cnSettings.ConnectionString)
      cn.Open()
      Using cmd As SqlCommand = cn.CreateCommand()
         cmd.CommandText = "raiserror ('Simulate an error in sql', 17,1)"
         cmd.ExecuteNonQuery()  'throws the SqlException
```

```
        End Using
    End Using
End Sub
```

C#

```
public void NoConnectionLeak()
{
    SqlConnectionStringBuilder cnSettings;
    cnSettings = new SqlConnectionStringBuilder(
        @"Data Source=.;"
            + "Database=PUBS;"
            + "Integrated Security=True;"
            + "Max Pool Size=5");
    using (SqlConnection cn = new SqlConnection(cnSettings.ConnectionString))
    {
        cn.Open();
        using (SqlCommand cmd = cn.CreateCommand())
        {
            cmd.CommandText = "raiserror ('Simulate an error in sql', 17,1)";
            cmd.ExecuteNonQuery();  //throws the SqlException
        }
    }
}
```

Notice that the *Close* method is no longer in the code because the *using* block automatically calls the *Dispose* method. Also, the *cmd* object has a *Dispose* method, so a *using* block was added for the command as well. This is a much more elegant way to code connections, commands, and anything else that implements the *Dispose* method. The code examples in the rest of this book implement *using* blocks instead of explicitly calling the *Close* or *Dispose* method unless code is required to conditionally close the connection.

When to Turn Off Pooling

It's a good idea to keep pooling on at all times, but if you need to troubleshoot connection-related problems, you might want to turn it off. Pooling is on by default, but you can change the *Pooling* setting in the connection string to *false* to turn off pooling. Remember that performance will suffer because each *Open* statement will create a new connection to the database and each *Close* statement will destroy the connection. Also, without any limits, the server might deny the requests for a connection if the licensing limit is exceeded or the administrator has set connection limits at the server.

Clearing the Pool

When you're working with a database server, it might not always be available–it might have been removed from a cluster, or you might have needed to stop and start the service. When a database server becomes unavailable, the connections in the pool become corrupted.

You can use two methods in your code to recover from a corrupted connection pool: *ClearPool* and *ClearAllPools*. These are static methods on the *SqlConnection* and *OracleConnection* classes.

The following code snippet works perfectly well and takes advantage of the connection pool until the database service is stopped and restarted.

Visual Basic

```
Private Sub Button3_Click( _
      ByVal sender As System.Object, _
      ByVal e As System.EventArgs) Handles Button3.Click
   Dim ver As String = Nothing
   Dim cnSettings As SqlConnectionStringBuilder
   cnSettings = New SqlConnectionStringBuilder( _
      "Data Source=.;" _
         + "Database=PUBS;" _
         + "Integrated Security=True;" _
         + "Max Pool Size=5")
   Using cn As SqlConnection = New SqlConnection(cnSettings.ConnectionString)
      cn.Open()
      Using cmd As SqlCommand = cn.CreateCommand()
         cmd.CommandText = "Select @@Version"
         ver = CType(cmd.ExecuteScalar(), String)
      End Using
   End Using
   MessageBox.Show(ver)
End Sub
```

C#

```
private void button3_Click(object sender, EventArgs e)
{
   string ver=null;
   SqlConnectionStringBuilder cnSettings;
   cnSettings = new SqlConnectionStringBuilder(
      @"Data Source=.;"
         + "Database=PUBS;"
         + "Integrated Security=True;"
         + "Max Pool Size=5");
   using (SqlConnection cn = new SqlConnection(cnSettings.ConnectionString))
   {
      cn.Open();
      using (SqlCommand cmd = cn.CreateCommand())
      {
         cmd.CommandText = "Select @@Version";
         ver = (string)cmd.ExecuteScalar();
      }
   }
   MessageBox.Show(ver);
}
```

If the database service is stopped and restarted, the previous code causes the following *SqlException* to be thrown.

```
A transport-
level error has occurred when receiving results from the server. (provider: Session Provid
er, error: 18 - Connection has been closed by peer)
```

To silently recover from this exception, you can clean the pools and then re-execute the code. The following code shows how to do this.

Visual Basic

```
Private Sub Button4_Click( _
      ByVal sender As System.Object,  _
      ByVal e As System.EventArgs) Handles Button4.Click
   try
      DisplayVersion()
   catch xcp as SqlException
      if xcp.Number <> 1236 then throw xcp 'first chance?
      System.Diagnostics.Debug.WriteLine("Clearing Pools")
      SqlConnection.ClearAllPools() 'recover
      DisplayVersion() 'retry
   end try
End Sub

public sub DisplayVersion()
   Dim ver As String = Nothing
   Dim cnSettings As SqlConnectionStringBuilder
   cnSettings = New SqlConnectionStringBuilder( _
      "Data Source=.;" _
         + "Database=PUBS;" _
         + "Integrated Security=True;" _
         + "Max Pool Size=5")
   Using cn As SqlConnection = New SqlConnection(cnSettings.ConnectionString)
      cn.Open()
      Using cmd As SqlCommand = cn.CreateCommand()
         cmd.CommandText = "Select @@Version"
         ver = CType(cmd.ExecuteScalar(), String)
      End Using
   End Using
   MessageBox.Show(ver)
End Sub
```

C#

```
private void button4_Click(object sender, EventArgs e)
{
   try
   {
      DisplayVersion();
   }
   catch (SqlException xcp)
   {
      if (xcp.Number != 1236) throw xcp; //first chance?
      System.Diagnostics.Debug.WriteLine("Clearing Pools");
      SqlConnection.ClearAllPools();//recover
      DisplayVersion();//retry
   }
}

public void DisplayVersion()
{
   string ver = null;
```

```
    SqlConnectionStringBuilder cnSettings;
    cnSettings = new SqlConnectionStringBuilder(
       @"Data Source=.;"
          + "Database=PUBS;"
          + "Integrated Security=True;"
          + "Max Pool Size=5");

    using (SqlConnection cn = new SqlConnection(cnSettings.ConnectionString))
    {
       cn.Open();
       using (SqlCommand cmd = cn.CreateCommand())
       {
          cmd.CommandText = "Select @@Version";
          ver = (string)cmd.ExecuteScalar();
       }
    }
    MessageBox.Show(ver);
}
```

Working with a Failover Partner

When you are ready to put your application into production, how can you know whether the database can withstand having many people bang on the application? What happens if the database server goes down? What happens if the database server needs to be quickly rebooted? How about that quick stop and start of the database service?

In the last example, you saw what happens when the database service is stopped and restarted. In that scenario, we caught the first chance exception, cleared the pools, and retried. How can you get the same result with essentially no down time if the database server needs to be rebooted? This is where a failover partner in SQL Server 2005 can come into play.

So here's the scenario: You have set up database mirroring by using three SQL Server 2005 machines. The first machine is a "principal" database owner, the second machine is a database partner "mirror," and the third machine is the "witness," as shown in Figure 4-2. (The database mirroring feature is not available in SQL Server Express Edition.) When database mirroring is implemented, the client application normally talks to the principal. The mirror database is in the recovering state, which means that you cannot use it for any data access activity, including read-only access. When a transaction successfully commits on the principal, it is sent to the mirror as a transaction. You can think of this as a continuous backup-and-restore operation. The witness is simply checking to see if the principal and mirror are running, but it's the witness's job to automate the reversal of roles–from principal to mirror and mirror to principal–if the principal goes down.

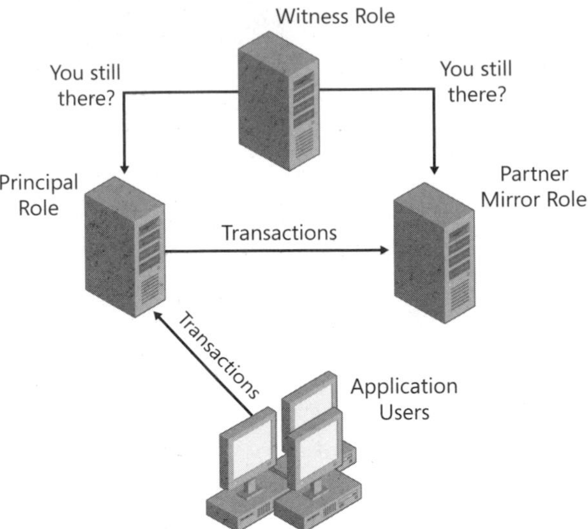

Figure 4-2 Database mirroring with initial role configuration

In this scenario, what happens if your application has a connection string that is configured to point to the principal? You might think that you have to write some fancy code to detect a transition and then start talking to the mirror, which just became the principal, and then do the same to switch back. However, you can simply use the *Failover Partner* setting in the connection string. This setting is new in ADO.NET 2.0 and works with SQL Server 2005. When *Failover Partner* is set, if the connection detects a problem connecting to the database server, it will automatically clear the pool for this connection string and switch to the failover server, as shown in Figure 4-3.

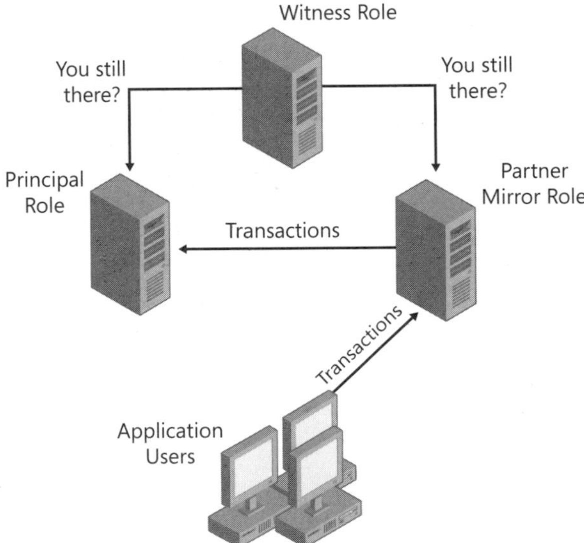

Figure 4-3 Database mirroring after the witness reverses the roles

To simulate this feature, I have three instances of SQL Server 2005 installed on a virtual machine. The principal is the default instance ("."), the mirror is the Partner instance (".\Partner"), and the witness is the Witness instance (".\Witness"). The following code inserts a row into the principal.

Visual Basic

```
Private Sub Button5_Click( _
   ByVal sender As System.Object, _
   ByVal e As System.EventArgs) Handles Button5.Click
 Dim ver As String = Nothing
   Dim cnSettings As SqlConnectionStringBuilder
   cnSettings = New SqlConnectionStringBuilder( _
      "Data Source=.;" _
         + "Database=FailTest;" _
         + "Integrated Security=True;" _
         + "Max Pool Size=5;" _
         + "Failover Partner=.\Partner")
   Using cn As SqlConnection = New SqlConnection(cnSettings.ConnectionString)
      cn.Open()
      Using cmd As SqlCommand = cn.CreateCommand()
         cmd.CommandText = string.Format( _
            "Insert into TestTable(Id, Name) Values('{0}','{1}')", _
            Guid.NewGuid(),DateTime.Now.ToLongTimeString())
         cmd.ExecuteNonQuery()
      End Using
      MessageBox.Show("Data entered into server: " + cn.DataSource)
   End Using
End Sub
```

C#

```
private void button5_Click(object sender, EventArgs e)
{
   SqlConnectionStringBuilder cnSettings;
   cnSettings = new SqlConnectionStringBuilder(
      "Data Source=.;"
         + "Database=FailTest;"
         + "Integrated Security=True;"
         + "Max Pool Size=5;"
         + @"Failover Partner=.\Partner");

   using (SqlConnection cn = new SqlConnection(cnSettings.ConnectionString))
   {
      cn.Open();
      using (SqlCommand cmd = cn.CreateCommand())
      {
         cmd.CommandText = string.Format(
            "Insert into TestTable(Id, Name) Values('{0}','{1}')",
            Guid.NewGuid(),DateTime.Now.ToLongTimeString());
         cmd.ExecuteNonQuery();
      }
      MessageBox.Show("Data entered into server: " + cn.DataSource);
   }
}
```

Notice that there is no fancy code, just the addition of the *Failover Partner* setting in the connection string. If the principal instance is shut down, the witness detects the shutdown and makes the mirror operational. The *SqlConnection* object gets a first-chance exception, clears the pool for this connection string, and replaces the *DataSource* with the *Failover Partner*. The resulting message indicates that the data was inserted into the ".\Partner" instance. If the original principal becomes available, it assumes the role of mirror until the current principal goes down and roles reverse again.

Asynchronous Data Access

Asynchronous access to data can greatly improve the performance or perceived performance (responsiveness) of your application. With asynchronous access, multiple commands can be executed simultaneously and notification of command completion can be accomplished by either polling, using *WaitHandles*, or delegates.

Synchronous vs. Asynchronous Access

Commands are normally executed synchronously, which causes the command to "block" program execution until the command has completed. Blocking execution keeps the program from continuing until the command has finished executing. This simplifies the writing of the code because the developer simply thinks about code execution in a rather procedural, step-by-step fashion, as shown in Figure 4-4. The problem arises with long-running commands because blocking inhibits the program's ability to do other work, such as performing additional commands or, more important, allowing the user to abort the command.

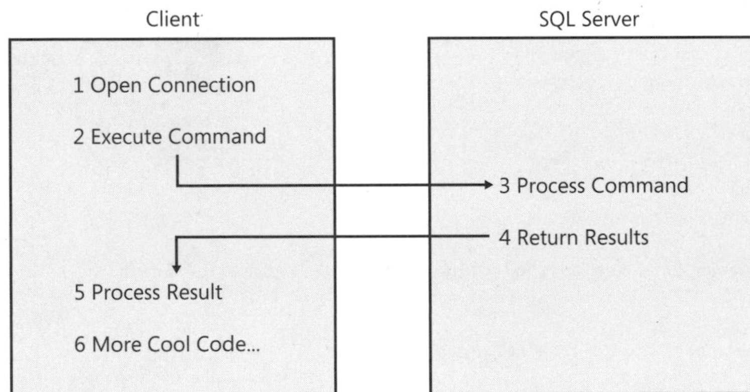

Figure 4-4 Synchronous data access

Asynchronous command execution does not block program execution because it takes place on a new thread. The new thread represents a new program execution path, which means the original thread can continue executing while the new thread is waiting for its command to complete, as shown in Figure 4-5. The original thread is free to repaint the screen or listen for other events, such as button clicks.

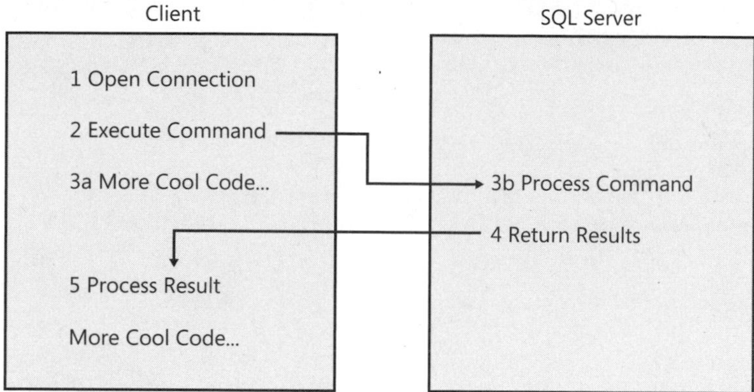

Figure 4-5 Asynchronous data access

Synchronous code is considered easier to write than asynchronous code because of its procedural nature, but the extra effort to write asynchronous code gives your users a much more responsive system.

To demonstrate the difference between synchronous and asynchronous data access, the following code uses synchronous data access. This code simulates a long-running query and then places a message in a label on the form.

Visual Basic

```
Private Sub Button1_Click( _
      ByVal sender As System.Object, _
      ByVal e As System.EventArgs) Handles Button1.Click
   Dim ver As String = nothing
   Dim cnSettings As SqlConnectionStringBuilder
   cnSettings = New SqlConnectionStringBuilder( _
      "Data Source=.;" _
         + "Database=PUBS;" _
         + "Integrated Security=True;" _
         + "Max Pool Size=5")
   Using cn As SqlConnection = New SqlConnection(cnSettings.ConnectionString)
      cn.Open()
      Using cmd As SqlCommand = cn.CreateCommand()
         cmd.CommandText = "WaitFor Delay '00:00:15' Select @@Version"
         ver = CType(cmd.ExecuteScalar(), String)
      End Using
   End Using
   Label1.Text = ver
End Sub
```

C#

```
private void button1_Click(object sender, EventArgs e)
{
   string ver = null;
   SqlConnectionStringBuilder cnSettings;
   cnSettings = new SqlConnectionStringBuilder(
      @"Data Source=.;"
         + "Database=PUBS;"
```

```
            + "Integrated Security=True;"
            + "Max Pool Size=5");
    using (SqlConnection cn = new SqlConnection(cnSettings.ConnectionString))
    {
        cn.Open();
        using (SqlCommand cmd = cn.CreateCommand())
        {
            cmd.CommandText = "WaitFor Delay '00:00:15' Select @@Version";
            ver = (string)cmd.ExecuteScalar();
        }
    }
    label1.Text = ver;
}
```

In this code, if you attempt to move or resize the window while the query is executing, the window does not respond. While you're waiting, if you want to look at another application, such as Microsoft Internet Explorer, you can open it on top of this application. If you minimize Internet Explorer while the query is still running, the application's form does not repaint until the query has completed.

To implement this application using asynchronous code, you must first set the connection string to have *Asynchronous Processing=true* or *async=true*. Otherwise, any attempt to execute a command asynchronously throws an exception. Next, one of the command object's *Begin* methods must be executed. The synchronous example just shown uses the *ExecuteScaler* method. Because there is no asynchronous version of this method, we'll use the closest equivalent, *BeginExecuteReader*, for our example. (The *SqlCommand* object provides the *BeginExecuteNoQuery*, *BeginExecuteReader*, and *BeginExecuteXmlReader* methods.) The following code shows the asynchronous implementation.

Visual Basic

```
Private Sub Button2_Click( ByVal sender As System.Object,  ByVal e As System.EventArgs) Hand
les Button2.Click
    Dim cnSettings as  SqlConnectionStringBuilder
    cnSettings = new SqlConnectionStringBuilder( _
        "Data Source=.;" _
            + "Database=PUBS;" _
            + "Integrated Security=True;" _
            + "Max Pool Size=5;" _
            + "async=true")
    Dim cn as new SqlConnection(cnSettings.ConnectionString)
    cn.Open()
    Dim cmd as SqlCommand = cn.CreateCommand()
    cmd.CommandText = "WaitFor Delay '00:00:15' Select @@Version"
    cmd.BeginExecuteReader(new AsyncCallback(AddressOf ProcessResult),cmd)
End Sub

public Sub ProcessResult(ar as IAsyncResult)
    Dim cmd as SqlCommand = ctype(ar.AsyncState, SqlCommand)
    using cmd.Connection
        using cmd
            dim ver as string = nothing
            dim rdr as SqlDataReader = cmd.EndExecuteReader(ar)
```

```
         if (rdr.Read()) then
            ver = ctype(rdr(0),string)
            label1.BeginInvoke(new LabelHandler( AddressOf UpdateLabel), ver)
         end if
      end using
   end using
End Sub

public delegate sub LabelHandler(text as string)

public sub UpdateLabel(text as string)
   label1.Text = text
End Sub
```

C#

```
private void button2_Click(object sender, EventArgs e)
{
   SqlConnectionStringBuilder cnSettings;
   cnSettings = new SqlConnectionStringBuilder(
      @"Data Source=.;"
         + "Database=PUBS;"
         + "Integrated Security=True;"
         + "Max Pool Size=5;"
         + "async=true");
   SqlConnection cn = new SqlConnection(cnSettings.ConnectionString);
   cn.Open();
   SqlCommand cmd = cn.CreateCommand();
   cmd.CommandText = "WaitFor Delay '00:00:15' Select @@Version";
   cmd.BeginExecuteReader(new AsyncCallback(ProcessResult),cmd);
}

public void ProcessResult(IAsyncResult ar)
{
   SqlCommand cmd = (SqlCommand)ar.AsyncState;
   using (cmd.Connection)
   {
      using (cmd)
      {
         string ver = null;
         SqlDataReader rdr = cmd.EndExecuteReader(ar);
         if (rdr.Read())
         {
            ver = (string)rdr[0];
            label1.BeginInvoke(new LabelHandler(UpdateLabel), ver);
         }
      }
   }
}

public delegate void LabelHandler(string text);

public void UpdateLabel(string text)
{
   label1.Text = text;
}
```

As you can see, the label is populated with the result of the query. The problem is that properties on Windows form controls must be set using the same thread as the thread that created the control. The *ProcessResult* method is always running with a different thread, so the result must be marshaled back to the original thread. You do this by executing the *BeginInvoke* method on the label and passing the text that needs to be placed into the label. The *BeginInvoke* method requires a delegate, so the delegate called *LabelHandler* is created and used. The *LabelHandler* delegate points to the *UpdateLabel* method, which is called by the thread that created the label.

In this asynchronous example, when the command is executed the form can still be resized or moved, and if another window temporarily covers this form, the form will be repainted as soon as the form is uncovered.

Working with SQL Server Provider Statistics

The SQL Server provider has built in run-time statistics that can be enabled on a valid connection object. Currently, there are more than 20 statistical values available that can help you understand what's happening in your application. They are described in Table 4-2.

Table 4-2 Available Statistical Values

Statistic Name	Description
BuffersReceived	The number of Tabular Data Stream (TDS) packets that this provider received from SQL Server after the application has started and statistics have been enabled.
BuffersSent	The number of TDS packets that this provider sent to SQL Server after statistics have been enabled.
BytesReceived	The number of data bytes that this provider received from SQL Server after the application has started and statistics have been enabled.
BytesSent	The number of data bytes that this provider sent to SQL Server after the application started and statistics have been enabled.
ConnectionTime	The time that the connection has been opened after statistics have been enabled.
CursorFetchCount	The number of fetches done against server cursors after the application has started and the statistics have been enabled.
CursorFetchTime	The total time it took fetches against server cursors to complete after the application has started and statistics have been enabled.
CursorOpens	Number of times a cursor was open through the connection after the application has started and statistics have been enabled.
CursorUsed	Number of rows actually retrieved through the driver from cursors after the application has started and statistics have been enabled.

Table 4-2 Available Statistical Values

Statistic Name	Description
ExecutionTime	The total time that the provider spent processing after the statistics have been enabled, including the time spent waiting for replies from the server as well as the time spent executing code in the provider itself.
IduCount	Total quantity of INSERT, DELETE, and UPDATE statements executed through the connection after the application has started and statistics have been enabled.
IduRows	Total quantity of rows affected by INSERT, DELETE, and UPDATE statements executed through the connection after the application has started and statistics have been enabled.
NetworkServerTime	The total time the provider spent waiting for replies from the server after the application has started and statistics have been enabled.
PreparedExecs	The number of prepared commands executed through the connection after the application has started and statistics have been enabled.
Prepares	The number of statements prepared through the connection after the application has started and statistics have been enabled.
SelectCount	Quantity of SELECT statements executed through the connection after the application has started and statistics have been enabled.
SelectRows	Quantity of rows selected after the application has started and statistics have been enabled. This includes all rows generated by SQL statements, even if they weren't consumed by the caller.
ServerRoundtrips	The number of times the connection sent commands to the server and got a reply back after the application has started and statistics have been enabled.
SumResultSets	Quantity of result sets that have been used after the application has started and statistics have been enabled.
Transactions	Quantity of user transactions started after the application has started and statistics have been enabled. This count includes rollbacks.
UnpreparedExecs	The number of unprepared statements executed through the connection after the application has started and statistics have been enabled.

To access the statistics, you must have a valid connection object, and the statistics must be enabled. To demonstrate the use statistics, create a Windows application, and add a *Button* control and two *DataGridView* controls. Change the *Text* property of the Button control to "Statistic Test". Double-click the *Button* control and add the following code to enable the statistics, run a simple query, and retrieve the statistics.

Visual Basic

```
Imports System.Configuration
Imports System.Data
Imports System.Data.SqlClient
```

```
Public Class Form1

    Private Sub Button1_Click(ByVal sender As System.Object, _
       ByVal e As System.EventArgs) Handles Button1.Click

        Dim authors As New DataTable()
        Dim pubSettings As ConnectionStringSettings = _
           ConfigurationManager.ConnectionStrings("PubsString")
        Using cn As New SqlConnection()
            cn.ConnectionString = pubSettings.ConnectionString
            cn.StatisticsEnabled = True
            Using cmd As SqlCommand = cn.CreateCommand()
                cn.Open()
                cmd.CommandText = "SELECT * FROM AUTHORS"
                authors.Load(cmd.ExecuteReader())
                DataGridView1.DataSource = authors
            End Using
            Dim stats As New ArrayList(cn.RetrieveStatistics())
            DataGridView2.DataSource = stats
        End Using

    End Sub
End Class
```

C#

```
using System;
using System.Data;
using System.Windows.Forms;
using System.Configuration;
using System.Data.SqlClient;
using System.Collections;

namespace StatisticsTest
{
    public partial class Form1 : Form
    {
        public Form1()
        {
            InitializeComponent();
        }

        private void Button1_Click(object sender, EventArgs e)
        {
            DataTable authors = new DataTable();
            ConnectionStringSettings pubSettings =
               ConfigurationManager.ConnectionStrings["PubsString"];
            using (SqlConnection cn = new SqlConnection())
            {
                cn.ConnectionString = pubSettings.ConnectionString;
                cn.StatisticsEnabled = true;
                using (SqlCommand cmd = cn.CreateCommand())
                {
                    cn.Open();
                    cmd.CommandText = "SELECT * FROM AUTHORS";
                    authors.Load(cmd.ExecuteReader());
```

```
                    DataGridView1.DataSource = authors;
                }
                ArrayList stats = new ArrayList(cn.RetrieveStatistics());
                DataGridView2.DataSource = stats;
            }
        }
    }
}
```

The result of the query was placed into the first *DataGridView* control, and the second *DataGridView* control contains the statistical information. The results are shown in Figure 4-6.

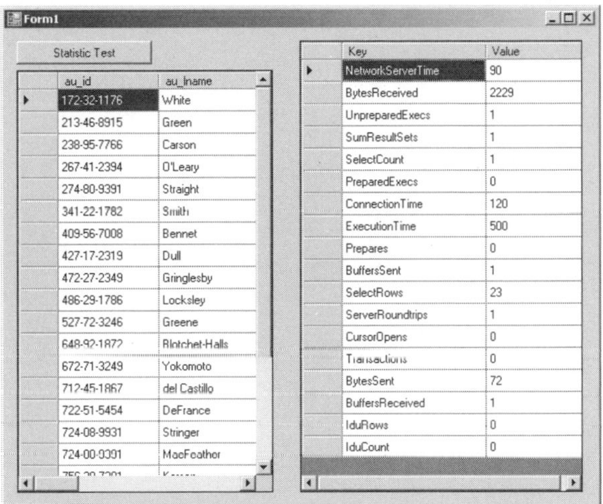

Figure 4-6 The statistics have been retrieved and are displayed in the second *DataGridView* control.

Summary

You can use the *ConnectionStringBuilder* object to accurately create connection strings because it provides validation of all of the available connection string settings. The *ConnectionStringBuilder* also plays an important role in the creation of database platform-independent code. You use the connection string to turn on advanced connectivity options such as connection pooling, clustered connections, and asynchronous access.

Connection pooling improves application responsiveness by allowing users to reuse existing active connections instead of creating new connections when a request is made to the database. A client-side connection manager maintains a list, or pool, of available connections that can be reused. Use the *using* statement to ensure that the *Dispose* method is called on the connection and command objects to avoid connection leaks.

Implementing a failover partner for clustered connections is as easy as setting the *Failover Partner* connection string setting. When a failover occurs, the server specified by the *Failover Partner* setting is used as the data source.

Asynchronous access to data can greatly improve the performance or perceived performance (responsiveness) of your application. To code asynchronous access in your application, use the *Asynchronous Processing* setting in the connection string and call one of the command object's *Begin* methods. And finally, the *SqlConnection* object provides statistical information that may be retrieved if the statistics have been enabled.

Chapter 5

Working with Disconnected Data

One challenge related to data access is that two or more users might need to access data in a given database simultaneously. For example, one user might be performing a task such as editing a customer record while another user is performing a different task, such as running a report of active customers. It is important to prevent two users from editing a record at the same time and to prevent reports from showing data that is half-complete.

Another data access issue is that users want the ability to access data from anywhere. We live in a mobile environment, where people want to access data on their laptops, cell phones, and PDAs. Many of these devices have limited communication capability, which adds to the challenge.

This chapter looks at the pros and cons of disconnected data access. It also explores how to implement unique row IDs as primary keys, such as Identity columns and Globally Unique Identifier (GUID) columns. These primary key types all have their advantages and problems, so we'll look at each type in detail.

Understanding Concurrency Issues

Concurrency is the ability to have multiple users accessing the database and seeing a consistent view of the data. You ensure a consistent view by locking rows, tables, and/or the database as necessary to keep users from accessing data that might be inconsistent. For example, let's say Mary is in the middle of a transaction that will transfer funds by debiting checking account A and crediting checking account B. At the same time, Joe might want to withdraw money from checking account A. What should Joe see as the current balance for account A if Mary is in the middle of her transaction? What should happen to Joe's transaction if Mary's transaction cannot be completed?

The database server addresses such situations by implementing database locking while a transaction is executing. If Mary is in the middle of a transaction that affects two checking accounts, both accounts should be locked until the transaction is complete. This means Joe's transaction should wait until Mary's transaction has been completed. The goal is to keep transactions as short as possible and to keep the lock wait time to a minimum.

Database locking allows concurrent access to the database in a connected environment where users are looking at and modifying live data, but what happens if you want to copy data to the client application, work on the data for a period of time, and then send all of the changes back to the database? If you start a transaction that lasts until you save your changes back to the database, you might cause severe locking issues for other users who need to access the database. On the other hand, if you don't start a transaction, the data won't be locked and another user might modify the data before you have a chance to save your changes. This latter approach is the least obtrusive and more desirable approach, but you have to deal with conflicts that arise from multiple updates taking place without locking.

To deal with concurrency conflicts, the wizards in Microsoft Visual Studio implement concurrency checking by default when you create *DbDataAdapter* objects. To understand the default operation of the *DbDataAdapter*, consider the following scenario.

The database contains a table named TblBookList that contains columns for the ISBN number (primary key), BookName, and Quantity. Joe and Mary have retrieved a complete list of all rows from the table and are making changes while offline. The following sequence of events takes place.

1. Joe and Mary read data into a *DataTable*. The data is in the *CurrentVersion* and *OriginalVersion* of the *DataRow*. At this point, Joe and Mary have started with the same data.
2. Joe changes the BookName of the book whose ISBN is 123 to "Test Book 123". Mary changes the Quantity of the same book to 999.
3. Joe updates his changes to the database, which performs an update only if the original version of the *DataRow* matches the data that is currently in the database (column for column). There is a match, so the update succeeds.
4. Mary updates her changes to the database, which again performs an update only if the original version of the *DataRow* matches the data that is currently in the database (column for column). There is no match because the BookName that is currently in the database is "Test Book 123", which Joe saved, so the update fails with a *ConcurrencyException*.

Should a concurrency error be thrown in this case? After all, Joe changed one column and Mary changed a different column. This is the default behavior of the *DbDataAdapter* object's update command, which you can modify to suit your needs. If you examine the SQL update command, it looks like the following:

SQL Update Command

```
UPDATE [dbo].[TblBookList]
   SET [ISBN] = @ISBN,
       [BookName] = @BookName,
       [Quantity] = @Quantity
   WHERE (([ISBN] = @Original_ISBN)
     AND ([BookName] = @Original_BookName)
     AND ([Quantity] = @Original_Quantity))
```

The SQL update command's *WHERE* clause dictates that the update takes place only if all of the current database column values are equal to the original column values. This is probably the safest and easiest generic approach to identifying concurrency conflicts. Also, notice that all of the columns will be set, regardless of the actual columns that have changed.

Resolving Concurrency Conflicts

When a concurrency conflict occurs, how should it be resolved? Should Joe's change override Mary's change? How you address concurrency conflicts is a business decision. Here are the main choices.

- *Prioritized on time; first update wins* Otherwise known as "first in wins." In this scenario, because Mary updated last, her changes are not persisted and Joe's changes are maintained. This approach is easy to implement because it is the default behavior of the *DataAdapter* Wizard.
- *Prioritized on time; last update wins* Otherwise known as "last in wins." In this scenario, because Mary updated last, her changes are persisted, which means Joe's changes are lost. This approach is easy to implement because it involves removing all of the extra conditions from the *WHERE* clause. In other words, the *WHERE* clause specifies only the primary key of the row to be updated.
- *Prioritized on role* Salespeople win over order entry people. If Joe is a salesperson and Mary is an order entry person, Joe has priority because it is assumed that salespeople are more knowledgeable about their customers. Thus, Joe's changes are kept and Mary's changes are rejected. This approach is a bit more difficult to implement because your application must know the role of each user. Also, if Joe and Mary have the same role, you still need to provide a fallback mechanism, such as prioritized on time.
- *Prioritized on location* Headquarters wins over branch offices. If Joe is in a branch office and Mary is at headquarters, Mary's changes are persisted and Joe's changes are overwritten. This approach is also a bit more difficult to implement because your application must know each user's location. Don't forget, if Joe and Mary are in the same location, you still need to provide a fallback mechanism, such as prioritized on time.
- *User resolves the conflict* When a conflict occurs, the user is presented with a conflict resolution screen with choices for how to resolve the conflict. Joe saves first, and at the time he saves there is no conflict. When Mary saves, a conflict is identified and she is presented with a conflict resolution screen that shows the original data that was retrieved from the database, the current data that is in the database (Joe's changes), and the current data that is in the application (Mary's changes). Mary can decide which data should be persisted.

How you should resolve concurrency conflicts depends entirely on the goals of your application and might also depend on the data you are working with. For example, with customer data the priority might be based on role, but with accounts receivable data the priority might be based on location. The automatic prioritization methods are rather straightforward; but allowing the user to resolve the conflict can be challenging to implement. I will show an implementation of this approach later in the chapter.

Designing for Disconnected Data

Before writing your code, you must make some key design decisions that will affect your ability to work with disconnected data: how much data should be loaded, how the data will be updated when many related tables are involved, and (probably the most important decision) which type of primary key you will implement. We will look at each of these in detail, using the following scenario.

Joe is a traveling salesperson who needs to maintain a list of customers and orders for his territory. While he is on the road, he can modify the data and store it to disk. When he returns to the office, he sends his changes to the main database server and retrieves updated information as well. If any concurrency conflicts arise, Joe is prompted to select the correct data. Our example uses a simplified order entry database that contains five related tables, as shown in Figure 5-1.

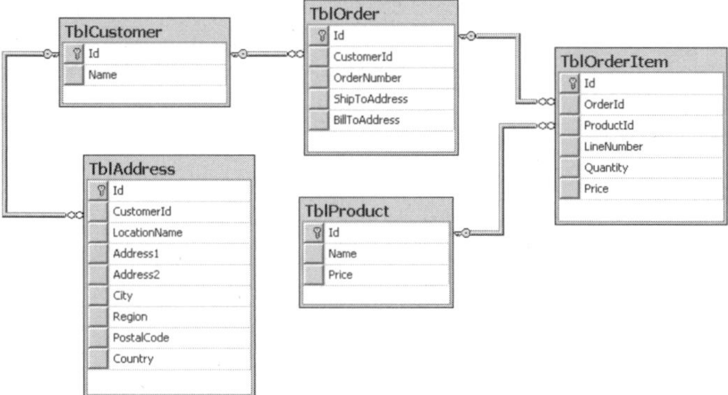

Figure 5-1 Simplified order entry database schema

What Data Should Be Loaded?

These factors affect the data that is to be loaded.

Data Selection

You should load only as much data as the user needs to work disconnected. If the user is a traveling salesperson, you might need to load his customer list and all of the information related to each customer. If you are building a Web site that uses disconnected data, you might only retrieve the data for the currently logged on customer. In almost all cases, you need to retrieve only a subset of the data in the database.

Data Size

The size of the data affects the load time, update time, and client memory requirements. Keep in mind that *DataSet* objects are memory based, so be careful about the amount of data you are retrieving. If you're not sure if you should retrieve certain data, don't retrieve it. This is a much better approach than arbitrarily retrieving data that might never be used.

Partitioning Data

It might be beneficial to break the data into multiple *DataSet* objects, based on what you think the *DataSet* object should represent. For example, you might think of a *DataSet* object as an object that contains all of the data for a single customer. In that case, the *DataSet* object might contain all five of the tables defined in Figure 5-1, but the TblCustomer and TblAddress tables contain only a single row with the information for a particular customer, and the TblOrder and TblOrderItem tables only have rows that relate to that customer.

What do you do with the TblProduct table? If the *DataSet* object is supposed to represent a complete snapshot of this customer at a point in time, you might want to include the TblProduct table but include only the product rows that relate to the TblOrderItem table. This would allow you to view all of the order information, including the products purchased. However, if you are going to allow products to be deleted from the TblProduct table, even if they have been used in orders, TblOrderItem should contain all of the data for the product being purchased, and the TblProduct table can be excluded from the customer *DataSet* object.

Similarly, if you need to be able to add more orders for different products, you must have the complete TblProduct table, so again you might want to place it into its own *DataSet* object. This would allow you to transfer product lists independently from the customer or customers. Remember that a foreign key constraint cannot be created between *DataTable* objects that are in different *DataSet* objects; however, in this case it's ok because you want to be able to delete obsolete products from the TblProduct table without being forced to delete references to them from the TblOrderItem table.

Therefore, the TblProduct table should be in its own *DataSet* object, and there should either be a *DataSet* object for each customer or one *DataSet* object that contains all of the customer data. In the scenario where Joe is a traveling salesperson, one *DataSet* object will contain the data for all of Joe's customers, and the second *DataSet* object will contain the products, as shown in Figure 5-2.

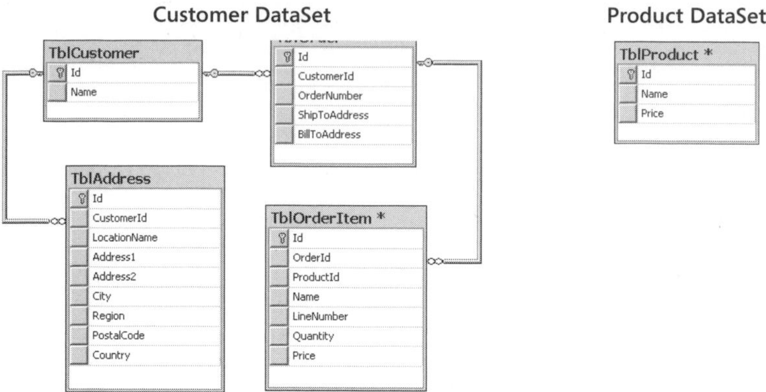

Figure 5-2 The customer data and product data should be in separate *DataSet* objects.

Choosing the Primary Key

The primary key is the column or combination of columns that uniquely defines a row. No column in the primary key can contain a null value. The primary key provides a means for the database engine to retrieve a specific row from a table in your database. The primary key is also used to enforce referential integrity. When you are working with disconnected data, you must eliminate any possibility of duplicate primary keys when multiple users are inserting data at the same time.

Intelligent, Natural Primary Keys vs. Surrogate Primary Keys

An intelligent key is a key that is based on the business data being represented. An example of an intelligent key is a Stock Keeping Unit (SKU) that is defined as a 10-character field (defined as CHAR(10) in the database). This SKU might be built as follows: the first four characters are the vendor code, the next three characters are a product type code, and the last three characters are a sequence number.

A natural key is a column or combination of columns that naturally exists in the business data and is chosen to uniquely identify records. For instance, an existing business process might define a social security number to identify a hospital patient.

Although intelligent and natural keys are different, they are both created from business-related columns that are normally viewed by the user, and the arguments for and against them are the same for the purposes of this discussion. I will refer to these keys collectively as *Intelligent-Keys*.

Surrogate primary keys are system-generated key values that have no relationship to the business data in the row, which makes them dumb keys. I'll refer to them generically as surrogate keys. One example of this kind of key is an auto-increment column where the value is set to 1, 2, 3, and so on as new rows are added. Auto-increment columns in Microsoft SQL Server are referred to as *identity columns*. I will refer to this key as an *Identity-Key*. Another example of system-generated key values is the use of a globally unique identifier (GUID) that is set to a value that is guaranteed to be unique based on the algorithm that creates these values. I will refer to this as a *GUID-Key*.

Which type of primary key do the experts recommend? It depends on which expert you ask. Each approach has major advantages and disadvantages that you should understand before you make your choice.

Figure 5-3 shows an example of *Intelligent-Key* and surrogate primary key implementation. This example contains a table for authors and books and a join (many-to-many) table because an author can write multiple books and a book can be written by multiple authors.

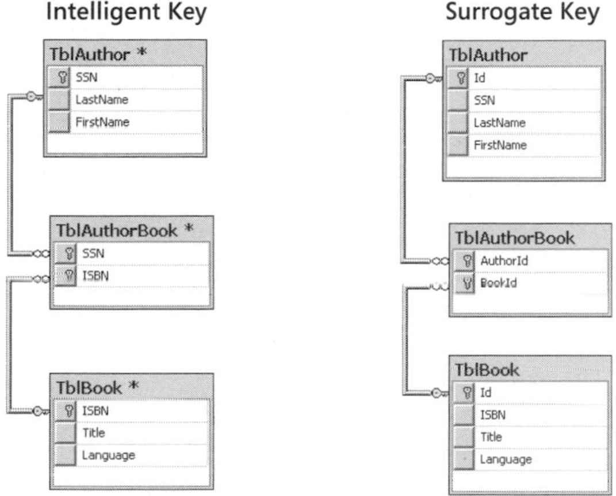

Figure 5-3 Example of intelligent and surrogate primary key implementations

Notice that the surrogate primary key implementation contains an extra Id column in the author and book tables because surrogate primary keys are system generated and have no relation to the row data. Surrogate primary keys should never be visible to the user. Here are the differences between the *Intelligent-Key* and surrogate key implementations.

Data Size Size itself is not too important, but the bandwidth that data consumes when it is transferred between the database and client is important. The surrogate implementation adds a column to each primary table. This can substantially increase data size. If the surrogate column is a GUID, the added column is 16 bytes per row. If the added column is an auto-increment column, the added column is based on the size of the numeric data type that you select (4 bytes for *int*, 8 bytes for *long*). It's common to see join tables that contain a very large quantity of rows, so be sure to consider the size difference between intelligent and surrogate keys when you analyze the overall database size difference. Also, the primary key enforces uniqueness by creating a unique index, so be sure to consider this as well. Table 5-1 compares the sizes that result when choosing each key type.

Table 5-1 Example Primary Key Sizes

Description	*Intelligent-Key*	*Identity-Key (int)*	*GUID-Key*
1000 Authors	9 bytes/SSN = 9,000 bytes	4 bytes/int = 4,000 bytes	16 bytes/GUID = 16,000 bytes
3000 Books	10 bytes/ISBN = 30,000 bytes	4 bytes/int = 12,000 bytes	16 bytes/GUID = 48,000 bytes
10,000 AuthorBooks	19 bytes/key = 190,000 bytes	8 bytes/key = 80,000 bytes	32 bytes/key = 320,000 bytes
Subtotal	229,000 bytes	96,000 bytes	384,000 bytes
Index	229,000 bytes	96,000 bytes + 9000 SSN + 30,000 ISBN = 135,000	384,000 bytes + 9000 SSN + 30,000 ISBN = 423,000
Total Size	**458,000 bytes**	**231,000 bytes**	**807,000 bytes**

The apparent winner in this scenario is the *Identity-Key*, but remember that the maximum value of the *int* is $2^{31} - 1$ = 2,147,483,647. This should be good for most applications, but you might need to use a *long* data type for large row quantities. Notice the size calculations for the index category. The implementation of a surrogate primary key still requires a unique index on the SSN and ISBN columns to enforce uniqueness on these columns.

Key Visibility Surrogate keys are not intended to be seen by the user, whereas intelligent keys are seen and understood by the user. Your custom applications can hide surrogate keys, but database tools cannot. This means that people who use database tools must understand the use of surrogate keys. The *Intelligent-Key* is therefore the winner in this category.

Modifying Keys Primary keys are difficult to change because if you modify the key, the change must be propagated to the child tables. This is where the surrogate key shines and the intelligent key suffers. Why? Surrogate keys are not intended to be displayed to the user, so there is never a need to modify them. Intelligent keys consist of business data that is visible to the user, so you must always allow this data to change.

Surrogate *int* primary keys also need to change to ensure uniqueness (as described shortly), but surrogate GUID primary keys never need to change. This is the primary reason why I like to use surrogate GUID keys.

Quantity of Joins In some cases, you can reduce the number of joins with intelligent keys. For example, if you want to run a report showing the books by each author and containing just the author's SSN and the book's ISBN fields, you can simply query the TblAuthorBook join table when intelligent primary keys are implemented. When surrogate primary keys are implemented, you have to join the TblAuthor, TblAuthorBook, and TblBook tables to get this information. The intelligent primary keys win in this category, but consider how seldom you need just these two columns without also needing additional information such as the author's name or book title.

SQL Complexity Intelligent primary keys are often implemented using multiple columns to achieve uniqueness. SQL queries can be much more complicated if such a compound intelligent key is involved. Although you might have more joins with surrogate keys, as described previously, surrogate keys can be easier to work with because they don't use compound keys (except possibly on join tables). If you compare the two surrogate key types, the *Identity-Key* implementation is easier to write queries for than the *GUID-Key*, but once you get familiar with some of the tricks of working with GUID data types (as described later), you'll find that the *GUID-Key* is only slightly more difficult to work with than the *Identity-Key*.

Ensuring Uniqueness When Disconnected It's essentially impossible to ensure uniqueness with intelligent keys when the user is entering data while disconnected. The problem is that someone else could enter matching information, resulting in a conflict when you attempt to send the added rows to the database server. One might argue that using surrogate keys can mask the problem, but don't forget that you still have the ability to create unique indexes on fields such as social security number or vehicle identification number, which can throw an exception if duplicate entries are added.

When surrogate *int* keys are used, the trick to managing the numbering on the primary key columns is to set the *AutoIncrement* property in the disconnected *DataSet* object to *true*, the *AutoIncrementStep* (increment) to *-1* (negative one), and the *AutoIncrementSeed* (starting value) to *-1*, which means that new rows will be added starting with a value of *-1* and will continue to increment by *-1*. The negative values are considered to be disconnected placeholders, and there is no chance of conflict with the server's identity column settings because the server assigns only positive numbers. The following SQL command shows the insertion followed immediately by querying for the inserted row. The information that is returned is used to update the placeholders (negative keys) with the value that the database created.

SQL Insert Command

```
INSERT INTO [TBLAUTHOR] ([SSN], [LastName], [FirstName])
   VALUES (@SSN, @LastName, @FirstName)
SELECT Id, SSN, LastName, FirstName FROM TblAuthor
   WHERE (Id = SCOPE_IDENTITY())
```

The *SCOPE_IDENTITY* function returns the value of the author's *Id* that was just inserted. Be careful not to use the *@@IDENTITY* function because this function returns an incorrect value if an insert trigger was fired and it inserted one or more rows into a table with an identity column.

Because the data must be retrieved from the server to update the placeholders in the disconnected data, you must consider the performance impact of updating the primary key values. What happens if you update the disconnected data key with the value that was created at the server? All of the child data must be updated to reflect the change as well; you can do this by enabling cascading updates on the relationships. This creates another performance hit, especially for large *DataSet* objects.

When surrogate GUID primary keys are used, there is no need to change the key once it has been set. The main problem is setting the value. The following code snippet shows how to initialize the GUID.

Visual Basic

```
Private Sub Form1_Load(ByVal sender As System.Object, _
      ByVal e As System.EventArgs) Handles MyBase.Load
   For Each dt As DataTable In salesSurrogateGuidKeyDs.Tables
      If (not dt.Columns("Id") Is Nothing) Then
         AddHandler dt.TableNewRow, addressof InitializeGuid
      End If
   Next
End Sub
Private Sub InitializeGuid(ByVal sender As Object, _
      ByVal e As DataTableNewRowEventArgs)
   If (TypeOf e.Row("Id") Is DBNull) Then
      e.Row("Id") = Guid.NewGuid()
   End If
End Sub
```

C#

```
public Form1() //constructor
{
   InitializeComponent();
   foreach (DataTable dt in sales_SurrogateGuidKeyDs.Tables)
   {
      if(dt.Columns["Id"] != null)
         dt.TableNewRow += new DataTableNewRowEventHandler(InitializeGuid);
   }
}
private void InitializeGuid(object sender, DataTableNewRowEventArgs e)
{
   if(e.Row["Id"] is DBNull)
      e.Row["Id"] = Guid.NewGuid();
}
```

Because *TblAuthor* and *TblBook* have primary keys with the same name ("Id"), a method called *InitializeGuid* is coded for creating new GUIDs and the *TableNewRow* event of these tables is wired to call this method. It's usually a good idea to give all surrogate primary keys the same name, as I did here. There is no need to create cascading relationships with this implementation. This is why surrogate GUID primary keys win in this category.

Migrating Data to Other Databases Migrating data from one database to another when the *Identity-Key* is implemented requires some work. Imagine that your tables have keys with values 1 through *n* and these values are also placed in foreign keys throughout the database. You want to take that data and merge it into a database with data that uses the same numbers. To solve this problem, you need to renumber all of the Identity columns.

With the *GUID-Key* implementation, migrating data is a simple matter of copying the data from one database to the other, which means the *GUID-Key* wins in this category.

And the Winner Is...

I just finished a very large project where the *GUID-Key* was implemented, and I have also worked on large projects using *Intelligent-Key* and *Identity-Key* implementations. Table 5-2 summarizes how each approach rates in a number of categories that are important in terms of performance, size, and ease of use. Based on my experience with these approaches, I assigned scores on a weight of 0 to 100 percent, where a weight of 100 is most important. Next I assigned a first-place (1), second-place (0.5), and third-place (0) score to the key types and multiplied that score by the weight to obtain a weighted score for each item.

Table 5-2 Final Scores Based on Categories and Weights

	Weighted Scores		
Category and Weight	***Intelligent-Key***	***Identity-Key***	***GUID-Key***
Data Size = 25%	12.5%	25%	0%
Key Visibility = 5%	5%	2.5%	0%
Modifying Keys = 20%	0%	10%	20%
Quantity of Joins = 5%	5%	2.5%	2.5%
SQL Complexity = 5%	0%	5%	2.5%
Ensuring Uniqueness = 25%	0%	12.5%	25%
Migration = 15%	7.5%	0%	15%
Total = 100%	**30%**	**57.5%**	**65%**

Based on my weighting, the *GUID-Key* best satisfies the greatest number of the most important categories. If you feel differently about any of the items, try modifying the weights to see whether you get a different result. Note that none of these primary key implementations gets a perfect, 100 percent rating. My general feeling is that the *GUID-Key* implementation is the best approach for disconnected data applications. Is there a place for the *Intelligent-Key* implementation? Yes, it might be the best approach for data warehouse applications because data warehouse applications are typically designed to provide high performance read-only access with minimum joins. Since the data is read-only, there is little concern regarding key modification. With a bit of tweaking, Table 5-3 provides the scores based on different weights.

Table 5-3 Data Warehouse Scores Based on Categories and Weights

	Weighted Scores		
Category and Weight	***Intelligent-Key***	***Identity-Key***	***GUID-Key***
Data Size = 25%	12.5%	25%	0%
Key Visibility = 10%	10%	0%	0%
Modifying Keys = 5%	0%	2.5%	5%
Quantity of Joins = 25%	25%	0%	0%

Table 5-3 Data Warehouse Scores Based on Categories and Weights

	Weighted Scores		
Category and Weight	*Intelligent-Key*	*Identity-Key*	*GUID-Key*
SQL Complexity = 10%	10%	5%	5%
Ensuring Uniqueness = 5%	0%	0%	5%
Migration = 20%	10%	0%	20%
Total = 100%	**67.5%**	**32.5%**	**35%**

Use these tables as guidelines, and be sure to consider any additional categories that your project may have.

Who's Afraid of the Big, Bad GUID?

Many people find the GUID to be quite intimidating when they attempt to use the *GUID-Key*. GUIDs might be big, but they aren't so bad. A few tips can help.

Copying/Pasting GUIDs

When you are debugging, you can select code that contains a GUID and IntelliSense will show the GUID (Figure 5-4). You can select the GUID value and copy it to the clipboard. Paste this value into a query window, replacing the curly braces with single quotation marks, as shown in the following SQL statement.

SQL Query Using a GUID

```
SELECT Id, SSN, LastName, FirstName
FROM   TblAuthor
WHERE  (Id = 'cbc8c64c-6ba6-4bec-baef-4c0e50e8b251')
```

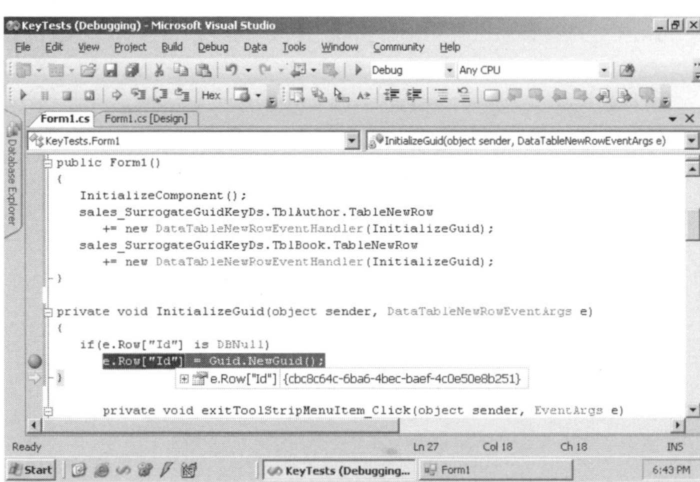

Figure 5-4 Using IntelliSense to copy a GUID for pasting into query tools

Using the Same Name for the Primary Key Column on Non-Join Tables

I strongly recommend that you use the same name (such as *Id*) for the primary key column of all of your non-join tables. This makes it easier to code stored procedures that work with GUIDs. Also, make it the first column in every table to help users understand the purpose of this field.

Finding a GUID in the Database

Depending on your database design, you might face situations where you are looking for a GUID in a foreign key column but have no idea where the data is for that GUID. An example of this is when you have an Exclusive-OR relationship, as shown in Figure 5-5. This type of relationship is typical in an object-oriented environment–you might have a book class with various child classes such as EBook, PaperBack, and HardCover. These classes will have fields that are not common to each other, so you must choose to either create a single table with lots of null column values, or create a separate table for each child class as shown in Figure 5-5.

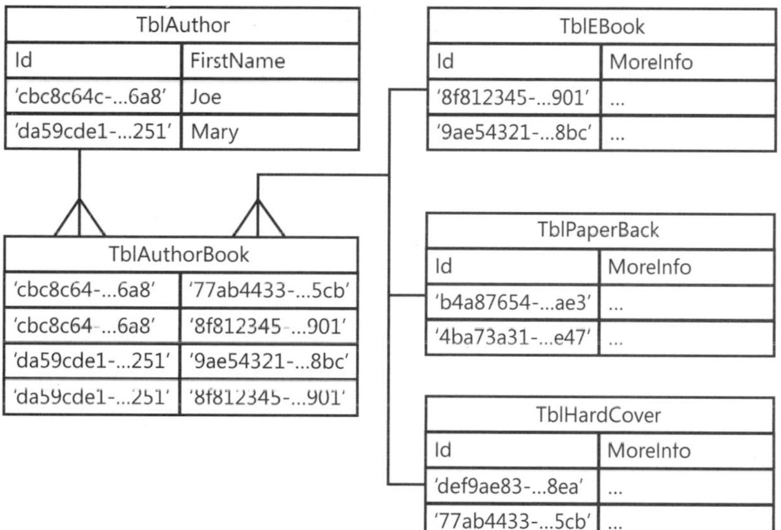

Figure 5-5 An example of an Exclusive-OR relationship

If you are trying to find out which table contains a specific GUID, you can use the following stored procedure to locate the table that has this GUID as a primary key value.

SQL uspGetDataForId

```
CREATE PROCEDURE dbo.uspGetDataForId
(
	@id uniqueidentifier
)
AS
```

```
SET NOCOUNT ON
--NOTE: This proc assumes that all user tables have 'Tbl' prefix
--Usage: in Query Analyser, type the following without the '--'
--exec uspGetDataForId '78257ec8-c8f9-4d35-a636-d58d8a67c3d4'
DECLARE @tbl varchar(2000)
DECLARE @sql varchar(2000)
IF OBJECT_ID('tempdb..#idTable') IS NOT NULL DROP TABLE #idTable
CREATE TABLE #idTable (
      Id uniqueidentifier,
      Count INT,
      TableName varchar(2000)
)
DECLARE tables_cursor CURSOR
   FOR SELECT TABLE_NAME FROM information_schema.Tables
      WHERE substring (TABLE_NAME,1,3)='Tbl'
OPEN tables_cursor
FETCH NEXT FROM tables_cursor INTO @tbl
WHILE @@FETCH_STATUS = 0
BEGIN
   IF EXISTS (SELECT * FROM information_schema.columns
            WHERE table_name=@tbl AND Column_Name='Id')
   BEGIN
      SET @sql = 'INSERT INTO #idTable SELECT id as ''Id'', '
         + 'count(*) as ''Count'',''' + @tbl +''' as ''TableName'' FROM '
         + @tbl + ' WHERE ID=''' + CONVERT(varchar(2000),@id)
         + ''' group by Id'
      EXEC(@sql)
   END
   FETCH NEXT FROM tables_cursor INTO @tbl
END
CLOSE tables_cursor
DEALLOCATE tables_cursor
SELECT Id, TableName FROM #idTable WHERE Count > 0
```

Note that this stored procedure relies on all primary key columns being named *Id* and the user tables having a *Tbl* prefix. This stored procedure does not attempt to find a GUID in any other column, but if you need to find all usages for a GUID, read on.

Finding All Usages of a GUID in the Database

You often want to find all usages of a GUID. The following SQL script enumerates all of the user tables with a *Tbl* prefix and queries all columns with a *uniqueidentifier* data type.

SQL uspGetUsagesForId

```
CREATE   PROCEDURE dbo.uspGetUsagesForId
(
      @id uniqueidentifier
)
AS
--NOTE: This proc assumes that all user tables have 'Tbl' prefix
--Usage: in Query Analyser, type the following without the '--'
--exec uspGetUsagesForId '78257ec8-c8f9-4d35-a636-d58d8a67c3d4'
SET NOCOUNT ON
```

```
DECLARE @tbl varchar(2000)
DECLARE @sql varchar(2000)
DECLARE @counter integer

IF OBJECT_ID('tempdb..#guidTable') IS NOT NULL DROP TABLE #guidTable
CREATE TABLE #guidTable (
      Id uniqueidentifier,
      Count INT,
      TableName varchar(2000)
)

DECLARE tables_cursor CURSOR
   FOR SELECT TABLE_NAME FROM information_schema.Tables
       WHERE SUBSTRING(TABLE_NAME,1,3)='Tbl'
OPEN tables_cursor
FETCH NEXT FROM tables_cursor INTO @tbl
WHILE @@FETCH_STATUS = 0
BEGIN
      SET @sql = 'INSERT INTO #guidTable SELECT id as ''Id'', '
            + 'count(*) as ''Count'',''' + @tbl +''' as ''TableName'' FROM '
            + @tbl + ' WHERE ' + dbo.fnGetGuidWhereClause(@tbl, @id)
            + ' GROUP BY ID'
      EXEC(@sql)
      SELECT @counter = COUNT(*) FROM #guidTable
      IF @counter > 0
      BEGIN
            SET @sql = 'SELECT ''' + @tbl + ''' as TABLE_NAME, * FROM ' + @tbl
                  + ' WHERE ' + dbo.fnGetGuidWhereClause(@tbl, @id)
            EXEC(@sql)
      END
      DELETE FROM #guidTable
FETCH NEXT FROM tables_cursor INTO @tbl
END
CLOSE tables_cursor
DEALLOCATE tables_cursor
```

If you think about the benefits of these stored procedure tricks, you will realize that you can't accomplish these tricks and get the same results with the other primary key implementations.

Building a Conflict Resolution Screen

The rest of this chapter focuses on building a conflict resolution screen that allows the user to resolve a conflict by selecting the current user value, the original database value, the current database value, or a typed-in value. To drive this conflict resolution screen, the application will display only the customer names and will allow the user to update the list. If a *DbConcurrency* exception occurs, the conflict resolution screen will be displayed.

Creating the Project

First we create the project for demonstrating conflict resolution when a *DbConcurrency* exception occurs after an update of the database server from disconnected data.

1. Create a Microsoft Windows application using the appropriate programming language.
2. Add a *MenuStrip* control to the form. Add the following menu items.

   MenuItem List

   ```
   &File
      &Sync With Database
      E&xit
   &Concurrency
      &Resolve Concurrency Errors
   ```

3. Add a status bar with a single status label called *status*.
4. Add a new database file to the application by right-clicking the project, choosing Add, choosing New Item, and then choosing SQL Database. Name the database *Customer.mdf,* and then click the Add button. This launches the Data Source Configuration Wizard. You haven't created any tables yet, so click Finished to add the empty customer *DataSet* to your project.
5. Add the tables as shown earlier in Figure 5-1 or, at a minimum, add a table called TblCustomer that has a column named Id that is a *uniqueidentifier* primary key and a column named Name that is a *varchar(50)* data type. Neither column should allow a null value. (You can edit the tables by right-clicking the database file and clicking Open.)
6. Open the DataSources window by choosing Data and then choosing Show Data Sources. The *CustomerDataSet* class is visible in this window, but it needs to be updated to show tables that you have added. Right-click the CustomerDataSet and choose Configure DataSet With Wizard, which will launch the Data Source Configuration Wizard. Select all the tables you have created in the database, as shown in Figure 5-6.

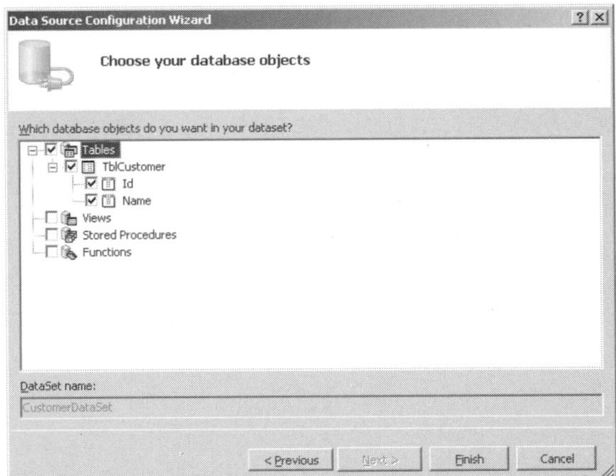

Figure 5-6 Adding tables to the *CustomerDataSet* using the Data Source Configuration Wizard

7. In the Data Sources window, drag and drop TblCustomer onto the form. This adds *TblCustomerDataGridView* to the form. Set the *TblCustomerDataGridView* object's *Dock* property to *Fill*. Set the *AutoSizeMode* of the Name column to *Fill*. Also note that Visual Studio automatically added *CustomerDataSet*, *TblCustomerBindingSource*, *TblCustomerTableAdapter*, and *TblCustomerBindingNavigator* to the designer tray (Figure 5-7).

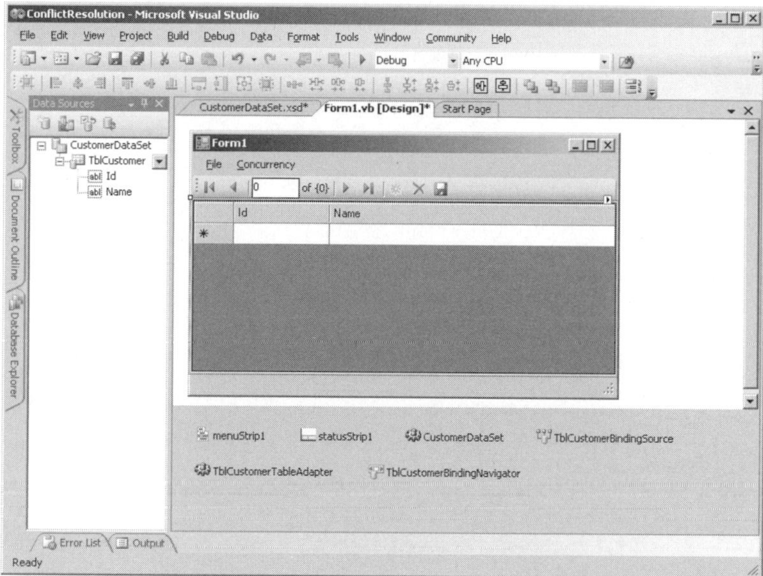

Figure 5-7 Adding *TblCustomer* to the form adds the necessary objects to the designer tray automatically.

Extending the Typed *DataSet* (*CustomerDataSet*) Class

We must extend this *CustomerDataSet* class so that there is one place to automatically generate new GUIDs for our primary key columns. Then we can forget about generating new GUIDs in the application.

1. Right-click the CustomerDataSet.xsd file and choose View Code. This adds a new file called CustomerDataSetExtension.vb or CustomerDataSetExtension.cs under the CustomerDataSet.xsd node.

2. Add the following code to this file.

Visual Basic

```
Imports System.Data
Partial Public Class CustomerDataSet
   Private createDefaultGuidForNewRows As Boolean = False
   Public Sub CreateDefaultGuids()
      If (createDefaultGuidForNewRows) Then Exit Sub
      createDefaultGuidForNewRows = True
      For Each dt As DataTable In Me.Tables
         If (Not dt.Columns("Id") Is Nothing) Then
```

```
            AddHandler dt.TableNewRow, AddressOf TableNewRow
         End If
      Next
   End Sub
   Private Sub TableNewRow(ByVal sender As Object, _
         ByVal e As DataTableNewRowEventArgs)
      If (TypeOf e.Row("Id") Is DBNull) Then
         e.Row("Id") = Guid.NewGuid()
      End If
   End Sub
End Class
```

C#

```
using System;
using System.Data;
namespace ConflictResolution
{
   public partial class CustomerDataSet
   {
      private bool createDefaultGuids = false;
      public void CreateDefaultGuids()
      {
         if (createDefaultGuids) return;
         createDefaultGuids = true;
         foreach (DataTable dt in this.Tables)
         {
            if (dt.Columns["Id"] != null)
               dt.TableNewRow += new DataTableNewRowEventHandler(TableNewRow);
         }
      }
      private void TableNewRow(object sender, DataTableNewRowEventArgs e)
      {
         if (e.Row["Id"] is DBNull)
            e.Row["Id"] = Guid.NewGuid();
      }
   }
}
```

3. This code needs to be called once from the application, so add the following code into the form object's *Load* method. You can then run the application and add new customers to the table.

   Visual Basic

   ```
   CustomerDataSet.CreateDefaultGuids()
   ```

   C#

   ```
   customerDataSet.CreateDefaultGuids();
   ```

Extending the *TableAdapter* (*TblCustomerTableAdapter*) Class to Expose the *ContinueUpdateOnError* Property

The *DataAdapter* object contains a property called *ContinueUpdateOnError*. If this property is set to *true*, multi-row updates continue when concurrency errors occur. The *TableAdapter* objects expose only the minimally required properties, and this application requires the *ContinueUpdateOnError* property of the underlying *TableAdapter* object's *DataAdapter* to be set to *true*. This means the *TblCustomerTableAdapter* must be extended.

1. In the file called CustomerDataSetExtension.vb or CustomerDataSetExtension.cs that you just added when you extended the *CustomerDataSet* class, add the following code to expose the *ContinueUpdateOnError* property. (Unfortunately, this code cannot easily be added in a single place for all *TableAdapter* objects. If you have additional *TableAdapter* objects, add code to extend each of them in a similar fashion.)

   Visual Basic

   ```
   Namespace CustomerDataSetTableAdapters
      Partial Public Class TblCustomerTableAdapter
         Public Property ContinueUpdateOnError() As Boolean
            Get
               Return Adapter.ContinueUpdateOnError
            End Get
            Set(ByVal value As Boolean)
               Adapter.ContinueUpdateOnError = Value
            End Set
         End Property
      End Class
   End Namespace
   ```

   C#

   ```
   namespace ConflictResolution.CustomerDataSetTableAdapters
   {
      public partial class TblCustomerTableAdapter
      {
         public bool ContinueUpdateOnError
         {
            get { return Adapter.ContinueUpdateOnError; }
            set { Adapter.ContinueUpdateOnError = value; }
         }
      }
   }
   ```

2. Add the following code to the form's *Load* method to set the *ContinueUpdateOnError* property of each *TableAdapter* object to *true*.

   Visual Basic

   ```
   TblCustomerTableAdapter.ContinueUpdateOnError=True
   ```

   C#

   ```
   tblCustomerTableAdapter.ContinueUpdateOnError = true;
   ```

Synchronizing the Disconnected *DataSet* with the Database Server

The application can now be run, but without any synchronization of the disconnected *CustomerDataSet* with the database server. The following step adds synchronization to your code.

- Place the following code into the Synchronize With Database menu item. This code attempts to send all changes back to the database server. If it is successful, the customer table is refilled from the database server to capture any changes that other users have made.

Visual Basic

```
Private Sub syncWithDatabaseToolStripMenuItem_Click( _
      ByVal sender As System.Object, _
      ByVal e As System.EventArgs) _
      Handles syncWithDatabaseToolStripMenuItem.Click
   TblCustomerTableAdapter.Update(CustomerDataSet.TblCustomer)
   If (CustomerDataSet.HasErrors) Then
      status.Text = "Partial synchronization with concurrency errors."
   Else
      'get current database data
      tblCustomerTableAdapter.Fill(CustomerDataSet.TblCustomer)
      status.Text = "Database synchronized."
   End If
   TblCustomerDataGridView.Refresh()
End Sub
```

C#

```
private void syncWithDatabaseToolStripMenuItem_Click(
      object sender, EventArgs e)
{
   tblCustomerTableAdapter.Update(customerDataSet.TblCustomer);
   if (customerDataSet.HasErrors)
   {
      status.Text = "Partial synchronization with concurrency errors.";
   }
   else
   {
      //get current database data
      this.tblCustomerTableAdapter.Fill(customerDataSet.TblCustomer);
      status.Text = "Database synchronized.";
   }
   tblCustomerDataGridView.Refresh();
}
```

Creating the Conflict Resolution Screen

The primary purpose of the conflict resolution screen is to allow you to select the final data values when a concurrency error occurs. It displays your current values, the original database values, and the current database values. The screen is somewhat generic, and you will probably want to tweak it to suit your needs. For reference, the form that you create is shown in Figure 5-8.

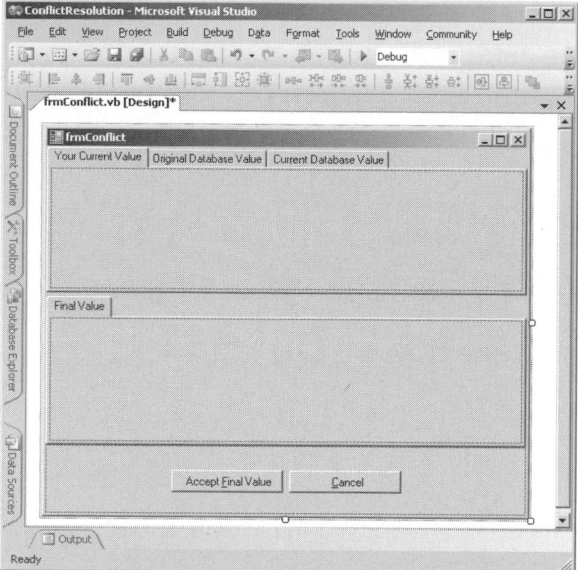

Figure 5-8 The completed conflict resolution screen

1. Add a new form to your project called frmConflict.vb or frmConflict.cs.
2. Add a *Panel* control to the form, and set its *Dock* property to *Bottom*.
3. Add two *Button* controls to the *Panel* control. Assign the *Name* properties, *btnAccept* and *btnCancel*, and set their *Text* property to *"Accept Final Value"* and *"Cancel"*. Set the *Anchor* property on both buttons to *Top*.
4. Add a *SplitContainer* control to the form. Set its *Dock* property to *Fill*, and set its *Orientation* property to *Horizontal*.
5. Add a *TabControl* to the top of *the SplitContainer*. Create three tab pages, with the *Name* property set to *tabCurrent*, *tabOriginal*, and *tabCurrentDb*. Set the *Text* property to *Your Current Value*, *Original Database Value*, and *Current Database Value*.
6. Add a *TabControl* to the bottom of the *SplitContainer*. Create a single tab page, with the *Name* property set to *tabFinal*. Set the *Text* property to *Final Value*.
7. The conflict resolution screen is created by passing two *DataRow* objects into a new constructor. The first *DataRow* object contains your current data values in the *Current DataRowVersion* and the original database data values in the *Original DataRowVersion*. The second *DataRow* object initially contains the current database data value in the *Original* and *Current DataRowVersion*. The *Current DataRowVersion* will contain the final result of your conflict resolution. These *DataRow* objects are stored in properties. Here is the code to accomplish this.

Visual Basic

```
Public Sub New(ByVal currentDataRow As DataRow, _
      ByVal currentDatabaseDataRow As DataRow)
   MyBase.New()
```

```
    InitializeComponent()
    Me.CurrentDataRow = currentDataRow
    FinalDatabaseDataRow = currentDatabaseDataRow
End Sub
Public Property FinalDatabaseDataRow() As DataRow
    Get
        Return m_finalDatabaseDataRow
    End Get
    Set(ByVal value As DataRow)
        m_finalDatabaseDataRow = value
    End Set
End Property
Private m_finalDatabaseDataRow As DataRow = Nothing
Public Property CurrentDataRow() As DataRow
    Get
        Return m_currentDataRow
    End Get
    Set(ByVal value As DataRow)
        m_currentDataRow = value
    End Set
End Property
Private m_currentDataRow As DataRow = Nothing
```

C#

```
public frmConflict(DataRow currentDataRow, DataRow currentDatabaseDataRow)
{
    InitializeComponent();
    CurrentDataRow = currentDataRow;
    FinalDatabaseDataRow = currentDatabaseDataRow;
}
public DataRow FinalDatabaseDataRow
{
    get { return m_finalDatabaseDataRow; }
    set { m_finalDatabaseDataRow = value; }
}
private DataRow m_finalDatabaseDataRow = null;
public DataRow CurrentDataRow
{
    get { return m_currentDataRow; }
    set { m_currentDataRow = value; }
}
private DataRow m_currentDataRow = null;
```

8. Create the *PopulateTab* and *CopyToFinal* methods. For each column in the *DataRow* object, the *PopulateTab* populates a tab page with a *Label* that shows the column name, a *TextBox* that shows the value of the column based on the *DataRowVersion*, and a *Button* that lets you copy the selected value to the final value by executing the *CopyToFinal* method. Here is the code for these two methods.

Visual Basic

```
Public Sub PopulateTab(ByVal tab As TabPage, ByVal dataRow As DataRow, _
        ByVal dataRowVersion As DataRowVersion, ByVal m_ReadOnly As Boolean)
    Const verticalSpacing As Integer = 30
    Const labelWidth As Integer = 50
```

```
    Const horizontalSpacing As Integer = 10
    Const buttonWidth As Integer = 100
    Const buttonHeight As Integer = 20
    For col As Integer = 0 To dataRow.ItemArray.Length - 1
       Dim val As Object = dataRow(col, dataRowVersion)
       Dim label As New Label()
       tab.Controls.Add(label)
       label.Text = dataRow.Table.Columns(col).ColumnName
       label.Top = (col + 1) * verticalSpacing
       label.Left = horizontalSpacing
       label.Width = labelWidth
       label.Visible = True
       Dim textBox As New TextBox()
       tab.Controls.Add(textBox)
       textBox.Text = val.ToString()
       textBox.Top = (col + 1) * verticalSpacing
       textBox.Left = (horizontalSpacing * 2) + labelWidth
       textBox.Width = tab.Width - textBox.Left _
          - buttonWidth - (horizontalSpacing * 2)
       textBox.Name = tab.Name + label.Text
       textBox.ReadOnly = m_ReadOnly
       textBox.Visible = True
       textBox.Anchor = AnchorStyles.Left _
          Or AnchorStyles.Top Or AnchorStyles.Right
       If (tab.Name = "tabFinal") Then Continue For
       Dim btn As New Button()
       tab.Controls.Add(btn)
       btn.Text = "Copy to Final"
       btn.Left = textBox.Left + textBox.Width _
          + horizontalSpacing
       btn.Top = (col + 1) * verticalSpacing
       btn.Height = buttonHeight
       btn.Visible = True
    btn.Anchor = AnchorStyles.Top OR AnchorStyles.Right
       AddHandler btn.Click, AddressOf CopyToFinal
       Dim propertyBag As New ArrayList()
       propertyBag.Add(dataRow.Table.Columns(col))
       propertyBag.Add(textBox)
       btn.Tag = propertyBag
    Next
End Sub
Private Sub CopyToFinal(ByVal sender As Object, ByVal e As EventArgs)
   Dim btn As Button = CType(sender, Button)
   Dim propertyBag As ArrayList = CType(btn.Tag, ArrayList)
   Dim dc As DataColumn = CType(propertyBag(0), DataColumn)
   Dim textBox As TextBox = CType(propertyBag(1), TextBox)
   tabFinal.Controls(tabFinal.Name + dc.ColumnName).Text = textBox.Text
End Sub
```

C#

```
public void PopulateTab(TabPage tab, DataRow dataRow,
      DataRowVersion dataRowVersion, bool readOnly)
{
   const int verticalSpacing = 30;
   const int labelWidth = 50;
```

```
    const int horizontalSpacing = 10;
    const int buttonWidth = 100;
    const int buttonHeight = 20;
    for (int col = 0; col < dataRow.ItemArray.Length; col++)
    {
        object val = dataRow[col, dataRowVersion];
        Label label = new Label();
        tab.Controls.Add(label);
        label.Text = dataRow.Table.Columns[col].ColumnName;
        label.Top = (col + 1) * verticalSpacing;
        label.Left = horizontalSpacing;
        label.Width = labelWidth;
        label.Visible = true;
        TextBox textBox = new TextBox();
        tab.Controls.Add(textBox);
        textBox.Text = val.ToString();
        textBox.Top = (col + 1) * verticalSpacing;
        textBox.Left = (horizontalSpacing * 2) + labelWidth;
        textBox.Width = tab.Width - textBox.Left
            - buttonWidth - (horizontalSpacing * 2);
        textBox.Name = tab.Name + label.Text;
        textBox.ReadOnly = readOnly;
        textBox.Visible = true;
        textBox.Anchor = AnchorStyles.Left | AnchorStyles.Top
            | AnchorStyles.Right;
        if (tab.Name == "tabFinal") continue;
        Button btn = new Button();
        tab.Controls.Add(btn);
        btn.Text = "Copy to Final";
        btn.Left = textBox.Left + textBox.Width + horizontalSpacing;
        btn.Top = (col + 1) * verticalSpacing;
        btn.Height = buttonHeight;
        btn.Visible = true;
        btn.Anchor = AnchorStyles.Top | AnchorStyles.Right;
        btn.Click += new EventHandler(CopyToFinal);
        ArrayList propertyBag = new ArrayList();
        propertyBag.Add(dataRow.Table.Columns[col]);
        propertyBag.Add(textBox);
        btn.Tag = propertyBag;
    }
}
```

9. Add code to call the *PopulateTab* method for each tab page when the form is loaded. The code is as follows.

Visual Basic

```
Private Sub frmConflict_Load( ByVal sender As System.Object, _
      ByVal e As System.EventArgs) Handles MyBase.Load
   PopulateTab(tabCurrent, CurrentDataRow, _
      DataRowVersion.Current, true)
   PopulateTab(tabOriginal, CurrentDataRow, _
      DataRowVersion.Original, true)
   PopulateTab(tabCurrentDb, FinalDatabaseDataRow, _
      DataRowVersion.Original, true)
   PopulateTab(tabFinal, FinalDatabaseDataRow, _
```

```
      DataRowVersion.Current, false)
End Sub
```

C#

```
private void frmConflict_Load(object sender, EventArgs e)
{
   PopulateTab(tabCurrent, CurrentDataRow,
      DataRowVersion.Current, true);
   PopulateTab(tabOriginal, CurrentDataRow,
      DataRowVersion.Original, true);
   PopulateTab(tabCurrentDb, FinalDatabaseDataRow,
      DataRowVersion.Original, true);
   PopulateTab(tabFinal, FinalDatabaseDataRow,
      DataRowVersion.Current, false);
}
```

10. Add code to collect the final data values from the *TextBox* objects in *tabFinal* and place the values into the *FinalDatabaseRow*, which will be retrieved by the calling form. This code will be placed into the *Click* event handler of *btnAccept* as follows.

Visual Basic

```
Private Sub btnAccept_Click( ByVal sender As System.Object, _
      ByVal e As System.EventArgs) Handles btnAccept.Click
   for each dc as DataColumn  in FinalDatabaseDataRow.Table.Columns
      FinalDatabaseDataRow(dc) = _
         tabFinal.Controls(tabFinal.Name + dc.ColumnName).Text
   next
End Sub
```

C#

```
private void btnAccept_Click(object sender, EventArgs e)
{
   foreach (DataColumn dc in FinalDatabaseDataRow.Table.Columns)
   {
      FinalDatabaseDataRow[dc] =
         tabFinal.Controls[tabFinal.Name + dc.ColumnName].Text;
   }
}
```

11. The final step is to configure the buttons. Set the *DialogResult* of *btnAccept* to *OK*, and set the *DialogResult* of *btnCancel* to *Cancel*. On the form's property screen, set the *AcceptButton* property to *btnAccept* and set the *CancelButton* property to *btnCancel*.

Calling the Conflict Resolution Screen

The conflict resolution screen deals with conflicts only on a *DataRow*-by-*DataRow* basis. This means you must loop through your concurrency errors, displaying the conflict resolution screen for each conflict.

- In the Resolve Concurrency Errors menu item, add the following code to retrieve the latest data from the database and call the conflict resolution screen for each conflict that has occurred since the last time you synchronized with the database.

Visual Basic

```
Private Sub resolveConcurrencyErrorsToolStripMenuItem_Click( _
      ByVal sender As System.Object,  ByVal e As System.EventArgs) _
      Handles resolveConcurrencyErrorsToolStripMenuItem.Click
   if (customerDataSet.TblCustomer.HasErrors) then
      'get data refresh with most current
      Dim refreshCustomer as new CustomerDataSet()
      tblCustomerTableAdapter.Fill(refreshCustomer.TblCustomer)
      'loop through the errors
      for each dr as DataRow in customerDataSet.TblCustomer.GetErrors()
         Dim currentDb as DataRow = _
            refreshCustomer.TblCustomer.Rows.Find(dr("Id"))
         using conflict as new frmConflict(dr, currentDb)
            if (conflict.ShowDialog(Me) = DialogResult.OK) then
               dr.ClearErrors()
               tblCustomerTableAdapter.Update(conflict.FinalDatabaseDataRow)
               customerDataSet.TblCustomer.LoadDataRow( _
                  conflict.FinalDatabaseDataRow.ItemArray, _
                  LoadOption.OverwriteChanges)
               status.Text = "Single row updated."
            else
               status.Text = "Single row update cancelled."
            end if
         end using
      next
      tblCustomerDataGridView.Refresh()
   end if
End Sub
```

C#

```
private void resolveConcurrencyErrorsToolStripMenuItem_Click(
   object sender, EventArgs e)
{
   if (customerDataSet.TblCustomer.HasErrors)
   {
      //get data refresh with most current
      CustomerDataSet refreshCustomer = new CustomerDataSet();
      this.tblCustomerTableAdapter.Fill(refreshCustomer.TblCustomer);
      //loop through the errors
      foreach (DataRow dr in customerDataSet.TblCustomer.GetErrors())
      {
         DataRow currentDb = refreshCustomer.TblCustomer.Rows.Find(dr["Id"]);
         using (frmConflict conflict = new frmConflict(dr, currentDb))
         {
            if (conflict.ShowDialog(this) == DialogResult.OK)
            {
               dr.ClearErrors();
               tblCustomerTableAdapter.Update(conflict.FinalDatabaseDataRow);
               customerDataSet.TblCustomer.LoadDataRow(
                  conflict.FinalDatabaseDataRow.ItemArray,
                  LoadOption.OverwriteChanges);
               status.Text = "Single row updated.";
            }
            else
            {
```

```
                    status.Text = "Single row update cancelled.";
                }
            }
        }
        tblCustomerDataGridView.Refresh();
    }
}
```

Correcting Concurrency Errors with the Conflict Resolution Screen

When it's time to test the conflict resolution screen, you must have two instances of the application running. When each instance starts, it loads a copy of the data from the database. If changes are made in both instances, the first instance that synchronizes with the database will succeed and the second instance will fail for each *DataRow* object that was also updated by the first instance.

Follow these steps to create and resolve concurrency errors.

1. Start two instances of the application. (Navigate to the ConflictResolution.exe file and double-click it twice, or right-click the project in the Solution Explorer window and choose Debug | Start New Instance twice.) You will see the contents of the *TblCustomer* table.
2. The first time the application is executed there is no data, so add data to both instances, as shown in Figure 5-9.

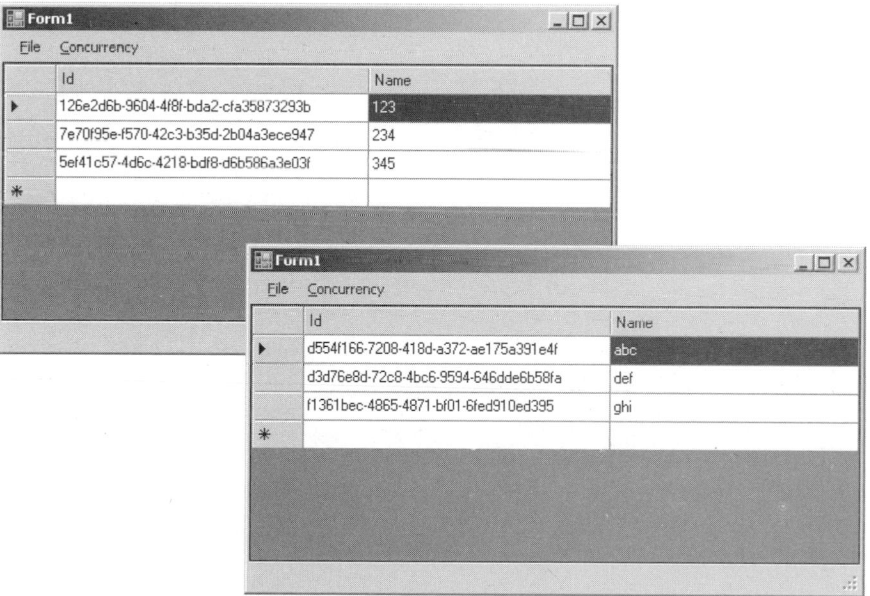

Figure 5-9 Different data has been entered into each instance of the application.

3. Synchronize with the database. When the first instance is synchronized, the only noticeable change is that the status bar displays a message indicating that the data is synchronized. When the second instance is synchronized, the same message is displayed, but the grid displays the data that was input into the first instance. Notice that both instances can synchronize with the new data because there are no conflicts. If the first instance is synchronized again, it will contain the data from the second instance, as shown in Figure 5-10.

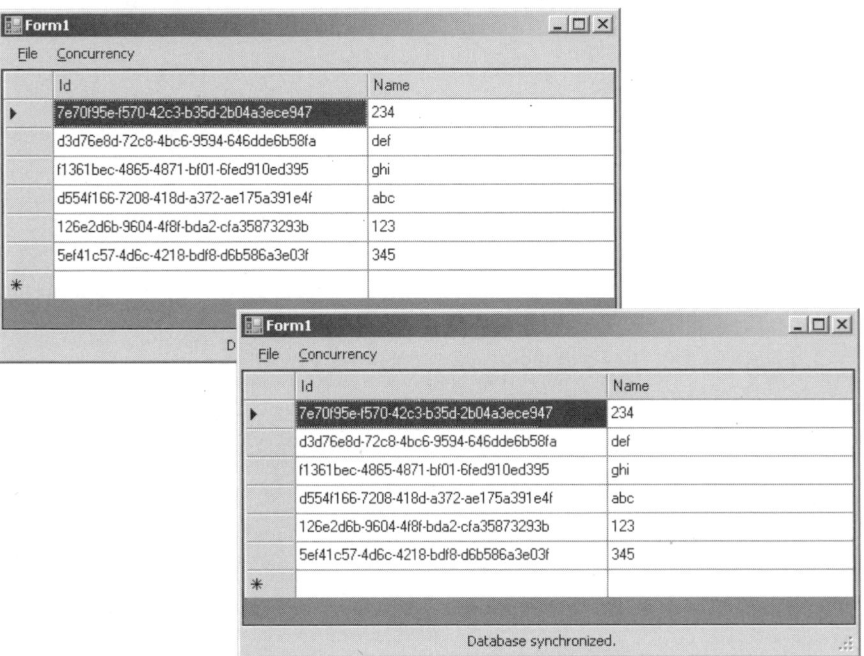

Figure 5-10 The two instances are synchronized with the database.

4. Make changes to the same name in both instances. For example, you can change the name *234* to *Joe* in one instance and to *Mary* in the other instance. Synchronize the instance with *Joe* as the name, and the synchronization will succeed. Next, synchronize the instance with *Mary* as the name; a concurrency error occurs because the data in the database was changed between the time this instance was previously synchronized and this attempt to synchronize. The grid displays the error, as shown in Figure 5-11.

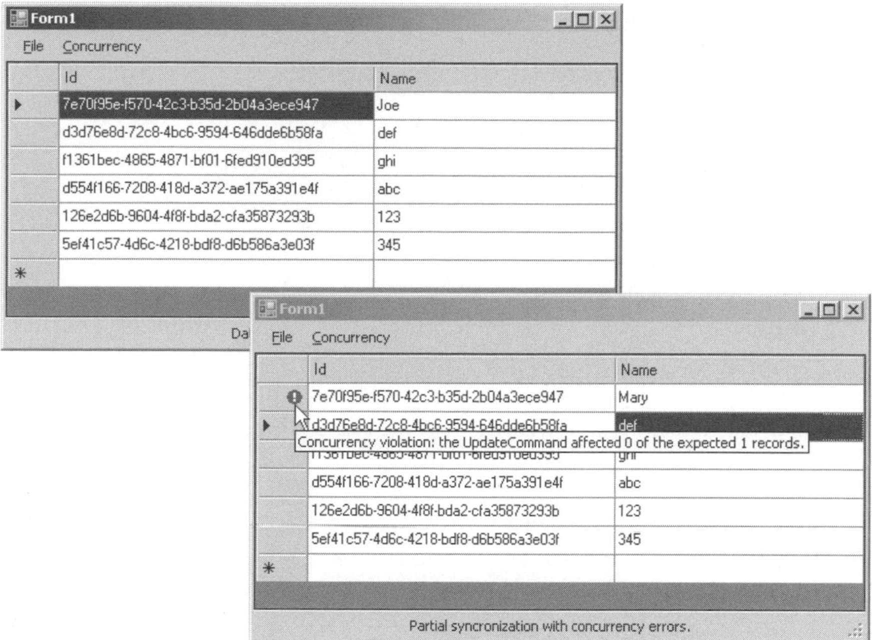

Figure 5-11 The concurrency error is displayed in the grid because the underlying data changed since we read the data.

5. Finally, test the conflict resolution screen. Click the Resolve Concurrency Errors menu item to launch the conflict resolution screen, as shown in Figure 5-12. The tab pages are populated with data. Move between the tab pages to see the current disconnected data values, the original database values, and the current database values. Note that the final data values are displayed at the bottom, and notice the button beside each *TextBox* that allows you to copy the value in the *TextBox* into the final data value.

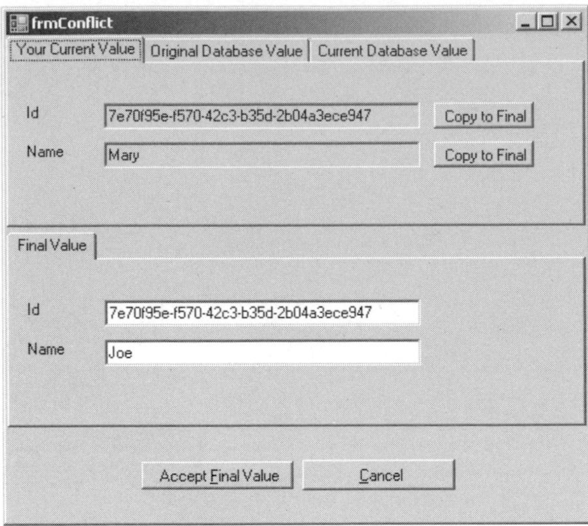

Figure 5-12 The conflict resolution screen allows you to resolve a concurrency error by selecting the current disconnected data values, the original database values, or the current database values.

Building a Better Conflict Resolution Screen

The conflict resolution screen was designed to let you generically resolve conflicts from concurrency errors. Most of the code can be reused in your application, but you might want to make some changes to make the screen more appealing to your users and to further encapsulate your code. Here are some changes to consider.

- *Pass two* DataSet *objects to the conflict resolution form instead of two* DataRow *objects.* The first *DataSet* object contains all of your data, along with the concurrency errors. The second *DataSet* object contains the data that is currently in the database. You can program the conflict resolution screen to loop through the errors so that users don't have to examine each error individually.
- *Hide surrogate keys.* Surrogate keys have no relationship with business data, so there is no need to show them. If you use *GUID-Keys*, you can simply hide all columns that are the GUID data type.
- *Provide Copy All buttons.* On each tab page, add a Copy All button that copies all of the data on the tab page to the final data values.

Summary

You must consider two important issues when you work with disconnected data: primary key implementation and concurrency error (conflict) resolution. The primary key is the column or combination of columns that uniquely defines a row. Intelligent and natural keys both contain business-related columns that are normally viewed by the user, but surrogate primary keys are system-generated key values that have no relationship to the business data in the row. The *GUID-Key* implementation is considered the best approach for disconnected data applications.

Concurrency is the ability for multiple users to access the database and be presented with a consistent view of the data. On connected database applications, locking rows and tables enforces concurrency, but disconnected database applications allow concurrency errors, so the application must be written to resolve conflicting data. How you resolve conflicts depends entirely on your business needs. You can choose to implement these strategies: *first update wins*, *last update wins*, *prioritized on role*, *prioritized on location*, or *user resolves the conflict*.

Chapter 6

Working with Relational Disconnected Data

The previous chapter identified some issues to consider when you implement disconnected data applications. The primary focus was on index selection and resolving concurrency conflicts, and the chapter concluded with the implementation of a concurrency conflict resolution screen in a simple application for viewing and modifying customer names.

This chapter expands on the disconnected data application by examining some issues you should address when you work with multiple related *DataTable* objects. First we review relationships and constraints, and then we dig deeply into the issues involved with updating the data. This is where you will see the need for a Data Access Layer (DAL) in your applications for performing updates.

Navigating Relationships

When you work with a *DataSet* object, you often need to navigate from one *DataTable* object to another. For example, when you work with a customer, you often start by retrieving that customer's *DataRow* object in the *TblCustomer DataTable*. To get to your customer's orders, you use the customer's primary key to search the *TblOrder DataTable* for orders that belong to that customer. This means the *TblOrder DataTable* must contain a customer foreign key, which is one or more columns that identify the customer who owns the order, based on a unique key in *TblCustomer*.

The unique key is usually the primary key, but it doesn't have to be. For example, the primary key on the employee table might be a *GUID*, but the employee table might also contain a social security number column that is configured as a unique key. Human resource records might be related to the employee table based on the social security number instead of the *GUID*.

A *DataRelation* object provides the means for navigating from one *DataTable* object to another by using the unique key value on the parent table to search for foreign keys in the child table. The *DataRelation* object can also use a specific foreign key value to find the parent *DataRow* object. The parent and child *DataTable* objects must be within the same *DataSet* object in order for you to create a *DataRelation* object that allows you to navigate between the parent and child *DataTable* objects. The *DataSet* object holds all of its *DataRelation* objects in the *Relationships* collection. Each *DataTable* object also contains a *ChildRelations* and *ParentRelations* collection. The following code snippet shows how you can create a *DataRelation* object and use it to navigate from a parent *DataRow* object to its child *DataRow* objects and from a child *DataRow* object to its parent *DataRow* object.

Visual Basic

```
'Create tables
Dim ds1 As New DataSet()
Dim dt1 As DataTable = ds1.Tables.Add("dt1")
Dim dt2 As DataTable = ds1.Tables.Add("dt2")
'Create columns
Dim parentPk As DataColumn = dt1.Columns.Add("pk", GetType(Integer))
dt2.Columns.Add("pk", GetType(Integer))
Dim childFk As DataColumn = dt2.Columns.Add("fk", GetType(Integer))
'Create relation
Dim rel As DataRelation = New DataRelation("dt1dt2", parentPk, childFk)
ds1.Relations.Add(rel)
'Add some data
dt1.Rows.Add(1)
dt1.Rows.Add(2)
dt1.Rows.Add(3)
dt1.Rows.Add(4)
dt1.Rows.Add(5)
dt2.Rows.Add(1, 1)
dt2.Rows.Add(2, 1)
dt2.Rows.Add(3, 2)
dt2.Rows.Add(4, 2)
dt2.Rows.Add(5, 2)
'get a parent row
Dim parentRow As DataRow = dt1.Rows(1)
'Get Children
Dim children As DataRow() = parentRow.GetChildRows(rel)
'Get Parent again
Dim myParent As DataRow = children(0).GetParentRow(rel)
```

C#

```
//Create tables
DataSet ds1 = new DataSet();
DataTable dt1 = ds1.Tables.Add("dt1");
DataTable dt2 = ds1.Tables.Add("dt2");
//Create columns
DataColumn parentPk = dt1.Columns.Add("pk", typeof(int));
dt2.Columns.Add("pk", typeof(int));
DataColumn childFk = dt2.Columns.Add("fk", typeof(int));
//Create relation
DataRelation rel = new DataRelation("dt1dt2", parentPk, childFk);
ds1.Relations.Add(rel);
//Add some data
dt1.Rows.Add(1);
dt1.Rows.Add(2);
dt1.Rows.Add(3);
dt1.Rows.Add(4);
dt1.Rows.Add(5);
dt2.Rows.Add(1,1);
dt2.Rows.Add(2,1);
dt2.Rows.Add(3,2);
```

```
dt2.Rows.Add(4,2);
dt2.Rows.Add(5,2);
//Get a parent row
DataRow parentRow = dt1.Rows[1];
//Get Children
DataRow[] children = parentRow.GetChildRows(rel);
//Get Parent Again
DataRow myParent = children[0].GetParentRow(rel);
```

Creating Constraints

What happens with the previous code snippet if *myParent* is deleted? What happens if the parent's *Pk* is changed from 2 to 10? What happens if another *DataRow* object is added to *dt2*, where its parent is set to 99 and there is no parent with a *Pk* of 99?

As it turns out, creating a *DataRelation* object also creates constraints to deal with these issues. It's important to understand that the creation of constraints is optional; the following line of code does not create the constraints.

Visual Basic

```
Dim rel As New DataRelation("dt1dt2", parentPk, childFk, False)
```

C#

```
DataRelation rel = new DataRelation("dt1dt2", parentPk, childFk, false);
```

The *DataRelation* object is used only for navigation between *DataTable* objects; the constraint provides enforcement of data integrity by ensuring that a child row has a parent when the child is added and that changing or deleting a parent does not orphan any children.

In this example, where the constraints are created automatically, if *myParent* is deleted, the child *DataRow* objects are deleted automatically. This is called a *cascading delete*, and it is turned on by default. If the parent's *Pk* field is changed from 2 to 10, the *Fk* field in the child *DataRow* objects is changed to 10 as well. This is called a *cascading update*, and it is also turned on by default. If an attempt is made to add a child *DataRow* object that has no parent, an *InvalidConstraintException* is thrown. Chapter 1 covers the constraint in more detail.

In most scenarios, it is appropriate to create relationships that create constraints with the default settings for cascading update and delete, but there are some scenarios where you want to create a relationship but you don't want the default constraints. For example, if you are holding data that is somewhat historical in nature, you might want to allow orphaned *DataRow* objects to exist. Here are a couple of examples:

- In an order entry application, if a customer places an order for a widget, the widget information is placed into the order item table. If the widget becomes obsolete, you might want to delete the widget from the product table. You don't want to delete child *DataRow* objects that exist in the order item table, so you might create a relationship without creating the constraints.

- In many applications, you might keep audit records for every insert, change, and delete that is sent to the database. The audit record identifies the change as well as the person who made the change. If a person is removed from the database, you would not want the audit records to be removed, so you might create a relationship without creating the constraints.

In both of these scenarios, you need the ability to delete a *DataRow* object without causing a cascading delete. Normally the child *DataRow* object contains only an identifier of the parent *DataRow* object, but in these cases, you also need to copy more information into the child *DataRow* object because the parent *DataRow* might not exist later. For the widget, you need to copy the name and price of the widget to the order item table. For the audit record, you need to copy the person's name to the audit table.

Another scenario in which you might not want the default constraint setting is when business rules dictate that a parent *DataRow* object cannot be deleted when child *DataRow* objects exist. For example, you might have a business rule dictating that you cannot delete a customer who has outstanding invoices. You can imagine the consequences of a cascading delete of the invoices if you delete a customer. To best address this situation, you should create the constraints but set the *DeleteRule* property to *None*, which causes an exception to be thrown if you try to delete a customer who has outstanding invoices.

Disconnected Data Access Scenario Revisited

Joe is a traveling salesperson who needs to maintain a list of customers and orders for his territory. Joe takes a subset of the data with him on the road, where he can modify the data and store it to disk. When he returns to the office, he sends his changes to the main database server and retrieves updated information. If any concurrency conflicts arise, Joe is prompted to select the correct data.

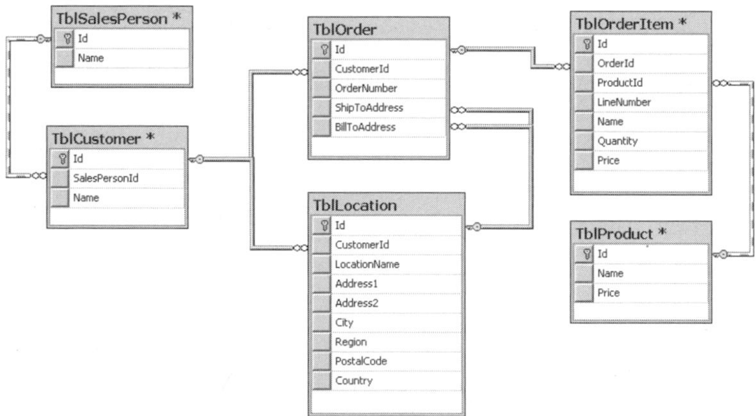

Figure 6-1 Modified order entry database schema

> This is the same scenario presented in Chapter 5, but here you look at how to retrieve all of Joe's customer data, make changes, and send all of the changes back to the database. The database schema has been tweaked a bit in this chapter, and it is shown in Figure 6-1.
>
> Notice that the *TblSalesperson/TblCustomer* and *TblProduct/TblOrderItem* relationships are represented using a dashed line, which is an indication of a relationship in the database that is unenforced. This means that salespeople and products can be removed without causing foreign key constraint errors.

Updating Data: The Beginning of the Data Access Layer

Concurrency conflicts that dealt with situations in which multiple people were editing the same data at the same time were discussed in the previous chapter. In addition to resolving concurrency errors, you need to understand how an update is accomplished.

When you set up constraints in the database, it takes a bit more work to send updates from many *DataTable* objects. The problem is that updates need to take place in a certain order. In this scenario, a customer must be added before an order can be added to that customer, and the order must be added before order items are added. When it's time to delete, the order items must be deleted before the orders, and the orders must be deleted before the customer. Do you see the problem? Normally, you perform an update on a *DataTable*-by-*DataTable* basis. When the *Customer DataTable* object is updated, all inserts, changes, and deletes are sent to the database, and then you update the next *DataTable* object, which might be the *Order DataTable* object. This order works for inserts, but it is backward for deletions because deletions must be done on the *Order DataTable* object first and then on the *Customer DataTable* object. (As long as changes are not modifying primary keys, the changes can be sent to the database in any order because the change does not affect data in any other *DataTable* object.)

You can solve the update problem by building an ordered table list based on the insert order, extracting the inserted and changed *DataRow* objects from each *DataTable* object, and submitting just the insert and changed *DataRow* objects to the database. Then you can reverse the ordered table list to get the delete order, extract the deleted *DataRow* objects from each *DataTable* object, and submit the deleted *DataRow* objects to the database. To build an ordered table list on a small database application, you can simply look at your database, and based on the relationships you can manually construct the list in your code. For large databases, it is much better to create a Data Access Layer to retrieve the list of relationships from Microsoft SQL Server and generate an ordered list of tables.

Retrieving the Relationships

The following code snippet creates a stored procedure called *uspGetSqlRelationships* that can be used on SQL Server 2000 or later to retrieve a list of relationships in a format that can be used to come up with an ordered table list.

SQL: uspGetSqlRelations

```
IF EXISTS (
   SELECT * FROM dbo.sysobjects
   WHERE id = object_id('dbo.uspGetSqlRelationships') AND
      OBJECTPROPERTY(id,'IsProcedure') = 1)
   DROP PROCEDURE dbo.uspGetSqlRelationships
GO

CREATE PROCEDURE dbo.uspGetSqlRelationships
AS
IF OBJECT_ID('tempdb..#temp') IS NOT NULL DROP TABLE #temp
SELECT  r_obj.name AS RelationshipName,
   parent_obj.name AS Parent,
   child_obj.name AS Child,
   CONVERT(nvarchar(1000),'') as PK,
   CONVERT(nvarchar(1000),'') as FK,
   r.fkeyid,
   r.rkeyid,
   r.constid
INTO #TEMP
FROM dbo.sysobjects r_obj
INNER JOIN dbo.sysreferences r  ON
   r_obj.id = r.constid
INNER JOIN dbo.sysobjects parent_obj ON
   r.rkeyid = parent_obj.id
INNER JOIN dbo.sysobjects child_obj ON
   r_obj.parent_obj = child_obj.id
INNER JOIN dbo.sysforeignkeys fkeys on
   fkeys.constid = r.constid
INNER JOIN dbo.syscolumns cols on
   cols.id = fkeys.fkeyid and
   cols.colid = fkeys.fkey
WHERE  (r_obj.xtype = 'F')
   AND ((r_obj.status & 0x100)=0)
-- OBTAIN TWO TABLE IDs
DECLARE @PK VARCHAR(1000), @FK VARCHAR(1000)
DECLARE @fkeyid INT, @rkeyid INT, @cnstid INT
DECLARE @keys NVARCHAR(2126)
DECLARE @cnstname SYSNAME
DECLARE @cnstdes NVARCHAR(4000)
DECLARE @cnsttype CHARACTER(2)
DECLARE @relName VARCHAR(1000)
DECLARE tempTable CURSOR local
   FOR SELECT RelationshipName, PK, FK, fkeyid, rkeyid, constid  FROM #temp
OPEN tempTable
FETCH tempTable INTO @relName, @PK, @FK, @fkeyid, @rkeyid, @cnstid
WHILE @@fetch_status >= 0
BEGIN
   -- USE CURSOR OVER FOREIGN KEY COLUMNS TO BUILD COLUMN LISTS
```

```
   -- (NOTE: @keys HAS THE FKEY AND @cnstdes HAS THE RKEY COLUMN LIST)
   DECLARE ms_crs_fkey CURSOR local
      FOR SELECT fkey, rkey FROM sysforeignkeys WHERE constid = @cnstid
   OPEN ms_crs_fkey
   DECLARE @fkeycol SMALLINT, @rkeycol SMALLINT
   FETCH ms_crs_fkey INTO @fkeycol, @rkeycol
   SELECT @keys = col_name(@fkeyid, @fkeycol),
         @cnstdes = col_name(@rkeyid, @rkeycol)
   FETCH ms_crs_fkey INTO @fkeycol, @rkeycol
   WHILE @@fetch_status >= 0
   BEGIN
      SELECT   @keys = @keys + ',' + col_name(@fkeyid, @fkeycol),
            @cnstdes = @cnstdes + ',' + col_name(@rkeyid, @rkeycol)
      FETCH ms_crs_fkey into @fkeycol, @rkeycol
   END
   DEALLOCATE ms_crs_fkey
   UPDATE #temp
   SET pk = @cnstdes,
      fk= @keys
   WHERE RelationshipName=@relName
   FETCH tempTable INTO @relName, @PK, @FK, @fkeyid, @rkeyid, @cnstid
END
DEALLOCATE tempTable
SELECT DISTINCT RelationshipName, Parent, Child, PK, FK FROM #temp
```

This procedure queries the *sysreferences* table to get the complete list of references between objects. The *sysreferences* table contains id columns, which are converted to the object name by several joins back to the *sysobjects* table. The *where* clause filters the references to foreign keys (*r_obj.xtype* = 'F') and filters out unenforced relationships (*(r_obj.status & 0x100)=0*). The results are placed into a temporary table called *#Temp*. Notice that the PK and FK columns are blank; the latter part of the stored procedure fills them by opening a cursor to the temporary table, performing a lookup of the primary and foreign key columns, and placing this information into the PK and FK fields. If you have composite keys, this procedure populates the PK and FK fields with a comma-delimited list of fields. The last thing this procedure does is return the relationship information.

You can use this stored procedure to construct the relationships in your *DataSet* object if you choose not to use typed *DataSet* objects in your application. Also, this procedure is not very fast, primarily due to its use of cursors. You can execute the stored procedure at application startup to retrieve the relationship list and cache the results. Figure 6-2 shows the result of this stored procedure when it is run on the *Customer* database.

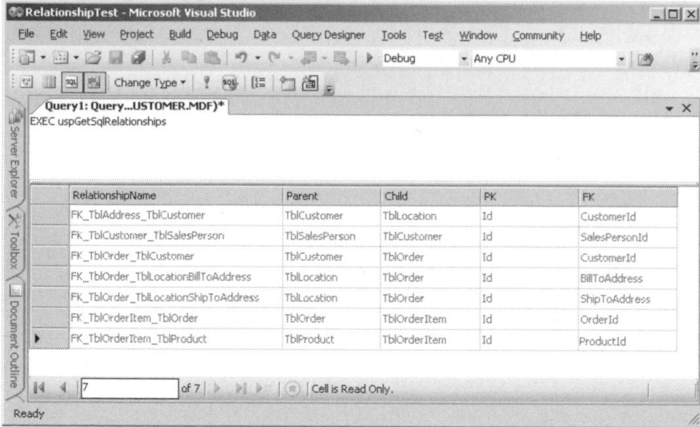

Figure 6-2 The output of the stored procedure *uspGetSqlRelationships* when run on the *Northwind* database

Retrieving the List of Tables

In addition to retrieving the list of relationships, you need to retrieve a complete list of tables in the database. There is a simple command that can accomplish this, but it should still be placed into a stored procedure. Here is the stored procedure:

SQL: uspGetSqlTables

```
IF EXISTS (SELECT * FROM dbo.sysobjects
      WHERE id = object_id('dbo.uspGetSqlTables')
      AND OBJECTPROPERTY(id, 'IsProcedure') = 1)
   DROP PROCEDURE dbo.uspGetSqlTables
GO

CREATE PROCEDURE dbo.uspGetSqlTables
AS
SELECT TABLE_NAME
FROM INFORMATION_SCHEMA.TABLES
WHERE (TABLE_TYPE = 'BASE TABLE') AND
   (TABLE_NAME <> 'dtproperties') AND
   (TABLE_NAME <> 'sysdiagrams')
```

Ordering the Table List

After creating these stored procedures, the next task is to write some code that builds the ordered table list. Create a new class called *DataAccess* in its own file; it can easily be copied to other projects as a more complete data access layer is created. The *DataAccess* class normally has a single instance that is referenced throughout the application, but you must create additional instances for each additional connection string in your application.

Add a property called *Instance* (the default instance) that is lazily initialized to an instance of the *DataAccess* class. Add a property called *OrderedTableList* that is lazily initialized when you request its value by calling a method called *BuildOrderedTableList*. Create a method called

LoadTable that accepts the name of a stored procedure to execute and returns a *DataTable* object that contains the results. This method will be used in the steps that follow.

Load a *DataTable* object called *sourceTableList* with the list of database tables, and load a *DataTable* object called *sourceRelationList* with the list of relationships. Clone the *sourceTableList* schema to the output *DataTable* object called *OrderedTableList*.

Remove self-relationships (relationships between fields in the same table). For example, the *Northwind* database has an *Employees* table that has a self-relationship between the *EmployeeId* and the *ReportsTo* fields. Self-relationships have no value when you are trying to calculate the table order. After that, you can continuously loop through the *sourceTableList*, performing the following steps.

1. See if the current table is a child in any relationship. If it isn't, remove relations where the current table is the parent in the relationship table and move the current table to the *OrderedTableList*.
2. Restart the loop by resetting the position in the *sourceTableList* to 0. If the end of the list is reached, the current count of rows in the *sourceTableList* is recorded and the loop is restarted by resetting the position to 0. If the end of the list is reached again and the current count of rows in the *sourceTableList* is the same as the count that was recorded previously, there is a circular reference error. The circular references are located by calling the *FindCircularErrors* method, and an *InvalidConstraintException* is thrown with this circular reference information.

The *FindCircularErrors* method loops through the remaining relationships that exist in *sourceRelationList* and tests to see if each one is part of a circular reference by calling the *IsCircular* method. The *IsCircular* method recursively follows each relationship until it ends or goes to a relationship that it has already visited.

Here is the complete *DataAccess* class.

Visual Basic

```
Imports System.Data
Imports System.Data.Common
Imports System.Data.SqlClient
Imports System.Configuration
Imports System.Text

Public Class DataAccess

   Public Shared ReadOnly Property Instance() As DataAccess
      Get
         If _instance Is Nothing Then
            _instance = New DataAccess()
         End If
         Return _instance
      End Get
   End Property
```

```
Private Shared _instance As DataAccess

Public Property OrderedTableList() As DataTable
   Get
      If _orderedTableList Is Nothing Then
         BuildOrderedTableList()
      End If
      Return _orderedTableList
   End Get
   Set(ByVal value As DataTable)
      _orderedTableList = value
   End Set
End Property
Private _orderedTableList As DataTable

'Builds an ordered list of tables and relationships.
'These lists will be used to determine the order of
'the updates that will be sent to the database.
Private Sub BuildOrderedTableList()
   Dim sourceTableList As DataTable = GetTable("dbo.uspGetSqlTables")
   Dim sourceRelationList As DataTable = _
      GetTable("dbo.uspGetSqlRelationships")
   OrderedTableList = sourceTableList.Clone()
   OrderedTableList.TableName = "OrderedTableList"
   'first delete circular references to self
   Dim iCounter As Integer = 0
   While (iCounter < sourceRelationList.Rows.Count)
      If sourceRelationList.Rows(iCounter)("Child").ToString() = _
            sourceRelationList.Rows(iCounter)("Parent").ToString() Then
         sourceRelationList.Rows.Remove(sourceRelationList.Rows(iCounter))
      Else
         iCounter += 1
      End If
   End While
   'continue looping through tables until there are none left.
   Dim position As Integer = 0
   Dim lastCount As Integer = sourceTableList.Rows.Count
   While (sourceTableList.Rows.Count <> 0)
      'for the current table, see if it is a child in a relationship
      'if no child relationship exists
      '1. remove relations where it is the parent in the
      '   relationship table.
      '2. move the table from the sourceTableList to the OrderedTableList.
      Dim findChild As String = String.Format("[Child]='{0}'", _
         sourceTableList.Rows(position)("TABLE_NAME"))
      If sourceRelationList.Select(findChild).Length = 0 Then
         Dim findParent As String = String.Format("[Parent]='{0}'", _
            sourceTableList.Rows(position)("TABLE_NAME"))
         For Each parent As DataRow In _
               sourceRelationList.Select(findParent)
            sourceRelationList.Rows.Remove(parent)
         Next
         'move table
         OrderedTableList.Rows.Add( _
            sourceTableList.Rows(position).ItemArray)
```

```
            'delete table row
            sourceTableList.Rows.RemoveAt(position)
            position = 0 'restart loop
         Else
            position += 1
            If (position = sourceTableList.Rows.Count) Then
               If (lastCount = sourceTableList.Rows.Count) Then
                  FindCircularErrors(sourceRelationList)
               End If
               lastCount = sourceTableList.Rows.Count
               position = 0
            End If
         End If
      End While
   End Sub

   Private Sub FindCircularErrors(ByVal sourceRelationList As DataTable)
      'this means that all of the tables that are left are children
      'so let's follow each relation to see if it is circular and
      'throw an exception.
      For Each currentRelation As DataRow In sourceRelationList.Rows
         Dim beenThere As New ArrayList()
         If (IsCircular(currentRelation, beenThere, sourceRelationList)) Then
            Dim pathBuilder As New StringBuilder()
            For Each relation As DataRow In beenThere
               pathBuilder.AppendFormat( _
                "Parent: {0,-35}  Child: {1,-35} Relationship:{2}{3}", _
                relation("Parent"), _
                relation("Child"), _
                relation("RelationshipName"), _
                vbCrLf)
            Next
            Throw New InvalidConstraintException( _
               "Circular relationships exist in the datbase." _
               + vbCrLf + pathBuilder.ToString())
         End If
      Next
   End Sub

   Private Function IsCircular(ByVal currentRelation As DataRow, _
         ByRef beenThere As ArrayList, _
         ByRef relations As DataTable) As Boolean
      beenThere.Add(currentRelation)
      'follow relation until it ends or been there...
      For Each childRelation As DataRow In relations.Rows
         If (childRelation("Parent").ToString() = _
               currentRelation("Child").ToString()) Then
            'have we been there? or do recursive check
            If (beenThere.Contains(childRelation)) Then
               Return True
            End If
            Dim currentPath As New ArrayList(beenThere)
            If (IsCircular(childRelation, currentPath, relations)) Then
               beenThere = currentPath
               Return True
```

```
            End If
         End If
      Next
      Return False
   End Function

   Public Shared Function GetTable(ByVal storedProcedure As String) _
         As DataTable
      Dim cnString As ConnectionStringSettings
      cnString = ConfigurationManager.ConnectionStrings("CustomerData")
      Dim dt As New DataTable()
      Using connection As DbConnection = New SqlConnection()
         connection.ConnectionString = cnString.ConnectionString
         Dim cmd As DbCommand = connection.CreateCommand()
         cmd.CommandType = CommandType.StoredProcedure
         cmd.CommandText = storedProcedure
         connection.Open()
         dt.Load(cmd.ExecuteReader())
      End Using
      Return dt
   End Function
End Class
```

C#

```
using System.Data;
using System.Data.Common;
using System.Data.SqlClient;
using System.Configuration;
using System.Text;
using System.Collections;

public class DataAccess
{
   public static DataAccess Instance
   {
      get {
         if ( _instance == null )
         {
            _instance = new DataAccess();
         }
         return _instance;
      }
   }
   private static DataAccess _instance;

   public DataTable OrderedTableList
   {
      get
      {
         if ( _orderedTableList == null )
         {
            BuildOrderedTableList();
         }
         return _orderedTableList;
      }
```

```
        set
        {
            _orderedTableList = value;
        }
    }
    private DataTable _orderedTableList;

    //Builds an ordered list of tables and relationships.
    //These lists will be used to determine the order of
    //the updates that will be sent to the database.
    private void BuildOrderedTableList()
    {
        DataTable sourceTableList = GetTable("dbo.uspGetSqlTables");
        DataTable sourceRelationList = GetTable("dbo.uspGetSqlRelationships");
        OrderedTableList = sourceTableList.Clone();
        OrderedTableList.TableName = "OrderedTableList";
        //first delete circular references to self
        int iCounter = 0;
        while (iCounter < sourceRelationList.Rows.Count)
        {
            if ( sourceRelationList.Rows[iCounter]["Child"].ToString() ==
                    sourceRelationList.Rows[iCounter]["Parent"].ToString() )
            {
                sourceRelationList.Rows.Remove(sourceRelationList.Rows[iCounter]);
            }
            else
            {
                iCounter += 1;
            }
        }
        //continue looping through tables until there are none left.
        int position  = 0;
        int lastCount = sourceTableList.Rows.Count;
        while (sourceTableList.Rows.Count != 0)
        {
            //for the current table, see if it is a child in a relationship
            //if no child relationship exists
            //1. remove relations where it is the parent in the
            //   relationship table.
            //2. move the table from the sourceTableList to the OrderedTableList.
            string findChild = string.Format("[Child]='{0}'",
                sourceTableList.Rows[position]["TABLE_NAME"]);
            if ( sourceRelationList.Select(findChild).Length == 0 )
            {
                string findParent = string.Format("[Parent]='{0}'",
                    sourceTableList.Rows[position]["TABLE_NAME"]);
                foreach ( DataRow parent in sourceRelationList.Select(findParent))
                {
                    sourceRelationList.Rows.Remove(parent);
                }
                //move table
                OrderedTableList.Rows.Add(
                    sourceTableList.Rows[position].ItemArray);
                //delete table row
                sourceTableList.Rows.RemoveAt(position);
```

```
            position = 0; //restart loop
         }
         else
         {
            position += 1;
            if ( position == sourceTableList.Rows.Count)
            {
               if ( lastCount == sourceTableList.Rows.Count)
               {
                  FindCircularErrors(sourceRelationList);
               }
              lastCount = sourceTableList.Rows.Count;
               position = 0;
            }
         }
      }
   }

   private void FindCircularErrors(DataTable sourceRelationList)
   {
      //this means that all of the tables that are left are children
      //so let's follow each relation to see if it is circular and
      //throw an exception.
      foreach ( DataRow currentRelation in sourceRelationList.Rows)
      {
         ArrayList beenThere = new ArrayList();
         if ( IsCircular(currentRelation,ref beenThere,
                 ref sourceRelationList))
         {
            StringBuilder pathBuilder = new StringBuilder();
            foreach ( DataRow relation in beenThere)
            {
               pathBuilder.AppendFormat(
                "Parent: {0,-35}  Child: {1,-35} Relationship:{2}{3}",
                relation["Parent"],
                relation["Child"],
                relation["RelationshipName"],
                "\r\n");
            }
            throw new InvalidConstraintException(
               "Circular relationships exist in the datbase.\r\n"
               + pathBuilder.ToString());
         }
      }
   }

   private bool IsCircular(DataRow currentRelation,
         ref ArrayList beenThere,
         ref DataTable relations)
   {
      beenThere.Add(currentRelation);
      //follow relation until it ends or been there...
      foreach (DataRow childRelation in relations.Rows)
      {
         if (childRelation["Parent"].ToString() ==
```

```
            currentRelation["Child"].ToString())
         {
            //have we been there? or do recursive check
            if ( beenThere.Contains(childRelation))
            {
               return true;
            }
            ArrayList currentPath = new ArrayList(beenThere);
            if (IsCircular(childRelation, ref currentPath, ref relations))
            {
               beenThere = currentPath;
               return true;
            }
         }
      }
      return false;
   }

   public static DataTable GetTable(string storedProcedure)
   {
      ConnectionStringSettings cnString;
      cnString = ConfigurationManager.ConnectionStrings["CustomerData"];
      DataTable dt = new DataTable();
      using(DbConnection connection = new SqlConnection())
      {
         connection.ConnectionString = cnString.ConnectionString;
         DbCommand cmd = connection.CreateCommand();
         cmd.CommandType = CommandType.StoredProcedure;
         cmd.CommandText = storedProcedure;
         connection.Open();
         dt.Load(cmd.ExecuteReader());
      }
      return dt;
   }
}
```

You can test this code by simply adding a *Button* object to a form and assigning the *OrderedTableList* to the *DataSource* property of a *DataGridView* object, as shown in the following code snippet.

Visual Basic

```
Private Sub btnGetOrderedTables_Click(ByVal sender As System.Object, _
      ByVal e As System.EventArgs) Handles btnGetOrderedTables.Click
   DataGridView1.DataSource = DataAccess.Instance.OrderedTableList
End Sub
```

C#

```
private void btnGetOrderedTables_Click(object sender, EventArgs e)
{
   dataGridView1.DataSource = DataAccess.Instance.OrderedTableList;
}
```

The *DataGridView* object displays the list of tables in the proper order for performing inserts. Modified *DataRow* objects can be sent to the database in any order provided they do not modify the primary key, so this is also the order that will be used for performing modifications, as shown in Figure 6-3.

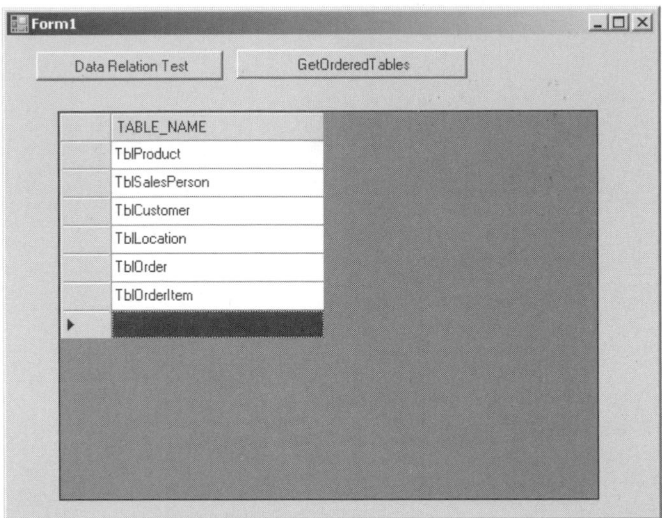

Figure 6-3 The ordered table list, based on the order for performing insertions

Using the *OrderedTableList* to Perform Updates

Now that you have an ordered list of all of the tables in the database, you can use this list when you have a *DataSet* object that needs to be updated. Ideally, you want to be able to have an *Update* method in the *DataAccess* class that accepts a *DataSet* with any combination of *DataTable* objects that map to the database, and you want the *DataSet* object's changes to always be sent to the database in the proper order. To accomplish this, you can add a new method called *BuildList* that accepts your *DataSet* object and an indicator of the SQL operation that is to be performed (insert, modification, or delete). The operation will be based on members of the *DataRowState* enumeration (*Added*, *Modified*, and *Deleted*). The following code shows the *BuildList* method.

Visual Basic

```
Public Function BuildList(ByVal state As DataRowState, ByVal ds As DataSet) _
      As ArrayList
   Dim list As New ArrayList()
   For Each drTable As DataRow In OrderedTableList.Rows
      Dim s As String = CType(drTable("TABLE_NAME"), String)
      Dim dt As DataTable = ds.Tables(s)
      If (Not dt Is Nothing) Then
         list.Add(dt)
      End If
   Next
   If (state = DataRowState.Deleted) Then
      list.Reverse()
   End If
   Return list
End Function
```

C#

```
public ArrayList BuildList(DataRowState state, DataSet ds)
{
   ArrayList list = new ArrayList();
   foreach (DataRow drTable in OrderedTableList.Rows)
   {
      string s = (string)drTable["TABLE_NAME"];
      DataTable dt = ds.Tables[s];
      if (dt != null) list.Add(dt);
   }
   if (state == DataRowState.Deleted)
   {
      list.Reverse();
   }
   return list;
}
```

The next step is to create the *Update* method in the *DataAccess* class. You essentially need to execute the same code for the inserts, modifications, and deletes, so a method called *UpdateOperation* is added that accepts the operation to be performed. To operate with the *TableAdapter* objects that are created by the *DataSet* designers, the *DataAccess* class must also hold a *Dictionary* of *TableAdapter* objects in a property called *TableAdapterMappings*, which is based on the name of the table. Here is the code.

Visual Basic

```
Public ReadOnly Property TableAdapterMappings() _
      As Dictionary(of string, TableAdapterBase)
   Get
      Return _tableAdapterMappings
   End Get
End Property
Private _tableAdapterMappings As _
      New Dictionary(of String, TableAdapterBase)

Public Sub Update(ds as DataSet)
   UpdateOperation(ds, DataRowState.Added)
   UpdateOperation(ds, DataRowState.Modified)
   UpdateOperation(ds, DataRowState.Deleted)
End Sub

Public Sub UpdateOperation(ds as DataSet, state as DataRowState)
   Dim _buildList as ArrayList = BuildList(state, ds)
   For Each table as DataTable in _buildList
      Using tempTable as DataTable = table.GetChanges(state)
         If (not tempTable is Nothing) then
            Dim ta as TableAdapterBase  = _
               TableAdapterMappings(table.TableName)
            ta.UpdateTable(tempTable)
         End If
      End Using
   Next
End Sub
```

C#

```
public Dictionary<string, TableAdapterBase> TableAdapterMappings
{
   get
   {
      return _tableAdapterMappings;
   }
}
private Dictionary<string, TableAdapterBase> _tableAdapterMappings =
      new Dictionary<string, TableAdapterBase>();

public void Update(DataSet ds)
{
   UpdateOperation(ds, DataRowState.Deleted);
   UpdateOperation(ds, DataRowState.Added);
   UpdateOperation(ds, DataRowState.Modified);
}

public void UpdateOperation(DataSet ds, DataRowState state)
{
   ArrayList buildList = BuildList(state, ds);
   foreach (DataTable table in buildList)
   {
      using (DataTable tempTable = table.GetChanges(state))
      {
         if (tempTable != null)
         {
            TableAdapterBase ta = TableAdapterMappings[table.TableName];
            ta.UpdateTable(tempTable);
         }
      }
   }
}
```

Why Is a *Dictionary* Object Required for the *TableAdapter* Objects?

The *Dictionary* object provides a list of key/value pairs. Since a *TableAdapter* object is used to fill and update a single table, creating a dictionary where the table name is the key and the *TableAdapter* object is the value lets you get to the *TableAdapter* object later by simply using the name of the table.

Wouldn't it be wonderful if a typed *DataSet* had a *Dictionary* of all of the *TableAdapter* objects that are required to fill and update the *DataSet*? The *TableAdapter* was designed to be used independently of the typed *DataSet* class that the Microsoft Visual Studio .NET *DataSet* Designer creates, so it's up to you to create this dictionary yourselves. You will use this *Dictionary* object in your data access layer, so that's where the *Dictionary* will be defined.

The last thing you need to make this code operate with *TableAdapter* objects is to create a base class from which all *TableAdapter* objects inherit and which contains code to perform the following operations.

- Set the *ContinueUpdateOnError* property of the *TableAdpater* object's underlying *DataAdapter* object to *true*.
- Add the *TableAdapter* to the *TableAdapterMappings Dictionary* object.
- Provide an *UpdateTable* method that uses the underlying *DataAdapter* to send inserts, modifications, and deletes to the database.

The following code block shows the new base class called *TableAdapterBase*. This code is placed in its own file.

Visual Basic

```
Imports System.Reflection
Imports System.Data.Common
Imports System.Data

Partial Public MustInherit Class TableAdapterBase
   Inherits System.ComponentModel.Component
   Public Sub New()
      ContinueUpdateOnError = True
      For Each tableMapping As DataTableMapping In ChildAdapter.TableMappings
         DataAccess.Instance.TableAdapterMappings(tableMapping.DataSetTable) _
            = Me
      Next
   End Sub

   Private ReadOnly Property ChildAdapter() As DbDataAdapter
      Get
         Dim myAdapter As PropertyInfo = Me.GetType().GetProperty("Adapter", _
           BindingFlags.GetProperty Or BindingFlags.NonPublic Or _
           BindingFlags.Instance)
         Return CType(myAdapter.GetValue(Me, Nothing), DbDataAdapter)
      End Get
   End Property

   Public Property ContinueUpdateOnError() As Boolean
      Get
         Return ChildAdapter.ContinueUpdateOnError
      End Get
      Set(ByVal value As Boolean)
         ChildAdapter.ContinueUpdateOnError = value
      End Set
   End Property

   Public Function UpdateTable(ByVal table As DataTable) As Integer
      Return ChildAdapter.Update(table)
   End Function

End Class
```

C#

```
using System;
using System.Collections.Generic;
using System.Text;
using System.Reflection;
using System.Data.Common;
using System.Data;

public abstract class TableAdapterBase : System.ComponentModel.Component
{

   public TableAdapterBase()
   {
      ContinueUpdateOnError = true;
      foreach (DataTableMapping tableMapping in ChildAdapter.TableMappings)
      {
         DataAccess.Instance.TableAdapterMappings[tableMapping.DataSetTable] =
            this;
      }
   }

   private DbDataAdapter ChildAdapter
   {
      get
      {
         PropertyInfo myAdapter = this.GetType().GetProperty("Adapter",
            BindingFlags.GetProperty | BindingFlags.NonPublic |
            BindingFlags.Instance);
         return (DbDataAdapter)myAdapter.GetValue(this, null);
      }
   }

   public bool ContinueUpdateOnError
   {
      get
      {
         return ChildAdapter.ContinueUpdateOnError;
      }
      set
      {
         ChildAdapter.ContinueUpdateOnError = value;
      }
   }

   public int UpdateTable(DataTable table)
   {
      return ChildAdapter.Update(table);
   }
}
```

All *TableAdapter* objects must be configured to inherit from this base class in order for this data access layer to function properly, as shown in Figure 6-4.

Figure 6-4 Every *TableAdapter* object must be configured to inherit from the *TableAdapterBase* class.

Testing the Relational Update

You can test the *Update* method of the data access layer by creating a new *DataSet* object and adding a button that has code to instantiate a new *TableAdapter* object for each *DataTable*. Then add more code in the button to add *DataRow* objects to each of the *DataTable* objects in the *Customer DataSet* object. Finally, call the *Update* method. The following code shows the *Update* test.

Visual Basic

```
Private custDataSet As New CustomerDataSet()
Private Sub btnUpdate1_Click(ByVal sender As System.Object, _
        ByVal e As System.EventArgs) Handles btnUpdate1.Click
   'initialize table adapters to get them into the
   'TableAdapterMappings collection
   Dim Adapter as TableAdapterBase
   Adapter = New CustomerDataSetTableAdapters.TblProductTableAdapter()
   Adapter = New CustomerDataSetTableAdapters.TblSalesPersonTableAdapter()
   Adapter = New CustomerDataSetTableAdapters.TblCustomerTableAdapter()
   Adapter = New CustomerDataSetTableAdapters.TblLocationTableAdapter()
   Adapter = New CustomerDataSetTableAdapters.TblOrderTableAdapter()
   Adapter = New CustomerDataSetTableAdapters.TblOrderItemTableAdapter()

   'Create the Guids for the objects
   Dim p1Id As Guid = Guid.NewGuid()
   Dim p2Id As Guid = Guid.NewGuid()
   Dim spId As Guid = Guid.NewGuid()
   Dim cId As Guid = Guid.NewGuid()
   Dim l1Id As Guid = Guid.NewGuid()
   Dim l2Id As Guid = Guid.NewGuid()
   Dim oId As Guid = Guid.NewGuid()
   Dim oi1Id As Guid = Guid.NewGuid()
   Dim oi2Id As Guid = Guid.NewGuid()
```

```
    'Create the DataRow
    custDataSet.TblProduct.LoadDataRow( _
       New Object() {p1Id, "Widget 1", 123.45}, False)
    custDataSet.TblProduct.LoadDataRow( _
       New Object() {p2Id, "Widget 2", 234.56}, False)
    custDataSet.TblSalesPerson.LoadDataRow( _
       New Object() {spId, "Joe"}, False)
    custDataSet.TblCustomer.LoadDataRow( _
       New Object() {cId, spId, "Joe's Customer"}, False)
    custDataSet.TblLocation.LoadDataRow( _
       New Object() {l1Id, cId, "HQ", "add1", "add2", "city", _
          "state", "12345", "US"}, False)
    custDataSet.TblLocation.LoadDataRow( _
       New Object() {l2Id, cId, "WAREHOUSE", "add1", "add2", _
          "city", "state", "12345", "US"}, False)
    custDataSet.TblOrder.LoadDataRow( _
       New Object() {oId, cId, "1", l2Id, l1Id}, False)
    custDataSet.TblOrderItem.LoadDataRow( _
       New Object() {oi1Id, oId, p1Id, 1, "Widget1", 1, 123.45}, False)
    custDataSet.TblOrderItem.LoadDataRow( _
       New Object() {oi2Id, oId, p2Id, 2, "Widget2", 2, 234.56}, False)

    'Do the update of the DataSet
    DataAccess.Instance.Update(custDataSet)
    MessageBox.Show("Customer Database Updated")
End Sub
```

C#

```
private CustomerDataSet custDataSet = new CustomerDataSet();
private void btnUpdate1_Click(object sender, EventArgs e)
{
    //initialize table adapters to get them into the
    //TableAdapterMappings collection
    TableAdapterBase Adapter;
    Adapter = new CustomerDataSetTableAdapters.TblProductTableAdapter();
    Adapter = new CustomerDataSetTableAdapters.TblSalesPersonTableAdapter();
    Adapter = new CustomerDataSetTableAdapters.TblCustomerTableAdapter();
    Adapter = new CustomerDataSetTableAdapters.TblLocationTableAdapter();
    Adapter = new CustomerDataSetTableAdapters.TblOrderTableAdapter();
    Adapter = new CustomerDataSetTableAdapters.TblOrderItemTableAdapter();

    //Create the Guids for the objects
    Guid p1Id = Guid.NewGuid();
    Guid p2Id = Guid.NewGuid();
    Guid spId = Guid.NewGuid();
    Guid cId = Guid.NewGuid();
    Guid l1Id = Guid.NewGuid();
    Guid l2Id = Guid.NewGuid();
    Guid oId = Guid.NewGuid();
    Guid oi1Id = Guid.NewGuid();
    Guid oi2Id = Guid.NewGuid();

    //Create the DataRow
    custDataSet.TblProduct.LoadDataRow(
       new Object[] { p1Id, "Widget 1", 123.45 }, false);
```

```
    custDataSet.TblProduct.LoadDataRow(
       new Object[] { p2Id, "Widget 2", 234.56 }, false);
    custDataSet.TblSalesPerson.LoadDataRow(
       new Object[] { spId, "Joe" }, false);
    custDataSet.TblCustomer.LoadDataRow(
       new Object[] { cId, spId, "Joe's Customer" }, false);
    custDataSet.TblLocation.LoadDataRow(
       new Object[] {l1Id, cId, "HQ", "add1", "add2", "city",
    "state", "12345", "US"}, false);
    custDataSet.TblLocation.LoadDataRow(
       new Object[] {l2Id, cId, "WAREHOUSE", "add1", "add2",
    "city", "state", "12345", "US"}, false);
    custDataSet.TblOrder.LoadDataRow(
       new Object[] { oId, cId, "1", l2Id, l1Id }, false);
    custDataSet.TblOrderItem.LoadDataRow(
       new Object[] { oi1Id, oId, p1Id, 1, "Widget1", 1, 123.45 }, false);
    custDataSet.TblOrderItem.LoadDataRow(
       new Object[] { oi2Id, oId, p2Id, 2, "Widget2", 2, 234.56 }, false);

    //Do the update of the DataSet
    DataAccess.Instance.Update(custDataSet);
    MessageBox.Show("Customer Database Updated");

}
```

DAL Update Caveats

The *Update* method works properly in most situations, but not all.

- *Self-references* If a SQL Server table has an enforced self-reference, such as an Employee table that has a ReportsTo column that points to the ID of a different Employee, you must come up with a way to send the inserts and deletes for that table. This means ordering the updates on a row-by-row basis that is similar to the table-by-table basis that has been presented.
- *Circular References* If a circular reference chain exists, the data access layer identifies this and throws an exception.

Summary

- A *DataRelation* object provides the means for navigating from one *DataTable* object to another by using the unique key value on the parent table to search for foreign keys in the child table.
- Constraints ensure data integrity by requiring that a child row has a parent when the child is added and that changing or deleting a parent does not orphan any children.
- Sending inserts to the database is a top-down action—for example, you must insert a customer before inserting an order for that customer.

- Sending deletes to the database is a bottom-up action—for example, you must delete the orders that belong to a particular customer before you can delete that customer.
- It is possible to extract the added *DataRow* objects separately from the deleted *DataRow* objects so that they can be sent to the database in opposite order.
- You can use a Data Access Layer (DAL) to provide the functionality required to send inserts, modifications, and deletes to a disconnected database that contains multiple related *DataTable* objects.

Chapter 7

Working with the Windows Data Grid Control

We're always looking for a way to display data in a manner that will allow the user to quickly browse and change data. Every version of Microsoft Visual Studio has had a data grid control that is meant to provide easy browse and change capability with minimal effort by the developer. This chapter will examine the Windows data grid control, called the *DataGridView*, which is available in Visual Studio 2005; the next chapter will examine the Web data grid control, called the *GridView*.

Understanding the *DataGridView* Control

The *DataGridView* control is used on Windows Forms applications to display data in a tabular, rows-and-columns format. Earlier grid controls were difficult to customize without diving deep into Windows handles and messages, but the *DataGridView* object exposes more than 160 events to make it much simpler to access the key area of the grid.

The basic structure of the *DataGridView* object is shown in Figure 7-1. The *DataGridView* object consists of collections of rows and columns. The *Rows* property provides a collection of *DataGridViewRow* objects. Each *DataGridViewRow* object contains a *Cells* collection, which is a collection of objects that derive from the *DataGridViewCell* class. The *Columns* property provides a collection of objects that derive from the *DataGridViewColumn* class. Although the *DataGridViewRow* object holds the collection of cells, each *DataGridViewColumn* provides an instance of a specific cell that is used as a template. The *DataGridViewRow* object can access the cell template to create clones of the correct cell type.

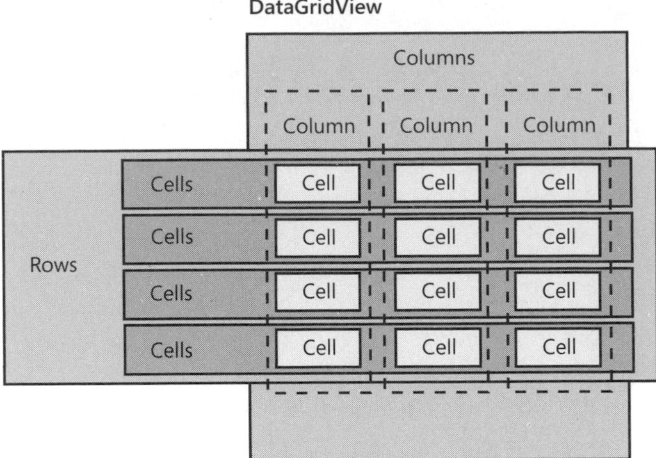

Figure 7-1 The basic structure of the *DataGridView* object

What do I mean by correct cell type? Figure 7-2 shows the class hierarchy of the *DataGridViewCell*. With the exception of the header types, the class hierarchy of the *DataGridViewColumn* class is similar to that of the *DataGridViewCell* class. You don't define cell types for your *DataGridView* object—you define columns, and each column object supplies a cell object to the row; the row uses the cells as templates for creating the proper cell types for the row.

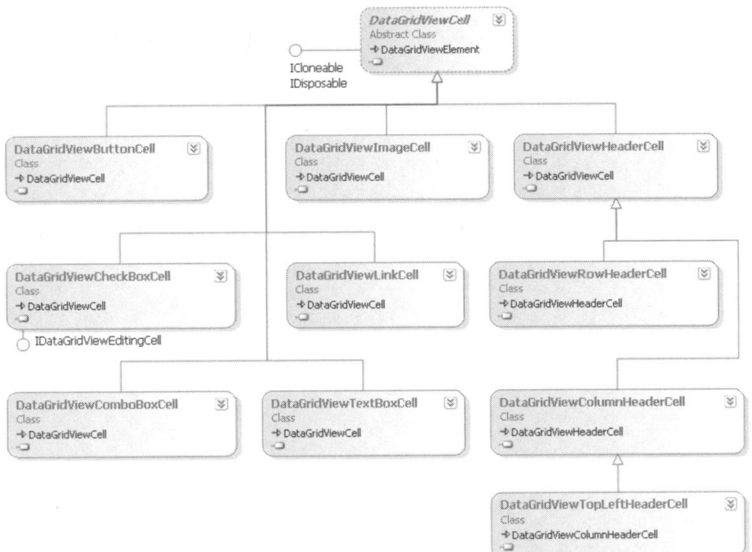

Figure 7-2 The *DataGridViewCell* class hierarchy

Formatting with Styles

You use styles to format the *DataGridView* object. You can assign styles to individual cells, rows, or columns or to the whole *DataGridView* object. The effective style of a cell is derived by evaluating from the least specific style (the *DataGridView* object) to the most specific style (the cell style). The style properties are additive, which means that when the *BackColor* property is set to red on the *DataGridView* object and the *Font* is set to Arial on the cell, the cell renders with the Arial font and a red background. When there is a conflict, such as different *BackColor* settings, the most specific setting prevails.

You can use the *CellFormatting* event to control the style programmatically. The benefit is that you can apply business rules to specify whether a cell should stand out from other cells (for example, making the negative "quantity on hand" number red, but only when the inventory item sells more than one item per month).

DataGridView Modes of Operation

The *DataGridView* supports three modes of operation: bound, unbound, and virtual. You are in bound mode when you bind, or connect, the *DataGridView* object to a data source. You are in unbound mode when you simply populate the row data programmatically. It is also possible to be in a "mixed" mode, where you bind to a data source but also add one or more unbound columns to the *DataGridView* object.

Virtual mode allows you to control the *DataGridView* object's interaction with your data cache. The primary benefit of virtual mode is that you can implement just-in-time data loading when you have large amounts of data to make available to the user but the user can select the data to be viewed. In other words, rather than filling a *DataSet* object with a couple of gigabytes of data, you can simply populate the *DataSet* with the data that is necessary when the user's interaction causes a request for specific data.

Binding to a Data Source

The *DataGridView* can be easily bound to a data source at design time; Visual Studio will read your data source and populate the columns collection. You can select or create the data source by using the Choose Data Source dialog box.

The data source can be one of the following:

- *Database* You can bind to an ODBC, OLEDB, SQL Server, Oracle, Microsoft Access, or other data source. You can even attach a SQL Server database file by simply including it in your project.
- *Web Service* You can browse to a Web service on your machine, you can locate UDDI (Universal Description, Discovery, and Integration) servers on the local area network, or you can use Microsoft's UDDI servers on the Web. This option opens the Add Web Ref-

erence dialog box, where you can create a connection to a Web service that returns the data for your application.

- *Object* This option lets you choose an object that can be used to bind to a *DataGridView* object or other data-bound controls.

Resource Sharing

The *DataGridView* object attempts to minimize resource usage by sharing *DataGridViewRow* instances wherever possible. A row can be shared if the state of all of its cells can be determined based on the state of the rows and columns that contain the cells. The state of a cell refers to a cell's appearance and behavior, which is typically derived from the column and row that the cell belongs to. Changing the state of a cell at the cell level so that its state cannot be determined via the row and column it belongs to causes a shared row to become unshared.

Here are some reasons that one or more rows can be unshared or can become unshared.

- Editing a cell in a row.
- Selecting a single cell in a row, where the cell's column is not selected.
- Assigning a *ToolTipText* or a *ContextMenuStrip* to a cell in the row.
- Populating the *Items* property of a *DataGridViewComboBoxCell* in the row.
- Creating an unbound row will always create an unshared row because the cell data is contained in the cell. You create unbound rows by calling the *DataGridViewRowCollection.Add(System.Object*[]) method or the *DataGridViewRowCollection.Insert(System.Object*[]) method.
- Using a "for each" command to enumerate the *Rows* collection of a *DataGridView* object causes the rows to become unshared. Use a "for" loop with an index number instead.
- Accessing a cell by using the *Cells* collection on the *DataGridView* object. When you work with the *DataGridView* events, the event arguments pass cell information that you can use to access the cell without causing the row to become unshared.
- Setting the *ReadOnly* property of a cell to *false* when the *ReadOnly* property of its column is set to *true* causes all rows to become unshared.
- Accessing the *List* property of the *DataGridViewRowCollection* causes all rows to become unshared.
- Calling the *Sort* method on the *DataGridView* with a custom *IComparer* causes all rows to become unshared. If you don't use a custom *IComparer*, calling the *Sort* method is OK.

- Calling the *AreAllCellsSelected* method on the *DataGridView* object using the overload that accepts a Boolean to include invisible cells causes all rows to become unshared. Calling other versions of *AreAllCellsSelected* is OK.
- Accessing the *SelectedCells* property of a *DataGridView* object when the selection mode is set to *FullColumnSelect*, *ColumnHeaderSelect*, *FullRowSelect*, or *RowHeaderSelect* causes all rows to become unshared.

DataGridView Setup

The following examples use the Employees table in the *Northwind* database; the *Northwind* database base files (Northwnd.mdf and Northwnd.ldf) were simply included in the project to create a typed *DataSet*.

Before working with a *DataGridView* object, you must configure a *DataSource*. For example, you can configure a *DataSource* by including a database in your project. When the *Northwind* database is added to the project, the Data Source Configuration Wizard starts. The first page prompts for the list of tables, views, functions, and stored procedures that should be included in the *DataSource*. Figure 7-3 shows all of the tables being selected except the sysdiagrams table because the sysdiagrams table holds metadata that is used by the database diagram tool. Also notice that the name of the *DataSet* to be created has been changed from *northwnd-DataSet* to *NorthwindDs*.

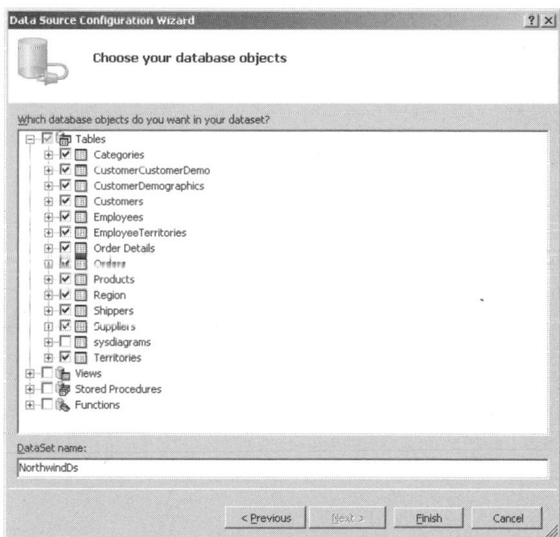

Figure 7-3 To set up the *Northwind DataSource*, you simply add the *Northwind* database to the project, which will start the Data Source Configuration Wizard.

After you create the *DataSource*, you can simply drag and drop the Employees table onto the form, which will add a *DataGridView* object to the form. The other objects that have been added to the form are as follows. These objects are shown in Figure 7-4.

- *northwindDs* An instance of the *NorthwindDs* typed *DataSet* that contains a populated *Employees DataTable* object.
- *employeesBindingSource* An instance of the *BindingSource* class, which acts as a *DataSource* for the *Employees* data. The *BindingSource* object simplifies the connection, or binding, of the data to one or more controls on the Windows Form.
- *employeesTableAdapter* An instance of the *EmployeesTableAdapter* class, which is used to populate the Employees *DataTable* object. The *employeesTableAdapter* object is also used to send changes back to the database server.
- *employeesBindingNavagator* An instance of the *BindingNavigator* class. The *BindingNavigator* object is a GUI control that allows you to move through a data source.

When the *DataGridView* is dropped onto a Windows form, the DataGridView Tasks window is displayed (Figure 7-4). This window gives you quick access to some of the common tasks for setting up the *DataGridView* quickly. Notice the little arrow button attached to the upper left corner of the DataGridView Tasks window, which you can use to hide or display the window.

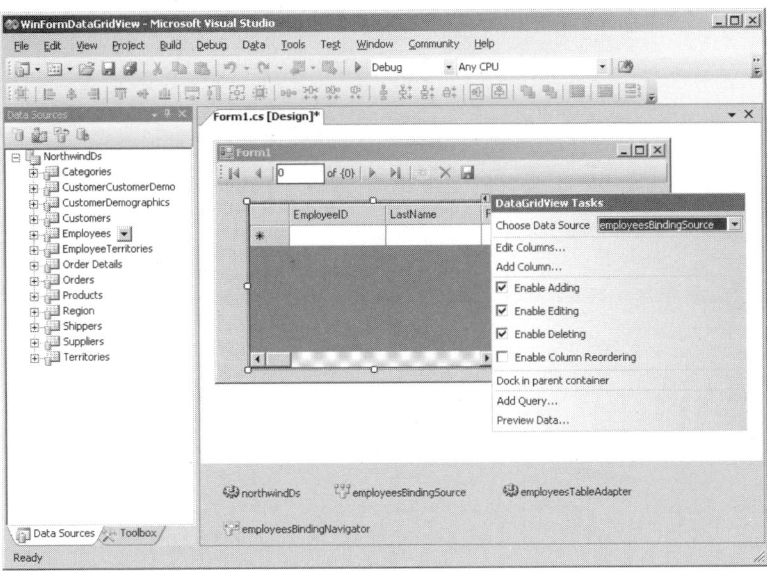

Figure 7-4 These objects are added to the tray when the Employees table is dragged onto the form.

Working with Cell Events

A cell can generate many events, which are bubbled up to the *DataGridView* object. These events substantially increase the flexibility of the *DataGridView* over data grid controls of the past. Table 7-1 lists the available cell events.

Table 7-1 Cell Events Available on the *DataGridView* Object

Event	Description
CellBeginEdit	A cell has entered edit mode.
CellBorderStyleChanged	The border style was changed for a cell.
CellClick	Any part of the cell has been clicked using the left mouse button.
CellContentClicked	The content of the cell has been clicked.
CellContentDoubleClick	The content of the cell has been double-clicked.
CellContextMenuStripChanged	The shortcut menu associated with a cell has been changed.
CellContextMenuStripNeeded	A shortcut menu is needed for a cell.
CellDoubleClick	Any part of a cell has been double-clicked using the left mouse button.
CellEndEdit	The currently selected cell has exited edit mode.
CellEnter	A cell has received focus and is becoming the currently selected cell.
CellErrorTextChanged	The error text of a cell has changed.
CellErrorTextNeeded	The error text of a cell is needed. At this time, the error text can be read or changed before it is displayed.
CellFormatting	A cell that is to be displayed needs to be formatted.
CellLeave	A cell has lost focus and is no longer the currently selected cell.
CellMouseClick	A mouse click has taken place anywhere on a cell using any mouse button. Use the *CellClick* event if you are only interested in left mouse button clicks.
CellMouseDoubleClick	A mouse double-click has taken place anywhere on a cell using any mouse button. Use the *CellDoubleClick* event if you are only interested in left mouse button double-clicks.
CellMouseDown	A mouse button was pressed while the mouse pointer was within a cell.
CellMouseEnter	The mouse pointer just entered a cell.
CellMouseLeave	The mouse pointer just left a cell.
CellMouseMove	The mouse pointer was moved over a cell.

Table 7-1 Cell Events Available on the *DataGridView* Object

Event	Description
CellMouseUp	A mouse button was released while the mouse pointer was within a cell.
CellPainting	A cell needs to be drawn.
CellParsing	A cell (either modified or not) is leaving edit mode.
CellStateChanged	A cell state has changed, typically to *Selected* or *None*.
CellStyleChanged	A style has been assigned to a cell. Note that this event does not fire if a property of the style, such as *BackColor*, changes.
CellStyleContentChanged	One of the properties of the style, such as *BackColor*, has changed.
CellToolTipTextChanged	A cell's *ToolTipText* has changed.
CellToolTipTextNeeded	A cell's *ToolTipText* is needed. At this time, the *ToolTipText* can be viewed or changed before it is displayed.
CellValidated	A cell has finished validation.
CellValidating	A cell is being validated, and the validation can be canceled.
CellValueChanged	The value of the cell has been changed.
CellValueNeeded	A value is needed for the cell to be formatted and displayed. This event fires only if *DataGridView.VirtualMode* is *true*.
CellValuePushed	A cell value has changed and needs to be stored in the underlying data source. This event fires only if *DataGridView.VirtualMode* is *true*.
CurrentCellChanged	A different cell is becoming the current cell.
CurrentCellDirtyStateChanged	The current cell's value has changed (for example, if a cell is in edit mode and a single character is typed). This event fires again when the dirty state has been cleared.
DefaultCellStyleChanged	A style has been assigned to the *DataGridView* object's *DefaultCellStyle* property.

You can view a list of the *DataGridView* object's events by clicking the *DataGridView* object and then clicking the event lightning bolt icon in the Properties window (Figure 7-5). You can add event handler stub code for any of the events by simply double-clicking the event.

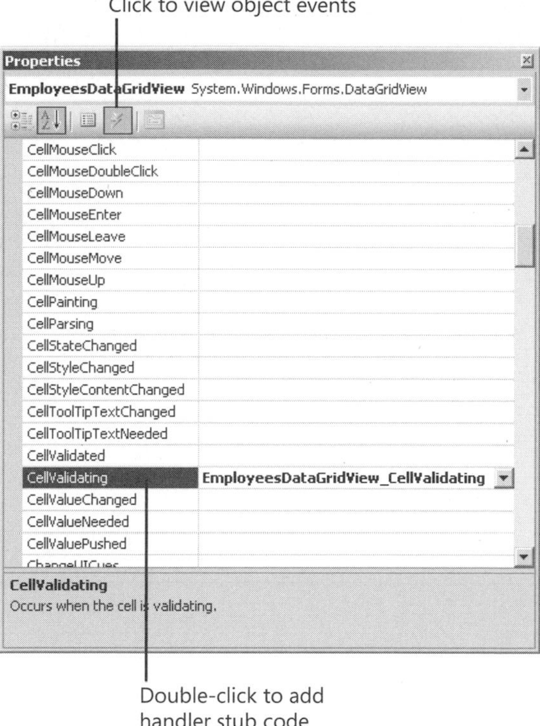

Figure 7-5 *DataGridView* object events

Event Sequence

Here are the events that take place when a cell is entered (the Current Cell) and edited, and then another cell is clicked (the Next Cell).

1. CellStateChanged (to Selected): Current Cell
2. CellEnter: Current Cell
3. CellFormatting: Current Cell
4. CellClick: Current Cell
5. CellMouseClick: Current Cell
6. CellFormatting: Current Cell
7. CellBeginEdit: Current Cell
8. CellFormatting: Current Cell

9. EditingControlShowing: Current Cell
10. CellDirtyStateChanged (to dirty): A character was typed into Current Cell
11. CellMouseLeave: Current Cell
12. CellMouseEnter: Next Cell
13. CellFormatting: Next Cell
14. CellMouseDown: Next Cell
15. CellLeave: Current Cell
16. CellValidating: Current Cell
17. CellParsing: Current Cell
18. CellValueChanged: Current Cell
19. CellDirtyStateChanged (to clear): Current Cell
20. CellValidated: Current Cell
21. CellFormatting: Current Cell
22. CellStateChanged (to None): Current Cell
23. CellStateChanged (to Selected): Next Cell
24. CellEndEdit: Current Cell

Now that you have a table of the cell events (Table 7-1) and the preceding sequential list of events, you can code the necessary event handlers to customize the *DataGridView* object. For example, if you want to keep a user from changing from one cell to another when the user does not enter an appropriate value into the first cell, you can set the *Cancel* property to *true* in the *CellValidating* event handler, as shown in the following code snippet.

Visual Basic

```
Private Sub EmployeesDataGridView_CellValidating( _
      ByVal sender As System.Object, _
      ByVal e As System.Windows.Forms.DataGridViewCellValidatingEventArgs) _
      Handles EmployeesDataGridView.CellValidating
   Debug.WriteLine("Cell Validating: " _
   + e.RowIndex.ToString() + ", " + e.ColumnIndex.ToString())
   'Check Last Name to see if last name has at least 1 character
   If (e.ColumnIndex = 1 _
   And e.FormattedValue.ToString().Trim().Length = 0) Then
      e.Cancel = True
   End If
End Sub
```

C#

```
private void employeesDataGridView_CellValidating(
   object sender, DataGridViewCellValidatingEventArgs e)
{
```

```
    Debug.WriteLine("Cell Validating: "
        + e.RowIndex.ToString() + ", " + e.ColumnIndex.ToString());
    //Check to see if last name has at least 1 character
    if (e.ColumnIndex==1 //Last Name
        && e.FormattedValue.ToString().Trim().Length==0)
    {
        e.Cancel = true;
    }
}
```

When the code is run and the user attempts to change the last name to an empty string or a string that consists of spaces, the *Cancel* property will be set to *true* and the user will not be allowed to leave the cell. Notice that the events will take place in the following order.

1. *CellLeave*: Current Cell
2. *CellFormatting*: Current Cell
3. *CellValidating*: Current Cell
4. *CellEnter*: Current Cell

You can see that the *CellLeave* event fired, and after *CellValidating* set the *Cancel* property to *true*, the *CellEnter* event fired as the user was placed back into the cell.

Working with *DataGridViewColumn* Objects

The *DataGridView* object has a *Columns* collection, which contains objects that inherit from the *DataGridViewColumn* class. The Microsoft .NET Framework contains several column types, but you can also create your own column types. Figure 7-6 shows the *DataGridView-Column* class hierarchy, with the available column types.

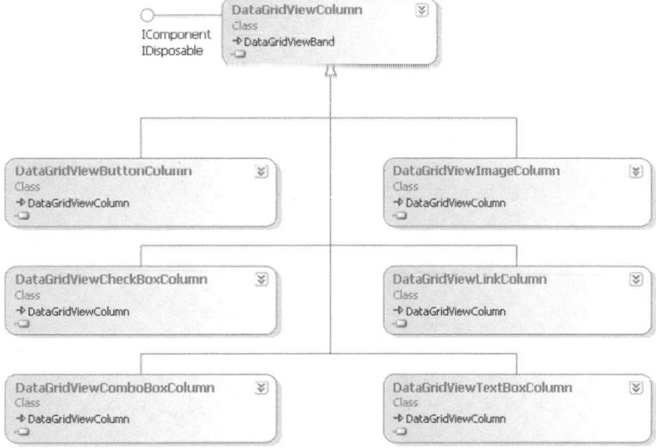

Figure 7-6 The *DataGridViewColumn* class hierarchy

Editing the Column List

The *DataGridView* designer lets you add and remove columns by using the Edit Columns dialog box. You can also populate the columns collection at runtime using your own code.

Working with Column Events

Many column-related events are available on the *DataGridView* object, as shown in Table 7-2. Notice that some of the events are based on individual column objects, while other events are based on a global column-related property being changed on the *DataGridView* object.

Table 7-2 Column Events on the *DataGridView* Object

Event	Description
AllowUserToOrderColumnsChanged	The *AllowUserToOrderColumns* property of the *DataGridView* object has been changed.
AllowUserToResizeColumnsChanged	The *AllowUserToResizeColumns* property of the *DataGridView* object has been changed.
AutoSizeColumnModeChanged	The *AutoSizeMode* property on a column object has been changed.
AutoSizeColumnsModeChanged	The *AutoSizeColumnsMode* property of the *DataGridView* object has been changed.
ColumnAdded	A column has been added to the *DataGridView* object.
ColumnContextMenuStripChanged	A column object's *ContextMenuStrip* property has been changed.
ColumnDataPropertyNameChanged	The *DataPropertyName* property of a column object has been changed.
ColumnDefaultCellStyleChanged	The *DefaultCellStyle* property of a column object has been changed.
ColumnDisplayIndexChanged	The *DisplayIndex* property of a column object has been changed.
ColumnDividerDoubleClick	A user double-clicked the divider between two columns.
ColumnDividerWidthChanged	The width of a column divider changed by setting the *DividerWidth* property on the column.
ColumnHeaderCellChanged	A column object's header cell contents have been changed.
ColumnHeaderMouseClick	A user clicked a column object's header.
ColumnHeaderMouseDoubleClick	A user double-clicked a column object's header.
ColumnHeadersBorderStyleChanged	The *ColumnHeadersBorderStyle* property of the *DataGridView* object has been changed.
ColumnHeadersDefaultCellStyleChanged	The *ColumnHeadersDefaultCellStyle* property of the *DataGridView* object has been changed.

Table 7-2 **Column Events on the *DataGridView* Object**

Event	Description
ColumnHeaderHeightChanged	The *ColumnHeaderHeight* property of the *DataGridView* object has been changed.
ColumnHeaderHeightSizeModeChanged	The *ColumnHeaderHeightSizeMode* property of the *DataGridView* object has been changed.
ColumnMinimumWidthChanged	The *ColumnMinimumWidth* property on a column object has been changed.
ColumnNameChanged	The *Name* property on a column has been changed.
ColumnRemoved	A column object has been removed from the *DataGridView* object.
ColumnSortModeChanged	The *SortMode* property of a column object has been changed.
ColumnStateChanged	A column object's state has changed (for example, from *Displayed* or *None* to indicate whether the column is currently being displayed).
ColumnToolTipTextChanged	The *ToolTipText* property of a column object has been changed.
ColumnWidthChange	The *Width* property of a column has been changed.

Using the *DataGridViewTextBoxColumn*

The default column type for string and numeric data is the *DataGridViewTextBoxColumn*, which supplies a *DataGridViewTextBoxCell*, as a cell template, to a row that is being created. The row queries the column for the cell template and clones the cell, which ensures that the template is not modified by the row.

The *DataGridViewTextBoxCell* simply renders data as text and accepts text input. For a given *DataGridViewTextBoxColumn* object, there is one *DataGridViewTextBoxCell* object for each *DataGridViewRow* object in the *DataGridView* object. When a cell becomes activated, a *DataGridViewTextBoxEditingControl* object is supplied so that the application user can edit the cell, provided that the cell's *ReadOnly* property is set to *false*.

Using the *DataGridViewCheckBoxColumn*

The default column type for Boolean data (Bit data type in SQL Server) is the *DataGridViewCheckBoxColumn*, which supplies a *DataGridViewCheckBoxCell*, as a cell template, to a row that is being created.

The *DataGridViewCheckBoxCell* renders data in a *CheckBox* and lets the user edit the value by selecting or deselecting the *CheckBox*. For a given *DataGridViewCheckBoxColumn* object, there is one *DataGridViewCheckBoxCell* object for each *DataGridViewRow* object in the *DataGridView* object. The *DataGridViewCheckBoxColumn* has a property called *ThreeState* that can be set to *true* to allow the *CheckBox* to have a selected (*true*), deselected (*false*), or indeterminate (null) state.

Probably the most common event you will be interested in is the *CellContentClick* event, which fires when the user clicks in the *CheckBox* to change the selected state.

Using the *DataGridViewImageColumn*

The *DataGridViewImageColumn* can be used to display images and icons in the *DataGridView* object. By default, the Visual Studio Data Source designer does not assign a data source image field to a *DataGridView* column, so images are not displayed, but a *DataGridViewImageColumn* can be added to the *DataGridView* object for displaying image and icon data. The *DataGrid-ViewImageColumn* supplies a *DataGridViewImageCell* as a cell template to a row that is being created.

The *DataGridViewImageCell* renders data directly into the cell. Figure 7-7 shows the photos from the *Employees* table rendered using a *DataGridViewImageColumn* object. In this example, the *AutoResizeRowsMode* of the *EmployeeDataGridView* object and the *AutoSizeMode* of the *DatagridViewImageColumn* have been set to *DisplayedCells*.

Figure 7-7 The Employees table contains a Photo column that can be rendered using the *DataGridViewImageCell*.

Loading a New Image into the *DataGridViewImageCell* from a File The *DataGrid-ViewImageColumn* easily displays an image, but if you want to replace the image with a new image, or if you are adding a new employee, you'll need to add some code to get the ability to replace the image. Using the current example project as shown in Figure 7-7, add a *Context-MenuStrip* to the form and set its *Name* property to *PhotoMenu*. Next, add a menu item and set the *Text* property to "&Insert Photo From File". Assign the *PhotoMenu* to the *ContextMenuStrip* property of the Photo column.

Add an event handler for the click event of the "&Insert Photo From File" menu item. Add the following code, which prompts the user for an image file and loads it.

Visual Basic

```
Dim currentPhotoCell as DataGridViewImageCell
Private Sub InsertPhotoFromFileToolStripMenuItem_Click( _
      ByVal sender As System.Object,  ByVal e As System.EventArgs) _
      Handles InsertPhotoFromFileToolStripMenuItem.Click
   dim dlg as new OpenFileDialog()
   dlg.Multiselect = false
   dlg.Filter = "GIF|*.gif|BMP|*.bmp|JPEG|*.jpg;*.jpeg|All Files|*.*"
   dlg.FilterIndex = 3
   dlg.Title = "Select a photo to insert"
   if Windows.Forms.DialogResult.OK <> dlg.ShowDialog() then return
   Dim bmp as new Bitmap(dlg.FileName)
   currentPhotoCell.Value = bmp
End Sub
```

C#

```
DataGridViewImageCell currentPhotoCell;
private void insertPhotoToolStripMenuItem_Click(object sender, EventArgs e)
{
   OpenFileDialog dlg = new OpenFileDialog();
   dlg.Multiselect = false;
   dlg.Filter = "GIF|*.gif|BMP|*.bmp|JPEG|*.jpg;*.jpeg|All Files|*.*";
   dlg.FilterIndex = 3;
   dlg.Title = "Select a photo to insert";
   if (DialogResult.OK != dlg.ShowDialog()) return;
   Bitmap bmp = new Bitmap(dlg.FileName);
   currentPhotoCell.Value = bmp;
}
```

Most of this code simply sets up the dialog box to prompt for an image file. The file is loaded into a new *Bitmap* object, and the *Bitmap* object is assigned to the *currentPhotoCell* object's *Value* property.

The only problem with this code is that the *currentPhotoCell* variable has not been set. You can make *currentPhotoCell* point to the cell that was right-clicked, by adding an event handler for the *CellContextMenuStripNeeded* event of the *employeesDataGridView* object and adding the following code.

Visual Basic

```
Private Sub EmployeesDataGridView_CellContextMenuStripNeeded( _
      ByVal sender As System.Object,  _
      ByVal e As _
 System.Windows.Forms.DataGridViewCellContextMenuStripNeededEventArgs) _
      Handles EmployeesDataGridView.CellContextMenuStripNeeded
   Dim dg as DataGridView = CType(sender,DataGridView)
   if typeof dg.Columns(e.ColumnIndex) is DataGridViewImageColumn then
      currentPhotoCell = _
         ctype(dg.Rows(e.RowIndex).Cells(e.ColumnIndex),DataGridViewImageCell)
   end if
End Sub
```

C#

```
private void employeesDataGridView_CellContextMenuStripNeeded(
   object sender, DataGridViewCellContextMenuStripNeededEventArgs e)
{
   DataGridView dg = (DataGridView)sender;
   if (dg.Columns[e.ColumnIndex] is DataGridViewImageColumn)
   {
      currentPhotoCell =
         (DataGridViewImageCell)dg.Rows[e.RowIndex].Cells[e.ColumnIndex];
   }
}
```

Run the project and right-click a photo, which will display the shortcut menu. Click the "Insert Item From File" menu item. Select an image file on your computer and click OK. The image will load into the cell as shown in Figure 7-8. Be sure to click the Save Data icon to store the new image into the database.

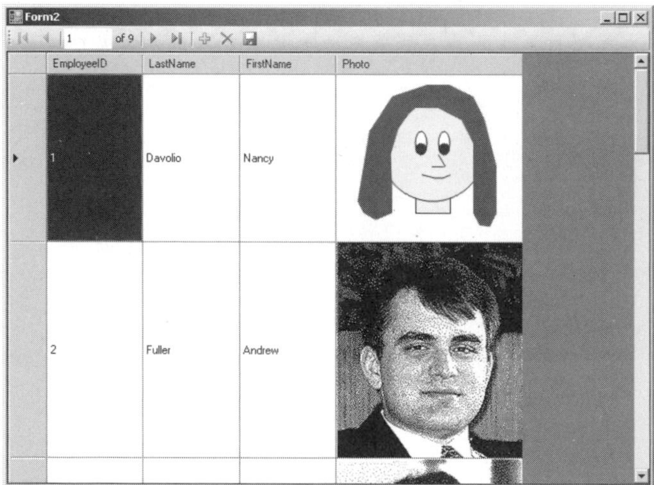

Figure 7-8 You can upload images to the *DataGridView* with a bit of code.

Saving an Image from the *DataGridViewImageCell* to a File To save an image that is in a *DataGridViewImageCell* object to a file, you can add a bit more code to your project. For starters, add another menu item to the *PhotoMenu* object and set its *Text* property to "Save Photo to File". Add a click event handler and add the following code.

Visual Basic

```
Private Sub SavePhotoToFileToolStripMenuItem_Click( _
      ByVal sender As System.Object, _
      ByVal e As System.EventArgs) _
      Handles SavePhotoToFileToolStripMenuItem.Click
   Const oleOffset As Integer = 78
   Const oleTypeStart As Integer = 20
   Const oleTypeLength As Integer = 12

   Dim imageBytes() As Byte = CType(currentPhotoCell.Value, Byte())
```

```
    If (imageBytes Is Nothing Or imageBytes.Length = 0) Then Return

    Dim dlg As New SaveFileDialog()
    dlg.AddExtension = True
    dlg.Filter = "GIF|*.gif|BMP|*.bmp|JPG|*.jpg"
    dlg.FilterIndex = 2
    dlg.Title = "Enter a file name for this photo"
    dlg.FileName = "EmployeePhoto.bmp"
    If (System.Windows.Forms.DialogResult.OK <> dlg.ShowDialog()) Then
        Return
    End If

    Dim tempStream As MemoryStream
    Dim type As String = System.Text.Encoding.ASCII.GetString( _
        imageBytes, oleTypeStart, oleTypeLength)
    If (type = "Bitmap Image") Then
        tempStream = New MemoryStream( _
            imageBytes, oleOffset, imageBytes.Length - oleOffset)
    Else
        tempStream = New MemoryStream( _
            imageBytes, 0, imageBytes.Length)
    End If
    Dim bmp As New Bitmap(tempStream)
    bmp.Save(dlg.FileName, ParseImageFormat(dlg.FileName))
End Sub

Public Function ParseImageFormat(ByVal fileName As String) As ImageFormat
    Dim ext As String = Path.GetExtension(fileName).ToLower()
    Select Case ext
        Case "bmp"
            Return ImageFormat.Bmp
        Case "jpg"
        Case "jpeg"
            Return ImageFormat.Jpeg
        Case "gif"
            Return ImageFormat.Gif
        Case Else
            Return ImageFormat.Bmp
    End Select
    Return Nothing
End Function
```

C#

```
private void savePhotoToFileToolStripMenuItem_Click(
      object sender, EventArgs e)
{
    const int oleOffset = 78;
    const int oleTypeStart = 20;
    const int oleTypeLength = 12;

    byte[] imageBytes = (byte[])currentPhotoCell.Value;
    if (imageBytes == null || imageBytes.Length == 0) return;

    SaveFileDialog dlg = new SaveFileDialog();
    dlg.AddExtension = true;
```

```
    dlg.Filter = "GIF|*.gif|BMP|*.bmp|JPG|*.jpg";
    dlg.FilterIndex = 2;
    dlg.Title = "Enter a file name for this photo";
    dlg.FileName = "EmployeePhoto.bmp";
    if (DialogResult.OK != dlg.ShowDialog()) return;

    MemoryStream tempStream;
    string type = System.Text.Encoding.ASCII.GetString(
        imageBytes, oleTypeStart, oleTypeLength);
    if (type == "Bitmap Image")
    {
        tempStream = new MemoryStream(
            imageBytes, oleOffset, imageBytes.Length - oleOffset);
    }
    else
    {
        tempStream = new MemoryStream(
            imageBytes, 0, imageBytes.Length);
    }
    Bitmap bmp = new Bitmap(tempStream);
    bmp.Save(dlg.FileName, ParseImageFormat(dlg.FileName));
}

public ImageFormat ParseImageFormat(string fileName)
{
    string ext = Path.GetExtension(fileName).ToLower();
    switch (ext)
    {
        case "bmp":
            return ImageFormat.Bmp;
        case "jpg":
        case "jpeg":
            return ImageFormat.Jpeg;
        case "gif":
            return ImageFormat.Gif;
        default:
            return ImageFormat.Bmp;
    }
}
```

There is a small problem with the employee photos that are embedded in the *Northwind* database. These photos were originally in a Microsoft Access database, which stored the photos with an OLE header. The OLE header occupies the first 78 bytes of the image byte array. If you want to save these as reuseable images, you need to strip off the OLE header. That's OK, but in the previous section, I showed you how to insert new images that were saved to the database into the *DataGridView* object. This means that some images may have the OLE header, while others don't, so you need a means for determining whether the OLE header exists. As it turns out, bytes 20 through 31 (12 total bytes) will hold the string "Bitmap Image" if the OLE header exists.

With that information, let's see what this code is doing. First, constants are declared that relate to the OLE header information. Next, a byte array variable called *imageBytes* is created to simplify access to the value that is in the *currentPhotoCell*. The *imageBytes* variable is tested to see if it contains an image. If it does not have an image, there is no need to go further.

The code then prompts the user to enter a filename. Notice that you have the option to save the image as a GIF, BMP, or JPG file, even if the image was originally stored in a different format. By the way, the original employee photos are in BMP format.

This code then looks for the "Bitmap Image" string, and if it exists, the OLE header will be stripped by creating a *MemoryStream* object from the *imageBytes*, starting at the OLE header offset.

Finally, a *Bitmap* object is created from the *MemoryStream* object. If the *MemoryStream* object contains a valid image, the Bitmap object will be successfully created in memory. If the *MemoryStream* object does not contain a valid image, or you didn't strip off the OLE header, an *ArgumentException* would be thrown with the message "Parameter is not valid". The Bitmap object is then saved to the file, using the format that you selected. Notice that a helper function was created to get the image format based on the file extension.

Using the *DataGridViewButtonColumn*

The *DataGridViewButtonColumn* supplies a *DataGridViewButtonCell* as a cell template to a row that is being created. The *DataGridViewButtonCell* renders the whole cell as a button. For a given *DataGridViewButtonColumn* object, there is one *DataGridViewButtonCell* object for each *DataGridViewRow* object in the *DataGridView* object. The *CellClick* and *CellContentClick* events fire when the button is clicked.

Using the *DataGridViewLinkColumn*

The *DataGridViewLinkColumn* functions like the *DataGridViewButtonColumn* but looks like a hyperlink instead of a button. It supplies a *DataGridViewLinkCell* as a cell template to a row that is being created. For a given *DataGridViewLinkColumn* object, there is one *DataGridViewLinkCell* object for each *DataGridViewRow* object in the *DataGridView* object. The *CellClick* and *CellContentClick* events fire when the button is clicked.

Using the *DataGridViewComboBoxColumn*

The *DataGridViewComboBoxColumn* supplies a *DataGridViewComboBoxCell* as a cell template to a row that is being created. For a given *DataGridViewComboBoxColumn* object, there is one *DataGridViewComboBoxCell* object for each *DataGridViewRow* object in the *DataGridView* object. The *DataGridViewComboBoxCell* renders the whole cell as a *ComboBox*. You can set the *DisplayStyleForCurrentCellOnly* property to *true*, which causes these cells to render as *TextBox* objects until you select one, and then the cell renders with a *ComboBox* (as shown in Figure 7-9). The *DataGridViewComboBoxColumn* can receive its pick list from another data source if you make assignments to the *DataSource*, *DisplayMember*, and *ValueMember* properties.

The *CellClick* fires every time the user activates the drop-down list; the *CellContentClick* event fires only when the user first clicks in the cell. The *CellValueChanged* event fires if the user changes the contents of the cell and leaves the cell.

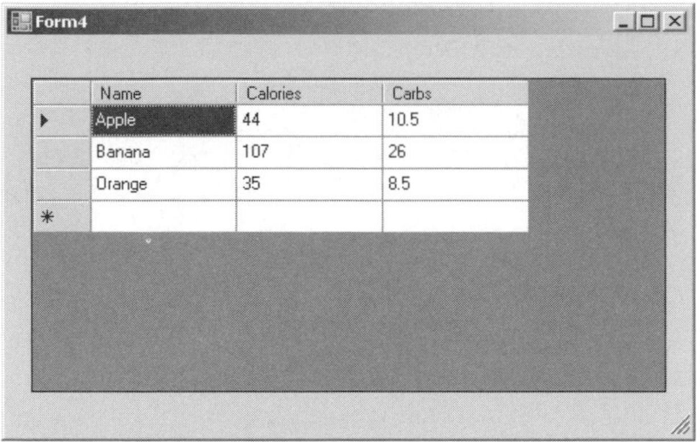

Figure 7-9 The *DisplayStyleForCurrentCellOnly* is set to *false* in the *CustomerID* column and is set to *true* in the *EmployeeID* column.

Working with *DataGridViewRow* Objects

A *DataGridViewRow* object is created for each row of data that needs to be rendered in the *DataGridView* object. Remember that the *DataGridViewRow* object contains a collection of cell objects that inherit from the *DataGridViewCell* class, where each of the columns supplies a cell template that the row clones when the row is created.

Table 7-3 shows the events that are related to the *DataGridViewRow*.

Table 7-3 Row Events on the *DataGridView* Object

Event	Description
AllowUserToAddRowsChanged	The *AllowUserToAddRows* property of the *DataGridView* object has been changed.
AllowUserToDeleteRowsChanged	The *AllowUserToDeleteRows* property of the *DataGridView* object has been changed.
AllowUserToResizeRowsChanged	The *AllowUserToResizeRows* property of the *DataGridView* object has been changed.
AlternatingRowsDefaultCellStyleChanged	The *AlternatingRowsDefaultCellStyle* property of the *DataGridView* object has been changed.
AutoSizeRowsModeChanged	The *AutoSizeRowsMode* property of the *DataGridView* object has been changed.
CancelRowEdit	The row edit is being canceled (fires only if the *DataGridView* object is in virtual mode).
NewRowNeeded	The user has navigated to the new row on the bottom of the *DataGridView* object (fires only if the *DataGridView* object is in virtual mode).

Table 7-3 Row Events on the *DataGridView* Object

Event	Description
RowContextMenuStripChanged	The *ContextMenuStrip* property of the *DataGridView* object has changed.
RowContextMenuStripNeeded	A shortcut menu strip needs to be displayed for the row.
RowDefaultCellStyleChanged	The *DefaultGridViewBand* object's *DefaultCellStyle* property has been changed. This event is typically triggered when the *RowTemplate* of the *DataGridView* object is changed.
RowDirtyStateNeeded	The *DataGridView* object is attempting to determine whether the row has uncommitted changes (fires only if the *DataGridView* is in virtual mode).
RowDividerDoubleClick	The row divider has been double-clicked.
RowDividerHeightChanged	The row divider's height has been changed.
RowEnter	A row gets the focus and becomes the current row.
RowErrorTextChanged	The error text of a row has changed.
RowErrorTextNeeded	The row error text is about to be displayed (fires only if the *DataGridView* object is in virtual mode).
RowHeaderCellChanged	A row object's header cell contents have been changed.
RowHeaderMouseClick	The user has clicked the row header.
RowHeaderMouseDoubleClick	The user has double-clicked the row header.
RowHeaderBorderStyleChanged	The *RowHeaderBorderStyle* property of the *DataGridView* object has been changed.
RowHeaderDefaultCellStyleChanged	The *RowHeaderDefaultCellStyle* property of the *DataGridView* object has been set.
RowHeadersWidthChanged	The *RowHeadersWidth* property of the *DataGridView* object has been changed
RowHeadersWidthSizeModeChanged	The *RowHeadersWidthSizeMode* property of the *DataGridView* object has been changed.
RowHeightChanged	The *Height* property of a *DataGridViewRow* object has been changed.
RowHeightInfoNeeded	The *Height* property of a *DataGridViewRow* has been requested.
RowHeightInfoPushed	The user has changed the height of a row.
RowLeave	The user has left the row, causing the row to lose focus and no longer be the current row.
RowMinimumHeightChanged	The *MinimumHeight* property on a *DataGridViewRow* object has been changed.
RowPostPaint	The row object's cells have been painted.
RowPrePaint	This event fires before any of the row object's cells are painted.

Table 7-3 Row Events on the *DataGridView* Object

Event	Description
RowsAdded	One or more rows have been added to the *DataGridView* object's *Rows* collection.
RowsDefaultCellStyleChanged	The *RowsDefaultCellStyle* property of the *DataGridView* object has been set.
RowsRemoved	One or more rows have been removed from the *DataGridView* object's *Rows* collection.
RowStateChanged	The state of the row has changed, typically to indicate that the row is being displayed.
RowUnshared	The row object's state has been changed from shared to unshared.
RowValidated	The row has been validated.
RowValidating	The row is being validated. This event also allows validation to fail by setting the *Cancel* property of *e* (the *DataGridViewCellCancelEventArgs*) to *true*.
UserAddedRow	The user has added a row.
UserDeletedRow	The user has deleted a row.
UserDeletingRow	The user is attempting to delete a row. The delete can be aborted by setting the *Cancel* property of *e* (the *DataGridViewRowCancelEventArgs*) to *true*.

Implementing Virtual Mode

You can implement virtual mode by setting the *VirtualMode* property of the *DataGridView* object to *true* and implementing event handlers to populate and edit cells as necessary. In a read-only scenario, the only event that needs to be handled is *CellValueNeeded*. Table 7-4 shows the other events that are available for use only when virtual mode is enabled.

Table 7-4 Virtual Mode Events on the *DataGridView* Object

Event	Description
CellValueNeeded	A request has been made for cell data to be displayed from the data cache.
CellValuePushed	Used to commit modified cell data back to the data cache.
NewRowNeeded	A request has been made for row data to be displayed from the data cache.
RowDirtyStateNeeded	A request has been made to retrieve the dirty state of a row from the data cache. A dirty row is a row with uncommitted changes.
CancelRowEdit	A request has been made to roll back changes in the cell to the original data cache values.
RowErrorTextNeeded	A request has been made for row error text. If the error text has changed, be sure to call the *UpdateRowErrorText* method to ensure that the proper error text is displayed in the *DataGridView* object.

To keep this example simple, we will work with a *Fruit* class and a *Fruit* collection. The *Fruit* class is shown in the following code snippet.

Visual Basic

```
Public Class Fruit

   Public Property Name() As String
      Get
         Return _name
      End Get
      Set(ByVal value As String)
         _name = value
      End Set
   End Property
   Private _name As String

   Public Property Calories() As Decimal
      Get
         Return _calories
      End Get
      Set(ByVal value As Decimal)
         _calories = value
      End Set
   End Property
   Private _calories As Decimal

   Public Property Carbs() As Decimal
      Get
         Return _carbs
      End Get
      Set(ByVal value As Decimal)
         _carbs = value
      End Set
   End Property
   Private _carbs As Decimal

   Public Sub New(ByVal name As String,
         ByVal calories As Decimal, _
         ByVal carbs As Decimal)
      Me.Name = name
      Me.Calories = calories
      Me.Carbs = carbs
   End Sub

End Class
```

C#

```
namespace WinFormDataGridView
{
   public class Fruit
   {
      public string Name
      {
         get { return _name; }
         set { _name = value; }
```

```
        }
        private string _name;

        public decimal Calories
        {
           get { return _calories; }
           set { _calories = value; }
        }
        private decimal _calories;

        public decimal Carbs
        {
           get { return _carbs; }
           set { _carbs = value; }
        }
        private decimal _carbs;

        public Fruit(string name, decimal calories, decimal carbs)
        {
           this.Name = name;
           this.Calories = calories;
           this.Carbs = carbs;
        }
     }
  }
```

The following steps are required to implement virtual mode.

1. Add a *DataGridView* object to a Windows form and set its *VirtualMode* property to *true*. Add three *DataGridViewTextBoxColumn* objects for *FruitName*, *Calories*, and *Carbs*. Rather than code this, right-click the *DataGridView* control in Visual Studio's form designer and choose Add Column to configure these settings.
2. Be sure to add the *Fruit* class as shown in the previous code example. Add an instance variable to the form that is a fruit list object. In the form constructor, add code to populate the fruit list. Set the *RowCount* of the *DataGridView* object to the count of items in the fruit list, plus one to provide the ability to add a new row. Lastly, add instance variables to hold a reference to the fruit being edited and its index number.
3. Add an event handler for the *DataGridView* object's *CellValueNeeded* event. This event fires when a cell needs to be painted, and this code populates the grid cell in a just-in-time fashion. What this means is that the *DataGridView* object will request this information when a cell needs to be displayed. This essentially lets the DataGridView object act as a sliding window into your data. The code for these steps is as follows:

   Visual Basic

```
Public Class Form4

   Private fruitList As New List(Of Fruit)
   Private rowInEdit As Integer = -1
   Private fruitInEdit As Fruit = Nothing

   Private Sub Form4_Load(ByVal sender As System.Object, _
         ByVal e As System.EventArgs) Handles MyBase.Load
```

```
        'populate sample data
        fruitList.Add(New Fruit("Apple", 44, 10.5))
        fruitList.Add(New Fruit("Banana", 107, 26))
        fruitList.Add(New Fruit("Orange", 35, 8.5))
        'Add 1 for new row
        DataGridView1.RowCount = fruitList.Count + 1
    End Sub

    'occurs when a cell needs to be painted
    Private Sub DataGridView1_CellValueNeeded(
          ByVal sender As System.Object, _
          ByVal e As _
          System.Windows.Forms.DataGridViewCellValueEventArgs) _
          Handles DataGridView1.CellValueNeeded
        'do not return anything on the "*" row
        If e.RowIndex = DataGridView1.RowCount - 1 Then
            'not needed for new row
            Return
        End If

        Dim tmpFruit As Fruit = Nothing
        ' if the row is being edited
        ' get the fruitInEdit else get
        ' the appropriate fruitList
        ' reference.
        If e.RowIndex = rowInEdit Then
            tmpFruit = Me.fruitInEdit
        Else
            tmpFruit = fruitList(e.RowIndex)
        End If

        ' Set the cell value based on mapping the
        ' column name to the property.
        Select Case Me.DataGridView1.Columns(e.ColumnIndex).Name
            Case "FruitName"
                e.Value = tmpFruit.Name
            Case "Calories"
                e.Value = tmpFruit.Calories
            Case "Carbs"
                e.Value = tmpFruit.Carbs
        End Select
    End Sub

End Class
```

C#

```
using System;
using System.Collections.Generic;
using System.Windows.Forms;

namespace WinFormDataGridView
{
    public partial class Form4 : Form
    {
        private List<Fruit> fruitList = new List<Fruit>();
```

```
        private int rowInEdit = -1;
        private Fruit fruitInEdit = null;

        public Form4()
        {
           InitializeComponent();
        }

        private void Form4_Load(object sender, EventArgs e)
        {
           //populate sample data
           fruitList.Add(new Fruit("Apple", 44M, 10.5M));
           fruitList.Add(new Fruit("Banana", 107M, 26M));
           fruitList.Add(new Fruit("Orange", 35M, 8.5M));
           // Add 1 for new row
           DataGridView1.RowCount = fruitList.Count + 1;
        }

        //occurs when a cell needs to be painted
        private void DataGridView1_CellValueNeeded(object sender,
              DataGridViewCellValueEventArgs e)
        {
           //don't return anything on the "*" row
           if (e.RowIndex == DataGridView1.RowCount - 1)
           {
              // not needed for new row
              return;
           }

           Fruit tmpFruit = null;
           // if the row is being edited
           // get the fruitInEdit else get
           // the appropriate fruitList
           // reference.         if (e.RowIndex == rowInEdit)
           {
              tmpFruit = fruitInEdit;
           }
           else
           {
              tmpFruit = fruitList[e.RowIndex];
           }

           // Set the cell value based on mapping the
           // column name to the property.
           switch (DataGridView1.Columns[e.ColumnIndex].Name)
           {
              case "FruitName":
                 e.Value = tmpFruit.Name; break;
              case "Calories":
                 e.Value = tmpFruit.Calories; break;
              case "Carbs":
                 e.Value = tmpFruit.Carbs; break;
           }
        }
     }
  }
```

With this code entered, the *DataGridView* object can be displayed with its contents, as shown in Figure 7-10. When the *CellValueNeeded* event handler is called, this code will return nothing if the cell to be painted is in the "*" (new) row. If the cell to be painted is in a row that is being edited, the column value from the *fruitInEdit* variable will be returned. If this is a column in a row that is not being edited, the fruit will be retrieved from the *fruitList* collection and its column value will be returned.

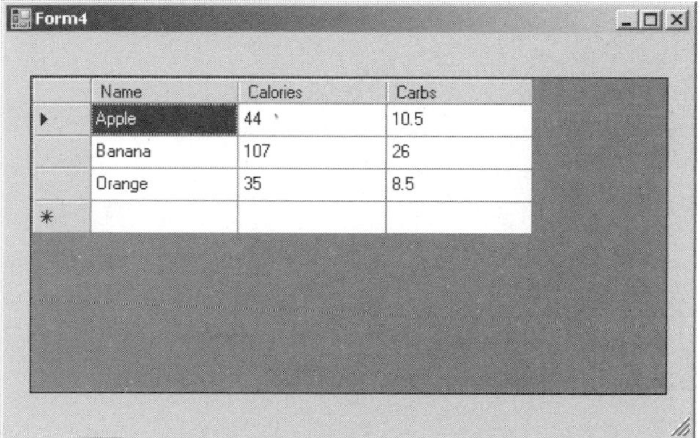

Figure 7-10 The *DataGridView* object was populated using the *CellValueNeeded* event.

The next step is to add code to handle the addition of a new row to the *DataGridView* object. The *NewRowNeeded* event must be implemented to create a new *Fruit* instance when a new row is created in the *DataGridView* object.

Code must also be added to commit cell changes back to the fruit list. This requires implementation of the *CellValuePushed* event and the *RowValidated* event. These events are implemented as shown in the following code snippets:

Visual Basic

```
Private Sub DataGridView1_NewRowNeeded( _
      ByVal sender As System.Object, _
      ByVal e As System.Windows.Forms.DataGridViewRowEventArgs) _
      Handles DataGridView1.NewRowNeeded
   ' Create a new Fruit object when the user
   ' moves the cursor into the "*" row
   fruitInEdit = New Fruit("", 0, 0)
   rowInEdit = DataGridView1.Rows.Count - 1
End Sub

Private Sub DataGridView1_CellValuePushed( _
      ByVal sender As System.Object, _
      ByVal e As _
      System.Windows.Forms.DataGridViewCellValueEventArgs) _
      Handles DataGridView1.CellValuePushed
   Dim tmpFruit As Fruit = Nothing
   ' Store a reference to the Fruit object for the row.
   If e.RowIndex < fruitList.Count Then
      ' If the user has started editing an
```

```
         ' existing row, create a clone to edit.
         If fruitInEdit Is Nothing Then
            fruitInEdit = New Fruit( _
               fruitList(e.RowIndex).Name, _
               fruitList(e.RowIndex).Calories, _
               fruitList(e.RowIndex).Carbs)
         End If
         tmpFruit = fruitInEdit
         rowInEdit = e.RowIndex
      Else
         ' get the row that's being edited
         tmpFruit = fruitInEdit
      End If
      ' Set the appropriate Fruit property to the cell
      ' value entered.
      Dim newValue As String = TryCast(e.Value, String)
      ' Set the appropriate Fruit property to the cell value entered.
      Select Case DataGridView1.Columns(e.ColumnIndex).Name
         Case "FruitName"
            tmpFruit.Name = newValue
         Case "Calories"
            tmpFruit.Calories = decimal.Parse(newValue)
         Case "Carbs"
            tmpFruit.Carbs = decimal.Parse(newValue)
      End Select
   End Sub

   Private Sub DataGridView1_RowValidated( _
         ByVal sender As System.Object, _
         ByVal e As _
         System.Windows.Forms.DataGridViewCellEventArgs) _
         Handles DataGridView1.RowValidated
      ' Save row changes if any were made and
      ' release edited Fruit object.
      If e.RowIndex >= fruitList.Count And _
            e.RowIndex <> DataGridView1.Rows.Count - 1 Then
         ' Add the new fruit object to the data store.
         fruitList.Add(fruitInEdit)
         fruitInEdit = Nothing
         rowInEdit = -1
      ElseIf Not (fruitInEdit Is Nothing) And _
            e.RowIndex < fruitList.Count Then
         ' Overwrite existing Fruit object
         ' with modified fruit.
         fruitList(e.RowIndex) = fruitInEdit
         fruitInEdit = Nothing
         rowInEdit = -1
      Else
         'clear the edit
         fruitInEdit = Nothing
         rowInEdit = -1
      End If
   End Sub
```

C#

```
private void DataGridView1_NewRowNeeded(object sender,
      DataGridViewRowEventArgs e)
{
   // Create a new Fruit object when the user
   // moves the cursor into the "*" row
   fruitInEdit = new Fruit("", 0, 0);
   rowInEdit = DataGridView1.Rows.Count - 1;
}

private void DataGridView1_CellValuePushed(object sender,
      DataGridViewCellValueEventArgs e)
{
   Fruit tmpFruit = null;
   // Store a reference to the Fruit object for the row.
   if (e.RowIndex < fruitList.Count)
   {
      // If the user is editing a new row, create
      // a new Fruit object.
      if (fruitInEdit == null)
      {
         fruitInEdit = new Fruit(
            fruitList[e.RowIndex].Name,
            fruitList[e.RowIndex].Calories,
            fruitList[e.RowIndex].Carbs);
      }
      tmpFruit = fruitInEdit;
      rowInEdit = e.RowIndex;
   }
   else
   {
      tmpFruit = fruitInEdit;
   }
   // Set the appropriate Fruit property to the
   // cell value entered.
   string newValue = e.Value as string;
   switch (DataGridView1.Columns[e.ColumnIndex].Name)
   {
      case "FruitName":
         tmpFruit.Name = newValue; break;
      case "Calories":
         tmpFruit.Calories = decimal.Parse(newValue); break;
      case "Carbs":
         tmpFruit.Carbs = decimal.Parse(newValue); break;
   }
}

private void DataGridView1_RowValidated(object sender,
      DataGridViewCellEventArgs e)
{
   // Save row changes if any were made and
   // release edited Fruit object.
   if (e.RowIndex >= fruitList.Count &&
   e.RowIndex != DataGridView1.Rows.Count - 1)
   {
```

```
      // Add the new fruit object to the data store.
      fruitList.Add(fruitInEdit);
      fruitInEdit = null;
      rowInEdit = -1;
   }
   else if ((fruitInEdit != null) &&
      (e.RowIndex < fruitList.Count))
   {
      // Overwrite existing Fruit object
      // with modified fruit.
      fruitList[e.RowIndex] = fruitInEdit;
      fruitInEdit = null;
      rowInEdit = -1;
   }
   else
   {
      // clear the edit
      fruitInEdit = null;
      rowInEdit = -1;
   }
}
```

The *NewRowNeeded* event handler fires when you move your cursor into the "*" row, which will create an empty *Fruit* object that can be edited.

This *CellValuePushed* event handler fires when you leave a cell, and this handler is responsible for saving a cell value into the appropriate property of the *Fruit* object that is being edited. This code tests to see if you have just started to edit an existing row, and if you have, the existing row is cloned. The clone is copied over the existing *Fruit* object when you leave the row, but if you press the Esc key twice, you will be able to cancel all column edits on the row, and the clone will be discarded without being committed.

The *RowValidated* event handler is used to commit an edited *Fruit* object to the *fruitList* collection. If the edited *Fruit* object was an existing *Fruit* object, the old *Fruit* object is overwritten. If the edited *Fruit* object is a new *Fruit* object, it's added to the *fruitList* collection.

If you run this code, adding rows and editing rows will appear to work, but more work is needed. To be able to delete rows and cancel edits, you must implement the *UserDeletingRow* event and the *CancelRowEdit* event, as shown in the following code.

Visual Basic

```
Private Sub DataGridView1_UserDeletingRow( _
      ByVal sender As System.Object, _
      ByVal e As _
      System.Windows.Forms.DataGridViewRowCancelEventArgs) _
      Handles DataGridView1.UserDeletingRow
   If e.Row.Index < fruitList.Count Then
      ' If the user has deleted an existing row, remove the
      ' corresponding Fruit object from the data cache.
      fruitList.RemoveAt(e.Row.Index)
   End If
   If e.Row.Index = Me.rowInEdit Then
```

```
        ' If the user has deleted a newly created row,
        ' simply release the corresponding Fruit object.
        rowInEdit = -1
        fruitInEdit = Nothing
    End If
End Sub

Private Sub DataGridView1_CancelRowEdit( _
        ByVal sender As System.Object, _
        ByVal e As System.Windows.Forms.QuestionEventArgs) _
        Handles DataGridView1.CancelRowEdit
    If rowInEdit = DataGridView1.Rows.Count - 2 And _
        rowInEdit = fruitList.Count Then
        ' If user canceled the edit of a new row,
        ' replace the corresponding Fruit object
        ' with a new empty Fruit.
        fruitInEdit = New Fruit("", 0, 0)
    Else
        ' If user cancels existing row edit,
        ' release the edited Fuit object.
        fruitInEdit = Nothing
        rowInEdit = -1
    End If
End Sub
```

C#

```
private void DataGridView1_UserDeletingRow(object sender,
    DataGridViewRowCancelEventArgs e)
{
    if (e.Row.Index < fruitList.Count)
    {
        // If the user has deleted an existing row, remove the
        // corresponding Fruit object from the data cache.
        fruitList.RemoveAt(e.Row.Index);
    }
    if (e.Row.Index == rowInEdit)
    {
        // If the user has deleted a newly created row,
        // simply release the corresponding Fruit object.
        rowInEdit = -1;
        fruitInEdit = null;
    }
}

private void DataGridView1_CancelRowEdit(object sender,
    QuestionEventArgs e)
{
    if ((rowInEdit == DataGridView1.Rows.Count - 2) &&
        (rowInEdit == fruitList.Count))
    {
        // If user canceled the edit of a new row,
        // replace the corresponding Fruit object
        // with a new empty Fruit.
        fruitInEdit = new Fruit("", 0, 0);
    }
```

```
    else
    {
        // If user cancels existing row edit,
        // release the edited Fuit object.
        fruitInEdit = null;
        rowInEdit = -1;
    }
}
```

You should now have a functioning *DataGridView* object that has virtual mode enabled and implemented. You might want to implement other events to expand the functionality of this example, but the example should give you a good idea of what is required to get an editable *DataGridView* object to operate in virtual mode.

Summary

- The *DataGridView* object represents a tabular (row-and-column format) display of data.
- *DataGridViewColumn* objects provide a *DataGridViewCell* object template for the *DataGridViewRow* objects.
- You use styles to change the look of the *DataGridView* object. You can assign styles to individual cells, rows, or columns, or to the complete *DataGridView* object.
- The *DataGridView* object has three modes of operation: bound mode, unbound mode, and virtual mode.
- In virtual mode, you can implement just-in-time data loading when large amounts of data need to be available to the user and the user will select the data to be viewed.
- The *DataGridView* object can be bound to a database, Web service, or object.
- Resource usage is minimized by sharing *DataGridViewRow* instances, but you must be careful with the calls that you make in your code because you can cause one or more rows to become unshared.
- The *DataGridView* object provides many events that are related to cells, columns, and rows.

Chapter 8

Working with the Web Data Grid Control

The Web is a collection of interesting but somewhat confusing technologies and innovations that have evolved over the last 20 or so years based on one key requirement: to deliver content in a platform-independent manner. The Web started as simple, platform-independent HTML and grew significantly with the addition of technologies such as JavaScript, Cascading Style Sheets (CSS), and XML. The driving force behind the Web has been that users and developers have expected the same robustness that a regular Windows-based application delivers.

The previous chapter examined the Windows *DataGridView* class in detail. Ideally, we want the *DataGridView* features to also be available in Web-based applications. This chapter examines the Web-based data grid control, the *GridView*. You will see that the *GridView* is more similar to the *DataGridView* than previous Web data grids were to the Windows data grids.

Understanding the *GridView* Control

The *GridView* control is used on Web form applications to display data in a tabular, rows-and-columns format. The *GridView* renders in the browser as an HTML table. Earlier grid controls were difficult to customize without having to dive deep into HTML and JavaScript, but the *GridView* greatly simplifies most customization tasks. The *GridView* even makes it easy to configure features such as paging, sorting, and editing without having to write much code, if any.

The basic structure of the *GridView* is similar to that of the *DataGridView* and is shown in Figure 8-1. The *GridView* object consists of a collection of rows and columns. The *Rows* property consists of a collection of *GridViewRow* objects. Each *GridViewRow* object inherits from the *TableRow* object, which contains a *Cells* collection. The *Cells* collection that the *GridViewRow* inherits is a collection of objects that derive from the *DataControlFieldCell* class. The *Columns* property consists of a collection of objects that inherit from the *DataControlField* class. Although the *GridViewRow* object holds the collection of cells, each *DataControlField* object provides the behavior to initialize cells of a specific type in its *InitializeCell* method. Inherited classes override the *InitializeCell* method. The *GridView* object has an *InitializeRow* method that makes calls to the overridden *InitializeCell* method when the row is being created.

GridView

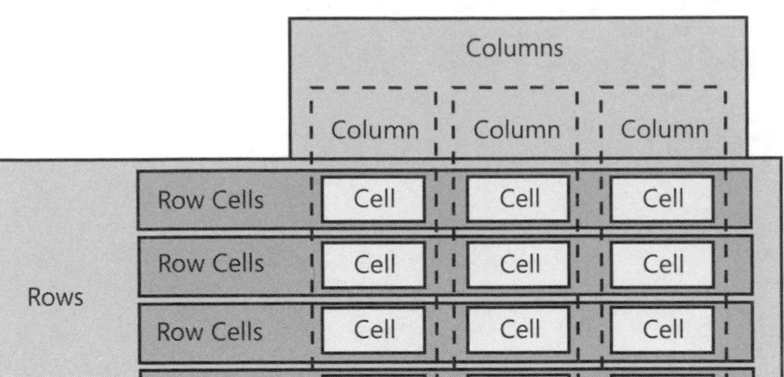

Row = GridView
Column = DataControlField
Cell = DataControlFieldCell

Figure 8-1 The basic structure of the *GridView* consists of a collection of rows and columns.

The *DataControlField* class hierarchy is shown in Figure 8-2. The derived classes are used to create a *DataControlFieldCell* with the proper contents. Remember that you don't define cell types for your *GridView* object, you define column types and your column object supplies a cell object to the row using the *InitializeCell* method.

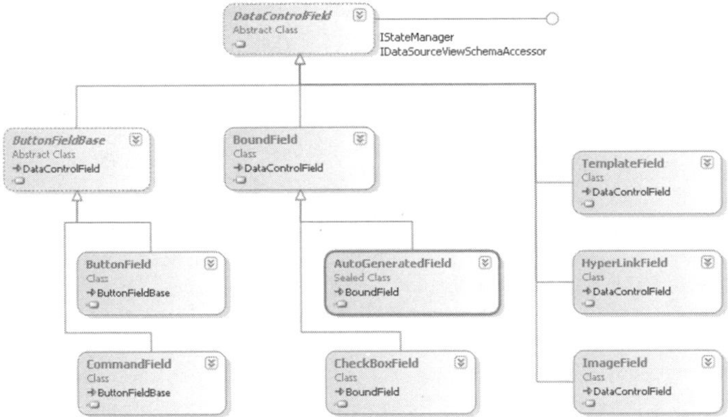

Figure 8-2 The *DataControlField* class hierarchy shows the different column types that are available in a *GridView* object.

Formatting with Styles

You use styles to format the *GridView* object the same way as discussed in the previous chapter for the *DataGridView* object. Figure 8-3 shows the style hierarchy.

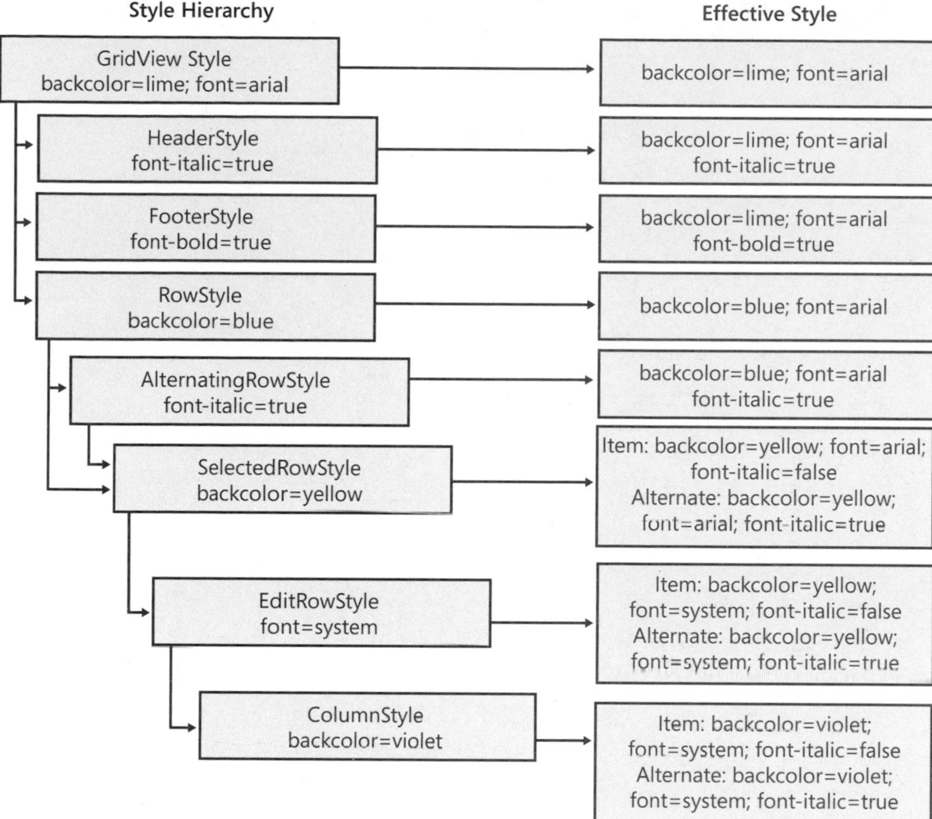

Figure 8-3 The *GridView* object style hierarchy

You can use the *RowCreated* and *RowDataBound* events to control the style programmatically. You can access the *Cells* collection on the newly created row to apply a style to a single cell in the row. The *RowCreated* event takes place first, but the data is not available at this time. Use the *RowDataBound* event when you need to apply a different style to a cell based on the data in the cell. These events fire after the styles have been applied, which means you can override any existing styles. Applying a different style to a cell based on the data in the cell allows you to apply business rules to determine whether a cell should stand out from other cells (such as making a negative "quantity on hand" number red, but only when the item sells more than one per month).

Binding to a Data Source

The *GridView* can be easily bound to a data source at design time. Microsoft Visual Studio reads your data source and populates the columns collection. You can select or create the data source by dragging a *GridView* object to the Web form and then clicking the smart tag arrow on the top right of the *GridView* object to reveal the GridView Tasks window (Figure 8-4). From the Choose Data Source drop-down list, you can select the New Data Source item.

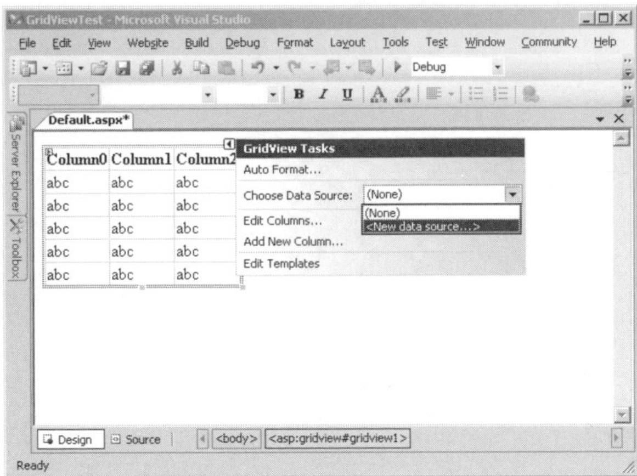

Figure 8-4 The GridView Tasks window, where you can create a new data source that will bind to the *GridView* object

The *GridView* object can bind, or connect, to the following data source types.

- *Microsoft Access database* An Access database file has the .mdb extension.
- *SQL database* You can bind to an ODBC, OLEDB, SQL Server, Oracle, or other database that uses Structured Query Language (SQL). You can even attach a SQL Server database file by simply including it in your project.
- *XML file* You can browse to an XML file in your project folder. You can specify a transform file that can be used to modify the XML file before it is bound to the *GridView* object. You can also provide an XPath expression to retrieve a subset of the data in the XML file.
- *Object* You can choose an object that can be used to bind to a *GridView* object. This connects to a middle-tier business object or *DataSet* object in the *Bin* or *App_Code* directory of your application. When using this option, you can select a class that you have access to, and an instance of the class is created for you when the data is required. In addition to selecting a class, you must choose the methods you want to execute to select, insert, update, and delete. The select method should return a single *DataTable* object or *DataSet* object. If the select method returns a *DataSet* object, the first *DataTable* object in the *DataSet* is used.
- *Sitemap* You can connect to the site navigation tree for your application. This option requires a valid sitemap file at the application root.

The following examples use the Employees table in the *Northwind* database.

GridView Setup

When you work with the *GridView*, you must have a *DataSource* configured. For example, you can add the *Northwind* database to the App_Data folder of your project, drag a *GridView* object to the Web form, and then click the smart tag arrow on the top right of the *GridView* object to reveal the *GridView Tasks* window (as shown earlier in Figure 8-4). From the Choose Data Source drop-down list, you can select the New Data Source item to launch the Data Source Configuration Wizard. Select the Database icon to create a new data source. Change the *DataSource* name from *SqlDataSource1* to *EmployeeList*. You can select the Northwnd.mdf file as the connection. Notice that the connection string is configured to connect to the file, as shown in Figure 8-5.

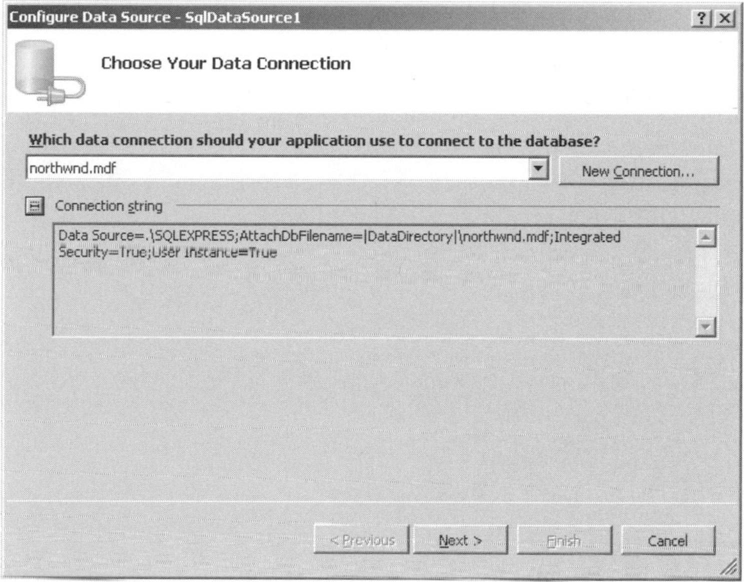

Figure 8-5 The connection string shows that your project will connect to the Northwnd.mdf file in the App_Data folder.

The next wizard page gives you the option of storing the connection string in the application configuration (Web.config) file. Accept the default setting to save the connection string in the Web.config file as a setting called *ConnectionString*.

The next page prompts you for the data you want to retrieve. You will be working with the Employees table and will retrieve a simple subset of columns: *EmployeedID*, *LastName*, *FirstName*, *BirthDate*, and *ReportsTo* (as shown in Figure 8-6). The *Photo* field will be retrieved as a separate query, which I will discuss later in this chapter.

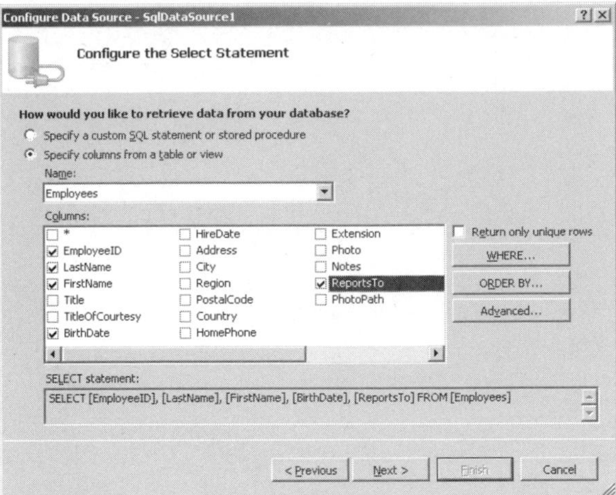

Figure 8-6 Retrieving a subset of columns in the Employees table

This page also contains an Advanced button, which displays an option to automatically generate insert, update, and delete statements that match the select statement, and an option to use optimistic concurrency. For this example, select the first option only, as shown in Figure 8-7, but note that in a production environment you should always use stored procedures instead of the generated statements.

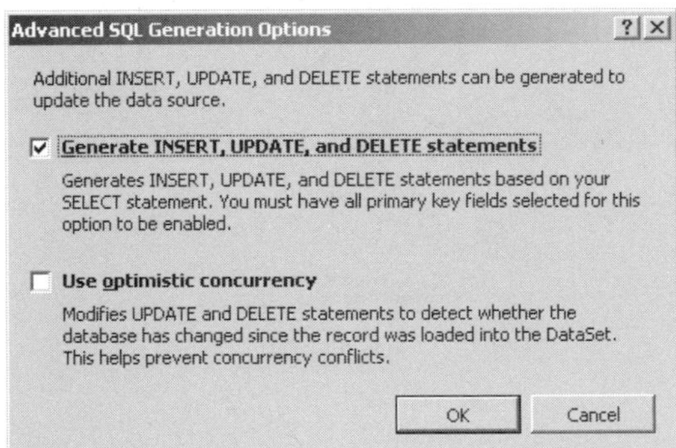

Figure 8-7 You can select both options to create INSERT, UPDATE, and DELETE statements using optimistic concurrency.

The last page of the Configure Data Source Wizard allows you to test your query to verify that you are retrieving the correct data. After you test the query, you can click Finish to complete the configuration.

Notice that adding a database to the project and configuring the data source for the *GridView* object did not automatically create a typed *DataSet* class in your project. The data source was created to operate with stateless controls on the current Web page, so you did not need to provide the extra functionality of a typed or untyped *DataSet* object. If you want to use typed or untyped *DataSet* objects, you should use the *ObjectDataSource* option. The *ObjectDataSource* option lets you select a class in your project and then prompts you to choose a method to be executed to select, insert, update, or delete data. The select method can return a *DataSet*, a *DataTable*, a *DataReader*, or a typed collection.

When the *GridView* was dropped onto the Web form and the data source was configured, the GridView Tasks window was displayed to give you access to some of the common tasks for setting up the *GridView* object quickly (Figure 8-8). In this example, we selected all of the options and used the Auto Format option to select the Brown Sugar theme. We set the column headers to *ID*, *Last Name*, *First Name*, *Birth Date*, and *Reports To* by using the Edit Columns option in the GridView Tasks window.

Note If you don't have the ability to enable editing and deleting in the GridView Tasks window, you probably did not configure the data source to generate insert, update, and delete statements.

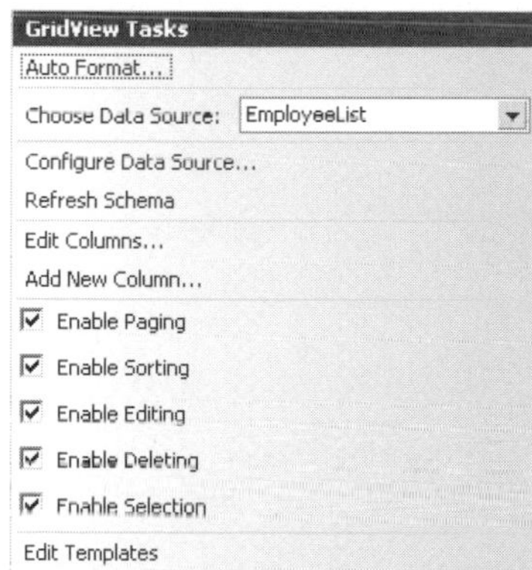

Figure 8-8 The options for the *GridView* object in the GridView Tasks window

In the Properties window for the *GridView* object, change the *PageSize* property from the default value of 10 to 3. You wouldn't be able to see the paging options with the default setting of 10 because the Employees table has only 9 rows.

After configuring the *GridView* object, you can press the F5 key to build and run the project. You can tell that paging is enabled because page numbers are displayed at the bottom of the *GridView* object. Because sorting is also enabled, the column headers are displayed as links that you can click to sort in ascending order or descending order.

If you click the Select link, the *SelectedRow* style is applied and you see a highlighted row. If you click the Edit link on a row, you see edit controls in any columns that can be modified. Figure 8-9 shows the *GridView* object with row 2 selected; row 3 is in edit mode.

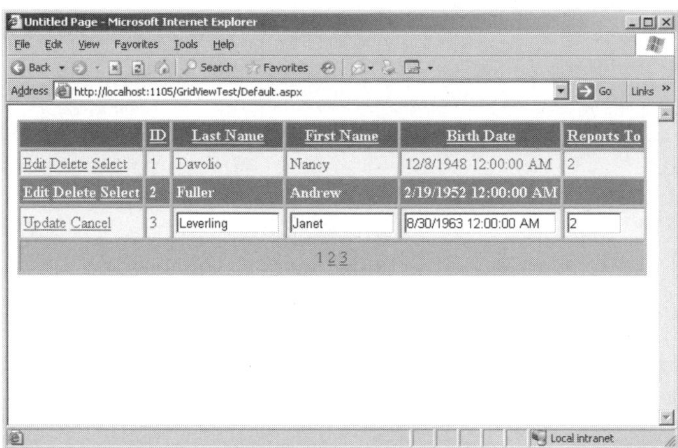

Figure 8-9 The configured *GridView* object with paging and sorting enabled

As you can see, the selected row and the row being edited are independent of each other. This might be a feature, but in most cases you will probably want these to be tied together; you can accomplish this by adding a bit of code to the *RowEditing* event handler, as shown in the following code snippet.

Visual Basic

```
Protected Sub GridView1_RowEditing( _
      ByVal sender As Object, _
      ByVal e As System.Web.UI.WebControls.GridViewEditEventArgs) _
      Handles GridView1.RowEditing
   GridView1.SelectedIndex = e.NewEditIndex
End Sub
```

C#

```
protected void GridView1_RowEditing(
   object sender, GridViewEditEventArgs e)
{
   GridView1.SelectedIndex = e.NewEditIndex;
}
```

When the Edit link is clicked on the *GridView* object, this code assigns the index of the line being edited to the *SelectedIndex* property of the *GridView* object. This results in the edited row being selected, as shown in Figure 8-10.

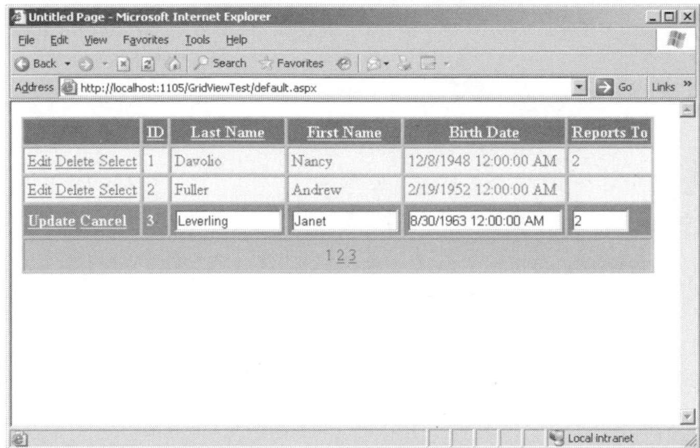

Figure 8-10 With a bit of code, the edited row is now selected when the Edit link is clicked.

Viewing the Declarative Markup in the HTML Source

Declarative markup is the HTML-like source that is inserted into the aspx page when the *GridView* object is dragged to the Web form. You can see this by clicking the Source tab of the Web form. You can configure the *GridView* object by typing the declarative markup directly into the body of the HTML source. The following declarative markup represents the *GridView* object that you created in this chapter.

GridView Object's Declarative Markup

```
<asp:GridView ID="GridView1" runat="server" AllowPaging="True"
      AllowSorting="True" AutoGenerateColumns="False"
      BackColor="#DEBA84" BorderColor="#DEBA84"
      BorderStyle="None" BorderWidth="1px" CellPadding="3"
      CellSpacing="2" DataKeyNames="EmployeeID"
      DataSourceID="EmployeeList"
      OnRowEditing="GridView1_RowEditing" PageSize="3">
   <FooterStyle BackColor="#F7DFB5" ForeColor="#8C4510" />
   <Columns>
      <asp:CommandField ShowDeleteButton="True"
            ShowEditButton="True" ShowSelectButton="True" />
      <asp:BoundField DataField="EmployeeID"
            HeaderText="ID" InsertVisible="False" ReadOnly="True"
            SortExpression="EmployeeID" />
      <asp:BoundField DataField="LastName"
            HeaderText="Last Name" SortExpression="LastName">
         <ControlStyle Width="100px" />
      </asp:BoundField>
      <asp:BoundField DataField="FirstName"
            HeaderText="First Name" SortExpression="FirstName">
         <ControlStyle Width="100px" />
      </asp:BoundField>
      <asp:BoundField DataField="BirthDate"
            HeaderText="Birth Date" SortExpression="BirthDate">
         <ControlStyle Width="150px" />
```

```
        </asp:BoundField>
        <asp:BoundField DataField="ReportsTo"
            HeaderText="Reports To" SortExpression="ReportsTo">
            <ControlStyle Width="50px" />
        </asp:BoundField>
    </Columns>
    <RowStyle BackColor="#FFF7E7" ForeColor="#8C4510" />
    <SelectedRowStyle BackColor="#738A9C"
            Font-Bold="True" ForeColor="White" />
    <PagerStyle ForeColor="#8C4510"
            HorizontalAlign="Center" />
    <HeaderStyle BackColor="#A55129"
            Font-Bold="True" ForeColor="White" />
</asp:GridView>
```

Notice that the *<asp:GridView>* tag contains many general settings, such as the data source and *GridView* style settings. This tag also contains the wiring of events to their event handler methods, such as the *RowEditing* event that was configured earlier.

Between the *<asp:GridView>* and *</asp:GridView>* tags are settings for the rows and columns. The footer, which is a row, has a style setting. After that, you see the columns collection. Finally, you see the other row styles, including the selected row style, the pager style, and the header style.

The columns collection is defined between the *<asp:Columns>* and *</asp:Columns>* tags. The first column is a *CommandField* object, and the rest of the columns are *BoundField* objects.

When the *GridView* object was configured, a new *SqlDataSource* was created called *EmployeeList*. The declarative markup for the *SqlDataSource* is shown in the following snippet.

SqlDataSource Object's Declarative Markup

```
<asp:SqlDataSource ID="EmployeeList" runat="server"
    ConnectionString="<%$ ConnectionStrings:ConnectionString %>"
    DeleteCommand="DELETE FROM [Employees]
        WHERE [EmployeeID] = @original_EmployeeID"
    InsertCommand="INSERT INTO [Employees] ([LastName],
        [FirstName], [BirthDate], [ReportsTo])
        VALUES (@LastName, @FirstName, @BirthDate, @ReportsTo)"
    OldValuesParameterFormatString="original_{0}"
    SelectCommand="SELECT [EmployeeID], [LastName],
        [FirstName], [BirthDate], [ReportsTo] FROM [Employees]"
    UpdateCommand="UPDATE [Employees] SET [LastName] = @LastName,
        [FirstName] = @FirstName, [BirthDate] = @BirthDate,
        [ReportsTo] = @ReportsTo
        WHERE [EmployeeID] = @original_EmployeeID">
    <DeleteParameters>
        <asp:Parameter Name="original_EmployeeID" Type="Int32" />
    </DeleteParameters>
    <UpdateParameters>
        <asp:Parameter Name="LastName" Type="String" />
        <asp:Parameter Name="FirstName" Type="String" />
```

```
        <asp:Parameter Name="BirthDate" Type="DateTime" />
        <asp:Parameter Name="ReportsTo" Type="Int32" />
        <asp:Parameter Name="original_EmployeeID" Type="Int32" />
    </UpdateParameters>
    <InsertParameters>
        <asp:Parameter Name="LastName" Type="String" />
        <asp:Parameter Name="FirstName" Type="String" />
        <asp:Parameter Name="BirthDate" Type="DateTime" />
        <asp:Parameter Name="ReportsTo" Type="Int32" />
    </InsertParameters>
</asp:SqlDataSource>
```

Notice that the *<asp:SqlDataSource>* tag contains the connection string and the SQL command information. Between the *<asp:SqlDataSource>* and *</asp:SqlDataSource>* tags are the parameters for the commands, each represented as a collection of parameters for each command.

Creating the *GridView* Object Programmatically

You have seen how to drag and drop the *GridView* object onto a Web form. You have also seen how you can create the *GridView* object by typing the declarative markup into the source window of the Web form. You can also create the *GridView* object at runtime in the code-behind file (as you can all other Web parts). In the following example, you add a new Web form to the project called Default2.aspx and add the following code to the code-behind page to create the *GridView* object and the *SqlDataSource* object. Note that you don't add anything to the Default.aspx file.

Visual Basic

```
Imports System.Drawing

Partial Class Default2
   Inherits System.Web.UI.Page

   Dim WithEvents GridView1 As New GridView()
   Dim EmployeeList As New SqlDataSource()

   Protected Sub Page_Init(ByVal sender As Object, _
         ByVal e As System.EventArgs) Handles Me.Init
      With GridView1
         .ID = "GridView1"
         .AllowPaging = True
         .AllowSorting = True
         .AutoGenerateColumns = False
         .BackColor = Color.FromArgb(&HDE, &HBA, &H84)
         .BorderColor = Color.FromArgb(&HDE, &HBA, &H84)
         .BorderStyle = BorderStyle.None
         .BorderWidth = New Unit("1px")
         .CellPadding = 3
         .CellSpacing = 3
         .DataKeyNames = New String() {"EmployeeID"}
         .DataSourceID = "EmployeeList"
```

```
.PageSize = 3
.RowStyle.BackColor = Color.FromArgb(&hFF, &hF7, &hE7)
.RowStyle.ForeColor = Color.FromArgb(&h8C, &h45, &h10)
.SelectedRowStyle.BackColor = Color.FromArgb(&h73, &h8A, &h9C)
.SelectedRowStyle.Font.Bold = True
.SelectedRowStyle.ForeColor = Color.White
.PagerStyle.ForeColor = Color.FromArgb(&h8C, &h45, &h10)
.PagerStyle.HorizontalAlign = HorizontalAlign.Center
.HeaderStyle.BackColor = Color.FromArgb(&hA5, &h51, &h29)
.HeaderStyle.Font.Bold=True
.HeaderStyle.ForeColor = Color.White
AddHandler .RowEditing, _
   New GridViewEditEventHandler(AddressOf GridView1_RowEditing)
Dim cmdColumn As New CommandField()
With cmdColumn
   .ShowDeleteButton = True
   .ShowEditButton = True
   .ShowSelectButton = True
End With
.Columns.Add(cmdColumn)
Dim bndColumn As New BoundField()
With bndColumn
   .DataField = "EmployeeID"
   .HeaderText = "ID"
   .InsertVisible = False
   .ReadOnly = True
   .SortExpression = "EmployeeID"
End With
.Columns.Add(bndColumn)
bndColumn = New BoundField()
With bndColumn
   .DataField = "LastName"
   .HeaderText = "Last Name"
   .SortExpression = "LastName"
   .ControlStyle.Width = New Unit("100px")
End With
.Columns.Add(bndColumn)
bndColumn = New BoundField()
With bndColumn
   .DataField = "FirstName"
   .HeaderText = "First Name"
   .SortExpression = "FirstName"
End With
.Columns.Add(bndColumn)
bndColumn = New BoundField()
With bndColumn
   .DataField = "BirthDate"
   .HeaderText = "Birth Date"
   .SortExpression = "BirthDate"
   .ControlStyle.Width = New Unit("150px")
End With
.Columns.Add(bndColumn)
bndColumn = New BoundField()
With bndColumn
   .DataField = "ReportsTo"
```

```
            .HeaderText = "Reports To"
            .SortExpression = "ReportsTo"
            .ControlStyle.Width = New Unit("50px")
        End With
        .Columns.Add(bndColumn)
    End With

    With EmployeeList
        .ID = "EmployeeList"
        .ConnectionString = _
            ConfigurationManager.ConnectionStrings("ConnectionString").ToString()
        .SelectCommand = "SELECT [EmployeeID], [LastName], [FirstName], " _
            + "[BirthDate], [ReportsTo] FROM [Employees]"
        .InsertCommand = "INSERT INTO [Employees] ([LastName], " _
            + "[FirstName], [BirthDate], [ReportsTo]) " _
            + "VALUES (@LastName, @FirstName, @BirthDate, @ReportsTo)"
        .UpdateCommand = "UPDATE [Employees] SET [LastName] = @LastName, " _
            + "[FirstName] = @FirstName, [BirthDate] = @BirthDate, " _
            + "[ReportsTo] = @ReportsTo " _
            + "WHERE [EmployeeID] = @original_EmployeeID"
        .DeleteCommand = "DELETE FROM [Employees] " _
            + "WHERE [EmployeeID] = @original_EmployeeID"
        .OldValuesParameterFormatString = "original_{0}"
        .DeleteParameters.Add( _
            New Parameter("original_EmployeeID",System.TypeCode.Int32))
        .UpdateParameters.Add( _
            New Parameter("LastName",System.TypeCode.String))
        .UpdateParameters.Add( _
            New Parameter("FirstName",System.TypeCode.String))
        .UpdateParameters.Add( _
            New Parameter("BirthDate",System.TypeCode.DateTime))
        .UpdateParameters.Add( _
            New Parameter("ReportsTo",System.TypeCode.Int32))
        .UpdateParameters.Add( _
            New Parameter("original_EmployeeID",System.TypeCode.Int32))
        .InsertParameters.Add( _
            New Parameter("LastName",System.TypeCode.String))
        .InsertParameters.Add( _
            New Parameter("FirstName",System.TypeCode.String))
        .InsertParameters.Add( _
            New Parameter("BirthDate",System.TypeCode.DateTime))
        .InsertParameters.Add( _
            New Parameter("ReportsTo",System.TypeCode.Int32))
    End With

    Dim frm As Control = Me.FindControl("form1")
    frm.Controls.Add(EmployeeList)
    frm.Controls.Add(GridView1)

End Sub

Protected Sub GridView1_RowEditing( _
        ByVal sender As Object, _
        ByVal e As System.Web.UI.WebControls.GridViewEditEventArgs) _
        Handles GridView1.RowEditing
```

```
      GridView1.SelectedIndex = e.NewEditIndex
   End Sub

End Class
```

C#

```
using System.Web.UI.WebControls;
using System.Drawing;
using System.Configuration;
using System.Web.UI;

public partial class Default2 : System.Web.UI.Page
{
   GridView GridView1 = new GridView();
   SqlDataSource EmployeeList = new SqlDataSource();

   protected void Page_Init(object sender, System.EventArgs e)
   {
      GridView1.ID = "GridView1";
      GridView1.AllowPaging = true;
      GridView1.AllowSorting = true;
      GridView1.AutoGenerateColumns = false;
      GridView1.BackColor = Color.FromArgb(0xDE, 0xBA, 0x84);
      GridView1.BorderColor = Color.FromArgb(0xDE, 0xBA, 0x84);
      GridView1.BorderStyle = BorderStyle.None;
      GridView1.BorderWidth = new Unit("1px");
      GridView1.CellPadding = 3;
      GridView1.CellSpacing = 3;
      GridView1.DataKeyNames = new string[] { "EmployeeID" };
      GridView1.DataSourceID = "EmployeeList";
      GridView1.PageSize = 3;
      GridView1.RowStyle.BackColor = Color.FromArgb(0xFF, 0xF7, 0xE7);
      GridView1.RowStyle.ForeColor = Color.FromArgb(0x8C, 0x45, 0x10);
      GridView1.SelectedRowStyle.BackColor
         = Color.FromArgb(0x73, 0x8A, 0x9C);
      GridView1.SelectedRowStyle.Font.Bold = true;
      GridView1.SelectedRowStyle.ForeColor = Color.White;
      GridView1.PagerStyle.ForeColor = Color.FromArgb(0x8C, 0x45, 0x10);
      GridView1.PagerStyle.HorizontalAlign = HorizontalAlign.Center;
      GridView1.HeaderStyle.BackColor = Color.FromArgb(0xA5, 0x51, 0x29);
      GridView1.HeaderStyle.Font.Bold = true;
      GridView1.HeaderStyle.ForeColor = Color.White;
      GridView1.RowEditing +=
         new GridViewEditEventHandler(GridView1_RowEditing);
      CommandField cmdColumn = new CommandField();
      cmdColumn.ShowDeleteButton = true;
      cmdColumn.ShowEditButton = true;
      cmdColumn.ShowSelectButton = true;
      GridView1.Columns.Add(cmdColumn);
      BoundField bndColumn = new BoundField();
      bndColumn.DataField = "EmployeeID";
      bndColumn.HeaderText = "ID";
      bndColumn.InsertVisible = false;
      bndColumn.ReadOnly = true;
      bndColumn.SortExpression = "EmployeeID";
```

```
GridView1.Columns.Add(bndColumn);
bndColumn = new BoundField();
bndColumn.DataField = "LastName";
bndColumn.HeaderText = "Last Name";
bndColumn.SortExpression = "LastName";
bndColumn.ControlStyle.Width = new Unit("100px");
GridView1.Columns.Add(bndColumn);
bndColumn = new BoundField();
bndColumn.DataField = "FirstName";
bndColumn.HeaderText = "First Name";
bndColumn.SortExpression = "FirstName";
GridView1.Columns.Add(bndColumn);
bndColumn = new BoundField();
bndColumn.DataField = "BirthDate";
bndColumn.HeaderText = "Birth Date";
bndColumn.SortExpression = "BirthDate";
bndColumn.ControlStyle.Width = new Unit("150px");
GridView1.Columns.Add(bndColumn);
bndColumn = new BoundField();
bndColumn.DataField = "ReportsTo";
bndColumn.HeaderText = "Reports To";
bndColumn.SortExpression = "ReportsTo";
bndColumn.ControlStyle.Width = new Unit("50px");
GridView1.Columns.Add(bndColumn);
EmployeeList.ID = "EmployeeList";
EmployeeList.ConnectionString =
   ConfigurationManager.ConnectionStrings["ConnectionString"].ToString();
EmployeeList.SelectCommand = "SELECT [EmployeeID], [LastName], "
   + "[FirstName], [BirthDate], [ReportsTo] FROM [Employees]";
EmployeeList.InsertCommand = "INSERT INTO [Employees] ([LastName], "
   + "[FirstName], [BirthDate], [ReportsTo]) "
   + "VALUES (@LastName, @FirstName, @BirthDate, @ReportsTo)";
EmployeeList.UpdateCommand = "UPDATE [Employees] "
   + "SET [LastName] = @LastName, "
   + "[FirstName] = @FirstName, [BirthDate] = @BirthDate, "
   + "[ReportsTo] = @ReportsTo "
   + "WHERE [EmployeeID] = @original_EmployeeID";
EmployeeList.DeleteCommand = "DELETE FROM [Employees] "
   + "WHERE [EmployeeID] = @original_EmployeeID";
EmployeeList.OldValuesParameterFormatString = "original_{0}";
EmployeeList.DeleteParameters.Add(
   new Parameter("original_EmployeeID", System.TypeCode.Int32));
EmployeeList.UpdateParameters.Add(
   new Parameter("LastName", System.TypeCode.String));
EmployeeList.UpdateParameters.Add(
   new Parameter("FirstName", System.TypeCode.String));
EmployeeList.UpdateParameters.Add(
   new Parameter("BirthDate", System.TypeCode.DateTime));
EmployeeList.UpdateParameters.Add(
   new Parameter("ReportsTo", System.TypeCode.Int32));
EmployeeList.UpdateParameters.Add(
   new Parameter("original_EmployeeID", System.TypeCode.Int32));
EmployeeList.InsertParameters.Add(
   new Parameter("LastName", System.TypeCode.String));
EmployeeList.InsertParameters.Add(
```

```
            new Parameter("FirstName", System.TypeCode.String));
        EmployeeList.InsertParameters.Add(
            new Parameter("BirthDate", System.TypeCode.DateTime));
        EmployeeList.InsertParameters.Add(
            new Parameter("ReportsTo", System.TypeCode.Int32));

        Control frm = this.FindControl("form1");
        frm.Controls.Add(EmployeeList);
        frm.Controls.Add(GridView1);
    }

    protected void GridView1_RowEditing(
        object sender, GridViewEditEventArgs e)
    {
        System.Diagnostics.Debug.WriteLine("GridView1_RowEditing");
        GridView1.SelectedIndex = e.NewEditIndex;
    }

}
```

This code looks straightforward: the *GridView* object named *GridView1* and the *SqlDataSource* object named *EmployeeList* are created as instance fields. You use the *Page_Init* event handler to initialize the properties of both objects. Finally, you add the *EmployeeList* and *GridView1* objects to the Web form by placing the objects into the *Controls* collection. But notice that you can't simply place the objects into the Web form object's *Controls* collection. Instead, you have to search for the *form1* object and put the controls into this object's *Controls* collection because these objects, which are *WebControl* objects, must be placed within a *form* element that is configured with the *runat="server"* attribute. The name of the default *form* element is *form1*, as shown in the following snippet of source HTML from Default2.aspx file.

HTML Source

```
<html xmlns="http://www.w3.org/1999/xhtml" >
<head runat="server">
    <title>Untitled Page</title>
</head>
<body>
    <form id="form1" runat="server">
    <div>

    </div>
    </form>
</body>
</html>
```

Working with the *GridView* Object Events

The *GridView* object has significantly fewer events than the Windows *DataGridView* object, but they allow you to accomplish most tasks. (See Table 8-1.)

Table 8-1 Events on the *GridView* Object

Event	Description
DataBinding	The *GridView* object's data binding expressions are to be evaluated.
DataBound	The *GridView* object has been data bound.
Disposed	The *GridView* object has been disposed.
Init	The *GridView* object has been initialized.
Load	The *GridView* object has been loaded.
PageIndexChanged	The current page index on the *GridView* object has changed.
PageIndexChanging	The current page index on the *GridView* object is going to change.
PreRender	The *GridView* object is about to be rendered.
RowCancelingEdit	The Cancel link has been clicked by the user to cancel editing of a row.
RowCommand	An event has taken place within the row.
RowCreated	A row has been created.
RowDataBound	A row has been data bound.
RowDeleted	The row has been deleted.
RowDeleting	The Delete link has been clicked by the user and the row is about to be deleted.
RowEditing	The Edit link has been clicked by the user.
RowUpdated	The Update link has been clicked by the user and the row has been updated.
Row Updating	The Update link has been clicked by the user and the row is about to be updated.
SelectedIndexChanged	The Select link has been clicked by the user and the index of the selected row has been changed.
SelectedIndexChanging	The Select link has been clicked by the user and the index of the selected row is about to be changed.
Sorted	The user clicked a column header sort link and the sort has completed.
Sorting	The user clicked a column header sort link and the sort is about to begin.
Unloaded	The *GridView* object has been unloaded.

You can use any of the *GridView* object's events by clicking the *GridView* object and then clicking the event lightning bolt in the Properties window (Figure 8-11). You can add event handler stub code for any of the events by simply double-clicking an event.

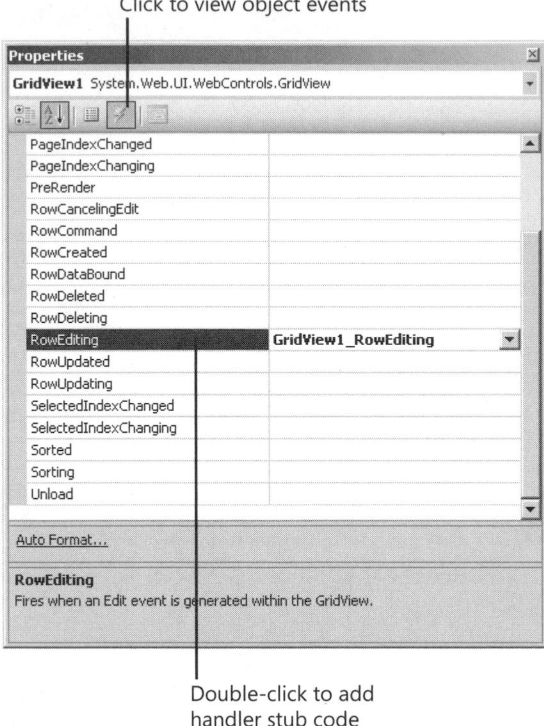

Figure 8-11 *GridView* object events

Event Sequence

It's always helpful to understand which events will be triggered when a Web page is loaded. The following *GridView* events take place when this sample project is run, which causes the Default2.aspx page to be loaded and sent to the browser.

1. *Init*
2. *Load*
3. *DataBinding*
4. *RowCreated*
5. *RowDataBound*
6. *RowCreated*
7. *RowDataBound*
8. *RowCreated*
9. *RowDataBound*
10. *RowCreated*

11. *RowDataBound*
12. *RowCreated*
13. *RowDataBound*
14. *RowCreated*
15. *RowDataBound*
16. *DataBound*
17. *PreRender*
18. *Unload*

Notice that single events fire for *Init*, *Load*, and *DataBinding*. After that, *RowCreated* and *RowDataBound* events fire for each row that is being created. Why did these events fire six times when only three rows are being displayed per page? In addition to the three rows of data that are being displayed, this pair of events fires for the header row, the footer row, and the pager row. These events give you access to the current row and its *Cells* collection. Be sure to use the *RowDataBound* event if you need to access the data in the cells, because the data is not yet available in the *RowCreated* event.

The last events to fire are the *DataBound*, *PreRender*, and *Unload* events. All of the data in the *GridView* object is available when the *DataBound* event fires. The *PreRender* event can be used for "last-minute" style changes based on business rules. This is the last event that fires before the *GridView* object is displayed. The *UnLoad* event can be used to clean up resources that are no longer required.

After the *GridView* object has been displayed, if the user clicks one of the links on a row, such as Edit, the following events are fired.

1. *Init*
2. *RowCreated*
3. *RowCreated*
4. *RowCreated*
5. *RowCreated*
6. *RowCreated*
7. *RowCreated*
8. *Load*
9. *RowCommand*
10. *SelectedIndexChanging*
11. *SelectedIndexChanged*

12. *PreRender*
13. *Unload*

Notice that the *RowCreated* events for all of the rows fire before the *Load* event. This means that the row objects are created so you can access them in the *Load* event handler. The *Row-Command* event fires for any of the row events, which allows you to examine the event and act on it. The *SelectedIndexChanging* event fires before the selected index is changed; the event arguments contain a *Cancel* property that can be set to true, which aborts the changing of the selected index. The *SelectedIndexChanged* event fires after the selected index has changed.

Working with Column Objects

The *GridView* object has a *Columns* collection, which contains objects that inherit from the *DataControlField* class. The .NET Framework contains several column types, and you can also create your own column types. Figure 8-6, shown earlier, depicts the *DataControlField* class hierarchy, which shows the available column types.

Editing the Column List

The Visual Studio *GridView* designer lets you add and remove columns by choosing Edit Columns in the GridView Task window, which displays the Fields dialog box (Figure 8-12). This dialog box is also used to access the properties of each column. For example, you can configure the first column, which is a *CommandField* object, to show a header, and you can set the header text.

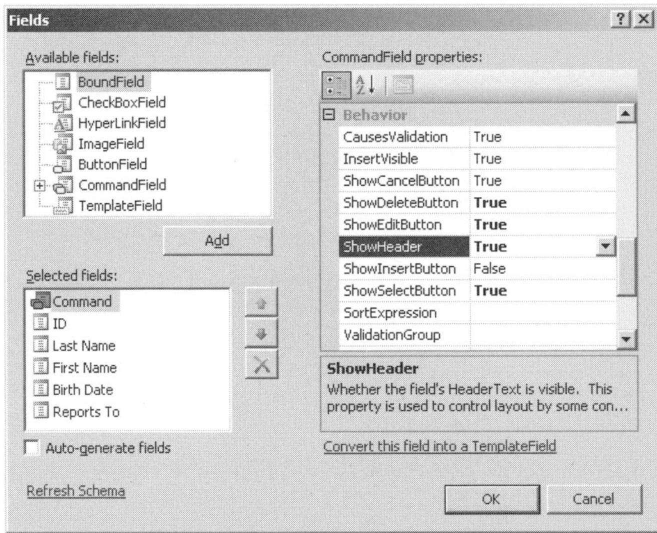

Figure 8-12 Choosing Edit Columns in the GridView Task menu displays the Fields dialog box, where you can add and remove columns as well as configure the column style and behavior.

You can also populate the columns collection at runtime using your own code, as shown previously in this chapter.

Working with Column Templates

You'll often want a column with different behavior than the available column types provide. For example, the Employees table contains a *ReportsTo* field, which contains the ID of the employee's boss. Wouldn't it be better to display the boss's name? In fact, wouldn't it be nice to be able to select the boss's name from a *DropDownList* object when the employee is in edit mode?

You could create a new column type by inheriting from the *DataControlField* class or one of its subclasses. This would work if you were creating the columns through code, but the *GridView* designer would not recognize your new column. A simpler approach is to use a template column. By default, a template column has no user interface–it simply provides the framework that the *GridView* object needs to create repeating rows. You have the flexibility of placing any declarative markup within each cell, which means you can include HTML, DHTML, server controls, and ASP.NET data binding code in the template.

You could create the template column by selecting the *TemplateField* object from the Available Fields list when you add columns to the *GridView* object. You can also create a template column by selecting an existing column and clicking the Convert This Field Into A TemplateField link, as shown in Figure 8-13.

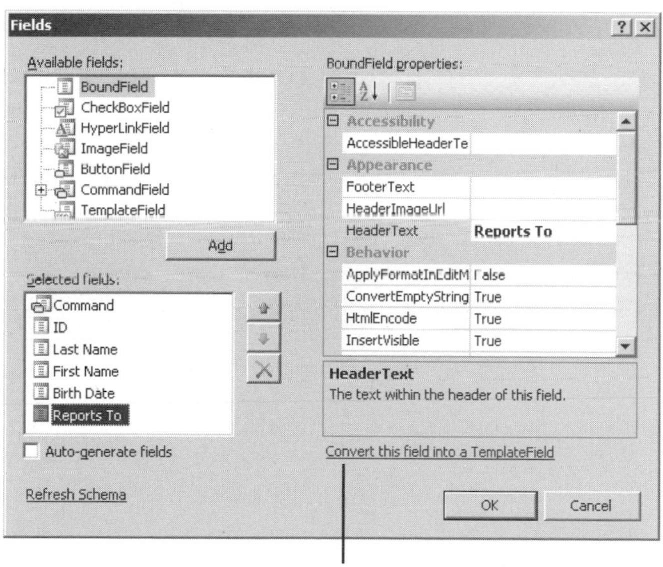

Figure 8-13 Click the Convert This Field Into A TemplateField link to create a template column that can be modified.

After a field has been converted to a template, you can edit the template by clicking the Edit Templates link in the GridView Tasks window. The *TemplateField* object can consist of any of the following templates.

- *HeaderTemplate* Renders as a cell at the top of the column.
- *FooterTemplate* Renders as a cell at the bottom of the column.
- *ItemTemplate* Repetitively renders cells for each row of data.
- *AlternatingItemTemplate* Repetitively renders cells for every other row of data.
- *EditItemTemplate* Renders for a cell that is in edit mode.

All of these templates are optional, but remember that if you don't supply an *ItemTemplate*, nothing will be rendered in the data cells. The good news is that when you convert a field to a template, the *ItemTemplate* will contain a default value. There is more information on modifying the template later. In addition to the preceding templates for a *TemplateField* object, you can provide the following templates for a *GridView* object.

- *EmptyDataTemplate* Renders instead of the *GridView* object where there is no data to be displayed. Previous versions of Web-based data grid controls were simply invisible when there was no data, which sometimes caused confusion because you didn't know if there was an error on the page or if there simply wasn't any data to be displayed.
- *PagerTemplate* Renders when you have paging enabled.

Converting the *ReportsTo* Column to a *TemplateField* Column

Before you convert the *ReportsTo* column to a *TemplateField* column that will normally display the boss's name but that in edit mode will provide a *DropDownList* object that you can use to select the boss, you need to set up one thing: a new *SqlDataSource* object that will contain the data you will use in this column. Drag a new *SqlDataSource* object to the Web form. Change its *ID* property to *ReportsToList*.

> **Note** This conversion will be done on the Default.aspx page, so you should verify that Default.aspx is set as your startup page.

Configure the data source by selecting the same connection string that the *EmployeeList* has, which was called *ConnectionString*. Instead of selecting the Employees table with its fields, select to use a custom query because the *ReportsTo* field can have a null value, and we want this to be displayed as "[Unassigned]". Use the following query to get the list of employee IDs and names, along with an extra row for unassigned.

ReportsToList Select Query

```
SELECT EmployeeID, LastName + ', ' + FirstName as Name FROM EMPLOYEES
UNION
SELECT null,'[Unassigned]'
ORDER BY Name ASC
```

Notice that this query returns only two columns: *ID* and *Name*. The name column comprises the last name, a comma and space, and then the first name. This format will work nicely in the *Label* object or *DropDownList* object that will be displayed. Because this list is read-only, there is no need for an insert, update, or delete query. On the next screen, you can test the query to see if you get the expected results.

OK, it's time to convert the *ReportsTo* column to a *TemplateField* column. Select the *ReportsTo* column in the Selected Fields list of the Fields dialog box, click the link shown earlier in Figure 8-13 to perform the conversion, and then click OK. The column is converted and you see the GridView Tasks window, which has a link at the bottom called Edit Templates. Click the link to see the available templates. Figure 8-14 shows the *ItemTemplate* for the *ReportsTo* column; it contains a simple *Label* control, but notice that the Display drop-down list includes all templates that can be edited.

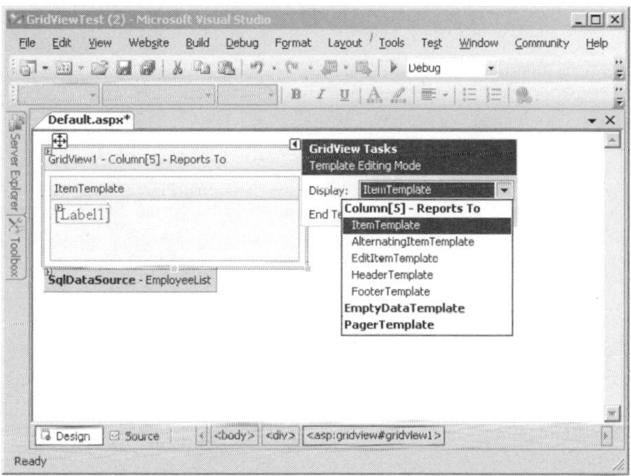

Figure 8-14 The templates that can be edited in this *GridView* object

If you click the *Label* object's smart tag, you will see that you can edit the data bindings for this control. The *Label* control has its *Text* property bound to the *ReportsTo* field. Instead of binding directly to the *ReportsTo* field, this expression will be replaced with a Custom Binding Code Expression that will pass the current *ID* of the boss to a method that you will use to look up the boss's name in the *ReportsToList* data source. Replace the binding with the following code snippet (which works with Visual Basic and C#), as shown in Figure 8-15.

```
GetReportsToName(Eval("ReportsTo"))
```

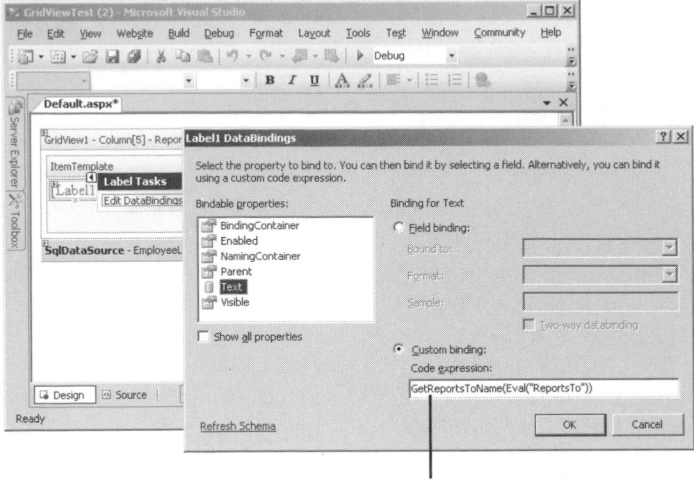

Figure 8-15 The data bindings can be edited for each control.

Next you'll create the *GetReportsToName* method, which can be added to the code-behind page.

Visual Basic

```
Public Function GetReportsToName(ByVal reportsToId As Object) As String
   For Each row As DataRowView In _
         ReportsToList.Select(DataSourceSelectArguments.Empty)
      If (reportsToId.Equals(row("EmployeeID"))) Then
         Return row("Name").ToString()
      End If
   Next
   Throw New ArgumentException("Employee with ID: " _
      + reportsToId.ToString() + " does not exist.")
End Function
```

C#

```
public string GetReportsToName(object reportsToId)
{
   foreach(DataRowView row in
      ReportsToList.Select(DataSourceSelectArguments.Empty))
   {
      if (reportsToId.Equals(row["EmployeeID"]))
      {
         return row["Name"].ToString();
      }
   }
   throw new ArgumentException( "Employee with ID: "
      + reportsToId.ToString() + " does not exist.");
}
```

This code executes the *Select* statement in the data source, which does not require any parameters. Next the code loops through the list of employees until an employee with a matching *ID* is found. If no match is found, an *ArgumentException* is thrown.

If you build and run the project, you will find that the bosses' names now appear instead of their IDs. Also notice that Andrew Fuller has no boss, so this shows as unassigned. What happens if you click the Edit link on one of the employees? Figure 8-16 shows that the editing template is still configured to allow you to edit the *ReportsTo* based on the ID number. This must be changed to a drop-down list of employee names.

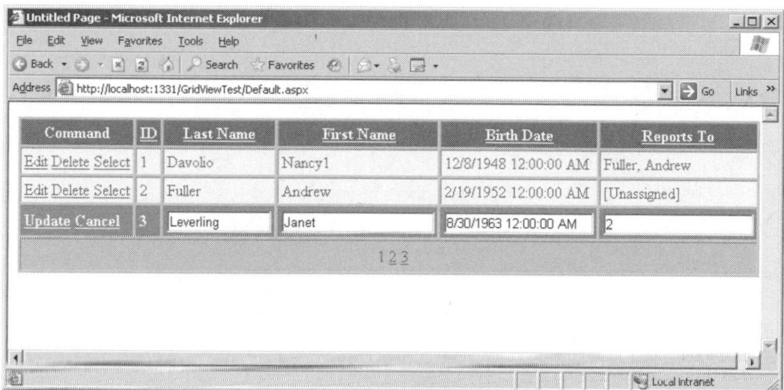

Figure 8-16 The list of employees now shows the boss's name, except when the Edit link is clicked.

If you look at the *EditItemTemplate* for the *ReportsTo* field, you will see that this template contains a *TextBox* control that is also bound to the *ReportsTo* field. You can see that this is the template that will be rendered for a cell that is in a row that is being edited. Delete the *TextBox* control and add a *DropDownList* control. Resize the *DropDownList* object to 150 pixels to make room for the name to be displayed.

Click the Choose DataSource link in the DropDownList Tasks window to connect the *DropDownList* to the *ReportsToList* data source that you created. Select the *Name* field to be displayed and select the *EmployeeID* field as the value field, as shown in Figure 8-17.

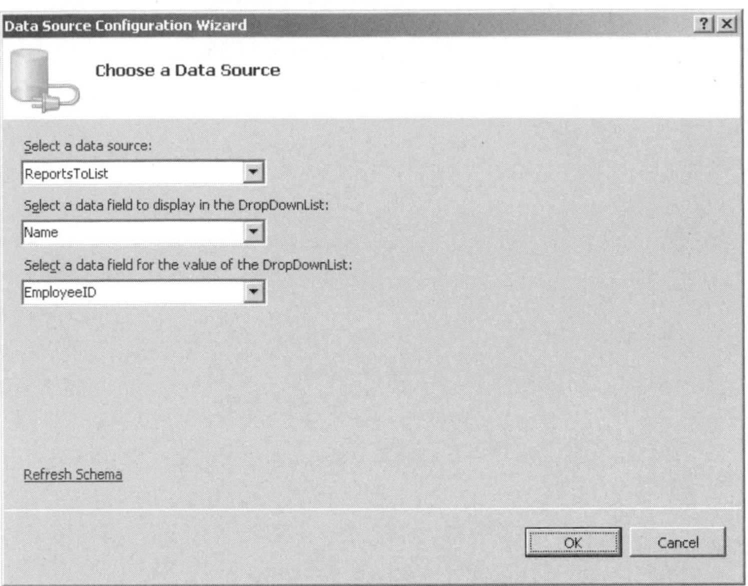

Figure 8-17 Set the *DataSource* of the *DropDownList* to the *ReportsToList* that you previously created, and configure the field to be displayed and the field to be used as the value.

Click the Edit DataBindings link and set the *SelectedValue* property to the *ReportsTo* field, as shown in Figure 8-18. If the Field Binding option is disabled, you might need to click the Refresh Schema link at the bottom of the form. Binding the value to this field causes the *ReportsTo* field to update with the correct *ID* when a different employee is selected. Further, when the cell is edited, it gets the proper name based on the current *ReportsTo* value.

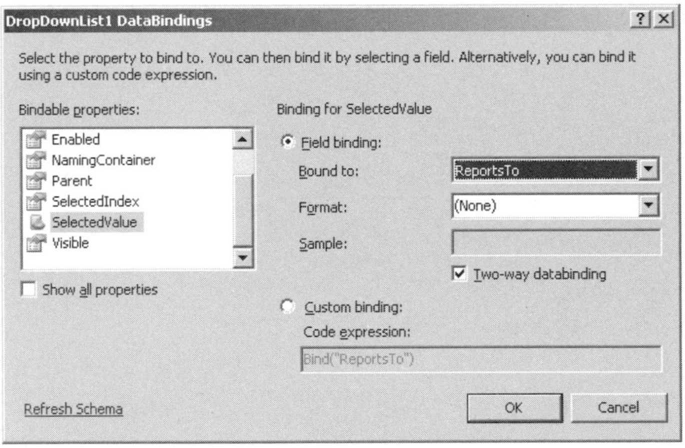

Figure 8-18 Binding the *SelectedValue* property of the *DropDownList* object to the *ReportsTo* field

If you build and run the project, you will see that when you edit an employee, the *ReportsTo* cell becomes a *DropDownList* object that is populated with the employee names and the correct boss is displayed. Figure 8-19 shows the browser window with the completed conversion of a *BoundField* column to a *TemplateField* column. Notice that you can set any employee's boss to unassigned, which puts a null value into the *ReportsTo* field.

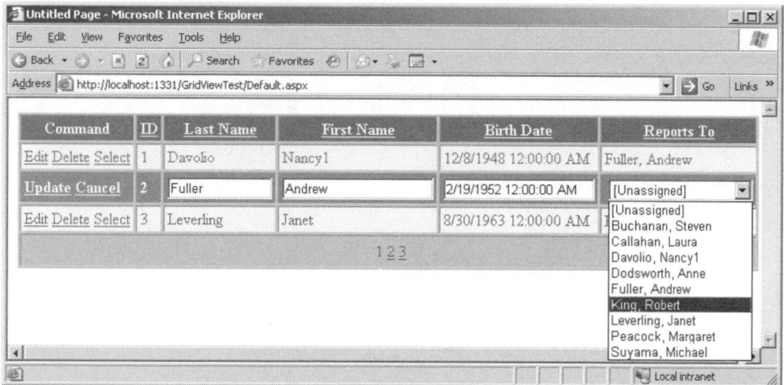

Figure 8-19 The completed conversion of a *BoundField* column to a *TemplateField* column

Displaying a Calendar Control for the *BirthDate* You have seen how to convert a *BoundField* column to a *TemplateField* column and how to use a *DropDownList* to display the employee names from a different data source. You can also convert the *BirthDate* field to use a *Calendar* control when in edit mode. You simply convert the *BirthDate* column from a *BoundField* to a *TemplateField*, and then replace the *TextBox* in the *EditItemTemplate* with a *Calendar* control.

In the data binding properties, you must set up two bindings. The first item to bind is the *SelectedDate* to the *BirthDate* field. Be sure that the Two-Way Databinding option is selected, to ensure that the *BirthDate* is updated when a new date is selected. The second item to bind is the *VisibleDate* to the *BirthDate* field. The Two-Way Databinding option should not be selected because the *Calendar* control will simply read the *BirthDate* into the *VisibleDate* property to ensure that the *BirthDate* is initially displayed when the row is edited.

Before running the project, you might also want to change the format of the *Label* control when the birth date is displayed normally (that is, not in edit mode). Edit the *ItemTemplate*, and edit the data bindings for the *Label* control. The *Text* property is bound to the *BirthDate* field; set its *Format* property to *Short date - {0:d}*.

If you build and run the project, you will see that the birth dates that are shown in a *Label* control when not editing appear with the correct formatting, but if a row is edited, you will be prompted with a *Calendar* control for selecting the date (Figure 8-20).

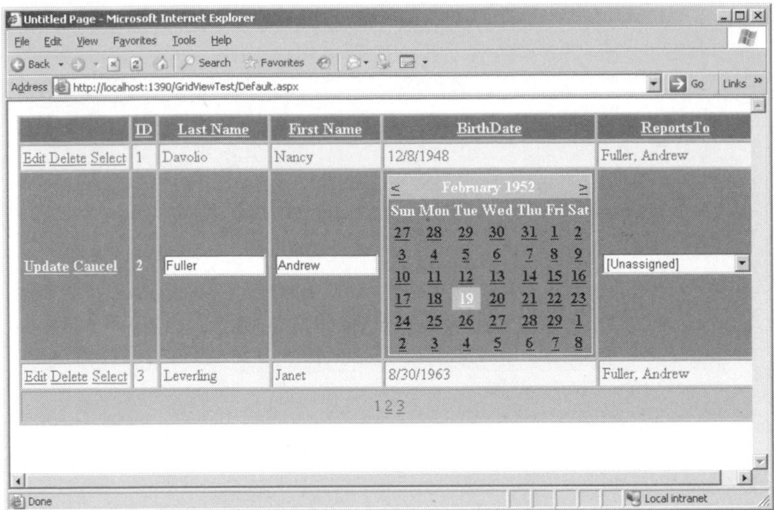

Figure 8-20 The *BirthDate* field has been converted to a *TemplateField*, and a *Calendar* control is displayed when a row is edited.

Retrieving and Displaying Images with the *ImageField* Column

The *ImageField* column can be used to display images and icons in the *GridView* object. The *ImageField* renders as an HTML <*IMG*> element in each cell, and you must provide the URL to each image that is to be displayed. Theoretically, you could bind to the *PhotoPath* field in the Employees table, but if you look at the URLs that are currently in the *PhotoPath* field, you will see that they point to a location that is not available. For example, Nancy Davolio's photo is located at the following URL, which is a LAN address.

```
http://accweb/employees/davolio.bmp
```

If you want to change the URLs and use this field, add the *PhotoPath* field to your *EmployeeList Select* statement and bind the *PhotoPath* field to the *DataImageUrlField* property, and you're done.

But how can you bind to the images that are embedded in the *Photo* field of the Employees table? This is a bit more challenging, but before I cover this, you need a clear understanding of the <*IMG*> element.

A user-requested Web page typically contains HTML content, which might also include <*IMG SRC="MyImage1.gif"*> elements. When the browser encounters the image element, it knows that the content isn't included in the Web page being received; it's in a different file, which must be retrieved in order to display the image. Figure 8-21 shows an example of the requests and responses between the browser and the Web server.

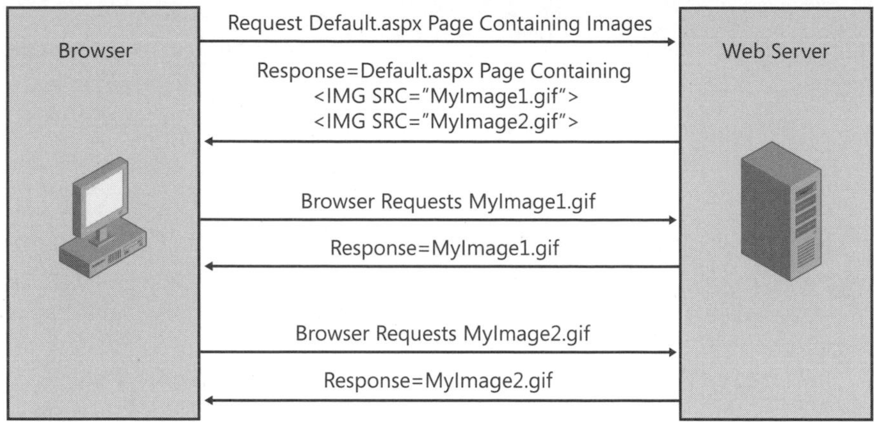

Figure 8-21 The typical communication between the browser and Web server, which is accomplished by a series of requests from the browser and responses from the server

As discussed earlier, the source (SRC) of the image element is typically a file, such as MyImage1.gif, but it doesn't have to be a file. The source can be set to a handler that locates the requested image and responds with the image. You can create a simple handler by adding another Web form to the project that has no HTML content, but the code-behind page retrieves the image from the *Photo* field in the Employees table and places the image into the response stream to the browser. You might think of this page as a sort of "image engine" for this project. The query string can contain the employee's *ID* of the image to be retrieved, and the image engine will locate and respond with the correct image, as shown in Figure 8-22.

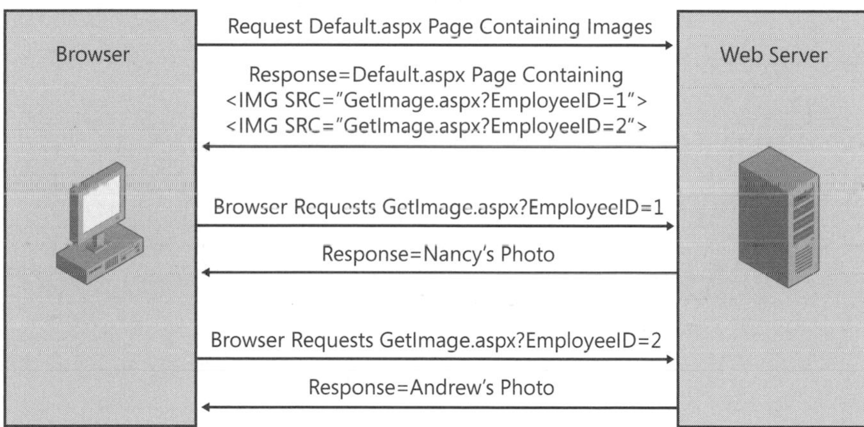

Figure 8-22 In this scenario, the URLs of the images are the same, but the *QueryString* is different for each image.

Creating the image engine has many advantages, which become more apparent as more graphics are added to the site. The advantages include:

- *Logging* All requests for images can be logged. This can be beneficial when the image is of an advertisement and you want to record how many times each advertisement is displayed.
- *Sizing* All images can be sized the same, usually to a thumbnail, and the browser will display the smaller image. Downsizing lowers the bandwidth requirements, but you can also add links to see the full-size image.
- *Storage* The images don't have to be stored on the file system. If they are stored in the database, the database can be easily moved as a unit, ensuring a consistent backup. Think of the situation in which the *PhotoPath* field points to a URL that is not accessible. Storing the image in the database solves this problem.

Building the Image Engine You should note a couple of things about the images stored in the *Photo* field of the Employees table. First, the images are in BMP format, so they are not considered compatible with the Web, which has standardized on formats such as GIF and JPG. The images must therefore be converted before they are sent to the browser. Second, the images were embedded into the database using Microsoft Access, which placed an OLE header on these files. This header occupies the first 78 bytes. The header must be stripped off before the image is usable. The image engine can handle both these problems.

You can build an image engine by adding a Web form to the project, called GetImage.aspx. In the code-behind page, add the following code.

Visual Basic

```
Imports System.IO
Imports System.Drawing
Imports System.Drawing.Imaging
Imports System.Data.SqlClient

Partial Class GetImage
   Inherits System.Web.UI.Page

   Protected Sub Page_Load(ByVal sender As Object, _
      ByVal e As System.EventArgs) Handles Me.Load
      Const oleOffset As Integer = 78
      Const oleTypeStart As Integer = 20
      Const oleTypeLength As Integer = 12
      Dim EmployeeID As String
      Dim sql As String
      Dim bmp As Bitmap
      Dim imageBytes() As Byte
      EmployeeID = CType(Me.Request.QueryString("EmployeeID"), String)
      If (EmployeeID Is Nothing) Then Return
      'eliminate injection threat
      EmployeeID = Integer.Parse(EmployeeID).ToString()
      sql = "Select Photo from Employees where EmployeeID=" + EmployeeID
      Dim cnSettings As ConnectionStringSettings = _
          ConfigurationManager.ConnectionStrings("ConnectionString")
      Using cn As New SqlConnection(cnSettings.ConnectionString)
         Using cmd As New SqlCommand(sql, cn)
```

```
            cn.Open()
            Using dr As SqlDataReader = cmd.ExecuteReader()
               dr.Read()
               imageBytes = CType(dr.GetValue(0), Byte())
            End Using
         End Using
      End Using
      If (imageBytes Is Nothing Or imageBytes.Length = 0) Then Return
      Dim tempStream As MemoryStream
      Dim type As String = System.Text.Encoding.ASCII.GetString( _
         imageBytes, oleTypeStart, oleTypeLength)
      If type = "Bitmap Image" Then
         tempStream = New MemoryStream(imageBytes, oleOffset, _
         imageBytes.Length - oleOffset)
      Else
         tempStream = New MemoryStream(imageBytes, 0, _
         imageBytes.Length)
      End If
      bmp = New Bitmap(tempStream)
      'if you want to resize the photos, uncomment next line and tweak...
      'bmp = New Bitmap(bmp, bmp.Height / 2, bmp.Width / 2)
      Response.ContentType = "image/gif"
      bmp.Save(Response.OutputStream, ImageFormat.Gif)
      Response.End()
   End Sub
End Class
```

C#

```
using System;
using System.Configuration;
using System.Web;
using System.Drawing;
using System.Data.SqlClient;
using System.IO;
using System.Drawing.Imaging;

public partial class GetImage : System.Web.UI.Page
{
   protected void Page_Load(object sender, EventArgs e)
   {
      const int oleOffset = 78;
      const int oleTypeStart = 20;
      const int oleTypeLength = 12;
      string EmployeeID;
      string sql;
      Bitmap bmp;
      byte[] imageBytes;
      EmployeeID = (string)this.Request.QueryString["EmployeeID"];
      if (EmployeeID == null) return;
      //eliminate injection threat
      EmployeeID = int.Parse(EmployeeID).ToString();
      sql = "Select Photo from Employees where EmployeeID=" + EmployeeID;
      ConnectionStringSettings cnSettings =
          ConfigurationManager.ConnectionStrings["ConnectionString"];
      using (SqlConnection cn =
```

```
            new SqlConnection(cnSettings.ConnectionString))
        {
            using (SqlCommand cmd = new SqlCommand(sql, cn))
            {
                cn.Open();
                using (SqlDataReader dr = cmd.ExecuteReader())
                {
                    dr.Read();
                    imageBytes = (byte[])dr.GetValue(0);
                }
            }
        }
        if (imageBytes == null || imageBytes.Length == 0) return;
        MemoryStream tempStream;
        string type = System.Text.Encoding.ASCII.GetString(
            imageBytes, oleTypeStart, oleTypeLength);
        if (type == "Bitmap Image")
        {
            tempStream = new MemoryStream(
                imageBytes, oleOffset, imageBytes.Length - oleOffset);
        }
        else
        {
            tempStream = new MemoryStream(
                imageBytes, 0, imageBytes.Length);
        }
        bmp = new Bitmap(tempStream);
        //if you want to resize the photos, uncomment next line and tweak...
        //bmp = new Bitmap(bmp, bmp.Height / 2, bmp.Width / 2);
        Response.ContentType = "image/gif";
        bmp.Save(Response.OutputStream, ImageFormat.Gif);
        Response.End();
    }
}
```

This code retrieves the *EmployeeID* from the *QueryString*. In some cases, the *EmployeeID* might be null or nothing, so a check is made to see if the code should continue.

Next, to make sure the *ID* does not have any invalid characters, we parse (convert) the *ID* to a numeric value and then convert it back to a string. If the *ID* has non-numeric characters, an exception is thrown. This also eliminates potential SQL injection attacks, which are caused when a hacker adds malicious code after the ID number that is showing in the browser's address.

You then use the *ID* to create a SQL query that will retrieve the *Photo* that matches the employee's *ID*. A connection is opened, and the command is executed, returning a byte array containing the image bytes.

Next we convert the byte array to a *MemoryStream* object and do a test to see if an OLE header exists by looking at the bytes, starting at offset 20, to see if they contain "Bitmap Image". If so, we strip off the OLE header by specifying that the stream start reading the byte array at offset 78.

The *MemoryStream* object can be passed into the Bitmap object's constructor, and the image is finally rendered in memory. Notice the comment on the subsequent line that shows how you can resize the bitmap as well.

Finally, you save the *Bitmap* to the *Response* object's *OutputStream*. By setting the content type to *image/gif*, the *Bitmap* object is converted to GIF format. Then you close the *Response* object's *OutputStream*.

Adding the *ImageField* Column to Display the Photos Now that you have done the prep work, you can add the *ImageField* column to the *GridView* object. Add the *ImageField* column and set its properties as shown in the following table.

ImageField Property	Setting
HeaderText	*Photo*
DataImageUrlField	*EmployeeID*
DataImageUrlFormatString	*GetImage.aspx?EmployeeID={0}*

Notice that the binding is set to the *EmployeeID* because that is what is being used to retrieve the photo. The *EmployeeID* is fed into the format string, replacing the placeholder. After you set the properties, build and run the project. You should see the photos of each employee as shown in Figure 8-23.

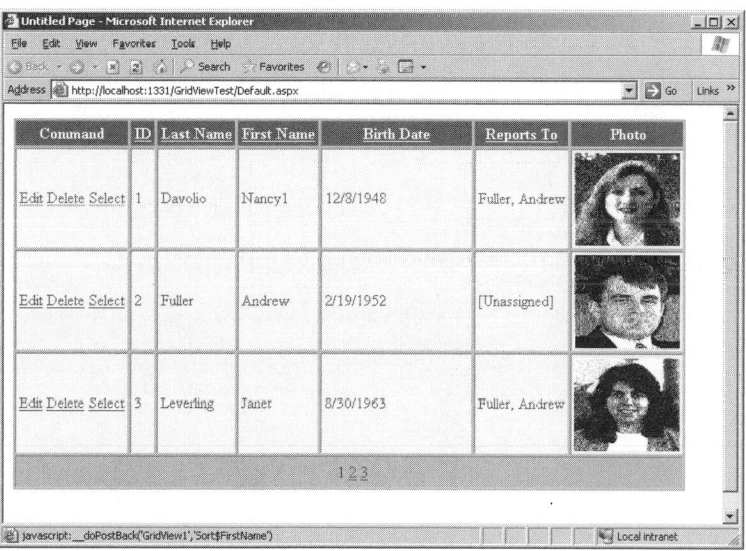

Figure 8-23 Retrieving the photos from the *Photo* field in the Employees table by using the GetImage.aspx Web form

Uploading New Employee Photos You have seen how to add the *ImageField* to the *GridView* object, but if you attempt to edit one of the rows, you will see a *TextBox* that contains the *EmployeeID* value. This serves little purpose. One option is to set the *ReadOnly* property of the

ImageField to *true*, which causes the employee's photo to be displayed while you are in edit mode. A better option is to convert the *ImageField* to a *TemplateField* and place a *FileUpload* control into the *EditItemTemplate*; this gives you the ability to upload new photos. Let's do that.

First convert the *ImageField* to a *TemplateField*. Remove the *TextBox* control from the *EditItemTemplate* and add a *FileUpload* control. Change the *ID* property of the *FileUpload* control from *FileUpload1* to *PhotoUpload*. Changing the *ID* property makes it easy to access the control later. Figure 8-24 shows what the *FileUpload* control looks like when it's rendered.

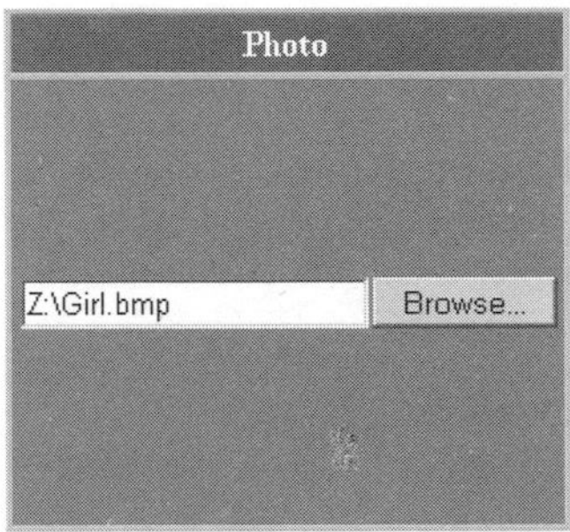

Figure 8-24 You can use the *FileUpload* control either to type the filename or to locate the file to be uploaded by clicking the Browse button.

Next add code to handle the uploaded file. When the file is uploaded to the Web server, it becomes available as a stream that can be sent directly to the database. This requires a bit of code, some of which is placed into the *RowUpdated* event handler; the rest is placed into a new method called *UpdatePhoto*. Create the *RowUpdated* event handler, and add the following code.

Visual Basic

```
Protected Sub GridView1_RowUpdated(ByVal sender As Object, _
      ByVal e As System.Web.UI.WebControls.GridViewUpdatedEventArgs) _
      Handles GridView1.RowUpdated
   Dim gridView As GridView = CType(sender, GridView)
   Dim employeeId As Integer = e.Keys("EmployeeID")
   Dim photoFile As FileUpload = _
      CType(gridView.Rows(gridView.EditIndex).FindControl("PhotoUpload"), _
      FileUpload)
   UpdatePhoto(employeeId, photoFile)
End Sub

Public Sub UpdatePhoto(ByVal employeeId As Integer, _
      ByVal photoFile As FileUpload)
   If (photoFile Is Nothing) Or (photoFile.HasFile = False) Then Return
   Dim imageStream As Stream = photoFile.PostedFile.InputStream
   Dim imageLength As Integer = photoFile.PostedFile.ContentLength
   Dim imageType As String = photoFile.PostedFile.ContentType
   Dim mStream As New MemoryStream()
   Dim imageData(1024) As Byte
   Dim count As Integer = 0
```

```
    count = imageStream.Read(imageData, 0, imageData.Length)
    While (0 < count)
       mStream.Write(imageData, 0, count)
       count = imageStream.Read(imageData, 0, imageData.Length)
    End While
    Dim cnSettings As ConnectionStringSettings = _
          ConfigurationManager.ConnectionStrings("ConnectionString")
    Using cn As New SqlConnection(cnSettings.ConnectionString)
       Using cmd As New SqlCommand()
          cmd.CommandText = _
             "Update Employees Set Photo = @Photo " + _
             "WHERE EmployeeID = @EmployeeID"
          Dim parm As New SqlParameter()
          parm.ParameterName = "@EmployeeID"
          parm.Value = employeeId
          cmd.Parameters.Add(parm)
          parm = New SqlParameter()
          parm.ParameterName = "@Photo"
          parm.Value = mStream.GetBuffer()
          cmd.Parameters.Add(parm)
          cmd.Connection = cn
          cn.Open()
          cmd.ExecuteNonQuery()
       End Using
    End Using
End Sub
```

C#

```
protected void GridView1_RowUpdated(object sender, GridViewUpdatedEventArgs e)
{
   GridView gridView = ((GridView)sender);
   int employeeId = (int)e.Keys["EmployeeID"];
   FileUpload photoFile =
      (FileUpload)gridView.Rows[gridView.EditIndex]
      .FindControl("PhotoUpload");
   UpdatePhoto(employeeId, photoFile);
}

public void UpdatePhoto(int employeeId, FileUpload photoFile)
{
   if (photoFile == null || photoFile.HasFile == false) return;
   Stream imageStream = photoFile.PostedFile.InputStream;
   int imageLength = photoFile.PostedFile.ContentLength;
   string imageType = photoFile.PostedFile.ContentType;
   MemoryStream mStream = new MemoryStream();
   byte[] imageData = new byte[1024];
   int count = 0;
   while (0 < (count = imageStream.Read(imageData, 0, imageData.Length)))
   {
      mStream.Write(imageData, 0, count);
   }
   ConnectionStringSettings cnSettings =
         ConfigurationManager.ConnectionStrings["ConnectionString"];
   using (SqlConnection cn =
      new SqlConnection(cnSettings.ConnectionString))
```

```
      {
         using (SqlCommand cmd = new SqlCommand())
         {
            cmd.CommandText =
               "Update Employees Set Photo = @Photo " +
               "WHERE EmployeeID = @EmployeeID";
            SqlParameter parm = new SqlParameter();
            parm.ParameterName = "@EmployeeID";
            parm.Value = employeeId;
            cmd.Parameters.Add(parm);
            parm = new SqlParameter();
            parm.ParameterName = "@Photo";
            parm.Value = mStream.GetBuffer();
            cmd.Parameters.Add(parm);
            cmd.Connection = cn;
            cn.Open();
            cmd.ExecuteNonQuery();
         }
      }
   }
```

This *RowUpdated* event handler simply retrieves the current *EmployeeID* and the *FileUpload* control and passes them to the *UpdatePhoto* method. You use the *FindControl* method to get the *FileUpoad* control by its ID, which is *PhotoUpload*, because the only way you can access the row's *Cell* collection is by index number, and if another column were inserted ahead of the *Photo* column, the index number would need to be updated.

The *UpdatePhoto* method tests the *FileUpload* control to verify that it is not null or nothing and that it has a file. A loop is then executed to retrieve the contents of the file from the network stream. The contents are placed into a *MemoryStream* object. Finally, a SQL update command is executed, which updates the *Photo* field based on the *EmployeeID*. If you build and run the code, you will see the *FileUpload* control when you are in edit mode. Find a picture to upload, and click the Update link on the row. The result might look something like that shown in Figure 8-25.

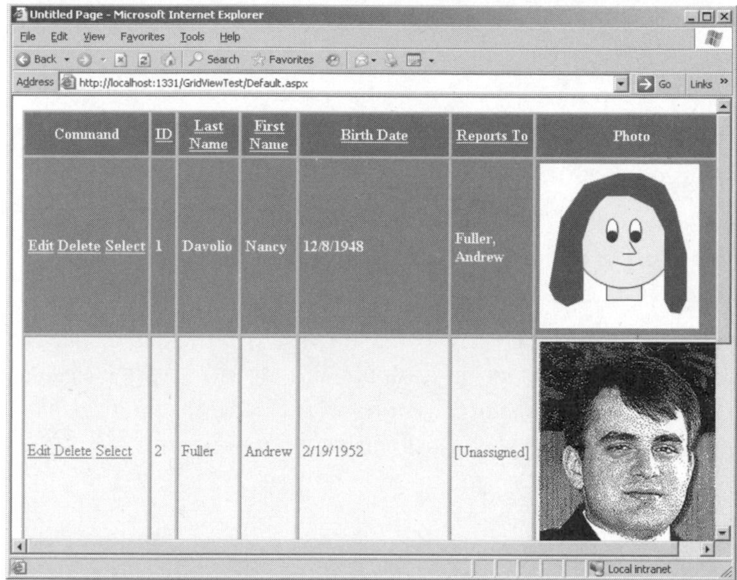

Figure 8-25 The *FileUpload* control lets you upload a new photo that will be placed into the database.

Summary

- The *GridView* object represents a tabular (rows-and-columns format) display of data on a Web form.
- *DataControlField* objects provide a *DataControlFieldCell* object template to the *GridViewRow* objects.
- You use styles to change the look of the *GridView* object. You can assign styles to individual rows or columns or to the entire *GridView* object.
- The *GridView* object can be bound to an Access database, a SQL-based database, an XML file, an object, or a site map.
- A *DataSource* must be configured and connected, or bound, to the *GridView* object.
- The *GridView* object can be configured to provide paging, sorting, and updating.
- You can create a *GridView* object by dragging it to the Web form, by typing the declarative markup, or by adding code in the code-behind file.

- The *GridView* object provides events that are related to rows, data binding, paging, sorting, initialization, and cleanup.
- The *TemplateField* column allows you to provide custom column behavior based on templates. Existing columns can be easily converted to *TemplateField* columns.
- The *GridView* object can display images by using the *ImageField* column.
- You can retrieve images from the database by creating a simple "image engine." The engine processes requests for images by retrieving the image from the database and writing it to the *Response* object's *OutputStream*.
- You can upload images to the Web server and store them in the database by converting the *ImageField* column to a *TemplateField* column and inserting a *FileUpload* control in the *EditItemTemplate*. The *RowUpdated* event handler can access the *FileUpload* control to retrieve the image stream and send the image to the database.

Chapter 9

Working with the SQLCLR

With the release of Microsoft SQL Server 2005, you can write .NET code that runs within SQL Server. Like Microsoft Internet Information Services (IIS), SQL Server hosts the .NET common language runtime (also known as the SQLCLR or Integrated CLR) and can run .NET code within its server process.

This chapter explores the advantages and disadvantages of running .NET code, which is also known as managed code, within SQL Server. You learn how to create stored procedures, user-defined functions, aggregates, triggers, and user-defined types (UDTs).

Note that Visual Studio 2005 Professional Edition is required to create and use the Database project template that is referenced in this chapter, but this chapter also shows you how to create, deploy, and use SQLCLR features using the command-line compiler.

Does the SQLCLR Replace T-SQL?

I remember the first time I heard that SQL Server would be able to run .NET code. My first thought was that this was great for developers because they wouldn't need to know Transact-SQL (T-SQL) and could use the same language for every tier of a large application. Well, I was wrong.

As it turns out, T-SQL is alive and well and is still the best-performing language for executing set-based queries. As a general rule, T-SQL is still the best choice for set-oriented tasks or for queries that don't need a SQL cursor or function.

The SQLCLR, which runs on all SQL Server 2005 versions, including SQL Server Express, offers the addition of the supported .NET Framework Class Libraries (FCL) as well as third-party libraries and any libraries you create. The SQLCLR is usually the best choice for implementing computation-intensive routines.

For example, you might have encountered situations in which you need to move a large amount of data across the network to perform a computation-intensive function or a function that simply cannot be done using T-SQL. Moving this data across the network almost always hurts performance.

I had a recent project that used large complex objects, about 4 MB each, that were stored in a relational fashion within SQL Server and spanned 125 tables. The objects were large because they contained many child objects–around 100,000. The application had a complex, multipurpose cloning framework because users rarely created these objects from scratch–they usually created a new object by copying and then modifying an existing object. They had to first load the object to the user's machine, clone it, and then save the new object to the database. To make matters worse, even though the server computers were connected with a gigabit bus, the network communication between the user's machine and the network switch was set to 10 megabits to ensure that no user could hog bandwidth.

Let's do some quick calculations. First, there are 8 bits to a byte, and when you factor in network overhead, communicating at 10 megabits/second is roughly 1 MB per second. This means it should (and did) take about 4 seconds to move the relational data from SQL Server to the application, which constructs the object in about 2 seconds.

You might think it would take 4 seconds to move the data back to SQL Server, but that's where the problem is. The data was in a *DataSet*, and the *DataAdapter* objects moved the data to SQL Server by essentially creating 100,000 INSERT statements. Just to jog your memory, here's what a typical SQL INSERT statement looks like:

```
INSERT TblCustomer(CustomerId, CustomerName, CreditLimit, ActiveCustomer)
   VALUES('69454446-24FE-48BE-A553-5AB44986C36A', 'Northwind', 5000.00, 1)
```

This has more than 150 characters, but the data is only about 50 characters. Obviously, every table is different, but you can see that even a simple SQL INSERT statement such as this one translates into three times as many bytes being sent to SQL Server as are received. The particular application I'm describing did not send INSERT statements to SQL Server; it executed stored procedures for the inserts. The typical stored procedure looked like this:

```
exec uspTblCustomerInsert @CustomerId='32F9AEC2-0E0C-4D29-BDFD-9885CC25E7D9',
   @CustomerName='Northwind',@CreditLimit=10,000.00,@ActiveCustomer=1
```

Not much better, huh? The actual application had about 8 times more bytes being transferred back to SQL Server because many of the tables and columns had verbose (better stated as "meaningful") names. It took 35 seconds to send the newly created object back to SQL Server, but about 3 seconds of the time was not related to network bandwidth–it was time that SQL needed to store the data.

The total time to create the cloned object and store it in the database was approximately 41 seconds. You can see that network bandwidth was the primary bottleneck, consuming 36 of the 41 seconds, so eliminating the network from the equation would result in a major performance gain.

Implementing the same complex cloning framework with T-SQL would be a nightmare, and because the application's C# cloning framework is used for many types of cloning, the framework could not be eliminated at the client even if a T-SQL implementation were possible. In other words, two cloning frameworks would need to be maintained.

This is where the SQLCLR can come to the rescue. At the time of this project I've described, SQL Server 2005 was not yet released; now the C# cloning framework libraries can be implemented in the SQLCLR to increase performance.

Creating a Stored Procedure Without Visual Studio

Let's start by creating a small stored procedure using Notepad. This approach exposes everything that needs to be done to get the stored procedure to operate. Then we'll look at what Microsoft Visual Studio .NET brings to the table to simplify the process. These examples run on SQL Server with the *Northwind* sample database attached. They also run on all other versions of SQL Server 2005 if you change your connection string appropriately.

Enabling the SQLCLR

To minimize resource usage and maximize security, the SQLCLR is disabled by default. To use the SQLCLR, you must first enable this server-wide setting, as shown in the following SQL script.

> **Note** All of the following SQL scripts can be executed from a New Query window. Although I prefer to use the Microsoft SQL Server Management Studio, you can use the Server Explorer in Visual Studio to open a New Query window by right-clicking your connection and clicking New Query. When using the Server Explorer, you can deselect the Show Diagram Pane and the Show Criteria Pane, and you are left with a window that has the SQL Pane and the Result Pane. With the Server Explorer, you cannot use the GO statement to separate batches, so you must execute the commands that are between each *GO* separately, without using GO.

SQL: Enabling the SQLCLR

```
EXEC sp_configure 'clr enabled', 1
RECONFIGURE WITH OVERRIDE
GO
```

To disable the SQLCLR, change the 1 to a 0 and execute the script. To view the status of the SQLCLR, simply execute the following SQL script.

SQL: Retrieving the SQLCLR State

```
EXEC sp_configure 'clr enabled'
```

This returns the minimum, maximum, configured, and currently running values for this setting.

You might also want to get other information about the SQLCLR, such as the version number. You do this by executing the following SQL script.

SQL: Retrieving SQLCLR Properties

```
SELECT * FROM sys.dm_clr_properties
```

Creating the Source Code

If you want to create a stored procedure in Visual Basic or C#, the class with the method that will become a stored procedure must be public. The method must be public as well. Also, the method must be static (shared in Visual Basic) because the SQLCLR makes no attempt to create an instance of the class.

Namespaces are allowed in your code but not required. I've seen many code samples that don't use namespaces, and although I question the value of using a namespace in this scenario, I have included one so you can see how it affects the registration of the stored procedure later.

The following code can be typed into Notepad or any other text editor and saved to a file called HiVbWorld.vb for Visual Basic or HiCsWorld.cs for C#.

Visual Basic: HiVbWorld.vb

```
imports Microsoft.SqlServer.Server
namespace VbTestNamespace
   public class VbTestClass
      public shared sub SayHi( )
         SqlContext.Pipe.Send("Hi VB World from SQL Server!")
      end sub
   end class
end namespace
```

C#: HiCsWorld.cs

```
using Microsoft.SqlServer.Server;
namespace CsTestNamespace
{
   public class CsTestClass
   {
      public static void SayHi( )
      {
         SqlContext.Pipe.Send("Hi C# World from SQL Server!");
      }
   }
}
```

Using the Context Object

Notice the use of *SqlContext*, which is commonly called the "context" object. This object gives you access to the environment where the SQLCLR has been activated. It also enables access to runtime information based on the type of SQLCLR object that is being executed. The *SqlContext* class is in the *Microsoft.SqlServer.Server* namespace, and the class is defined in the System.Data.dll file. You normally need to add a reference to the System.Data.dll file, but the Visual Basic and C# compilers add the reference for you when they find the *SqlContext* class in your code.

The *Pipe* property lets you send data back to the client. In SQL, the PRINT statement is the equivalent of the *Pipe.Send* method. In your application, you can access the sent data by retrieving data from the *SqlConnection* object's *InfoMessages* collection.

Compiling the Code

Open the Visual Studio 2005 Command Prompt. Next, change your default directory to the directory that contains your source file and compile the file by executing the following command.

Visual Basic

```
vbc /t:library HiVbWorld.vb
```

C#

```
csc /t:library HiCsWorld.cs
```

Nothing fancy happens here. The output of a compile is an assembly, and this command simply created an assembly that consists of either the HiVbWorld.dll or HiCsWorld.dll file.

Loading the Assembly

The next step is to install the assembly into SQL Server. Installing the assembly gives the assembly a logical name that is usable in SQL Server and sets the permissions. Note that the assembly installs into the database that you are currently connected to. If the assembly is installed and the database is backed up, the assembly is included in the backup. When the database is restored, the assembly is restored as well, even if you deleted the file that you used to install the assembly. The following SQL script installs the assembly into SQL Server. It can be executed in a query window, or you can use the SqlCmd.exe command-line utility. Be sure to verify the path to the assembly.

SQL: Install the Visual Basic Assembly

```
CREATE ASSEMBLY VbProcs FROM 'C:\Projects\Vb\Chapter09\HiVbWorld.dll'
WITH PERMISSION_SET=SAFE
GO
```

SQL: Install the C# Assembly

```
CREATE ASSEMBLY CsProcs FROM 'C:\Projects\Cs\Chapter09\HiCsWorld.dll'
WITH PERMISSION_SET=SAFE
GO
```

The permission can be set at the time that the assembly is registered. By default, the assembly is installed with the permission set to SAFE. The SQLCLR has three levels of execution permissions that are enforced at the assembly level:

- *SAFE* Access only to CLR code and the database data. Access to unmanaged code, external resources, or thread management is not allowed.
- *EXTERNAL_ACCESS* Allows access to external systems, such as the file system, the event log, the network, and other database servers. Access to unmanaged code is not allowed.

- *UNSAFE* Access is not limited in any way. Obviously, this option is not recommended but is sometimes necessary, especially if you need to access unmanaged code. For example, you may need to access a COM component, and this would require UNSAFE execution access.

Changing the Execution Permission

Before you can set the execution permission to either EXTERNAL_ACCESS or UNSAFE, you must have permission to change this access permission, and the database must be configured as TRUSTWORTHY. If these items aren't addressed, you receive the following exception when you attempt to change the execution permission.

```
CREATE ASSEMBLY for assembly 'AssemblyName' failed because assembly 'AssemblyName' is no
t authorized for PERMISSION_SET = EXTERNAL_ACCESS.  The assembly is authorized when eith
er of the following is true: the database owner (DBO) has EXTERNAL ACCESS ASSEMBLY permi
ssion and the database has the TRUSTWORTHY database property on; or the assembly is sign
ed with a certificate or an asymmetric key that has a corresponding login with EXTERNAL
ACCESS ASSEMBLY permission.
```

You can correct this exception by executing the following SQL script to set the database TRUSTWORTHY property.

SQL: Enabling the Database as Trustworthy

```
USE master
ALTER DATABASE Northwind SET TRUSTWORTHY ON
GO
```

This is all that you need to do if you are the SQL Server administrator, but if you aren't, you need to get permission to set the execution permission. This can be granted using the appropriate SQL script that follows for external access or unsafe execution permission.

SQL: Granting External Access Permissions

```
USE master
GRANT EXTERNAL ACCESS ASSEMBLY TO [loginName]
GO
```

SQL: Granting Unsafe Permissions

```
USE master
GRANT UNSAFE ASSEMBLY TO [loginName]
GO
```

Registering the Stored Procedure

Your method is not available as a stored procedure until you register it. You do this using the following command.

SQL: Register the Visual Basic Stored Procedure

```
CREATE PROCEDURE SayVbHi
AS EXTERNAL NAME VbProcs.[VbTestNamespace.VbTestClass].SayHi
GO
```

SQL: Register the C# Stored Procedure

```
CREATE PROCEDURE SayCsHi
AS EXTERNAL NAME CsProcs.[CsTestNamespace.CsTestClass].SayHi
GO
```

Notice that the external name is in *assembly.class.method* format. The class has been defined within a namespace, so the namespace must also be included, but including the namespace means additional dots in the format, and SQL Server gets confused. The use of the square brackets around the *namespace.class* tells SQL Server that the middle section represents the full path to the class.

Executing the Stored Procedure

The stored procedure can be executed like any other stored procedure—from within a query window, from the SqlCmd.exe console utility, or from your application. Figure 9-1 shows the query window output after the assemblies have been installed in the *Northwind* database and the stored procedures have been executed.

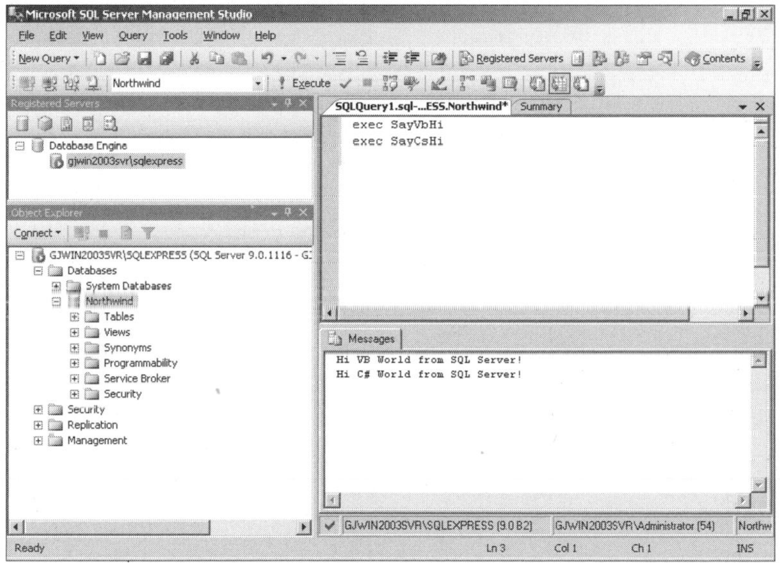

Figure 9-1 Executing the stored procedures in a query window from within SQL Management Studio displays the output.

Refreshing the Assembly

If you need to make changes to your source code and recompile your assembly, you must refresh the SQL Server installation as follows.

SQL: Refresh the Visual Basic Assembly

```
ALTER ASSEMBLY VbProcs FROM 'C:\Projects\Vb\Chapter09\HiVbWorld.dll'
GO
```

SQL: Refresh the C# Assembly

```
ALTER ASSEMBLY CsProcs FROM 'C:\Projects\CS\Chapter09\HiCsWorld.dll'
GO
```

Note that if you execute this statement without first recompiling your assembly, you get the message that states that the command failed because the source has the same MVID (module ID) as the assembly that is currently registered.

Using the *ALTER* statement means you don't lose the current security setting.

Viewing Installed Assemblies and Their Permissions

You can view the loaded assemblies and their permissions by executing the following SQL script. Remember that this script lists the assemblies that are loaded into the current database.

SQL: List Assemblies in Current Database

```
SELECT * FROM sys.assemblies
```

Using Parameters to Transfer Data

The previous sample application shows the steps required for getting your code to operate in the SQLCLR, but when data is transferred between SQL Server and the client, it's typically done using parameter and rowsets. This section explores the use of parameters to pass data; the subsequent section examines rowset-based data movement.

To use parameters, you simply add a method to your assembly that accepts parameters and/or returns a value. The return value can be either *SqlInt32 System.Int32* or *void*. If you attempt to return a string, for example, you can compile and load the assembly, but when you attempt to register the stored procedure, an exception is thrown. If you need to return a string value to the client, you can pass parameters as reference parameters using the *ref* (C#) or *ByRef* (Visual Basic) keywords, or you can pass parameters as output parameters using the *out* (C# only) keyword. For example, we'll add the following method to the previous assembly.

Visual Basic

```
public shared Sub GetGreeting(name as string, _
      ByRef greeting as string)
   greeting = "Hello from VB, " + name
End Sub
```

C#

```
public static void GetCsGreeting(string name,
      ref string greeting)
{
   greeting = "Hello from C#, " + name;
}
```

After saving the source code, recompile and refresh the assembly. Registering the stored procedure is a bit different because the parameters must be specified when the stored procedure is registered. You don't need to identify the return value as a parameter if you are planning to use the RETURN statement in your stored procedure, however. The following SQL snippet shows how the parameters are defined in SQL Server.

SQL: Registering the Visual Basic Stored Procedure with Parameters

```
CREATE PROCEDURE GetVbGreeting
 @name nvarchar(50),
 @greeting nvarchar(100) OUTPUT
AS EXTERNAL NAME VbProcs.[VbTestNamespace.VbTestClass].GetGreeting
```

SQL: Registering the C# Stored Procedure with Parameters

```
CREATE PROCEDURE GetCsGreeting
 @name nvarchar(50),
 @greeting nvarchar(100) OUTPUT
AS EXTERNAL NAME CsProcs.[CsTestNamespace.CsTestClass].GetGreeting
```

After registering the stored procedure, you can execute it using the following SQL snippet.

SQL: Executing the Visual Basic Stored Procedure

```
DECLARE @result nvarchar(100)
EXEC GetVbGreeting 'Glenn', @result OUTPUT
PRINT @result
```

SQL: Executing the C# Stored Procedure

```
DECLARE @result nvarchar(100)
EXEC GetCsGreeting 'Glenn', @result OUTPUT
PRINT @result
```

The output is displayed as shown in Figure 9-2. Notice that an empty variable called *@result* is created to hold the greeting. After the store procedure is run, *@result* is printed and the greeting is displayed.

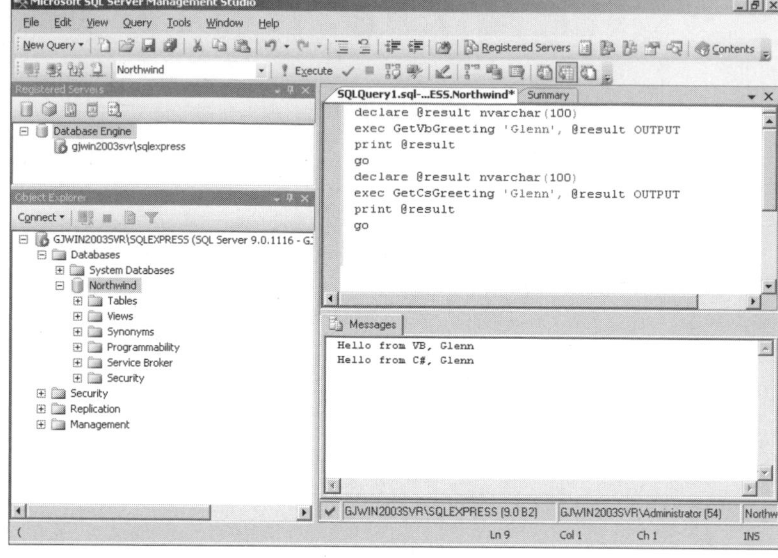

Figure 9-2 The output window when you use parameters to pass data between SQL Server and the client

Creating a Stored Procedure by Using Visual Studio

If you have been using Notepad up to this point as I have, you'll certainly be ready to move over to Visual Studio .NET before continuing. Visual Studio .NET Professional Edition offers a Database project template that you can use to create assemblies that run in SQL Server. For example, Figure 9-3 shows the Database project template that is available for Visual Basic projects.

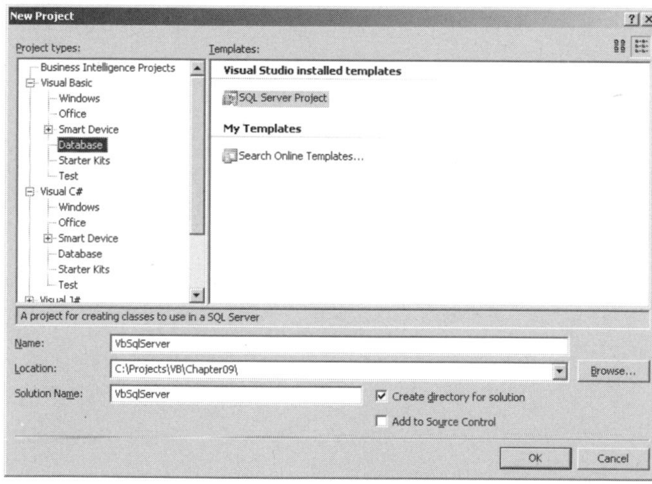

Figure 9-3 Visual Studio .NET has Database project templates for each language.

Using Visual Studio means that you use the same robust environment that you normally write code in, complete with IntelliSense. The Database project template also gives you the ability to easily deploy and debug your projects.

Create a Database project called SqlServerVb or SqlServerCs, depending on your language. You are prompted to select the database to connect to. If the database isn't attached, you can opt to attach a new database. For these examples, we'll select the *Northwind* database.

You can add stored procedures, user-defined functions, aggregates, triggers, and user-defined types to the database project. All of these are covered in this chapter, but at this time, add a stored procedure called HelloVb.vb or HelloCs.cs. The following code is included in the stored procedure template when it is added.

Visual Basic

```
Imports System
Imports System.Data
Imports System.Data.Sql
Imports System.Data.SqlTypes
Imports Microsoft.SqlServer.Server


Partial Public Class StoredProcedures
    <Microsoft.SqlServer.Server.SqlProcedure()> _
    Public Shared Sub  HelloVb ()
        ' Add your code here
    End Sub
End Class
```

C#

```
using System;
using System.Data;
using System.Data.Sql;
using System.Data.SqlTypes;
using Microsoft.SqlServer.Server;


public partial class StoredProcedures
{
   [Microsoft.SqlServer.Server.SqlProcedure]
   public static void HelloCs()
   {
      // Put your code here
   }
};
```

The *Imports* (Visual Basic) or *using* (C#) statement saves you typing. No namespace has been defined because there is little benefit to doing so. Also, Visual Studio has created a partial class called *StoredProcedures* because there really isn't any benefit to creating a separate class for each stored procedure. Notice the use of the *SqlProcedure* attribute, which tells Visual Studio how to register this method in SQL Server. Modify the method to display a simple message as follows.

Visual Basic

```
<Microsoft.SqlServer.Server.SqlProcedure(Name:="HiVb")> _
   Public Shared Sub HelloVb()
   SqlContext.Pipe.Send("Hello from VB!")
End Sub
```

C#

```
[Microsoft.SqlServer.Server.SqlProcedure(Name="HiCs")]
public static void HelloCs()
{
   SqlContext.Pipe.Send("Hello from C#!");
}
```

The *SqlProcedure* attribute has a property called *Name* that has been assigned to create the stored procedure with a different name. If you try to build and run the project by pressing F5, the project builds but it doesn't appear to run because what actually runs is a test script in the Test Scripts folder. Notice that there is only one test script in the folder, called Test.sql. You can add script files, and you can modify the existing test script. Open the existing Test.sql file, and add the following SQL to the end of the file.

Visual Basic

```
EXEC HiVb
```

C#

```
EXEC HiCs
```

Note that the SQLCLR needs to be enabled first. If you don't enable the SQLCLR, you get an error message that states that the SQLCLR must be enabled first.

The *Name* property that was assigned in the *SqlProcedure* attribute is used to execute the stored procedure. Press F5 and the result is sent to the output window. The main benefit is that you can make a change to the stored procedure and press F5 to recompile and refresh the assembly. You can also add breakpoints in your code to debug your stored procedures.

Passing Rowset Data

Stored procedures frequently need to return rowset data. You pass rowset data in different ways depending on whether you are producing the rowset data in your .NET code or simply returning database data from a SQL query. Let's start by producing the data.

Passing Data as a Produced Rowset

Let's add a stored procedure to our database project called *GetWords*. The procedure accepts a string of words and splits the string into a rowset with two columns. The first column contains the index number of the word, and the second column contains the word. The stored procedure code is as follows.

Visual Basic

```
Imports System
Imports System.Data
Imports System.Data.Sql
Imports System.Data.SqlTypes
Imports Microsoft.SqlServer.Server

Partial Public Class StoredProcedures
   <Microsoft.SqlServer.Server.SqlProcedure(Name:="GetVbWords")> _
   Public Shared Sub GetWords(ByVal sentence As String)
      Dim rec As New SqlDataRecord( _
         New SqlMetaData("Index", SqlDbType.Int), _
         New SqlMetaData("Word", SqlDbType.NVarChar, 50))
      SqlContext.Pipe.SendResultsStart(rec)

      Dim i As Integer = 0
      For Each word As String In sentence.Split(" "c)
         rec.SetInt32(0, i)
         i += 1
         rec.SetString(1, word)
         SqlContext.Pipe.SendResultsRow(rec)
      Next
      SqlContext.Pipe.SendResultsEnd()
   End Sub
End Class
```

C#

```
using System;
using System.Data;
using System.Data.Sql;
using System.Data.SqlTypes;
using Microsoft.SqlServer.Server;

public partial class StoredProcedures
{
   [Microsoft.SqlServer.Server.SqlProcedure(Name = "GetCsWords")]
   public static void GetWords(string sentence)
   {
      SqlDataRecord rec = new SqlDataRecord(
         new SqlMetaData("Index", SqlDbType.Int),
         new SqlMetaData("Word", SqlDbType.NVarChar, 50));
      SqlContext.Pipe.SendResultsStart(rec);

      int i = 0;
      foreach (string word in sentence.Split(' '))
      {
         rec.SetInt32(0, i++);
         rec.SetString(1, word);
         SqlContext.Pipe.SendResultsRow(rec);
      }
      SqlContext.Pipe.SendResultsEnd();
   }
}
```

This code introduces the *SqlDataRecord* object, which is used to define a tabular row of column data. The columns are *SqlMetaData* objects that consist of the column name and the data type. Strings must be defined in SQL Server terminology, so the string is defined as a Unicode variable character (*NVarChar*) field with a maximum length of 50 characters. Next, the *SendResultsStart* method is executed to open the stream and send the metadata down the pipe. In the loop that processes each row, *rec* is populated with current data consisting of the index number and the current word. Finally, the *SendResultsEnd* method is executed to close the stream.

Add the following script into the Test.sql script file and run the project.

Visual Basic

```
EXEC GetVbWords 'This is a test of the GetWords stored procedure'
```

C#

```
EXEC GetCsWords 'This is a test of the GetWords stored procedure'
```

When you look at the results in the output window, you see the following returned data.

```
Index       Word
----------- ---------
0           This
1           is
2           a
3           test
4           of
5           the
6           GetWords
7           stored
8           procedure
```

Using the *SqlConnection* Object in the SQLCLR

You can use the *SqlConnection* object in the SQLCLR just as you would normally use the *SqlConnection* object, but for data within the current database you can set the connection string to be a context connection for better performance. The context connection does not carry the overhead of the network protocol stack, and it communicates directly with SQL Server without leaving the process, as shown in Figure 9-4. Would you use a regular connection in the SQLCLR? Sure. You'll often want to retrieve data that is on a different server, so you can simply use a regular connection to get the data.

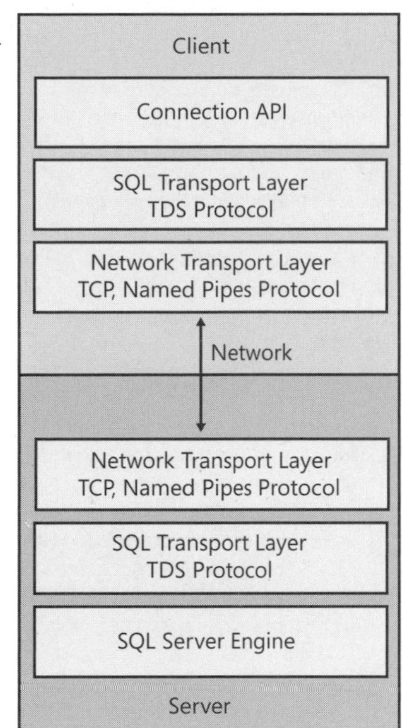

Figure 9-4 The network protocol stack is eliminated when you communicate using a context connection.

As an example of using a context connection, someone once asked me to create something that looked like the following: A rowset containing a column called *EmployeeId* that represented the employee IDs in the Employees table, and another column called *Last3Orders* that represented the last three order IDs, comma separated in a single field. To do this without the SQLCLR, I might come up with a solution that implements a SQL cursor. Using the SQLCLR, the following stored procedure solves the problem.

Visual Basic

```
Imports System
Imports System.Data
Imports System.Data.Sql
Imports System.Data.SqlTypes
Imports Microsoft.SqlServer.Server
Imports System.Data.SqlClient

Partial Public Class StoredProcedures
   <Microsoft.SqlServer.Server.SqlProcedure()> _
   Public Shared Sub LastEmployeeOrdersVb()
      Dim rec As New SqlDataRecord( _
```

```
            New SqlMetaData("EmployeeID", SqlDbType.Int), _
            New SqlMetaData("Last3Orders", SqlDbType.NVarChar, 50))

        Dim employees As New DataTable("Employees")
        Using cn As New SqlConnection()
            cn.ConnectionString = "context connection=true"
            Using cmd As SqlCommand = cn.CreateCommand()
                cmd.CommandText = "Select EmployeeID From Employees" _
                    + " ORDER BY EmployeeId ASC"
                cn.Open()
                Using rdr As SqlDataReader = cmd.ExecuteReader()
                    employees.Load(rdr)
                End Using
            End Using
            SqlContext.Pipe.SendResultsStart(rec)
            For Each dr As DataRow In employees.Rows
                Dim empId As Integer = CType(dr("EmployeeID"), Integer)
                Using cmd As SqlCommand = cn.CreateCommand()
                    cmd.CommandText = String.Format( _
                        "Select TOP 3 OrderID From Orders " _
                        + "WHERE EmployeeId = {0} " + _
                        "Order By OrderDate DESC", _
                        empId)
                    Using rdr As SqlDataReader = cmd.ExecuteReader()
                        Dim orders As String = ""
                        While (rdr.Read())
                            If orders.Length > 0 Then orders += ", "
                            orders += rdr(0).ToString()
                        End While
                        rec.SetInt32(0, empId)
                        rec.SetString(1, orders)
                        SqlContext.Pipe.SendResultsRow(rec)
                    End Using
                End Using
            Next
        End Using
        SqlContext.Pipe.SendResultsEnd()
    End Sub
End Class
```

C#

```
using System;
using System.Data;
using System.Data.Sql;
using System.Data.SqlTypes;
using Microsoft.SqlServer.Server;
using System.Data.SqlClient;

public partial class StoredProcedures
{
   [Microsoft.SqlServer.Server.SqlProcedure]
   public static void LastEmployeeOrdersCs()
   {
```

```
        SqlDataRecord rec = new SqlDataRecord(
           new SqlMetaData("EmployeeID", SqlDbType.Int),
           new SqlMetaData("Last3Orders", SqlDbType.NVarChar, 50));

        DataTable employees = new DataTable("Employees");
        using (SqlConnection cn = new SqlConnection())
        {
           cn.ConnectionString = "context connection=true";
           using (SqlCommand cmd = cn.CreateCommand())
           {
              cmd.CommandText = "Select EmployeeID From Employees"
                 + " ORDER BY EmployeeId ASC";
              cn.Open();
              using (SqlDataReader rdr = cmd.ExecuteReader())
              {
                 employees.Load(rdr);
              }
           }
           SqlContext.Pipe.SendResultsStart(rec);
           foreach (DataRow dr in employees.Rows)
           {
              int empId = (int)dr["EmployeeID"];
              using (SqlCommand cmd = cn.CreateCommand())
              {
                 cmd.CommandText = string.Format(
                    "Select TOP 3 OrderID From Orders "
                    + "WHERE EmployeeId = {0} " +
                    "Order By OrderDate DESC",
                    empId);
                 using (SqlDataReader rdr = cmd.ExecuteReader())
                 {
                    string orders = "";
                    while (rdr.Read())
                    {
                       if (orders.Length > 0) orders += ", ";
                       orders += rdr[0].ToString();
                    }
                    rec.SetInt32(0, empId);
                    rec.SetString(1, orders);
                    SqlContext.Pipe.SendResultsRow(rec);
                 }
              }
           }
        }
        SqlContext.Pipe.SendResultsEnd();
    }
}
```

This code retrieves the list of employee IDs into a *DataTable* object. The code then loops through the employee IDs and retrieves the last three order IDs for each employee. We can add code to Test.sql to execute the stored procedure, and the results can be viewed in the output window as shown here.

```
EmployeeID  Last3Orders
----------- ------------------------------------------------
1           11077, 11071, 11067
2           11070, 11073, 11060
3           11063, 11057, 11052
4           11076, 11072, 11061
5           11043, 10954, 10922
6           11045, 11031, 11025
7           11074, 11066, 11055
8           11075, 11068, 11065
9           11058, 11022, 11017
```

Context and Regular Connection Restrictions

The context connection is very much like a regular connection, but with some limitations:

- Multiple Active Result Sets (MARS) is not supported. In the previous example, the coding could have been somewhat simplified if MARS could have been used.
- On a given connection to SQL Server from the client, otherwise known as a Server Process ID (SPID), only one context connection can be open at a time.
- The *SqlBulkCopy* object is not supported.
- Update batching is not supported.
- *SqlNotificationRequest* is not supported.
- *SqlCommand.Cancel* is not supported. A call to this method is silently ignored.
- No other keywords can exist in the connection string with *context connection=true*.

Some of these restrictions might be limitations for the current release only, while other restrictions might be by design. So they will not change in future releases.

The only restrictions on a regular connection are the following:

- Asynchronous access is not supported within the SQLCLR.
- The *SqlDependency* framework is not supported within the SQLCLR.

Connection Credentials for Regular Connections

When you use a regular connection within the SQLCLR, if you use integrated authentication, the credentials used are those of the SQL Server service account, not the credentials you used to connect to SQL Server. This might be desirable in some scenarios, but at other times you probably want to use the same credentials you used to connect to SQL Server.

If the SQL Server service account is running using the "local system" account, the effective permissions for accessing anything on the local machine are similar to those of an administrator, but the "local system" account has no effective permissions for accessing anything on a remote server. If you attempt to access a remote server using the "local system" account, an exception is thrown that states "Login failed for user '(null)'. Reason: Not associated with a trusted SQL Server connection."

It is possible to get your credentials from your connection to SQL Server by using the *SqlContext.WindowsIdentity* property. You can use your credentials to impersonate your account while on the local machine, but Windows security keeps you from impersonating across the network. Impersonation across the network is called *delegation*; an administrator can enable delegation on an account-by-account basis, but most Windows domain administrators will not want to do this. Chapter 13, which covers security, covers delegation in more detail.

One solution is to use a Windows domain account for the SQL Server service and make sure the account has permission to access the remote database. Another solution is to use standard SQL Server security to access the remote database server, which means that you have a user name and password embedded in your connection string to the remote server.

Remember that you can impersonate to get access to local resources (as you'll see later in this chapter when we cover the streaming table valued functions).

Passing Data from a Database Rowset

You used the *Pipe.Send* method to return string data that can be viewed as *InfoMessage* objects. You have also used the *Pipe.Send* method to return a rowset that you produced. You can also return a rowset that contains database data by passing a *SqlDataReader* object to the .*Pipe.Send* method. The following code snippet gets the list of customers from the database and passes the *SqlDataReader* object to the *Pipe.Send* method.

Visual Basic

```
Imports System
Imports System.Data
Imports System.Data.Sql
Imports System.Data.SqlTypes
Imports Microsoft.SqlServer.Server
Imports System.Data.SqlClient

Partial Public Class StoredProcedures
   <Microsoft.SqlServer.Server.SqlProcedure()> _
   Public Shared Sub GetCustomersVb()
      Using cn As New SqlConnection()
         cn.ConnectionString = "context connection=true"
         Using cmd As SqlCommand = cn.CreateCommand()
            cmd.CommandText = "Select * From Customers"
            cn.Open()
            Using rdr As SqlDataReader = cmd.ExecuteReader()
               SqlContext.Pipe.Send(rdr)
            End Using
         End Using
      End Using
   End Sub
End Class
```

C#

```
using System;
using System.Data;
using System.Data.Sql;
using System.Data.SqlTypes;
using Microsoft.SqlServer.Server;
using System.Data.SqlClient;

public partial class StoredProcedures
{
   [Microsoft.SqlServer.Server.SqlProcedure]
   public static void GetCustomersCs()
   {
      using (SqlConnection cn = new SqlConnection())
      {
         cn.ConnectionString = "context connection=true";
         using (SqlCommand cmd = cn.CreateCommand())
         {
            cmd.CommandText = "Select * From Customers";
            cn.Open();
            using (SqlDataReader rdr = cmd.ExecuteReader())
            {
               SqlContext.Pipe.Send(rdr);
            }
         }
      }
   }
}
```

When you run this stored procedure, you see the customer list in the output window. You can further simplify this code by using the *Pipe.ExecuteAndSend* method, as shown in the next code snippet.

Visual Basic

```
Imports System
Imports System.Data
Imports System.Data.Sql
Imports System.Data.SqlTypes
Imports Microsoft.SqlServer.Server
Imports System.Data.SqlClient

Partial Public Class StoredProcedures
   <Microsoft.SqlServer.Server.SqlProcedure()> _
   Public Shared Sub GetCustomers2Vb()
      Using cn As New SqlConnection()
         cn.ConnectionString = "context connection=true"
         Using cmd As SqlCommand = cn.CreateCommand()
            cmd.CommandText = "Select * From Customers"
            cn.Open()
            SqlContext.Pipe.ExecuteAndSend(cmd)
         End Using
      End Using
   End Sub
End Class
```

C#

```
using System;
using System.Data;
using System.Data.Sql;
using System.Data.SqlTypes;
using Microsoft.SqlServer.Server;
using System.Data.SqlClient;

public partial class StoredProcedures
{
   [Microsoft.SqlServer.Server.SqlProcedure]
   public static void GetCustomers2Cs()
   {
      using (SqlConnection cn = new SqlConnection())
      {
         cn.ConnectionString = "context connection=true";
         using (SqlCommand cmd = cn.CreateCommand())
         {
            cmd.CommandText = "Select * From Customers";
            cn.Open();
            SqlContext.Pipe.ExecuteAndSend(cmd);
         }
      }
   }
}
```

Notice that this code returns the customer list by simply passing the *SqlCommand* object to the *Pipe.ExecuteAndSend* method, which executes the command and passes the resulting *SqlDataReader* object to the *Send* method.

Creating User-Defined Functions

Previous versions of SQL Server have had only a T-SQL version of user-defined functions. As with stored procedures, you can now create user-defined functions using managed code and the SQLCLR.

A user-defined function is a T-SQL or managed code routine that is stored in the database and returns a scalar value or table value. User-defined functions can be called from within T-SQL statements.

A user-defined function should never attempt to alter database data or schema. This rule is enforced with T-SQL and with the context connection, but if you use a regular connection to modify data, no exception is thrown. In any case, you should always avoid modifying the database from within a user-defined function.

We examine the scalar function first, and then we look at the table value function.

Using Scalar Functions

Scalar functions return a single scalar value. The type can be any SQL scalar type except *text*, *ntext*, *image*, or *timestamp*. You can specify managed data types but not alias data types. Also, for SQLCLR functions, you can specify *nchar* and *nvarchar* but not *char* and *varchar*.

One example of a scalar function is a function that puts leading zeros in front of numbers so they line up properly in a report. Add a function to your example project as follows:

Visual Basic

```
Imports System
Imports System.Data
Imports System.Data.Sql
Imports System.Data.SqlTypes
Imports Microsoft.SqlServer.Server

Partial Public Class UserDefinedFunctions
   <Microsoft.SqlServer.Server.SqlFunction()> _
   Public Shared Function PadVb( _
         ByVal inputValue As integer, _
         ByVal width As Integer) As SqlString
      Return New SqlString(inputValue.ToString().PadLeft(width, "0"c))
   End Function
End Class
```

C#

```
using System;
using System.Data;
using System.Data.Sql;
using System.Data.SqlTypes;
using Microsoft.SqlServer.Server;

public partial class UserDefinedFunctions
{
   [Microsoft.SqlServer.Server.SqlFunction]
   public static SqlString PadCs(int inputValue, int width)
   {
      return new SqlString(inputValue.ToString().PadLeft(width, '0'));
   }
}
```

Add the following SQL script to the Test.sql file that will use this scalar function to pad the *SupplierID* field with leading zeros for a total width of five characters. Notice the use of *dbo* to access the function. User-defined functions always require the owner prefix when you access them.

Visual Basic

```
Select Top dbo.PadVb(supplierid,5) as ID,CompanyName from  suppliers
```

C#

```
Select dbo.PadCs(supplierid,5) as ID,CompanyName from  suppliers
```

In your output window, you will notice that the ID column is very wide; the function was registered in SQL Server with a return type of *nvarchar(4000)*, so the output window doesn't know how wide the column really is. You could alter the registration to set the return data type to *nvarchar(5)*, but you would have a problem if you passed a width other than 5 into the function. The good news is that the values returned were only 5 characters long. The output window will look like the following (except I removed the extra spaces in the ID column).

```
ID     CompanyName
------ ----------------------------------------
00018  Aux joyeux ecclésiastiques
00016  Bigfoot Breweries
00005  Cooperativa de Quesos 'Las Cabras'
00027  Escargots Nouveaux
00001  Exotic Liquids
00029  Forêts d'érables
00014  Formaggi Fortini s.r.l.
00028  Gai pâturage
00024  G'day, Mate
00003  Grandma Kelly's Homestead
00011  Heli Süßwaren GmbH & Co. KG
00023  Karkki Oy
00020  Leka Trading
00021  Lyngbysild
00025  Ma Maison
00006  Mayumi's
00019  New England Seafood Cannery
00002  New Orleans Cajun Delights
00013  Nord-Ost-Fisch Handelsgesellschaft mbH
00015  Norske Meierier
00026  Pasta Buttini s.r.l.
00007  Pavlova, Ltd.
00009  PB Knäckebröd AB
00012  Plutzer Lebensmittelgroßmärkte AG
00010  Refrescos Americanas LTDA
00008  Specialty Biscuits, Ltd.
00017  Svensk Sjöföda AB
00004  Tokyo Traders
00022  Zaanse Snoepfabriek
No rows affected.
(29 row(s) returned)
```

You can view the function registration information in Server Explorer in Visual Studio. Figure 9-5 shows the Server Explorer window and the functions we created. Clicking a function or one of the parameters displays its properties in the Properties window.

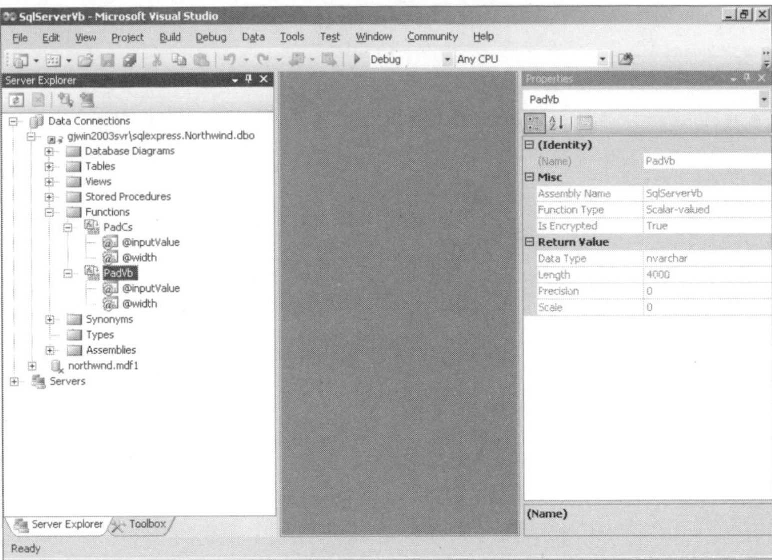

Figure 9-5 You can view the function registration information in Server Explorer and the Properties window.

Sometimes you will want to manually register the function in SQL Server. The following SQL script shows the syntax.

SQL: Scalar Function Registration

```
CREATE FUNCTION <function name>
(
<parameter list>
)
RETURNS <return type>
AS EXTERNAL NAME <assembly identifier>.<type name>.<method name>
```

Using a Streaming Table-Valued Function (TVF)

You can also create a user-defined function that returns a table. When you use the SQLCLR to create one of these functions, it is called a *streaming table-valued function*, or streaming TVF. Streaming TVFs don't return rowsets to the client, as stored procedures do. Instead, you can use streaming TVFs in a SQL statement where a table is expected. For example, you can use a streaming TVF after the word FROM in a SQL SELECT statement.

Streaming TVFs are so named because a typical T-SQL TVF temporarily stores its results in a work table, whereas the SQLCLR TVF is capable of streaming the results it produces–the results don't need to be fully materialized before returning from the function.

The streaming TVF requires a return type of *IEnumerable*, and you must set the *FillRow-MethodName* property to the name of a method that will be used to break an object into the columns required for a row in the returning rowset. The method signature for the fill row method is based on the schema of the row that is being returned.

An example of a streaming TVF is one that accepts a folder name as a parameter and a filter pattern as a parameter and returns a list of file information as a table that can be filtered with a WHERE clause or sorted with the ORDER BY clause (as shown in the following code sample).

Visual Basic

```
Imports System
Imports System.Data
Imports System.Data.Sql
Imports System.Data.SqlTypes
Imports Microsoft.SqlServer.Server
Imports System.IO
Imports System.Collections
Imports System.Security.Principal

Partial Public Class UserDefinedFunctions
   <Microsoft.SqlServer.Server.SqlFunction( _
    FillRowMethodName:="FillRow", _
    TableDefinition:="Name nvarchar(32), Length bigint, Modified DateTime")> _
   Public Shared Function FileListVb( _
         ByVal directoryName As String, ByVal pattern As String) _
         As IEnumerable
      Dim files As FileInfo()
      Dim OriginalContext As WindowsImpersonationContext
      OriginalContext = SqlContext.WindowsIdentity.Impersonate()
      Try
         Dim di As New DirectoryInfo(directoryName)
         files = di.GetFiles(pattern)
      Finally
         If Not (OriginalContext Is Nothing) Then
            OriginalContext.Undo()
         End If
      End Try
      Return files
   End Function

   ' The fill row method that cracks the FileRecord
   ' and returns the individual columns.
   Public Shared Sub FillRow(ByVal Obj As Object, _
         ByRef fileName As SqlString, _
         ByRef fileLength As SqlInt64, _
         ByRef fileModified As SqlDateTime)
      If Not (Obj Is Nothing) Then
         Dim file As FileInfo = CType(Obj, FileInfo)
         fileName = file.Name
         fileLength = file.Length
         fileModified = file.LastWriteTime
      Else
         fileName = SqlString.Null
         fileLength = SqlInt64.Null
         fileModified = SqlDateTime.Null
```

```
      End If
   End Sub
End Class
```

C#

```
using System;
using System.Data;
using System.Data.Sql;
using System.Data.SqlTypes;
using Microsoft.SqlServer.Server;
using System.Collections;
using System.IO;
using System.Security.Principal;

public partial class UserDefinedFunctions
{
   [Microsoft.SqlServer.Server.SqlFunction(FillRowMethodName = "FillRow",
    TableDefinition = "Name nvarchar(32), Length bigint, Modified DateTime")]
   public static IEnumerable FileListCs(string directoryName, string pattern)
   {
      FileInfo[] files;
      WindowsImpersonationContext OriginalContext;
      OriginalContext = SqlContext.WindowsIdentity.Impersonate();
      try
      {
         DirectoryInfo di = new DirectoryInfo(directoryName);
         files = di.GetFiles(pattern);
      }
      finally
      {
         if (OriginalContext != null)
         {
            OriginalContext.Undo();
         }
      }
      return files;
   }

   // The fill row method that cracks the FileRecord
   // and returns the individual columns.
   public static void FillRow(object Obj,
         ref SqlString fileName,
         ref SqlInt64 fileLength,
         ref SqlDateTime fileModified)
   {
      if (Obj != null)
      {
         FileInfo file = (FileInfo)Obj;
         fileName = file.Name;
         fileLength = file.Length;
         fileModified = file.LastWriteTime;
      }
      else
      {
         fileName = SqlString.Null;
```

```
            fileLength = SqlInt64.Null;
            fileModified = SqlDateTime.Null;
        }
    }
}
```

The *FileList* function is a streaming TVF, and streaming TVFs are required to return an *IEnumerator* type. The easiest way to satisfy this requirement is to return an array or some other collection that already implements the *IEnumerator* interface. An array of *FileInfo* objects works well.

The *FileList* function uses impersonation to access the file system, using the credentials of the caller rather the credentials of the SQL service account. After the file information is retrieved, impersonation is undone. This works as long as the directory you are accessing is on the SQL Server machine. Remember that access to a remote machine requires delegation, which must be enabled on an account-by-account basis by the Windows domain administrator and is described in detail in Chapter 13.

The *FillRow* method is responsible for filling a row of data based on the object being passed in. Notice that the parameters are specific to this function, so the method signature varies based on your function.

You must specify the *SqlFunction* attribute's *TableDefinition* and *FillRowMethodName* when you create streaming TVFs. The *TableDefinition* is simply the schema information for the rowset that will be returned. (Note that the file name is set to a measly 32 characters for the purpose of rendering in this book.)

To test this function, add the following script to the Test.sql file.

Visual Basic

```
Select * from dbo.FileListVb('C:\','*.*')
```

C#

```
Select * from dbo.FileListCs('C:\','*.*')
```

Here is the output of this function when executed on my SQL Server machine. Your results will vary.

```
Name                             Length               Modified
-------------------------------- -------------------- -----------------------
AUTOEXEC.BAT                     0                    4/16/2005 12:19:06 PM
boot.ini                         210                  5/1/2005 5:17:26 PM
CONFIG.SYS                       0                    4/16/2005 12:19:06 PM
IO.SYS                           0                    4/16/2005 12:19:07 PM
MSDOS.SYS                        0                    4/16/2005 12:19:07 PM
NTDETECT.COM                     47772                5/1/2005 3:02:40 PM
ntldr                            295536               5/1/2005 3:02:40 PM
pagefile.sys                     943718400            7/26/2005 8:26:32 PM
No rows affected.
(8 row(s) returned)
```

Working with User-Defined Aggregates

SQL Server has aggregate functions for such things as MAX, MIN, COUNT, and SUM, but what if you want to create a new aggregate function? You can create user-defined aggregates using managed code, which means you can create a function that will be executed once for every row in your rowset, using the column of your choice.

To create a user-defined aggregate in Visual Studio .NET, simply add an Aggregate template to your project. This template consists of a structure (C# *struct*), not a partial class. The structure has the *SqlUserDefinedAggregate* attribute, which tells Visual Studio .NET how to deploy the structure. The user-defined aggregate must implement the following four methods.

- *Init* Executes when the aggregate is initialized. You must initialize your fields in this method because SQL Server might choose to reuse your aggregate instead of creating a new one, and this method will be called with the expectation that the aggregate will be "like new" and ready for use.
- *Accumulate* Called once for each row that is to be aggregated.
- *Merge* If SQL Server decides to use multiple threads to perform the aggregation, each thread uses its own aggregate object. The accumulated results of the objects are merged to get the combined result. Notice that *Merge* is handed an aggregate object, not a value, which makes it possible to access the object's member variables.
- *Terminate* Used to return the results.

The *Format* property on the *SqlUserDefinedAggregate* attribute tells SQL Server how to handle serialization. If all members of the class are value types, you can use *Format.Native*. To serialize more complex data, you must do your own serialization.

You should be careful to always test the value parameter (that is passed to the *Accumulate* method) for null values because SQL data types are nullable. There is also an optimizer hint that is called *IsInvariantToNulls*, which is a property of the *SqlUserDefinedAggregate* attribute that you can set to *true* when you don't need the *Accumulate* to be called with null values. In many cases, you will want to ignore nulls, but if you are counting the total number of items, you might want to use null as part of the count. For example, the COUNT aggregate that SQL Server has does not count nulls if you are performing a count on a field, but you can create an aggregate that does count the nulls.

You can also choose the data type to pass into the *Accumulate* method, and the type to be returned from the *Terminate* method.

The *SqlUserDefinedAggregate* attribute also contains a property called *IsNullIfEmpty*. If you set *IsNullIfEmpty* to *true*, the aggregate returns null when there are no values to aggregate.

An example of an aggregate is one that gets the minimum date/time and the maximum date/time and returns the time span, as shown in the following code.

Visual Basic

```
Imports System
Imports System.Data
Imports System.Data.Sql
Imports System.Data.SqlTypes
Imports Microsoft.SqlServer.Server

<Serializable()> _
<Microsoft.SqlServer.Server.SqlUserDefinedAggregate( _
   Format.Native, IsNullIfEmpty:=True, IsInvariantToNulls:=True)> _
Public Structure DateTimeSpanVb

   Private minDate As SqlDateTime
   Private maxDate As SqlDateTime

   Public Sub Init()
      minDate = SqlDateTime.Null
      maxDate = SqlDateTime.Null
   End Sub

   Public Sub Accumulate(ByVal value As SqlDateTime)
      If value.IsNull Then Return
      If ((minDate.IsNull) Or (value.CompareTo(minDate) < 0)) Then
         minDate = value
      End If
      If ((maxDate.IsNull) Or (value.CompareTo(maxDate) > 0)) Then
         maxDate = value
      End If
   End Sub

   Public Sub Merge(ByVal Group As DateTimeSpanVb)
      Accumulate(Group.minDate)
      Accumulate(Group.maxDate)
   End Sub

   Public Function Terminate() As SqlString
      If (maxDate.IsNull Or minDate.IsNull) Then
         Return SqlString.Null
      End If
      Dim ts As TimeSpan
      ts = maxDate.Value - minDate.Value
      Return ts.ToString()
   End Function
End Structure
```

C#

```
using System;
using System.Data;
using System.Data.Sql;
using System.Data.SqlTypes;
using Microsoft.SqlServer.Server;

[Serializable]
[Microsoft.SqlServer.Server.SqlUserDefinedAggregate(
   Format.Native, IsNullIfEmpty=true, IsInvariantToNulls=true)]
```

```
public struct DateTimeSpanCs
{
   private SqlDateTime minDate;
   private SqlDateTime maxDate;

   public void Init()
   {
      minDate = SqlDateTime.Null;
      maxDate = SqlDateTime.Null;
   }

   public void Accumulate(SqlDateTime Value)
   {
      if (Value.IsNull) return;
      if ((minDate.IsNull)||(Value.CompareTo(minDate) < 0))
         minDate = Value;
      if ( (maxDate.IsNull)||(Value.CompareTo(maxDate) > 0))
         maxDate = Value;
   }

   public void Merge(DateTimeSpanCs Group)
   {
      Accumulate(Group.minDate);
      Accumulate(Group.maxDate);
   }

   public SqlString Terminate()
   {
      if (maxDate.IsNull || minDate.IsNull)
         return SqlString.Null;
      TimeSpan  ts;
      ts=maxDate.Value - minDate.Value;
     return  ts.ToString();
   }
}
```

In this sample, two fields are defined: *minDate* and *maxDate*. These fields are set to null in the *Init* method, which ensures that these values are initialized properly even if SQL Server reuses this structure. The *Accumulate* method signature accepts a *SqlDateTime* type for the *Value* parameter. You can test this aggregate by adding the following script to the Test.sql file.

Visual Basic

```
SELECT dbo.DateTimeSpanVb(ShippedDate) AS TimeSpan
   FROM orders
```

C#

```
SELECT dbo.DateTimeSpanCs(ShippedDate) AS TimeSpan
   FROM orders
```

The output should look like the following, which shows 665 days between the first ship date and the last ship date.

Output Window: User-Defined Aggregate

```
TimeSpan
-----------------------
665.00:00:00
No rows affected.
(1 row(s) returned)
```

Sometimes you want to manually register the aggregate in SQL Server. The following SQL script shows the syntax.

SQL: User-Defined Aggregate Registration

```
CREATE AGGREGATE <user defined aggregate name>
(
   @Value <data type of value>
)
RETURNS <data type of return value>
   EXTERNAL NAME <assembly name>.<aggregate name>'
```

Working with Triggers

A *trigger* is a function that is executed in response to an insert, update, or delete of one or more rows from a table; it's an event handler. Coding the trigger is similar to coding a stored procedure, except you typically want to access the rows that are being inserted or deleted. Notice that I didn't mention updated rows, because an update looks like a delete of the original row and an insert of a new row with changes.

You can use a single trigger for insert, update, and delete, which makes sense if you are going to perform the same function. In most cases, it probably makes more sense to use separate triggers for each. You can also assign more than one trigger to a table, but be careful: their firing order is not guaranteed.

Like the stored procedure, the trigger is capable of sending rowsets to the client. For example, a trigger can return the product ID and the amount by which the price changed if the unit price has been updated on a product.

Visual Basic

```
Imports System
Imports System.Data
Imports System.Data.Sql
Imports System.Data.SqlTypes
Imports Microsoft.SqlServer.Server
Imports System.Data.SqlClient

Partial Public Class Triggers
   <Microsoft.SqlServer.Server.SqlTrigger( _
      Name:="ReturnDifferenceVb", Target:="Products", Event:="FOR UPDATE")> _
    Public Shared Sub ReturnDifferenceVb()
```

```
      Using cn As New SqlConnection()
         cn.ConnectionString = "context connection=true"
         cn.Open()
         Using cmd As SqlCommand = cn.CreateCommand()
           cmd.CommandText = _
           "Select i.ProductID,(i.UnitPrice - d.UnitPrice) as AmountChanged " _
           + "from INSERTED i JOIN DELETED d ON i.ProductID = d.ProductID " _
           + "ORDER BY ProductID ASC"
            SqlContext.Pipe.ExecuteAndSend(cmd)
         End Using
      End Using
   End Sub
End Class
```

C#

```
using System;
using System.Data;
using System.Data.Sql;
using Microsoft.SqlServer.Server;
using System.Data.SqlClient;

public partial class Triggers
{
   [Microsoft.SqlServer.Server.SqlTrigger (
      Name="ReturnDifferenceCs", Target="Products",
      Event="FOR UPDATE")]
   public static void ReturnDifferenceCs()
   {
      using (SqlConnection cn = new SqlConnection())
      {
         cn.ConnectionString = "context connection=true";
         cn.Open();
         using (SqlCommand cmd = cn.CreateCommand())
         {
            cmd.CommandText =
             "Select i.ProductID,(i.UnitPrice - d.UnitPrice) as AmoutChanged "
             + "from INSERTED i JOIN DELETED d ON i.ProductID = d.ProductID "
             + "ORDER BY ProductID ASC";
            SqlContext.Pipe.ExecuteAndSend(cmd);
         }
      }
   }
}
```

Notice that the trigger template creates a partial class for all triggers to join. The *SqlTrigger* attribute tells Visual Studio .NET how to register this method. If you had to manually register this method, you would use the following syntax.

SQL: Trigger Registration

```
CREATE TRIGGER <trigger name>
ON <table name>
FOR <INSERT, UPDATE, DELETE>
AS EXTERNAL NAME <assembly name>.<trigger name>'
```

This example uses the context connection to access the INSERTED virtual table, which is aliased as *i*, and DELETED virtual tables, which is aliased as *d*. These tables are populated with the rows that have changed. Because this is an update trigger, there is a matching inserted row for every deleted row. The inserted and deleted rows are joined together to calculate the price change.

Add the following script to the Test.sql file to update the prices on products whose product ID is less than 5.

Visual Basic

```
--10% increase in prices
UPDATE products
SET unitprice = unitprice * 1.1
WHERE ProductID < 5
```

C#

```
--10% increase in prices
UPDATE products
SET unitprice = unitprice * 1.1
WHERE ProductID < 5
```

When you run this script, products 1 through 4 are updated, and you see the returned results in the output window, as follows. Note that because this modifies data, every time you run this script your results are different.

```
ProductID   AmoutChanged
----------- ------------
1           1.8
2           1.9
3           1
4           2.2
(4 row(s) affected)
(4 row(s) returned)
```

If you wanted to add a conditional check to display the output only if the UnitPrice column data has changed, you could use the *IsUpdatedColumn* method on the *TriggerContext* property of the *SqlContext* class. Be aware that the *IsUpdatedColumn* method is similar to its T-SQL counterpart in that it requires an ordinal column position as a parameter instead of a column name. This means that adding a column might change the ordinal position of the column you are monitoring.

Transactions in Triggers

A trigger is always part of an ongoing transaction, either because you have explicitly begun a transaction or because an implicit transaction was created for you. This means you can abort the transaction to prevent the data modification. For example, you can use a trigger to perform validation. If you inspect the inserted row and the data is not valid, you can add the following statement to abort the change. Transactions are covered in more detail in the next chapter.

Visual Basic

```
System.Transactions.Transaction.Current.Rollback()
```

C#

```
System.Transactions.Transaction.Current.Rollback();
```

Working with User-Defined Types

You can create user-defined types (UDTs) in SQL Server to extend the existing scalar type system in the database. In addition to using the existing scalar types, such as *int*, *char*, *nvarchar*, and *uniqueidentifier*, you can create your own atomic data types for creating tables and return values. The benefit is that you can store your data in a more natural way and access the properties and methods of the data type from within T-SQL or your .NET code.

Many people incorrectly conclude that SQL Server is now an object database server, but the UDT feature doesn't come close to fulfilling this fantasy. When you want to store data in a more natural format, however, this feature fulfills the need. For example, it might be advantageous to create a custom date type and time type to be used instead of the built in *datetime* type. Or you might want to store a distance given in feet and inches as a single value rather than two separate values. Remember that the UDT should be an atomic value and should be created only when it is appropriate to display your UDT value in a column.

A UDT must have a string representation for input and display of the data. It must also have a binary representation (for being persisted to disk) that cannot exceed 8000 bytes, and it must have a null representation because all scalars in SQL Server must be able to have a null value.

UDTs must be implemented on every database that uses them. For example, if you are planning to explicitly create temporary tables based on data that is in your current database and that data includes UDTs, the UDTs must also be registered in the *tempdb* database. As a side note, there is no need to register all of your types in the tempdb database even though SQL Server often implicitly creates temporary tables in tempdb that are used to help the SQL engine do its work.

A UDT can be created using a structure (C# struct) or a class, and the Visual Studio .NET template creates a structure. If you decide to change this to a class, you must add the *StructLayout* attribute with the *LayoutKind.Sequential* setting to the class to ensure that the fields in the class remain in the defined order when the object is serialized.

When creating a UDT in Visual Studio .NET, you use the *SqlUserDefinedType* attribute to tell Visual Studio how to register the type. This attribute has a property called *Format* that can be set to *Native* or *UserDefined*. If you set the format to *Native*, the SQLCLR provides the code to read and write the binary data, but all of your fields in this structure must be *blittable*. (Blittable fields are those whose managed and unmanaged byte representations are the same, so no conversion is required to marshal between managed and unmanaged code.) Here are the blittable types and other types you can use with *Format.Native*. Notice that *string* is not in the list. If you want to use a *string* field, you must set the *Format* property to *UserDefined* and you must provide the code to read and write the byte representation to disk.

- *System.Byte*
- *System.SByte*
- *System.Int16*
- *System.UInt16*
- *System.Int32*
- *System.UInt32*
- *System.Int64*
- *System.IntPtr*
- *System.UIntPtr*
- One-dimensional arrays of blittable types, such as an array of integers
- *System.Float*
- *System.Double*
- *SqlSingle*
- *SqlDouble*
- *SqlByte*
- *SqlInt16*
- *SqlUInt16*
- *SqlInt32*
- *SqlUInt32*
- *SqlInt64*
- *SqlUInt64*
- *SqlDateTime*

Another requirement when you use *Format.Native* is that you must assign the *Serializable* attribute to the UDT.

User-defined types can be sorted, indexed, and used in magnitude comparisons if the *IsByteOrdered* property of the *SqlUserDefinedType* attribute is set to *true*. The comparisons are always done using the binary representation of the UDT, so it's important to order your fields in your

UDT so that comparisons can be made. Doing comparisons across the binary representations can be a big limitation if you are attempting to store many fields in the UDT, but if the UDT is implemented properly—that is, implemented for truly atomic values—this should not be a limitation.

The following code sample shows a UDT for a *distance* data type. The distance is atomic in that it is a single value called *totalInches* (but it is represented as feet and inches when it is displayed).

Visual Basic

```
Imports System
Imports System.Data
Imports System.Data.Sql
Imports System.Data.SqlTypes
Imports Microsoft.SqlServer.Server

<Serializable()> _
<Microsoft.SqlServer.Server.SqlUserDefinedType(Format.Native)> _
Public Structure DistanceVb
   Implements INullable, IComparable

   Public ReadOnly Property Feet() As Integer
      Get
         Return CInt(totalInches / 12)
      End Get
   End Property

   Public ReadOnly Property Inches() As Integer
      Get
         Return totalInches Mod 12
      End Get
   End Property


   Public Overrides Function ToString() As String
      Return String.Format("{0} ft. {1} in.", Feet, Inches)
   End Function

   Public ReadOnly Property IsNull() As Boolean Implements INullable.IsNull
      Get
         ' Put your code here
         Return m_Null
      End Get
   End Property

   Public Shared ReadOnly Property Null() As DistanceVb
      Get
         Dim h As DistanceVb = New DistanceVb
         h.m_Null = True
         Return h
      End Get
   End Property
```

```
    Public Shared Function Parse(ByVal s As SqlString) As DistanceVb
        If s.IsNull Then
            Return Null
        End If
        Dim u As DistanceVb = New DistanceVb
        Dim distance As String = s.Value
        If distance = "null" Then Return Null
        distance = distance.ToLower()
        Dim feet As Integer = 0
        Dim inches As Integer = 0
        Dim parts() As String = distance.Split(" "c)
        Dim feetLocation As Integer = Array.IndexOf(parts, "ft.")
        If (feetLocation > 0) Then
            feet = Integer.Parse(parts(feetLocation - 1))
        End If
        Dim inchesLocation As Integer = Array.IndexOf(parts, "in.")
        If (inchesLocation > 0) Then
            inches = Integer.Parse(parts(inchesLocation - 1))
        End If
        u.totalInches = (feet * 12) + inches
        Return u
    End Function

    Public Function CompareTo(ByVal obj As Object) As Integer _
            Implements IComparable.CompareTo
        Dim other As DistanceVb = CType(obj, DistanceVb)
        Return totalInches - other.totalInches
    End Function

    Public totalInches As Integer
    Private m_Null As Boolean
End Structure
```

C#

```
using System;
using System.Data;
using System.Data.Sql;
using System.Data.SqlTypes;
using Microsoft.SqlServer.Server;

[Serializable]
[Microsoft.SqlServer.Server.SqlUserDefinedType(Format.Native)]
public struct DistanceCs : INullable, IComparable
{
    public int Feet
    {
        get
        {
            return totalInches / 12;
        }
    }

    public int Inches
    {
        get
```

```
        {
            return totalInches % 12;
        }
    }

    public override string ToString()
    {
        return string.Format("{0} ft. {1} in.", Feet, Inches);
    }

    public bool IsNull
    {
        get
        {
            return m_Null;
        }
    }

    public static DistanceCs Null
    {
        get
        {
            DistanceCs h = new DistanceCs();
            h.m_Null = true;
            return h;
        }
    }

    public static DistanceCs Parse(SqlString s)
    {
        if (s.IsNull)
            return Null;
        DistanceCs u = new DistanceCs();
        string distance = s.Value;
        if (distance == "null") return Null;
        distance = distance.ToLower();
        int feet = 0;
        int inches = 0;
        string[] parts = distance.Split(' ');
        int feetLocation = Array.IndexOf(parts, "ft.");
        if (feetLocation > 0)
        {
            feet = int.Parse(parts[feetLocation-1]);
        }
        int inchesLocation = Array.IndexOf(parts,"in.");
        if (inchesLocation > 0)
        {
            inches = int.Parse(parts[inchesLocation - 1]);
        }
        u.totalInches = (feet * 12) + inches;
        return u;
    }

    public int CompareTo(object obj)
    {
```

```
        DistanceCs other = (DistanceCs)obj;
        return totalInches - other.totalInches;
    }

    private int totalInches;
    private bool m_Null;
}
```

Notice the use of the *SqlUserDefinedType* attribute, which tells Visual Studio .NET how to deploy this structure. If you need to manually register a UDT with SQL Server, you can use the following SQL syntax.

The *IComparable* interface was also implemented on this UDT, which was not a UDT requirement, but you will want the ability to display and sort this UDT in a *DataGridView* control. For this, the *IComparable* must be implemented.

SQL: UDT Registration

```
CREATE TYPE <UDT name>
FROM <assembly name>.<UDT name>
```

The only data being persisted is *totalInches*, followed by *m_Null*. This means it is easy to provide sorting and comparisons based on the byte representation. Read-only properties were created to access the feet and inches independently. These properties are available in your .NET code as well as your T-SQL statements.

This sample also implements the *INullable* interface methods, *IsNull* and *Null*. Anywhere that a null is required for this data type, the *Null* method is used to generate it.

To test this UDT, add the following SQL script to the Test.sql file.

Visual Basic

```
create table UdtTestVb (Id int not null, distance distanceVb not null)
insert into UdtTestVb values(1, '2 ft. 5 in.')
insert into UdtTestVb values(2, '15 in.')
insert into UdtTestVb values(3, '10 ft.')
insert into UdtTestVb values(4, '1 ft. 23 in.')
select id, convert(nvarchar(25),distance) from UdtTestVb
drop table UdtTestVb
```

C#

```
create table UdtTestCs (Id int not null, distance distanceCs not null)
insert into UdtTestCs values(1, '2 ft. 5 in.')
insert into UdtTestCs values(2, '15 in.')
insert into UdtTestCs values(3, '10 ft.')
insert into UdtTestCs values(4, '1 ft. 23 in.')
select id, convert(nvarchar(25),distance) from UdtTestCs
drop table UdtTestCs
```

Output Window: UDT

```
id          Column1
----------- ------------------------
1           2 ft. 5 in.
2           1 ft. 3 in.
3           10 ft. 0 in.
4           2 ft. 11 in.
(8 row(s) affected)
(4 row(s) returned)
```

When Not to Use a UDT

You should never use a UDT to model business objects such as customers, employees, orders, or products. Remember that in a relational database, these objects are usually represented by rows in one or more tables, whereas the UDT is represented as a single value in a single column. The 8000-byte limit is much higher than you should ever need. Indexing, sorting, and magnitude comparisons are done only one way, across the entire binary representation. This is workable if the UDT is truly atomic, but if you need different indexes, the UDT is not for you.

Any operation on a UDT except comparisons causes the UDT value to be deserialized and a method to be invoked. You should therefore consider performance implications when evaluating the use of a UDT.

When to Use a UDT

If you have atomic data, typically represented as a single field, and you have many complex methods that need to be associated with the data, the UDT might be the answer.

Also, it's worth noting that if you simply want to create a library of functions for use in T-SQL, you can create a type that has no data and comprises static methods. This is equivalent to creating user-defined functions, but the benefit is that these methods are grouped inside your type. Beware that you cannot assign execute permissions to the methods on a UDT. The following code shows how you can package a *PadLeft* and *PadRight* method into a UDT.

Visual Basic

```
Imports System
Imports System.Data
Imports System.Data.Sql
Imports System.Data.SqlTypes
Imports Microsoft.SqlServer.Server

<Serializable()> _
<Microsoft.SqlServer.Server.SqlUserDefinedType(Format.Native)> _
Public Structure StringStuffVb
   Implements INullable

   Public Shared Function PadLeft( _
```

```
        ByVal inputString As SqlString, _
        ByVal totalWidth As SqlInt32) As SqlString
      Return New SqlString( _
        inputString.Value.PadLeft(totalWidth.Value))
   End Function

   Public Shared Function PadRight( _
        ByVal inputString As SqlString, _
        ByVal totalWidth As SqlInt32) As SqlString
      Return New SqlString( _
        inputString.Value.PadRight(totalWidth.Value))
   End Function

   Public Overrides Function ToString() As String
      ' Put your code here
      Return ""
   End Function

   Public ReadOnly Property IsNull() As Boolean Implements INullable.IsNull
      Get
         ' Put your code here
         Return m_Null
      End Get
   End Property

   Public Shared ReadOnly Property Null() As StringStuffVb
      Get
         Dim h As StringStuffVb = New StringStuffVb
         h.m_Null = True
         Return h
      End Get
   End Property

   Public Shared Function Parse(ByVal s As SqlString) As StringStuffVb
      If s.IsNull Then
         Return Null
      End If

      Dim u As StringStuffVb = New StringStuffVb
      ' Put your code here
      Return u
   End Function

   ' Private member
   Private m_Null As Boolean
End Structure
```

C#

```
using System;
using System.Data;
using System.Data.Sql;
using System.Data.SqlTypes;
using Microsoft.SqlServer.Server;

[Serializable]
```

```
[Microsoft.SqlServer.Server.SqlUserDefinedType(Format.Native)]
public struct StringStuffCs : INullable
{
   public static SqlString PadLeft(
      SqlString inputString, SqlInt32 totalWidth)
   {
      return new SqlString(
         inputString.Value.PadLeft(totalWidth.Value));
   }

   public static SqlString PadRight(
   SqlString inputString, SqlInt32 totalWidth)
   {
      return new SqlString(
         inputString.Value.PadRight(totalWidth.Value));
   }

   public override string ToString()
   {
      // Replace the following code with your code
      return "";
   }

   public bool IsNull
   {
      get
      {
         // Put your code here
         return m_Null;
      }
   }

   public static StringStuffCs Null
   {
      get
      {
         StringStuffCs h = new StringStuffCs();
         h.m_Null = true;
         return h;
      }
   }

   public static StringStuffCs Parse(SqlString s)
   {
      if (s.IsNull)
         return Null;
      StringStuffCs u = new StringStuffCs();
      // Put your code here
      return u;
   }

   // Private member
   private bool m_Null;
}
```

The UDT in this code sample has no fields for user data. The *PadLeft* and *PadRight* methods are added as static (Visual Basic shared) methods. The trick to using these methods in a T-SQL statement is to know the calling syntax. Here is the code you can add to your Test.sql file.

Visual Basic

```
select '<' + StringStuffVb::PadLeft('Hi',10) + '>'
select '<' + StringStuffVb::PadRight('Hi',10) + '>'
```

C#

```
select '<' + StringStuffCs::PadLeft('Hi',10) + '>'
select '<' + StringStuffCs::PadRight('Hi',10) + '>'
```

The output looks like this:

```
Column1
-----------------------
<        Hi>
(8 row(s) affected)
(1 row(s) returned)
Column1
-----------------------
<Hi        >
(8 row(s) affected)
(1 row(s) returned)
```

Note that the affected value of the row(s) may differ based on where you placed this T-SQL script command in your test file. In reality, no rows were affected by this T-SQL script, but the number was carried down from a previous T-SQL command.

Accessing SQLCLR Features from the Client

Accessing most of the SQLCLR features from a client application is rather straightforward. Stored procedures, for example, are executed exactly in the same fashion as their T-SQL counterparts.

One difference you will find is using the User Defined Types that you created in SQL Server from the client. To test this, you need to add a new project to your existing solution. In Visual Studio, click File | Add | New Project. Select a Windows application in C# or Visual Basic and name the project *UdtTest*.

Add a reference to the SqlServerCs or SqlServerVb project by right-clicking the UdtTest project and clicking Add Reference. Click the Projects tab, and you will see your SqlServerCs or SqlServerVb project. Select it to add the reference.

If you are working with Visual Basic, you will want to add an imports statement for the *SqlServerVb* namespace because Visual Basic adds this by default, whereas C# does not add a namespace.

You need to change the UdtTest project to be the startup project. Do this by right-clicking the UdtTest project and clicking Set as StartUp Project.

Add a *Button* control and *DataGridView* control to the default form. Set the *Button* control's *Text* property to "UDT Test". Double-click the button to add a click handler, and add the following code.

Visual Basic

```
Imports System.Data
Imports System.Data.SqlClient
Imports SqlServerVb

Public Class Form1

    Private Sub button1_Click(ByVal sender As System.Object, _
            ByVal e As System.EventArgs) Handles button1.Click
        Using cn As New SqlConnection()
            cn.ConnectionString = _
                    "server=.;database=northwind;integrated security=true"
            Using cmd As SqlCommand = cn.CreateCommand()
                cmd.CommandText = _
                     "create table UdtTestCs (" _
                       + "Id int not null, " _
                       + "Distance DistanceVb not null)"
                cn.Open()
                cmd.ExecuteNonQuery()
                cmd.CommandText = _
                        "insert into UdtTestCs values(@Id, @distance)"
                Dim id As SqlParameter = cmd.CreateParameter()
                id.ParameterName = "@id"
                id.DbType = DbType.Int32
                Dim distance As SqlParameter = cmd.CreateParameter()
                distance.ParameterName = "@distance"
                distance.SqlDbType = SqlDbType.Udt
                distance.UdtTypeName = "DistanceVb"
                cmd.Parameters.Add(id)
                cmd.Parameters.Add(distance)
                id.Value = 1
                distance.Value = DistanceVb.Parse("2 ft. 5 in.")
                cmd.ExecuteNonQuery()
                id.Value = 2
                distance.Value = DistanceVb.Parse("15 in.")
                cmd.ExecuteNonQuery()
                id.Value = 3
                distance.Value = DistanceVb.Parse("10 ft.")
                cmd.ExecuteNonQuery()
                id.Value = 4
                distance.Value = DistanceVb.Parse("1 ft. 23 in.")
                cmd.ExecuteNonQuery()

                cmd.CommandText = "Select * from UdtTestCs"
                cmd.Parameters.Clear()
                Dim testTable As New DataTable()
```

```
                testTable.Load(cmd.ExecuteReader())
                dataGridView1.DataSource = testTable

                cmd.CommandText = "DROP TABLE UdtTestCs"
                cmd.ExecuteNonQuery()
            End Using
        End Using
    End Sub
End Class
```

C#

```
using System;
using System.Data;
using System.Windows.Forms;
using System.Data.SqlClient;


namespace UdtTest
{
    public partial class Form1 : Form
    {
        public Form1()
        {
            InitializeComponent();
        }

        private void button1_Click(object sender, EventArgs e)
        {
            using (SqlConnection cn = new SqlConnection())
            {
                cn.ConnectionString =
                    "server=.;database=northwind;integrated security=true";
                using (SqlCommand cmd = cn.CreateCommand())
                {
                    cmd.CommandText =
                         "create table UdtTestCs ("
                       + "Id int not null, "
                       + "Distance DistanceCs not null)";
                    cn.Open();
                    cmd.ExecuteNonQuery();
                    cmd.CommandText =
                        "insert into UdtTestCs values(@Id, @distance)";
                    SqlParameter id = cmd.CreateParameter();
                    id.ParameterName = "@id";
                    id.DbType = DbType.Int32;
                    SqlParameter distance = cmd.CreateParameter();
                    distance.ParameterName = "@distance";
                    distance.SqlDbType = SqlDbType.Udt;
                    distance.UdtTypeName = "DistanceCs";
                    cmd.Parameters.Add(id);
                    cmd.Parameters.Add(distance);
                    id.Value = 1;
                    distance.Value = DistanceCs.Parse("2 ft. 5 in.");
                    cmd.ExecuteNonQuery();
                    id.Value = 2;
```

```
                    distance.Value = DistanceCs.Parse("15 in.");
                    cmd.ExecuteNonQuery();
                    id.Value = 3;
                    distance.Value = DistanceCs.Parse("10 ft.");
                    cmd.ExecuteNonQuery();
                    id.Value = 4;
                    distance.Value = DistanceCs.Parse("1 ft. 23 in.");
                    cmd.ExecuteNonQuery();

                    cmd.CommandText = "Select * from UdtTestCs";
                    cmd.Parameters.Clear();
                    DataTable testTable = new DataTable();
                    testTable.Load(cmd.ExecuteReader());
                    dataGridView1.DataSource = testTable;

                    cmd.CommandText = "DROP TABLE UdtTestCs";
                    cmd.ExecuteNonQuery();
                }
            }
        }
    }
}
```

This code creates a connection to the database and then executes a series of T-SQL commands using the same *SqlCommand* object. The first command creates a table. After that, there are four commands to insert data. Notice that the parameter needed to have its *SqlDbType* set to *SqlDbType.Udt* and *UdtTypeName* was set to either *DistanceCs* or *DistanceVb*. To create an instance of the appropriate distance, the *Parse* method was executed. Finally, the last command retrieved the data that was placed into the table and placed the results into the *DataGridView* control. The result is shown in Figure 9-6. Notice that the distance is sortable because the *IComparable* interface was implemented on the distance UDT.

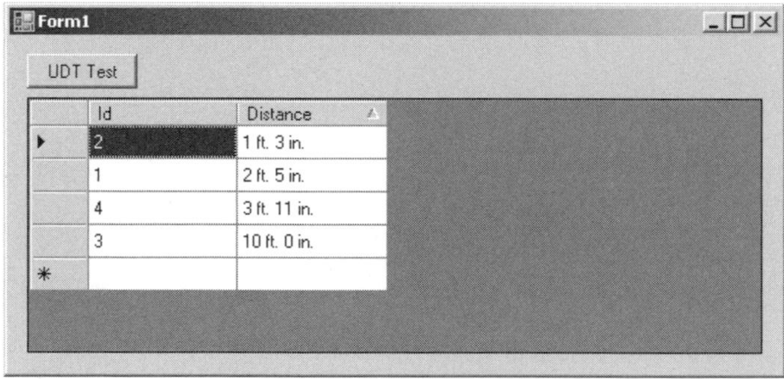

Figure 9-6 The result after adding distance objects to the database and then retrieving them into a *DataGridView* control.

Summary

- You can write stored procedures, user-defined functions, aggregates, triggers, and UDTs using managed code hosted by the SQLCLR.
- The SQLCLR does not replace Transact-SQL. Set-based operations are best accomplished using T-SQL, whereas computation-intensive operations are best done using the SQLCLR.
- You must enable the SQLCLR to use it on the SQL Server instance.
- The *SqlContext* object provides access to the SQLCLR environment. This object has the *Pipe* property, which sends messages and data to the client.
- The *SqlContext* object's *Pipe* property also contains the *SendResultsStart*, *SendResultsRow*, and *SendResultsEnd* methods that are used for sending rowset data back to the client.
- You can write your SQLCLR source code with a text editor, compile it using the command-line compiler, and load and register the SQLCLR code using SQL scripts. Visual Studio .NET provides a developer-friendly interface that simplifies coding, deployment, and debugging.
- You should use the context connection to access data within the current database because the context connection runs in-process and does not use any of the protocol stacks to communicate with the database server.
- You should use a UDT only to define an atomic value that will be viewed in a column, not to represent business objects such as customers and employees.

Chapter 10

Understanding Transactions

The previous chapters covered ways to access and modify data, but they barely mentioned transactions because transactions are so important they deserve their own chapter. This chapter explains what a transaction is and how you can use different types of transactions with your ADO.NET data access, starting with the simplest type, the implicit transaction.

You will find that this chapter quickly moves beyond ADO.NET to a new namespace called *System.Transactions*. That's right: the *System.Transactions* namespace is not part of ADO.NET. It was developed by the Enterprise Services team at Microsoft. We will cover this namespace in detail because it offers a consistent, flexible programming model that's simply too significant to overlook.

What Is a Transaction?

A transaction is an atomic unit of work that must be completed in its entirety. The transaction succeeds if it is committed and it fails if it is aborted. Transactions have four essential attributes: atomicity, consistency, isolation, and durability (known as the ACID attributes).

- *Atomicity* The work cannot be broken into smaller parts. Although a transaction might contain many SQL statements, they must be run as an all-or-nothing proposition, which means that if a transaction is half complete when an error occurs, the work reverts to its state prior to the start of the transaction.
- *Consistency* A transaction must operate on a consistent view of the data and must also leave the data in a consistent state. Any work in progress must not be visible to other transactions until the transaction has been committed.
- *Isolation* A transaction should appear to be running by itself—the effects of other ongoing transactions must be invisible to this transaction, and the effects of this transaction must be invisible to other ongoing transactions.
- *Durability* When a transaction is committed, it must be persisted so it will not be lost in the event of a power failure or other system failure. Only committed transactions are recovered during power-up and crash recovery; uncommitted work is rolled back.

Concurrency Models and Database Locking

The attributes of consistency and isolation are implemented by using the database locking mechanism, which keeps one transaction from affecting another. If one transaction needs access to data that another transaction is working with, the data is locked until the first transaction is committed or rolled back. Transactions that need to access locked data are forced to wait until the lock is released, which means that long-running transactions can affect performance and scalability. The use of locks to prevent access to the data is known as a "pessimistic" concurrency model.

In an "optimistic" concurrency model, locks are not used when the data is read. Instead, when updates are made, the data is checked to see if the data has changed since it was read. If the data has changed, an exception is thrown and the application applies business logic to recover.

Transaction Isolation Levels

Complete isolation can be great, but it comes at a high cost. Complete isolation means that any data that is read or written during a transaction must be locked. Yes, even data that is read is locked because a query for customer orders should yield the same result at the beginning of a transaction and at the end of the transaction.

Depending on your application, you might not need complete isolation. By tweaking the transaction isolation level, you can reduce the amount of locking and increase scalability and performance. The transaction isolation level affects whether you experience the following.

- *Dirty Read* Being able to read data that has not been committed. This can be a big problem if a transaction that has added data is rolled back.
- *Nonrepeatable Read* When a transaction reads the same row more than once and a different transaction modifies the row between reads.
- *Phantom Read* When a transaction reads a rowset more than once and a different transaction inserts or deletes rows between the first transaction's reads.

Table 10-1 lists the transaction isolation levels along with their effects. It also shows the concurrency model that the isolation level supports.

Table 10-1 Isolation Levels in SQL Server 2005

Level	Dirty Read	Nonrepeatable Read	Phantom Read	Concurrency Model
Read Uncommitted	Yes	Yes	Yes	None
Read Committed with Locks	No	Yes	Yes	Pessimistic
Read Committed with Snapshots	No	Yes	Yes	Optimistic
Repeatable Read	No	No	Yes	Pessimistic
Snapshot	No	No	No	Optimistic
Serializable	No	No	No	Pessimistic

Here are details on each concurrency level.

- *Read Uncommitted* Queries inside one transaction are affected by uncommitted changes in another transaction. No locks are acquired, and no locks are honored when data is read.
- *Read Committed With Locks* The default setting in SQL Server. Committed updates are visible within another transaction. Long-running queries and aggregations are not required to be point-in-time consistent.
- *Read Committed With Snapshots* Committed updates are visible within another transaction. No locks are acquired, and row versioning is used to track row modifications. Long-running queries and aggregates are required to be point-in-time consistent. This level comes with the overhead of the version store (discussed further at the end of this list). The version store provides increased throughput with reduced locking contention.
- *Repeatable Read* Within a transaction, all reads are consistent—other transactions cannot affect your query results because they cannot complete until you finish your transaction and release your locks. This level is used primarily when you read data with the intention of modifying the data in the same transaction.
- *Snapshot* Used when accuracy is required on long-running queries and multi-statement transactions but there is no plan to update the data. No read locks are acquired to prevent modifications by other transactions because the changes will not be seen until the snapshot completes and the data modification transactions commit. Data can be modified within this transaction level at the risk of conflicts with transactions that have updated the same data after the snapshot transaction started.
- *Serializable* Places a range lock, which is a multirow lock, on the complete rowset that is accessed, preventing other users from updating or inserting rows into the data set until the transaction is complete. This data is accurate and consistent through the life of the transaction. This is the most restrictive of the isolation levels. Because of the large amount of locking in this level, you should use it only when necessary.

The version store retains row version records after the UPDATE or DELETE statement has committed, until all active transactions have committed. The version store essentially retains row version records until all of the following transaction types have committed or ended:

- Transactions that are running under Snapshot isolation
- Transactions that are running under Read Committed with Snapshot isolation
- All other transactions that started before the current transaction committed

Single Transactions and Distributed Transactions

A transaction is a unit of work that must be done with a single durable resource (such as a database or a message queue). In the .NET Framework, a transaction typically represents all of the work that can be done on a single open connection.

A distributed transaction is a transaction that spans multiple durable resources. In the .NET Framework, if you need a transaction to include work on multiple connections, you must perform a distributed transaction. A distributed transaction uses a two-phase commit protocol and a dedicated transaction manager. In Windows, the dedicated transaction manager for managing distributed transactions is the Distributed Transaction Coordinator (DTC). (This is covered in more detail later in the chapter.)

Creating a Transaction

The two types of transactions are *implicit* and *explicit*. Each SQL statement runs in its own implicit transaction. This means if you don't explicitly create a transaction, a transaction is implicitly created for you on a statement-by-statement basis. This ensures that a SQL statement that updates many rows is either completed as a unit or rolled back.

Creating a Transaction Using T-SQL

An explicit transaction is one that you create in your program. You can explicitly create a transaction in T-SQL by using the following script.

SQL: Explicit Transaction

```
SET XACT_ABORT ON
BEGIN TRY
   BEGIN TRANSACTION
   --work code here
   COMMIT TRANSACTION
END TRY
BEGIN CATCH
   ROLLBACK TRANSACTION
   --cleanup code
END CATCH
```

The SQL TRY/CATCH block is used to catch any errors and roll back the transaction. This code sets *XACT_ABORT* to on, which ensures that all errors under severity level 21 are handled as transaction abort errors. Severity level 21 and higher is considered fatal and stops code execution, which also rolls back the transaction.

The scope of the transaction is limited to the statements in the TRY block, which can include calls to other stored procedures.

Creating a Transaction Using the ADO.NET *DbTransaction* Object

Another way to create an explicit transaction is to put the transaction logic in your .NET code. The *DbConnection* object has the *BeginTransaction* method, which creates a *DbTransaction* object. The following code snippet shows how this is done.

Visual Basic

```
Private Sub Button1_Click(ByVal sender As System.Object, _
      ByVal e As System.EventArgs) Handles Button1.Click
   Dim cnSetting As ConnectionStringSettings = _
      ConfigurationManager.ConnectionStrings("NorthwindString")
   Using cn As New SqlConnection()
      cn.ConnectionString = cnSetting.ConnectionString
      cn.Open()
      Using tran As SqlTransaction = cn.BeginTransaction()
         Try
            'work code here
            Using cmd As SqlCommand = cn.CreateCommand()
               cmd.Transaction = tran
               cmd.CommandText = "SELECT count(*) FROM employees"
               Dim count As Integer = CInt(cmd.ExecuteScalar())
               MessageBox.Show(count.ToString())
            End Using
            'if we made it this far, commit
            tran.Commit()
         Catch xcp As Exception
            tran.Rollback()
            'cleanup code
            MessageBox.Show(xcp.Message)
         End Try
      End Using
   End Using
End Sub
```

C#

```
private void button1_Click(object sender, EventArgs e)
{
   ConnectionStringSettings cnSetting =
      ConfigurationManager.ConnectionStrings["NorthwindString"];
   using (SqlConnection cn = new SqlConnection())
   {
      cn.ConnectionString = cnSetting.ConnectionString;
      cn.Open();
      using (SqlTransaction tran = cn.BeginTransaction())
      {
         try
         {
            //work code here
            using (SqlCommand cmd = cn.CreateCommand())
            {
               cmd.Transaction = tran;
               cmd.CommandText = "SELECT count(*) FROM employees";
               int count = (int)cmd.ExecuteScalar();
               MessageBox.Show(count.ToString());
            }
            //if we made it this far, commit
            tran.Commit();
         }
         catch (Exception xcp)
         {
            tran.Rollback();
```

```
                //cleanup code
                MessageBox.Show(xcp.Message);
            }
        }
    }
}
```

In this code, a *SqlConnection* object is created and opened, and then the connection object is used to create a transaction object by executing the *BeginTransaction* method. The try block does the work and commits the transaction. If an exception is thrown, the catch block rolls back the transaction. Also notice that the *SqlCommand* object must have its *Transaction* property assigned to the connection's transaction.

The scope of the transaction is limited to the code within the try block, but the transaction was created by a specific connection object, so the transaction cannot span to a different connection object.

Setting the Transaction Isolation Level

Each SQL Server connection (SQL session) can have its transaction isolation level set. The setting you assign remains until the connection is closed or until you assign a new setting. One way to assign the transaction isolation level is to add the SQL statement to your stored procedure. For example, to set the transaction isolation level to Repeatable Read, add the following SQL statement to your stored procedure.

SQL

```
SET TRANSACTION ISOLATION LEVEL REPEATABLE READ
```

Another way to set the transaction isolation level is to add a query hint to your SQL statement. For example, the following SQL statement overrides the current session's isolation setting and uses the Read Uncommitted isolation level to perform the query.

SQL

```
SELECT * FROM CUSTOMERS WITH (NOLOCK)
```

The transaction isolation level can also be set on the *DbTransaction* class, which the *SqlTransaction* class inherits from. Simply pass the desired transaction isolation level to the *BeginTransaction* method, as shown in the following code.

Visual Basic

```
Private Sub Button2_Click(ByVal sender As System.Object, _
      ByVal e As System.EventArgs) Handles Button3.Click
   Dim cnSetting As ConnectionStringSettings = _
      ConfigurationManager.ConnectionStrings("NorthwindString")
   Using cn As New SqlConnection()
      cn.ConnectionString = cnSetting.ConnectionString
      cn.Open()
      Using tran As SqlTransaction = _
         cn.BeginTransaction(System.Data.IsolationLevel.Serializable)
```

```
            Try
               'work code here
               Using cmd As SqlCommand = cn.CreateCommand()
                  cmd.Transaction = tran
                  cmd.CommandText = "SELECT count(*) FROM employees"
                  Dim count As Integer = CInt(cmd.ExecuteScalar())
                  MessageBox.Show(count.ToString())
               End Using
               'if we made it this far, commit
               tran.Commit()
            Catch xcp As Exception
               tran.Rollback()
               'cleanup code
               MessageBox.Show(xcp.Message)
            End Try
         End Using
      End Using
   End Sub
```

C#

```
private void button2_Click(object sender, EventArgs e)
{
   ConnectionStringSettings cnSetting =
      ConfigurationManager.ConnectionStrings["NorthwindString"];
   using (SqlConnection cn = new SqlConnection())
   {
      cn.ConnectionString = cnSetting.ConnectionString;
      cn.Open();
      using (SqlTransaction tran =
         cn.BeginTransaction(System.Data.IsolationLevel.Serializable))
      {
         try
         {
            //work code here
            using (SqlCommand cmd = cn.CreateCommand())
            {
               cmd.Transaction = tran;
               cmd.CommandText = "SELECT count(*) FROM employees";
               int count = (int)cmd.ExecuteScalar();
               MessageBox.Show(count.ToString());
            }
            //if we made it this far, commit
            tran.Commit();
         }
         catch (Exception xcp)
         {
            tran.Rollback();
            //cleanup code
            MessageBox.Show(xcp.Message);
         }
      }
   }
}
```

Introducing the *System.Transactions* Namespace

The *System.Transactions* namespace offers enhanced transactional support for managed code and makes it possible to handle transactions in a rather simple programming model. *System.Transactions* is designed to integrate well with SQL Server 2005 and offers automatic promotion of standard transactions to fully distributed transactions. Figure 10-1 shows the hierarchy of the *Transaction* class in the *System.Transactions* namespace. The *TransactionScope* class was added to the diagram to show that it is not related to the *Transaction* class but is used to create transactions.

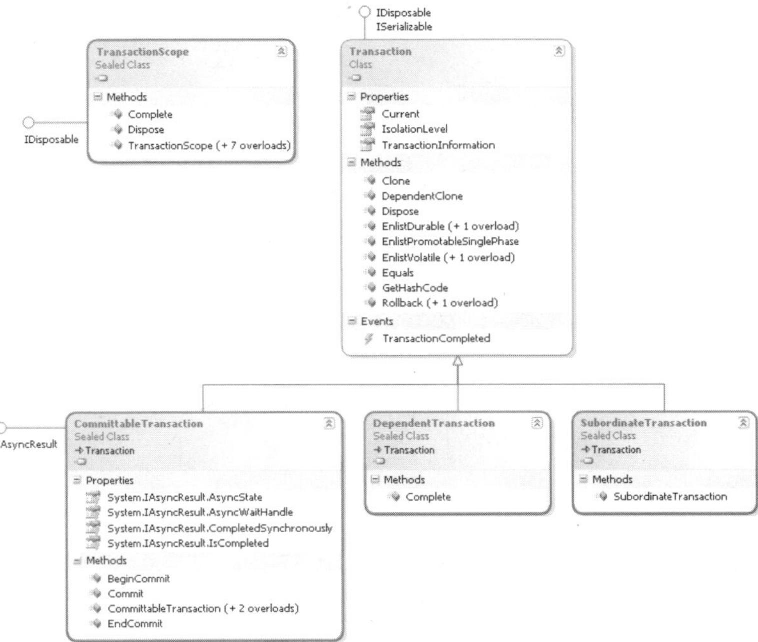

Figure 10-1 The *System.Transactions.Transaction* class hierarchy

Creating a Transaction Using the *TransactionScope* Class

You can also create a transaction in your .NET code by using classes in the *System.Transaction* namespace. The most commonly used class is the *TransactionScope* class; it creates a standard transaction called a "local lightweight transaction" that is automatically promoted to a full-fledged distributed transaction if required. Note that this automatically promoted transaction is commonly referred to as an *implicit transaction*. This is certainly worth mentioning because it seems to give a somewhat different meaning to this term. You should note that even in this context, you are not explicitly creating the transaction for the work and explicitly issuing a commit or rollback. Instead, you are creating a scope where a transaction will exist and will automatically commit or roll back.

Visual Basic

```
Private Sub Button3_Click(ByVal sender As System.Object, _
      ByVal e As System.EventArgs) Handles Button2.Click
   Dim cnSetting As ConnectionStringSettings = _
      ConfigurationManager.ConnectionStrings("NorthwindString")
   Using ts As TransactionScope = New TransactionScope()
      Using cn As New SqlConnection()
         cn.ConnectionString = cnSetting.ConnectionString
         cn.Open()
         'work code here
         Using cmd As SqlCommand = cn.CreateCommand()
            cmd.CommandText = "SELECT count(*) FROM employees"
            Dim count As Integer = CInt(cmd.ExecuteScalar())
            MessageBox.Show(count.ToString())
         End Using
         'if we made it this far, commit
         ts.Complete()
      End Using
   End Using
End Sub
```

C#

```
private void button3_Click(object sender, EventArgs e)
{
   ConnectionStringSettings cnSetting =
      ConfigurationManager.ConnectionStrings["NorthwindString"];
   using (TransactionScope ts = new TransactionScope())
   {
      using (SqlConnection cn = new SqlConnection())
      {
         cn.ConnectionString = cnSetting.ConnectionString;
         cn.Open();
         //work code here
         using (SqlCommand cmd = cn.CreateCommand())
         {
            cmd.CommandText = "SELECT count(*) FROM employees";
            int count = (int)cmd.ExecuteScalar();
            MessageBox.Show(count.ToString());
         }
         //if we made it this far, commit
         ts.Complete();
      }
   }
}
```

This code starts by creating a *TransactionScope* object in a *using* block. If a connection is created, the *TransactionScope* object assigns a transaction to this connection, so you don't need to add anything to your code to enlist this connection into the transaction. Notice that the *SqlCommand* object doesn't need to have the *Transaction* property assigned, but the *SqlCommand* object joins the transaction. If an exception is thrown within the *TransactionScope* object's *using* block, the transaction aborts and all work is rolled back. The last line of the *TransactionScope* object's *using* block calls the *Complete* method to commit the transaction. This method sets an internal flag called *Complete*. The *Complete* method can be called only once. This is a design decision that ensures that you don't continue adding code after a call to *Complete* and then try calling *Complete* again. A second call to *Complete* throws an *InvalidOperationException*.

The scope of the transaction is limited to the code within the *TransactionScope* object's *using* block, which includes any and all connections created within the block, even if the connections are created in methods called within the block. You can see that the *TransactionScope* object offers more functionality than ADO.NET transactions and is easy to code.

Note The code in this example performs as well as the previous examples showing ADO.NET transactions, so you should consider standardizing your code to use this programming model whenever you need transactional behavior, as long as you are using SQL Server 2005. If you are using SQL Server 2000, you should continue to use the existing ADO.NET transaction because SQL Server 2000 does not know how to create a local lightweight transaction.

Setting the Transaction Options

You can set the isolation level and the transaction's timeout period on the *TransactionScope* object by creating a *TransactionOptions* object. The *TransactionOptions* class has an *IsolationLevel* property that you can use to deviate from the default isolation level of Serializable and employ another isolation level (such as Read Committed). The isolation level is merely a suggestion (hint) to the database. Most database engines try to use the suggested level if possible. The *TransactionOptions* class also has a *TimeOut* property that can be used to deviate from the default of one minute.

The *TransactionScope* object's constructor also takes a *TransactionScopeOption* enumeration parameter. This parameter can be set to any of the following.

- *Required* If your application has already started a transaction, this *TransactionScope* joins it. If there is no ongoing transaction, a new transaction is created. To help you understand the benefit of this setting, consider a *BankAccount* class that has *Deposit*, *WithDraw*, and *Transfer* methods. You want to create a *TransactionScope* in all three methods, but when you get to the *Transfer* method, it calls the *WithDraw* and the *Deposit* methods that already have a *TransactionScope* defined. This means that the *Deposit* and *WithDraw* will be nested within the *Transfer*. You can't remove the *TransactionScope* from the *WithDraw* and *Deposit* because you need the ability to call these methods directly, and you want these methods to execute within a transaction. With the *Required* setting, the *WithDraw* and *Deposit* join the *Transfer* transaction. This is the default setting.
- *RequiresNew* Always starts a new transaction, even if there is an ongoing transaction. Expanding on the previous *BankAccount* scenario, you may want an audit record to be written, regardless of the outcome of the overall transaction. If you simply try to write an audit record and the transaction aborts, the audit record is rolled back as well. Use the *RequiresNew* setting to write the audit record regardless of the overall transaction state.

- *Suppress* Suppresses any transaction activity in this block. This setting provides a way to do non-transactional work while there is an ongoing transaction. The execution of the *Complete* method is not required in this block and has no effect.

The following code creates and configures a *TransactionOptions* object, which is passed to the constructor of the *TransactionScope* object.

Visual Basic

```
Private Sub Button4_Click(ByVal sender As System.Object, _
      ByVal e As System.EventArgs) Handles Button4.Click
   Dim cnSetting As ConnectionStringSettings = _
      ConfigurationManager.ConnectionStrings("NorthwindString")
   Dim opt as New TransactionOptions()
   opt.IsolationLevel = IsolationLevel.Serializable
   Using ts As TransactionScope = _
         New TransactionScope(TransactionScopeOption.Required, opt)
      Using cn As New SqlConnection()
         cn.ConnectionString = cnSetting.ConnectionString
         cn.Open()
         'work code here
         Using cmd As SqlCommand = cn.CreateCommand()
            cmd.CommandText = "SELECT count(*) FROM employees"
            Dim count As Integer = CInt(cmd.ExecuteScalar())
            MessageBox.Show(count.ToString())
         End Using
      End Using
      'if we made it this far, commit
      ts.Complete()
   End Using
End Sub
```

C#

```
private void button4_Click(object sender, EventArgs e)
{
   ConnectionStringSettings cnSetting =
      ConfigurationManager.ConnectionStrings["NorthwindString"];
   TransactionOptions opt = new TransactionOptions();
   opt.IsolationLevel = System.Transactions.IsolationLevel.Serializable;
   using (TransactionScope ts =
      new TransactionScope(TransactionScopeOption.Required, opt))
   {
      using (SqlConnection cn = new SqlConnection())
      {
         cn.ConnectionString = cnSetting.ConnectionString;
         cn.Open();
         //work code here
         using (SqlCommand cmd = cn.CreateCommand())
         {
            cmd.CommandText = "SELECT count(*) FROM employees";
            int count = (int)cmd.ExecuteScalar();
            MessageBox.Show(count.ToString());
         }
      }
```

```
        //if we made it this far, commit
        ts.Complete();
    }
```

Working with Distributed Transactions

Before the release of the classes in the *System.Transactions* namespace, developers had to create classes that inherited from the *ServicedComponent* class in the *System.EnterpriseServices* namespace to perform distributed transactions, as shown in the following snippet.

Visual Basic

```
Imports System.EnterpriseServices

<Transaction> _
Public Class MyClass
      Inherits ServicedComponent
   <AutoComplete()> _
   Public Sub MyMethod()
      ' calls to other serviced components
      ' and resource managers like SQL Server
   End Sub
End Class
```

C#

```
using System.EnterpriseServices;

[Transaction]
public class MyClass : ServicedComponent
{
   [AutoComplete]
   public void MyMethod()
   {
      // calls to other serviced components
      // and resource managers like SQL Server
   }
}
```

Notice the use of the *Transaction* and *AutoComplete* attributes to ensure that any method called within the class is in a transactional context. The use of the *AutoComplete* attribute makes it simple to commit a transaction in a declarative way, but you can also use the *ContextUtil* class for better control of the transaction from within your code.

The problem with this old approach is that you must inherit from the *ServicedComponent* class–that is, you lose the flexibility of inheriting from a class that might be more appropriate to your internal application's class model. This also means that the DTC is always used, which is too resource intensive if you don't really need to execute a distributed transaction. Ideally, the DTC should be used only when necessary. This approach uses the COM+ hosting model, in which your component must be loaded into Component Services.

The *System.Transactions* namespace includes the Lightweight Transaction Manager (LTM) in addition to the DTC. The LTM is used to manage a single transaction to a durable resource manager, such as SQL Server 2005. Volatile resource managers, which are memory based, can also be enlisted in a single transaction. The transaction managers are intended to be invisible to the developer, who never needs to write code to access them.

Using the *TransactionScope* object and the same programming model that we used for single transactions, you can easily create a distributed transaction. When you access your first durable resource manager, a lightweight committable transaction is created to support the single transaction. When you access a second durable resource manager, the transaction is promoted to a distributed transaction. When a distributed transaction is executed, the DTC manages the two-phase commit protocol to commit or roll back the transaction.

The LTM and the DTC represent their transaction using the *System.Transactions.Transaction* class, which has a static (Visual Basic shared) property called *Current* that gives you access to the current transaction. The current transaction is known as the *ambient transaction*. This property is null if there is no ongoing transaction. You can access the *Current* property directly to change the transaction isolation level, roll back the transaction, or view the transaction status.

Promotion Details

When a transaction is first created, it always attempts to be a lightweight committable transaction, managed by the LTM. The LTM lets the underlying durable resource manager, such as SQL Server 2005, manage the transaction. A transaction that is managed by the underlying manager is known as a *delegated transaction*. The only thing the LTM does is monitor the transaction for a need to be promoted. If promotion is required, the LTM tells the durable resource manager to provide an object that is capable of performing a distributed transaction. To support the notification, the durable resource manager must implement the *IPromotableSinglePhaseNotification* interface. This interface, and its parent interface, the *ITransactionPromoter*, are shown here.

Visual Basic

```
Imports System
Namespace System.Transactions
   Public Interface IPromotableSinglePhaseNotification
         Inherits ITransactionPromoter
      Sub Initialize()
      Sub Rollback(ByVal singlePhaseEnlistment As _
         SinglePhaseEnlistment)
      Sub SinglePhaseCommit(ByVal singlePhaseEnlistment As _
         SinglePhaseEnlistment)
   End Interface
   Public Interface ITransactionPromoter
      Function Promote() As Byte()
   End Interface
End Namespace
```

C#
```
using System;
namespace System.Transactions
{
   public interface IPromotableSinglePhaseNotification :
      ITransactionPromoter
   {
      void Initialize();
      void Rollback(SinglePhaseEnlistment
         singlePhaseEnlistment);
      void SinglePhaseCommit(SinglePhaseEnlistment
         singlePhaseEnlistment);
   }
   public interface ITransactionPromoter
   {
      byte[] Promote();
   }
}
```

For example, the System.Data.dll assembly contains an internal class called *SqlDelegatedTransaction* that implements these interfaces for use with SQL Server 2005. SQL Server 2005 uses delegated transactions whenever possible. This means that on the *SqlConnection.Open* method, a local promotable transaction is created using the *SqlDelegatedTransaction* class, not a distributed transaction, and it remains a local transaction with its accompanying performance implications until you require a distributed transaction.

A transaction can be promoted from a lightweight committable transaction to a distributed transaction in the following three scenarios:

- When a durable resource manager is used that doesn't implement the *IPromotableSinglePhaseNotification* interface, such as SQL Server 2000
- When two durable resource managers are enlisted in the same transaction
- When the transaction spans multiple application domains

Viewing Distributed Transactions

The DTC is available through Component Services (choose Start | Control Panel | Administrative Tools | Component Services | Computers | My Computer | Distributed Transaction Coordinator | Transaction Statistics). When Component Services starts, the Transaction Statistics node is blank, as shown in Figure 10-2. If you run any of the previous code examples, the screen will remain blank because the examples use standard transactions; when a transaction is promoted to a distributed transaction, however, you will see a change to the total transaction count as well as the other counters.

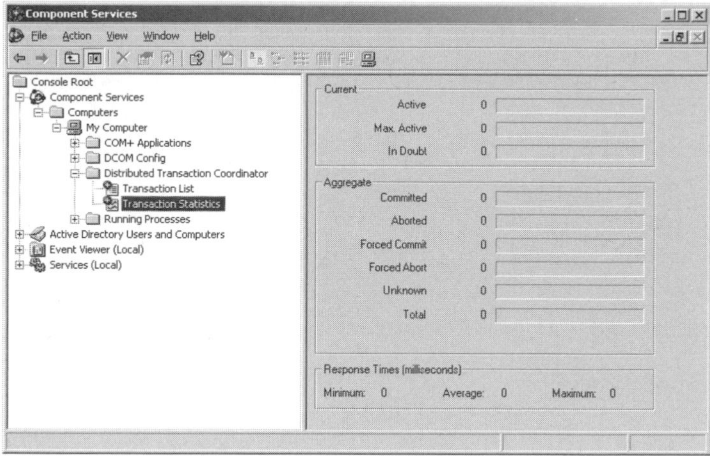

Figure 10-2 The DTC is used to monitor distributed transactions.

Creating a Distributed Transaction

To create a distributed transaction, you can use the same *TransactionScope* programming model that we used to create a standard transaction, but you add work to be performed on a different connection. The following code example uses two connections. Even though these connection objects use the same connection string, they are two different connection objects, which will cause the single transaction to be promoted to a distributed transaction.

> **Note** Before running this code, make sure that the DTC is running or you will get an exception stating that the MSDTC is not available.

Visual Basic

```
Private Sub Button5_Click(ByVal sender As System.Object, _
   ByVal e As System.EventArgs) Handles Button5.Click
   Dim cnSetting As ConnectionStringSettings = _
      ConfigurationManager.ConnectionStrings("NorthwindString")
   Using ts As TransactionScope = New TransactionScope()
      Using cn As New SqlConnection()
         cn.ConnectionString = cnSetting.ConnectionString
         cn.Open()
         'work code here
         Using cmd As SqlCommand = cn.CreateCommand()
            cmd.CommandText = "SELECT count(*) FROM employees"
            Dim count As Integer = CInt(cmd.ExecuteScalar())
            MessageBox.Show(count.ToString())
         End Using
      End Using
      Using cn As New SqlConnection()
         cn.ConnectionString = cnSetting.ConnectionString
         cn.Open()
         'work code here
```

```
         Using cmd As SqlCommand = cn.CreateCommand()
            cmd.CommandText = "SELECT count(*) FROM employees"
            Dim count As Integer = CInt(cmd.ExecuteScalar())
            MessageBox.Show(count.ToString())
         End Using
      End Using
      'if we made it this far, commit
      ts.Complete()
   End Using
End Sub
```

C#

```
private void button5_Click(object sender, EventArgs e)
{
   ConnectionStringSettings cnSetting =
      ConfigurationManager.ConnectionStrings["NorthwindString"];
   using (TransactionScope ts = new TransactionScope())
   {
      using (SqlConnection cn = new SqlConnection())
      {
         cn.ConnectionString = cnSetting.ConnectionString;
         cn.Open();
         //work code here
         using (SqlCommand cmd = cn.CreateCommand())
         {
            cmd.CommandText = "SELECT count(*) FROM employees";
            int count = (int)cmd.ExecuteScalar();
            MessageBox.Show(count.ToString());
         }
      }
      using (SqlConnection cn = new SqlConnection())
      {
         cn.ConnectionString = cnSetting.ConnectionString;
         cn.Open();
         //work code here
         using (SqlCommand cmd = cn.CreateCommand())
         {
            cmd.CommandText = "SELECT count(*) FROM employees";
            int count = (int)cmd.ExecuteScalar();
            MessageBox.Show(count.ToString());
         }
      }
      //if we made it this far, commit
      ts.Complete();
   }
}
```

Because this code uses multiple connections, the connections appear to the LTM as requiring multiple durable resource managers, and the transaction that was originally delegated to SQL Server 2005 is promoted to a distributed transaction.

Building Your Own Transactional Resource Manager

You can build your own transactional resource manager classes that can participate in a transaction that is within the *TransactionScope*. Remember that your resource manager can be a volatile resource manager that is memory based or it can be a durable resource manager that is persisted to disk or other media. In your class, you must implement the *IEnlistmentNotification* interface, which has methods that are invoked on objects enlisted in a transaction, and you must also add code to enlist in the transaction.

We start by creating a simple *Employee* class that enlists in an ongoing transaction if one exists. If a change is made to one of the *Employee* properties while in a transaction, the value is stored in a working variable. If there is no ongoing transaction, the change is immediately stored to a committed variable.

Creating the *Employee* Class

The following code creates a simple *Employee* class containing *EmployeeID*, *LastName*, and *FirstName* properties. This class also contains private variables to hold the working and committed values for each of the properties. The *ToString* method is overridden to provide an easy means to get the state of the object, and internal methods are created for committing and rolling back the transaction.

Visual Basic

```
Imports System.Transactions

Public Class Employee
   Private workingEmployeeId As Integer
   Private workingLastName As String
   Private workingFirstName As String
   Private committedEmployeeId As Integer
   Private committedLastName As String
   Private committedFirstName As String

   public Sub New(employeeId as Integer, lastName as String, _
         firstName as String)
      Me.EmployeeID = employeeId
      Me.LastName = lastName
      Me.FirstName = firstName
   End Sub

   Public Property EmployeeID() As Integer
      Get
         Return workingEmployeeId
      End Get
      Set(ByVal value As Integer)
         workingEmployeeId = value
      End Set
   End Property

   Public Property LastName() As String
```

```
      Get
         Return workingLastName
      End Get
      Set(ByVal value As String)
         workingLastName = value
      End Set
   End Property

   Public Property FirstName() As String
      Get
         Return workingFirstName
      End Get
      Set(ByVal value As String)
         workingFirstName = value
      End Set
   End Property

   Public Overrides Function ToString() As String
      Return String.Format( _
         "  Employee WorkingVal   {0} {1}, {2}" + vbCrLf + _
         "           CommittedVal {3} {4}, {5}", _
         workingEmployeeId, workingLastName, workingFirstName, _
         committedEmployeeId, committedLastName, committedFirstName)
   End Function

   Public Sub internalCommit()
      committedEmployeeId = workingEmployeeId
      committedFirstName = workingFirstName
      committedLastName = workingLastName
   End Sub

   Public Sub internalRollback()
      workingEmployeeId = committedEmployeeId
      workingFirstName = committedFirstName
      workingLastName = committedLastName
   End Sub
End Class
```

C#

```
using System;
using System.Transactions;

namespace TransactionTest
{
   class Employee
   {
      private int workingEmployeeId;
      private string workingLastName;
      private string workingFirstName;
      private int committedEmployeeId;
      private string committedLastName;
      private string committedFirstName;

      public Employee(int employeeId, string lastName, string firstName)
      {
```

```
         EmployeeID = employeeId;
         LastName = lastName;
         FirstName = FirstName;
      }

      public int EmployeeID
      {
         get{ return workingEmployeeId; }
         set{ workingEmployeeId = value; }
      }

      public string LastName
      {
         get{ return workingLastName; }
         set{ workingLastName = value; }
      }

      public string FirstName
      {
         get{ return workingFirstName; }
         set{ workingFirstName = value; }
      }

      public override string ToString()
      {
         return string.Format(
              "  Employee WorkingVal   {0} {1}, {2}\r\n" +
              "            CommittedVal {3} {4}, {5}",
              workingEmployeeId, workingLastName, workingFirstName,
              committedEmployeeId, committedLastName, committedFirstName);
      }

      private void  internalCommit()
      {
         committedEmployeeId = workingEmployeeId;
         committedFirstName = workingFirstName;
         committedLastName = workingLastName;
      }

      private void internalRollback()
      {
        workingEmployeeId =  committedEmployeeId;
        workingFirstName =  committedFirstName;
        workingLastName = committedLastName;
      }
   }
}
```

This code makes use of the working values in the properties and in the *internalRollback* method. The committed values are set in the *internalCommit* method, and they are displayed in the *ToString* method. To test the class, add a button containing the following code to a form.

Visual Basic

```
Private Sub button6_Click(ByVal sender As System.Object, _
      ByVal e As System.EventArgs) Handles button6.Click
   Dim e1 As New Employee(1, "JoeLast", "JoeFirst")
   Dim e2 As New Employee(2, "MaryLast", "MaryFirst")
   Try
      Using scope As New TransactionScope()
         e1.LastName = "JoeTranLast"
         e2.LastName = "MaryTranLast"
         scope.Complete()
      End Using
   Catch xcp As Exception
      System.Diagnostics.Debug.WriteLine("Exception:" + xcp.Message)
   End Try
      System.Diagnostics.Debug.WriteLine( _
         "Final Answer:" + vbCrLf + e1.ToString())
      System.Diagnostics.Debug.WriteLine( _
         "Final Answer:" + vbCrLf + e2.ToString())
End Sub
```

C#

```
private void button6_Click(object sender, EventArgs e)
{
   Employee e1 = new Employee(1, "JoeLast", "JoeFirst");
   Employee e2 = new Employee(2, "MaryLast", "MaryFirst");
   try
   {
      using (TransactionScope scope = new TransactionScope())
      {
         e1.LastName = "JoeTranLast";
         e2.LastName = "MaryTranLast";
         scope.Complete();
      }
   }
   catch (Exception xcp)
   {
      System.Diagnostics.Debug.WriteLine("Exception: " + xcp.Message);
   }
   System.Diagnostics.Debug.WriteLine(
      "Final Answer:\r\n" + e1.ToString());
   System.Diagnostics.Debug.WriteLine(
      "Final Answer:\r\n" + e2.ToString());
}
```

The output window displays the following information when the button is clicked.

Output Window

```
Final Answer:
  Employee WorkingVal   1 JoeTranLast, JoeFirst
           CommittedVal 0 ,
Final Answer:
  Employee WorkingVal   2 MaryTranLast, MaryFirst
           CommittedVal 0 ,
```

Notice that each employee displays the working and committed values, but the committed values have not been set because there is no code to commit the objects.

Implementing the *IEnlistmentNotification* Interface

You must implement the *IEnlistmentNotification* interface to get notification of changes to the transaction. This interface has the following methods that must be implemented.

- *Commit* Executed by the transaction manager during the second phase of a transaction, when the transaction manager instructs participants to commit the transaction. This method is passed an *Enlistment* object, which needs to have its *Done* method executed if the commitment is okay.
- *Prepare* Called by the transaction manager during the first phase of a transaction, when the transaction manager asks participants whether they can commit the transaction.
- *Rollback* Called by the transaction manager if the transaction is rolled back.
- *InDoubt* Called by the Lightweight Transaction Manager only on volatile resources when the transaction manager has invoked a single-phase commit operation to a single durable resource and then the connection to the durable resource is lost before the transaction result is obtained. At that point, the transaction outcome cannot be safely determined. The volatile resource that receives a call to its *InDoubt* method should perform whatever recovery or containment operation it understands on the affected data. This method is called to represent the final state of this object (volatile resource), so neither *Commit* nor *Rollback* will be called on this object.

In addition to adding the implementation of these methods, you must add code to enlist in any ongoing transaction. When a change is made to a property, if there is no ongoing transaction, the committed value is immediately updated. If there is an ongoing transaction, this object enlists in it and the committed value is not updated until the transaction is committed. The following code shows how the *Employee* class has been updated to add automatic enlistment and a simple implementation of the *IEnlistmentNotification* interface methods.

Visual Basic

```
Imports System.Transactions

Public Class Employee
   Implements IEnlistmentNotification
   Private currentTransaction As Transaction
   Private workingEmployeeId As Integer
   Private workingLastName As String
   Private workingFirstName As String
   Private committedEmployeeId As Integer
   Private committedLastName As String
   Private committedFirstName As String

   Public Sub New(ByVal employeeId As Integer, ByVal lastName As String, _
         ByVal firstName As String)
      Me.EmployeeID = employeeId
```

```
      Me.LastName = lastName
      Me.FirstName = firstName
   End Sub

   Public Property EmployeeID() As Integer
      Get
         Return workingEmployeeId
      End Get
      Set(ByVal value As Integer)
         workingEmployeeId = value
         If Not Enlist() Then committedEmployeeId = value
      End Set
   End Property

   Public Property LastName() As String
      Get
         Return workingLastName
      End Get
      Set(ByVal value As String)
         workingLastName = value
         If Not Enlist() Then committedLastName = value
      End Set
   End Property

   Public Property FirstName() As String
      Get
         Return workingFirstName
      End Get
      Set(ByVal value As String)
         workingFirstName = value
         If Not Enlist() Then committedFirstName = value
      End Set
   End Property

   Public Overrides Function ToString() As String
      Return String.Format( _
         "  Employee WorkingVal   {0} {1}, {2}" + vbCrLf + _
         "             CommittedVal {3} {4}, {5}", _
         workingEmployeeId, workingLastName, workingFirstName, _
         committedEmployeeId, committedLastName, committedFirstName)
   End Function

   Public Sub internalCommit()
      committedEmployeeId = workingEmployeeId
      committedFirstName = workingFirstName
      committedLastName = workingLastName
   End Sub

   Public Sub internalRollback()
      workingEmployeeId = committedEmployeeId
      workingFirstName = committedFirstName
      workingLastName = committedLastName
   End Sub
   Public Function Enlist() As Boolean
      If Not (currentTransaction Is Nothing) Then
```

```
         Return True
      End If
      currentTransaction = Transaction.Current
      If currentTransaction Is Nothing Then
         Return False
      End If
      currentTransaction.EnlistVolatile(Me, EnlistmentOptions.None)
      Return True
   End Function
   Public Sub Commit(ByVal enlistment As System.Transactions.Enlistment) _
         Implements System.Transactions.IEnlistmentNotification.Commit
      System.Diagnostics.Debug.WriteLine("Commit(before):" + vbCrLf _
         + Me.ToString())
      internalCommit()
      currentTransaction = Nothing
      enlistment.Done()
   End Sub
   Public Sub InDoubt(ByVal enlistment As System.Transactions.Enlistment) _
         Implements System.Transactions.IEnlistmentNotification.InDoubt
      System.Diagnostics.Debug.WriteLine("InDoubt:" + vbCrLf + Me.ToString())
      currentTransaction = Nothing
      Throw New TransactionAbortedException( _
         "Commit results cannot be determined")
   End Sub
   Public Sub Prepare(ByVal preparingEnlistment As _
         System.Transactions.PreparingEnlistment) _
         Implements System.Transactions.IEnlistmentNotification.Prepare
      System.Diagnostics.Debug.WriteLine("Prepare(before):" + vbCrLf _
         + Me.ToString())
      preparingEnlistment.Prepared()
   End Sub
   Public Sub Rollback(ByVal enlistment As System.Transactions.Enlistment) _
         Implements System.Transactions.IEnlistmentNotification.Rollback
      System.Diagnostics.Debug.WriteLine("Rollback(before):" + vbCrLf _
         + Me.ToString())
      currentTransaction = Nothing
      Me.internalRollback()
   End Sub
End Class
```

C#

```
using System;
using System.Transactions;

namespace TransactionTest
{
   class Employee : IEnlistmentNotification
   {
      private Transaction currentTransaction;
      private int workingEmployeeId;
      private string workingLastName;
      private string workingFirstName;
      private int committedEmployeeId;
      private string committedLastName;
      private string committedFirstName;
```

```
public Employee(int employeeId, string lastName, string firstName)
{
   EmployeeID = employeeId;
   LastName = lastName;
   FirstName = firstName;
}

public int EmployeeID
{
   get{ return workingEmployeeId; }
   set
   {
      workingEmployeeId = value;
      if (!Enlist()) committedEmployeeId = value;
   }
}

public string LastName
{
   get{ return workingLastName; }
   set
   {
      workingLastName = value;
      if (!Enlist()) committedLastName = value;
   }
}

public string FirstName
{
   get{ return workingFirstName; }
   set
   {
      workingFirstName = value;
      if (!Enlist()) committedFirstName = value;
   }
}

public override string ToString()
{
   return string.Format(
        "  Employee WorkingVal   {0} {1}, {2}\r\n" +
        "            CommittedVal {3} {4}, {5}",
        workingEmployeeId, workingLastName, workingFirstName,
        committedEmployeeId, committedLastName, committedFirstName);
}

private void internalCommit()
{
   committedEmployeeId = workingEmployeeId;
   committedFirstName = workingFirstName;
   committedLastName = workingLastName;
}

private void internalRollback()
{
```

```
            workingEmployeeId = committedEmployeeId;
            workingFirstName = committedFirstName;
            workingLastName = committedLastName;
        }
        public bool Enlist()
        {
            if (currentTransaction != null)
            {
                return true;
            }
            currentTransaction = Transaction.Current;
            if (currentTransaction == null)
            {
                return false;
            }
            currentTransaction.EnlistVolatile(this,
                EnlistmentOptions.None);
            return true;
        }
        #region IEnlistmentNotification Members
        public void Commit(Enlistment enlistment)
        {
            System.Diagnostics.Debug.WriteLine("Commit(before):\r\n"
                + this.ToString());
            internalCommit();
            currentTransaction = null;
            enlistment.Done();
        }
        public void InDoubt(Enlistment enlistment)
        {
            System.Diagnostics.Debug.WriteLine("InDoubt:\r\n"
                + this.ToString());
            currentTransaction = null;
            throw new TransactionAbortedException(
                "Commit results cannot be determined");
        }
        public void Prepare(PreparingEnlistment
            preparingEnlistment)
        {
            System.Diagnostics.Debug.WriteLine("Prepare(before):\r\n"
                + this.ToString());
            preparingEnlistment.Prepared();
        }
        public void Rollback(Enlistment enlistment)
        {
            System.Diagnostics.Debug.WriteLine("Rollback(before):\r\n"
                + this.ToString());
            currentTransaction = null;
            this.internalRollback();
        }
        #endregion
    }
}
```

This code implements the interface along with its methods. Notice that we simply made calls to the *internalCommit* and *internalRollback* methods as required. We added a new field called *currentTransaction* to hold the transaction that this object is enlisted in. We also added the *Enlist* method, which returns *true* if this object is enlisted in a transaction and *false* if it is not. If this is the first time the *Enlist* method is entered after a transaction starts, the *Enlist* method sets the *currentTransaction* field and enlists in the current transaction. Additional calls to the *Enlist* method will quickly return *true* because the *currentTransaction* field is set.

The *currentTransaction* field is cleared when the transaction completes, which is when the *Commit*, *RollBack*, or *InDoubt* method is called.

Notice that every property setter contains a call to the *Enlist* method to ensure automatic enlistment. If the object is not in a transaction, the committed value is immediately set.

If you run the same test, the output window will look like the following. Notice that the *Prepare* method is called on both of the *Employee* objects before the *Commit* method is called on the *Employee* objects.

Output Window

```
Prepare(before):
  Employee WorkingVal   1 JoeTranLast, JoeFirst
           CommittedVal 1 JoeLast, JoeFirst
Prepare(before):
  Employee WorkingVal   2 MaryTranLast, MaryFirst
           CommittedVal 2 MaryLast, MaryFirst
Commit(before):
  Employee WorkingVal   1 JoeTranLast, JoeFirst
           CommittedVal 1 JoeLast, JoeFirst
Commit(before):
  Employee WorkingVal   2 MaryTranLast, MaryFirst
           CommittedVal 2 MaryLast, MaryFirst
Final Answer:
  Employee WorkingVal   1 JoeTranLast, JoeFirst
           CommittedVal 1 JoeTranLast, JoeFirst
Final Answer:
  Employee WorkingVal   2 MaryTranLast, MaryFirst
           CommittedVal 2 MaryTranLast, MaryFirst
```

You can see that the initial creation of the *Employee* objects immediately commits the values because these objects were created prior to entering the transaction scope and there is no ongoing transaction. Notice that the working value and committed value are different in the *Prepare* and *Commit* output because the transaction has not committed yet. You can see that in the final answer output, the objects are committed, so their working and committed values have been updated properly.

Implementing the *ISinglePhaseNotification* Interface

The *ISinglePhaseNotification* interface provides a quick commit when only a single resource needs to be committed. It only has one method, called *SinglePhaseCommit*, which can be easily implemented. The following code shows the addition of this method to the previous code example.

Visual Basic

```
Public Class Employee
   Implements IEnlistmentNotification, ISinglePhaseNotification
' . . . Existing code
Public Sub SinglePhaseCommit(ByVal singlePhaseEnlistment As _
      System.Transactions.SinglePhaseEnlistment) Implements _
      System.Transactions.ISinglePhaseNotification.SinglePhaseCommit
   System.Diagnostics.Debug.WriteLine("SinglePhaseCommit(before):" + vbCrLf _
      + Me.ToString())
   internalCommit()
   currentTransaction = Nothing
   singlePhaseEnlistment.Done()
End Sub
```

C#

```
class Employee : IEnlistmentNotification,
   ISinglePhaseNotification
// . . . Existing code
public void SinglePhaseCommit(
   SinglePhaseEnlistment singlePhaseEnlistment)
{
   System.Diagnostics.Debug.WriteLine("SinglePhaseCommit(before):\r\n"
         + this.ToString());
   internalCommit();
   currentTransaction = null;
   singlePhaseEnlistment.Done();
}
```

If you run the code, you won't see a change to the output window because the previous examples have updated two volatile resource managers (two *Employee* objects). Comment out the code that changes the second employee, and run the example code. The output window will show that the prepare phase was skipped and the single-phase commit was executed as shown below.

Output Window: Single-Phase Commit

```
SinglePhaseCommit(before):
  Employee WorkingVal   1 JoeTranLast, JoeFirst
           CommittedVal 1 JoeLast, JoeFirst
Final Answer:
  Employee WorkingVal   1 JoeTranLast, JoeFirst
           CommittedVal 1 JoeTranLast, JoeFirst
Final Answer:
  Employee WorkingVal   2 MaryLast, MaryFirst
           CommittedVal 2 MaryLast, MaryFirst
```

You can see that although the code worked before the implementation of this interface, for greater efficiency when you are working with a single resource manager, you should always implement the *ISinglePhaseNotification* interface when you implement the *IEnlistmentNotification* interface.

Using *System.Transactions* with the SQLCLR

When we invoke managed stored procedures within a database transaction, we flow the transaction context down into the CLR code. The context connection is the same connection, so the same transaction applies and no extra overhead is involved.

If you're opening a connection to a remote server from within the SQLCLR, you use a new connection, so the existing database transaction that came with the context is promoted to a distributed transaction.

The notion of a "current transaction" that is available in the *System.Transactions* namespace is also available in the SQLCLR. If a transaction is active when your code enters the SQLCLR, you will see that *Transaction.Current* contains the transaction within the SQLCLR.

If you want to abort the external transaction from within your stored procedure or function, you can call the *Transaction.Current.Rollback* method.

If you use the *TransactionScope* object in the SQLCLR, you must use a distributed transaction. This means that if you are in a lightweight transaction, the use of the *TransactionScope* causes a promotion, which means additional overhead. If you will need a distributed transaction anyway, because you need to access remote servers from the SQLCLR, there is no difference in overhead.

Best Practices

Regardless of how you implement transactions, you must get in and out of your transactions quickly because transactions lock valuable resources. Use the "just-in-time" approach to create a transaction just before you need it, open your connections, execute your commands, and complete the transaction. Avoid running lots of non-database code inside the transaction so that other resources aren't locked any longer than absolutely necessary.

Transactions also affect connection pooling. When a connection is enlisted in an active transaction scope, even if the connection is closed, it is not fully released to the connection pool to be reused right away. The closed connection is still enlisted in the active transaction scope, so it remains in a special subpool until the active transaction is completed. Once the transaction has completed, all connections are released back to their appropriate connection pools.

Summary

- Transactions have ACID attributes: atomicity, consistency, isolation, and durability. Data locking gives transactions their ACID properties. Locking is costly; in some applications, you can adjust the extent of the locking by setting the transaction isolation level.
- A transaction is a unit of work that is done with a single durable resource, and a distributed transaction is a unit of work that is done with multiple durable resources.
- Transactions can be initiated from T-SQL statements, the *DbConnection* object's *BeginTran* method, or the *TransactionScope* object (which is in the *System.Transactions* namespace). The *System.Transactions* namespace is not part of ADO.NET but provides a programming model for transactions that should always be used when working with SQL Server 2005.
- You can view distributed transactions by using the Distributed Transaction Coordinator (DTC), which displays the committed, aborted, and total transaction counts, as well as other information.
- Using the *TransactionScope* object, you can create delegated transactions, which are lightweight transactions managed by the resource manager. If another durable resource enlists in the same transaction, the lightweight transaction is promoted to a distributed transaction.
- You can build your own transactional resource manager by implementing the *IEnlistmentNotification* interface. Add the *ISinglePhaseNotification* interface for better performance when there is only one resource in the transaction.
- The SQLCLR also has access to the current transaction through its *Transaction.Current* property. If you create a *TransactionScope* object within the SQLCLR while a lightweight transaction is active, the lightweight transaction is promoted to a distributed transaction.
- Transactions should always be coded using the just-in-time approach, where you create the transaction just before it is needed, do the work, and commit as quickly as possible.

Chapter 11

Retrieving Metadata

Imagine that you've written an order entry application that is highly dependent on a backend database server. All of your code gains access to the data through stored procedures that you have written. The application is deployed, and a couple hundred users enter customer and order information all day long.

Now imagine that you need to add a new field that contains the customer's credit limit. You must add this field to the customer screen in the application and add business logic to ensure that new orders cannot be entered if the customer's credit limit has been exceeded. Of course, you must add this field to the customer table in the database and modify the stored procedures for retrieving and modifying the customer table to deal with the new field. Oh, yeah: you also have to modify your data access code that calls these stored procedures.

In addition to all of the work that you have to do to accomplish this task, some important questions will arise: How can you be sure that the database is in sync with the code? What should you do if a user is running an older version of the application? Do the database changes need to be deployed at exactly the same time as the application changes?

The answers to these questions might be different for every application, but if your code can get information from the database that describes its tables and stored procedures, you can programmatically decide to abort the application if it's not in sync with the database or to adapt it to the database.

As data stores add new features and schemas change, it becomes increasingly important to have a means of finding out about the data store's capabilities. Exposing metadata–data that describes data–is important in applications that need the ability to identify and possibly adjust to changes in the backend data store.

You can use metadata in an application to enable users to create new tables or fields on the fly. Developers also create tools that generate data access layer code based on the metadata that the database provides. Microsoft Visual Studio and other development tools make heavy use of metadata when running data access wizards.

Although most data access technologies allow you to query for database schema information, the query method depends on the data provider. This chapter examines the schema API and its metadata capabilities.

Getting Started

The metadata capabilities in Microsoft ADO.NET are exposed through a generic API using the *DbConnection* object. The *DbConnection* object's *GetSchema* method has overloads that allow you to pass the name of the schema information, called the *metadata collection*, that you are interested in. You can also pass filter information. Table 11-1 shows the overloads.

Table 11-1 The *GetSchema* Overloads

Overload	Description
GetSchema( )	Gets a *DataTable* with a row for each metadata collection that is available with this provider. This option is the same as calling *GetSchema("MetaDataCollections")*.
GetSchema(string)	Passes a metadata collection name and gets a *DataTable* containing a row for each item found in that metadata collection in the database.
GetSchema(string, string array)	Passes a metadata collection name and an array of string values that specify how to filter the results, and gets a *DataTable* containing a row for each filtered item found in the metadata collection in the database.

You need an open connection to execute the *GetSchema* method. You can start by calling the *GetSchema* method with no parameters; it returns a list of the available metadata collections.

Our sample project is a Windows Forms application that contains both a Microsoft Access version and a SQL Server version of the *Northwind* database. It also has a copy of the *Northwind* database attached (mounted) to SQL Server Express that is used with the OLEDB and ODBC providers. The App.config file contains a clear statement first, which clears all connection strings that may have been defined in the machine.config file. Next, the following connection strings were added into the App.config file to provide connectivity to each database as needed.

App.config File

```
<?xml version="1.0" encoding="utf-8" ?>
<configuration>
   <connectionStrings>
      <clear />
      <add name="NorthwindSqlClient" connectionString=
         "Data Source=.\SQLEXPRESS;
         AttachDbFilename=|DataDirectory|\northwnd.mdf;
         Integrated Security=True;User Instance=True"
         providerName="System.Data.SqlClient" />
      <add name="NorthwindSqlOleDb"
         connectionString=
         "Provider=SQLOLEDB.1;
         Integrated Security=SSPI;
         Persist Security Info=False;
```

```
      Initial Catalog=Northwind;
      Data Source=.\SQLEXPRESS"
      providerName="System.Data.OleDb" />
    <add name="NorthwindSqlOdbc"
        connectionString=
      "DRIVER=SQL Server;
      SERVER=.\SQLEXPRESS;
      DATABASE=Northwind;Trusted_Connection=Yes"
      providerName="System.Data.Odbc" />
    <add name="NorthwindAccess"
      connectionString=
      "Provider=Microsoft.Jet.OLEDB.4.0;
      Data Source=|DataDirectory|\Northwind.mdb;
      Persist Security Info=True"
      providerName="System.Data.OleDb" />
  </connectionStrings>
</configuration>
```

Set a reference to System.Configuration.dll and add the *using* (C#) and *imports* (Visual Basic) statements for the *System.Configuration* namespace.

The connection strings are selectable by reading the *ConnectionStringSettings* collection and populating a combo box with the name of each connection. This application will be looking in SQL Express for a permanently mounted copy of the *Northwind* database. Rather than manually mounting the *Northwind* database, you can add code to check for the existence of the *Northwind* database and, if it is not found, mount the database. This is done in the form's *Load* event handler, as shown in the following code sample.

Visual Basic

```
Private Sub Form1_Load(ByVal sender As System.Object, _
      ByVal e As System.EventArgs) Handles MyBase.Load
   For Each cnSetting As ConnectionStringSettings In _
         ConfigurationManager.ConnectionStrings
      comboBox1.Items.Add(cnSetting.Name)
   Next
   'mount northwind if it isn't mounted
   Using cn As New SqlConnection()
      Using cmd As SqlCommand = cn.CreateCommand()
         cmd.CommandText = "SELECT COUNT(*) FROM sysdatabases" _
            + "WHERE name='Northwind'"
         cn.ConnectionString = "Server=.\SQLEXPRESS;" _
            + "Database=master;" _
            + "integrated security=true"
         cn.Open()
         Dim count As Integer = CType(cmd.ExecuteScalar(), Integer)
         If (count = 1) Then
            Return
         End If
         cn.Close()
      End Using
      cn.ConnectionString = "Server=.\SQLEXPRESS;" _
```

```
            + "AttachDbFilename=|DataDirectory|\MountedNorthwnd.mdf;" _
            + "Database=Northwind;" _
            + "integrated security=true;" _
            + "user instance=false"
        cn.Open()
        cn.Close()
        MessageBox.Show("Northwind Mounted")
    End Using
End Sub
```

C#

```
private void Form1_Load(object sender, EventArgs e)
{
    foreach (ConnectionStringSettings cnSetting in
        ConfigurationManager.ConnectionStrings)
    {
        comboBox1.Items.Add(cnSetting.Name);
    }
    //mount northwind if it isn't mounted
    using (SqlConnection cn = new SqlConnection())
    {
        using (SqlCommand cmd = cn.CreateCommand())
        {
            cmd.CommandText = "SELECT COUNT(*) FROM sysdatabases"
                + "WHERE name='Northwind'";
            cn.ConnectionString = @"Server=.\SQLEXPRESS;"
                + "Database=master;"
                + "integrated security=true";
            cn.Open();
            int count = (int)cmd.ExecuteScalar();
            if (count == 1)
            {
                return;
            }
            cn.Close();
            cn.ConnectionString = @"Server=.\SQLEXPRESS;"
                + @"AttachDbFilename=|DataDirectory|\MountedNorthwnd.mdf;"
                + "Database=Northwind;"
                + "integrated security=true;"
                + "user instance=false";
            cn.Open();
            cn.Close();
            MessageBox.Show("Northwind Mounted");
        }
    }
}
```

The code to mount the *Northwind* database is proactively checking the sysdatabases table, which is located in the master database, to see whether the *Northwind* database exists. If the database does not exist, the connection is closed and a new connection string is assigned that will mount the file called MountedNorthwnd.mdf as a database called *Northwind*. This database is used for the OLEDB and ODBC connections that will be tested.

Retrieving the Metadata Collections

We'll add a *DataGridView* object to the form, which will be used to display data when an option is selected. We'll also add a button to the form and add the following code, which retrieves the metadata collections for the database connection we selected.

Visual Basic

```
Private Sub button1_Click(ByVal sender As System.Object, _
      ByVal e As System.EventArgs) Handles button1.Click
   If comboBox1.Text.Trim().Length = 0 Then
      MessageBox.Show("Select a connection")
      Return
   End If
   dataGridView1.DataSource = GetSchemaDataTable(Nothing, Nothing)
End Sub

Public Function GetSchemaDataTable(ByVal collectionName As String, _
      ByVal restrictions As String()) As DataTable
   Dim cnSettings As ConnectionStringSettings = _
      ConfigurationManager.ConnectionStrings(comboBox1.Text)
   Dim provider As DbProviderFactory = _
      DbProviderFactories.GetFactory(cnSettings.ProviderName)
   Using cn As DbConnection = provider.CreateConnection()
      cn.ConnectionString = cnSettings.ConnectionString
      cn.Open()
      If (collectionName Is Nothing) Then
         Return cn.GetSchema()
      End If
      Return cn.GetSchema(collectionName, restrictions)
   End Using
End Function
```

C#

```
private void button1_Click(object sender, EventArgs e)
{
   if (comboBox1.Text.Trim().Length == 0)
   {
      MessageBox.Show("Select a connection");
      return;
   }
   dataGridView1.DataSource = GetSchemaDataTable(null, null);
}

public DataTable GetSchemaDataTable(string collectionName,
   string[] restrictions)
{
   ConnectionStringSettings cnSettings =
      ConfigurationManager.ConnectionStrings[comboBox1.Text];
   DbProviderFactory provider =
      DbProviderFactories.GetFactory(cnSettings.ProviderName);
   using (DbConnection cn = provider.CreateConnection())
   {
```

```
            cn.ConnectionString = cnSettings.ConnectionString;
            cn.Open();
            if (collectionName == null)
            {
                return cn.GetSchema();
            }
            return cn.GetSchema(collectionName, restrictions);
        }
    }
```

This code simply uses the name of the current connection string to create and open a connection to the database. The *GetSchema* method runs next, and the resultant *DataTable* object is assigned directly to the *DataSource* property of the *DataGridView* object. The *GetSchema* method cannot be called with a null *collectionName* parameter, so the *collectionName* is checked; if it is null, the parameterless overload is executed. Figure 11-1 shows the form when the code is run and the SqlClient and Access versions are selected.

Microsoft Access Metadata Collections

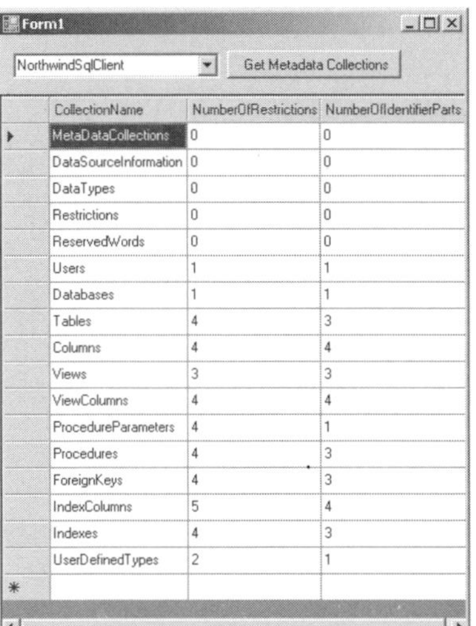

CollectionName	NumberOfRestrictions	NumberOfIdentifierParts
MetaDataCollections	0	0
DataSourceInformation	0	0
DataTypes	0	0
Restrictions	0	0
ReservedWords	0	0
Users	1	1
Databases	1	1
Tables	4	3
Columns	4	4
Views	3	3
ViewColumns	4	4
ProcedureParameters	4	1
Procedures	4	3
ForeignKeys	4	3
IndexColumns	5	4
Indexes	4	3
UserDefinedTypes	2	1

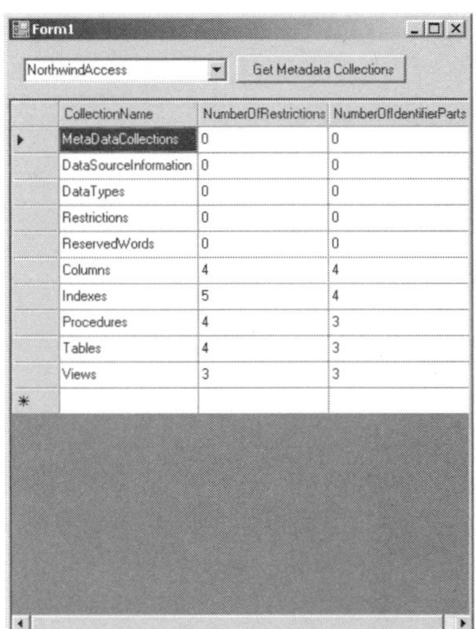

CollectionName	NumberOfRestrictions	NumberOfIdentifierParts
MetaDataCollections	0	0
DataSourceInformation	0	0
DataTypes	0	0
Restrictions	0	0
ReservedWords	0	0
Columns	4	4
Indexes	5	4
Procedures	4	3
Tables	4	3
Views	3	3

Figure 11-1 The SQL Server metadata collections using the SqlClient versus the Microsoft Access metadata collection

Figure 11-2 shows the form when the code is run and the OLEDB and ODBC versions are selected. Notice that the SQL Server database has the most metadata available and the Access database has the least. Every provider has different metadata collections, but you can start here and drill down into each collection as needed.

SQL Server Metadata Collections Using OleDb Provider

CollectionName	NumberOfRestrictions	NumberOfIdentifierParts
MetaDataCollections	0	0
DataSourceInformation	0	0
DataTypes	0	0
Restrictions	0	0
ReservedWords	0	0
Users	1	1
Databases	1	1
Tables	4	3
Columns	4	4
Views	3	3
ViewColumns	4	4
ProcedureParameters	4	1
Procedures	4	3
ForeignKeys	4	3
IndexColumns	5	4
Indexes	4	3
UserDefinedTypes	2	1

SQL Server Metadata Collections Using Odbc Provider

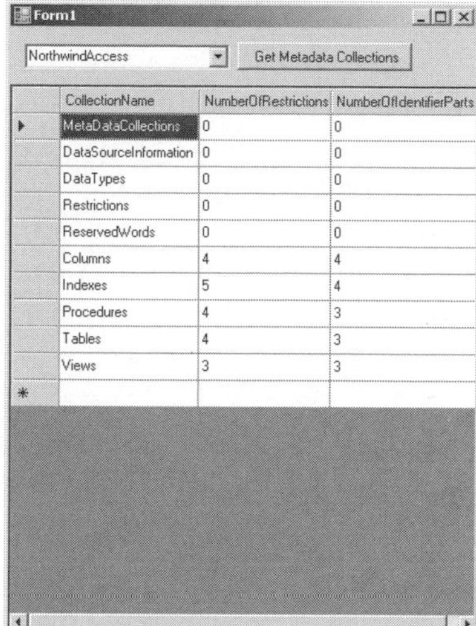

CollectionName	NumberOfRestrictions	NumberOfIdentifierParts
MetaDataCollections	0	0
DataSourceInformation	0	0
DataTypes	0	0
Restrictions	0	0
ReservedWords	0	0
Columns	4	4
Indexes	5	4
Procedures	4	3
Tables	4	3
Views	3	3

Figure 11-2 The SQL Server metadata collections using the OleDb provider versus the Odbc provider.

Navigating the Schema

If every provider has a different schema, you might have a problem navigating the various metadata collections. In the ADO.NET schema API, regardless of the provider you select to query, the following common collections must be implemented by each provider.

- *MetaDataCollections* Contains a list of all the available collections and is the default collection when you execute *GetSchema* with no parameters, as shown earlier in Figure 11-1. This also returns the number of restrictions (filters) that can be applied to each collection.
- *DataSourceInformation* Contains a single row that provides the name, version, and other details about the database.
- *DataTypes* Contains a list of all the supported data types. Also provides metadata about each data type, such as the size and whether it is incrementing, case sensitive, and nullable.
- *ReservedWords* Contains a list of all the words reserved for use by the database and code that runs within it, including code in stored procedures and SQL statements.
- *Restrictions* Contains a list of the restrictions you can apply to filter the results when querying any of the metadata collections.

If you look at the four connection samples, you will see that they contain these five metadata collections. Other than these five collections, no other collections are required. This means provider writers can implement other collections as they see fit, but there is no standard even for common collections such as the table collection.

Navigating a Metadata Collection

We added a *CellDoubleClick* event handler to the *DataGridView* object that reads the collection name and navigates into the collection if the row that was clicked has a *CollectionName* column. The following code shows the use of *GetSchema* when passing a collection name.

Visual Basic

```
Private Sub dataGridView1_CellDoubleClick( _
      ByVal sender As System.Object, _
      ByVal e As System.Windows.Forms.DataGridViewCellEventArgs) _
      Handles dataGridView1.CellDoubleClick
   If dataGridView1.Columns("CollectionName") Is Nothing Then
      MessageBox.Show("No CollectionName column")
      Return
   End If
   Dim collectionName As String = CStr(dataGridView1.Rows( _
        e.RowIndex).Cells("CollectionName").Value)
   dataGridView1.DataSource = GetSchemaDataTable(collectionName, Nothing)
End Sub
```

C#

```
private void dataGridView1_CellDoubleClick(
   object sender, DataGridViewCellEventArgs e)
{
   if (dataGridView1.Columns["CollectionName"] == null)
   {
      MessageBox.Show("No CollectionName column");
      return;
   }
   string collectionName = (string)dataGridView1.Rows[
      e.RowIndex].Cells["CollectionName"].Value;
   dataGridView1.DataSource =
      GetSchemaDataTable(collectionName, null);
}
```

This code simply gets the collection that matches the collection name in the row that was double-clicked. Figure 11-3 shows the table collection when you use the *NorthwindSqlClient* connection string. Notice that this collection contains the user-defined tables and views, not the system tables and views. Also notice that the SqlClient provider returns only four columns: TABLE_CATALOG, TABLE_SCHEMA, TABLE_NAME, and TABLE_TYPE. Notice that TABLE_CATALOG, which is the database name, contains the complete path and database filename. This is the default naming when you use SQL Server Express and set *User Instance=True* in the connection string.

Form1

NorthwindSql

Get Metadata Collections

TABLE_CATALOG	TABLE_SCHEMA	TABLE_NAME	TABLE_TYPE
C:\PROJECTS\VB\CHAPTER11\CHAPTER11\BIN\DEBUG\NORTHWND.MDF	dbo	Customers	BASE TABLE
C:\PROJECTS\VB\CHAPTER11\CHAPTER11\BIN\DEBUG\NORTHWND.MDF	dbo	Shippers	BASE TABLE
C:\PROJECTS\VB\CHAPTER11\CHAPTER11\BIN\DEBUG\NORTHWND.MDF	dbo	Suppliers	BASE TABLE
C:\PROJECTS\VB\CHAPTER11\CHAPTER11\BIN\DEBUG\NORTHWND.MDF	dbo	Orders	BASE TABLE
C:\PROJECTS\VB\CHAPTER11\CHAPTER11\BIN\DEBUG\NORTHWND.MDF	dbo	Products	BASE TABLE
C:\PROJECTS\VB\CHAPTER11\CHAPTER11\BIN\DEBUG\NORTHWND.MDF	dbo	Order Details	BASE TABLE
C:\PROJECTS\VB\CHAPTER11\CHAPTER11\BIN\DEBUG\NORTHWND.MDF	dbo	Customer and Suppliers by City	VIEW
C:\PROJECTS\VB\CHAPTER11\CHAPTER11\BIN\DEBUG\NORTHWND.MDF	dbo	Alphabetical list of products	VIEW
C:\PROJECTS\VB\CHAPTER11\CHAPTER11\BIN\DEBUG\NORTHWND.MDF	dbo	Current Product List	VIEW
C:\PROJECTS\VB\CHAPTER11\CHAPTER11\BIN\DEBUG\NORTHWND.MDF	dbo	Orders Qry	VIEW
C:\PROJECTS\VB\CHAPTER11\CHAPTER11\BIN\DEBUG\NORTHWND.MDF	dbo	Products Above Average Price	VIEW
C:\PROJECTS\VB\CHAPTER11\CHAPTER11\BIN\DEBUG\NORTHWND.MDF	dbo	Products by Category	VIEW
C:\PROJECTS\VB\CHAPTER11\CHAPTER11\BIN\DEBUG\NORTHWND.MDF	dbo	Quarterly Orders	VIEW
C:\PROJECTS\VB\CHAPTER11\CHAPTER11\BIN\DEBUG\NORTHWND.MDF	dbo	Invoices	VIEW
C:\PROJECTS\VB\CHAPTER11\CHAPTER11\BIN\DEBUG\NORTHWND.MDF	dbo	Order Details Extended	VIEW
C:\PROJECTS\VB\CHAPTER11\CHAPTER11\BIN\DEBUG\NORTHWND.MDF	dbo	Order Subtotals	VIEW
C:\PROJECTS\VB\CHAPTER11\CHAPTER11\BIN\DEBUG\NORTHWND.MDF	dbo	Product Sales for 1997	VIEW
C:\PROJECTS\VB\CHAPTER11\CHAPTER11\BIN\DEBUG\NORTHWND.MDF	dbo	Category Sales for 1997	VIEW
C:\PROJECTS\VB\CHAPTER11\CHAPTER11\BIN\DEBUG\NORTHWND.MDF	dbo	Sales by Category	VIEW
C:\PROJECTS\VB\CHAPTER11\CHAPTER11\BIN\DEBUG\NORTHWND.MDF	dbo	Sales Totals by Amount	VIEW
C:\PROJECTS\VB\CHAPTER11\CHAPTER11\BIN\DEBUG\NORTHWND.MDF	dbo	Summary of Sales by Quarter	VIEW
C:\PROJECTS\VB\CHAPTER11\CHAPTER11\BIN\DEBUG\NORTHWND.MDF	dbo	Summary of Sales by Year	VIEW

Figure 11-3 When you use the SqlClient provider, the table collection contains a list of user-defined tables and user-defined views.

If you switch to the *NorthwindOleDb* connection string and list the tables, you see that this collection returns the list of system tables, system views, user-defined tables, and user-defined views. Figure 11-4 shows this collection. Some of the columns can't be seen in the figure, but nine columns are returned: TABLE_CATALOG, TABLE_SCHEMA, TABLE_NAME, TABLE_TYPE, TABLE_GUID, DESCRIPTION, TABLE_PROPID, DATE_CREATED, and DATE_MODIFIED. This connection string references a mounted copy of the *Northwind* database, so TABLE_CATALOG simply says Northwind.

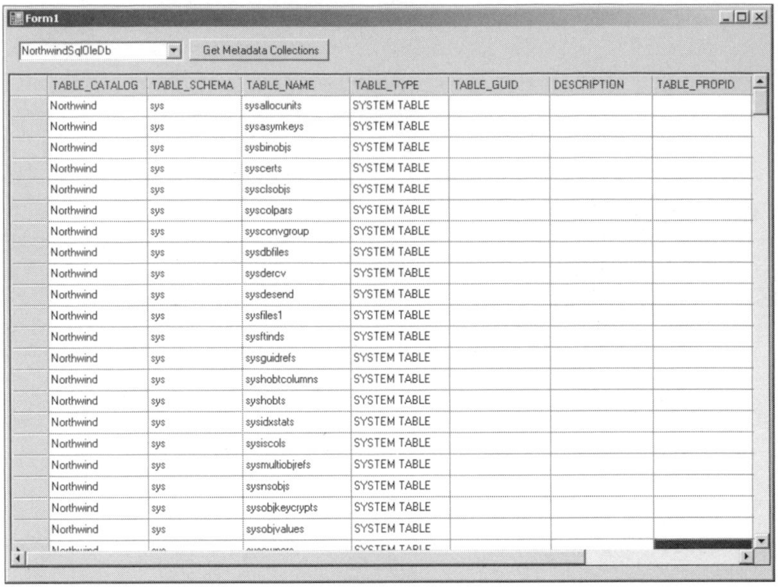

Form1

NorthwindSqlOleDb | Get Metadata Collections

TABLE_CATALOG	TABLE_SCHEMA	TABLE_NAME	TABLE_TYPE	TABLE_GUID	DESCRIPTION	TABLE_PROPID
Northwind	sys	sysallocunits	SYSTEM TABLE			
Northwind	sys	sysasymkeys	SYSTEM TABLE			
Northwind	sys	sysbinobjs	SYSTEM TABLE			
Northwind	sys	syscerts	SYSTEM TABLE			
Northwind	sys	sysclsobjs	SYSTEM TABLE			
Northwind	sys	syscolpars	SYSTEM TABLE			
Northwind	sys	sysconvgroup	SYSTEM TABLE			
Northwind	sys	sysdbfiles	SYSTEM TABLE			
Northwind	sys	sysdercv	SYSTEM TABLE			
Northwind	sys	sysdesend	SYSTEM TABLE			
Northwind	sys	sysfiles1	SYSTEM TABLE			
Northwind	sys	sysftinds	SYSTEM TABLE			
Northwind	sys	sysguidrefs	SYSTEM TABLE			
Northwind	sys	syshobtcolumns	SYSTEM TABLE			
Northwind	sys	syshobts	SYSTEM TABLE			
Northwind	sys	sysidxstats	SYSTEM TABLE			
Northwind	sys	sysiscols	SYSTEM TABLE			
Northwind	sys	sysmultiobjrefs	SYSTEM TABLE			
Northwind	sys	sysnsobjs	SYSTEM TABLE			
Northwind	sys	sysobjkeycrypts	SYSTEM TABLE			
Northwind	sys	sysobjvalues	SYSTEM TABLE			

Figure 11-4 When you use the OLEDB provider, the table collection contains a list of system tables, system views, user-defined tables, and user-defined views.

Working with the Restrictions

Retrieving the metadata is easy, as long as you know how to open a connection and you know the name of the metadata collection name to pass to the *GetSchema* method, but you must be wondering about the restriction parameter that has not been set when you call the *GetSchema* method. The restriction parameter is an array of string values that are used to filter the collection rows so you get only the information you want.

When you get the list of metadata collection names, you also get the number of restrictions you can specify. If the number is zero, you cannot apply a filter to this collection. If the number is greater than zero, you can query the restriction collection for the available filters for this collection. You must provide a restriction array to the *GetSchema* method that has the same number of elements as filters. The filters are position sensitive, so unused filter values should be set to *null* (Visual Basic *Nothing*).

In the sample application, when you double-click a cell, instead of immediately displaying the collection, the code is modified to display a filter prompt that can be used to narrow the displayed results. We want to build this form dynamically, displaying a combo box for each restriction that will be populated with valid filter values. We'll add a new method called *GetRestrictions* that dynamically populates a form and prompts the user for filter restrictions. We'll also add a new method called *GetComboValues* that gets all of the existing values in a column for display in a combo box. The code looks like the following.

Visual Basic

```
Dim restrictionDataTable As DataTable
Dim unselected As String = "<unselected>"

Public Function GetRestrictions(ByVal collectionName As String) _
      As String()
   'Display form with filter selections
   Dim frm As New Form()
   Dim filters As New ArrayList()
   Dim completeCollection As DataTable = _
      GetSchemaDataTable(collectionName, Nothing)

   restrictionDataTable.DefaultView.RowFilter = _
      "CollectionName='" + collectionName + "'"
   restrictionDataTable.DefaultView.Sort = "RestrictionNumber ASC"

   Dim labelX As Integer = 10
   Dim comboX As Integer = 150
   Dim labelWidth As Integer = comboX - labelX
   Dim comboWidth As Integer = 150
   Dim formWidth As Integer = comboWidth + comboX + 10
   Dim y As Integer = 20
   frm.Text = "Select Filter Values"
   frm.Width = formWidth
   Dim containsFilters As Boolean = False
   For Each dv As DataRowView In restrictionDataTable.DefaultView
      Dim lbl As New Label()
      lbl.Location = New Point(labelX, y)
      lbl.Width = labelWidth
      lbl.Text = CStr(dv("RestrictionName"))
      Dim cmb As New ComboBox()
      cmb.DropDownStyle = ComboBoxStyle.DropDownList
      cmb.Location = New Point(comboX, y)
      cmb.Width = comboWidth
      cmb.Anchor = AnchorStyles.Left Or AnchorStyles.Right _
         Or AnchorStyles.Top
      cmb.Items.Add(unselected)
      cmb.Items.AddRange(GetComboValues( _
         dv, completeCollection))
      frm.Controls.Add(lbl)
      frm.Controls.Add(cmb)
      filters.Add(cmb)
      cmb.Text = unselected
      cmb.Visible = True
      lbl.Visible = True
      y += 30
      containsFilters = True
   Next
   If (containsFilters) Then
      Dim ok As New Button()
      ok.Text = "&Ok"
      ok.DialogResult = Windows.Forms.DialogResult.OK
      ok.Location = New Point(labelX, y)
      frm.Controls.Add(ok)
      ok.Visible = True
```

```
         frm.AcceptButton = ok
         Dim cancel As New Button()
         cancel.Text = "&Cancel"
         cancel.DialogResult = Windows.Forms.DialogResult.Cancel
         cancel.Location = New Point(comboX, y)
         frm.Controls.Add(cancel)
         cancel.Visible = True
         frm.CancelButton = cancel
      Else
         Return Nothing
      End If
      frm.Height = y + 60
      If (frm.ShowDialog() <> Windows.Forms.DialogResult.OK) Then
         Return Nothing
      End If
      Dim results(filters.Count - 1) As String
      For i As Integer = 0 To filters.Count - 1
         Dim cmb As ComboBox = CType(filters(i), ComboBox)
         If (cmb.Text = unselected) Or (cmb.Text Is Nothing) _
               Or (cmb.Text.Length = 0) Then
            results(i) = Nothing
         Else
            results(i) = cmb.Text
         End If
      Next
      Return results
   End Function

   Public Function GetComboValues(ByVal dv As DataRowView, _
         ByVal list As DataTable) As Object()
      Dim ret As New Hashtable()

      Dim columnName As String
      columnName = CStr(dv("RestrictionName"))

      For Each dr As DataRow In list.Rows
         Dim currentValue As String = CStr(dr(columnName))
         ret(currentValue) = currentValue
      Next
      Dim comboValues As New ArrayList(ret.Keys)
      comboValues.Sort()
      Return comboValues.ToArray()
   End Function
```

C#

```
   DataTable restrictionDataTable;
   string unselected = "<unselected>";

   public string[] GetRestrictions(string collectionName)
   {
      //Display form with filter selections
      Form frm = new Form();
      ArrayList filters = new ArrayList();
      DataTable completeCollection =
         GetSchemaDataTable(collectionName, null);
```

```
restrictionDataTable.DefaultView.RowFilter =
   "CollectionName='" + collectionName + "'";
restrictionDataTable.DefaultView.Sort = "RestrictionNumber ASC";

int labelX = 10;
int comboX = 150;
int labelWidth = comboX - labelX;
int comboWidth = 150;
int formWidth = comboWidth + comboX + 10;
int y = 20;
frm.Text = "Select Filter Values";
frm.Width = formWidth;
bool containsFilters = false;
foreach (DataRowView dv in restrictionDataTable.DefaultView)
{
   Label lbl = new Label();
   lbl.Location = new Point(labelX, y);
   lbl.Width = labelWidth;
   lbl.Text = (string)dv["RestrictionName"];
   ComboBox cmb = new ComboBox();
   cmb.DropDownStyle = ComboBoxStyle.DropDownList;
   cmb.Location = new Point(comboX, y);
   cmb.Width = comboWidth;
   cmb.Anchor = AnchorStyles.Left | AnchorStyles.Right
      | AnchorStyles.Top;
   cmb.Items.Add(unselected);
   cmb.Items.AddRange(GetComboValues(
      dv, completeCollection));
   frm.Controls.Add(lbl);
   frm.Controls.Add(cmb);
   filters.Add(cmb);
   cmb.Text = unselected;
   cmb.Visible = true;
   lbl.Visible = true;
   y += 30;
   containsFilters = true;
}
if (containsFilters)
{
   Button ok = new Button();
   ok.Text = "&Ok";
   ok.DialogResult = DialogResult.OK;
   ok.Location = new Point(labelX, y);
   frm.Controls.Add(ok);
   ok.Visible = true;
   frm.AcceptButton = ok;
   Button cancel = new Button();
   cancel.Text = "&Cancel";
   cancel.DialogResult = DialogResult.Cancel;
   cancel.Location = new Point(comboX, y);
   frm.Controls.Add(cancel);
   cancel.Visible = true;
   frm.CancelButton = cancel;
}
else
```

```
    {
       return null;
    }
    frm.Height = y + 60;
    if (frm.ShowDialog() != DialogResult.OK)
    {
       return null;
    }
    string[] results = new string[filters.Count];
    for (int i = 0; i < filters.Count; i++)
    {
       ComboBox cmb = (ComboBox)filters[i];
       if (cmb.Text == unselected || cmb.Text == null || cmb.Text.Length == 0)
       {
          results[i] = null;
       }
       else
       {
          results[i] = cmb.Text;
       }
    }
    return results;
}

public object[] GetComboValues(DataRowView dv, DataTable list)
{
    Hashtable ret = new Hashtable();

    string columnName;
    columnName = (string)dv["RestrictionName"];

    foreach (DataRow dr in list.Rows)
    {
       string currentValue = (string)dr[columnName];
       ret[currentValue] = currentValue;
    }
    ArrayList comboValues = new ArrayList(ret.Keys);
    comboValues.Sort();
    return comboValues.ToArray();
}
```

This code starts by declaring a *DataTable* variable called *restrictionDataTable*, which is used to hold the restriction list when you get the metadata collection list for a connection. A variable called *unselected* holds the value to be displayed when you don't want to make a selection on a filter.

The *GetRestrictions* method accepts a collection name parameter and returns an array of strings that contains the filters the user selected. In this method, a form is dynamically created and populated with a combo box for each restriction filter. A call is made to get the complete collection, even though we might want a filtered list. This is done in this example to get a list of valid values to use when populating the combo boxes.

Next, the *restrictionDataTable* object's default data view is filtered and sorted so it shows only the restrictions for the currently selected collection, sorted by restriction number. We define variables for the layout of the restriction labels and combo boxes and loop through the restriction values, creating a label and combo box for each restriction and populating the combo box's values by calling the *GetComboValues* method. The *GetComboValues* method typically expects to find the filter column name in the *RestrictionName* value.

After the loop has completed, the code checks to see if any filters were added to the form; if so, an OK and a Cancel button are added to the form and the form is displayed. If no filters were added to the form, this method returns with no restrictions.

After the OK button is clicked, the results are collected from each combo box and selected values are copied into a string array of restrictions, which is returned.

We need to make a couple of changes to the existing code: the button's click event handler must fill the *restrictionDataTable* object, and the cell's double-click event handler must be modified to prompt the user for restriction filters. We'll modify these methods as follows.

Visual Basic

```
Private Sub button1_Click(ByVal sender As System.Object, _
      ByVal e As System.EventArgs) Handles button1.Click
   restrictionDataTable = GetSchemaDataTable("Restrictions", Nothing)
   dataGridView1.DataSource = GetSchemaDataTable(Nothing, Nothing)
End Sub

Private Sub dataGridView1_CellDoubleClick( _
      ByVal sender As System.Object, _
      ByVal e As System.Windows.Forms.DataGridViewCellEventArgs) _
      Handles dataGridView1.CellDoubleClick
   If dataGridView1.Columns("CollectionName") Is Nothing Then
      MessageBox.Show("No CollectionName column")
      Return
   End If
   Dim collectionName As String = CStr(dataGridView1.Rows(
      e.RowIndex).Cells("CollectionName").Value)
   dataGridView1.DataSource = GetSchemaDataTable(collectionName, _
      GetRestrictions(collectionName))
End Sub
```

C#

```
private void button1_Click(object sender, EventArgs e)
{
   restrictionDataTable = GetSchemaDataTable("Restrictions", null);
   dataGridView1.DataSource = GetSchemaDataTable(null, null);
}

private void dataGridView1_CellDoubleClick(
 object sender, DataGridViewCellEventArgs e)
{
   if (dataGridView1.Columns["CollectionName"] == null)
   {
```

```
        MessageBox.Show("No CollectionName column");
        return;
    }
    string collectionName = (string)dataGridView1.Rows[
        e.RowIndex].Cells["CollectionName"].Value;
    dataGridView1.DataSource =
        GetSchemaDataTable(collectionName,
        GetRestrictions(collectionName));
}
ByVal e As System.Windows.Forms.DataGridViewCellEventArgs) _
```

Run the application and get the metadata collection list for a connection such as the *NorthwindSqlClient*. Double-click the *Tables* collection and you will be prompted for restriction filters, as shown in Figure 11-5.

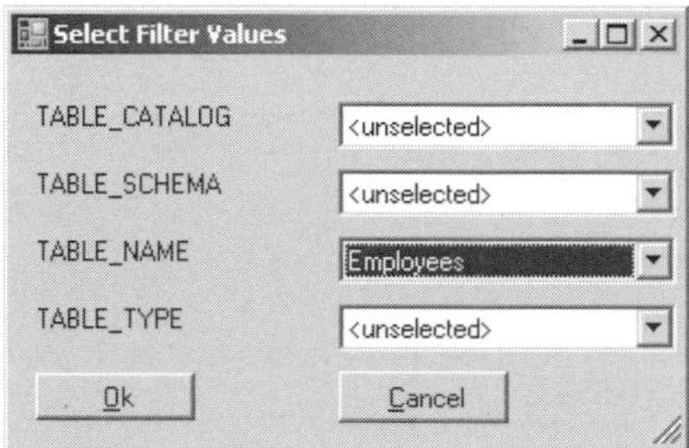

Figure 11-5 The restriction filters for the *Tables* collection with the Employees table selected

In the figure, the Employees table is selected. Clicking OK causes the filter to be applied to the *GetSchema* query, and only Employees table data is displayed.

Note Depending on the release of the .NET Framework, you might receive an *ArgumentException* in the *GetComboValues* method when you double-click on some of the collections. The problem is that this sample code assumes that the restriction names matches the collection's field names. Microsoft did not match these names, which means that you cannot link a restriction to a collection field. For example, the Tables collection has a field that is called *TABLE_CATALOG*, but its restriction is called *Catalog*. The following section shows how you can change the names to make them match.

Changing and Extending the Metadata

The metadata that you have been using comes from embedded XML resources in the System.Data.dll file. This information can be extracted very easily by launching the IL Disassembler (ILDasm.exe) from the Visual Studio 2005 Command Prompt, and dumping its contents to an empty folder. You can try the following steps, or you can use the XML files that are included in the sample code.

Choose Start | Programs | Microsoft Visual Studio 2005 | Visual Studio Tools | Visual Studio 2005 Command Prompt. At the command prompt, type **ILDasm** and press Enter. Open the

System.Data.dll file, which is located in the %WinDir%\Microsoft.NET\Framework\vX.X.XXXXX folder, where X.X.XXXXX is the latest version of the .NET Framework that is installed on your machine.

Dump the contents of this assembly to a new folder by choosing File | Dump | OK. When the SaveAs dialog is displayed, click the New Folder icon to create a new folder, give the folder a name, double-click on the folder to navigate into it, and finally save the contents of the assembly as System.Data.IL. Close ILDasm.exe and use Windows Explorer to navigate to this new folder. Notice that the following XML files exist, which contain the metadata information that you have been using.

System.Data.Odbc.OdbcMetaData.xml

System.Data.OleDb.OleDbMetaData.xml

System.Data.SqlClient.SqlMetaData.xml

If you open these files, you'll find that these files contain a serialized *DataSet* object with its schema embedded. Scrolling through the file you'll find that each metadata collection is defined in the XML file using the following format:

```
<MetaDataCollections>
   <CollectionName>Databases</CollectionName>
   <NumberOfRestrictions>1</NumberOfRestrictions>
   <NumberOfIdentifierParts>1</NumberOfIdentifierParts>
   <PopulationMechanism>SQLCommand</PopulationMechanism>
   <PopulationString>select name as database_name, dbid, crdate
      as create_date from master..sysdatabases
      where (name = @Name or (@Name is null))</PopulationString>
</MetaDataCollections>
```

You can see that the *CollectionName*, *NumberOfRestrictions*, and *NumberOfIdentifierParts* properties are directly defined in this file. To populate the metadata collection, the *PopulationMechanism* specifies how this will be done, and the *PopulationString* is the actual command to populate the collection.

If the *PopulationMechanism* is set to *DataTable* then the *PopulationString* must be the name of one of the *DataTable* objects that are in this *DataSet* object. For example, the collection called *MetaDataCollections* has its *PopulationMechanism* set to *DataTable* and the *PopulationString* is set to *MetaDataCollections* to return the *MetaDataCollections DataTable* object in this *DataSet* object.

If the *PopulationMechanism* is set to *SQLCommand*, the *PopulationString* must be a SQL query that will return a *DataTable* object as shown in the XML snippet for the *Databases* collection. Notice that the SELECT statement aliases (renames) the *name* column as *database_name*, which causes an exception to be thrown when you double-click the *Databases* collection because the restriction for the *Databases* collection is called *name*, not *database_name*.

If the *PopulationMechanism* is set to *PrepareCollection*, the *PopulationString* is not used; instead, the data for the collection is embedded in the XML document.

You edit these files to make the names match and fix other problems that may exist, and you can extend the metadata by adding your own collection. The following XML snippet could be inserted into the System.Data.SqlClient.SqlMetaData.xml file to add a new *SystemMessages* collection, which contains information about the SQL Server's error messages.

Note The sample code contains the XML files. The System.Data.SqlClient.SqlMetaData.xml file has been modified to match the collection field names to the restriction names, and the *SystemMessages* collection is included. You should use these files instead of keying this snippet into the file. Remember that only the SqlClient metadata file has been fixed, so if you use the ODBC or OLEDB files, you may still get errors.

XML – SystemMessages Collection

```
<!--new SystemMessages collection -->
<MetaDataCollections>
  <CollectionName>SystemMessages</CollectionName>
  <NumberOfRestrictions>5</NumberOfRestrictions>
  <NumberOfIdentifierParts>2</NumberOfIdentifierParts>
  <PopulationMechanism>SQLCommand</PopulationMechanism>
  <PopulationString>
    SELECT * FROM sys.messages
    WHERE
       ((message_id=@message_id) OR (@message_id is null))
     AND ((language_id = @language_id) OR (@language_id is null))
     AND ((severity = @severity) OR (@severity is null))
     AND ((is_event_logged = @is_event_logged) OR
       (@is_event_logged is null))
     AND (([text] = @text) OR (@text is null))
  </PopulationString>
</MetaDataCollections>
<Restrictions>
  <CollectionName>SystemMessages</CollectionName>
  <RestrictionName>message_id</RestrictionName>
  <ParameterName>@message_id</ParameterName>
  <RestrictionDefault>message_id</RestrictionDefault>
  <RestrictionNumber>1</RestrictionNumber>
</Restrictions>
<Restrictions>
  <CollectionName>SystemMessages</CollectionName>
  <RestrictionName>language_id</RestrictionName>
  <ParameterName>@language_id</ParameterName>
  <RestrictionDefault>language_id</RestrictionDefault>
  <RestrictionNumber>2</RestrictionNumber>
</Restrictions>
```

```
<Restrictions>
  <CollectionName>SystemMessages</CollectionName>
  <RestrictionName>severity</RestrictionName>
  <ParameterName>@severity</ParameterName>
  <RestrictionDefault>severity</RestrictionDefault>
  <RestrictionNumber>3</RestrictionNumber>
</Restrictions>
<Restrictions>
  <CollectionName>SystemMessages</CollectionName>
  <RestrictionName>is_event_logged</RestrictionName>
  <ParameterName>@is_event_logged</ParameterName>
  <RestrictionDefault>is_event_logged</RestrictionDefault>
  <RestrictionNumber>4</RestrictionNumber>
</Restrictions>
<Restrictions>
  <CollectionName>SystemMessages</CollectionName>
  <RestrictionName>text</RestrictionName>
  <ParameterName>@text</ParameterName>
  <RestrictionDefault>text</RestrictionDefault>
  <RestrictionNumber>5</RestrictionNumber>
</Restrictions>
```

You will need to get your application to read the data in this file instead of the XML resource file that is embedded in the System.Data.dll assembly. To do this, these XML files must be located in the %WinDir%\Microsoft.NET\Framework\vX.X.XXXXX\CONFIG folder, where X.X.XXXXX is the latest version of the .NET Framework that is installed on your machine.

After the XML files are saved to the proper location, edit your app.config and add commands to tell the runtime to load your XML files as follows.

XML – app.config

```
<?xml version="1.0" encoding="utf-8" ?>
<configuration>
   <system.data.odbc>
      <settings>
         <add name="MetaDataXml"
            value="System.Data.Odbc.OdbcMetaData.xml" />
      </settings>
   </system.data.odbc>
   <system.data.oledb>
      <settings>
         <add name="MetaDataXml"
           value="System.Data.OleDb.OleDbMetaData.xml" />
      </settings>
   </system.data.oledb>
   <system.data.sqlclient>
      <settings>
         <add name="MetaDataXml"
           value="System.Data.SqlClient.SqlMetaData.xml" />
      </settings>
   </system.data.sqlclient>
   <connectionStrings>
```

```
      <clear/>
      <add name="NorthwindSqlClient" connectionString=
         "Data Source=.\SQLEXPRESS;
         AttachDbFilename=|DataDirectory|\northwnd.mdf;
         Integrated Security=True;User Instance=True"
         providerName="System.Data.SqlClient" />
      <add name="NorthwindSqlOleDb"
         connectionString=
         "Provider=SQLOLEDB.1;
         Integrated Security=SSPI;
         Persist Security Info=False;
         Initial Catalog=Northwind;
         Data Source=.\SQLEXPRESS"
         providerName="System.Data.OleDb" />
      <add name="NorthwindSqlOdbc"
          connectionString=
         "DRIVER=SQL Server;
         SERVER=.\SQLEXPRESS;
         DATABASE=Northwind;Trusted_Connection=Yes"
         providerName="System.Data.Odbc" />
      <add name="NorthwindAccess"
         connectionString=
         "Provider=Microsoft.Jet.OLEDB.4.0;
         Data Source=|DataDirectory|\Northwind.mdb;
         Persist Security Info=True"
         providerName="System.Data.OleDb" />
   </connectionStrings>
</configuration>
```

If you run the sample code, you will find that the new XML files are used instead of the internal resource files, and when using the SqlClient, all of the metadata functions will work properly. Remember that you can also modify the other XML files as well.

Understanding the Unique Identifier Parts

The metadata collection list also contains a column called *NumberOfIdentifierParts*, which is the number of identifier parts that are required to make up a unique restriction on each metadata collection. This number will be either the same as the *NumberOfRestrictions* count or lower. If you look at the number of restrictions for the *Tables* collection, you'll see that it's 4, but the number of identifier parts is 3. This is because the last restriction filter is just a filter on table type—BASE TABLE or VIEW—but you can't have a table and a view that have the same name in a single database. This means you only need to use the first three restriction filters to uniquely identify or retrieve a table or view.

You can still filter based on any combination of the restrictions, including those that are not part of the set of unique identifiers. In Chapter 6, we created a stored procedure to get a list of the base tables, but we could have also retrieved the list of base tables by supplying a filter restriction based on the table type being BASE TABLE.

Summary

- Metadata is data that describes other data. It is important in applications that need the ability to identify and possibly adjust to changes in the backend data store.
- In ADO.NET, metadata is exposed through the *DbConnection* object's *GetSchema* method, which you can call with no parameters to get a metadata collection list.
- The *GetSchema* method contains an overload that accepts a collection name, such as *Tables* or *Databases*.
- You can use a *GetSchema* overload that accepts a collection name and an array of restriction filter strings to narrow the scope of the returned data.
- The metadata can be changed to get the behavior that you desire, or extended to add more metadata options.
- The unique identifier parts are the restrictions you are required to pass to the *GetSchema* method to retrieve a single unique value.

Chapter 12
Data Caching for Performance

One of the most common methods of increasing performance in an application is to provide data caching. Having the data available locally keeps you from repeatedly opening a database connection and making roundtrips to the server. Reducing the number of trips to the server means that more database resources and network bandwidth are available for other users and additional functionality. Caching can thus increase your overall performance.

Writing effective caching code can be quite a challenge because you need to know when the cache should expire (when the data is stale). For read-only data, this isn't too difficult to determine because you can simply choose to refresh the data when the application is restarted. For data that is updated occasionally, you can use timed expiration, such as at a specific time every day or after the cache hasn't been used for a certain amount of time. The problem with implementing timed expiration on a data cache is that one user might enter data that another user expects to see immediately and then doesn't see (or worse, the second user then attempts to reenter the data).

Microsoft ASP.NET offers many ways to cache Web pages, partial Web pages, and data. This chapter focuses on data caching only, but if you are a Web developer, I strongly suggest that you look at the other ASP.NET caching mechanisms.

This chapter explores some of the ways you can optimize performance by caching data and how you can minimize the effects of stale data.

Using the *SqlDependency* Class

What everyone wants is cached data that is always current. This might sound like a contradiction or impossible dream, but the *SqlDependency* class can deliver this. The *SqlDependency* class provides a way for your application to be notified when the data in a Microsoft SQL Server database changes. You can use the notification to expire the cache and reload the data from the database server.

What to Cache

You should consider three factors when deciding what data to cache.

- Frequency of change
- Reuse
- Size

Data that never changes can easily be cached. Because this data is read-only, you don't even need to use the *SqlDependency* class to refresh it. An example of read-only data is the list of states in the United States. Sure, the data could change, but in the unlikely event that it did, you could simply make the change and have users restart their application to get refreshed data. We'll look more closely at the *SqlDependency* class in a bit, but you can imagine that sending notifications to remote machines can be resource intensive for the database server, so adding a notification request for such read-only data would waste database resources.

Data that can be changed by a user but is not changed often is read-mostly data. You can cache read-mostly data and use the *SqlDependency* class to keep it fresh. An example of read-mostly data is a territory list for salespeople, or even a list of salespeople. Depending on where you work, this data can change several times a day, but it is still relatively stable.

Data should also be cached if you are likely to reuse it many times. The salesperson list might be cached for order entry people who need to assign a salesperson to each order received. Data that is relatively stable but not reused often should not be cached–for example, the list of orders that a salesperson received.

Caching small lists, such as a territory list or a category list, makes sense; caching large lists, such as the complete customer list or order list, does not. The problem with caching a complete order list is that the list changes all day long and you probably don't need to see all orders at once. A traveling salesperson might want to cache the list of her customer's orders, though. Be careful about overloading the memory in your computer by caching large items that are not frequently used.

Is the *SqlDependency* Class for You?

Sending notifications to clients can be a resource-intensive task–and the situation would be worse if the query notification were to result in 1000 clients re-querying a large table at the same time. When a notification is sent to the client, it is simply a message that states that the table changed, but you don't know what data changed. This means that you have to refresh the entire table. If you are writing an application that caches all of the sales orders for 1000 order entry people, you might end up generating large amounts of database activity because the clients will re-query the database for fresh data every time a new order is entered. Therefore, you should keep the client count and the data size to a minimum.

The *SqlDependency* class is best suited for Web applications or middle-tier components with a handful of clients (Web farm servers or component servers) that service hundreds or thousands of users at any given time. You can therefore cache large tables, but you might want to stagger the reload of these tables by simply expiring the cache when your application receives a change notification and reload the cache the next time a user references the data.

How Does *SqlDependency* Work?

The *SqlDependency* object does not work until you execute the static (Visual Basic shared) *Start* method, which starts a client-side process to communicate with SQL Server. The *Start* method requires a valid connection string and needs to be executed only once at the beginning of your application. When the application is closing, you can execute the *Stop* method to discontinue the client-side process.

The *SqlCommand* object has a *Notification* property that you can set by passing the *SqlCommand* object to the constructor of a *SqlDependency* object. When the command is sent to the database server, additional packets are sent to SQL Server to request a query notification. You can see these packets by using the SQL Profiler and monitoring query notification events. Figure 12-1 shows the SQL Profiler trace when a SQL dependency is set.

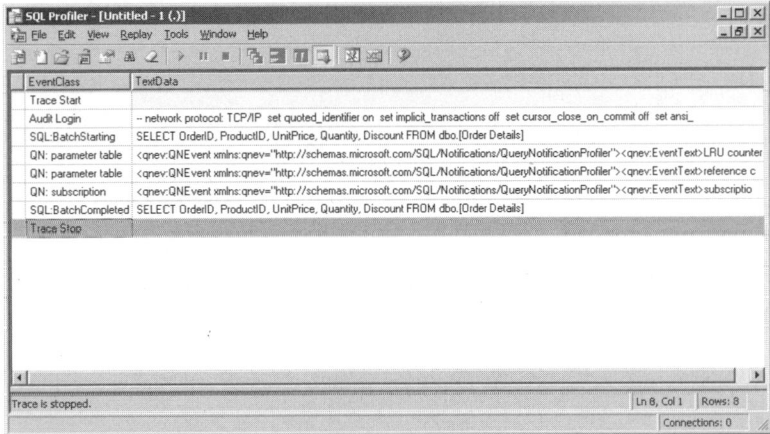

Figure 12-1 The SQL Profiler trace when a SQL command is sent to the database that has its *Notification* property set

When SQL receives the request for query notification, it sends a subscription request to the query notification infrastructure and executes the SQL command, as shown in Figure 12-2. SQL Server then watches the DML (Data Manipulation Language) statements for any changes that might affect the query results. If a change to the data affects this query result, a message is sent to the Service Broker and the subscription is removed from the query notification infrastructure. With the *SqlDependency* object, this message fires back to the application through the *sp_DispatcherProc* stored procedure. The message is received by the client application in the form of the *OnChange* event on the *SqlDependency* object.

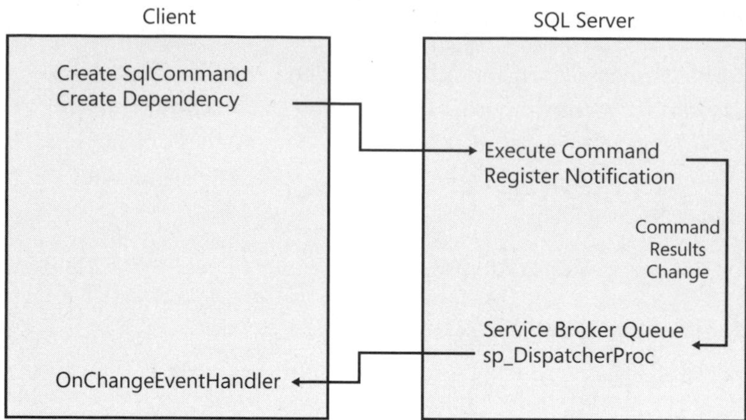

Figure 12-2 The *SqlDependency* object operation

When the *OnChange* event is fired, no data is sent that tells you what row was modified. You have to execute the *SqlCommand* object again to get the data, and you also have to re-create the *SqlDependency* object to be notified of more changes at the database.

Note that SQL Server is set up to be proactive about the notification you receive, which means that sometimes you might get a notification when no data has changed. For example, if the database server is restarted or if there is a schema change, you will receive a notification.

Query Considerations

For a query to work properly with *SqlDependency*, it must be written correctly. Here is a typical example of a *Northwind* database query that does *not* work.

Incorrect SQL Statement

```
SELECT * FROM [Order Details]
```

One problem with the preceding query is that you cannot use the asterisk (*) in it. Instead, you must spell out the field names. Another problem is that the table name is defined using a one-part name, but two-part table names are required. The corrected query looks like the following.

Correct SQL Query Statement

```
SELECT OrderID, ProductID, UnitPrice, Quantity, Discount
FROM dbo.[Order Details]
```

SqlDependency Setup in SQL Server

To get the *SqlDependency* object to work, you must use SQL Server 2005. The SQL *QueryNotificationService* does not exist on SQL Server Express. Perform the following configuration changes using Microsoft SQL Server Management Studio with a New Query window.

Granting Permissions

You must grant send permissions to the Guest user on the *QueryNotificationService* in the MSDB database because the *SqlDependency* object uses the Service Broker to post messages to the *QueryNotificationService* when a data change occurs.

```
USE MSDB
GRANT SEND ON SERVICE::
[http://schemas.microsoft.com/SQL/Notifications/QueryNotificationService]
TO GUEST
```

Note that the complete URL-like name for the *QueryNotificationService* is case sensitive, which database administrators might not be accustomed to.

Enabling CLR Execution on the Database Server

When a message arrives at the service queue, it is dispatched by a stored procedure with a queue named *sp_DispatcherProc* that contains .NET code, so you must have the common language runtime (CLR) enabled on this instance of SQL Server. The command to enable the CLR is as follows.

```
USE MASTER
EXEC sp_configure 'clr enabled', 1
RECONFIGURE
```

Enabling the Service Broker

You must verify and possibly enable the Service Broker on your database. To verify that the Service Broker is enabled on your database, you can use the following command.

```
SELECT DATABASEPROPERTYEX('Northwind', 'IsBrokerEnabled')
```

This command returns 1 for true and 0 for false (or null if you misspell the database name). To enable the Service Broker, you run this code.

```
USE MASTER
ALTER DATABASE Northwind SET ENABLE_BROKER
```

Using the *SqlDependency* Object

The following code sample is a simple Windows Forms application with a *DataGridView* object on the form. When the form is loaded, the *SqlDependency.Start* method is executed, and then a call is made to the *UpdateGrid* method, which populates the grid. The *UpdateGrid* method creates *SqlConnection*, *SqlCommand*, and *SqlDependency* objects. The *SqlCommand* object is then executed to load a *DataTable* that is bound to the *DataGridView* object. Notice that the *DataTable* object is assigned using the *DataGridView* object's *Invoke* method because the *UpdateGrid* method is also called from the *OnChange* event of the *SqlDependency* object, which is executed on a different thread than the form's thread. When the form is closed and the application is ending, the *SqlDependency.Stop* method is executed to discontinue the client-side services.

Visual Basic

```
Imports System.Data
Imports System.Data.SqlClient

Public Class Form1
   'requires Northwind to be installed
   'on default SQL Server instance
   Dim connect As String = _
      "Server=.;Database=Northwind;Integrated Security=True"
   Delegate Sub GridDelegate(ByVal table As DataTable)
   Dim WithEvents dep As SqlDependency

   Private Sub Form1_Load(ByVal sender As System.Object, _
         ByVal e As System.EventArgs) Handles MyBase.Load
      SqlDependency.Start(connect)
      UpdateGrid()
   End Sub

   Private Sub Form1_FormClosed(ByVal sender As System.Object, _
         ByVal e As System.Windows.Forms.FormClosedEventArgs) _
         Handles MyBase.FormClosed
      SqlDependency.Stop(connect)
   End Sub

   Private Sub UpdateGrid()
      Dim sql As String = _
         "SELECT OrderID, ProductID, UnitPrice, Quantity, " _
            + "Discount FROM dbo.[Order Details]"
      Dim dt As New DataTable()
      Using cn As New SqlConnection(connect)
         Using cmd As New SqlCommand(sql, cn)
            cn.Open()
            dep = New SqlDependency(cmd)
            Dim rdr As SqlDataReader = cmd.ExecuteReader()
            dt.Load(rdr)
         End Using
      End Using
      'Use anonymous method to assure
      're-assignment is done by the form's thread
      DataGridView1.Invoke(New GridDelegate(AddressOf assignDataSource), dt)
   End Sub

   Private Sub dep_OnChange(ByVal sender As Object, _
         ByVal e As SqlNotificationEventArgs) Handles dep.OnChange
      System.Diagnostics.Debug.WriteLine("Received OnChange Event")
      If (e.Info = SqlNotificationInfo.Invalid) Then
         MessageBox.Show("Invalid Statement")
         Return
      End If
      UpdateGrid()
   End Sub
```

```
   Private Sub assignDataSource(ByVal dt As DataTable)
      DataGridView1.DataSource = dt
   End Sub
End Class
```

C#

```
using System;
using System.Windows.Forms;
using System.Data;
using System.Data.SqlClient;

namespace SqlDependencyTest
{
   public partial class Form1 : Form
   {
      //requires Northwind to be installed
      //on default SQL Server instance
      private string connect =
        @"Server=.;Database=Northwind;Integrated Security=True";
      private delegate void GridDelegate(DataTable table);
      private SqlDependency dep;

      public Form1()
      {
         InitializeComponent();
      }

      private void Form1_Load(object sender, EventArgs e)
      {
         SqlDependency.Start(connect);
         UpdateGrid();
      }

      private void Form1_FormClosed(object sender, FormClosedEventArgs e)
      {
         SqlDependency.Stop(connect);
      }

      private void UpdateGrid()
      {
         string sql = "SELECT OrderID, ProductID, UnitPrice, Quantity, "
               + "Discount FROM dbo.[Order Details]";
         DataTable dt = new DataTable();
         using (SqlConnection cn = new SqlConnection(connect))
         {
            using (SqlCommand cmd = new SqlCommand(sql, cn))
            {
               cn.Open();
               dep = new SqlDependency(cmd);
               dep.OnChange += dep_OnChange;
               using (SqlDataReader rdr = cmd.ExecuteReader())
               {
                  dt.Load(rdr);
               }
            }
```

```
         }
         //Use anonymous method to assure
         //reassignment is done by the form's thread
         dataGridView1.Invoke(
            (GridDelegate)delegate(DataTable table)
            { dataGridView1.DataSource = table; }, dt);
      }

      private void dep_OnChange(object sender, SqlNotificationEventArgs e)
      {
         System.Diagnostics.Debug.WriteLine("Received OnChange Event");
         if (e.Info == SqlNotificationInfo.Invalid)
         {
            MessageBox.Show("Invalid Statement");
            return;
         }
         UpdateGrid();
      }
   }
}
```

To test this code, start the application, which loads the *DataGridView* object with the *Order Details* table in the *Northwind* database. Next, run a program that is capable of modifying the data in the *Order Details* table, such as Microsoft SQL Management Studio (as shown in Figure 12-3). Try changing the quantity field in the *Order Details* table (be sure to navigate to a different row after you change the quantity), and you should see the *DataGridView* object update accordingly.

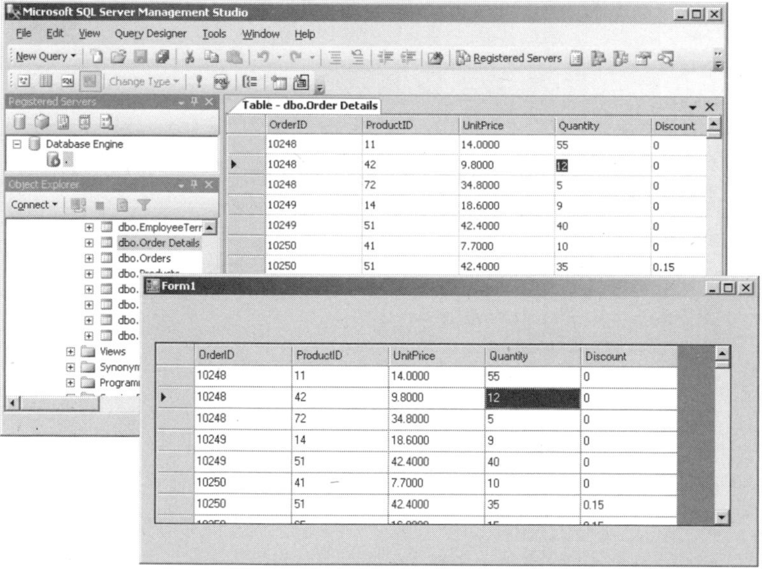

Figure 12-3 Changing data in Microsoft SQL Management Studio triggers the *OnChange* event, which refreshes the data.

Selecting the Communication Transport

The *SqlDependency* object constructor can have a parameter that sets the notification transport to a member of the *SqlNotificationTransports* enumeration. The default setting is *SqlNotificationTransports.Any*, which attempts to use the HTTP protocol by default if you have kernel mode HTTP support (which is available on Windows 2003 Server and Windows XP with SP2). If HTTP cannot be used, TCP is used. You can also try forcing the dependency to use TCP for notifications by using the following overload of the *SqlDependency* object constructor.

Visual Basic

```
Dim d As New SqlDependency(command, Nothing, _
   SqlNotificationAuthType.None, SqlNotificationTransports.Tcp, 0)
```

C#

```
SqlDependency d = new SqlDependency(command, null,
   SqlNotificationAuthType.None, SqlNotificationTransports.Tcp, 0);
```

ASP.NET SQL Cache Invalidation

ASP.NET offers various forms of data caching, but invalidating the cache has always been the biggest problem when you cache data from a backend database. Now you have an option to invalidate the cache by using a polling technique, which works on SQL Server 7 and later, or by using query notification, which works only on SQL Server 2005. The rest of this chapter looks at both techniques.

Cache Invalidation by Polling

Although cache invalidation by polling works on SQL Server 7 and later, you will want to poll SQL Server only if you have SQL Server 7 or SQL Server 2000. If you have SQL Server 2005, you should skip ahead to the later section on query notification. My general feeling about techniques that use polling instead of being event driven is that they tend to be a bit clunky, although they work well.

Preparing SQL Server for Polling

To configure polling, you configure each SQL Server database that will be polled, and then configure each table that will be polled. We'll configure the *Customers* table in the *Northwind* database in our example. We'll use the aspnet_regsql.exe utility, which is run from the Visual Studio 2005 Command Prompt. Configure the *Northwind* database on the local default SQL Server instance by issuing the following command.

```
aspnet_regsql.exe -S "." -E -d "Northwind" -ed
```

This command needs to be executed only once for each database, and it displays a message stating that the database has been enabled. If you look at the *Northwind* database, you'll see that this command adds a new table called AspNet_SqlCacheTablesForChangeNotification to the database. It has three columns: *tableName*, *notificationCreated*, and *changeId*. It has no rows yet. This command also adds the following stored procedures to the database.

- *AspNet_SqlCachePollingStoredProcedure* Selects *tableName* and *changeId* from the AspNet_SqlCacheTablesForChangeNotification table.
- *AspNet_SqlCacheQueryRegisteredTablesStoredProcedure* Selects *tableName* from the AspNet_SqlCacheTablesForChangeNotification table.
- *AspNet_SqlCacheRegisterTableStoredProcedure* Performs the table registration, which enables cache notification. You use the aspnet_regsql.exe utility to execute this stored procedure after the database has been registered. This stored procedure adds a row to the AspNet_SqlCacheTablesForChangeNotification table and adds a trigger to the table that is being registered.
- *AspNet_SqlCacheUnRegisterTableStoredProcedure* Undoes everything the *AspNet_SqlCacheRegisterTableStoredProcedure* did when the table was registered by removing the table trigger and removing the row from the AspNet_SqlCacheTablesForChangeNotification table.
- *AspNet_SqlCacheUpdateChangeIdStoredProcedure* Accepts a *tableName* parameter and increments its *changeId* in the AspNet_SqlCacheTablesForChangeNotification table.

Note The aspnet_regsql.exe utility is used to configure other SQL Server functionality, such as membership, personalization, and session state. If you run this utility without parameters, a wizard will start that takes you through the configuration of some of the options. Be sure to use the *-?* parameter to see all of the available options.

To configure the Customers table for cache invalidation, use the following command, which executes *AspNet_SqlCacheRegisterTableStoredProcedure*.

```
aspnet_regsql.exe -S "." -E -d "Northwind" -t "Customers" -et
```

This command adds a row to the AspNet_SqlCacheTablesForChangeNotification table and also adds the following trigger to the Customers table.

```
SET ANSI_NULLS ON
SET QUOTED_IDENTIFIER ON
GO

ALTER TRIGGER [dbo].[Customers_AspNet_SqlCacheNotification_Trigger]
ON [dbo].[Customers]
   FOR INSERT, UPDATE, DELETE AS
BEGIN
   SET NOCOUNT ON
   EXEC dbo.AspNet_SqlCacheUpdateChangeIdStoredProcedure N'Customers'
END
```

This trigger fires on any customer INSERT, UPDATE, or DELETE statement and simply increments the *changeId* of the table.

Creating a Web Site That Uses Polling

Now that the database server is configured for polling, it's time to set up a Web site that uses it. Create a Web site project called *SqlCacheDependency*. Add a *Button* control and a *GridView* control to the form. Set the *Text* property of the *Button* control to *"Refresh"*.

Use the GridView Tasks window to configure a new data source. Use the SQL Server instance that you configured for polling and name the connection string *NorthwindConnectionString*. In the Advanced options for the connection string, set the *Application Name* property to *SqlCacheDependency* (as shown in Figure 12-4), which will make it easier for you to view this application in the SQL Profiler utility.

To keep this example simple, select the Customers table, but only select the *CustomerID* and the *CompanyName* fields. In the Advanced options, select the option that automatically generates the INSERT, UPDATE, and DELETE statements. Use the GridView Tasks window to enable editing. Finally, set the *GridView* control's *EnableViewState* property to *false*.

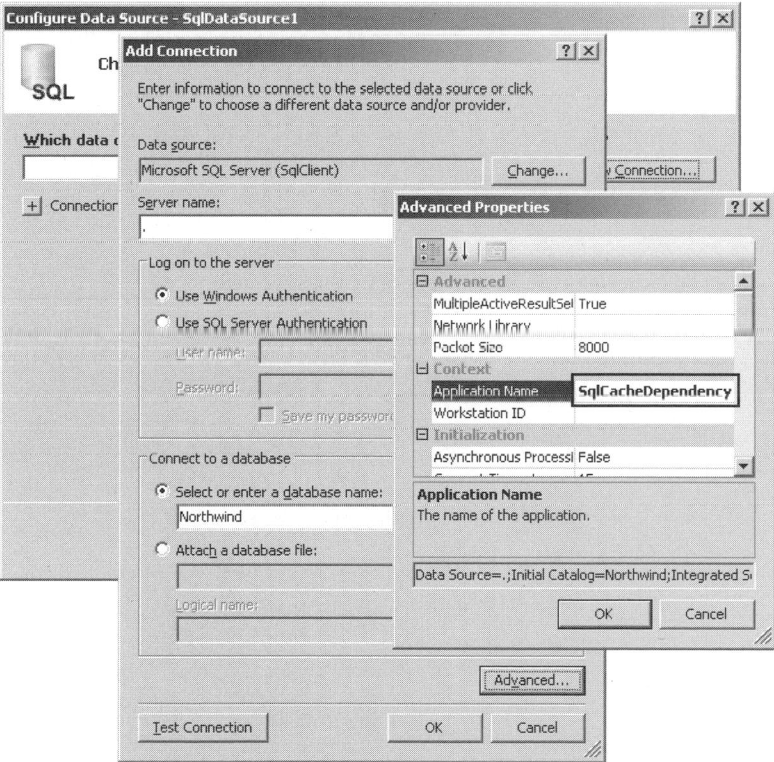

Figure 12-4 Use the Advanced settings on the connection to set the Application Name to SqlCacheDependency, which will make it easier to monitor in the SQL Profiler.

Testing the Application Before Enabling Polling

To test the application, start the SQL Server Profiler by clicking Start | All Programs | Microsoft SQL Server 2005 | Performance Tools | SQL Server Profiler and create a new SQL trace. In the Trace Properties window of the new trace, click the Events Selection tab, and then click the Column Filters button. In the ApplicationName filter, add *SqlCacheDependency* under the Like setting (as shown in Figure 12-5), and then click Run to start the trace.

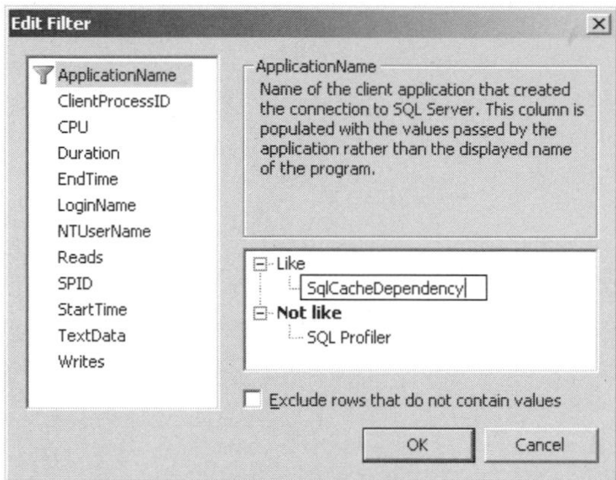

Figure 12-5 Add the SqlCacheDependency to the ApplicationName filter of the new trace.

Next, run the Web application. Notice that every time you click the Refresh button, the SELECT statement is executed. You can see the results in the SQL Profiler trace window.

Enabling Polling in the Web Application

To enable polling in the Web application, you must modify the Web.config file by adding the following settings.

Web.config File Settings for Polling

```
<system.web>
   <caching>
      <sqlCacheDependency enabled="true" pollTime="3600000" >
         <databases>
            <add name="NW"
               connectionStringName="NorthwindConnectionString"
               pollTime="60000" />
         </databases>
      </sqlCacheDependency>
   </caching>
</system.web>
```

I intentionally placed two *pollTime* attributes in these settings just to make sure that you know you can set this twice. The first *pollTime* attribute defines the default *pollTime* if you don't identify a time at the database level. This is set to one hour, which is the 3,600,000-millisecond setting. The second setting is at the specific database, and this setting overrides the default. This is set to 1 minute, which is the 60,000-millisecond setting.

Notice that the connection string setting points to the connection string that was created earlier, which connects to the *Northwind* database.

The last thing to do is to set up the *SqlDataSource* object to use caching and to use the polling you configured. Click the *SqlDataSource1* object on your Web form, modify the properties by enabling caching, and set *SqlCacheDependency* property to *NW:Customers*, as shown in Figure 12-6.

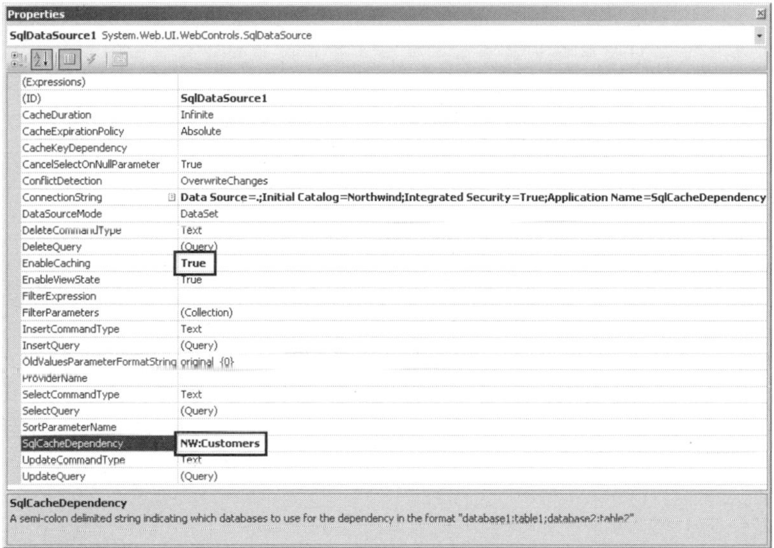

Figure 12-6 Enable caching and set the *SqlCacheDependency* on the *SqlDataSource1* object.

Testing the Application with Polling Enabled

Clear the SQL Profiler trace window by clicking the Clear Trace Window button (or Ctrl+Shift+Del). Run the application, and you'll see that the cache was filled by calling the SELECT statement. You can click the Refresh button on the Web browser many times, but you won't see a call to the SELECT statement. Once a minute, you will see a call to the stored procedure named *dbo.AspNet_SqlCachePollingStoredProcedure*, which retrieves the table names and their change ID numbers for all tables that are being polled in the *Northwind* database. If this change ID has changed on any table since the data was updated, the cache is invalidated and the next request for this data results in issuing the SELECT statement to the database.

Try opening SQL Server Management Studio and changing one of the company names. Then watch the SQL Profiler window until you see the call to the *dbo.AspNet_SqlCache-PollingStoredProcedure* stored procedure. Refresh your Web page, and you should see that the SELECT statement was issued to the database and the change shows on the Web page.

One last thing: in addition to enabling caching on the *SqlDataSource* object, you can use the output cache directive on the Web form as follows.

```
<%@ OutputCache Duration="999999"
   SqlDependency="NW:Customers" VaryByParam="none" %>
```

This caches all of the HTML output for this Web form until the data changes. Because you want to use *SqlDependency* instead of using time to expire the cache, the *Duration* attribute is set to the maximum value of 999,999.

Cache Invalidation by Command Notification

The command notification mechanism uses the *SqlDependency* class that was defined at the beginning of this chapter to receive change notifications when the result of a command changes. Command notification is also known as change notification and is supported only on SQL Server 2005.

Command notification is simple to set up, but you have to first perform all of the setup explained earlier in the "Using the *SqlDependency* Object" section of this chapter.

There is no need to register the *<sqlCacheDependency>* in the Web.config file, and you don't need to use the aspnet_regsql.exe utility to set up anything.

The command notification dependency is configured with the *OutputCache* directive, using the string *CommandNotification*. This value indicates to ASP.NET that a command notification dependency should be created for the page or *SqlDataSource* object.

Preparing SQL Server for Command Notification

This example uses the *pubs* database so you can be certain you are working with a fresh database. The following script can be run in SQL Server Management Studio to enable command notification on the *pubs* database. Note that if you have been executing the scripts in the "Using the *SqlDependency* Object" section of this chapter, you need to execute only the last line, which enables the service broker on the pubs database.

SQL: Enabling Command Notification

```
USE MSDB
GRANT SEND ON SERVICE::
[http://schemas.microsoft.com/SQL/Notifications/QueryNotificationService]
GO
USE MASTER
EXEC sp_configure 'clr enabled', 1
RECONFIGURE
ALTER DATABASE Pubs SET ENABLE_BROKER
```

Creating a Web Site That Uses Command Notification

Now that the database server is configured for command notification, it's time to set up a Web site that uses it. Create a Web site project, and add a *Button* control and a *GridView* control to the form. Set the *Button* control's *Text* property to *"Refresh"*.

Use the GridView Tasks window to configure a new data source. Use the SQL Server instance that you configured for polling, and name the connection string *PubsConnectionString*. In the Advanced options for the connection string, set the Application Name property to *CommandNotification*, which will make it easier for you to view this application in the SQL Profiler utility. To keep this example simple, select the Stores table, but select only the *stor_id* and the *stor_name* fields. In the Advanced options, select the option that automatically generates the insert, update, and delete statements. Use the GridView Tasks window to enable editing. Finally, set the *GridView* control's *EnableViewState* property to *false*.

Testing the Application Before Enabling Command Notification

Start the SQL Profiler and create a new SQL trace. In the Trace Properties window of the new trace, click the Events Selection tab, and then click the Column Filters button. In the ApplicationName filter, add CommandNotification under the Like setting, and then click Run to start the trace.

As with the polling application, when you run the Web application, every time you click the Refresh button, the SELECT statement is executed. You can see the results in the SQL Profiler trace window.

Enabling Command Notification in the Web Application

You don't need to modify the Web.config file. All you need to do is set up the *SqlDataSource* to use the caching you configured. Click the *SqlDataSource1* object on your Web form, modify the properties by enabling caching, and set *SqlCacheDependency* to *CommandNotification*, as shown in Figure 12-7.

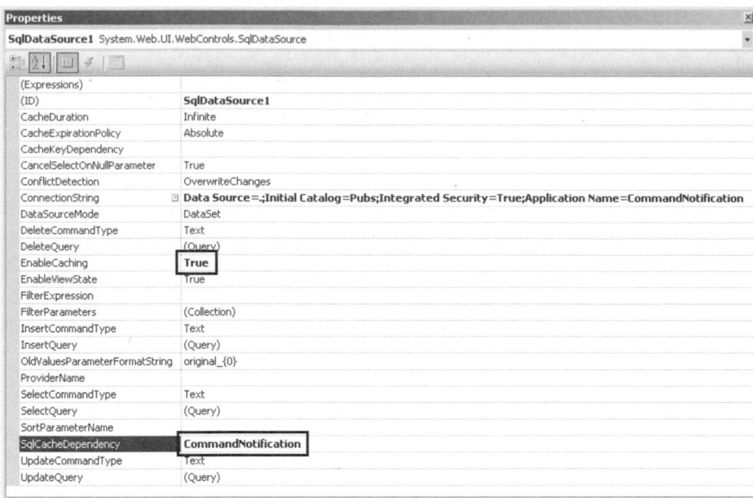

Figure 12-7 Enable caching and set the *SqlCacheDependency* on the *SqlDataSource1* object.

You must make one more property change to the *SqlDataSource1* object. As with the *SqlDependency* class described at the beginning of this chapter, you must change the SELECT query to use a two-part name for the table by adding the *dbo* prefix to the Stores table in the SELECT statement. You can do this in the properties window by clicking the *SelectQuery* property and editing the query as shown in Figure 12-8.

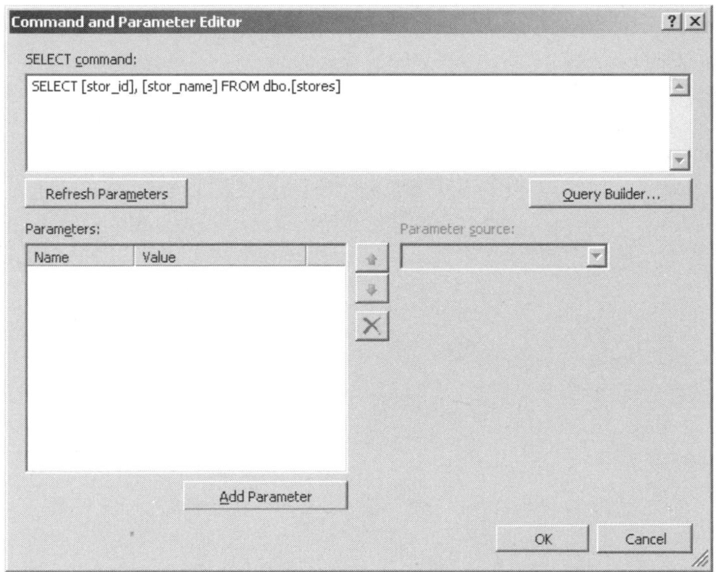

Figure 12-8 Command notification requires the use of two-part names to identify the table.

Testing the Application with Command Notification Enabled

Clear the SQL Profiler trace window and run the application. You will see that the cache was filled by calling the SELECT statement. You can click the Refresh button on the Web browser many times, but you won't see a call to the SELECT statement.

Try opening SQL Server Management Studio and changing one of the company names. Then refresh your Web page, and you should see that the SELECT statement was issued to the database. The change shows on the Web page.

Just as with polling, in addition to enabling the caching on the *SqlDataSource* object, you can also use the output cache directive on the Web form as follows.

```
<%@ OutputCache Duration="999999"
   SqlDependency="CommandNotification" VaryByParam="none" %>
```

This caches all of the HTML output for this Web form until the data changes. Because you want to use *SqlDependency* instead of using time to expire the cache, you set the *Duration* attribute to the maximum value of 999,999.

Summary

- The primary reason for caching data is performance, but caching data requires a means to expire the cache when the data is stale.
- The decision to cache different types of data should be based on frequency of change, the amount of reuse, and the size of the data.
- The *SqlDependency* object allows you to cache data and be notified when the data changes. This object is best suited for Web applications and middle-tier components with a small number of subscribers to the change notification event.
- When you use the *SqlDependency* object, your queries cannot contain the asterisk (*) to retrieve all fields, and the table names must use two-part naming (for example, dbo.Customers).
- You must set up the database server properly for the notification events to work properly, by granting send permissions to the guest account on the SQL *QueryNotificationService* service that is in the MSDB database, enabling the SQLCLR, and enabling the service broker for each database that will use the *SqlDependency* object.
- For SQL Server 7 and later, ASP.NET can perform cache invalidation by using polling. The database and each table must be configured using the aspnet_regsql.exe utility.
- ASP.NET also provides cache invalidation by command notification when you use SQL Server 2005. Command notification, which is also called change notification, uses the *SqlDependency* object; queries must be written using the same guidelines.

Chapter 13
Implementing Security

Application security is something most of us want to ignore. We just want to focus on the functionality of the application, and we wish hackers would just leave us alone. The problem is that we must be aware of security issues and we need to write our programs in a responsible way to spare ourselves the embarrassment and losses that hackers can cause.

Staying current with the latest security patches, running antivirus software, and providing firewalls with logging software are great starting points for implementing security, but writing secure code is equally, if not more, important.

This chapter is not meant to be a complete lesson on application security; entire books are available on this topic. It does, however, offer a lengthy application security overview, which includes Microsoft Windows security and code access security (CAS). This will give you enough information to understand Microsoft ADO.NET security, which is covered later in this chapter.

If you already feel comfortable with Windows security and CAS, skip to the last part of this chapter, which covers ADO.NET security issues, general tips, and ideas for how to make your data more secure.

Application Security Overview

The Microsoft .NET Framework implements a two-layer defense against security vulnerabilities. The first layer, called *role-based security*, allows you to control a user's access to application resources and operations; the second layer, called *code access security*, can control the code's access to resources and ability to perform privileged operations.

Before we plunge into ADO.NET security, you should understand some basic terms and the layers of security provided by Windows and the .NET Framework. These are the foundation for understanding ADO.NET security.

Authentication

Authentication is the process of obtaining the user's credentials, such as name and password, to identify and validate against an authority. Figure 13-1 shows a typical Web site authentication scenario in which Joe proves that he is Joe by providing a password that only Joe should know. The credentials typically contain an identifier and proof of identity. These can be a user name and password, an e-mail address and password, a user name and digital certificate, and so forth.

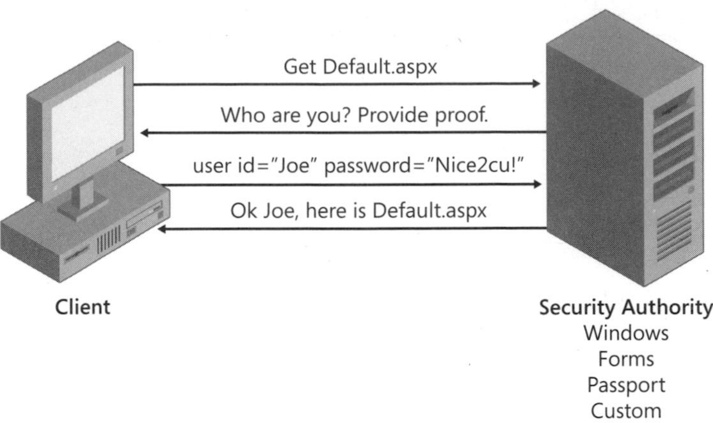

Figure 13-1 Authentication requires an identifier and proof of identity.

Authorization doesn't happen only when you enter an application; it also happens when you cross application boundaries to access resources such as the database server or an e-mail server.

Note that being authenticated means only that the authority believes that you are who you say you are; it does not include the granting of any permission to access resources. This is done though authorization.

Authorization

Authorization is the process of determining whether a user should be granted a specific type of access to a resource. The resource might be a file, a database, the registry, or any other controlled resource. The type of access can be read, write, add, or delete, or it can be resource specific, such as insert, update, or delete. Figure 13-2 shows that Joe, who is already trusted to be Joe based on being authenticated, is attempting to delete an order from the database. If Joe is authorized, he will succeed, but if he doesn't have Delete permission on the Orders table, his attempt will fail.

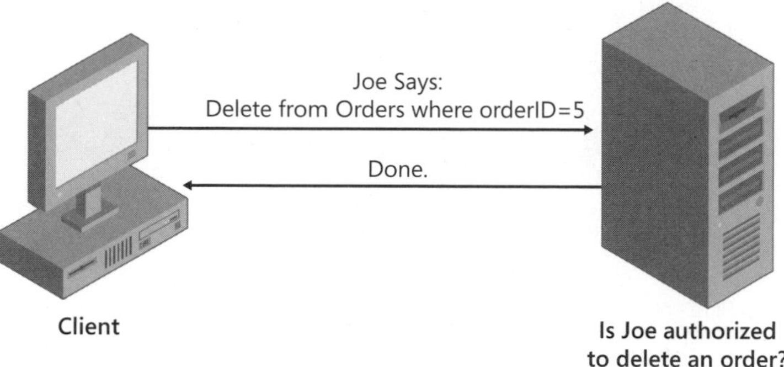
Typical Authorization
Joe Says:
Delete from Orders where orderID=5
Done.
Client
Is Joe authorized
to delete an order?

Figure 13-2 Authorization means determining whether a user should have a specific type of access to a resource.

Authorization can be performed on a user basis or a role basis, or a combination of the two. Using roles can simplify management of permissions. If a role is created for salespeople, it is easy to assign write permissions to that role instead of assigning permissions separately to each salesperson.

Impersonation

Impersonation means allowing code to execute with the identity of the client. In Chapter 9, the managed code uses the identity of the SQL Server service when executing, which means that the access level you have to resources such as files on the local hard drive might be unacceptable. If authorization is based on permissions granted to the user, you must impersonate the user's credentials. This was also demonstrated in Chapter 9.

Delegation

Impersonation across computers is called *delegation*. Impersonation works fine on a single machine, but it will fail if you attempt to access resources on a remote computer. Figure 13-3 shows an example in which delegation is used to delete order items from a remote database server, using Joe's credentials, but the call is coming from a database server, not directly from the user. To enable this scenario, the Windows Domain Administrator must enable Joe's account for delegation.

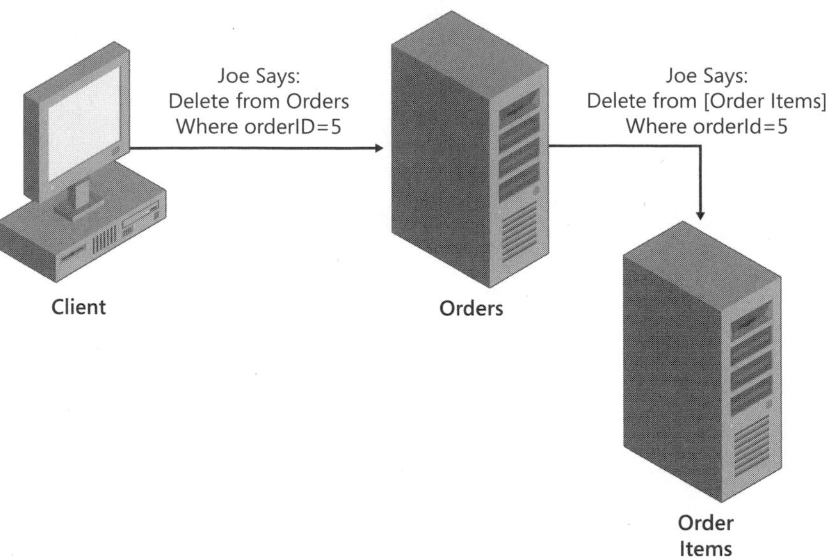

Figure 13-3 A typical delegation scenario in which a user must access a single server to perform an action but part of the work must be executed on a different server, using the user's credentials

You can implement delegation on Windows 2000 and later, but a Windows Domain Administrator must configure delegation for each user account, which can create security issues. Figure 13-4 shows Joe's user account settings, as viewed from the Active Directory Users And Computers tool. The Account Is Trusted For Delegation setting is selected. If the user is currently logged in when the setting is changed, the user must log off and log back on to receive this setting.

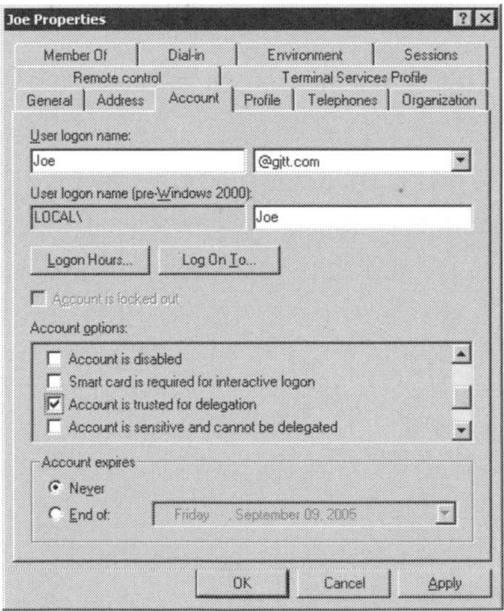

Figure 13-4 You must set the Account Is Trusted For Delegation setting for each user who needs to use delegation.

In addition to configuring delegation on the user account, each computer that is participating in delegation must be trusted for delegation. This can also be configured from the Active Directory Users And Computers tool by opening the Computers node and double-clicking the computer. This computer's properties will be opened as shown in Figure 13-5. Set the Trust Computer For Delegation option. You will need to reboot the computer to activate this setting.

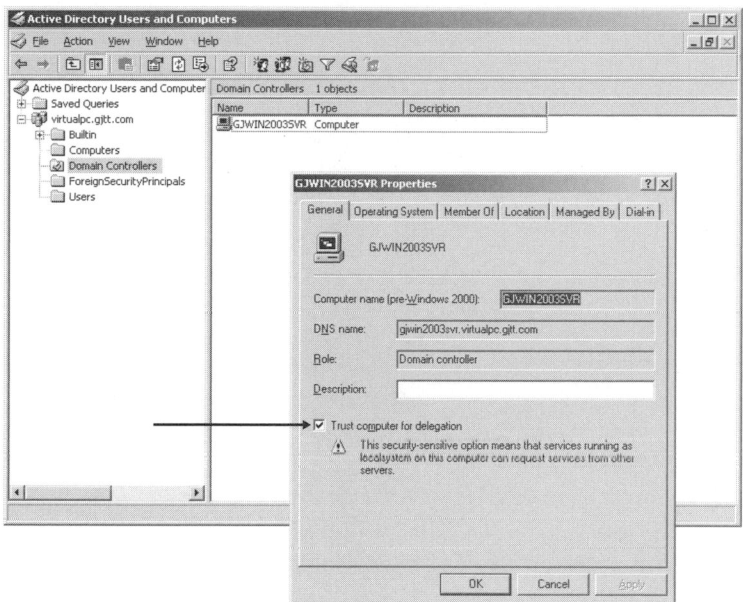

Figure 13-5 The computers that are performing delegation must be trusted for delegation.

Role-Based Security

Windows provides a directory that lists users and user roles. This list defines all users who are allowed to access the computer, domain, or enterprise.

Workgroup Environment

In a workgroup environment, each computer has its own directory of users who need to access the computer (Figure 13-6). If you have 10 users and each user needs access to all of the computers, matching accounts (with matching passwords) must be created on all computers. As the user and computer count grows, this environment will become unmanageable. You can also create roles or groups on each machine to simplify the assignment of users to resources. For example, you can create a group called salespeople and assign it to all resources that salespeople need access to. When a salesperson is hired, she can be simply placed into the salespeople group. This is much quicker than assigning permissions to each user on a resource-by-resource basis.

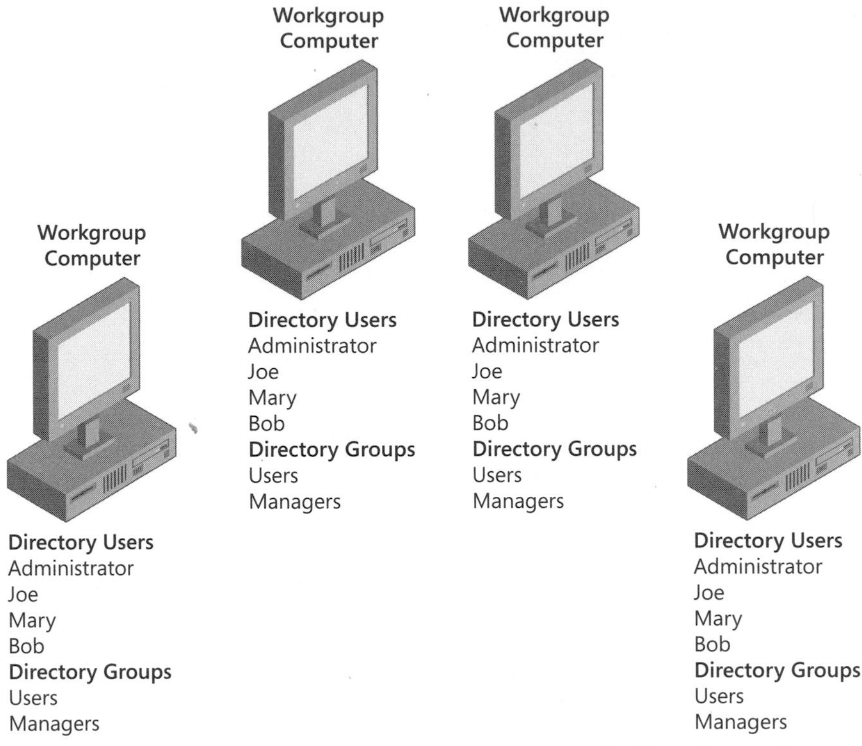

Figure 13-6 In a workgroup environment, accounts are duplicated on each computer, which means account maintenance (such as password changes) must be done on all of the computers.

The Local Users And Groups program in Windows allows you to create new users and add them to groups. In a workgroup environment, account maintenance, such as a password change, must be done on all machines.

Domain Environment

In a domain environment, servers that are configured as domain controllers contain a directory, called Active Directory, that lists users who have access to the domain. Although workstation computers still contain a directory, it should contain only groups, called local groups, which are assigned to resources as shown in Figure 13-7.

Accounts that are created in Active Directory automatically replicate to other domain controllers, which means that account maintenance, such as changing a password or adding or deleting users, needs to be done at only one location.

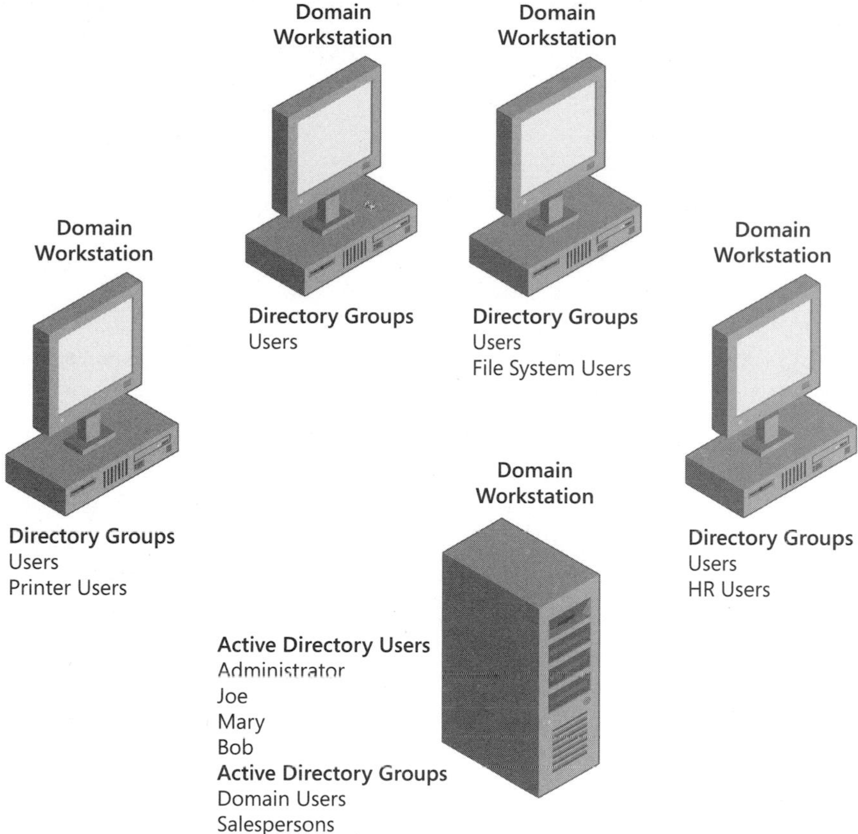

Figure 13-7 In a domain environment, account maintenance needs to be done only once within Active Directory and is replicated to all domain controllers.

The Windows Server operating system contains a tool called Active Directory Users And Computers, which is used to edit Active Directory. Active Directory is very extensible and can store other information, such as certificates, user preferences, printer location information, and e-mail information. Although Active Directory is intended to hold thousands of users, it's usually best suited to providing intranet authentication, not performing Internet Web site authentication.

Code Access Security

If you are logged on to your machine and have Administrator permissions, you can do virtually anything on your machine. If you allow me to log on to your machine, I might have little or no permissions. This looks and feels right, until I find a way for you to unknowingly execute malicious code that I have written or to unknowingly give me permission to do something malicious.

This scenario might seem far-fetched, but every time you open a Web page in your browser, you are executing code that has been written by someone else—and that someone could be me, the hacker.

I'm not a hacker, but I hope I've made my point. It's relatively easy to get someone to unknowingly run malicious code from the Web, and that code will execute with your permissions, which might be Administrator permissions.

Code access security (CAS) helps to minimize the problem of users unintentionally executing unsafe code. With CAS, you can limit the resources that code has access to. Even if a hacker finds a way to get into the code, no damage can be done if the code has limited access to resources. CAS is implemented by using permissions and permission sets, providing evidence of the code's origin, and applying security policies. Permissions are granted based on a security policy, using *evidence*—information about an assembly and its origin. This granting of permissions is analogous to authorization, and the use of evidence is analogous to authentication. When code needs to access a resource, it issues a request for the appropriate permissions, and the .NET Framework security system determines whether the code can perform the desired operation.

Evidence

Evidence includes the following.

- *Strong name* The combination of the assembly's public key, friendly name, and version.
- *Publisher* The Microsoft Authenticode signature.
- *Zone* The origin of the assembly, such as the local computer, intranet, or Internet zone.
- *Location* The current location of the assembly, which can be expressed as a URL, universal naming convention (UNC) path, or local computer folder.
- *Cryptographic hash* The cryptographic hash of the assembly, which is essentially a "digital fingerprint" of the assembly. The purpose of the cryptographic hash is to provide a means to detect changes to an assembly after it has been created. The assembly could change if bytes were somehow lost during the transfer of the assembly across a troublesome network. The assembly could also change if someone were maliciously attempting to alter the assembly. The cryptographic hash is a small, fixed-size byte sequence, also known as a hash code, based on running an algorithm on an assembly of any length.

Authentication types have varying strength in proving that you are who you say you are. For example, requiring a three-digit PIN is much weaker than requiring an eight-character password that includes lowercase alphabetic characters, uppercase alphabetic characters, numbers, and special characters. The same is true for the types of evidence. For example, having an assembly with a strong name that came from a UNC path but now resides on the local computer is certainly stronger than an assembly with a strong name that came from the Internet, even if it is currently on the local computer. You can create security policies based on the strength of the evidence.

Code Access Permissions

Code access permissions define the rights to access specific resources. Many of these permissions are implemented within the .NET Framework to secure the system resources. Table 13-1 lists the code access permissions in the .NET Framework.

Table 13-1 Code Access Permissions in the .NET Framework

Permission	Description
AspNetHostingPermission	Controls access permissions in ASP.NET-hosted environments
DataProtectionPermission	Controls the ability to access data and memory
DirectoryServicesPermission	Allows control of code access permissions for the *System.DirectoryServices* namespace
DistributedTransactionPermission	Controls the ability to access resources in a distributed transaction
DnsPermission	Controls the ability to access DNS servers
EnvironmentPermission	Controls access to the system and user environment variables
EventLogPermission	Controls access to the event logs
FileDialogPermission	Controls access to file dialog boxes in the user interface
FileIOPermission	Controls access to files and folders on the file system
GacIdentityPermission	Defines the identity permission for files originating in the global assembly cache (GAC)
IsolatedStorageFilePermission	Controls access to isolated storage
KeyContainerPermission	Controls the ability to access key containers
MessageQueuePermission	Controls access to message queues
NetworkInformationPermission	Controls access to network information and traffic statistics for the local computer
OdbcPermission	Controls database access by the ODBC data access provider
OleDbPermission	Controls database access by the OLEDB data access provider
OraclePermission	Controls database access by the Oracle data access provider
PerformanceCounterPermission	Controls access to performance counters
PrintingPermission	Controls access to printers
PublisherIdentityPermission	Represents the identity of a software publisher

Table 13-1 Code Access Permissions in the .NET Framework

Permission	Description
ReflectionPermission	Controls access to type metadata by reflection, which is a mechanism for discovering public and private class information at runtime
RegistryPermission	Controls access to the registry
SecurityPermission	Controls ability to execute code, assert permissions, and call unmanaged code
ServiceControllerPermission	Controls the ability to start or stop services
SiteIdentityPermission	Defines the identity permission for the Web site from which the code originates
SmtpPermission	Controls access to Simple Mail Transport Protocol (SMTP) servers
SocketPermission	Controls the ability to connect to other computers by means of sockets
SqlClientPermission	Controls database access by the Microsoft SQL client
SqlNotificationPermission	Controls whether the user can use SQL notifications
StorePermission	Controls access to stores containing X509 certificates
StrongNameIdentityPermission	Defines the identity permission for strong names
UIPermission	Controls access to windows and other user interface elements
UrlIdentityPermission	Defines the identity permission for the URL from which the code originates
WebBrowserPermission	Obsolete—will be removed soon because *WebBrowser* will not be available in semitrust (see *http://go.microsoft.com/fwlink/?linkid=14202*)
WebPermission	Controls the ability to connect to other computers by means of HTTP
ZoneIdentityPermission	Defines the identity permission for the zone from which the code originates

Working with CAS

The .NET Framework grants a set of permissions to every assembly when the assembly loads. Permission sets are used to determine when the assembly needs to access resources. The security policy uses the assembly's evidence to determine the permissions that should be assigned to the assembly.

Code Groups

Code groups are used to define the permissions that an assembly should receive. An assembly can be a member of many code groups. When a code group is created, it is assigned a membership condition and a set of permissions that its members should receive. For example, the code group called Internet_Zone has the membership condition that the assembly must be located on the Internet. It has no permissions. Another code group, My_Computer_Zone, has a membership condition that the assembly must be located on the current user's computer. This code group has several permissions assigned to it. Permissions are cumulative across code groups, which means that the assembly receives the union of all the permissions assigned to every code group that it is a member of.

Permission Sets

Permission sets are groupings of permissions that can be assigned to code groups as needed. The .NET Framework has built-in permission sets, and you can create custom permission sets. Table 13-2 describes the built-in permission sets.

Table 13-2 Built-in Permission Sets

Permission Set	Description
Everything	Contains all standard permissions except the permission to skip validation.
Execution	Permission for code to run.
FullTrust	Full access to all resources.
Internet	Allows code to execute and create top-level windows and file dialog boxes. This code can also make Internet connections to the same site that the assembly came from and use Isolated Storage with a quota.
LocalIntranet	Allows code to execute and provides unrestricted creation of user interface elements. This permission set allows unrestricted use of Isolated Storage with no quota. It also allows DNS usage and the reading of *USERNAME*, *TEMP*, and *TMP* environment variables. The code can make Internet connections to the same site that the assembly came from. This permission set also allows files to be read that are in the same folder.
Nothing	Provides no permissions; code cannot run with this setting.

Runtime Security Policy Levels

Runtime security policy levels are levels of security that you can apply to the Enterprise, the Local Machine, the User, and the Application Domain. Each policy level contains its own hierarchy of code groups and permission sets, as shown in Figure 13-8. Enterprise policies can be set by the network administrator, and they affect all managed code in the Windows domain.

Local Machine policies can be set by the local computer administrator. User policies can be set by the local user or local administrator. Application Domain policies can be programmatically or declaratively defined by a host, such as ASP.NET. Application Domain policies are never skipped during policy evaluation. Notice that in Figure 13-8, this policy is not displayed because the Application Domain policy is not an administrable policy level, whereas the other policies exist in a persisted policy file that administrators can alter using an administration tool like the .NET Framework 2.0 Configuration tool. Application Domain policies are optional and provide isolation, unloading, and security boundaries that are used for managed code execution.

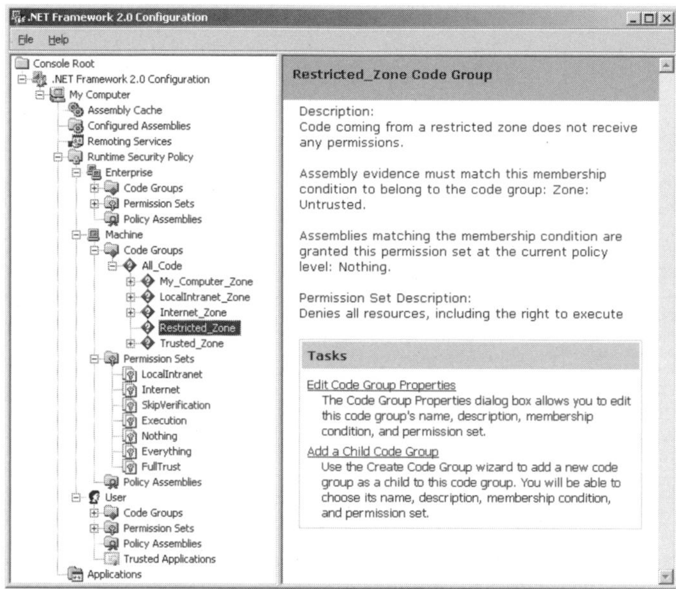

Figure 13-8 The .NET Framework 2.0 Configuration tool shows the hierarchy of runtime security policy levels, code groups, and permission sets.

An assembly's effective permissions are calculated by looping through all of the runtime security policy levels. Within each policy level, the assembly's evidence is collected and code group membership is evaluated. Permissions accumulate based on code group membership. The assembly receives the union of the permissions, based on code group membership. The resultant permissions are then intersected with the permissions of the next policy (Enterprise, Local Computer, User, or Application Domain), as shown in Figure 13-9.

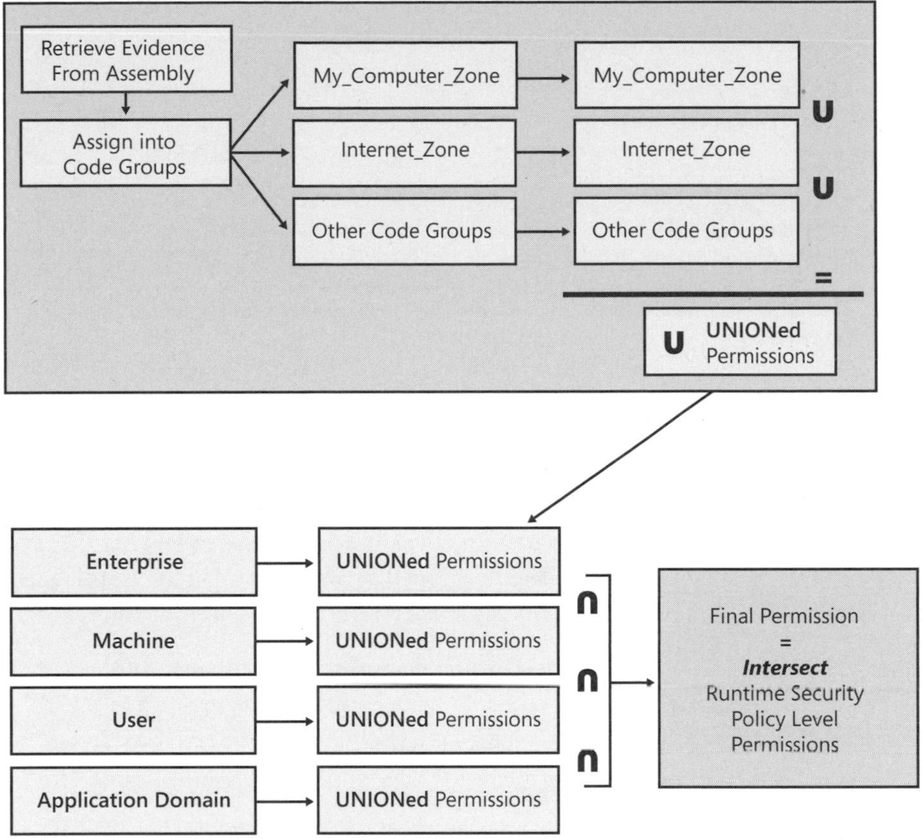

Figure 13-9 An assembly's effective permissions are based on the intersection of the permissions in each level, and each level is evaluated based on the union of the code group permissions.

As you can tell, the ability to change the security on different levels and in different code groups means that an assembly's effective security permissions can be different on every computer, depending on the user.

Changing the Application Domain Security

Application Domain security is defined by the host. You will probably need to work with two CLR hosts: ASP.NET and SQL Server 2005.

Changing ASP.NET Application Domain Security The Application Domain security settings for ASP.NET are in the Web.config file (which is in the same folder as the machine.config file), typically the following location.

```
%WinDir%\Microsoft.NET\Framework\version\CONFIG\
```

The Web.config file is an XML file that contains the settings for ASP.NET. In the Web.config file, you will see a section that looks like the following.

Web.config Security Policy

```
<location allowOverride="true">
   <system.web>
      <securityPolicy>
         <trustLevel name="Full" policyFile="internal" />
         <trustLevel name="High" policyFile="web_hightrust.config" />
         <trustLevel name="Medium" policyFile="web_mediumtrust.config" />
         <trustLevel name="Low"  policyFile="web_lowtrust.config" />
         <trustLevel name="Minimal" policyFile="web_minimaltrust.config" />
      </securityPolicy>
      <trust level="Full" originUrl="" />
   </system.web>
</location>
```

Notice that different security policy trust levels are defined by default, and each trust level has an associated policy file that contains an XML definition of the policy level. The actual setting that ASP.NET uses is defined with the *trust* element, which is set to *Full* here, but you can easily change this to one of the defined settings, such as *Medium* or *Minimal*, and you can look at the policy files to find out what permissions each level has.

Changing the SQLCLR Application Domain Security The other host of the CLR is SQL Server 2005. In Chapter 9, we used the following commands to create a SQLCLR assembly with an Application Domain setting that uses a permission set called SAFE.

SQL: Installing the Visual Basic Assembly

```
CREATE ASSEMBLY VbProcs FROM 'C:\Projects\Vb\Chapter09\HiVbWorld.dll'
WITH PERMISSION_SET=SAFE
GO
```

SQL: Installing the C# Assembly

```
CREATE ASSEMBLY CsProcs FROM 'C:\Projects\CS\Chapter09\HiCsWorld.dll'
WITH PERMISSION_SET=SAFE
GO
```

The SQLCLR has three levels of execution permissions that are enforced at the assembly level:

- *SAFE* Allows access only to CLR code and the database data. Access to unmanaged code, external resources, or thread management is not allowed.
- *EXTERNAL_ACCESS* Allows access to external systems, such as the file system, the event log, the network, and other database servers. Access to unmanaged code is not allowed.
- *UNSAFE* Does not limit access in any way. Obviously, this option is not recommended but is sometimes necessary.

Creating a Security Test Project

This chapter explores and tests many aspects of .NET security, so we'll need a test project. We'll create a simple Windows project called SecurityTest. Add a button to the form, double-click the button, and add the following code.

Visual Basic

```
Imports System.Security.Permissions
Imports System.IO

Public Class Form1

   Private Sub button1_Click(ByVal sender As System.Object, _
         ByVal e As System.EventArgs) Handles button1.Click
      Using stream As New StreamReader("CarList.xml")
         MessageBox.Show(stream.ReadToEnd())
      End Using
   End Sub

End Class
```

C#

```
using System;
using System.Collections.Generic;
using System.ComponentModel;
using System.Data;
using System.Drawing;
using System.Text;
using System.Windows.Forms;
using System.Security.Permissions;
using System.IO;

namespace SecurityTest
{
   public partial class Form1 : Form
   {
      public Form1()
      {
         InitializeComponent();
      }

      private void button1_Click(object sender, EventArgs e)
      {
         using (StreamReader stream = new StreamReader("CarList.xml"))
         {
            MessageBox.Show(stream.ReadToEnd());
         }
      }
   }
}
```

Creating an XML Test File This code simply attempts to open a file called CarList.xml and display its contents in a message box. You can add the file to your project by adding an XML file to the project and placing the following XML into that file. Also change the XML file's *Copy to Output Directory* property to *Copy if Newer*.

CarList.xml File

```
<?xml version="1.0" encoding="utf-8" ?>
<CarList>
   <Car Make="Chevy" Model="Impala"/>
   <Car Make="Ford" Model="Taurus"/>
   <Car Make="Dodge" Model="Caravan"/>
   <Car Make="BMW" Model="Z-4"/>
   <Car Make="Mazda" Model="Miata"/>
</CarList>
```

Assigning a Strong-Name Key File Next you must configure the project as a strong-named assembly. If you have a strong-name key file, use that or create a new strong-name file by using the project's Properties menu to create and assign the strong-name file, as shown in Figure 13-10. This creates a strong-name key file called myKey.pfx.

> **Note** The strong-name file provides evidence that the assembly was created by you. In the sample, the password assigned to the assembly is *Hello2u*. You should create a single strong-name key file with an assigned password that you use for all assemblies that you sign.

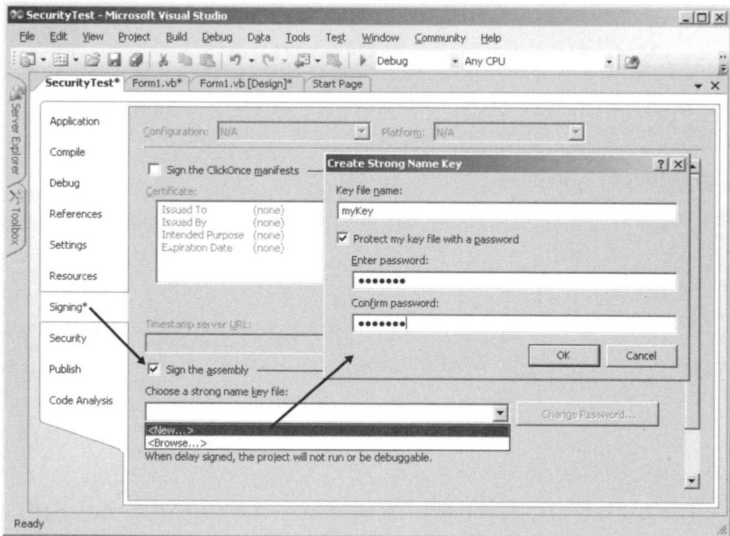

Figure 13-10 Creating a new strong-name file and assigning it to the project

Reducing Permissions Granted to the Assembly Using this strong-named assembly, we will reduce the permissions that this assembly gets without interfering with the rest of the .NET Framework security settings. First be sure to build the SecurityTest application with the key file assigned. Open the .NET Framework 2.0 Configuration tool (from the Start | Control Panel | Administrative Tools menu). Open the My Computer | Runtime Security Policy | User | Code Groups node. Right-click the All Code node, and click New. Set the name of the new code group to *SecurityTest* and click Next. Set the membership condition type to *Strong Name*. Click Import, and select the SecurityTest.exe file. This reads the strong-name key. Click Next, and change the permission set to LocalIntranet, which limits access to the file system. Click Next, and then click Finish. This creates a node called Copy Of SecurityTest. Right-click this node, and click Properties. On the General tab, select the two options at the bottom that limit the security policy evaluation, as shown in Figure 13-11, to be sure that only these permissions are set for assemblies with this strong-name key. Click OK or Apply to accept and immediately apply the changes.

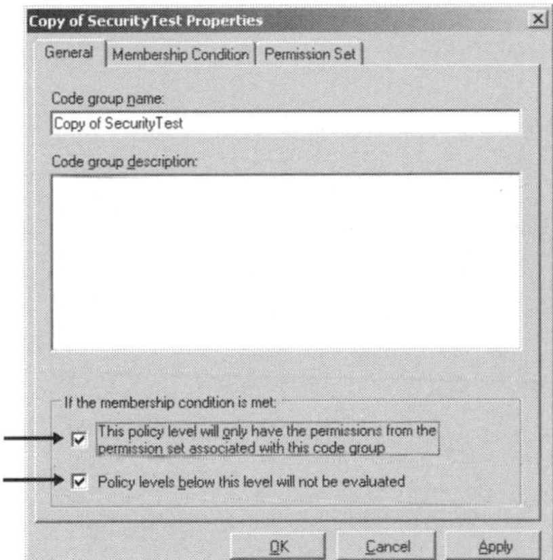

Figure 13-11 Select the bottom options to limit the policy evaluation, which ensures that only the permissions that are defined in this policy are assigned.

Testing the Assembly When you run the SecurityTest application and click the button, the following exception is thrown because the code is trying to surpass its permissions.

```
Request for the permission of type 'System.Security.Permissions.FileIOPermission,
mscorlib, Version=2.0.0.0, Culture=neutral, PublicKeyToken=b77a5c561934e089' failed.
```

The exception is thrown on the line of code that opens the stream. At this point, you know how to create a code group and assign tight security to an assembly. You also have a test project that has a limited permission set assigned.

Requested Permissions

In the previous section, we assigned permissions administratively to any assemblies having the same strong-name key as our test project. If this application were run with the default security permissions, it would have FullTrust because it would be running on the local computer. As a developer, you might not want your application to receive full trust permissions, so one thing you can do is configure your assembly to run with the least amount of permissions that are necessary and request additional permissions as required.

You can implement permission requests to make your code security-aware. You should include permission requests in applications that access protected resources. Permission requests do two things: they request the minimum permissions that your code must receive to run, and they ensure that your code receives only the permissions it actually needs.

Requests are applied as assembly-level attributes in the AssemblyInfo file, where your code tells the runtime about permissions that it needs in order to run or specific permissions that it does not want. The security requests are evaluated when your code is loaded into memory. Requests cannot obtain more permissions than the runtime would have given your code had the request not been made. In our SecurityTest example, requesting file permissions would fail because the User configuration did not give the assembly File permissions.

The assembly permission request requires a *SecurityAction* enumeration, which can be *RequestMinimum*, *RequestOptional*, or *RequestRefuse*. These actions are evaluated when the assembly is loaded and operate as follows.

- *RequestMinimum* Defines the minimum permissions required for the assembly to operate effectively. If these permissions are not granted, the .NET runtime throws a policy exception and the assembly is not loaded. If a request is not made for minimum permissions, the permissions granted are the equivalent to a *RequestMinimum* of Nothing.
- *RequestOptional* Allows you to request a set of permissions while refusing all other permissions that the runtime might otherwise be willing to grant you. If the requested permission cannot be granted, the code stills executes until it gets to the code that needs the permission, at which point a security exception is thrown. If you don't make a request using *RequestOptional*, the permissions granted to your assembly are equivalent to a *RequestOptional* of FullTrust. This is an important point because your code will end up requesting, and possibly receiving, full permissions by default. It's better to add code for a *RequestOptional* of Nothing, which won't give the assembly any extra permissions. It will force the assembly to run with the least permissions.
- *RequestRefuse* Identifies permissions that the assembly should never be granted, even if the security policy allows the permissions to be granted. If a request is not made for the *RequestRefuse* permission, the permissions granted are equivalent to a *RequestRefuse* of Nothing.

Implementing the Request for Permissions The SecurityTest project is currently not working because we added a code group without file input/output permissions. Delete this code group in the .NET Framework 2.0 Configuration tool to allow the application to run with FullTrust permissions. In the following example, we will ask for the minimum permissions to run the project, by adding the following code to the AssemblyInfo file (in the Properties folder of Solution Explorer).

Visual Basic

```
Imports System.Security.Permissions

<Assembly: UIPermission(SecurityAction.RequestMinimum, _
   Unrestricted:=True)>
<Assembly: FileIOPermission(SecurityAction.RequestMinimum, _
   Unrestricted:=True)>
<Assembly: PermissionSet(SecurityAction.RequestOptional, _
   Unrestricted:=False)>
```

C#

```
using System.Security.Permissions;

[assembly: UIPermission(SecurityAction.RequestMinimum,
   Unrestricted=true)]
[assembly: FileIOPermission(SecurityAction.RequestMinimum,
   Unrestricted=true )]
[assembly: PermissionSet(SecurityAction.RequestOptional,
   Unrestricted = false)]
```

This attribute requests user interface (UI) and file input/output (FileIO) permissions from the .NET security system. If these permissions are not granted, the assembly does not load. The last line requests a set of permissions, and you can specify the name of a particular permission set. In this example, no permission set name is given, so the Nothing permission set is assigned, and all other permissions not explicitly requested are refused. The permissions explicitly requested were the UI and FileIO permissions.

The permissions requested by the assembly are the union of *RequestMinimum* (M) and *RequestOptional* (O) minus *RequestRefuse* (R). The permissions that are finally granted (F) to the assembly are based on the runtime security policy permissions (RS) intersected with the permissions that were requested, as shown here.

$F = RS \cap ((M \cup O) - R)$

Testing the Permission Requests To test the code we just added to the SecurityTest project, run the application and click the button. You should see that the file is opened and the message box displays its contents.

Next try commenting out the statement in the AssemblyInfo file that requests FileIO permissions, and run the SecurityTest project again. You will see the same exception as earlier.

This exception is thrown because the last statement, *PermissionSet(SecurityAction.Request-Optional, Unrestricted = false)*, tells the runtime that no permissions should be given except permissions that are explicitly requested, and the FileIO permission is no longer being requested. If you comment out this last statement, the application will receive the FullTrust permission set and the project will run even with the FileIO permission request commented out.

Placing Demands on the Callers

Your code can demand that callers have specific permissions in order to execute your code. Any method that calls your method, directly or indirectly, is a caller, or more specifically, an upstream caller in the call stack, as shown in Figure 13-12. When you demand that the caller have specific permissions, the complete call stack is walked to verify that the permissions exist. Your code can place demands on the caller either declaratively or imperatively. Declarative demands are implemented by using attributes before the method or class that needs to access a specific resource, or by using an assembly-level attribute. Imperative permissions are implemented in code and can be more granular, but they are not as visible to tools that can identify the permissions that your assembly requires.

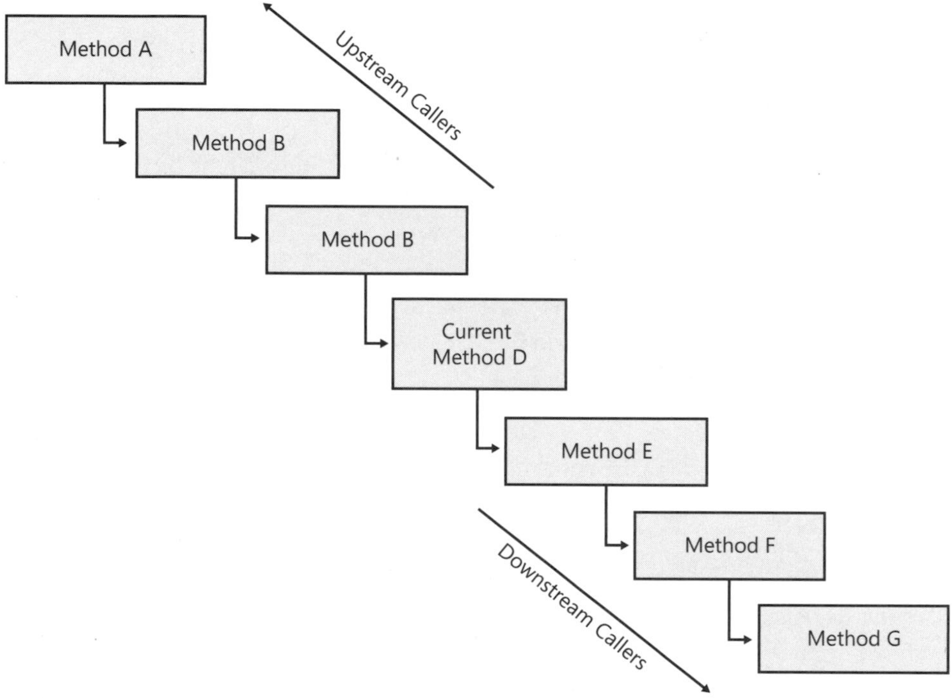

Figure 13-12 Looking at the call stack, upstream callers are direct and indirect callers of the current method, whereas downstream callers are calls that are directly and indirectly made from the current method.

Declarative Demands Declarative permission demands are assigned using attributes, which can be placed at the assembly, class, or class member. Declarative permissions assigned at the class level apply to all class members. If a class has a declarative demand and a class member has a declarative demand, the class member's declarative demand overrides the class-level declarative demand.

Implementing Declarative Permission Demands In the SecurityTest project, we'll add another button that performs the same action as the first button but has a declarative demand for FileIO permissions. Add a button to the form, double-click the button, and add the following code, which has a declarative demand for the *Button* object's event handler.

Visual Basic

```
<FileIOPermission(SecurityAction.Demand, Unrestricted:=True)> _
Private Sub Button2_Click(ByVal sender As System.Object, _
      ByVal e As System.EventArgs) Handles Button2.Click
   Using stream As New StreamReader("CarList.xml")
      MessageBox.Show(stream.ReadToEnd())
   End Using
End Sub
```

C#

```
[FileIOPermission(SecurityAction.Demand,Unrestricted=true)]
private void button2_Click(object sender, EventArgs e)
{
   using (StreamReader stream = new StreamReader("CarList.xml"))
   {
      MessageBox.Show(stream.ReadToEnd());
   }
}
```

This code places a declarative demand on this method only. The difference between this button and the previous button is that the previous button's method is entered and the security exception is thrown on the line of code that opens the file, whereas this button throws the security exception before the method is entered.

Using PermCalc.exe to Find Required Permissions PermCalc is a tool that estimates the permissions that callers must be granted to call the public entry points of an assembly. PermCalc is available in the .NET Framework SDK and can be accessed using the .NET Command Prompt. You can get help on PermCalc by calling *PermCalc* with the -? option. To view the permissions required for any caller into the SecurityTest project, change to the directory containing your executable and run PermCalc as follows.

```
PermCalc SecurityTest.exe -Show -Stacks -Under
```

The PermCalc tool produces the following XML output, which is normally directed to a file but can be displayed using the *-Show* option.

PermCalc Output

```
<?xml version="1.0"?>
<Assembly>
   <Namespace Name="SecurityTest">
      <Type Name="Form1">
         <Method Sig="instance void .ctor()">
            <Demand>
               <PermissionSet version="1"
                  class="System.Security.PermissionSet">
               <IPermission version="1"
                  class="System.Security.Permissions.FileIOPermission,
                  mscorlib, Version=2.0.0.0, Culture=neutral,
                  PublicKeyToken=b77a5c561934e089" Unrestricted="true" />
               </PermissionSet>
            </Demand>
            <Sandbox>
               <PermissionSet version="1"
                  class="System.Security.PermissionSet">
               <IPermission version="1"
                  class="System.Security.Permissions.FileIOPermission,
                  mscorlib, Version=2.0.0.0, Culture=neutral,
                  PublicKeyToken=b77a5c561934e089" Unrestricted="true" />
               </PermissionSet>
            </Sandbox>
            <Stacks>
               <CallStack>
                  <IPermission version="1"
                     class="System.Security.Permissions.FileIOPermission,
                     mscorlib, Version=2.0.0.0, Culture=neutral,
                     PublicKeyToken=b77a5c561934e089" Unrestricted="true" />
                  <Method Type="System.IO.StreamReader"
                     Sig="instance void .ctor(string )" Asm="mscorlib" />
                  <Method Type="SecurityTest.Form1"
                     Sig="instance void button1_Click(object ,
                        class EventArgs )" Asm="SecurityTest" />
                  <Method Type="SecurityTest.Form1"
                     Sig="instance void InitializeComponent()"
                        Asm="SecurityTest" />
                  <Method Type="SecurityTest.Form1"
                     Sig="instance void .ctor()"
                     Asm="SecurityTest" />
               </CallStack>
            </Stacks>
         </Method>
      </Type>
   </Namespace>
</Assembly>
```

This output shows that FileIO permissions are required to call into this assembly.

Imperative Demands You make imperative permission demands in your code by creating a new instance of the permission object you want to demand. You should generally avoid imperative demands in favor of declarative demands, but imperative demands give you the flexibility of being as granular as you need to be.

Implementing Imperative Permission Demands In the SecurityTest project, we'll add yet another button that performs the same action as the previous button but has an imperative demand for FileIO permissions. Add a button to the form, double-click the button, and add the following code.

Visual Basic

```
Private Sub button3_Click(ByVal sender As System.Object, _
      ByVal e As System.EventArgs) Handles button3.Click
   Dim filePerm As New FileIOPermission( _
      PermissionState.Unrestricted)
   filePerm.Demand()
   Using stream As New StreamReader("CarList.xml")
      MessageBox.Show(stream.ReadToEnd())
   End Using
End Sub
```

C#

```
private void button3_Click(object sender, EventArgs e)
{
   FileIOPermission filePerm = new FileIOPermission(
      PermissionState.Unrestricted);
   filePerm.Demand();
   using (StreamReader stream = new StreamReader("CarList.xml"))
   {
      MessageBox.Show(stream.ReadToEnd());
   }
}
```

When you run this code, the security exception is thrown on the line that demands the permission. The advantage is that you can place this code in a try/catch block. If the specific exception is thrown, you can display a more user-friendly exception message and/or gracefully recover from the exception.

Being Assertive on Downstream Callers

Assert is a downstream call that you can make on a permission to enable your code and downstream caller's code to execute code that your code has permission to do but your callers might not have permission to do. Any call to a method, directly or indirectly, by your code is considered to be a downstream caller, as shown previously in Figure 13-12. By calling the *Assert* method on a permission, you are telling the security system to not check the downstream callers for the asserted permission. When your code reaches the *Assert*, there is a stack walk to verify that you have permission to make the *Assert*, but if a downstream caller places a demand for a permission that you asserted, no stack walk is made to verify permissions.

Why is the *Assert* necessary? Sometimes your code needs to call code that is in a component that you didn't write, and you don't have the source code to change. This code might not have requested the permissions that are necessary for the action that you are trying to perform. Your code has the appropriate permission but the component does not. The *Assert* opens the door for you. Think of the *Assert* as being a "Just do it!" command.

When you are done with the assertion, call the *RevertAssert* method, which undoes the assertion. Using the *Assert* method can create security holes, so think twice about implementing this approach.

Using the *AllowPartiallyTrustedCallersAttribute* Attribute

By default, strong-named assemblies can be called only by other assemblies that are granted full trust by the runtime security policy. You enforce this restriction by placing a *LinkDemand* for FullTrust on every public or protected method on every publicly accessible class in the assembly.

A *LinkDemand* is a permission demand to the assembly that attempts to make a call. *LinkDemand* causes a security check during just-in-time compilation and checks only the immediate caller of your code. Linking occurs when your code is bound to a type reference, including function pointer references and method calls. If the caller does not have sufficient permission to link to your code, the link is not allowed and a runtime exception is thrown when the code is loaded and run. Note that a stack walk is not performed with a *LinkDemand*.

Strong-named assemblies that are intended to be called by partially trusted code can declare their intent through the use of the *AllowPartiallyTrustedCallersAttribute* (APTCA). The attribute is declared at the assembly level. The following is an example of adding the declaration to a strong-named assembly.

Visual Basic

```
<assembly:AllowPartiallyTrustedCallers>
```

C#

```
[assembly:AllowPartiallyTrustedCallers]
```

If a strong-named assembly does not explicitly apply this attribute at the assembly level, only assemblies that are granted FullTrust by the runtime security policy can call the assembly. If this attribute is present, all other security checks function as intended, including any class-level or method-level declarative security attributes.

SQL Server Security

To use SQL Server, you must be authenticated within SQL Server and then authorized to execute any T-SQL statement that you pass through the connection. Authentication is done using the connection string information when you open the connection. Authorization is done when you execute a command on the connection. This section provides a brief overview of authentication and authorization in SQL Server.

SQL Server Authentication

You can configure SQL Server to provide authentication by using its own security system (SQL Server authentication) and/or by using integrated Windows authentication. In SQL Server, authentication uses login accounts. If you match a login, you can get into SQL Server. However, you still have no permissions until you have been authorized to access a resource.

Using SQL Server Authentication

When SQL Server is configured for SQL Server authentication, you can create login accounts in SQL Server. A login consists of a user name and a password, which are maintained by the SQL Server administrator. You can turn on SQL Server authentication by editing the SQL Server security properties, as shown in Figure 13-13. Notice that this option, Mixed Mode, does not turn off integrated Windows authentication, because integrated Windows authentication cannot be turned off. The Mixed Mode option requires a restart of SQL Server before the change takes effect.

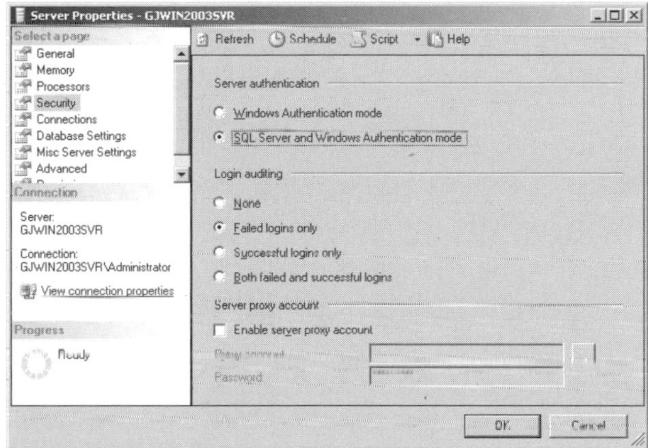

Figure 13-13 Setting SQL Server to use SQL Server authentication, which still uses Windows authentication

SQL Server Management Studio lets you add logins through the Security node. Figure 13-14 shows a login named Joe being added. Notice that adding the SQL Server login requires a name and a password.

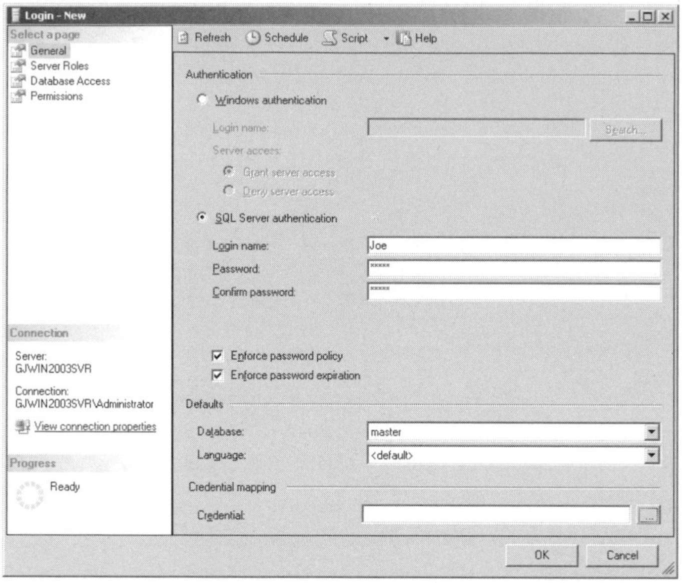

Figure 13-14 The login screen, where Joe's name and password are entered to create a new login

If SQL Server authentication is turned on, your connection string must contain a valid user name and password. This can become a security issue because you must deal with storing and passing the user and password information without someone discovering a way to read it. A typical connection string might look like the following.

```
Data Source=.;Initial Catalog=Northwind;User ID=Joe;Password=hi2u2
```

In SQL Server 2000 and earlier, the SQL Server authentication lacks strong controls such as password complexity, expiration, lockout, and history when you use SQL Server logins. SQL Server 2005 has all these controls, and they inherit from the Windows operating system policy. You should be aware, however, that SQL Server authentication is provided for backward compatibility and for use with Windows 98/Me installations where Windows authentication isn't an option.

Using SQL Server Authentication as a Form of Delegation

SQL Server 2005 can map Windows credentials to a SQL Server login. In some cases, you can use this instead of delegation. In Figure 13-14, shown earlier, notice that the bottom of the screen lets you specify credential mapping. If you map a Windows user account to this login, you can use this SQL login to connect to SQL Server and execute SQLCLR code that can access remote SQL Servers using this mapped account.

You should make every attempt to accomplish your tasks using integrated Windows authentication because no user credentials are exposed. If you must use SQL Server authentication with a Web application, be sure to read the "Storing Encrypted Connection Strings in Web Applications" section later in this chapter.

Using Integrated Windows Security

Integrated Windows authentication requires the user to be authenticated by the Windows operating system before attempting to connect to SQL Server. This is the default setting for SQL Server 2005. If you have changed to Mixed Mode, both SQL Server and Windows Authentication Mode logins are allowed access.

To access SQL Server using integrated Windows authentication, you must make sure your Windows credentials match one of the logins in SQL Server. In SQL Server, you can create a login that maps directly to a single user, but it's common to create a login that maps to a Windows role. You can grant access to all of your users by adding a couple of logins that map to the user roles.

If you want to use integrated Windows authentication, your connection string must contain the command to use a trusted connection or to use integrated security, as shown in the following sample connection strings.

```
Server=.;Database=Northwind;Trusted_Connection=Yes
Server=.;Database=Northwind;Integrated Security=SSPI
```

These connection strings are synonymous; notice that there is no user name or password. You should always try to use integrated Windows authentication.

SQL Server Authorization

In SQL Server, the login is used for authentication, but each database contains its own table of users. The database user is granted permissions to access resources. For a stored procedure, the only permission is *execute*. For tables, the permissions include *select*, *insert*, *update*, and *delete*. The login is mapped to a user in the tables that the login needs access to, and the login has the permissions of the user, as shown in Figure 13-15.

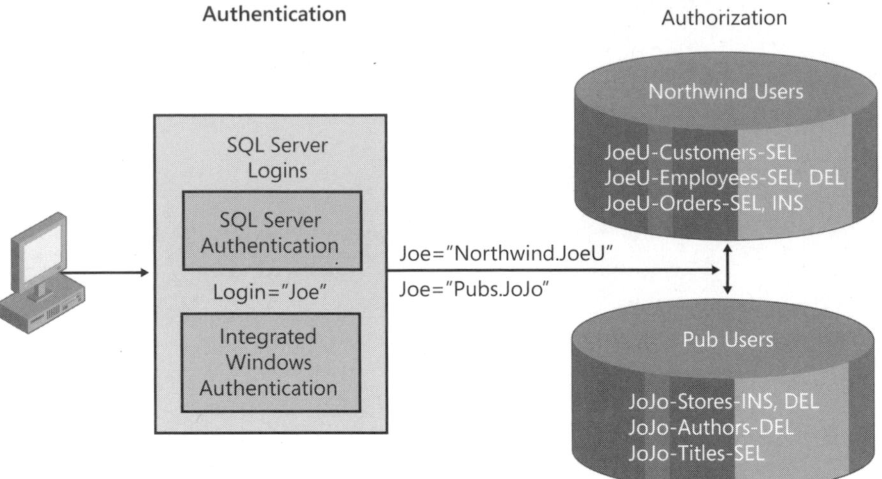

Figure 13-15 SQL Server authentication uses logins; authorization looks up users in each database to check their permissions.

The complexity of mapping the correct permissions to a user in a large application can be overwhelming, especially if you are trying to figure out how someone should have SELECT permissions on a table in some scenarios but not in others. This is why it's generally a good idea to remove all permissions that are assigned to tables and to create stored procedures for each action, assigning *execute* permissions to the appropriate users. As long as the stored procedure owner is the same as the table owner, no check is made to see if the user has access to the table when the stored procedure is executing, and permission assignment is greatly simplified.

ADO.NET Security

Several areas in ADO.NET let you achieve improved security. The rest of this chapter focuses on these areas.

Partial Trust Support

AllowPartiallyTrustedCallersAttribute is fully implemented in the System.Data.dll assembly. Previous releases of the ADO.NET supported only *System.Data.SqlClient*, with partially trusted applications. In ADO.NET 2.0, the SQL Server, OLEDB, ODBC, and Oracle providers can all run in partially trusted environments.

To use SQL Server in a partially trusted environment, your application must have *SqlClientPermission* permissions. You can also use *SqlClientPermissionAttribute* members to further restrict the capabilities of the SQL Server provider, as shown in Table 13-3.

Table 13-3 *SqlClientPermissionAttribute* Properties

Property	Description
AllowBlankPassword	Controls the use of a blank password in a connection string.
ConnectionString	Restricts the permitted connection strings to the set specified by this property. Do not include user names and passwords.
KeyRestrictions	Sets connection string parameters that are allowed or disallowed. Parameters are assigned in the form <*parameter name*>=. You can specify multiple, semicolon (;) delimited parameters. You can use the *KeyRestrictionBehavior* property with this property to set the keys as allowed or disallowed.
KeyRestrictionBehavior	Specifies that the connection string parameters identified by the *KeyRestrictions* property are the only additional connection string parameters allowed (*AllowOnly*) or are not allowed (*PreventUsage*). The default is *AllowOnly*.

If you don't specify any *KeyRestrictions* and the *KeyRestrictionBehavior* property is set to *AllowOnly*, no additional connection string parameters are allowed. If you don't specify any *KeyRestrictions* and the *KeyRestrictionBehavior* property is set to *PreventUsage*, no additional connection string parameters are allowed.

Testing ADO.NET with a Partially Trusted Caller

To test ADO.NET in a partially trusted environment, create a Windows application project called PartialTrustTest. Add a reference to the System.Configuration.dll library. Add the *Northwind* database to the project, and add a button to the form. Change the button text to *Get Version*. Double-click the button, and add the following code.

Visual Basic

```
Imports System.Data.SqlClient
Imports System.Configuration

Public Class Form1

   Private Sub button1_Click(ByVal sender As System.Object, _
         ByVal e As System.EventArgs) Handles button1.Click
      Dim cnSetting As ConnectionStringSettings = _
         ConfigurationManager.ConnectionStrings("nwString")
      Using cn As New SqlConnection(cnSetting.ConnectionString)
         cn.Open()
         MessageBox.Show(cn.ServerVersion)
      End Using
   End Sub
End Class
```

C#

```
using System;
using System.Windows.Forms;
using System.Configuration;
using System.Data.SqlClient;

namespace PartialTrustTest
{
   public partial class Form1 : Form
   {
      public Form1()
      {
         InitializeComponent();
      }

      private void button1_Click(object sender, EventArgs e)
      {
         ConnectionStringSettings cnSetting =
            ConfigurationManager.ConnectionStrings["nwString"];
         using (SqlConnection cn =
            new SqlConnection(cnSetting.ConnectionString))
         {
            cn.Open();
            MessageBox.Show(cn.ServerVersion);
         }
      }
   }
}
```

This code simply reads the connection information from the app.config file, opens the connection, and gets the current server version. To make the code work, add an app.config file to the project that contains the following connection string information.

App.config File

```
<?xml version="1.0" encoding="utf-8" ?>
<configuration>
   <connectionStrings>
      <add name="nwString" connectionString=
         "Data Source=.\SQLEXPRESS;
            AttachDbFilename=|DataDirectory|\northwnd.mdf;
            Integrated Security=True;User Instance=True"
          providerName="System.Data.SqlClient" />
      <add name="badString" connectionString=
         "Data Source=.;AttachDbFilename=|DataDirectory|\northwnd.mdf;
         Integrated Security=True;User Instance=True"
          providerName="System.Data.SqlClient" />
   </connectionStrings>
</configuration>
```

This file contains a valid connection string and a connection string that will be disallowed. After you add the app.config file, run the application and click the button; you should see the SQL Server version. At this point, the application is running with FullTrust permissions.

Add the following attributes to the AssemblyInfo file to make this application partially trusted.

Visual Basic

```
Imports System.Security.Permissions
Imports System.Data.SqlClient

<Assembly: SqlClientPermission(SecurityAction.RequestMinimum, _
   Unrestricted:=True)>
<Assembly: FileIOPermission(SecurityAction.RequestMinimum, _
   Unrestricted:=True)>
<Assembly: UIPermission(SecurityAction.RequestMinimum, _
   Unrestricted:=True)>
<Assembly: PermissionSet(SecurityAction.RequestOptional, _
   Unrestricted:=false)>
```

C#

```
using System.Security.Permissions;
using System.Data.SqlClient;

[assembly: SqlClientPermission(SecurityAction.RequestMinimum,
   Unrestricted = true)]
[assembly: FileIOPermission(SecurityAction.RequestMinimum,
   Unrestricted = true)]
[assembly: UIPermission(SecurityAction.RequestMinimum,
   Unrestricted = true)]
[assembly: PermissionSet(SecurityAction.RequestOptional,
   Unrestricted = false)]
```

If you run the application, it will still run properly as a partially trusted application. To prove that you are in a partially trusted environment, comment out the SQL Client permission request and restart the application; a *SqlClientPermission* exception is thrown. Uncomment the SQL Client permission request.

To test the *ConnectionString*, *KeyRestriction*, and *KeyBehavior* properties, add another button and change the button's text to *Get Bad Version*. Double-click the button, and copy the code from the first button and paste it into the second button. In the second button's code, change the name of the retrieved connection string to *badString*. If you have a default instance of SQL Server installed and you run the code, it will work.

Change the *SqlClientPermission* to add the *ConnectionString*, *KeyRestriction*, and *KeyRestriction-Behavior*, which will allow connections only to SQLEXPRESS and will limit the keys that can be used in the connection string. Also change the *Unrestricted* property to *false* to enable the other properties, as shown in the following code.

Visual Basic

```
<Assembly: SqlClientPermission(SecurityAction.RequestMinimum, _
   Unrestricted:=False, _
   ConnectionString:="Data Source=.\SQLEXPRESS", _
   KeyRestrictionBehavior:=KeyRestrictionBehavior.AllowOnly, _
   KeyRestrictions:="Data Source=;AttachDbFilename=;" + _
      "Integrated Security=;User Instance=")>
```

C#

```
[assembly: SqlClientPermission(SecurityAction.RequestMinimum,
   Unrestricted = false,
   ConnectionString = @"Data Source=.\SQLEXPRESS",
   KeyRestrictionBehavior = KeyRestrictionBehavior.AllowOnly,
   KeyRestrictions = "Data Source=;AttachDbFilename=;" +
      "Integrated Security=;User Instance=")]
```

If you test the application, clicking the first button displays the version and clicking the second button causes a *SecurityException* to be thrown, stating "Request for the permission of type 'System.Data.SqlClient.SqlClientPermission, System.Data, Version=2.0.0.0, Culture=neutral, PublicKeyToken=b77a5c561934e089' failed."

Storing Encrypted Connection Strings in Web Applications

It's common practice to store connection strings in the App.config file. This makes it easy to change the connection string without requiring a recompile of the application. The problem is that connection strings can contain login information such as user names and passwords. Quite frankly, I don't even want people to be able to see the location of the database server and the database name, but I also don't want to embed this information in my application.

In Web applications, the solution is to encrypt the connection string. You can do this by using the aspnet_regiis.exe utility to encrypt the *connectionStrings* section. You can use the */?* option to get help on the utility.

You encrypt and decrypt the contents of a Web.config file by using the *System.Configuration.DPAPIProtectedConfigurationProvider*, which uses the Windows Data Protection API (DPAPI) to encrypt and decrypt data, or the *System.Configuration.RSAProtectedConfigurationProvider*, which uses the RSA encryption algorithm to encrypt and decrypt data.

When you use the same encrypted configuration file on many computers in a Web farm, only the *System.Configuration.RSAProtectedConfigurationProvider* allows you to export the encryption keys used to encrypt the data and import them on another server. This is the default setting.

Note For information on exporting and importing RSA encryption keys, see the ReadMe.txt file in the sample code for this chapter. The sample code has encrypted connection strings that use an RSA key that was generated on my computer. You will need to import the RSA key, just as you would need to do when working with Web farms

Implementing an Encrypted *ConnectionString*

Create an ASP.NET Web site called EncryptWebSite, and add the *Northwind* database to the App_Data folder. Add a *GridView* control to the Web form. Use the GridView Tasks menu to add a new data source. The new data source will be the northwnd.mdf file that you added to the App_Data folder. For the query, select all fields in the Customers table.

Try running the application–it should run, and the Web.config file that Visual Studio generates will contain the connection string shown here.

Unencrypted Web.config

```
<?xml version="1.0"?>
<configuration xmlns="http://schemas.microsoft.com/.NetConfiguration/v2.0">
    <appSettings/>
    <connectionStrings>
        <add name="ConnectionString"
            connectionString="Data Source=.\SQLEXPRESS;
            AttachDbFilename=|DataDirectory|\northwnd.mdf;
            Integrated Security=True;User Instance=True"
            providerName="System.Data.SqlClient" />
    </connectionStrings>
    <system.web>
      ...
    </system.web>
</configuration>
```

Next you can encrypt the Web.config file by running the Visual Studio .NET command prompt and executing the following command, specifying the full path to your Web site folder.

```
aspnet_regiis -pef "connectionStrings" "C:\...\EncryptWebSite"
```

Note that the *–pef* switch requires you to pass the physical Web site path, which is the last parameter. Be sure to verify the path to your Web.config file. The encrypted Web.config file will look like the following.

Encrypted Web.config File

```
<?xml version="1.0"?>
<configuration xmlns="http://schemas.microsoft.com/.NetConfiguration/v2.0">
   <protectedData>
      <protectedDataSections>
         <add name="connectionStrings"
            provider="RsaProtectedConfigurationProvider"
            inheritedByChildren="false" />
      </protectedDataSections>
   </protectedData>
   <appSettings/>
   <connectionStrings>
      <EncryptedData Type="http://www.w3.org/2001/04/xmlenc#Element"
       xmlns="http://www.w3.org/2001/04/xmlenc#">
         <EncryptionMethod
            Algorithm="http://www.w3.org/2001/04/xmlenc#tripledes-cbc" />
         <KeyInfo xmlns="http://www.w3.org/2000/09/xmldsig#">
            <EncryptedKey Recipient=""
               xmlns="http://www.w3.org/2001/04/xmlenc#">
               <EncryptionMethod
                  Algorithm="http://www.w3.org/2001/04/xmlenc#rsa-1_5" />
               <KeyInfo xmlns="http://www.w3.org/2000/09/xmldsig#">
                  <KeyName>Rsa Key</KeyName>
               </KeyInfo>
```

```
                    <CipherData>
<CipherValue>PPWA1TkWxs2i698Dj07iLUberpFYIj6wBhbmqfmNK/plarau4i1k+xq5bZzB4VJW8
OkhwzcIIdZIXff6INJ1wlZz76ZV1DIbRzbH71t6d/L/qJtuOexXxTi2LrepreK/q3svMLpsJycnDPa
t9xaGoaLq4Cg3P19Z1J6HquFILeo=</CipherValue>
                    </CipherData>
                </EncryptedKey>
            </KeyInfo>
            <CipherData>
<CipherValue>Q1re8ntDDv7/dHsvWbnIKdZF6COA1y3S91hmnhUN3nxYfrjSc7FrjEVyJfJhl5EDX
4kXd8ukAjrqwuBNnQbsh1PAXNFDflzB4FF+jyPKP/jm1Q9mDnmiq+NCuo3KpKj8F4vcHbcj+f3GYqq
B4pYbblAvYnjPyPrrPmxLNT9KDtDr8pDbtGnKqAfcMnQPvA815w3BzPM4a73Vtt2kL/z9QJRu3Svd9
33taxOO/HufRJEnE2/hcBq30WcBmEuXx3LFNjV+xVmuebrInhhxQgM2froBKYxgjwWiWNjIIjIeTI2
FQ8nZ8V8kzAVohmDYkZpCj4NQGdrjD996h97phI6NnHZYZHJ7oPRz</CipherValue>
            </CipherData>
        </EncryptedData>
    </connectionStrings>
    <system.web>
        ...
    </system.web>
</configuration>
```

If changes are made to the *connectionStrings* section—for example, if another connection is added using the GUI tools—the new connection will be encrypted, that is, you won't have to run the aspnet_regiis utility again.

You can decrypt the *connectionStrings* section by using the following command.

```
aspnet_regiis -pdf "connectionStrings" "C:\...\EncryptWebSite"
```

After the *connectionStrings* section is decrypted, it will look just as it did before it was encrypted.

Preventing SQL Injection Attacks

A SQL injection attack occurs when an attacker finds a way to insert additional SQL statements into commands that are sent to the database server. The inserted commands can be used to destroy, modify, or retrieve private data. The inserted commands come from user input, so it's important to take steps to ensure that user input is validated and cannot contain inserted commands.

Your code is susceptible to SQL injection attacks if it builds a SQL statement by concatenating strings that come from user input. If the resultant SQL statement is syntactically correct and the caller has the appropriate permissions, SQL Server executes the commands.

Creating the SqlInjectionTest Project

To show how SQL injection works, create a Windows application called SqlInjectionTest. Add the *Northwind* database to the project, and set its *Copy To Output Directory* property to *Copy Always*. This will ensure that we use a clean copy of the database every time the application is run in Visual Studio .NET. Add a *Label* control, a *Button* control, and a *DataGridView* control to the form. Set the label's *Text* property to *Enter Last Name:* and set the button's *Text* property to *Run Query*. Double-click the button, and add the following code.

Visual Basic

```
Imports System.Data
Imports System.Data.SqlClient
Imports System.Configuration

Public Class Form1

   Private Sub Button1_Click(ByVal sender As System.Object, _
         ByVal e As System.EventArgs) Handles Button1.Click
      Dim cnSetting As ConnectionStringSettings = _
         ConfigurationManager.ConnectionStrings("nwString")
      Dim employees As New DataTable()
      Using cn As New SqlConnection()
         cn.ConnectionString = cnSetting.ConnectionString
         Dim cmd As SqlCommand = cn.CreateCommand()
         Dim sql As String = _
            "SELECT * FROM employees WHERE LastName LIKE '" _
            + TextBox1.Text.Trim() + "%'"
         cmd.CommandText = sql
         cn.Open()
         employees.Load(cmd.ExecuteReader())
         DataGridView1.DataSource = employees
      End Using
   End Sub

End Class
```

C#

```
using System;
using System.Data;
using System.Windows.Forms;
using System.Configuration;
using System.Data.SqlClient;

namespace SqlInjectionTest
{
   public partial class Form1 : Form
   {
      public Form1()
      {
```

```
            InitializeComponent();
        }

        private void Button1_Click(object sender, EventArgs e)
        {
            ConnectionStringSettings cnSetting =
                ConfigurationManager.ConnectionStrings["nwString"];
            DataTable employees = new DataTable();
            using (SqlConnection cn = new SqlConnection())
            {
                cn.ConnectionString = cnSetting.ConnectionString;
                SqlCommand cmd = cn.CreateCommand();
                string sql =
                    "SELECT * FROM employees WHERE LastName LIKE '"
                    + TextBox1.Text.Trim() + "%'";
                cmd.CommandText = sql;
                cn.Open();
                employees.Load(cmd.ExecuteReader());
                dataGridView1.DataSource = employees;
            }
        }
    }
}
```

The button click code gets a list of employees based on the characters you type in the text box.

Add the following app.config file to the project, which has a connection string for the *Northwind* database.

App.config File

```
<?xml version="1.0" encoding="utf-8" ?>
<configuration>
   <connectionStrings>
      <add name="nwString" connectionString=
         "Data Source=.\SQLEXPRESS;
         AttachDbFilename=|DataDirectory|\northwnd.mdf;
         Integrated Security=True;User Instance=True"
          providerName="System.Data.SqlClient" />
   </connectionStrings>
</configuration>
```

Run the application, type the letter *S*, and run the query, which yields a single employee. If you clear the text box and run the query again, all employees are returned.

What's wrong with this code? The problem is that it uses user input to build the query. There is no validation that the user has typed an appropriate input string. What happens if the user types the following text and runs the query?

```
%'; UPDATE employees SET lastname = 'you been hacked'; --
```

At first glance, you might not notice anything strange. The query returns the complete list of employees. If you clear the text from the text box and run the query again, you will see the results shown in Figure 13-16. Fortunately, you configured the *Northwind* database to be copied to the output folder on every build, but that overwrites all changes that might have been made, including the changes that you want to keep.

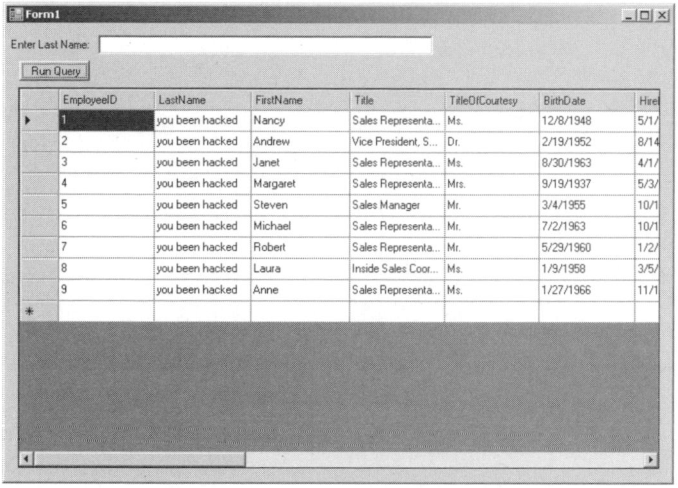

Figure 13-16 The last name was hacked using SQL injection

The user input that caused this problem starts with the %';, which closes the WHERE clause in the query, retrieving all employees, and the semicolon is a statement separator that is optional in SQL Server but might be required in other database servers. Next is the hack, which is an UPDATE statement to change the last name of the Employees table. Note that this could be any SQL statement, as long as the statement has the required permissions to run. So the deletion of table data can also happen if the deletion does not cause foreign key constraint exceptions. The hacker's text ends with comment syntax, --, which comments any existing text that is being added after the user input in the button click method. This is needed by the hacker to ensure that an exception is not thrown.

Protecting Against SQL Injection

You can imagine that this code opens the door for a hacker to do almost anything to your database. The scope of the damage depends on the permissions granted to the calling process. Running under a least-privilege account and validating user input is essential.

You can also pass column values as parameters instead of concatenating values. Add another button to the form, and add the following code to the new button, which uses a parameter with the command.

Visual Basic

```
Private Sub button2_Click(ByVal sender As System.Object, _
      ByVal e As System.EventArgs) Handles button2.Click
   Dim cnSetting As ConnectionStringSettings = _
      ConfigurationManager.ConnectionStrings("nwString")
   Dim employees As New DataTable()
   Using cn As New SqlConnection()
```

```
        cn.ConnectionString = cnSetting.ConnectionString
        Dim cmd As SqlCommand = cn.CreateCommand()
        Dim sql As String = _
           "SELECT * FROM employees WHERE LastName LIKE @name + '%'"
        cmd.CommandText = sql
        cmd.Parameters.AddWithValue("@name", TextBox1.Text.Trim())
        cn.Open()
        employees.Load(cmd.ExecuteReader())
        DataGridView1.DataSource = employees
    End Using
End Sub
```

C#

```
private void button2_Click(object sender, EventArgs e)
{
    ConnectionStringSettings cnSetting =
        ConfigurationManager.ConnectionStrings["nwString"];
    DataTable employees = new DataTable();
    using (SqlConnection cn = new SqlConnection())
    {
        cn.ConnectionString = cnSetting.ConnectionString;
        SqlCommand cmd = cn.CreateCommand();
        string sql =
           "SELECT * FROM employees WHERE LastName LIKE @name + '%'";
        cmd.CommandText = sql;
        cmd.Parameters.AddWithValue("@name", TextBox1.Text.Trim());
        cn.Open();
        employees.Load(cmd.ExecuteReader());
        dataGridView1.DataSource = employees;
    }
}
```

Notice that it was not too difficult to change the query to use a parameter. In fact, this SQL statement might be easier to read in complex queries. In the SQL statement, the parameter is a SQL variable. In the .NET code, the parameter can be quickly initialized by using the *AddWithValue* method.

Try running the same tests again, using the second button. Everything works as expected, and when the would-be attacker tries to inject the same SQL, the resultant data is empty because the complete input was used to find an employee named *"%'; update employees set lastname = 'you been hacked'; --* ". If you rerun the query with an empty text box, you see all employees with their correct last name–the attack failed.

This was a quick and easy fix, but you should also consider limiting the size of the text input passed into the parameter by setting the *Size* property on the parameter. After all, if the *LastName* field is only 20 characters long, you don't need to allow more than 20 characters in the parameter value.

Using Regular Expressions to Protect Against SQL Injection You can also protect against SQL injection attacks by using regular expressions to validate the data before placing the data into a parameter. Regular expressions offer a very powerful means to test for valid sequences of characters. Table 13-4 contains a small list of common regular expressions, and a search for "Regular Expressions" on the Web will yield many more.

Table 13-4 Common Regular Expressions

<table>
<tr><th>Description</th><th>Regular Expression</th><th>Sample</th></tr>
<tr><td>Name—Up to 40 uppercase and lowercase characters, spaces, dashes, and apostrophes that are common to some names</td><td>^[a-zA-Z''-'\s]{1,40}$</td><td>Joe O'Boy</td></tr>
<tr><td>Social Security Number—Consists of 3 numeric characters, a dash, 2 numeric characters, another dash, and 4 numeric characters</td><td>^\d{3}-\d{2}-\d{4}$</td><td>123-45-6789</td></tr>
<tr><td>U.S. Phone Number—Consists of 3 numeric characters that can optionally be enclosed in parentheses, followed by 3 numeric characters, a dash, and 4 numeric characters</td><td>^[01]?[- .]?(\([2-9]\d{2}\)|[2-9]\d{2})[- .]?\d{3}[- .]?\d{4}$</td><td>555 555-5555
-555 555-5555
-(555) 555-5555
555-555-5555</td></tr>
<tr><td>E-mail Address—Allows sets of alphanumeric characters delimited by the dot or dash, followed by the at symbol (@), and then more sets of alphanumeric characters (not starting with a dash), delimited with a dot, where the length of the last set of characters must be between 2 and 9 characters</td><td>^([0-9a-zA-Z]([-.\w]*[0-9a-zA-Z])*@([0-9a-zA-Z][-\w]*[0-9a-zA-Z]\.)+[a-zA-Z]{2,9})$</td><td>Glenn@GJTT.com
Glenn.Johnson@GJTT.com
G-Johnson@Local.GJTT.com</td></tr>
</table>

To test regular expression validation, add another *Button* control to the form and set its *Text* property to *"Run Query with Regular Expression and Parameter"*. Copy the code from the previous *Button* control's event handler to this *Button* control's *Click* event handler, and add regular expression code to validate the user input as follows.

Visual Basic

```
Private Sub Button3_Click(ByVal sender As System.Object, _
      ByVal e As System.EventArgs) Handles Button3.Click
   If (TextBox1.Text.Length > 0) Then
      If Not (System.Text.RegularExpressions.Regex.IsMatch( _
         TextBox1.Text, "^[a-zA-Z'.]{1,40}$")) Then
         MessageBox.Show( _
          "Invalid Query. Must contain only characters (max 40)")
         Return
      End If
   End If
   Dim cnSetting As ConnectionStringSettings = _
      ConfigurationManager.ConnectionStrings("nwString")
   Dim employees As New DataTable()
   Using cn As New SqlConnection()
```

```
        cn.ConnectionString = cnSetting.ConnectionString
        Dim cmd As SqlCommand = cn.CreateCommand()
        Dim sql As String = _
           "Select * from employees where LastName like @name + '%'"
        cmd.CommandText = sql
        cmd.Parameters.AddWithValue("@name", TextBox1.Text.Trim())
        cn.Open()
        employees.Load(cmd.ExecuteReader())
        DataGridView1.DataSource = employees
    End Using
End Sub
```

C#

```
private void Button3_Click(object sender, EventArgs e)
{
   if (TextBox1.Text.Length > 0)
   {
      if (!System.Text.RegularExpressions.Regex.IsMatch(
         TextBox1.Text,"^[a-zA-Z'.]{1,40}$"))
      {
         MessageBox.Show(
          "Invalid Query. Must contain only characters (max 40)");
         return;
      }
   }
   ConnectionStringSettings cnSetting =
      ConfigurationManager.ConnectionStrings["nwString"];
   DataTable employees = new DataTable();
   using (SqlConnection cn = new SqlConnection())
   {
      cn.ConnectionString = cnSetting.ConnectionString;
      SqlCommand cmd = cn.CreateCommand();
      string sql =
         "Select * from employees where LastName like @name + '%'";
      cmd.CommandText = sql;
      cmd.Parameters.AddWithValue("@name", TextBox1.Text.Trim());
      cn.Open();
      employees.Load(cmd.ExecuteReader());
      dataGridView1.DataSource = employees;
   }
}
```

Try running the tests again, using this button. You will find that you will not pass the regular expression validation because the length is more than 40 characters and special characters were used.

Last, if you are working on a Web application, you can easily implement regular expression validation by using the *RegularExpressionValidator* control, which can be attached to a *TextBox* control to perform client- and server-side validation using regular expressions.

Using Stored Procedures

Stored procedures provide an efficient way to execute T-SQL or SQLCLR code on the database server. If your data changes can be made without first moving the data to the client, performance will benefit.

Stored procedures also provide a simple means of assigning permissions. Consider situations in which a single stored procedure is performing inserts, updates, and deletes to multiple tables. You might want the user to have permission to execute this action, but you might not want the user to be able to execute ad hoc statements directly to the same tables. You can assign execute permissions to the stored procedure without assigning permissions at the table level, and the store procedure will execute, as long as the owner of the stored procedure is the same as the owner of the tables.

Although you can eliminate SQL injection attacks without implementing stored procedures, you would not have had any threat of SQL injection if you implemented stored procedures from the start, because parameters are the mechanism for passing user criteria to a stored procedure.

Summary

- The .NET Framework implements a two-layer defense against security vulnerabilities: role-based security and code access security.
  - Role-based security allows you to control a user's access to application resources and operations.
  - Code access security can control the code's access to resources and ability to perform privileged operations.
- *Authentication* is the process of obtaining the user's credentials, such as name and password, that will be identified and validated against an authority.
- *Authorization* is the process of determining, based on credentials, whether a user should be granted a specific type of access to a resource.
- *Impersonation* is the process of allowing code to execute with the identity of the client. Impersonation across computers is called *delegation*.
- *Evidence* is the collection of information about an assembly and its origin that is used to authenticate the assembly with the .NET Framework.
- Code access permissions represent the rights to access specific resources.
- Code groups are used to define the permissions that an assembly should receive, providing authorization of the code.

- Runtime security policy levels are levels of security that can be applied to the Enterprise, Local Computer, User, and Application Domain. Each of these policy levels has its own hierarchy of code groups and permission sets.
- Permission requests should be included in applications that access protected resources. Permission requests should request the minimum permissions that your code must receive to run, and they can ensure that your code receives only the permissions that it actually needs.
- Your code can place demands on the caller either declaratively or imperatively. When you demand that the caller have a specific permission, the complete call stack is walked to verify that those permissions exist.
- *Assert* is a downstream call that you can make on a permission to enable your code and downstream caller's code to execute code that your code has permission to do but that the downstream callers might not have permission to do.
- Strong-named assemblies that are intended to be called by partially trusted code can declare their intent through the use of the *AllowPartiallyTrustedCallersAttribute* (APTCA) attribute.
- SQL Server can be configured to provide authentication using its own security system (SQL Server authentication) and/or integrated Windows authentication.
- In SQL Server, the login is used for authentication, but each database contains its own table of users. The database user is granted permissions to access resources.
- The *AllowPartiallyTrustedCallersAttribute* is fully implemented in the System.Data.dll assembly in ADO.NET 2.0.
- In Web applications, you can easily encrypt the connection strings by using the aspnet_regiis.exe utility to encrypt the *connectionStrings* section of the Web.config file.
- You can eliminate the threat of SQL injection attacks by passing values as parameters instead of concatenating the values to create a SQL statement.
- Stored procedures inherently eliminate SQL injection attacks because the mechanism for passing data to the stored procedure is the parameter.

Chapter 14

Working with Large Objects (LOBs, BLOBs, and CLOBs)

When you work with data, one challenge you might face is moving large objects between the client application and the database server. In some scenarios, you might be able to treat large-object data just like any other data, but in many cases you might be forced to look at alternative approaches.

Chapter 7 and Chapter 8 both contain an example of reading employee photos from the *Northwind* database and displaying a photo in a Windows *DataGridView* or Web *GridView* control. These chapters include sample code for storing the photo to disk, as well as uploading a photo from a disk file to the database. These samples function properly with the small photos in the database, but if the photos were large and you wanted to simply read the photos and write them to a disk file using the least amount of memory, you would be better off using streaming techniques to handle the data in chunks.

Note that if you know the maximum size of your data and it's acceptable to load all of this data into memory, you don't need to use streaming techniques to access the data. This chapter explores the reading and writing of large objects using streaming techniques, as well as examples of retrieving and storing large objects.

What Are LOBs, BLOBs, and CLOBs?

Large objects, or LOBs, come in different flavors. If a large object is to be stored in the database in binary format, it's commonly referred to as a binary large object (BLOB). If a large object is to be stored in the database as textual data, it's commonly referred to as a character large object (CLOB). Table 14-1 shows the data types for each of these large object types.

Table 14-1 Large Object Data Types

Large Object Type	SQL Server Data Type	Maximum Size	.NET Data Type
BLOB	*varbinary(MAX)* *Image*	2,147,483,647	*Byte Array*
CLOB	*varchar(MAX)* *Text*	2,147,483,647	*String*
Unicode CLOB (NCLOB)	*nvarchar(MAX)* *NText*	1,073,741,823	*String*
XML Document	*xml*	2,147,483,647	*String*

SQL Server 2005 has new data types for working with large objects: *varbinary(MAX)*, *varchar(MAX)*, *nvarchar(MAX)*, and *xml*. Note that the *Image*, *Text*, and *NText* data types are used with earlier versions of SQL Server and will be removed in the next release of SQL Server. The *xml* data type is covered in detail in Chapter 15.

Where Should LOBs Be Stored?

Opinions have always differed on where LOBs should be stored. Some people believe they should be stored as files on the file system, while others believe that LOBs belong in the database. From a performance perspective, storing LOBs as files is definitely faster. If the LOBs are images, it might be easier for graphic artists to access them as files when the images need to be edited.

The biggest problem with storing LOBs as files shows up when databases are moved from one machine to another; it's easy for the files to get disconnected from the database. Even in the *Northwind* sample database, the Employees table has a field called *PhotoPath* that contains invalid paths to the employee's photo, and the photo files are nowhere to be found. On the other hand, the Employees table does contain a column called *Photo* that has the employee's photo embedded in it. When the LOBs are embedded in the database, you can be sure that backups contain synchronized copies of the data. In short, storing the LOB in the database helps you keep your data together at all times, which is why I prefer using the database for storing LOBs.

Working with LOBs

In ADO.NET, you can work with LOBs by using a *SqlDataReader* object to return a result set, by using a *SqlDataAdapter* object to fill a *DataTable* object, or by using a large object *SqlParameter*.

When you work with CLOBs, most operations work the same with large objects as they do with their smaller counterparts, as long as the large object can be loaded into memory.

If a large object is so large that you can't load it without running out of memory, you must deal with it by reading and processing a chunk at a time.

Also, when you work with BLOBs, you might not have a lot of experience working with binary data, which can be a problem. Most of our examples in this chapter use BLOBs, so you can get up to speed quickly.

Reading BLOB Data

The normal operation of the *DataReader* object is to read one row at a time. When the row is available, all of the columns are buffered and available for you to access, in any order.

To access the *DataReader* object in a stream fashion, you can change the *DbCommand* object's behavior to a sequential stream when you execute the *ExecuteReader* method. In this mode, you must get the bytes from the stream, in the order of each column that is being returned, and you can't retrieve the data more than once. You essentially have access to the underlying *DataReader* object's stream.

To work with chunks of data, you should understand the operation of a stream object. When you read from a stream, you pass a byte array buffer that the stream populates. The stream does not have an obligation to populate the buffer, however. The stream's only obligation is to populate the buffer with at least 1 byte if the stream is not at its end. If the end has been reached, no bytes are read. When you use slow streams, such as a slow Internet network stream, data might not be available when you attempt to read the stream. In this case, the stream is not at its end but no bytes are available, and the thread will block (wait) until 1 byte has been received. Based on the stream operation described, you should always perform stream reading in a loop that continues until no more bytes are read.

To try reading BLOB data from the database and writing to a file, create a Windows application called LobTest and add a button to the form. Change the button's *Text* property to *Photos To File*. Add the *Northwind* database to the project. Add an App.config file with the following connection string.

App.config

```
<?xml version="1.0" encoding="utf-8" ?>
<configuration>
   <connectionStrings>
      <add name="NwString"
         connectionString="Data Source=.\SQLEXPRESS;
         AttachDbFilename=|DataDirectory|\northwnd.mdf;
         Integrated Security=True;User Instance=True"
         providerName="System.Data.SqlClient" />
   </connectionStrings>
</configuration>
```

Double-click the button, and add the following code that opens a connection to the database, retrieves all of the employee photos, and stores each one to a disk file.

Visual Basic

```
Imports System.Configuration
Imports System.Data
Imports System.Data.SqlClient
Imports System.IO

Public Class Form1

   Private Sub button1_Click(ByVal sender As System.Object, _
      ByVal e As System.EventArgs) Handles button1.Click
         const  employeeIdColumn as integer = 0
         const  employeePhotoColumn as integer= 1
         'bufferSize must be bigger than oleOffset
         const  bufferSize as integer = 100
         Dim buffer(bufferSize) as  byte
         Dim  byteCountRead as integer
```

```
        Dim  currentIndex as long = 0

        Dim nwSetting as ConnectionStringSettings  = _
           ConfigurationManager.ConnectionStrings("NwString")
        using cn as  new SqlConnection()
           cn.ConnectionString = nwSetting.ConnectionString
           cn.Open()

           using cmd as SqlCommand = cn.CreateCommand()
              cmd.CommandText = _
                 "SELECT EmployeeID, Photo FROM Employees"
              Dim rdr as SqlDataReader = cmd.ExecuteReader( _
                 CommandBehavior.SequentialAccess)
              while (rdr.Read())

                 dim employeeId as integer = _
                     rdr.GetInt32(employeeIdColumn)
                 dim fileName as string = "c:\Employee" _
                    + employeeId.ToString().PadLeft(2, "0"c) _
                    + ".bin"

                 ' Create a file to hold the output.
                 using fs as new FileStream( _
                    fileName, FileMode.OpenOrCreate, _
                    FileAccess.Write)
                    currentIndex = 0
                    byteCountRead = _
                       cint(rdr.GetBytes(employeePhotoColumn, _
                       currentIndex, buffer, 0, bufferSize))
                    while (byteCountRead <> 0)
                       fs.Write(buffer, 0, byteCountRead)
                       currentIndex += byteCountRead
                       byteCountRead = _
                        cint(rdr.GetBytes(employeePhotoColumn, _
                        currentIndex, buffer, 0, bufferSize))
                    end while
                 end using
              end while
           end using
        end using
        MessageBox.Show("Done")
    End Sub
End Class
```

C#

```
using System;
using System.Data;
using System.Text;
using System.Windows.Forms;
using System.Configuration;
using System.Data.SqlClient;
using System.IO;

namespace LobTest
{
```

```
public partial class Form1 : Form
{
   public Form1()
   {
      InitializeComponent();
   }

   private void button1_Click(object sender, EventArgs e)
   {
      const int employeeIdColumn = 0;
      const int employeePhotoColumn = 1;
      //bufferSize must be bigger than oleOffset
      const int bufferSize = 100;
      byte[] buffer = new byte[bufferSize];
      int byteCountRead;
      long currentIndex = 0;

      ConnectionStringSettings nwSetting =
         ConfigurationManager.ConnectionStrings["NwString"];
      using (SqlConnection cn = new SqlConnection())
      {
         cn.ConnectionString = nwSetting.ConnectionString;
         cn.Open();

         using (SqlCommand cmd = cn.CreateCommand())
         {
            cmd.CommandText =
               "SELECT EmployeeID, Photo FROM Employees";
            SqlDataReader rdr = cmd.ExecuteReader(
               CommandBehavior.SequentialAccess);
            while (rdr.Read())
            {
               int employeeId =
                  rdr.GetInt32(employeeIdColumn);
               string fileName = @"c:\Employee"
                  + employeeId.ToString().PadLeft(2, '0')
                  + ".bin";

               // Create a file to hold the output.
               using (FileStream fs = new FileStream(
                  fileName, FileMode.OpenOrCreate,
                  FileAccess.Write))
               {
                  currentIndex = 0;
                  byteCountRead =
                    (int)rdr.GetBytes(employeePhotoColumn,
                    currentIndex, buffer, 0, bufferSize);
                  while (byteCountRead != 0)
                  {
                     fs.Write(buffer, 0, byteCountRead);
                     currentIndex += byteCountRead;
                     byteCountRead =
                       (int)rdr.GetBytes(employeePhotoColumn,
                       currentIndex, buffer, 0, bufferSize);
                  }
```

```
                    }
                }
            }
        }
        MessageBox.Show("Done");
    }
  }
}
```

This code gives you the pattern for reading the BLOB and writing it to a file. The *ExecuteReader* method is executed with the *CommandBehavior.SequentialAccess* parameter. Next, a loop runs to read row data, and within the loop and for each row, the employee's ID is read to create the filename. A new *FileStream* object is created, which opens the file for writing.

Next, a loop reads bytes into a byte array buffer and then writes the bytes to the file. The buffer size is set to 100 bytes, which keeps the amount of data in memory to a minimum.

Notice that the filename has a .bin extension. In Chapter 7 and Chapter 8, I explained that the employee photos were stored in the database with an OLE header. To retrieve the photos and strip off the OLE header, add a second button and add the following code, which reads the header and tests it to verify that the OLE header exists.

Visual Basic

```
Private Sub button2_Click(ByVal sender As System.Object, _
      ByVal e As System.EventArgs) Handles button2.Click

   Const oleOffset As Integer = 78
   Const oleTypeStart As Integer = 20
   Const oleTypeLength As Integer = 12
   Const employeeIdColumn As Integer = 0
   Const employeePhotoColumn As Integer = 1
   Const bufferSize As Integer = 100 'must be bigger than oleOffset
   Dim buffer(bufferSize) As Byte
   Dim bufferStart As Integer = 0
   Dim byteCountRead As Integer
   Dim currentIndex As Long = 0

   Dim nwSetting As ConnectionStringSettings = _
      ConfigurationManager.ConnectionStrings("NwString")
   Using cn As New SqlConnection()
      cn.ConnectionString = nwSetting.ConnectionString
      cn.Open()

      Using cmd As SqlCommand = cn.CreateCommand()
         cmd.CommandText = _
            "SELECT EmployeeID, Photo FROM Employees"
         Dim rdr As SqlDataReader = cmd.ExecuteReader( _
            CommandBehavior.SequentialAccess)
         While (rdr.Read())

            Dim employeeId As Integer = _
               rdr.GetInt32(employeeIdColumn)
            Dim fileName As String = "c:\Employee" + _
```

```
               employeeId.ToString().PadLeft(2, "0"c) + ".bmp"

            ' Create a file to hold the output.
            Using fs As New FileStream( _
               fileName, FileMode.OpenOrCreate, FileAccess.Write)

               currentIndex = 0
               'read until we have the oleheader, if possible
               While (currentIndex < oleOffset)
                  byteCountRead = _
                     CInt(rdr.GetBytes(employeePhotoColumn, _
                     currentIndex, buffer, CInt(currentIndex), _
                     bufferSize - CInt(currentIndex)))
                  If (byteCountRead = 0) Then Exit While
                  currentIndex += byteCountRead
               End While
               byteCountRead = CInt(currentIndex)

               'process oleheader, if it exists
               If (byteCountRead >= oleOffset) Then
                  Dim type As String = Encoding.ASCII.GetString( _
                     buffer, oleTypeStart, oleTypeLength)
                  If (type = "Bitmap Image") Then
                     bufferStart = oleOffset
                     byteCountRead = byteCountRead - oleOffset
                  End If
               End If

               While (byteCountRead <> 0)
                  fs.Write(buffer, bufferStart, byteCountRead)
                  bufferStart = 0
                  byteCountRead = _
                     CInt(rdr.GetBytes(employeePhotoColumn, _
                     currentIndex, buffer, 0, bufferSize))
                  currentIndex += byteCountRead
               End While
            End Using
         End While
      End Using
   End Using
   MessageBox.Show("Done")
End Sub
```

C#

```
private void button2_Click(object sender, EventArgs e)
{
   const int oleOffset = 78;
   const int oleTypeStart = 20;
   const int oleTypeLength = 12;
   const int employeeIdColumn = 0;
   const int employeePhotoColumn = 1;
   const int bufferSize = 100; //must be bigger than oleOffset
   byte[] buffer = new byte[bufferSize];
   int bufferStart = 0;
   int byteCountRead;
```

```
long currentIndex = 0;

ConnectionStringSettings nwSetting =
   ConfigurationManager.ConnectionStrings["NwString"];
using (SqlConnection cn = new SqlConnection())
{
   cn.ConnectionString = nwSetting.ConnectionString;
   cn.Open();

   using (SqlCommand cmd = cn.CreateCommand())
   {
      cmd.CommandText =
         "SELECT EmployeeID, Photo FROM Employees";
      SqlDataReader rdr = cmd.ExecuteReader(
         CommandBehavior.SequentialAccess);
      while (rdr.Read())
      {
         int employeeId = rdr.GetInt32(employeeIdColumn);
         string fileName = @"c:\Employee" +
            employeeId.ToString().PadLeft(2, '0') + ".bmp";

         // Create a file to hold the output.
         using (FileStream fs = new FileStream(
            fileName, FileMode.OpenOrCreate,
            FileAccess.Write))
         {
            currentIndex = 0;
            //read until we have the oleheader, if possible
            while (currentIndex < oleOffset)
            {
               byteCountRead =
                  (int)rdr.GetBytes(employeePhotoColumn,
                  currentIndex, buffer, (int)currentIndex,
                  bufferSize - (int)currentIndex);
               if (byteCountRead == 0) break;
               currentIndex += byteCountRead;
            }
            byteCountRead = (int)currentIndex;

            //process oleheader, if it exists
            if (byteCountRead >= oleOffset)
            {
               string type = Encoding.ASCII.GetString(
                  buffer, oleTypeStart, oleTypeLength);
               if (type == "Bitmap Image")
               {
                  bufferStart = oleOffset;
                  byteCountRead = byteCountRead - oleOffset;
               }
            }

            while (byteCountRead != 0)
            {
               fs.Write(buffer, bufferStart, byteCountRead);
               bufferStart = 0;
```

```
                    byteCountRead =
                        (int)rdr.GetBytes(employeePhotoColumn,
                        currentIndex, buffer, 0, bufferSize);
                    currentIndex += byteCountRead;
                }
            }
        }
    }
  }
  MessageBox.Show("Done");
}
```

This code still takes into account that when the stream is read, it might not fill the buffer. This means a loop is created to read enough bytes to get the complete OLE header, if one exists. This code also has checks to verify that the photo is at least as large as the OLE header, in case a very small photo is loaded into the database. After the code tests for the OLE header, the main read/write loop starts, but the first time through, the writing might start after the OLE header, if it exists.

Writing BLOB Data

You can write BLOB data to a database by issuing the appropriate INSERT or UPDATE statement and passing the BLOB value as an input parameter. Because the BLOB is stored in binary format, you can pass an array of type *byte* as a binary parameter.

BLOBs that are quite large will consume too many system resources; your application performance will suffer and possibly throw out-of-memory exceptions.

You can use the SQL Server *UPDATETEXT* function to write the BLOB data in chunks of a specified size. The *UPDATETEXT* function requires a pointer to the BLOB field being updated, so the SQL Server *TEXTPTR* function is first called to get a pointer to the field of the record to be updated.

The following code example updates the Employees table, replacing a photo with a new one from a file.

Visual Basic

```
Private Sub button3_Click(ByVal sender As System.Object, _
        ByVal e As System.EventArgs) Handles button3.Click
    Const bufferSize As Integer = 100
    Dim buffer(bufferSize) As Byte
    Dim currentIndex As Long = 0
    Dim photoPtr() As Byte

    Dim nwSetting As ConnectionStringSettings = _
        ConfigurationManager.ConnectionStrings("NwString")
    Using cn As New SqlConnection()
        cn.ConnectionString = nwSetting.ConnectionString
        cn.Open()
```

```
      Using cmd As SqlCommand = cn.CreateCommand()
         cmd.CommandText = _
            "SELECT TEXTPTR(Photo) FROM Employees WHERE EmployeeID = 1"
         photoPtr = CType(cmd.ExecuteScalar(), Byte())
      End Using
      Using cmd As SqlCommand = cn.CreateCommand()
         cmd.CommandText = _
            "UPDATETEXT Employees.Photo @Pointer @Offset null @Data"
         Dim ptrParm As SqlParameter = _
            cmd.Parameters.Add("@Pointer", SqlDbType.Binary, 16)
         ptrParm.Value = photoPtr
         Dim photoParm As SqlParameter = _
            cmd.Parameters.Add("@Data", SqlDbType.Image)
         Dim offsetParm As SqlParameter =  _
            cmd.Parameters.Add("@Offset", SqlDbType.Int)
         offsetParm.Value = 0
         Using fs As New FileStream("Girl.gif", _
               FileMode.Open, FileAccess.Read)
            Dim count As Integer = fs.Read(buffer, 0, bufferSize)
            While (count <> 0)
               photoParm.Value = buffer
               photoParm.Size = count
               cmd.ExecuteNonQuery()
               currentIndex += count
               offsetParm.Value = currentIndex
               count = fs.Read(buffer, 0, bufferSize)
            End While
         End Using
      End Using
   End Using
   MessageBox.Show("Done")
End Sub
```

C#

```
private void button3_Click(object sender, EventArgs e)
{
   const int bufferSize = 100;
   byte[] buffer = new byte[bufferSize];
   long currentIndex = 0;
   byte[] photoPtr;

   ConnectionStringSettings nwSetting =
      ConfigurationManager.ConnectionStrings["NwString"];
   using (SqlConnection cn = new SqlConnection())
   {
      cn.ConnectionString = nwSetting.ConnectionString;
      cn.Open();
      using (SqlCommand cmd = cn.CreateCommand())
      {
         cmd.CommandText =
            "SELECT TEXTPTR(Photo) FROM Employees WHERE EmployeeID = 1";
```

```
            photoPtr = (byte[])cmd.ExecuteScalar();
         }
         using (SqlCommand cmd = cn.CreateCommand())
         {
            cmd.CommandText =
               "UPDATETEXT Employees.Photo @Pointer @Offset null @Data";
            SqlParameter ptrParm =
               cmd.Parameters.Add("@Pointer", SqlDbType.Binary, 16);
            ptrParm.Value = photoPtr;
            SqlParameter photoParm =
               cmd.Parameters.Add("@Data", SqlDbType.Image);
            SqlParameter offsetParm =
               cmd.Parameters.Add("@Offset", SqlDbType.Int);
            offsetParm.Value = 0;
            using (FileStream fs = new FileStream("Girl.gif",
               FileMode.Open, FileAccess.Read))
            {
               int count = fs.Read(buffer, 0, bufferSize);
               while (count != 0)
               {
                  photoParm.Value = buffer;
                  photoParm.Size = count;
                  cmd.ExecuteNonQuery();
                  currentIndex += count;
                  offsetParm.Value = currentIndex;
                  count = fs.Read(buffer, 0, bufferSize);
               }
            }
         }
      }
      MessageBox.Show("Done");
   }
```

This code opens a connection and retrieves a pointer to the photo that is to be updated by calling the *TEXTPTR* function using a *SqlCommand* object. Then a new *SqlCommand* object is created, and its *CommandText* property is set to the following.

```
"UPDATETEXT Employees.Photo @Pointer @Offset null @Data "
```

Note that the *null* parameter defines the quantity of bytes to delete. Passing *null* indicates that all existing data should be deleted. Passing a 0 (zero) indicates that no data should be deleted; the new data simply overwrites the exist data. (You pass a number if you want to delete some of the data.) The other parameters represent the pointer to the start of the photo, the current offset to insert data, and the data being sent to the database.

After the file is opened, a loop starts that reads chunks of the file into the buffer and then sends the chunk to the database.

Summary

- Large objects are known as LOBs. CLOBs are character large objects, and BLOBs are binary large objects.
- You can work with LOBs using the same techniques you use for smaller data types, unless the objects are too large to fit into memory. When a LOB is too large to fit into memory, you must use streaming techniques to move the data.
- Streaming involves "chunking" data, which means moving data in chunks to keep from using too much memory.

Chapter 15

Working with XML Data

Companies began trying to communicate in an automated fashion some time ago, but they always encountered issues related to the type of data being exchanged. There are many variations of structured file formats for exchanging data, including fixed-width files and delimited files. Fixed-width files and delimited files cannot easily reflect a relational or hierarchical structure, however, and the alternative of structured data files typically resulted in monolithic implementations that were not reusable. It became obvious that a structured file format was needed for communicating data—a format that everyone could use, that would support relational and other types of structured data, and that would include features such as validation support, extensibility, and the ability to pass through firewalls.

The World Wide Web Consortium (W3C) was created in October 1994 to help further the Web's potential by developing common protocols to ensure interoperability. In February 1998, the W3C published the XML 1.0 Recommendation. XML, or Extensible Markup Language, provides a foundation for text-based data communication that supports the features that many companies were looking for.

XML and its supporting technologies are growing rapidly. Most large companies have embraced it, and the W3C envisions the future Web as being completely based on XML technologies. As a developer, you can't escape XML—even application configuration files are XML based.

This chapter looks at XML as it relates to Microsoft ADO.NET. We start by briefly introducing XPath and XQuery technologies. After that, we examine the implementation of XML in Microsoft SQL Server 2005, and then we explore the use of XML with ADO.NET.

Introducing XPath and XQuery

Before jumping into SQL Server and ADO.NET features, it's important to briefly introduce two XML technologies that are used throughout this chapter: XPath and XQuery.

XPath, which is also known as XML Path Language, is an XML technology that was created to provide a common syntax and semantics to address parts of an XML document. XPath has been a W3C (*http://www.w3c.org*) recommendation since November 1999.

XPath uses a path notation for navigating through the hierarchical structure of an XML document; the notation is similar to the way you navigate the folder hierarchy on your disk drive when you are locating a file. Just as you can locate a file by specifying a relative or explicit path, you can locate parts of an XML document by supplying a relative or explicit path. Even the asterisk (*) is useable as the "all" wildcard when locating parts of an XML document.

XQuery, which is also known as XML Query, provides flexible query facilities to extract data from real and virtual XML documents. XQuery 1.0 is an extension of XPath 2.0, which means that any pattern-matching expression that you use in XPath to locate parts of an XML document can also be used in XQuery. XQuery also provides variables, functions, and operators that can be used with the XML data, plus XML serialization and a Data Model. The Data Model precisely defines the information that can be contained in the input to the XQuery processor. In addition, the Data Model also defines all permissible values of expressions in the XQuery language.

Why Store XML Data in SQL Server 2005?

One key feature added to SQL Server 2005 is the support for native XML data. SQL Server 2005 is an integrated platform for both XML and relational data, providing core database services such as concurrency, recovery, query and update language, and an execution engine and optimizer.

Here are some of the benefits of storing XML data in SQL Server 2005.

- You can run queries directly against the XML data. In versions before SQL Server 2005, XML data is stored as CLOBs, which have limited search capabilities.
- You can index the XML data and show query plans in the Showplan output.
- Many applications have stored XML data as files on a server, separate from the relational data. Keeping the XML and relational data in sync could be a problem, especially when dealing with failover issues and backup and restore issues. Storing XML directly in SQL Server 2005 eliminates this problem.
- The elements in an XML document are inherently part of the XML document, and their order is preserved in query results. Relational data is unordered, which means you must add order columns to enforce ordering. For example, for an estimating system, the items on each estimate must be stored with a line number column to keep them in the order in which they were entered by the estimator. Another example is an XML document containing paragraphs of text, such as a manuscript. In a relational database, a position column would be required to maintain order, but that's not necessary if you store the data as XML in SQL Server.
- With relational data, a highly normalized design often means a high quantity of tables to join to retrieve the data. These joins hurt performance.
- XML data can more easily represent recursive data and graphs.
- From a transactional perspective, XML data that is stored in SQL Server 2005 is durable, consistent, and recoverable.

In most cases, structured data should be stored in relational tables with columns, whereas the *xml* data type is suited for semi-structured and markup data.

The *xml* Data Type

SQL Server 2005 defines a new data type called *xml*. This data type can be the data type for a column when you create a table. It can also be the data type for a parameter that is passed to a stored procedure or a function. It works in much the same way as the other built-in data types in SQL Server. An *XML instance* is the value assigned to a variable, parameter, or column value that has an *xml* data type.

When XML data comes into SQL Server, SQL Server parses it to ensure that it is XML data, based on the SQL ANSI 2003 standard of an XML data type. This means the XML can be an XML document or a fragment containing more than one top-level element, and it can even have top-level text.

After parsing, the data is placed into the *xml* data type, which provides a logical view of the XML data that has been parsed into binary XML representation of the XQuery data model. The binary XML is used by SQL Server to provide efficient processing of queries.

Using the Schema Collection to Implement "Typed" *xml* Columns

You can also place a set of XML schemas into the SQL Server Schema Collection. The Schema Collection is a metadata object that is used to manage schema validation information, which can be associated with an *xml* data type to provide automatic validation of the type. An *xml* column that has no schema assigned is called an "untyped" *xml* column; an *xml* column that has a schema assigned is called a "typed" *xml* column, as shown in Figure 15-1.

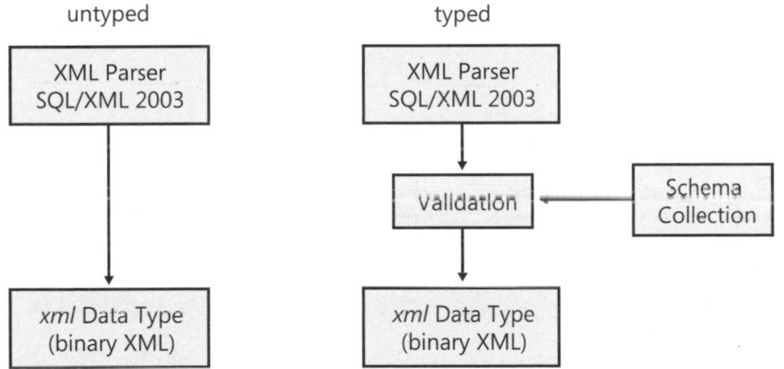

Figure 15-1 Untyped vs. typed XML data storage to the *xml* data type

The Schema Collection contains XML schemas that might be related using *<xs:import>* or might be unrelated. Each typed XML instance specifies the target namespace from the Schema Collection it conforms to. The database engine validates the instance according to its schema during data assignment and modification. To provide efficient processing of typed XML data, the schema information is also used in storage and query optimizations.

Retrieving and Modifying XML Data

You can easily query for the complete XML data instance in the *xml* column, but the *xml* data type has five methods that are used to retrieve and modify XML data:

- *query* Extracts parts of an XML instance. An XQuery expression is provided that evaluates to a list of XML nodes. The complete subtree root of these nodes is returned in document order. The result type is untyped *xml*.
- *value* Extracts a scalar value from an XML instance. An XQuery expression is provided that evaluates to a node value. This value is cast to the T-SQL type specified as the second argument of the *value* method.
- *exist* Provides an existential check on an XML instance. An XQuery expression is provided that returns 1 if the expression evaluates to a non-null node list; otherwise, it returns 0.
- *nodes* Yields instances of a special *xml* data type, each with its context set to a different node than the XQuery expression evaluates to. The special *xml* data type supports *query*, *value*, *nodes*, and *exist* methods and can be used in *count*(*) aggregations and *NULL* checks. All other uses result in an error.
- *modify* Permits modifying parts of an XML instance, such as adding or deleting subtrees or replacing scalar values (such as replacing the inventory count of a widget from 5 to 4).

Indexing the *xml* Column

Executing a query processes each XML instance at runtime—which can be expensive if the XML instance values are large or the query needs to be evaluated on many rows in a table. In these situations, you can increase performance by implementing an index.

You can create a primary XML index on an *xml* column, which creates an index on all tags, values, and paths of the XML instances in the *xml* column. The primary XML index provides efficient evaluation of queries on XML data, and it can efficiently reassemble an XML result from the index while preserving document order and document structure.

The following secondary XML indexes, shown also in Figure 15-2, can also be created on an *xml* column to improve performance on different types of queries.

- *PATH* Used for path-based queries.
- *PROPERTY* Used for *property bag* scenarios. A property bag is a container that can store any value and that is usually implemented as a dictionary, where a name, or key, is used to retrieve or set a value. This is how you locate XML parts when you work with untyped XML documents.
- *VALUE* Used for value-based queries.

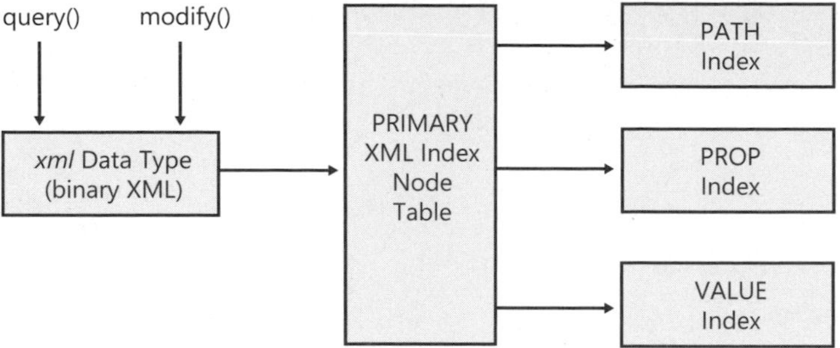

Figure 15-2 The primary index must be created before the secondary indexes are created, and these indexes can increase performance when you work with large XML instances.

Getting Started with the *xml* Data Type

The following examples show how to access the data in an *xml* data type. This is not intended to be an all-inclusive tutorial on XQuery and XPath; however, the examples should give you an understanding of how to write basic queries for data.

The simplest example is a variable that is an *xml* data type and has an XML instance value assigned to it. The following SQL snippet creates a variable and populates it with XML data. Note that this populated variable is used for the samples that follow. You can open a new query window in SQL Server Management Studio and put this SQL script before any of the examples that require the *@myXPath* variable.

SQL: Populating the *@myXPath* Variable

```
DECLARE @myXPath xml
SET @myXPath =
'<vehicles>
   <car vin="123" make="Ford" model="Mustang">
      <repair>
        <id>3</id>
        <description>Replace Supercharger.</description>
        <cost>4000.34</cost>
      </repair>
      <repair>
        <id>45</id>
        <description>Front end alignment.</description>
        <cost>45.67</cost>
      </repair>
   </car>
   <car vin="234" make="Mazda" model="Miata">
      <repair>
        <id>7</id>
        <description>Repair top.</description>
        <cost>123.45</cost>
      </repair>
      <repair>
        <id>22</id>
        <description>Oil Change.</description>
```

```
            <cost>29.99</cost>
         </repair>
      </car>
      <truck vin="567" make="Nissan" model="Pathfinder">
         <repair>
            <id>2</id>
            <description>Replace air filter.</description>
            <cost>34.95</cost>
         </repair>
         <repair>
            <id>6</id>
            <description>Oil Change.</description>
            <cost>39.99</cost>
         </repair>
      </truck>
   </vehicles>'
```

Using the *query* Method with XPath

XQuery includes XPath 2.0 as a navigation language. XPath gets its name from its *path* expression, which provides a means of efficiently searching and hierarchically addressing the nodes in an XML tree.

For example, you can search for all occurrences of the *car* element in the XML tree by using *//car* in your query. The *//* means *descendent or self*, and when the query expression starts with the double slashes, it means the document's *descendent or self*. So *//car* means find any *descendent or self* in the XML document that is a car. XQuery also supports abbreviated syntax for specifying the axis. Table 15-1 lists the axes with their corresponding abbreviated syntax.

Table 15-1 Axes Supported by XQuery

Axis	Abbreviated Form
Attribute	@
Child	NA
descendant-or-self::node()	//
parent::node()	..
self::node()	.

You can also include filter expressions by using the *[expression]* syntax, as shown in the next example. Note that any node referenced in the filter expression is relative to the current node being evaluated. When you need to access an XML attribute, the attribute name must have the @ prefix.

Now that the variable is populated, you can query it as shown in the following SQL snippet.

SQL

```
SELECT @myXPath.query('//car[@vin="234"]')
```

When you execute this script, you get the following results.

```
<car vin="234" make="Mazda" model="Miata">
  <repair>
    <id>7</id>
    <description>Repair top.</description>
    <cost>123.45</cost>
  </repair>
  <repair>
    <id>22</id>
    <description>Oil Change.</description>
    <cost>29.99</cost>
  </repair>
</car>
```

The SELECT statement returns the XML node using an XPath query expression that locates car elements at any level in the document with a *vin* attribute of *234*.

One problem with this query is that the data includes cars and trucks, and you might want to locate any vehicle that has a specific *vin* attribute. Instead of using the word *car*, you can specify *self*, which is represented as a period. Here is the query for a *vin* of *567* that will return a truck.

SQL

```
SELECT @myXPath.query('//.[@vin="567"]')
```

This query now looks for any descendent of the XML document that has a *vin* of *567*. The result is as follows.

```
<truck vin="567" make="Nissan" model="Pathfinder">
  <repair>
    <id>2</id>
    <description>Replace air filter.</description>
    <cost>34.95</cost>
  </repair>
  <repair>
    <id>6</id>
    <description>Oil Change.</description>
    <cost>39.99</cost>
  </repair>
</truck>
```

You can change the filter expression to search for the *vin* of a car, and the query will then return a car as well.

Using a SQL Variable in the Filter Expression

You might want to use a SQL variable to retrieve a car or truck instead of using a constant. This approach is helpful if you are working with parameters in a stored procedure. It is shown in the following script.

SQL

```
DECLARE @findvar nvarchar(20)
SET @findvar = '567'
SELECT @myXPath.query('//.[@vin=sql:variable("@findvar")]')
```

When you execute the script, the same results are returned as in the previous example, but here you can use a SQL variable to filter the output of the query.

The SELECT statement returns an *xml* data type. If you want to retrieve the make of the car as a string, you can use the *value* method, as shown in the following SQL snippet.

SQL

```
DECLARE @findvar nvarchar(20)
SET @findvar = '567'
SELECT @myXPath.query(
   '//.[@vin=sql:variable("@findvar")]')
   .value('(//@make)[1]','nvarchar(max)')
```

When the SQL script is run, it displays *Nissan* as an *nvarchar(max)*. Notice that the *value* method requires your query expression to return only a single item, so we added parentheses around the query and a *[1]* to specify that only the first result be used, even if you know that only one item will be returned from the *//@make* query expression.

You can perform a search based on the text in a node by using the *text* method. This method returns the text in the node. If the node has child nodes, their text is included, but the child element tags are not. The following code returns the car or truck whose repair *id* is equal to 7.

SQL

```
SELECT @myXPath.query('//.[repair/id/text()="7"]')
```

The following is returned from the query. Notice that the query returns the complete car with all of its repairs.

```
<car vin="234" make="Mazda" model="Miata">
  <repair>
    <id>7</id>
    <description>Repair top.</description>
    <cost>123.45</cost>
  </repair>
  <repair>
    <id>22</id>
    <description>Oil Change.</description>
    <cost>29.99</cost>
  </repair>
</car>
```

Notice that one of the repairs has an *id* of 7. If you want to retrieve only the repair whose *id* is 7, you can tweak the query as follows.

SQL

```
SELECT @myXPath.query('//repair[id/text()="7"]')
```

This query locates all repairs in the document with a matching *id*. The following is the result.

```
<repair>
  <id>7</id>
  <description>Repair top.</description>
  <cost>123.45</cost>
</repair>
```

You can use information from the parent node in your filter expression by using .. to specify *parent*. For example, if you want to retrieve the description of the repair whose *id* is *7*, you can use the following script.

```
SELECT @myXPath.query('//repair/description[../id/text()="7"]')
```

This script locates all descriptions, where the *parent* element has an *id* element and the *id* is *7*. The result is as follows.

```
<description>Repair top.</description>
```

Although we haven't covered every variation, these examples should give you enough information to get going with XPath queries.

Performing General Comparisons

XPath provides general comparison operators to compare atomic values, sequences, or a combination of the two. The general comparison operators are =, !=, <, >, <=, and >=. These comparisons return *true* on any match.

The following example returns all the repair elements whose *id* node is *40* or greater.

SQL

```
SELECT @myXPath.query('//repair[id>=40]')
```

The results are as follows.

```
<repair>
  <id>45</id>
  <description>Front end alignment.</description>
  <cost>45.67</cost>
</repair>
```

Be careful not to use quotation marks when you work with numeric types; the following script yields an entirely different result.

SQL

```
SELECT @myXPath.query('//repair[id>="40"]')
```

Notice the results.

```
<repair>
  <id>45</id>
  <description>Front end alignment.</description>
  <cost>45.67</cost>
</repair>
<repair>
  <id>7</id>
  <description>Repair top.</description>
  <cost>123.45</cost>
</repair>
<repair>
  <id>6</id>
  <description>Oil Change.</description>
  <cost>39.99</cost>
</repair>
```

What happened here? This query performed a string comparison instead of a numeric comparison, which resulted in additional matches because 7 and 6 are greater than 4, which is the first character in 40.

Using Value Comparison Operators

You can also use value comparison operators to compare atomic values. The value comparison operators supported by SQL Server 2005 are *eq*, *ne*, *lt*, *gt*, *le*, and *ge*. You use the value comparison operators when you want to strictly type an atomic value for the comparison operation. This ensures that the correct type is used for the comparison.

The following snippet uses a value comparison operator to return repair elements whose cost is greater than or equal to 45.

SQL

```
SELECT @myXPath.query('//repair[ xs:decimal(cost[1]) ge 45]')
```

Notice that the explicit cast to *xs:decimal* is required when you use the value comparison operator, and the cost must be a single atomic value, so *[1]* is used to get the first cost result.

The output looks like the following.

```
<repair>
  <id>3</id>
  <description>Replace Supercharger.</description>
  <cost>4000.34</cost>
</repair>
<repair>
  <id>45</id>
  <description>Front end alignment.</description>
  <cost>45.67</cost>
</repair>
<repair>
  <id>7</id>
  <description>Repair top.</description>
  <cost>123.45</cost>
</repair>
```

Using Node Comparison Operators

You use the node comparison operator to determine whether two nodes are actually the same node. The following example performs a node test on two cars to see if they are the same node.

SQL

```
SELECT @myXPath.query('
if( (/vehicles/*[@vin="123"])[1] is (/vehicles/*[@make="Ford"])[1])
then
<result>These nodes are actually the same node.</result>
else
<result>These nodes are different nodes.</result>
')
```

In this example, two XPath queries first get all child nodes under the vehicle node, using the asterisk. The first expression filters the children by finding a matching *vin* attribute, while the second expression filters the child nodes by finding a matching *make* attribute. You want to test to see if the node returned from each query is actually the same node. The result is as follows:

```
<result>These nodes are actually the same node.</result>
```

Using Node Order Comparisons

You can use the node comparison operators to compare two nodes in the XML data to find out which node is first. The >> operator means "is after," and the << operator means "is before." Each operator takes two operands. The following example shows how to use the >> operator to find out if the repair whose *id* is *7* is after the repair whose *id* is 2.

SQL

```
SELECT @myXPath.query('
if( (/vehicles/*/repair[./id="7"])[1] >> (/vehicles/*/repair[./id="2"])[1])
then
   <result>repair 7 is after repair 2</result>
else
   <result>repair 2 is after repair 7</result>
')
```

Notice that both parameters execute an XPath query to get a node set and that the first result is selected. The result of the comparison is as follows:

```
<result>repair 2 is after repair 7</result>
```

Using Logical Operators

You can use the *and* and *or* logical operators in your queries to combine logical expressions. The following example returns any car or truck whose *vin* is *567* or *234*.

SQL

```
SELECT @myXPath.query('
/vehicles/*[@vin="567" or @vin="234"]
')
```

The output is as follows.

```
<car vin="234" make="Mazda" model="Miata">
  <repair>
    <id>7</id>
    <description>Repair top.</description>
    <cost>123.45</cost>
  </repair>
  <repair>
    <id>22</id>
    <description>Oil Change.</description>
    <cost>29.99</cost>
  </repair>
</car>
<truck vin="567" make="Nissan" model="Pathfinder">
  <repair>
    <id>2</id>
    <description>Replace air filter.</description>
    <cost>34.95</cost>
  </repair>
  <repair>
    <id>6</id>
    <description>Oil Change.</description>
    <cost>39.99</cost>
  </repair>
</truck>
```

Notice that both vehicles were found and a car and a truck are returned because of the use of the asterisk (*) to select any child of vehicles.

Using the *query* Method with XQuery

XQuery is a superset of XPath 2.0 and extends the navigational and filtering aspects of XPath 2.0 by providing the FLWOR expression syntax. FLWOR stands for for-let-where-order-return and is pronounced *flower*. These clauses are defined as follows.

- *for* Generates an ordered list of bindings that is assigned to a variable.
- *let* Associates a single variable with the results of an expression. **Note that this clause is not supported in SQL Server 2005.**
- *where* Filters the list to retain only the results.
- *order* Sorts the query results on given criteria.
- *return* For each query result, construct and return a resulting value.

Learning the XQuery FLWOR syntax is relatively easy if you already know T-SQL and XPath. All of the XPath information covered in this chapter also applies when you use XQuery.

When you work with typed *xml* values, XQuery works as a strongly typed language. Strong typing improves query performance by providing type assurances that you can use when you perform query optimization. When you work with untyped *xml* values, XQuery works as a weak typed language for untyped data.

You use the *return* clause to construct the resulting value, which means you can use XQuery to provide a transformation of the XML data. Queries written in XQuery usually require less code compared with queries written in XSLT (Extensible Stylesheet Language Transformations), which is another XML technology for transforming data. Transforming data is also known as repurposing data.

The following SQL snippet populates a variable called *@myXQuery* with data that will be used in the upcoming XQuery examples. You can open a new query window in SQL Server Management Studio and put this SQL script before any of the examples that require the *@myXQuery* variable.

SQL: Populating the *@myXQuery* Variable

```
DECLARE @myXQuery xml
SET @myXQuery = '
<owners>
   <owner name="Joe">
      <vehicle vin="567"/>
      <vehicle vin="234"/>
   </owner>
   <owner name="Mary">
      <vehicle vin="123"/>
   </owner>
```

```
</owners>
<vehicles>
   <car vin="123" make="Ford" model="Mustang">
      <repair>
        <id>3</id>
        <description>Replace Supercharger.</description>
        <cost>4000.34</cost>
      </repair>
      <repair>
        <id>45</id>
        <description>Front end alignment.</description>
        <cost>45.67</cost>
      </repair>
   </car>
   <car vin="234" make="Mazda" model="Miata">
      <repair>
        <id>7</id>
        <description>Repair top.</description>
        <cost>123.45</cost>
      </repair>
      <repair>
        <id>22</id>
        <description>Oil Change.</description>
        <cost>29.99</cost>
      </repair>
   </car>
   <truck vin="567" make="Nissan" model="Pathfinder">
      <repair>
        <id>2</id>
        <description>Replace air filter.</description>
        <cost>34.95</cost>
      </repair>
      <repair>
        <id>6</id>
        <description>Oil Change.</description>
        <cost>39.99</cost>
      </repair>
   </truck>
</vehicles>'
```

The following SQL snippet provides an XQuery sample that uses all of the FLWOR clauses available in SQL Server 2005.

SQL

```
SELECT @myXQuery.query('
for $r in /vehicles/*/repair
where $r/cost >= 100
order by $r/cost[1] ascending
return $r
')
```

The *for* clause provides a loop that iterates over each repair element belonging to each vehicle. The *for* clause uses an XPath query to locate the repairs. Each time through the loop, the variable, *$r*, is assigned an element from the XPath query result. In this case, *$r* iterates through the repair elements. The *where* clause is used to provide a filter for the repair elements. This filter is set to ignore all repair elements with a cost less than 100, by using *$r/cost* to get the repair cost. The *order* clause changes the order of the result set instead of using the default document order. In this example, the order is by repair cost. If you are ordering on a child node such as cost, you must specify using the first cost node that is found. The *return* clause lets you decide what to return; it is currently set to return the repair element. The returned results are as follows.

```
<repair>
  <id>7</id>
  <description>Repair top.</description>
  <cost>123.45</cost>
</repair>
<repair>
  <id>3</id>
  <description>Replace Supercharger.</description>
  <cost>4000.34</cost>
</repair>
```

Notice that the repairs are in order of cost—a different order than in the XML data, and the repair elements are returned with their child elements.

You can use the *return* clause to reshape the result data. For example, if you want to provide a list of high-cost repairs that also include the *vin* attribute of the vehicle, you can shape the output as follows.

SQL

```
SELECT @myXQuery.query('
for $r in /vehicles/*/repair
where $r/cost >= 100
return
<high-cost-repair repair-id="{$r/id}">
   <vehicle vin="{$r/../@vin}"/>
   {$r/description}
   {$r/cost}
</high-cost-repair>
')
```

The *return* clause defines a new element called *high-cost-repair* that is returned for each repair in the result set. This element has an attribute called *repair-id* that contains the *id* of the repair. Notice the use of the braces to get the repair's *id*. Next, we added a new element called *vehicle*, which has a *vin* attribute set to the value of the *vin* attribute of the parent of the repair. Notice that the parent is accessible by using the .. syntax. Finally, the complete description and cost nodes are returned, and the result is as follows.

```
<high-cost-repair repair-id="3">
  <vehicle vin="123" />
  <description>Replace Supercharger.</description>
  <cost>4000.34</cost>
</high-cost-repair>
<high-cost-repair repair-id="7">
  <vehicle vin="234" />
  <description>Repair top.</description>
  <cost>123.45</cost>
</high-cost-repair>
```

You might also want the result to include the owner information for each repair. You can do this in a couple of ways. One way is to create a nested loop that iterates through the owner's vehicles to find a vehicle that has a matching *vin*, as shown in the following SQL snippet.

SQL

```
SELECT @myXQuery.query('
for $r in /vehicles/*/repair
for $o in /owners/*/vehicle[@vin=$r/../@vin]/..
where $r/cost >= 100
return
<high-cost-repair repair-id="{$r/id}">
   <owner name="{$o/@name}" />
   <vehicle vin="{$r/../@vin}" />
   {$r/description}
   {$r/cost}
</high-cost-repair>
')
```

When the vehicle is found, the .. syntax is used to get the parent element, which is the owner of the vehicle. Although the second loop actually iterates through the *owners/owner/vehicle* elements, it returns the *owners/owner* of the vehicle that has the matching *vin*.

The *return* clause defines a new element called *owner* and contains a *name* attribute that is populated with the current owner name. (Note that if you simply returned *$o*, you would see the *owner* element and its vehicle child elements in the result.) The following is returned.

```
<high-cost-repair repair-id="3">
  <owner name="Mary" />
  <vehicle vin="123" />
  <description>Replace Supercharger.</description>
  <cost>4000.34</cost>
</high-cost-repair>
<high-cost-repair repair-id="7">
  <owner name="Joe" />
  <vehicle vin="234" />
  <description>Repair top.</description>
  <cost>123.45</cost>
</high-cost-repair>
```

Another way to retrieve the same information, with better performance, is to use an XPath query to populate the owner information without adding a second *for* clause, as shown in the following SQL script.

SQL

```
SELECT @myXQuery.query('
for $r in /vehicles/*/repair
where $r/cost >= 100
return
<high-cost-repair repair-id="{$r/id}">
   <owner name="{/owners/*/vehicle[@vin=$r/../@vin]/../@name}" />
   <vehicle vin="{$r/../@vin}"/>
   {$r/description}
   {$r/cost}
</high-cost-repair>
')
```

Notice the XPath query for the owner's *name* attribute. This approach performs much better than the previous example because nested *for* loops create joins to the *iterator* variable.

Using Data Accessors

XQuery supports two data accessor functions that you can use to extract values of nodes as strings or typed values. To extract a node as a string, use the *string* function; to extract a node as a typed value, use the *data* function. When you use the *data* function, the node must be a text node, attribute node, or element node. If the node is a document node of an untyped XML instance, the *data* function returns a string value of the document. The next section includes an example of data accessor usage.

Using Computed Element Constructors

Instead of scripting the XML tag information where the angle brackets are in your code as in the previous example, you can instruct XQuery to create element and attribute objects and then you can call their constructors using the *element name { }* and *attribute name { }* syntax. This technique is significantly faster than the previous example.

The following example demonstrates the implementation of data accessors and computed element constructors to create the same output as in the previous example.

SQL

```
SELECT @myXQuery.query('
for $r in /vehicles/*/repair
where $r/cost >= 100
return
element high-cost-repair
{
   attribute repair-id {$r/id},
   element owner
   {
      attribute name {/owners/*/vehicle[@vin=$r/../@vin]/../@name}
```

```
   },
   element vehicle
   {
      attribute vin {$r/../@vin}
   },
   element description {data($r/description)},
   element cost { data($r/cost)}
}
')
```

You should favor this approach over the previous examples because it is significantly faster.

Using String Functions

SQL Server 2005 does not support all of the XQuery 1.0 string functions. Here are the string functions you can use in your XQuery statements, along with brief examples.

- *string-length* Used to calculate the length of a string.

  ```
  SELECT @myXQuery.query('
  <result>
  {(//owners/owner/@name)[1]}
  {string-length((//owners/owner/@name)[1])}
  </result>
  ')
  ```

  Returns:

  ```
  <result name="Joe">3</result>
  ```

- *substring* Extracts part of a string from the source string. Note that the length can be omitted to return the rest of the source string.

  ```
  SELECT @myXQuery.query('
  <result>{substring((//vehicles/truck/@model)[1], 4, 5)}</result>
  ')
  ```

  Returns the following based on *Pathfinder*:

  ```
  <result>hfind</result>
  ```

- *concat* Concatenates two or more strings.

  ```
  SELECT @myXQuery.query('
  <result>
  {
     concat
     (
        (//owners/owner/@name)[1],
        " has a ",
  ```

```
        (//vehicles/truck[@vin=(//owners/owner)[1]/vehicle/@vin]/@make)[1],
        " ",
        (//vehicles/truck[@vin=(//owners/owner)[1]/vehicle/@vin]/@model)[1]
    )
}
</result>
')
```

Returns:

```
<result>Joe has a Nissan Pathfinder</result>
```

- *contains* Determines whether one string is contained within another string. Note that this function is case sensitive.

```
SELECT @myXQuery.query('
for $r in /vehicles/*/repair
where contains(($r/description)[1],"Super")
return $r
')
```

Returns:

```
<repair>
  <id>3</id>
  <description>Replace Supercharger.</description>
  <cost>4000.34</cost>
</repair>
```

Note Here is a list of XQuery 1.0 string functions that are not supported in SQL Server 2005 but might be added in a future release: *codepoints-to-string, string-to-codepoints, compare, string-join, normalize-space, normalize-unicode, upper-case, lower-case, translate, escape-uri, starts-with, ends-with, substring-before, substring-after, matches, replace,* and *tokenize.*

Using Aggregate Functions

An aggregate function operates on a sequence of items and returns the aggregated value of the sequence. The following is a list of aggregate functions, with brief examples, that you can use in your XQuery statements.

- *count* Returns the number of items in a sequence.

```
SELECT @myXQuery.query('
<result>{ count(/vehicles/*/repair) }</result>
')
```

Returns the following:

```
<result>6</result>
```

- *min* Returns the minimum value in a range. Works with base types that support the *gt* operator. Mixed types are not supported.

```
SELECT @myXQuery.query('
<result>{ min(/vehicles/*/repair/cost) }</result>
')
```

Returns the following:

```
<result>29.99</result>
```

- *max* Returns the maximum value in a range. Works with base types that support the *gt* operator. Mixed types are not supported.

```
SELECT @myXQuery.query('
<result>{ max(/vehicles/*/repair/cost) }</result>
')
```

Returns the following:

```
<result>4000.34</result>
```

- *avg* Returns the average value of the sequence. Works with the any of the numeric base types or *untypedAtomic*, which is the text node of an untyped element, but cannot be mixed.

```
SELECT @myXQuery.query('
<result>{ avg(/vehicles/*/repair/cost) }</result>
')
```

Returns the following:

```
<result>712.398333333333</result>
```

- *sum* Returns the sum value of the sequence. Works with any of the numeric base types or *untypedAtomic*, but cannot be mixed.

```
SELECT @myXQuery.query('
<result>{ sum(/vehicles/*/repair/cost) }</result>
')
```

Returns the following:

```
<result>4274.39</result>
```

Using Context Functions

Context functions are based on your location in an XML tree. SQL Server 2005 implements the following context functions, which are shown here with small example scripts.

- *last* Used to determine the number of items in a sequence.

```
SELECT @myXQuery.query('
<result>{ (/vehicles/*/repair/cost)[last()] }</result>
')
```

Returns the last repair cost:

```
<result>
  <cost>39.99</cost>
</result>
```

To get the last repair of each vehicle and then get its cost, use the following:

```
SELECT @myXQuery.query('
<result>{ /vehicles/*/repair[last()]/cost }</result>
')
```

The results:

```
<result>
  <cost>45.67</cost>
  <cost>29.99</cost>
  <cost>39.99</cost>
</result>
```

- *position* Obtains your current position in a sequence.

```
SELECT @myXQuery.query('
<result>{ (/vehicles/*/repair)[last() - position() < 3] }</result>
')
```

The parentheses around the */vehicles/*/repair* expression indicate that this expression should be fully executed, and its result is fed into the last function to get the last three repair elements in the document. If the parentheses were used, the last three repairs of each vehicle would be returned instead. The expression returns the last three repairs in the document as follows:

```
<result>
  <repair>
    <id>22</id>
    <description>Oil Change.</description>
    <cost>29.99</cost>
  </repair>
  <repair>
    <id>2</id>
    <description>Replace air filter.</description>
    <cost>34.95</cost>
  </repair>
  <repair>
    <id>6</id>
    <description>Oil Change.</description>
    <cost>39.99</cost>
  </repair>
</result>
```

Using XQuery FLWOR vs. XPath

You should always try to use an XPath expression over a FLWOR expression because the *for* statement in the FLWOR expression creates a query plan with a join operation between the *for* variable and the body of the *for* clause, and this join results in poorer performance compared to the XPath expression.

You should use the FLWOR expression when you need to do any of the following.

- Filter the result sequence of the *for* clause based on something that cannot be defined using simple XPath expressions.
- Sort the result set based on a sorting expression. Sorting is defined on the result set using the *order by* clause.
- Construct the returned result using the results obtained from the *for* clause.

Using Namespaces in Your Queries

In SQL Server 2005, XQuery expressions consist of a prolog and a body. You can use the prolog to declare namespaces. A namespace declaration is used to map a prefix to a namespace Uniform Resource Identifier (URI), which is a compact string of characters that identify a resource. You use the prefix when a namespace is required, instead of using the complete URI.

Remember that in XML, the default namespace for attributes is always the *null* namespace and the only way to get an attribute into a different namespace is to explicitly assign the attribute to the namespace. XQuery is consistent with this behavior, and you should be aware that XQuery uses the same namespaces for searching and constructing XML.

The examples in this section use a variable called *@myXQueryNs*, which is populated with the following XML data. Note that the namespace assignments are intentionally inconsistent.

SQL: Populating the *@myXQueryNs* Variable

```
DECLARE @myXQueryNs xml
SET @myXQueryNs = '
<work xmlns="default.gjtt.com"
      xmlns:OWN="owner.gjtt.com"
      xmlns:VEH="vehicle.gjtt.com" >
  <OWN:owners>
     <OWN:owner name="Joe">
        <OWN:vehicle OWN:vin="567"/>
        <OWN:vehicle vin="234"/>
     </OWN:owner>
     <OWN:owner name="Mary">
        <OWN:vehicle vin="123"/>
     </OWN:owner>
  </OWN:owners>
  <VEH:vehicles>
     <car vin="123" make="Ford" model="Mustang">
        <VEH:repair>
          <id>3</id>
          <description>Replace Supercharger.</description>
          <cost>4000.34</cost>
        </VEH:repair>
        <repair>
          <id>45</id>
          <description>Front end alignment.</description>
          <cost>45.67</cost>
        </repair>
     </car>
     <car vin="234" make="Mazda" model="Miata">
        <repair>
          <id>7</id>
          <description>Repair top.</description>
          <cost>123.45</cost>
        </repair>
        <repair>
          <id>22</id>
          <description>Oil Change.</description>
          <cost>29.99</cost>
        </repair>
     </car>
     <truck vin="567" make="Nissan" model="Pathfinder">
        <repair>
          <id>2</id>
          <description>Replace air filter.</description>
          <cost>34.95</cost>
        </repair>
        <repair>
          <id>6</id>
          <description>Oil Change.</description>
          <cost>39.99</cost>
        </repair>
     </truck>
  </VEH:vehicles>
</work>'
```

What is the result if you perform a simple query for the last repair using the following SQL snippet?

```
SELECT @myXQueryNs.query('
<result>{ (//repair)[last()] }</result>
')
```

This snippet is returned:

```
<result />
```

No repairs were found because the repairs defined in *@myXQueryNs* are actually in the *default.gjtt.com* namespace, which is the default namespace. The search for *//repair* looks for a repair in the empty namespace.

One way to correct the problem is to define a namespace in the prolog of the XQuery statement and use it for the search, as shown in the following SQL script.

```
SELECT @myXQueryNs.query('
declare namespace ns1 = "default.gjtt.com";
<result>{ (//ns1:repair)[last()] }</result>
')
```

In this code, a namespace is declared in the prolog section of the XQuery expression and is referenced in the search for the repair. This returns the following repair.

```
<result>
  <ns1:repair xmlns:ns1="default.gjtt.com">
    <ns1:id>6</ns1:id>
    <ns1:description>Oil Change.</ns1:description>
    <ns1:cost>39.99</ns1:cost>
  </ns1:repair>
</result>
```

The first thing to verify is whether you got the repair you expected. You should have, because this is the last repair element in the XML document.

Notice that the *ns1* prefix is on the repair and its elements and that the namespace declaration in the result maps *ns1* to the correct namespace. This means the namespace mapping you defined for the search is the same namespace mapping used in the result.

Although the result is technically accurate, if you want these elements to be in a default namespace, you can use the following SQL snippet.

```
SELECT @myXQueryNs.query('
declare default element namespace "default.gjtt.com";
<result>{ (//repair)[last()] }</result>
')
```

This code declares a default element namespace in the prolog of the XQuery expression, which means the search for the repair will use the default namespace without requiring a prefix. The result is as follows:

```
<result xmlns="default.gjtt.com">
  <repair>
    <id>6</id>
    <description>Oil Change.</description>
    <cost>39.99</cost>
  </repair>
</result>
```

The result and its elements are all in the default namespace. Once again, notice that the same namespace definitions used for the query were also used in the output.

Do You Really Want to Set the Default Namespace? Wait. This output isn't the same as the previous output. The previous output placed the result element in the *null* namespace, and this output places the result in the *default.gjtt.com* namespace. Try to change the namespace of the *result* element, as shown in the following snippet.

```
SELECT @myXQueryNs.query('
declare default element namespace "default.gjtt.com";
<result xmlns="">{ (//repair)[last()] }</result>
')
```

This code looks like it should work, but here's the output:

```
<p1:result xmlns="" />
```

What happened? The namespace declaration added to the *result* element changed the namespace used for the search, so no repairs were found. You can make a quick fix to the search to retrieve repairs that are in any namespace, as follows.

```
SELECT @myXQueryNs.query('
declare default element namespace "default.gjtt.com";
<result xmlns="">{ (//*:repair)[last()] }</result>
')
```

The asterisk is used as a wildcard to search all namespaces for repair elements, but here's the output:

```
<result xmlns=""
  <p1:repair xmlns:p1="default.gjtt.com">>
    <p1:id>6</p1:id>
    <p1:description>Oil Change.</p1:description>
    <p1:cost>39.99</p1:cost>
  </p1:repair>
</result>
```

This output looks the same as the original, where the result element is in the default namespace. This exercise demonstrates three key points.

- If you change a namespace in your element construction, that new namespace will be used for searching.
- When you change the default element namespace from the default *null* namespace, you have a way to set namespace back to the *null* namespace.
- Consider never using a *null* namespace; this will also eliminate the problem.

Using the SQL WITH *XMLNAMESPACES* Clause You can also use the SQL *WITH XML-NAMESPACES* clause to set the namespaces for your XQuery expression. This clause is an extension to the SQL *WITH* clause that you can use to define locking hints. (Locking hints are not related to this subject, however.) To eliminate any ambiguities, you must end the previous T-SQL statement with a semicolon (;) before using this clause.

The following SQL snippet retrieves the last repair using the *WITH XMLNAMESPACES* clause.

```
; --semicolon required on previous statement
WITH XMLNAMESPACES
(
  'default.gjtt.com' AS "ns1"
)
SELECT @myXQueryNs.query('
<result>{ (//ns1:repair)[last()] }</result>
')
```

Here is the result:

```
<result>
  <ns1:repair xmlns:ns1="default.gjtt.com">
    <ns1:id>6</ns1:id>
    <ns1:description>Oil Change.</ns1:description>
    <ns1:cost>39.99</ns1:cost>
  </ns1:repair>
</result>
```

You can also set the default namespace. Note that setting the default namespace using the WITH XMLNAMESPACES clause works the same way as the *declare default element namespace* clause that we looked at previously. The following SQL snippet sets the default namespace.

```
; --semicolon required on previous statement
WITH XMLNAMESPACES
(
   DEFAULT 'default.gjtt.com'
)
SELECT @myXQueryNs.query('
<result>{ (//repair)[last()] }</result>
')
```

This code returns the following:

```
<p1:result xmlns:p1="default.gjtt.com">
  <p1:repair>
    <p1:id>6</p1:id>
    <p1:description>Oil Change.</p1:description>
    <p1:cost>39.99</p1:cost>
  </p1:repair>
</p1:result>
```

The output is a bit different than with the *declare default element namespace* clause. Although all of the constructed elements have the proper namespace, the output still has a *null* default namespace, which might work well if you are combining this output with other output.

Another benefit to using the *WITH XMLNAMESPACES* clause over the *declare default element namespace* clause is that you can define the namespaces once for a single SELECT statement. Consider the following example that retrieves a column for the last repair and a column for the first repair.

```
SELECT @myXQueryNs.query('
declare namespace ns1 = "default.gjtt.com";
<result>{ (//ns1:repair)[last()] }</result>
') as LastRepair,
@myXQueryNs.query('
declare namespace ns1 = "default.gjtt.com";
<result>{ (//ns1:repair)[1] }</result>
') as FirstRepair
```

Notice that the namespace is defined for each XQuery expression. Instead, you can use the *WITH XMLNAMESPACES* clause as follows and define the namespace only once.

```
; --semicolon required on previous statement
WITH XMLNAMESPACES
(
   DEFAULT 'default.gjtt.com'
)
SELECT @myXQueryNs.query('
```

```
<result>{ (//repair)[last()] }</result>
') as LastRepair,
@myXQueryNs.query('
<result>{ (//repair)[1] }</result>
') as FirstRepair
```

Using Namespaces with Attributes When you work with namespaces and attributes, remember that the attribute is in the *null* namespace unless you explicitly specify a namespace. The following snippet is one example of how to query using an attribute.

```
SELECT @myXQueryNs.query('
declare namespace ns1 = "owner.gjtt.com";
<result>{ //ns1:vehicle[@vin="234"] }</result>
')
```

This code returns the following:

```
<result>
  <ns1:vehicle xmlns:ns1="owner.gjtt.com" vin="234" />
</result>
```

Notice that no namespace is needed for the *vin* because the attribute is in the *null* namespace even though the XML document sets the default namespace. If you try to search for the *vin* with a value of *567*, you need the namespace identifier, as shown in the following snippet.

```
SELECT @myXQueryNs.query('
declare namespace ns1 = "owner.gjtt.com";
<result>{ //ns1:vehicle[@ns1:vin="567"] }</result>
')
```

This returns:

```
<result>
  <ns1:vehicle xmlns:ns1="owner.gjtt.com" ns1:vin="567" />
</result>
```

Using Schemas to Work with Typed XML Data

The previous examples use a variable that is an "untyped" *xml* data type. Untyped *xml* data types are stored as raw text data with their elements and attributes, and they are checked to verify that they are well formed. Untyped *xml* data types are ideal when the data in each *xml* instance is in a different, or varied, format–when you want to ensure that the data is well formed but the field can contain any kind of XML data.

You can also create a "typed" *xml* data type, which requires the use of an XML schema that has been registered with SQL Server. To register schemas with SQL Server, you add the schemas to SQL Server Schema Collections. The use of schemas offers the following benefits.

- Provides early error detection based on type checking.
- Provides increased performance in *for* queries by eliminating much of the type inspection and providing a better query plan.
- Validates XML instances during inserts.
- Validates XML instances during updates.
- Optimizes SQL Server storage.

Why Add Schemas to a Schema Collection? You add schemas to a Schema Collection, and you assign the Schema Collection to an *xml* type to allow schema versioning. Let's say you create a schema for sales orders that has a target namespace of *Orders-V1*. You add the schema to a new Schema Collection and assign this schema to the applicable *xml* types. Later, you realize that you need to add an *OrderDate* element. You can create the new schema with the changes and set the target namespace to *Orders-V2*. You can add this new schema to the Schema Collection, and the *xml* types will work with both *Orders-V1* and *Orders-V2*.

The following SQL script adds an abbreviated schema of the *Northwind* database's Orders table to a new Schema Collection called *OrdersSchemas*.

SQL: Creating the Schema Collection

```
CREATE XML SCHEMA COLLECTION OrdersSchemas
AS '<?xml version="1.0" standalone="yes"?>
<xs:schema id="northwindDataSet"
      targetNamespace="orders-v1"
      xmlns:mstns="orders-v1"
      xmlns="orders-v1"
      xmlns:xs="http://www.w3.org/2001/XMLSchema"
      xmlns:msdata="urn:schemas-microsoft-com:xml-msdata"
      attributeFormDefault="qualified"
      elementFormDefault="qualified">
  <xs:element name="northwindDataSet" msdata:IsDataSet="true"
      msdata:UseCurrentLocale="true">
    <xs:complexType>
      <xs:choice minOccurs="0" maxOccurs="unbounded">
        <xs:element name="Orders">
          <xs:complexType>
            <xs:sequence>
              <xs:element name="OrderID" msdata:ReadOnly="true"
                 msdata:AutoIncrement="true" type="xs:int" />
              <xs:element name="CustomerID" minOccurs="0">
                <xs:simpleType>
                  <xs:restriction base="xs:string">
                    <xs:maxLength value="5" />
                  </xs:restriction>
                </xs:simpleType>
              </xs:element>
              <xs:element name="Freight" type="xs:decimal" minOccurs="0" />
              <xs:element name="ShipName" minOccurs="0">
                <xs:simpleType>
                  <xs:restriction base="xs:string">
```

```
                    <xs:maxLength value="40" />
                  </xs:restriction>
                </xs:simpleType>
              </xs:element>
            </xs:sequence>
          </xs:complexType>
        </xs:element>
      </xs:choice>
    </xs:complexType>
  </xs:element>
</xs:schema>'
```

You can view your registered schemas by using the *xml_schema_namespace* function and passing the name of the Schema Collection, as shown in the following SQL snippet.

```
SELECT xml_schema_namespace('dbo', 'OrdersSchemas')
```

This code lists all of the schemas in the Schema Collection, but you can use the *query* method to filter the list of schemas that are returned, based on the *targetNamespace* attribute in the schema element:

```
SELECT xml_schema_namespace('dbo', 'ordersSchemas').query('
   /xs:schema[@targetNamespace="orders-v1"]
')
```

After this schema has been added, you can create *xml* data types that are typed based on this Schema Collection. The following SQL snippet declares and initializes a typed *xml* variable called *@myTypedXml*.

SQL: Populating the *@myTypedXml* Variable

```
DECLARE @myTypedXml xml(OrdersSchemas)
SET @myTypedXml =
'<northwindDataSet xmlns="orders-v1">
  <Orders>
    <OrderID>10248</OrderID>
    <CustomerID>VINET</CustomerID>
    <Freight>32.3800</Freight>
    <ShipName>Vins et alcools Chevalier</ShipName>
  </Orders>
</northwindDataSet>'
```

This XML data conforms to the schema, so it will be successfully validated and you can use this variable.

If you realize that you want an order date and you simply try to add the order date to the data, you will receive an error stating that the *OrderDate* element was not expected. You must create a new version of the schema that identifies the *OrderDate* as shown in the following SQL snippet.

SQL: Adding Version 2 of the Schema

```
ALTER XML SCHEMA COLLECTION OrdersSchemas
ADD '<?xml version="1.0" standalone="yes"?>
<xs:schema id="northwindDataSet"
      targetNamespace="orders-v2"
      xmlns:mstns="orders-v2"
      xmlns="orders-v2"
      xmlns:xs="http://www.w3.org/2001/XMLSchema"
      xmlns:msdata="urn:schemas-microsoft-com:xml-msdata"
      attributeFormDefault="qualified"
      elementFormDefault="qualified">
  <xs:element name="northwindDataSet" msdata:IsDataSet="true"
      msdata:UseCurrentLocale="true">
    <xs:complexType>
      <xs:choice minOccurs="0" maxOccurs="unbounded">
        <xs:element name="Orders">
          <xs:complexType>
            <xs:sequence>
              <xs:element name="OrderID" msdata:ReadOnly="true"
                 msdata:AutoIncrement="true" type="xs:int" />
              <xs:element name="CustomerID" minOccurs="0">
                <xs:simpleType>
                  <xs:restriction base="xs:string">
                    <xs:maxLength value="5" />
                  </xs:restriction>
                </xs:simpleType>
              </xs:element>
              <xs:element name="OrderDate" type="xs:dateTime" minOccurs="0" />
              <xs:element name="Freight" type="xs:decimal" minOccurs="0" />
              <xs:element name="ShipName" minOccurs="0">
                <xs:simpleType>
                  <xs:restriction base="xs:string">
                    <xs:maxLength value="40" />
                  </xs:restriction>
                </xs:simpleType>
              </xs:element>
            </xs:sequence>
          </xs:complexType>
        </xs:element>
      </xs:choice>
    </xs:complexType>
  </xs:element>
</xs:schema>'
```

Notice that *targetNamespace* and the default namespace have been changed to *orders-v2*. Also, the order data has been added between the *CustomerID* and *Freight*, and its type is *xs:dateTime*. Try to use the following code to initialize the *@myTypedXml* variable.

```
DECLARE @myTypedXml xml(OrdersSchemas)
SET @myTypedXml =
'<northwindDataSet xmlns="orders-v2">
  <Orders>
    <OrderID>10248</OrderID>
    <CustomerID>VINET</CustomerID>
```

```
    <OrderDate>1996-07-04T00:00:00.0000000-04:00</OrderDate>
    <Freight>32.3800</Freight>
    <ShipName>Vins et alcools Chevalier</ShipName>
  </Orders>
</northwindDataSet>'
```

If you want to query for the *OrderID* of an *Order* with a specific *OrderDate*, you can use the following SQL script.

```
SELECT @myTypedXml.query('
declare default element namespace "orders-v2";
<result>
  {//Orders[OrderDate=xs:dateTime("1996-07-04T04:00:00Z")]/OrderID}
</result>')
```

Notice that the filter value must be cast to *xs:dateTime*. Without the explicit cast, an error will occur stating that the = operator cannot be applied to operators of type *dateTime* and *string*. (Note that you don't need to include the milliseconds in your query.) Here is the result:

```
<result xmlns="orders-v2">
  <OrderID>10248</OrderID>
</result>
```

You now have two schema versions in your Schema Collection, and you can use either version, or, to state it more accurately, both versions of the schema and data can co-exist. This is a nice feature that you don't have with standard relational data, which has a much more rigid schema and requires all data to be upgraded to the latest schema when the schema is changed.

Using the *xml* Data Type in SQL Tables

Up to this point, all of our sample code has been based on assigning XML data to a variable that is an *xml* data type, but the XML data can also be used as a column type in a database table. This means that you can use relational data with XML data, and everything covered in this chapter is applicable to *xml* columns.

You can create a table with typed and untyped *xml* columns. You can have many *xml* columns in a table, and each *xml* value (XML instance) that is inserted has a maximum size of 2 GB. To insert a row into the table, use the T-SQL INSERT command, which is used in the following SQL script that creates a table called MyXmlTable in the *Northwind* database and populates it with data.

SQL: Creating and Populating MyXmlTable

```
USE Northwind
CREATE TABLE MyXmlTable(id int NOT NULL, ownername varchar(50), vehicles xml )
GO
ALTER TABLE dbo.MyXmlTable ADD CONSTRAINT
   PK_MyXmlTable PRIMARY KEY CLUSTERED
```

```
   (
   id
   )
WITH( STATISTICS_NORECOMPUTE = OFF, IGNORE_DUP_KEY = OFF,
   ALLOW_ROW_LOCKS = ON, ALLOW_PAGE_LOCKS = ON) ON [PRIMARY]
GO
INSERT MyXmlTable VALUES(1, 'Joe',
'<vehicles>
   <car vin="234" make="Mazda" model="Miata">
      <repair>
        <id>7</id>
        <description>Repair top.</description>
        <cost>123.45</cost>
      </repair>
      <repair>
        <id>22</id>
        <description>Oil Change.</description>
        <cost>29.99</cost>
      </repair>
   </car>
   <truck vin="567" make="Nissan" model="Pathfinder">
      <repair>
        <id>2</id>
        <description>Replace air filter.</description>
        <cost>34.95</cost>
      </repair>
      <repair>
        <id>6</id>
        <description>Oil Change.</description>
        <cost>39.99</cost>
      </repair>
   </truck>
</vehicles>')
INSERT MyXmlTable VALUES(2, 'Mary',
'<vehicles>
   <car vin="123" make="Ford" model="Mustang">
      <repair>
        <id>3</id>
        <description>Replace Supercharger.</description>
        <cost>4000.34</cost>
      </repair>
      <repair>
        <id>45</id>
        <description>Front end alignment.</description>
        <cost>45.67</cost>
      </repair>
   </car>
</vehicles>')
INSERT MyXmlTable VALUES( 3, 'Bob', null)
```

This script inserts a row for Joe and his vehicles, another row for Mary and her vehicles, and another row for Bob, who has no vehicles. In the past, you would have converted (or "shredded") the *xml* data to relational data, which meant that you would have created a vehicles table and a repairs table to hold the shredded data. But you know that the structure of this data might be very different depending on the vehicle and/or the repair. In addition, the XML data might be coming from an external XML source, so storing this data as an *xml* column makes sense.

Now that you have some table data, you can run all of the same SELECT statements that we ran earlier in the chapter. For example, the following SQL script returns the ID, the owner's name, and the last repair for each owner.

SQL

```
SELECT id, ownername,
   vehicles.query('(/vehicles/*/repair)[last()]') as lastrepair
FROM MyXmlTable
```

The result is shown in Figure 15-3.

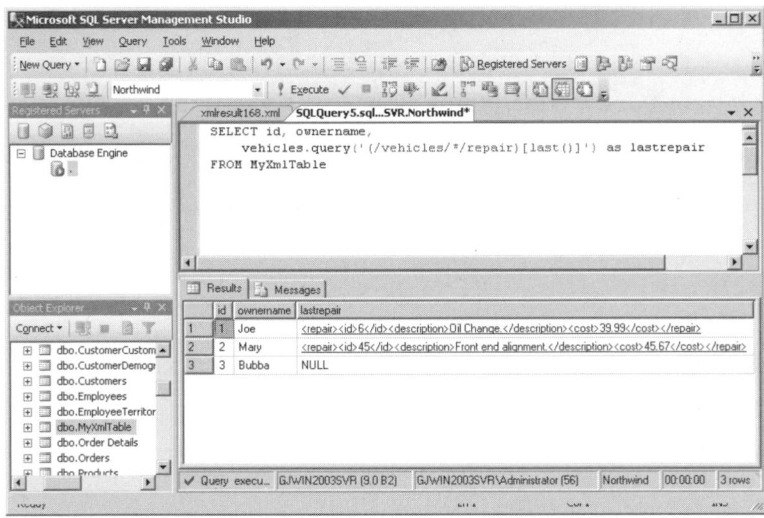

Figure 15-3 The result of querying for each owner's last repair

Using Column Data in the XQuery Expression

Sometimes you will want to access column data from within your XQuery expression. For example, when you run your query, you might want to return a single *xml* column that contains XML data that has been constructed and includes the owner's name and ID. For this, you can use the *sql:column* method, as shown in the following SQL snippet.

SQL

```
SELECT vehicles.query('
for $e in /*
return
element owner
{
   attribute ownerid {sql:column("id")},
   attribute name {sql:column("ownername")},
```

```
    $e
}
')
FROM MyXmlTable
```

This code creates an outer element for the owner, creates attributes for the ownerid and name columns, and embeds the existing XML data into this element. Three rows are returned, but Bob has no cars, so his XML data is null. The following shows the XML data for Joe.

```
<owner ownerid="1" name="Joe">
  <vehicles>
    <car vin="234" make="Mazda" model="Miata">
      <repair>
        <id>7</id>
        <description>Repair top.</description>
        <cost>123.45</cost>
      </repair>
      <repair>
        <id>22</id>
        <description>Oil Change.</description>
        <cost>29.99</cost>
      </repair>
    </car>
    <truck vin="567" make="Nissan" model="Pathfinder">
      <repair>
        <id>2</id>
        <description>Replace air filter.</description>
        <cost>34.95</cost>
      </repair>
      <repair>
        <id>6</id>
        <description>Oil Change.</description>
        <cost>39.99</cost>
      </repair>
    </truck>
  </vehicles>
</owner>
```

Using the *exist* Method with XQuery

In the previous example, MyXmlTable was queried for each owner's last repair, but you might also want to use the *xml* column in the T-SQL WHERE clause to filter the result. Consider the following SQL script that retrieves all owners and their trucks.

SQL

```
SELECT id, ownername,
    vehicles.query('//truck') as trucks
FROM MyXmlTable
```

This query returns all owners, even if the owner has no trucks. If you want to see only the owners who have at least one truck, you can use the *exist* method to search the *xml* column value in each row. If the row has a match, the *exist* function returns true as a value of 1. If no match is found, the function returns false as a value of 0. If the *xml* column is null, the *exist* function returns null. The following SQL script retrieves owners and trucks only if the owner has at least one truck.

SQL

```
SELECT id, ownername,
    vehicles.query('//truck') as trucks
FROM MyXmlTable
WHERE vehicles.exist('//truck')= 1
```

The results are shown in Figure 15-4. Notice that Joe is the only truck owner, so he is the only owner that is displayed.

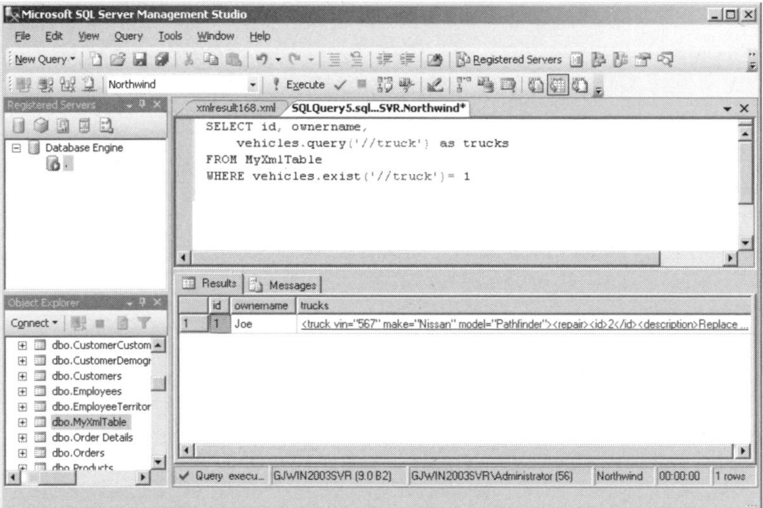

Figure 15-4 Using the *exist* method to filter the query output

Using the *modify* Method to Change Data

You can use the *modify* method with XML instances to replace the value of a single node, insert one or more nodes, or delete nodes. This means you don't need to retrieve the complete XML instance, modify it, and replace it when you need to make a small change.

Note In these examples, literal strings are used to perform modifications. You get an error if you try to modify by using a SQL variable. The use of SQL variables in the *modify* statement is not yet implemented but might be implemented in a future release. For a workaround, see the upcoming section titled "Moving Part of XML Data from One Row to Another."

Replacing the Value of a Node

If you want to modify the value that is in a single node, you can use the *replace value of* clause of the *modify* method. This clause requires a search expression that returns a single node, plus a replacement expression. If the node is not found, no replacement is made. The replacement uses the following format in the *modify* method.

```
replace value of
   SearchExpression
with
   NewExpression
```

Any attempt to execute the *modify* method on a null XML instance generates an error, so you must add a WHERE clause to your SQL statement to filter out null rows. The following SQL script searches for the repair whose *id* is 6 and replaces the repair description with an updated description.

SQL

```
update MyXmlTable
SET vehicles.modify('
replace value of (//repair[id=6]/description/text())[1]
with "Oil change. Took 5 Quarts of oil."')
WHERE vehicles is not null
```

When this update is executed, the description's text node is modified.

If you want to simply change the value of a node in an *xml* variable, you can use the following syntax to execute the *modify* method.

SQL

```
DECLARE @myXmlVar xml
SET @myXmlVar = '
<meats>
   <meat>beef</meat>
   <meat>pork</meat>
   <meat>chicken</meat>
</meats>' --initialize

SET @myXmlVar.modify('
replace value of (//meat/text()[.="pork"])[1]
with "fish"
') --replace node

SELECT @myXmlVar --show change
```

This script declares a variable, initializes it, modifies it, and displays it.

Inserting a New Node

You can insert nodes into the XML instance by using the *insert* clause of the *modify* method. This clause requires a search expression that returns a single node, a location indicator, and the *insert* expression. If the node is not found, no insert is made. You can't use the *insert* clause to modify a null XML instance. Doing so results in the following exception.

```
Msg 5302, Level 16, State 1, Line 1
Mutator 'modify()' on 'vehicles' cannot be called on a null value.
```

The *insert* clause has the following format.

```
insert
   NewExpression
      as first into | as last into | after | before
   SearchExpression
```

An example of the *insert* method is when additional repairs are made to a vehicle. In this scenario, Mary has had her wiper blades replaced and the repair must be inserted after the last repair. The following script modifies the data by adding an additional repair to Mary's car and then displays the resulting XML instance.

SQL

```
UPDATE MyXmlTable
SET vehicles.modify('
insert <repair><id>102</id>
<description>Replace wiper blades.</description>
<cost>24.95</cost>
</repair>
as last into
(//car[@vin="123"])[1]
')
WHERE id=2 --Mary's id

SELECT vehicles FROM MyXmlTable WHERE id=2
```

The first item of interest is the WHERE clause that returns Mary's row. This means that the only XML instance that will be included in the query is Mary's XML instance. The search expression locates the node of the car that was repaired. The new repair is inserted into the car node, as the last node within the car. The result of this query is as follows.

```
<vehicles>
  <car vin="123" make="Ford" model="Mustang">
    <repair>
      <id>3</id>
      <description>Replace Supercharger.</description>
      <cost>4000.34</cost>
```

```
      </repair>
      <repair>
        <id>45</id>
        <description>Front end alignment.</description>
        <cost>45.67</cost>
      </repair>
      <repair>
        <id>102</id>
        <description>Replace wiper blades.</description>
        <cost>24.95</cost>
      </repair>
    </car>
</vehicles>
```

Deleting a Node

You can delete nodes in the XML instance by using the *delete* clause of the *modify* method. This clause requires a search expression that can return multiple nodes, and those nodes are deleted. If no nodes are found, no nodes are deleted. The format of the *delete* clause is as follows.

```
delete
   SearchExpression
```

If Joe sells his car, you must delete it from his XML instance. You can do this by using the following SQL script.

SQL

```
UPDATE MyXmlTable
SET vehicles.modify('
delete
//car[@vin="234"]
')
WHERE id=1 --Joe's id
```

Moving Part of XML Data from One Row to Another

Now we will put everything together and also show the workaround to deal with not being able to use SQL variables with the *modify* method.

Here is the scenario: if Joe sells his truck to Bob, you must retrieve the truck from Joe's XML instance and insert it into Bob's XML instance. Remember that you must check to see if Bob's XML instance is null before attempting the insert, and you must delete the truck from Joe's XML instance as well.

The following SQL script is an example of how you might move a vehicle based on its *vin* (567) from a source owner (Joe) to a destination owner (Bob).

SQL

```
DECLARE @SourceOwner int
DECLARE @DestinationOwner int
DECLARE @vin varchar(50)
SET @SourceOwner = 1
SET @DestinationOwner = 3
SET @vin = '567'

BEGIN TRY
  BEGIN TRAN
  DECLARE @sourceVehicle xml
  DECLARE @destinationVehicle xml
  --get the source vehicle
  SELECT @sourceVehicle = vehicles.query('
      //vehicles/*[@vin=sql:variable("@vin")]
      ')
  FROM MyXmlTable
  WHERE id = @SourceOwner
  AND vehicles is not null

  --was source vehicle retrieved?
  IF @sourceVehicle.exist('
      /*[@vin=sql:variable("@vin")]
      ') <> 1
  BEGIN
    RAISERROR ('Vehicle with VIN: %s not owned by owner: %d',
      16, 1, @vin, @SourceOwner)
  END

  --get destination xml
  SELECT @destinationVehicle = vehicles
  FROM MyXmlTable
  WHERE id = @destinationOwner

  --null? add root
  IF @destinationVehicle is null
  BEGIN
    UPDATE MyXmlTable
    SET vehicles = '<vehicles/>'
    WHERE id = @destinationOwner
  END
  ELSE
  BEGIN
    --not null, but no vehicles element; add one
    IF @destinationVehicle.exist('/vehicles') <> 1
    BEGIN
      UPDATE MyXmlTable
      SET vehicles.modify('
         insert <vehicles/> as last into /
      ')
      WHERE id = @destinationOwner
    END
  END
  --add to destination owner
  --Yuk, can't use xml type variable
```

```
  --Work around by building and executing string
  DECLARE @sql nvarchar(MAX)
  SET @sql = 'UPDATE MyXmlTable
    SET vehicles.modify(''insert '
    + CAST( @sourceVehicle as nvarchar(MAX))
    + ' as last into  (/vehicles)[1]'')
    WHERE id = ' + CONVERT(varchar(MAX),@destinationOwner)
  EXEC (@sql)

  --delete from source owner
  UPDATE MyXmlTable
  SET vehicles.modify('
      delete //vehicles/*[@vin=sql:variable("@vin")]
      ')
  WHERE id=@SourceOwner

  --done
  COMMIT TRAN
END TRY
BEGIN CATCH
  ROLLBACK TRAN
  PRINT ERROR_MESSAGE()
END CATCH

--show results
SELECT * FROM MyXmlTable
```

This script starts by declaring SQL variables to hold the source owner, destination owner, and *vin*. Next it enters a try/catch block and starts a transaction. It creates temporary variables for the source vehicle and the destination vehicle. It then loads the source vehicle variable from the source owner's table row and checks to see if the vehicle was indeed loaded. It loads the destination vehicle's *xml* column from the destination owner's table row and checks to make sure it isn't null and that it has a *vehicles* element to hold the newly purchased vehicle.

After performing all of the validations, the script creates a variable that contains a SQL UPDATE statement that executes the *modify* method, and then the script executes the contents of the variable. It's a bit of a kludge, but it works.

Using the *nodes* Method to Change Data

The *nodes* method accepts an XPath search expression and returns a collection of instances of *xml* data types, each with its context set to the node that its XPath expression evaluates to. This collection supports the *query*, *value*, *nodes*, and *exist* methods, and it can be used in *count*(*) aggregations and null checks. The collection can also be used to build a database table with a single column that contains the XML data. All other uses result in an error.

To understand how this method works, it's best to start by examining how it works with a variable, and then look at its operation with a table.

Earlier in this chapter, we populated a variable called *@myXPath* with a list of three vehicles, each with two repairs (for a total of six repairs). How can you view these repairs in a tabular format that is similar to a database table format? You can try running an XPath query for the repair elements like the following.

```
SELECT @myXPath.query('//repair')
```

This query yields a single row with a single column, but you want to see one row for each repair (six total rows) with a column for the *id*, *description*, and *cost* (three columns). This is where the *nodes* method can help. By itself, the *nodes* method breaks up the results into six rows of one column, each containing the XML data for a repair. The *nodes* method is a table-valued function, so it is used after the FROM clause in a SELECT statement, as follows.

```
SELECT T.myRepair.query('.') FROM @myXPath.nodes('//repair') AS T(myRepair)
```

Notice that the FROM clause contains a call to the *nodes* method on the *@myXPath* variable, which uses the same XPath search expression that we previously used. This method returns a table with a single column, both unnamed, so you must create an alias for the table and for the column. In this case, we created a table alias called *T* and a column alias called *myRepair* by using the AS clause. The *myRepair* column cannot be directly viewed, but a simple query for *self* will display its contents, as shown in Figure 15-5.

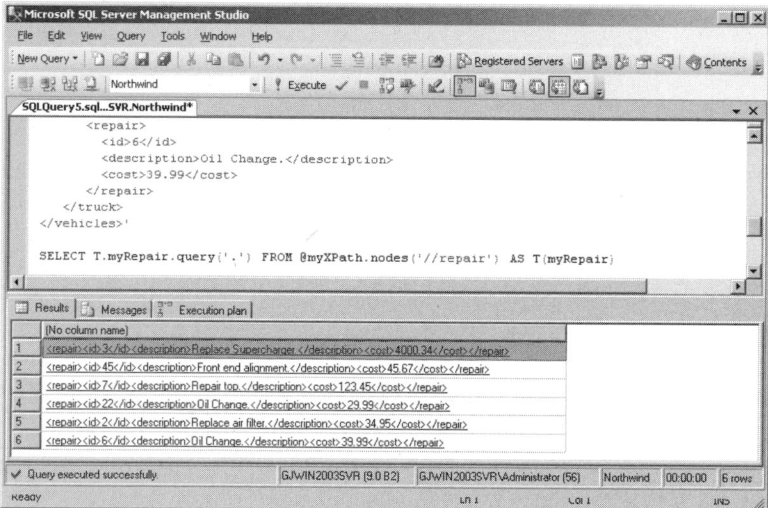

Figure 15-5 Using the *nodes* method to produce a table with a single column containing the XML data for each item matching the search

Now that we have a table with six rows, we can use the *value* method to extract single values from our column of XML data, which we will use to produce the three columns that are required. Also, it's not necessary to display the column of XML data, so we will eliminate this from the column list. The following SQL snippet shows how this is done.

SQL

```
SELECT
  T.myRepair.value('(./id)[1]','int') as id,
  T.myRepair.value('(./description)[1]','nvarchar(max)') as description,
  T.myRepair.value('(./cost)[1]','money') as cost
FROM @myXPath.nodes('//repair') AS T(myRepair)
```

For each of the columns, we use the *value* method to extract the single value and cast it to the desired SQL data type. Each column is also given an alias, and the result of this query produces six repair rows, each containing an *id*, *description*, and *cost*, as shown in Figure 15-6.

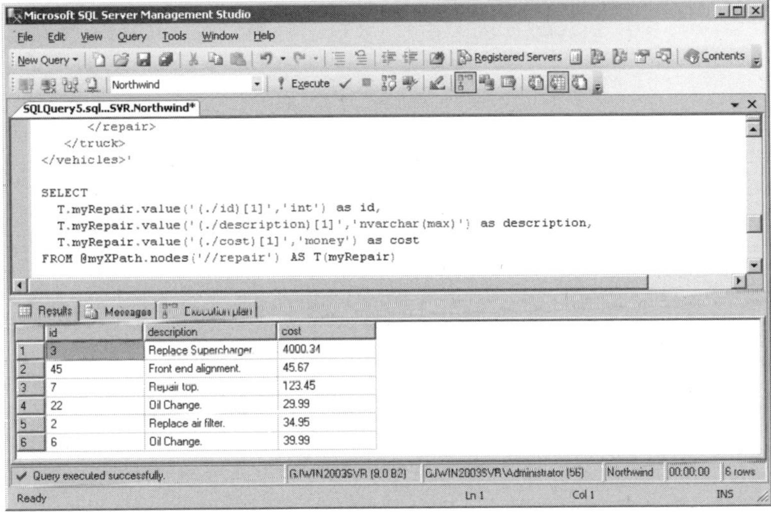

Figure 15-6 Converting XML data to tabular data by using the *nodes* and *value* methods

Now that you understand how to easily convert a single variable to a tabular form, it's time to see how the *nodes* method works when you use table data.

Let's say we have a database table called MyXmlTable that contains three rows that identify owners of vehicles: Joe, Mary, and Bob. Each row has an *xml* column containing vehicles, and each vehicle has repairs. We want the list of all repairs in a tabular format, similar to the previous example when we worked with a single variable, but we also want a column for the owner's name and the *vin* of the vehicle, and we want to sort the list on the repair cost.

Locate the SQL script, shown on pages 444 and 445, titled "SQL: Creating and Populating MyXmlTable," and run it. If you already have the table but have made changes to it, drop the table and run the script.

SQL Server provides a relational operator called APPLY that allows you to execute a table-valued function once per each row of an outer table expression. The *nodes* method is a table-valued function. The APPLY operator is essentially a join to the table-valued function. You specify APPLY after the FROM clause of a query, much as you do the JOIN operator. With the APPLY operator, you can refer to a table-valued function in a correlated subquery. APPLY has two flavors: CROSS APPLY and OUTER APPLY.

CROSS APPLY executes the table-valued function for each row in an outer table expression. It returns a single result set that represents the union of all of the results returned by the individual executions of the table-valued function. For a given outer row, if the table-valued function returns an empty set, the outer row is not returned in the result. This is much like an inner join.

OUTER APPLY is like an outer join in that all outer rows are included even if the table-valued function returns an empty set.

For this example, we will use the CROSS APPLY relational operator to retrieve the results because we don't want to display owners who have no repairs. The following is a SQL script that retrieves the tabular data.

SQL

```
SELECT
  OwnerName,
  T.myRepair.value('(../@vin)[1]','nvarchar(max)') as VIN,
  T.myRepair.value('(./id)[1]','int') as RepairId,
  T.myRepair.value('(./description)[1]','nvarchar(max)') as Description,
  T.myRepair.value('(./cost)[1]','money') as Cost
FROM MyXmlTable CROSS APPLY vehicles.nodes('//repair') as T(myRepair)
ORDER BY Cost
```

The SELECT statement retrieves the *OwnerName* as a column. Next, the script displays the *vin*, which is interesting because you might have thought that the resultant XML data for the nodes would be rooted to the repair, but you can still retrieve the parent and get its *vin* attribute. The same three columns are then retrieved, as in the previous example. Notice the use of the CROSS APPLY relational operator, which joins the source table to the *nodes* method's output. Just as in the previous example, the table and its column must be aliased. The output of this script is shown in Figure 15-7.

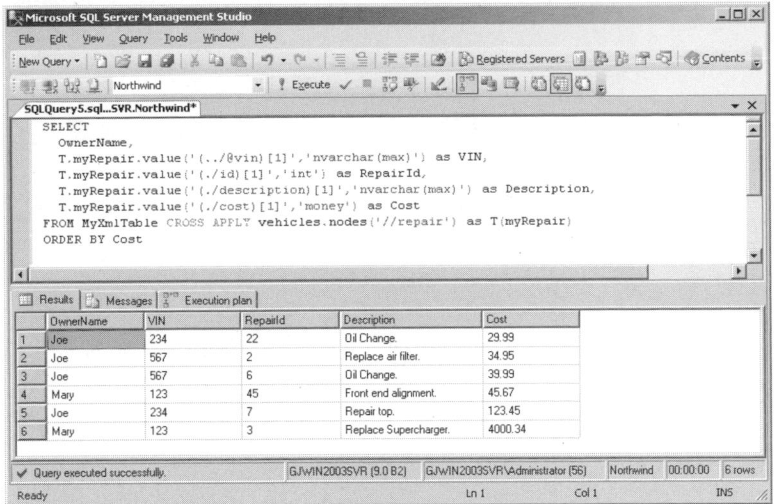

Figure 15-7 Using the *nodes* method with CROSS APPLY creates a new row for each element.

Using the FOR XML Clause

The FOR XML clause was introduced in SQL Server 2000, which provides various options for retrieving data as XML. The FOR XML clause is still available in SQL Server 2005, and it has been extended with the FOR XML PATH option. The following options are available.

- *FOR XML AUTO* Returns nested XML elements, based on the tables listed in the *FROM* clause of the query, and the fields listed in the *SELECT* clause.
- *FOR XML RAW* Returns repeating XML elements from a table with a tag name of "row", and each table column value is represented as an attribute in the row element. Null column values aren't included.
- *FOR XML EXPLICIT* Returns a user-defined XML shape. This mode provides complete control of the shape of the returned XML by allowing you to mix attributes and elements as needed and even create space-separated value lists and mixed content.
- *FOR XML PATH* Returns a user-defined XML shape. This mode allows you to provide XPath syntax as a column name that can be mapped into an attribute, element, subelement structure, element content, text, or data value.

You can easily combine non-*xml* columns with *xml* columns by using one of the FOR XML clauses. For example, you can execute the following SQL snippet to retrieve an XML document that represents MyXmlTable, which contains the owners and their vehicles.

```
SELECT * FROM MyXmlTable FOR XML PATH
```

Here is the result:

```
<row>
  <id>1</id>
  <ownername>Joe</ownername>
  <vehicles>
    <vehicles>
      <car vin="234" make="Mazda" model="Miata">
        <repair>
          <id>7</id>
          <description>Repair top.</description>
          <cost>123.45</cost>
        </repair>
        <repair>
          <id>22</id>
          <description>Oil Change.</description>
          <cost>29.99</cost>
        </repair>
      </car>
      <truck vin="567" make="Nissan" model="Pathfinder">
        <repair>
          <id>2</id>
          <description>Replace air filter.</description>
          <cost>34.95</cost>
        </repair>
        <repair>
          <id>6</id>
          <description>Oil Change.</description>
          <cost>39.99</cost>
        </repair>
      </truck>
    </vehicles>
  </vehicles>
</row>
<row>
  <id>2</id>
  <ownername>Mary</ownername>
  <vehicles>
    <vehicles>
      <car vin="123" make="Ford" model="Mustang">
        <repair>
          <id>3</id>
          <description>Replace Supercharger.</description>
          <cost>4000.34</cost>
        </repair>
        <repair>
          <id>45</id>
          <description>Front end alignment.</description>
          <cost>45.67</cost>
        </repair>
      </car>
    </vehicles>
  </vehicles>
</row>
```

```
<row>
  <id>3</id>
  <ownername>Bob</ownername>
</row>
```

This default output looks good, but the benefit of the FOR XML PATH clause is that you can control the look of the generated XML by assigning XPath expressions to the column names. For example, if you want the XML output to be an XML fragment having a root node for each owner with the vehicles nested in each owner element and attributes of the owner element giving the owner information, you can use the following SQL snippet.

```
SELECT id 'owner/@id',
  ownername 'owner/@name',
  vehicles 'owner'
 FROM MyXmlTable FOR XML PATH('')
```

Notice that an XPath-like expression is assigned to the column alias for ID and owner name, indicating that attributes will be created on an owner element for this data. The vehicle's *xml* column has *owner* as its location, which means the vehicles will be nested inside each owner. The empty string after PATH specifies the name of the root element, which will be omitted because we've specified an empty string. The following XML fragment is the result:

```
<owner id="1" name="Joe">
  <vehicles>
    <car vin="234" make="Mazda" model="Miata">
      <repair>
        <id>7</id>
        <description>Repair top.</description>
        <cost>123.45</cost>
      </repair>
      <repair>
        <id>22</id>
        <description>Oil Change.</description>
        <cost>29.99</cost>
      </repair>
    </car>
    <truck vin="567" make="Nissan" model="Pathfinder">
      <repair>
        <id>2</id>
        <description>Replace air filter.</description>
        <cost>34.95</cost>
      </repair>
      <repair>
        <id>6</id>
        <description>Oil Change.</description>
        <cost>39.99</cost>
      </repair>
    </truck>
  </vehicles>
</owner>
```

```
<owner id="2" name="Mary">
  <vehicles>
    <car vin="123" make="Ford" model="Mustang">
      <repair>
        <id>3</id>
        <description>Replace Supercharger.</description>
        <cost>4000.34</cost>
      </repair>
      <repair>
        <id>45</id>
        <description>Front end alignment.</description>
        <cost>45.67</cost>
      </repair>
    </car>
  </vehicles>
</owner>
<owner id="3" name="Bob" />
```

You can see that the FOR XML PATH clause makes it easy to repurpose the relational and XML data.

Indexing the *xml* Column

Every time you execute the *query* method, you parse the *xml* data type one or more times for each row in the table. With a large row count and/or large XML data BLOBs, this can hurt performance. To speed up *query* method performance, you can index the *xml* columns–but be sure to take into account the cost of maintaining the index if the data changes frequently.

You can create indexes on typed and untyped *xml* columns; this creates a B+ tree, which is a tree structure that is used to perform quick lookups, for each instance in the column. The first index you create on an *xml* column is called the *primary XML index*. You can create three types of secondary XML indexes to speed up common types of queries.

To create the primary XML index, you must make the primary key of the table a clustered index. The following SQL script creates the clustered primary key on MyXmlTable and then creates an XML index called *idx_vehicles* on the *xml* column vehicles of table MyXmlTable.

```
CREATE PRIMARY XML INDEX idx_vehicles on MyXmlTable (vehicles)
```

After you create the primary XML index, you can create secondary XML indexes for different classes of queries. The three classes of secondary XML indexes are PATH, PROPERTY, and VALUE.

The PATH index is used to speed up path-based queries by building a B+ tree on the path and value columns of the primary XML index. Probably the most noticeable performance increase will be when you use the *exist* method of the *xml* column in the WHERE clause of a SELECT statement. To create this index, use the following SQL snippet.

SQL: Creating the *PATH* Index

```
CREATE XML INDEX idx_vehicles_Path on MyXmlTable(vehicles)
   USING XML INDEX idx_vehicles FOR PATH
```

The PROPERTY index creates a B+ tree on the primary key, path, and value columns of the primary XML index. This index speeds up performance on value lookups within an XML instance.

SQL: Creating the PROPERTY Index

```
CREATE XML INDEX idx_vehicles_Property on MyXmlTable(vehicles)
   USING XML INDEX idx_vehicles FOR PROPERTY
```

The VALUE index creates a B+ tree on the value and path columns of the primary XML index. This index increases performance on queries that search for a node based on the descendent axes (that use //) and wildcard queries that use the asterisk.

SQL: Creating the VALUE Index

```
CREATE XML INDEX idx_vehicles_Value on MyXmlTable(vehicles)
   USING XML INDEX idx_vehicles FOR VALUE
```

The *xml* column cannot be part of a primary or foreign key, but you can create an index on the XML data in a table. Here are the limitations.

- An index can be created only on a table; indexing on a view is not supported.
- Only a single column can be specified in an *xml* index. Compound indexes are not supported.
- The primary key of the table must be a clustered index. You cannot modify the primary clustered index without first dropping the *xml* index.

Using XML with ADO.NET

To help you take advantage of the *xml* data type and XQuery in SQL Server 2005, ADO.NET and the classes in the *System.Xml* namespace provide you with helpful tools. Here is a list of some changes that have been made to the ADO.NET classes to enable or enhance the SQL Server XML experience.

- The *System.Data.SqlTypes* namespace contains a new class called *SqlXml*. This is a nullable data type that contains a method called *CreateReader*, which returns a derived instance of *XmlReader* that you can use to read the XML data contained in the instance.
- The *System.Data.SqlDbType* enumeration contains a new value called *xml* that indicates the *SqlXml* data type (described earlier).
- The *SqlDataReader* class contains a method called *GetSqlXml* that returns a *SqlXml* data type instance based on the column index that you pass to this function. The *SqlDataReader* object can also read the schema information of the *xml* columns by using the

GetSchemaTable method, which has three new columns called *XmlSchemaCollectionDatabase*, *XmlSchemaCollectionOwningSchema*, and *XmlSchemaCollectionName*.

- The *System.Data.Common.DataAdapter* class contains a method called *ReturnProviderSpecificTypes* that is set to true to read in XML data as a *SqlXml* type. If you use the default value of false, XML data is read into a string field.

Getting Started with the *SqlXml* Class

You can access instances of the *SqlXml* class by using the *DataReader* object's *GetSqlXml* method. After you have a *SqlXml* object, you can execute its *CreateReader* method to retrieve an object that derives from the *XmlReader* object.

To see how this works, create a Windows application named XmlTest and add a *Button* control and a *DataGrid* control to the form. Note that the *DataGrid* control is being used because it supports hierarchical data, whereas the *DataGridView* does not. If the *DataGrid* control is not in your ToolBox, you will need to add it by right-clicking in the ToolBox, clicking Choose Items, and selecting the *DataGrid* control from the .NET Framework Components tab. On the *Button* control, change the *Text* property to *Get Vehicles*. We are using the *DataGrid* control instead of the *DataGridView* control because the *DataGrid* control can display many tables by assigning a *DataSet* object to its *DataSource* property and leaving the *DataMember* property empty. Add the *Northwind* database to your project, and add the following App.config file to your project.

App.config File

```
<?xml version="1.0" encoding="utf-8" ?>
<configuration>
    <connectionStrings>
        <add name="NwString"
            connectionString="Data Source=.\SQLEXPRESS;
            AttachDbFilename=|DataDirectory|\northwnd.mdf;
            Integrated Security=True;User Instance=True"
            providerName="System.Data.SqlClient" />
    </connectionStrings>
</configuration>
```

Run the script to add MyXmlTable to the *Northwind* database. The script, titled "SQL: Creating and Populating MyXmlTable," can be found earlier in the chapter.

Next, add a reference to the System.Configuration.dll, System.Data.dll, and System.Xml.dll assemblies. Double-click the button, and add the following code to read the vehicles into the *DataSet* object.

Visual Basic

```
Imports System.Data
Imports System.Data.SqlClient
Imports System.Data.SqlTypes
Imports System.Configuration
```

```
Public Class Form1

   Private Sub button1_Click(ByVal sender As System.Object, _
         ByVal e As System.EventArgs) Handles button1.Click
      Dim ds As New DataSet()
      Dim nwSetting As ConnectionStringSettings = _
         ConfigurationManager.ConnectionStrings("NwString")
      Using cn As New SqlConnection()
         cn.ConnectionString = nwSetting.ConnectionString
         Using cmd As SqlCommand = cn.CreateCommand()
            cmd.CommandText = "SELECT vehicles FROM MyXmlTable"
            cn.Open()
            Using rdr As SqlDataReader = cmd.ExecuteReader()
               While (rdr.Read())
                  Dim vehicles As SqlXml = rdr.GetSqlXml(0)
                  If (Not vehicles.IsNull) Then
                     ds.ReadXml(vehicles.CreateReader())
                  End If
               End While
            End Using
         End Using
      End Using
      dataGrid1.DataSource = ds
   End Sub
End Class
```

C#

```
using System;
using System.Data;
using System.Windows.Forms;
using System.Data.SqlClient;
using System.Configuration;
using System.Data.SqlTypes;

namespace XmlTest
{
   public partial class Form1 : Form
   {
      public Form1()
      {
         InitializeComponent();
      }

      private void button1_Click(object sender, EventArgs e)
      {
         DataSet ds = new DataSet();
         ConnectionStringSettings nwSetting =
            ConfigurationManager.ConnectionStrings["NwString"];
         using (SqlConnection cn = new SqlConnection())
         {
            cn.ConnectionString = nwSetting.ConnectionString;
            using (SqlCommand cmd = cn.CreateCommand())
            {
               cmd.CommandText = "SELECT vehicles FROM MyXmlTable";
               cn.Open();
```

```
                using (SqlDataReader rdr = cmd.ExecuteReader())
                {
                    while (rdr.Read())
                    {
                        SqlXml vehicles = rdr.GetSqlXml(0);
                        if (!vehicles.IsNull)
                            ds.ReadXml(vehicles.CreateReader());
                    }
                }
            }
        }
        dataGrid1.DataSource = ds;
    }
  }
}
```

When you run this code, a connection is opened to the database and a query is executed to retrieve the vehicles. Using the *SqlDataReader* object, you can read each row and execute the *GetSqlXml* method to retrieve an instance of the *SqlXml* class. As long as the *SqlXml* object is not null, the XML data is read into the *DataSet* object by executing the *CreateReader* method on the *SqlXml* object, which creates an *XmlSqlBinaryReader* object. The *XmlSqlBinaryReader* object is passed into the *ReadXml* method on the *DataSet* object. Each *SqlXml* object that is read into the *DataSet* object appends to existing XML data. Finally, the *DataSet* object is assigned to the *DataSource* property of the *DataGrid* control. The resulting *DataGrid* object displays a plus sign indicating that tables are available. If you click the plus sign, you'll see that the *DataSet* object converted the XML data into *DataTable* objects for cars, trucks, and repairs (as shown in Figure 15-8).

Figure 15-8 The XML data that was read into the *DataSet* object was automatically converted to *DataTable* objects.

Assigning and Retrieving the Schema

Working with typed and untyped *xml* data is essentially the same on the client by default, because typed *xml* columns do not automatically transfer their schema to the client. This means that schema validation does not occur until the modified XML data is sent to SQL

Server. The problem is that in the previous example, the XML data was loaded into a *DataSet* object and all of the data types were inferred to be string data types. If you navigate to the repair table and change a code to a nonnumeric value, the new value is accepted. This probably isn't the behavior you want.

You can get the schema from SQL Server, which gives you the opportunity to perform client-side validation. You do this by using the *SqlDataReader* object's *GetSchemaTable* method to discover the schema information, and then you can retrieve the schema.

To prepare the SQL Server data for this example, we must add a schema to SQL Server for the vehicles and then alter MyXmlTable to use a typed *xml* column based on the new schema. Start by executing the following SQL script to create the Schema Collection called *VehicleSchema* in SQL Server.

SQL: Creating the *VehicleSchema*

```
CREATE XML SCHEMA COLLECTION VehicleSchema AS
'<?xml version="1.0" standalone="yes"?>
<xs:schema id="vehicles" xmlns=""
      xmlns:xs="http://www.w3.org/2001/XMLSchema"
      xmlns:msdata="urn:schemas-microsoft-com:xml-msdata">
  <xs:element name="repair">
    <xs:complexType>
      <xs:sequence>
        <xs:element name="id" type="xs:int" />
        <xs:element name="description" type="xs:string" minOccurs="0" />
        <xs:element name="cost" type="xs:decimal" minOccurs="0" />
      </xs:sequence>
    </xs:complexType>
  </xs:element>
  <xs:element name="car">
    <xs:complexType>
      <xs:sequence>
        <xs:element ref="repair" minOccurs="0" maxOccurs="unbounded" />
      </xs:sequence>
      <xs:attribute name="vin" type="xs:string" />
      <xs:attribute name="make" type="xs:string" />
      <xs:attribute name="model" type="xs:string" />
    </xs:complexType>
  </xs:element>
  <xs:element name="truck">
    <xs:complexType>
      <xs:sequence>
        <xs:element ref="repair" minOccurs="0" maxOccurs="unbounded" />
      </xs:sequence>
      <xs:attribute name="vin" type="xs:string" />
      <xs:attribute name="make" type="xs:string" />
      <xs:attribute name="model" type="xs:string" />
    </xs:complexType>
  </xs:element>
```

```
  <xs:element name="vehicles"
      msdata:IsDataSet="true" msdata:UseCurrentLocale="true">
    <xs:complexType>
      <xs:choice minOccurs="0" maxOccurs="unbounded">
        <xs:element ref="repair" />
        <xs:element ref="car" />
        <xs:element ref="truck" />
      </xs:choice>
    </xs:complexType>
  </xs:element>
</xs:schema>'
```

This schema is somewhat generic, but it contains an *IsDataSet* attribute set to indicate that this schema can be loaded into a *DataSet* object before the data is loaded, to enable type checking on numeric columns (such as the repair cost).

If you retrieve the schema you just added, you will find that the *IsDataSet* attribute was not stored. Try the following command.

```
SELECT xml_schema_namespace('dbo', 'VehicleSchema')
```

This command returns the following schema information.

Retrieved Schema: Missing *IsDataSet* Attribute

```
<xsd:schema xmlns:xsd="http://www.w3.org/2001/XMLSchema">
   <xsd:element name="car">
      <xsd:complexType>
         <xsd:complexContent>
            <xsd:restriction base="xsd:anyType">
               <xsd:sequence>
                  <xsd:element ref="repair" minOccurs="0"
                     maxOccurs="unbounded" />
               </xsd:sequence>
               <xsd:attribute name="vin" type="xsd:string" />
               <xsd:attribute name="make" type="xsd:string" />
               <xsd:attribute name="model" type="xsd:string" />
            </xsd:restriction>
         </xsd:complexContent>
      </xsd:complexType>
   </xsd:element>
   <xsd:element name="repair">
      <xsd:complexType>
         <xsd:complexContent>
            <xsd:restriction base="xsd:anyType">
               <xsd:sequence>
                  <xsd:element name="id" type="xsd:int" />
                  <xsd:element name="description"
                     type="xsd:string" minOccurs="0" />
                  <xsd:element name="cost" type="xsd:decimal" minOccurs="0" />
```

```
            </xsd:sequence>
          </xsd:restriction>
        </xsd:complexContent>
      </xsd:complexType>
    </xsd:element>
    <xsd:element name="truck">
      <xsd:complexType>
        <xsd:complexContent>
          <xsd:restriction base="xsd:anyType">
            <xsd:sequence>
              <xsd:element ref="repair"
                minOccurs="0" maxOccurs="unbounded" />
            </xsd:sequence>
            <xsd:attribute name="vin" type="xsd:string" />
            <xsd:attribute name="make" type="xsd:string" />
            <xsd:attribute name="model" type="xsd:string" />
          </xsd:restriction>
        </xsd:complexContent>
      </xsd:complexType>
    </xsd:element>
    <xsd:element name="vehicles">
      <xsd:complexType>
        <xsd:complexContent>
          <xsd:restriction base="xsd:anyType">
            <xsd:choice minOccurs="0" maxOccurs="unbounded">
              <xsd:element ref="repair" />
              <xsd:element ref="car" />
              <xsd:element ref="truck" />
            </xsd:choice>
          </xsd:restriction>
        </xsd:complexContent>
      </xsd:complexType>
    </xsd:element>
  </xsd:schema>
```

The problem is that the schema was parsed and stored based on what SQL Server needed. The original schema is not stored in the Schema Collection, so you must store it to a file or to a text field in the database. In this example, we want to use the same schema that SQL Server is using, so we will add code to insert the *IsDataSet* attribute into the schema when it is retrieved from the database.

Now that the schema is loaded into SQL Server, we can modify MyXmlTable to use the schema. Open the table definition, and change the *XmlTypeSpecification* to use *dbo.Vehicle-Schema*, as shown in Figure 15-9.

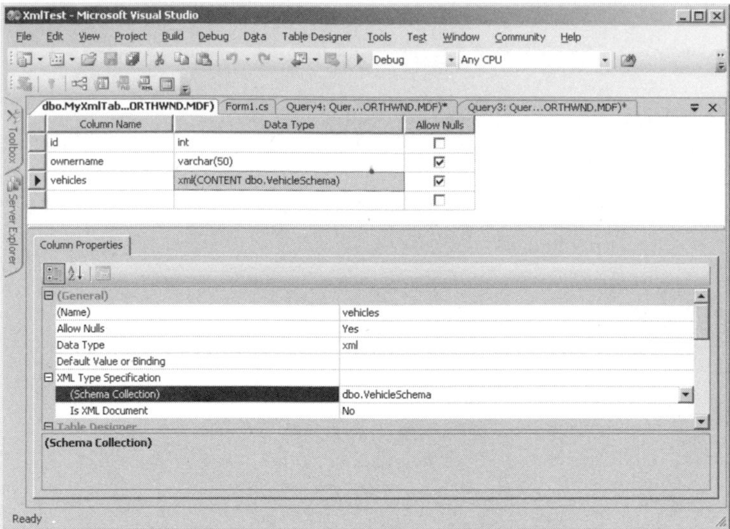

Figure 15-9 Changing MyXmlTable to use the *VehicleSchema*

You can add code to discover the schema information and retrieve it. The code that discovers the schema and retrieves it uses the same connection object, which means you must enable the *MultipleActiveResultSets* (MARS) option in the connection string, as follows.

App.config File

```
<?xml version="1.0" encoding="utf-8" ?>
<configuration>
    <connectionStrings>
        <add name="NwString"
            connectionString="Data Source=.\SQLEXPRESS;
            AttachDbFilename=|DataDirectory|\northwnd.mdf;
            Integrated Security=True;User Instance=True;
            MultipleActiveResultSets=True"
            providerName="System.Data.SqlClient" />
    </connectionStrings>
</configuration>
```

To discover the schema information and retrieve it, we will add a new method, called *GetSchema*, which reads the schema from the database and adds the *IsDataSet* attribute, as shown in the following code.

Visual Basic

```
Imports System.Data
Imports System.Data.SqlClient
Imports System.Data.SqlTypes
Imports System.Configuration
Imports System.Xml
Imports System.IO

Public Class Form1
```

```
    Private Sub button1_Click(ByVal sender As System.Object, _
          ByVal e As System.EventArgs) Handles button1.Click
       Dim ds As New DataSet()
       Dim nwSetting As ConnectionStringSettings = _
          ConfigurationManager.ConnectionStrings("NwString")
       Using cn As New SqlConnection()
          cn.ConnectionString = nwSetting.ConnectionString
          Using cmd As SqlCommand = cn.CreateCommand()
             cmd.CommandText = "Select vehicles from MyXmlTable"
             cn.Open()
             Using rdr As SqlDataReader = cmd.ExecuteReader()
                GetSchema("vehicles", ds, cn, rdr)
                While (rdr.Read())
                   Dim vehicles As SqlXml = rdr.GetSqlXml(0)
                   If (Not vehicles.IsNull) Then
                      ds.ReadXml(vehicles.CreateReader())
                   End If
                End While
             End Using
          End Using
       End Using
       dataGrid1.DataSource = ds
    End Sub

    Private Sub GetSchema(ByVal xmlColumn As String, _
          ByVal ds As DataSet, ByVal cn As SqlConnection, _
          ByVal rdr As SqlDataReader)
       'discover and retrieve schema
       Dim schema As DataTable = rdr.GetSchemaTable()
       Dim row As DataRow = schema.Select("columnName='" + xmlColumn + "'")(0)
       Using schemaCmd As SqlCommand = cn.CreateCommand()
          schemaCmd.CommandText = _
             "SELECT xml_schema_namespace(@owner, @name) FOR XML PATH('')"
          schemaCmd.Parameters.AddWithValue( _
             "@owner", row("XmlSchemaCollectionOwningSchema"))
          schemaCmd.Parameters.AddWithValue( _
             "@name", row("XmlSchemaCollectionName"))
          'load into XmlDocument to fix IsDataSet attribute
          Dim doc As New XmlDocument()
          doc.Load(schemaCmd.ExecuteXmlReader())
          Dim mgr As New XmlNamespaceManager(doc.NameTable)
          mgr.AddNamespace("xsd", "http://www.w3.org/2001/XMLSchema")
          Dim vehicles As XmlNode = doc.SelectSingleNode( _
             "//xsd:element[@name=""" + xmlColumn + """ ]", mgr)
          Dim dataSetAtt As XmlAttribute = doc.CreateAttribute("msdata", _
             "IsDataSet", "urn:schemas-microsoft-com:xml-msdata")
          dataSetAtt.Value = "true"
          vehicles.Attributes.Append(dataSetAtt)
          Dim tempStream As New MemoryStream()
          doc.Save(tempStream)
          tempStream.Position = 0
          ds.ReadXmlSchema(tempStream)
       End Using
    End Sub
 End Class
```

C#

```
using System;
using System.Data;
using System.Windows.Forms;
using System.Data.SqlClient;
using System.Configuration;
using System.Data.SqlTypes;
//using System.Collections;
using System.Collections.Generic;

using System.Xml;
using System.Xml.XPath;
using System.IO;

namespace XmlTest
{
   public partial class Form1 : Form
   {
      public Form1()
      {
         InitializeComponent();
      }

      private void button1_Click(object sender, EventArgs e)
      {
         DataSet ds = new DataSet();
         ConnectionStringSettings nwSetting =
            ConfigurationManager.ConnectionStrings["NwString"];
         using (SqlConnection cn = new SqlConnection())
         {
            cn.ConnectionString = nwSetting.ConnectionString;
            using (SqlCommand cmd = cn.CreateCommand())
            {
               cmd.CommandText = "SELECT vehicles FROM MyXmlTable WHERE id=1";
               cn.Open();
               using (SqlDataReader rdr = cmd.ExecuteReader())
               {
                  GetSchema("vehicles", ds, cn, rdr);
                  while (rdr.Read())
                  {
                     SqlXml vehicles = rdr.GetSqlXml(0);
                     if (!vehicles.IsNull)
                        ds.ReadXml(vehicles.CreateReader());
                  }
               }
            }
         }
         dataGrid1.DataSource = ds;
      }

      private static void GetSchema(string xmlColumn,
         DataSet ds, SqlConnection cn, SqlDataReader rdr)
      {
```

```
            //discover and retrieve schema
            DataTable schema = rdr.GetSchemaTable();
            DataRow row = schema.Select("columnName='" + xmlColumn + "'")[0];
            using (SqlCommand schemaCmd = cn.CreateCommand())
            {
               schemaCmd.CommandText =
                  "SELECT xml_schema_namespace(@owner, @name) FOR XML PATH('')";
               schemaCmd.Parameters.AddWithValue(
                  "@owner", row["XmlSchemaCollectionOwningSchema"]);
               schemaCmd.Parameters.AddWithValue(
                  "@name", row["XmlSchemaCollectionName"]);
               //load into XmlDocument to fix IsDataSet attribute
               XmlDocument doc = new XmlDocument();
               doc.Load(schemaCmd.ExecuteXmlReader());
               XmlNamespaceManager mgr = new XmlNamespaceManager(doc.NameTable);
               mgr.AddNamespace("xsd", "http://www.w3.org/2001/XMLSchema");
               XmlNode vehicles = doc.SelectSingleNode(
                  "//xsd:element[@name=\"" + xmlColumn + "\"]", mgr);
               XmlAttribute dataSetAtt = doc.CreateAttribute("msdata",
                  "IsDataSet", "urn:schemas-microsoft-com:xml-msdata");
               dataSetAtt.Value = "true";
               vehicles.Attributes.Append(dataSetAtt);
               MemoryStream tempStream = new MemoryStream();
               doc.Save(tempStream);
               tempStream.Position = 0;
               ds.ReadXmlSchema(tempStream);
            }
         }
      }
   }
```

The new *GetSchema* method discovers the schema name by calling the *GetSchemaTable* method and then selecting the metadata row for the column we are interested in (in this case, the vehicles column). This information is plugged into the call to *xml_schema_namespace*, which retrieves the schema from the database. Instead of loading the schema directly into the *DataSet* object, we load it into an *XmlDocument* object and perform a search for the *vehicles* element, and then we add the *IsDataSet* attribute to it, along with its required namespace. The *DataSet* object can read the schema from either a file or a stream, so the *XmlDocument* object is saved to a temporary *MemoryStream* object and the *DataSet* object uses the *MemoryStream* object to read the schema.

If you run this sample application and click the button to load the vehicles data, the schema is retrieved from the database and then the schema is loaded into the *DataSet* object. Then the data is loaded and displayed.

With the schema information at the client, navigate to the repair table and try to change one of the cost values to a nonnumeric value. When you leave the cost field, it is validated. Validation will fail, and the value will revert to its original numeric value.

Passing an *SqlXml* Object Parameter to Update the Database

When it's time to update the database, you can create a parameter that is an *SqlXml* type and issue an UPDATE statement to the database with this object.

For the following example, add a *Button* control to the form. Change the *Text* property to *Update Vehicles*, and add the following code to its *Click* event handler.

Visual Basic

```
Private Sub button2_Click(ByVal sender As System.Object, _
      ByVal e As System.EventArgs) Handles button2.Click
   Dim ds As DataSet = CType(dataGrid1.DataSource, DataSet)
   Dim nwSetting As ConnectionStringSettings = _
      ConfigurationManager.ConnectionStrings("NwString")
   Using cn As New SqlConnection()
      cn.ConnectionString = nwSetting.ConnectionString
      Using cmd As SqlCommand = cn.CreateCommand()
         cmd.CommandText = _
            "UPDATE MyXmlTable SET vehicles = @veh WHERE id=1"
         Dim ms As New MemoryStream()
         ds.WriteXml(ms)
         ms.Position = 0
         Dim r As XmlReader = XmlReader.Create(ms)
         Dim x As New SqlXml(r)
         cmd.Parameters.AddWithValue("@veh", x)
         cn.Open()
         cmd.ExecuteNonQuery()
      End Using
   End Using
   MessageBox.Show("Done.")
End Sub
```

C#

```
private void button2_Click(object sender, EventArgs e)
{
   DataSet ds = (DataSet)dataGrid1.DataSource;
   ConnectionStringSettings nwSetting =
      ConfigurationManager.ConnectionStrings["NwString"];
   using (SqlConnection cn = new SqlConnection())
   {
      cn.ConnectionString = nwSetting.ConnectionString;
      using (SqlCommand cmd = cn.CreateCommand())
      {
         cmd.CommandText =
            "UPDATE MyXmlTable SET vehicles = @veh WHERE id=1";
         MemoryStream ms = new MemoryStream();
         ds.WriteXml(ms);
         ms.Position = 0;
         XmlReader r = XmlReader.Create(ms);
         SqlXml x = new SqlXml(r);
         cmd.Parameters.AddWithValue("@veh", x);
         cn.Open();
         cmd.ExecuteNonQuery();
      }
```

```
    }
    MessageBox.Show("Done.");
}
```

Summary

- SQL Server 2005 supports native XML data by using the *xml* data type.
- You can store XML data into a "typed" or "untyped" *xml* data type.
- "Typed" *xml* data types require the assignment of a Schema Collection–one or more schemas that have been stored in the SQL Server XML Schema Collection repository.
- Using a Schema Collection allows you to provide multiple versions of a schema.
- The *query* method extracts parts of an XML instance.
- The *value* method extracts a scalar value from an XML instance.
- The *exist* method provides an existential check on an XML instance.
- The *nodes* method yields instances of a special XML data type, each with its context set to a different node than the XQuery expression evaluates to.
- The *modify* method permits modifying parts of an XML instance.
- You can create a primary XML index on an *xml* column.
- The secondary PATH index is used for path-based queries.
- The secondary PROPERTY index is used for property bag scenarios.
- The secondary VALUE index is used for value-based queries.
- XQuery provides the FLWOR expression syntax, which is an acronym for for-let-where-order-return and is pronounced *flower*.
- You can still use the FOR XML clause to produce XML data, and FOR XML PATH lets you control the combination of XML data and non-XML data.
- The ADO.NET *SqlXml* class lets you work with the SQL Server *xml* data type.
- The *SqlDataReader* class contains a *GetSqlXml* method to retrieve XML data.
- When you assign a schema to the SQL Server XML Schema Collection, the schema is parsed and stored. Non-schema data and annotations are not stored.

Index

B

C

D

E

F

G

H

I

N

O

P

Q

R

S

T

Z

About the Author

Glenn Johnson is a professional trainer whose experience spans the years from COBOL and assembly language to Microsoft .NET. Formerly the director of information technologies and technical support for Tyco International, Johnson now runs his own training, consulting, and development business. This is Glenn's second .NET-related book, and he has also developed courseware for and taught classes in many countries on the topics of Microsoft ASP.NET, Microsoft Visual Basic, .NET, C#, and .NET internals. Glenn holds the following Microsoft certifications: MCT, MCAD, MCSD, MCDBA, MCP + Site Building, MCSE + Internet, MCP + Internet, and MCSE.

Glenn's Web site can found at *http://GJTT.com*.

Additional Resources for Visual Basic Developers

Published and Forthcoming Titles from Microsoft Press

Microsoft® Visual Basic® 2005 Express Edition: Build a Program Now!

Patrice Pelland • ISBN 0-7356-2213-2

Featuring a full working edition of the software, this fun and highly visual guide walks you through a complete programming project—a desktop weather-reporting application—from start to finish. You'll get an introduction to the Microsoft Visual Studio® development environment and learn how to put the lightweight, easy-to-use tools in Visual Basic Express to work right away—creating, compiling, testing, and delivering your first ready-to-use program. You'll get expert tips, coaching, and visual examples each step of the way, along with pointers to additional learning resources.

Microsoft Visual Basic 2005 *Step by Step*

Michael Halvorson • ISBN 0-7356-2131-4

With enhancements across its visual designers, code editor, language, and debugger that help accelerate the development and deployment of robust, elegant applications across the Web, a business group, or an enterprise, Visual Basic 2005 focuses on enabling developers to rapidly build applications. Now you can teach yourself the essentials of working with Visual Studio 2005 and the new features of the Visual Basic language—one step at a time. Each chapter puts you to work, showing you how, when, and why to use specific features of Visual Basic and guiding as you create actual components and working applications for Microsoft Windows®. You'll also explore data management and Web-based development topics.

Programming Microsoft Visual Basic 2005 *Core Reference*

Francesco Balena • ISBN 0-7356-2183-7

Get the expert insights, indispensable reference, and practical instruction needed to exploit the core language features and capabilities in Visual Basic 2005. Well-known Visual Basic programming author Francesco Balena expertly guides you through the fundamentals, including modules, keywords, and inheritance, and builds your mastery of more advanced topics such as delegates, assemblies, and My Namespace. Combining in-depth reference with extensive, hands-on code examples and best-practices advice, this *Core Reference* delivers the key resources that you need to develop professional-level programming skills for smart clients and the Web.

Programming Microsoft Visual Basic 2005 Framework Reference

Francesco Balena • ISBN 0-7356-2175-6

Complementing *Programming Microsoft Visual Basic 2005 Core Reference*, this book covers a wide range of additional topics and information critical to Visual Basic developers, including Windows Forms, working with Microsoft ADO.NET 2.0 and ASP.NET 2.0, Web services, security, remoting, and much more. Packed with sample code and real-world examples, this book will help developers move from understanding to mastery.

Programming Microsoft Windows Forms
Charles Petzold • ISBN 0-7356-2153-5

Programming Microsoft Web Forms
Douglas J. Reilly • ISBN 0-7356-2179-9

Debugging, Tuning, and Testing Microsoft .NET 2.0 Applications
John Robbins • ISBN 0-7356-2202-7

Microsoft ASP.NET 2.0 *Step by Step*
George Shepherd • ISBN 0-7356-2201-9

Microsoft ADO.NET 2.0 *Step by Step*
Rebecca Riordan • ISBN 0-7356-2164-0

Programming Microsoft ASP.NET 2.0 *Core Reference*
Dino Esposito • ISBN 0-7356-2176-4

For more information about Microsoft Press® books and other learning products, visit: **www.microsoft.com/books** *and* **www.microsoft.com/learning**

Microsoft Press products are available worldwide wherever quality computer books are sold. For more information, contact your book or computer retailer, software reseller, or local Microsoft Sales Office, or visit our Web site at **www.microsoft.com/mspress**. To locate your nearest source for Microsoft Press products, or to order directly, call 1-800-MSPRESS in the United States. (In Canada, call **1-800-268-2222**.)

Additional Resources for C# Developers

Published and Forthcoming Titles from Microsoft Press

Microsoft® Visual C#® 2005 Express Edition: Build a Program Now!

Patrice Pelland • ISBN 0-7356-2229-9

In this lively, eye-opening, and hands-on book, all you need is a computer and the desire to learn how to program with Visual C# 2005 Express Edition. Featuring a full working edition of the software, this fun and highly visual guide walks you through a complete programming project—a desktop weather-reporting application—from start to finish. You'll get an unintimidating introduction to the Microsoft Visual Studio® development environment and learn how to put the lightweight, easy-to-use tools in Visual C# Express to work right away—creating, compiling, testing, and delivering your first, ready-to-use program. You'll get expert tips, coaching, and visual examples at each step of the way, along with pointers to additional learning resources.

Microsoft Visual C# 2005 *Step by Step*

John Sharp • ISBN 0-7356-2129-2

Visual C#, a feature of Visual Studio 2005, is a modern programming language designed to deliver a productive environment for creating business frameworks and reusable object-oriented components. Now you can teach yourself essential techniques with Visual C#—and start building components and Microsoft Windows®–based applications—one step at a time. With *Step by Step*, you work at your own pace through hands-on, learn-by-doing exercises. Whether you're a beginning programmer or new to this particular language, you'll learn how, when, and why to use specific features of Visual C# 2005. Each chapter puts you to work, building your knowledge of core capabilities and guiding you as you create your first C#-based applications for Windows, data management, and the Web.

Programming Microsoft Visual C# 2005 Framework Reference

Francesco Balena • ISBN 0-7356-2182-9

Complementing *Programming Microsoft Visual C# 2005 Core Reference*, this book covers a wide range of additional topics and information critical to Visual C# developers, including Windows Forms, working with Microsoft ADO.NET 2.0 and Microsoft ASP.NET 2.0, Web services, security, remoting, and much more. Packed with sample code and real-world examples, this book will help developers move from understanding to mastery.

Programming Microsoft Visual C# 2005 *Core Reference*

Donis Marshall • ISBN 0-7356-2181-0

Get the in-depth reference and pragmatic, real-world insights you need to exploit the enhanced language features and core capabilities in Visual C# 2005. Programming expert Donis Marshall deftly builds your proficiency with classes, structs, and other fundamentals, and advances your expertise with more advanced topics such as debugging, threading, and memory management. Combining incisive reference with hands-on coding examples and best practices, this *Core Reference* focuses on mastering the C# skills you need to build innovative solutions for smart clients and the Web.

CLR via C#, Second Edition

Jeffrey Richter • ISBN 0-7356-2163-2

In this new edition of Jeffrey Richter's popular book, you get focused, pragmatic guidance on how to exploit the common language runtime (CLR) functionality in Microsoft .NET Framework 2.0 for applications of all types—from Web Forms, Windows Forms, and Web services to solutions for Microsoft SQL Server™, Microsoft code names "Avalon" and "Indigo," consoles, Microsoft Windows NT® Service, and more. Targeted to advanced developers and software designers, this book takes you under the covers of .NET for an in-depth understanding of its structure, functions, and operational components, demonstrating the most practical ways to apply this knowledge to your own development efforts. You'll master fundamental design tenets for .NET and get hands-on insights for creating high-performance applications more easily and efficiently. The book features extensive code examples in Visual C# 2005.

Programming Microsoft Windows Forms
Charles Petzold • ISBN 0-7356-2153-5

CLR via C++
Jeffrey Richter with Stanley B. Lippman
ISBN 0-7356-2248-5

Programming Microsoft Web Forms
Douglas J. Reilly • ISBN 0-7356-2179-9

Debugging, Tuning, and Testing Microsoft .NET 2.0 Applications
John Robbins • ISBN 0-7356-2202-7

For more information about Microsoft Press® books and other learning products, visit: **www.microsoft.com/books** *and* **www.microsoft.com/learning**

What do you think of this book? We want to hear from you!

Do you have a few minutes to participate in a brief online survey? Microsoft is interested in hearing your feedback about this publication so that we can continually improve our books and learning resources for you.

To participate in our survey, please visit:
www.microsoft.com/learning/booksurvey

And enter this book's ISBN, 0-7356-2141-1. As a thank-you to survey participants in the United States and Canada, each month we'll randomly select five respondents to win one of five $100 gift certificates from a leading online merchant.* At the conclusion of the survey, you can enter the drawing by providing your e-mail address, which will be used for prize notification *only.*

Thanks in advance for your input. Your opinion counts!

Sincerely,

Microsoft Learning

Microsoft | Learning

Learn More. Go Further.

To see special offers on Microsoft Learning products for developers, IT professionals, and home and office users, visit: *www.microsoft.com/learning/booksurvey.*

* No purchase necessary. Void where prohibited. Open only to residents of the 50 United States (includes District of Columbia) and Canada (void in Quebec). Sweepstakes ends 6/30/2006. For official rules, see: *www.microsoft.com/learning/booksurvey.*